The Rough Guide BOOK OF

Playlists

Edited by
Mark Ellingham

Contributing editors
**Al Spicer, Nigel Williamson,
Garth Cartwright**

ROUGH
GUIDES

Contributors

This second edition of our Playlists book is – we're confident in saying – bigger and better than ever. Some of the first edition's dodgier opinions have been corrected, many of our more alarming omissions have been addressed, and – well, there's been an awful lot of new music over the past couple of years that has found its way into these pages.

Thanks, once again, to in-house editors Duncan Clark and Peter Buckley, for taking on large tracks of the alphabet, and to our contributing editors, Al Spicer, Nigel Williamson and Garth Cartwright, for downloading much of their strange and encyclopedic knowledge. We're also very grateful to Neil Foxlee, who went over the old edition like a hound dog.

And finally, a thousand thanks to our cast of writer and musician contributors:

WRITER CONTRIBUTORS

Ian Anderson
Dave Atkinson
Richard Baker
Frank Barrett
Clem Bastow
Essi Berelian
Steve Birt
George Bradley
Lloyd Bradley
Simon Broughton
Peter Buckley
Tom Bullough
Garth Cartwright
Duncan Clark
Chris Coe
Nik Cohn
Rachel Coldicutt
Geoff Colquitt
Kaz Cooke

Ian Cranna
Daniel Crewe
R. Crumb
Nat Defriend
John Duhigg
Martin Dunford
Nick Edwards
Mark Ellen
Mark Ellingham
Lisa-Jane Ellis
Robert Evers
Graeme Ewens
Jan Fairley
Claire Fogg
Neil Foxlee
Ben Garfield
Simon Garfield
Charlie Gillett
Doug Hall
Link Hall
Pete Hogan
David Honigmann
Nick Hornby
Chris Ingham
Colin Irwin
Peter Labella
Paul Laidlaw
Butch Lazorchak
Andrew Lockett
Jon Lusk
Toby Manning
Rhodri Marsden
Dan May
Gavin McNamara
Phil Meadley
Barry Miles
Matt Milton
Greg Neale
Chris Nickson
George Pelecanos
Werner Pieper
Tim Pollard
Peter Really
DJ Ritu

MUSICIAN CONTRIBUTORS

Carl Barat
Peter Blegvad
Dennis Bovell
Billy Bragg
Peter Buck
Tim Burgess
Eric Clapton
Elvis Costello
Dr John
Marianne Faithfull
Dani Filth
David Gray
Al Green
David Harrington
Emmylou Harris
Robyn Hitchcock
Hugh Hopper
Liam Howlett
Bert Jansch
Jazzy B
Gary Lightbody

Stephen Malkmus
Phil Manzanera
Mariza
Danny McNamara
Moby
Charlie Musselwhite
Sinead O'Connor
Andrew Loog Oldham
Mark Perry
Robert Plant
Keith Richards
Mykaell S Riley
Michael Stipe
Richard Thompson
KT Tunstall
Tom Waits
James Walsh
Paul Weller
Lucinda Williams
Brian Wilson
Robert Wyatt

Alastair Rolfe
Andrew Rosenberg
Madelyn Rosenberg
Rough Trade, Portobello
Greg Salter
Martin Sealby
Peter Shapiro
Lesley Simpson
Paul Simpson
Hunter Slaton
Ed Smith
AnneLise Sorensen
Al Spicer
Sue Steward

Mike Symons
Geoff Travis
Jean Trouillet
Richie Unterberger
Brendan Waller
Geoff Wallis
Greg Ward
Neil Way
Alex Webb
Tony Wheeler
Rowland White
Nigel Williamson
Ed Wright

Introduction

You're reading this book, so you know the deal. Albums aren't everything anymore. Sure, they're a handy format for symphonies and concertos, but when it comes to rock, soul, pop, reggae, hip-hop, jazz, world music – the terrain of this book – it's individual tracks that matter. It's all about assembling those tracks for yourself, or for your friends, in **playlists**.

You can do anything with a playlist. Historic overviews of artists, restrospectives of a micro-genre that passed everyone else by, lists of the greatest soul songs ever, classic hip-hop, or prog rock that stands the test of time. Or something more flip, like the weirdest covers ever recorded, or songs about the moon, or rain, or stars, or chickens and insects, or jelly, or getting drunk.

That's what this book is all about. Not the drunk thing, especially, though we do have lists for drinking songs (and sex, and drugs, and most conceivable forms of of rock'n'roll). But this is a book about enthusiasms, obsessions and sharing. It's a collection of playlists that will burst into life as you download the tracks, reflecting a fantastic depth of knowledge from a myriad of contributors, who have scrutinized their iPods or MP3 players and set out their stores.

Most of these contributors are professional music writers, but there are some first-timers, too, who got to hear about the project and sent in their ideas. And it's a pleasure to be able to say that the book is chock-full of playlists from legends such as Tom Waits, Keith Richards and Robert Plant. In these pages you'll find the songs that turned Eric Clapton on to blues, the tracks that move Al Green or Emmylou Harris.

But as the cliché goes, this is a book that needs no introduction. Just get browsing – and start downloading. And if you think we've got it all wrong, let us know. This second edition has added more artists, genres and quirks, and we are already looking at plans for an even bigger, ever more mad, third book.

Meantime, see what you think of this lot…

Mark Ellingham, Editor

"There's always the possibility that you're going to come across a record that transforms your life. And it happens weekly. It's like a leaf on the stream. There are little currents and eddies and sticks lying in the water that nudge you in a slightly different direction. And then you break loose and carry on down the current. There's nothing that actually stops you and lifts you out of the water and puts you on the bank but there are diversions and distractions and alarums and excursions which is what makes life interesting really. Not in a Roman Emperor kind of way where you have an *excess* of stimulation – I forget which Emperor it was that used to have animal skins thrown over him and then scamper into an arena and claw the testicles off naked slaves with his bare hands, not quite *that* level – but a little excitement here and there. And music provides that. It's fantastic."

JOHN PEEL

Contents

ABBA

You didn't have to hear an ABBA song twice to get it: they hit you square in the heart and the head first time.

❶ KNOWING ME, KNOWING YOU from ARRIVAL
The synths and acoustic guitars are crisp and clean as the snow in the video, but there's nothing cold about that climactic whisper ("baaad days"). Alan Partridge notwithstanding, still the stuff of goosebumps.

❷ S.O.S. from ABBA
ABBA in excelsis: coat-grabbingly immediate piano riff, plaintive verse suddenly gives way to instantly anthemic chorus.

❸ THE WINNER TAKES IT ALL from SUPER TROUPER
Agnetha's accent rarely sounded thicker, yet this somehow adds to the emotional impact of another great break-up ballad that had poignant parallels in real life.

❹ THE NAME OF THE GAME from ABBA THE ALBUM
Even The Fugees' pillaging of the riff has done the song no harm: curiously complex for something so immediate – simultaneously fragile, forlorn, hopeful and happy.

❺ DANCING QUEEN from ARRIVAL
Frida famously burst into tears when she first heard the backing track for this song: rarely has disco exuberance had such an undercurrent of melancholy.

❻ MAMMA MIA from ABBA
Only consummate pop craftsmen understand the glory of the glockenspiel, which takes equal billing to the girls' glorious voices here.

❼ MONEY MONEY MONEY from ARRIVAL
Pounding, piano-fuelled paean to 1970s excess. Wonderfully disingenuous use of English slang too: "I bet he wouldn't fancy me." Yeah, right!

❽ WATERLOO from WATERLOO
Where it all started: this 1974 Eurovision winner may be lyrically daft, but it's musically deft, reeling you in with hook after hook after hook.

Toby Manning

AC/DC

Australia's finest – the smutty schoolboys who went on forever. Scroll that volume wheel all the way round to 11…

❶ WHOLE LOTTA ROSIE from LET THERE BE ROCK
A song of ballsy brilliance – loose, raw and very, very fast. Just listen to Angus shredding his fingers on the solo.

❷ DOWN PAYMENT BLUES from POWERAGE
One of the all time great rock'n'roll penury lyrics from Bon Scott. He's so poor he can't even feed his cat!

❸ OVERDOSE from LET THERE BE ROCK
Who said things ever had to be perfect? Angus fumbles the intro and creates timeless magic.

❹ JAILBREAK from DIRTY DEEDS DONE DIRT CHEAP (AUSSIE RELEASE)
Featuring an immaculate mid-song pause – and a top riff to boot.

❺ DIRTY DEEDS DONE DIRT CHEAP from DIRTY DEEDS DONE DIRT CHEAP
Bon Scott at his menacing best, over a riff built to smash concrete.

❻ RIFF RAFF from IF YOU WANT BLOOD…
If the hum of juiced-up amps at the start doesn't hook you then you must be deaf or dead. The best live album opener. Ever.

❼ ROCK'N'ROLL AIN'T NOISE POLLUTION from BACK IN BLACK
A spot-on, two-finger salute to critica as new boy Brian Johnson sleazes through the song like he'd been in the band for years.

❽ FOR THOSE ABOUT TO ROCK (WE SALUTE YOU) from FOR THOSE ABOUT TO ROCK…
Amazing solos and great big feckin' cannons at the end! What more do you need?

Essi Berelian

a

Acid Jazz

Take a dash of acid house, a slice of jazz-funk, sprinkle with lounge – and you have a movement. For a while in the 1990s it ruled.

❶ LONG TIME GONE GALLIANO from THE PLOT THICKENS
Acid jazz at its most inventive on an urbanized version of David Crosby's song from the first CSN album.

❷ STONED WOMAN MOTHER EARTH from STONED WOMAN
Funky, Hammond-led title track from the debut album from Matt Deighton's band.

❸ MIDNIGHT AT THE OASIS BRAND NEW HEAVIES from BROTHER SISTER
Great, jazzy vocal from N'Dea Davenport on a reinvention of the old Maria Muldaur song.

❹ VIRTUAL INSANITY JAMIROQUAI from TRAVELLING WITHOUT MOVING
A simple groove and clever, complex arrangement on a track from the most successful band to earn – and then transcend – the acid jazz tag.

❺ SO WHAT RONNY JORDAN from THE ANTIDOTE
The Miles Davis classic reworked with a modern groove by the British guitarist, with Arnie Somejee on superb acoustic bass.

❻ LOUNGIN' JAZZMATAZZ from JAZZMATAZZ VOL 1
An experimental fusion of hip-hop and doctored jazz-funk beats courtesy of Guru of Gang Starr and jazz veteran Donald Byrd.

❼ SKIRT ALERT CORDUROY from DAD MAN CAT
Swinging but playful organ-led grooves from the post-modern Booker T & The MGs.

❽ STARSKY AND HUTCH THEME JAMES TAYLOR QUARTET from WAIT A MINUTE
One of the key records that kicked off the Acid Jazz movement in the late 1980s, complete with ex-James Brown horn section.

Nigel Williamson

Adam & The Ants

The sweaty, leather-clad champions of Art-Punk sleaze who grew into dandy highwaymen, and blossomed as kings of the wild frontier. Adam and his Ants always had designs on your underwear.

❶ STAND AND DELIVER from PRINCE CHARMING
Adam's campest, most hook-laden hit lays out the Ants' plan to rob you blind and spend the money on flash clothing. Perfect pop, heavy on the drums and drama-queen guitar riffs.

❷ KINGS OF THE WILD FRONTIER from KINGS OF THE WILD FRONTIER
More of the same, all pomp and swagger, plus a neat line-dance you can use to clear the floor at weddings.

❸ STRIP from THE VERY BEST OF
All tease and swagger as Adam bumps and grinds his 1980s magnificence in your face like… well, like some overly made-up stripper.

❹ DEUTSCHER GIRLS from THE VERY BEST OF
Vintage Ant music looked back to the Weimar decadence glorified in *Cabaret*, then added a dash of shiny leather. This is the result, a tango about masochism.

❺ WONDERFUL from THE VERY BEST OF
No-nonsense love ballad crooned by a mature and oh-so-experienced Ant whose days as a pirate highwayman have eased into decadent middle age. If Tom Jones recorded it, they could both retire on the profits.

❻ WHIP IN MY VALISE from DIRK WEARS WHITE SOX
The Ants play dungeon master to Adam's master of debauch. Great title, painful puns ("who taught you to torture, who taught ya?").

❼ PHYSICAL (YOU'RE SO) from KINGS OF THE WILD FRONTIER
Sounding as if the gag has just been ripped from between his jaws, Adam gasps through a tune so sleazy it could be in a nudie show.

❽ CLEOPATRA from DIRK WEARS WHITE SOX
According to the Ants, history's best stories were the dirty ones. This is gleeful dirty sex, celebrated.

Al Spicer

Ryan Adams

Erratic, unpredictable and at times infuriating – but at his best, Ryan Adams is clearly touched by genius.

❶ COME PICK ME UP from HEARTBREAKER
"Fuck me up, steal my records, screw all my friends" – the highlight of his first and most potent solo album to date.

❷ OH MY SWEET CAROLINA from HEARTBREAKER
On the road and homesick with suitably aching backing vocals from Emmylou Harris.

❸ TO BE YOUNG (IS TO BE SAD, IS TO BE HIGH) from HEARTBREAKER
Sure it sounds like "Subterranean Homesick Blues". But then Dylan borrowed *his* song from Chuck Berry's "Too Much Monkey Business"…

❹ NEW YORK, NEW YORK from GOLD
Ryan lifts the opening riff of Pinball Wizard but takes it somewhere all his own on an exuberant hymn to the Big Apple.

❺ WHEN THE STARS GO BLUE from GOLD
Deliciously cracked vocals and a tune to die for on one of Gold's more reflective moments.

❻ MAGNOLIA MOUNTAIN from COLD ROSES
Whiskeytown-sounding opener from 2005 album that marked a major return to form.

Nigel Williamson

Aerosmith

Big, bad-ass rockers in the 1970s, Aerosmith went off the rails, then returned as one of the slickest mega-bands of the MTV era and beyond.

❶ DREAM ON from AEROSMITH
A ballad devoid of schmaltz. The build-up is masterful and singer Steven Tyler sounds suitably frayed at the edges.

❷ DUDE (LOOKS LIKE A LADY) from PERMANENT VACATION
MTV loved this one. This lady-boy identity crisis is both funny and irritatingly catchy, plus Joe Perry delivers one hell of a twangy guitar solo.

❸ HANGMAN JURY from PERMANENT VACATION
A tale of drunken murder and retribution down in the bayou. You can almost smell the stale hooch and stagnant swamp water.

❹ LAST CHILD from ROCKS
A streetwise and funky riff bounces off some of Tyler's sassiest vocals. And a great guitar solo.

❺ MAMA KIN from AEROSMITH
A salutary lesson for would-be sleazesters everywhere. This is how you write great gutter-level rockers with balls.

❻ RAG DOLL from PERMANENT VACATION
Smokin' slide guitar and Technicolor New Orleans brass collide with a monster drum track. This sounds simply immense.

❼ RATS IN THE CELLAR from ROCKS
When they hit the gas there's no stopping them. Tyler's schizophrenic vocals ricochet all over the place and the honking blues harp just adds to the chaos.

❽ SWEET EMOTION from TOYS IN THE ATTIC
A Vocoder classic. Weird wobbly voices make the intro sound like a descent into some sort of erotic nightmare. Great riff too.

Essi Berelian

Africa calling

A playlist for a whole continent? Tall order, mad idea, etc. Still, here are ten tracks that wear the classic tag with some ease.

❶ PATA PATA
MIRIAM MAKEBA from THE VERY BEST OF
They call her "Mama Africa" and her biggest hit really does transcend its South African township origins to create a joyous soundtrack for the entire continent.

❷ SOUL MAKOSSA
MANU DIBANGO from SOUL MAKOSSA
Africa doesn't get much funkier than this crossover hit from the Cameroonian veteran.

❸ LADY FELA KUTI from THE BLACK PRESIDENT
Classic Afrobeat from Nigeria's late, legendary rebel. The man who invented the whole genre.

❹ MONIE
KANDA BONGO MAN from THE VERY BEST OF
A prime slice of Congolese soukous from one of its most ebullient performers.

❺ BIRIMA YOUSSOU N'DOUR from JOKO
His biggest hit in the West was Seven Seconds, but back home in Senegal this is his best-loved anthem.

❻ LASIDAN ALI FARKA TOURE
from TALKING TIMBUKTU
One of the finest guitarists in Africa, the Malian here teams up with Ry Cooder.

❼ DIDI KHALED from KHALED
A thrilling international hit for Algeria's "king of raï" in the early 1990s.

❽ TEKERE SALIF KEITA from FOLON – THE PAST
The golden voice of Mali at his imperious best…

❾ SHUMBA THOMAS MAPFUMO from THE BEST OF
Mapfumo created the soundtrack for Zimbabwe's independence struggle with hits like this.

❿ YEKE YEKE MORY KANTÉ from THE BEST OF
Monster 1980s dancefloor hit from the singer from Guinea, and one of the records that first put African music on a global stage.

Nigel Williamson

Alice Cooper

Matching pop sensibility with house-of-horror theatrics and heavy metal thunder, Alice spat in the face of the love'n'peace generation… and his spirit spawned bastard child Marilyn Manson.

❶ HALO OF FLIES from KILLER
Alice as modern day Rasputin. And below the schlock is serious music – mad-monk dance moves and an extremely tight rhythm section.

❷ DESPERADO from KILLER
Alice as gunslinger-for-hire. He's a killer. He's a clown. His shots are clean. His shots are final.

❸ SCHOOL'S OUT from SCHOOL'S OUT
Alice as school-leaver drunkenly marching towards the principal's office. Was there ever anything more pure delinquent rock'n'roll?

❹ ELECTED from BILLION DOLLAR BABIES
Alice as demented politician, egomania laid bare. Fabulous tune, too.

❺ NO MORE MR NICE GUY
from BILLION DOLLAR BABIES
Alice plays… Alice. Only tongue in cheek, of course.

❻ ONLY WOMEN BLEED from WELCOME TO MY NIGHTMARE
Alice sings sensitive ballad shock. And it was a #1 hit for Julie Covington.

Chris Coe

Alt.country

Known by many names, this bastard, rebellious mini-genre channels a world where Nashville doesn't exist and Hank Williams had no progeny.

❶ NO DEPRESSION UNCLE TUPELO from NO DEPRESSION
According to many, the song that started it all, an updated-for-latter-times (at least by implication) Carter Family classic from the 1930s.

❷ WINDFALL SON VOLT from TRACE
Rising from Uncle Tupelo's ashes, Jay Farrar's Son Volt was soon eclipsed by Wilco – but not before releasing this alt.country classic.

❸ EMMA RICHARD BUCKNER from BLOOMED
One of many character-study gems by the oft-over-looked Buckner, delivered in his gloriously deep, sorrowful trademark drawl.

❹ HIGHWAY PATROLMAN BRUCE SPRINGSTEEN from NEBRASKA
Though technically Nebraska predates alt.country, the album shares its spirit; this tale of two brothers is its heartbreaking highlight.

❺ SUNKEN WALTZ CALEXICO from FEAST OF WIRE
Too Southwest for some, Calexico mines a rich seam of end-of-century Americana here, praying for rain "to cover the whole Western states".

❻ JOHN WALKER'S BLUES
STEVE EARLE from JERUSALEM
Written from the POV of the "American Taliban'" John Walker Lindh, Earle growls about being "Just an American boy, raised on MTV".

❼ OH MY SWEET CAROLINA
RYAN ADAMS from HEARTBREAKER
Adams was an alt.country darling before he got too big for his britches; you'll see why on this duet with the inimitable Emmylou Harris.

❽ PORTLAND, OREGON LORETTA LYNN & JACK WHITE from VAN LEAR ROSE
Timeless Loretta teams up with White Stripe Jack, hollering "Portland, Oregon and sloe gin fizz – if that ain't love then tell me what is".

❾ ATONEMENT LUCINDA WILLIAMS
from WORLD WITHOUT TEARS
Lucinda shows why she's on the outs with the Nashville establishment, howling fire and brimstone toward preachers and their flock.

❿ MISUNDERSTOOD WILCO from BEING THERE
Before Wilco got all art-rock, they turned in this furious milestone. Tweedy would like to thank you all for "nothing, nothing, nothing at all".

Hunter Slaton

Classic American Songbook

"The fundamental things apply, as time goes by…" Here is the essential canon from the American Songbook: the great popular-song composers of the 1930s and 40s.

❶ FOOLS RUSH IN BROOK BENTON from BEST OF THE DEFINITIVE AMERICAN SONGBOOK VOL 1
Early rock'n'roll? Sounds like it. But this song, with lyrics by Johnny Mercer (co-founder of Capitol Records) and music by Rube Bloom, first appeared in 1940.

❷ SMOKE GETS IN YOUR EYES SARAH VAUGHAN from AMERICAN SONGBOOK SERIES: JEROME KERN
Written by Jerome Kern (music) and Otto Harbach (lyrics), this made its debut in the 1933 musical Roberta, which starred a pre-movies Bob Hope. The song "swept the dancefloors, radio stations, and glee clubs of the country," noted the Herald Tribune.

❸ I'VE GOT YOU UNDER MY SKIN PEGGY LEE from AMERICAN SONGBOOK SERIES: COLE PORTER
This evergreen favourite of Franks Sinatra and Valli was written by Cole Porter for Born To Dance (1936), where it's sung by a Broadway star pursuing a young sailor on shore leave.

❹ NIGHT AND DAY FRANK SINATRA from BEST OF THE DEFINITIVE AMERICAN SONGBOOK VOL 2
Another by Cole Porter. The song was inspired by dancer-choreographer Nelson Barclift, with whom Porter had an intense affair. Written, appropriately enough, for the 1932 musical comedy Gay Divorce.

❺ I'LL BE SEEING YOU BING CROSBY from BEST OF THE DEFINITIVE AMERICAN SONGBOOK VOL 1
Written by Sammy Fain and Irving Kahal for the 1938 Broadway production Right This Way, this classic has demonstrated considerably more staying power than the show, which lasted all of fourteen performances.

❻ STORMY WEATHER LENA HORNE from BEST OF THE DEFINITIVE AMERICAN SONGBOOK VOL 2
Harold Arlen wrote this for the 1933 Cotton Club Revue. And it sounded just as great half a century later in Derek Jarman's movie of Shakespeare's Tempest, where it is sung by the wonderful Elizabeth Welch.

❼ BLUE MOON MEL TORME from BEST OF THE DEFINITIVE AMERICAN SONGBOOK VOL 1
It was third time lucky for this Richard Rodgers and Lorenz Hart song, composed for a Rita Hayworth project, but discarded, then re-worked as "The Bad In Every Man" (for the Clark Gable movie Manhattan Melodrama), before at last emerging as "Blue Moon".

❽ OVER THE RAINBOW JUDY GARLAND from AMERICAN SONGBOOK SERIES: HAROLD ARLEN
You have to have this Harold Arlen song on your iPod. If you've got a heart. Everybody has covered it – notably Chet Baker on horn – but the original is essential.

❾ EMBRACEABLE YOU NAT KING COLE from AMERICAN SONGBOOK SERIES: GEORGE GERSHWIN
Gershwin wrote this as an instrumental for An American in Paris, but it took flight with lyrics, becoming a #1 hit for Nat King Cole.

❿ MY FUNNY VALENTINE CHET BAKER from BEST OF THE DEFINITIVE AMERICAN SONGBOOK VOL 2
Rodgers & Hart again: a sublime creation for the kids-in-showbiz musical, Babes In Arms, starring Judy Garland and Mickey Rooney.

Ian Cranna

New American Songbook

The American Songbook refreshes each decade. Here are ten fine revisitings from the 1960s on.

❶ THESE FOOLISH THINGS BRYAN FERRY from THESE FOOLISH THINGS
Ferry looked strangely menacing in Lounge Lizard gear, but this 1973 cover of a 1936 musical revue song started a new appreciation of standards.

❷ MY HEART STOOD STILL THE MAMAS & THE PAPAS from THE MAMAS & THE PAPAS
Were harmonies ever so thrilling? It's just 1.43 mins long but this 1966 rendition of a Rodgers & Hart song was the group's finest moment.

❸ HAPPY TALK CAPTAIN SENSIBLE single
An irresistible tune, the incontrovertible logic of "If you don't have a dream, how you gonna have a dream come true?", and the punk Captain's genial looning gave this classic from South Pacific new life.

❹ I'M AN OLD COW HAND DAN HICKS & HIS HOT LICKS from RETURN TO HICKSVILLE
Johnny Mercer's witty dissection of a 1936-style cowboy who learns his songs from the radio is perfect for Hicks' eccentric vision and acoustic swing. Beautifully delivered by Lickette Naomi Eisenberg.

❺ I GET A KICK OUT OF YOU GARY SHEARSTON from ONLY LOVE SURVIVES

An inspired, sweeping violin accompaniment helped send this memorable Cole Porter cover (by an Australian singer-songwriter) up the UK charts in 1974.

❻ ANYTHING GOES HARPERS BIZARRE
from ANYTHING GOES

This Cole Porter song might have been written for the Californian quintet's close harmonies, though some of his waspish wit does get lost.

❼ I ONLY HAVE EYES FOR YOU ART GARFUNKEL from GARFUNKEL

Beautiful song, beautifully sung. Written for the 1934 musical *Dames*, this Harry Warren/Al Dubin composition launched Art's solo career with a worldwide #1.

❽ SUMMERTIME BILLY STEWART
from ONE MORE TIME: THE CHESS YEARS

R&B singer Stewart's unforgettable, Force-10 performance of this George Gershwin song (from *Porgy & Bess*) is full of soulful brrrs and chucks… guess nobody told him it's supposed to be a lullaby.

❾ MISS OTIS REGRETS KIRSTY MACCOLL
from RED HOT & BLUE

Cole Porter again, the man who told Frank Sinatra to stop singing his songs unless he stuck to the tune. He'd have had no problem with Kirsty MacColl's melancholy treatment of his 1934 melody.

❿ IT NEVER ENTERED MY MIND PEGGY LEE
from MISS WONDERFUL/DREAM STREET

Were it not for the Rodgers & Hart writing credit (1940), you would swear that Ms Lee's 1952 reworking was a Pet Shop Boys' song. A classic of wistful regret.

Ian Cranna

Tori Amos

Tori Amos often appears to be off with the fairies, but her extraordinary voice, combined with her gift for melody and a startlingly original line, has made her a Kate Bush for her generation.

❶ ME AND A GUN from LITTLE EARTHQUAKES

A harrowingly autobiographical tale of rape that is not for the squeamish.

❷ SILENT ALL THESE YEARS
from LITTLE EARTHQUAKES

Has there ever been a more startling exploration of a dysfunctional relationship?

❸ CORNFLAKE GIRL from UNDER THE PINK

Some people thought this one *was* Kate Bush when they first heard this 1994 Top 10 hit.

❹ PAST THE MISSION from UNDER THE PINK

Featuring Nine Inch Nails' nihilist Trent Reznor and recorded in the house where Manson's mob murdered Sharon Tate. Was she by any chance trying to shock us?

❺ LOSING MY RELIGION
from THE SOUNDTRACK TO HIGHER LEARNING

Amos has made a secondary career out of quirky versions of other people's songs, culminating in the all-covers album *Strange Little Girl* in 2001. This extraordinary take on an R.E.M. song was recorded for the movie *Higher Learning*.

❻ PROFESSIONAL WIDOW from BOYS FOR PELE

A striking remix by Armand Van Helden gave Amos a British #1 single with this in 1997.

❼ DOWN BY THE SEASIDE from ENCOMIUM: A TRIBUTE TO LED ZEPPELIN

Another cover, but this time as a duet with her teenage hero and the man who originally sang the song on Zep's *Physical Graffiti*, Mr Robert Plant.

❽ JAMAICA INN from THE BEEKEEPER

From her most recent 2005 album and inspired by Daphne Du Maurier's book of the same name, set in Cornwall, where Amos now lives.

Nigel Williamson

Laurie Anderson

At her best, performance artist Laurie Anderson makes the familiar strange again with a precise ear for a telling banality.

❶ FROM THE AIR from BIG SCIENCE

Whip-cracking drums and robotic saxophone lead into an in-flight announcement that morphs into a demented game of Simon Says: "Jump out of the plane. There is… no… pilot."

❷ O SUPERMAN (FOR MASSENET)
from LIVE IN NEW YORK

Back in the 1980s, we had hit singles which lasted for eight minutes and whose lyrics consisted largely of the repeated word "Ah". Tell the kids nowadays, and they won't believe you. This live version, just a week after 9/11, adds a new chill to "Here come the planes/ They're American planes/Made in America".

❸ GRAVITY'S ANGEL from MISTER HEARTBREAK
Opens in near hysteria with a tintinnabulation of bells and keening, high-pitched singing, and then pays oblique homage to Thomas Pynchon's *Gravity's Rainbow*, or at least to that book's central parabola.

❹ KOKOKU from MISTER HEARTBREAK
Hypnotic Japanoiserie, patterned with woodblock and kayagum and parrot noises.

❺ BLUE LAGOON from MISTER HEARTBREAK
A sampled voice barks like a tropical frog amid quotations from *The Tempest* and *Moby Dick*. Melville remained an obsession: Anderson would later devote an entire show and album to the Great White Whale.

❻ LANGUAGE IS A VIRUS from UNITED STATES LIVE
One of the only moments when this eight-hour performance piece broke into something that resembled a song; short, sharp, funky and driven by the theories of William Burroughs.

❼ STRANGE ANGELS from STRANGE ANGELS
Anderson's work is never actually pretty, but this comes close, with a tinkling keyboard trill and swooning pedal steel. The lyrics were inspired by a conversation with Wim Wenders about *Wings Of Desire*.

❽ SAME TIME TOMORROW from TIGHTROPE
"Is time long? Or is it wide?" It sounds like an editorial from the heyday of *Wired* magazine.

David Honigmann

Animal magic

What with all the fuss about monkeys these days, it's easy to forget that there's a whole world of exciting animals out there to sing about; fortunately, pop stars exist to remind us of the important things in life.

❶ PIGGIES THE BEATLES from THE BEATLES WHITE ALBUM
The Beatles' song of choice for Charles Manson.

❷ PINK ELEPHANTS ON PARADE SUN RA AND HIS ORCHESTRA from STAY AWAKE
In *Dumbo*, the polychromatic pachyderms were rather endearing; Sun Ra found them a whole lot scarier.

❸ TIGER MAN ELVIS PRESLEY from '68 COMEBACK SPECIAL
Elvis proclaims himself the King of the Jungle, in a song that's distantly descended from "Hound Dog".

❹ EFFERVESCING ELEPHANT SYD BARRETT from WOULDN'T YOU MISS ME?
Syd is said to have written this charming piece of doggerel in his early teens.

❺ SEE YOU LATER ALLIGATOR BOBBY CHARLES from THE CHESS BLUES-ROCK SONGBOOK
Bobby Charles never learned to play an instrument, but by setting this overheard conversational snippet to music he wrote an enduring classic.

❻ HOLY COW LEE DORSEY from THE BEST OF LEE DORSEY
Batman used to invoke sacred quadrupeds too, but he never sounded quite so funky.

❼ MONKEY MAN THE ROLLING STONES from LET IT BLEED
Mick Jagger at his prancing poutiest, proclaiming himself on this Toots & the Maytals song to be a great big monkey; who could possibly disagree?

❽ THE MONKEY DAVE BARTHOLOMEW from HIGHLIGHTS FROM CRESCENT CITY SOUL
An amazingly outspoken proto-rap from the dawn of the civil rights era, recorded in 1957.

❾ ALL THE TIRED HORSES BOB DYLAN from SELF PORTRAIT
Bizarre even by the Bobster's standards; a song that consists of a single line, endless repeated by a female chorus, whom he never deigns to join.

❿ GET READY TO RIDE THE LION TO ZION CULTURE from TWO SEVENS CLASH
Actually, I think it's going to take me a while to get ready. Why don't you ride this one, and I'll see if I can get another one later?

Greg Ward

Anti-Flag

Pittsburgh's agit-punk outfit has been churning out politically charged sounds for a decade and has upped the ante since the Bush Führer's coup d'état. They can kick up a storm, too.

❶ DIE FOR YOUR GOVERNMENT from DIE FOR YOUR GOVERNMENT
Popular live chant-along with the right mixture of mangled chords and simple chorus: "Die for your country? That's shit!".

❷ RANK-N-FILE from THE TERROR STATE
The catchy harmonies and clipped guitars with rocket flashes summon up early Clash.

❸ YOU CAN KILL THE PROTESTER BUT YOU CAN'T KILL THE PROTEST from THE TERROR STATE

Another anthem for the disillusioned and disenfranchised as guitars and vocals race each other for the cause.

❹ STARS AND STRIPES
from UNDERGROUND NETWORK

A delicious loping bass underlies the chunky chords and chanted vocals in this high-energy tirade against America's obsession with Old Glory.

❺ MIND THE G.A.T.T. from THE TERROR STATE

The band turn their anger on corporate globalization to a punk/reggae beat with a couple of brilliant pop hooks, introduced by Mr Bush himself.

Nick Edwards

Aphex Twin

A one-man case for an independent Cornwall, Richard D James makes for some fantastically uneasy listening.

❶ COME TO DADDY from COME TO DADDY EP

Play this at bedtime and you'll never be asked to babysit again. Loud, dirty, bad, scary music.

❷ WINDOWLICKER from WINDOWLICKER EP

Aphex get a bit funky. Exploring hip-hop beats, deconstructing them into their component parts and building them back up like a transformer robot, this instrumental packs more menace than a thousand lines of cheap rap boasts.

❸ CORNISH ACID from RICHARD D JAMES

You know, I think the secret of his inspiration might be in the title. Another madcap, high-speed dash round Richard's neurones.

❹ MOUNT SAINT MICHEL MIX from DRUKQS

Includes pretty much all the effects, including police sirens and, somewhere deep down, the kitchen sink.

❺ VORDHOSBN from DRUKQS

Lovely delicious acidity, maddening beats and crazy rhythms.

❻ DIDGERIDOO (LIVE IN CORNWALL 1990) from CLASSICS

It sounds like a didgeridoo at first, then before you know it, you're on your feet dancing, screaming at the dawn and throwing your clenched fists high into the sky. You might need a sit-down afterwards.

❼ FOUR from RICHARD D JAMES

Aphex drifts off into a dreamy, lost-concentration drum'n'breaks reverie before a voice from the real world drops in and calls us all suddenly back into pin-sharp focus.

❽ XTAL from SELECTED AMBIENT WORKS 85–92

Aphex Twin's most beautiful chill-out track.

Al Spicer

Arab world

Arab world music offers everything from epic string orchestras to genre-crossing rai stars.

❶ AICHA KHALED from SAHRA

Algeria's Khaled is the planet's most popular Arab singer and this 1990s hit is his most seductive.

❷ AL WARD GAMIL OUM KALTHOUM from CAIRO ROAD

Oum Kalthoum was the great diva of Egyptian music and her 1975 funeral brought millions of mourners onto the streets of Cairo. Here is a classic from her extensive songbook.

❸ YA BAHJAT ARROH SABUH FAKHRI from CAIRO ROAD

A famous song from Syria's most famous singer, who holds a *Guinness Book of Records* slot for the longest non-stop singing performance (10 hours).

❹ GAFNOUHOU MOHAMED ABDELWAHAB from CAIRO ROAD

A modernizer of Egyptian music, Abdelwahab introduced Western classical styles into Arabic music.

❺ ISHAR FAIRUZ from ISHAR

Fairuz is Lebanon's greatest singer and stands today as the acknowledged diva of the Arab world.

❻ YA BANI INSANE NASS EL GHIWANE from NASS EL GHIWANE

Fine number from a legendary Moroccan group who were to the Arab world what The Rolling Stones were to the West.

❼ NSALFIK CHEB SAHRAOUI & FADELA from RAÏ: THE BEST OF THE ORIGINAL NORTH AFRICAN GROOVES

This duo were Algeria's answer to Motown's Marvin & Tammi in the 1980s and this song remains one of rai's greatest hits.

❽ CHAB RASSI CHEIKHA REMITTI from RAÏ: THE BEST OF THE ORIGINAL NORTH AFRICAN GROOVES

Until her death aged 83 in May 2006, Cheikha Remitti was the relentless voice of Algerian roots raï.

⑨ HELALISA (NUBIAN SONG) HAMZA EL DIN from ECLIPSE

Egyptian-born Hamza El Din helped popularize Arabic oud music in the West and this meditative music demonstrates his cross-cultural appeal.

⑩ HABIBI ALI HASSAN KUBAN from THE ROUGH GUIDE TO ALI HASSAN KUBAN

The late-Egyptian musician took Nubian culture to the world, blending ancient styles with contemporary influences from Cairo pop and jazz.

Garth Cartwright

Arabesque

"Arabesque" refers to a heavily stylized type of Arabic decoration, or something that is "strangely mixed" or "fantastic". That sums up dance music's new-found love affair with contemporary Arabic music pretty much perfectly.

❶ EYE OF THE DUCK NATACHA ATLAS from MARRAKESH MISSION

An insistently funky mix of Jamaican dancehall and Egyptian bellydance, featuring ragga toasting.

❷ KALZOOM U-CEF FEATURING AMINA ANNABI from MARRAKESH MISSION

Amina covers the great Umm Kalthum, the Arab world's legendary singer, while U-Cef adds a powerful, string-laden drum & bass backdrop.

❸ ALAOUI (DIGITAL BLED DANCE MIX) L'ORCHESTRE NATIONAL DE BARBÈS from FLYING CARPET BY CLAUDE CHALLE

An epic remix from Paris-based DJ Pedro of this French–Maghrebi outfit, creating a track that manages to encapsulate Westernized Arabic dance music.

❹ BEYROUTH ÉCOEURÉE CLOTAIRE K from LEBANESE

A poignant tale of Beirut's wartorn heart played out amid hard hip-hop beats and automatic weapon fire.

❺ CHICKY OOJAMI from BELLYDANCING BREAKBEATS

A supremely funky slice of Turkish break-beat featuring the rapping of Samir Bouchakara.

❻ SOUTANBI GNAWA NJOUM EXPERIENCE FEATURING AIWA from AIWA

The gutsiest slice of *gnawa* this side of the Rif Mountains, this hypnotic track sees the Iraqi brothers hooking up with the hot new French–Moroccan collective.

Phil Meadley

Arcade Fire

The skilled songsmiths from Montréal encase perceptive, sometimes barbed, observational lyrics in a deluxe bedding of indie thrash. Passionate, intense, short on laughs.

❶ NO CARS GO from ARCADE FIRE EP

Beating several colours of surprise out of a backline of acoustic instruments, and twinning Win Butler's plaintive vocals with a cheery upbeat "Hey!" from the guitar wranglers at front of stage, this early track sums up what the band does best.

❷ HEADLIGHTS LOOK LIKE DIAMONDS from ARCADE FIRE EP

Butler booms away like the reincarnation of Joy Division's Ian Curtis on this powerful rocker that spits in the face of death.

❸ NEIGHBORHOOD 3 (POWER CUT) from FUNERAL

One of the debut album's four "Neighborhood" pieces that helped build the band's reputation as saviours of the album format. Tense and nerve-jangling as only a sudden plunge into the dark can be.

❹ WAKE UP from FUNERAL

A rousing call to action that moves from trot to canter to gallop with deceptive swiftness. A sure-fire hit at the indie disco that knocks the live crowd out, too.

❺ IN THE BACKSEAT from FUNERAL

Stunning vocals from Régine Chassagne and husband Win Butler bring the recording to a shuddering climax before drifting away into the distance.

❻ BLACK MIRROR from NEON BIBLE

Reminiscent of The Pixies at their most melancholy, "Black Mirror" pulls the last sparks of defiance from a tragically beaten body, then staggers to its feet with an air of brooding danger in its eyes. The struggle continues…

❼ KEEP THE CAR RUNNING from NEON BIBLE

Builds from a simple drone plus mandolin riff into a hard-stomping folk anthem from a country yet to be discovered.

❽ INTERVENTION from NEON BIBLE

A huge, stadium-thrilling roar of a song, with doom-laden vocals and magnificent keyboard flourishes.

❾ NEON BIBLE from NEON BIBLE

Haunting to the extent of inspiring bad dreams, this title track from the second album somehow manages to depress and inspire at the same time.

⑩ MY BODY IS A CAGE from NEON BIBLE

Terrifyingly intense, thanks again to the power of the mighty church organ, this track seals the end of the album like the lid closing on a coffin.

Al Spicer

Arctic Monkeys

Testament to the instant career-building power of the internet, Sheffield's Arctic Monkeys gate-crashed the music world in a welter of indie punk riffing and cool John-Cooper-Clark style lyrics. And it all still worked on the difficult second album.

❶ DESPAIR IN THE DEPARTURE LOUNGE from THE WHO THE FUCK ARE ARCTIC MONKEYS? EP

Just one lonesome guitar and Alex Turner's voice cracking under the emotional pressure. A perfect and achingly melancholy snapshot.

❷ FAKE TALES OF SAN FRANCISCO from WHATEVER PEOPLE SAY I AM, THAT'S WHAT I'M NOT

The Monkeys just don't like fakers. Counterfeit garage rockers from Rotheram get it in the neck in some of Turner's funniest gig-time observations.

❸ I BET YOU LOOK GOOD ON THE DANCEFLOOR from WHATEVER PEOPLE SAY I AM, THAT'S WHAT I'M NOT

"Oh there int no love no, Montague's or Capulets just banging tunes in DJ sets!" A shock chart topper boasting some impossible-to-resist lyrics.

❹ THE VIEW FROM THE AFTERNOON from WHATEVER PEOPLE SAY I AM, THAT'S WHAT I'M NOT

Surely the result of too much caffeine? Dig that terrifically edgy rhythm, not to mention the cunning gets-you-every-time false ending.

❺ WHO THE FUCK ARE ARCTIC MONKEYS? from THE WHO THE FUCK ARE ARCTIC MONKEYS? EP

The band try to engineer their own backlash. An ace riff and some enjoyably menacing playground chanting power this ironic attempt at commercial suicide.

❻ BRIANSTORM from FAVOURITE WORST NIGHTMARE

The Monkeys' difficult second album boots open the doors with this, the true tale of Brian. Dripping purest vitriol while rolling along on a wave of deep sarcasm, "Brian" gets the treatment – screaming guitars and intense drumming, hanging from the brilliant lyrical hook "Well, seeya later, innovator!"

❼ BALACLAVA from FAVOURITE WORST NIGHTMARE

More of the lads' patented sound – all clattering drums fighting it out with the guitar section.

❽ FLUORESCENT ADOLESCENT from FAVOURITE WORST NIGHTMARE

A disturbingly addictive tune, this was the main rival to "Brianstorm" for the new album's most delicious and witty track.

❾ THIS HOUSE IS A CIRCUS from FAVOURITE WORST NIGHTMARE

Welcome to the arctic monkey enclosure, where it sounds as if the party's been going on for just a few days too long. Any song that dares rhyme "circus" with "berserk as" deserves inclusion here.

⑩ THE BAD THING from FAVOURITE WORST NIGHTMARE

A sleazy, misbehaving grower detailing the joys and fears of extramarital malarky. Clever words and a seductive rhythm add to its charms.

Essi Berelian

Louis Armstrong

The first instrumental genius of jazz and the father of jazz singing, ladies and gentlemen: The Great Satchmo…

❶ HEEBIE JEEBIES from THE COMPLETE HOT FIVE AND HOT FIVE SEVEN RECORDINGS

A risky, joyful, note-perfect, wordless vocal chorus in 1926 heralds the birth of scat singing.

❷ POTATO HEAD BLUES from THE COMPLETE HOT FIVE AND HOT FIVE SEVEN RECORDINGS

Astonishingly intrepid trumpet-playing from 1927, especially in the celebrated stop-time chorus.

❸ WEST END BLUES from THE COMPLETE HOT FIVE AND HOT FIVE SEVEN RECORDINGS

This 1928 track featured a solo trumpet fanfare whose daring virtuosity bewitched jazz fans and musicians for generations to come.

❹ WEATHER BIRD from THE COMPLETE HOT FIVE AND HOT FIVE SEVEN RECORDINGS

A veritable joust in 1928 between Armstrong and pianist Earl Hines, in which there's no clear winner but much thrilling improvised music.

❺ TIGHT LIKE THIS from THE COMPLETE HOT FIVE AND HOT FIVE SEVEN RECORDINGS

Offbeat verbal exchanges between Louis and arranger Don Redman don't distract from Armstrong's powerful trumpet choruses on this 1928 track.

⑥ MAHOGANY HALL STOMP from THE COMPLETE HOT FIVE AND HOT FIVE SEVEN RECORDINGS

By 1929 Armstrong had settled into commercial routines somewhat removed from the New Orleans jazz feeling of his earlier work, but this rollicking track is an exception.

⑦ (WHAT DID I DO TO BE SO) BLACK AND BLUE from LOUIS ARMSTRONG IN NEW YORK

Lyricist Andy Razaf's modest cry for racial equality ("my only sin is in my skin") delivered to plaintive perfection by Louis in 1929.

⑧ ROCKIN' CHAIR from COMPLETE LOUIS ARMSTRONG ON RCA

An amusing, highly musical call-and-response vocal routine between Louis and the brilliantly laconic trombonist Jack Teagarden.

⑨ HESITATING BLUES from PLAYS W.C. HANDY

A highlight of a great later-period album from 1954, in which Louis eschews commercial settings for a gutsy examination of classic material close to his roots.

⑩ THERE'S NO YOU from LOUIS ARMSTRONG MEETS OSCAR PETERSON

Accompanied only by guitarist Herb Ellis in 1957, Louis shows how affecting his cement-mixer voice could be on a delicate pop melody.

Chris Ingham

Art for art's sake

When it comes to creativity, the canvas and the stave are virtually kindred spirits, so it is no surprise that songwriters often highlight the lives and works of painters.

❶ VINCENT (STARRY, STARRY NIGHT) DON MCLEAN from AMERICAN PIE

Reading a biography of Van Gogh prompted McLean to pen this poignant tribute. Nigh on every line in the verses points to one of the artist's works.

❷ PICASSO VISITA EL PLANETA DE LOS SIMIOS ADAM & THE ANTS from PRINCE CHARMING

A spaced-out slice of punky kitsch – kudos for that title – that stomps through 31/2 minutes of barminess. The hero-worship has since come full circle with Floridian artist Beatriz Monteavaro basing works on Adam and Pablo's intergalactic exploits. An English-language version of the track, as on the original demo, was released on 2000's *Antbox*.

❸ INTERIORS (SONG FOR WILLEM DE KOONING)/ HIS LAST PAINTING/DOOR TO THE RIVER MANIC STREET PREACHERS from EVERYTHING MUST GO/KNOW YOUR ENEMY/FOREVER DELAYED

Nicky Wire has penned a clutch of lyrics about the Dutch-born abstract expressionist painter. De Kooning continued to paint even as his health degenerated from Alzheimer's, an aspect of his work that "His Last Painting" discusses in melodious fashion.

❹ MICHELANGELO EMMYLOU HARRIS from RED DIRT GIRL

Influenced by the poetry of Carl Sandburg, Harris said the scenes she unravels in this haunting piece came to her in a dream.

❺ ANDY WARHOL DAVID BOWIE from HUNKY DORY

The spoken studio intro yields to a wonderfully moody acoustic riff and Bowie's musings on his artist friend. Warhol supposedly replied "I like your shoes" when Bowie asked what he thought of the track.

❻ MONA LISA NAT KING COLE from THE WORLD OF NAT KING COLE

Comparing the singer's love to the painting, this Oscar-winning song appeared in 1950 Alan Ladd flick *Captain Carey, USA*. The ode was made famous by Cole, but covered by Elvis Presley and Willie Nelson.

❼ PICASSO'S LAST WORDS (DRINK TO ME) WINGS from BAND ON THE RUN

Actor Dustin Hoffman told McCartney that in his final hours Picasso asked those with him to "drink to me, drink to my health – you know I can't drink any longer", a refrain adopted in this bouncy song.

❽ MAX ERNST/MAX ERNST'S DREAM MISSION OF BURMA from SIGNALS, CALLS & MARCHES EP/ONOFFON

Post-punk agit-rockers MoB's two tributes to the pioneer of surrealism, weaving shouty indignance with cut-and-paste feedback experimentation on the former, and spun floaty guitar loops on the latter.

Ed Wright

The Associates

Supernaturally talented singer and lyricist Billy MacKenzie and multi-instrumentalist Alan Rankine created intoxicating, epic music.

❶ PARTY FEARS TWO from SULK

This four-minute melodrama with its memorable keyboard hook showcases Billy's voice at the height of its expressive power.

❷ SKIPPING from SULK
A vocal intro gallops into this energetic track, with chords blooming from unidentified instruments and a Sean Connery impersonation from Billy.

❸ LOVE HANGOVER from SULK
Billy sprawls and soars through this Diana Ross cover, hitting impossible notes with langourous ease.

❹ PAPER HOUSE from AFFECTIONATE PUNCH (1982 REMIX)
Piano arpeggios burst like sunshine through fidgetting guitars, while Billy meanders caressingly towards octave-straddling, goosebumps-inducing coda.

❺ A SEVERE BOUT OF CAREER INSECURITY from RADIO 1 SESSIONS
Deranged kitchen-sink drama set to a loose but insistently energetic musical backdrop.

❻ A GIRL NAMED PROPERTY
from FOURTH DRAWER DOWN
Operatic, intensely emotional track of bleak beauty.

Doug Hall

Atlantic soul

Thanks largely to Jerry Wexler, Atlantic became one of the great soul labels.

❶ DROWN IN MY OWN TEARS RAY CHARLES from RAY CHARLES LIVE
As Peter Guralnick observes in his classic book, *Sweet Soul Music*, this is it.

❷ I FOUND A LOVE THE FALCONS from ATLANTIC R&B VOL 5
Wilson Pickett on incendiary lead vocals, Robert Ward on blistering Magnatone guitar: now just what more do you need?

❸ UP ON THE ROOF THE DRIFTERS from ATLANTIC R&B VOL 5
When this old world start's getting you down, all you have to do is put on this Gerry Goffin/Carole King classic.

❹ YOU DON'T MISS YOUR WATER WILLIAM BELL from ATLANTIC R&B VOL 5
Before there was Otis Redding, there was the understated and underrated Bell, a fine balladeer.

❺ MAKING LOVE AT THE DARK END OF THE STREET
CLARENCE CARTER from TESTIFYIN'/THIS IS CLARENCE CARTER
Carter's mainly spoken take on this classic Dan Penn/Chips Moman song is as comical, dirty and special.

❻ MERCY MERCY DON COVAY from MERCY!/SEE-SAW
Vocal model for Mick Jagger on a self-penned song with an unforgettable hook.

❼ SOME KIND OF WONDERFUL SOUL BROTHERS SIX from SOCK IT TO 'EM SOUL
Not the Drifters' tune, this is classic high-octane stomping soul. It has been covered by, among others, Grand Funk Railroad and Joss Stone.

❽ MEMPHIS SOUL STEW KING CURTIS from ATLANTIC R&B VOL 7
The regal sax supremo talks through the musical ingredients in a recipe for soul. Just give me some of that fatback bass.

❾ THE GHETTO DONNY HATHAWAY from ATLANTIC R&B VOL 7
The title is simply repeated over a moody electric-keyboard groove, but the music speaks volumes.

❿ CLEAN UP WOMAN BETTY WRIGHT from ATLANTIC R&B VOL 8
Wright warns women against taking their man for granted over an irresistible Little Beaver guitar riff.

Neil Foxlee

Australian iconic

These are the songs instantly recognizable to Australians as "theirs": the songs that conjure a shared sense of place, of time, of feeling. As opposed to "Waltzing Matilda", say, written around 32 BC about a sheep-stealing hobo.

❶ CATTLE AND CANE THE GO BETWEENS from BELLAVISTA TERRACE: THE BEST OF THE GO BETWEENS
Grant McLennan's memory wasn't wasted: his lyrics gorgeously evoke a tropical Queensland childhood with "I recall a schoolboy coming home through fields of cane to a house of tin and timber and in the sky a rain of falling cinders."

❷ MY ISLAND HOME CHRISTINE ANU from STYLIN' UP
Neil Murray's homesick song for the Aboriginal Warumpi Band from the red sand of the western desert takes on new meaning with Anu, a Torres Strait islander from the deep North.

❸ THROW YOUR ARMS AROUND ME HUNTERS AND COLLECTORS from HUMAN FRAILTY
One of the blokiest, hard-driving bands of all time slow-builds to an anthemic chorus and the failproof line "I will kiss you in four places." If you insist, big boy.

④ FROM ST KILDA TO KINGS CROSS PAUL KELLY from SONGS FROM THE SOUTH.
Musical poet Paul Kelly's tribute to Melbourne would "give you all of Sydney Harbour, all that land and all that water, for that one sweet promenade (The Esplanade, St Kilda)".

⑤ BETTER BE HOME SOON CROWDED HOUSE from TEMPLE OF LOW MEN
Perfect yearning ballad from the part-Aussie outfit led by Kiwi Neil Finn.

⑥ SOUNDS OF THEN THIS IS AUSTRALIA GANGGAJANG from THE ESSENTIAL GANGGAJANG
Moody ode to humidity.

⑦ POWER AND THE PASSION MIDNIGHT OIL from POWER AND THE PASSION: BEST OF MIDNIGHT OIL
The Oils' full-on wake-up call to a complacent Australia warning against sunbaking while "wasting away in paradise" as a new state of the USA.

⑧ WIDE OPEN ROAD THE TRIFFIDS from BORN SANDY DEVOTIONAL
The title is about the melancholy of being alone, but also nods at long drives (the band was from Western Australia). From one side of Australia to the other is about the same distance as Dublin to Moscow.

⑨ I STILL CALL AUSTRALIA HOME PETER ALLEN from THE VERY BEST OF PETER ALLEN THE BOY FROM DOWN UNDER
The Australian national anthem is so crap, people turned to this harmless, piano-pounding piffle. It can still rouse pissed expats.

⑩ EAGLE ROCK DADDY COOL from EAGLE ROCK
Irresistible 1970s hippy blues-pop, so old the video's in black and white. Still, it consistently tops Australian song polls.

Kaz Cooke

Awopbopaloobop alopbambboom

As Little Richard knew so well, if you can't think of the right words for your song, you can always just make some up.

① BE-BOP-A-LULA GENE VINCENT from ONLY ROCK'N'ROLL
Assuming Alvin Stardust hasn't permanently spoilt the black leather look for you , Gene Vincent's panting 1959 anthem remains the essence of rock'n'roll.

② DA DOO RON RON THE CRYSTALS from LEADERS OF THE PACK 1963
Phil Spector could pack plenty of punch and a timeless teen saga into two minutes and twenty seconds, though it's still not entirely clear what went on "when he walked me home".

③ DIDDY WAH DIDDY CAPTAIN BEEFHEART from THE CALIFORNIA CONNECTION
She may have told him her name was "Diddy Wah Diddy", but what's the betting he'll be able to find her in the phone book?

④ DIGA DIGA DOO THE MILLS BROTHERS WITH DUKE ELLINGTON & HIS ORCHESTRA from POP MUSIC – THE EARLY YEARS
A delightfully ditzy Jazz-Age ditty, from 1932, decked out with some nice wahs-wahs on the trumpet for good measure.

⑤ DOO WAH DIDDY MANFRED MANN from AGES OF MANN
So let's get this straight? You say there you were, just walking down the street, when she came up and walked next to you singing "Doo Wah Diddy"? Do you honestly expect the jury to believe that?

⑥ MAHNA MAHNA THE MUPPETS from MUPPET HITS
Has anyone, anywhere, ever been able to resist this song?

⑦ OB-LA-DI, OB-LA-DA THE BEATLES from THE BEATLES WHITE ALBUM
And has anyone, anywhere, ever been able to stand this one?

⑧ FA-FA-FA-FA-FA OTIS REDDING from THE OTIS REDDING ANTHOLOGY
Otis could of course make absolutely anything sound heart-wrenching – and it proves it here, kicking off the song with seventeen "fa"s in succession and barely letting up thereafter.

⑨ UM, UM, UM, UM, UM, UM MAJOR LANCE from THE SOUND OF THE CITY – CHICAGO
Though Northern Soul favorite Major Lance couldn't outdo Otis in every respect, the chorus here undeniably consists of 24 "um"s in a row.

⑩ ZUNGGUZUNGG-UGUZUNGGUZENG YELLOWMAN from ZUNGGUZUNGG-UGUZUNGGUZENG
Reggae DJ Yellowman was so called because he was a yellow man; this 1984 dancehall smash is a little harder to decipher.

Greg Ward

Kevin Ayers

He was Bryan Ferry with cool, Noël Coward on acid. Yet in an age that liked its big rock numbers, fame steadfastly eluded Kevin Ayers, the cultish hippy, with his songs of hedonistic, psychedelic whimsy. He's worth rediscovering, not least to hear the guitar work from a young Mike Oldfield.

❶ THE LADY RACHEL from JOY OF A TOY
Ah, 1968: shades of the time, when earnest Pre-Raphaelite young men invested would-be lovers with such titles. But this was a lovely song, on Ayers' first solo album, and would become one of his live standards.

❷ MAY I from SHOOTING AT THE MOON
A sensuous crooner that opened an unusually experimental and jazz-fuelled album. A seductive French version appeared on the *Odd Ditties* album.

❸ THE OYSTER AND THE FLYING FISH
from SHOOTING AT THE MOON
A duet with Bridget St John, with peculiar folk overtones, this retains heaps of charm.

❹ WHATEVERSHEBRINGSWESING
from WHATEVERSHEBRINGSWESING
Mike Oldfield's staggeringly beautiful guitar solo is a delight to behold.

❺ STRANGER IN BLUE SUEDE SHOES
from WHATEVERSHEBRINGSWESING
A ramshackle slice of wit on the joys of herbal indulgence, when it seemed revolutionary.

❻ DIDN'T FEEL LONELY TILL I THOUGHT OF YOU from
THE CONFESSIONS OF DR DREAM
A last bid for stardom, the *Dr Dream* album stands up nicely, and nowhere better than on this song, with its doo-wop chorus, swaggering lyrics and Ollie Halsall's virtuoso guitar break.

Greg Neale

B

Bacharach & David

Burt Bacharach and Hal David – one of the great songwriting partnerships – met working at New York's legendary Brill Building (for more on which see the Brill Building list). There are numerous Bacharach/David anthologies, and you get a whole raft on classic Dionne Warwick compilations. But here's a medley of gems.

❶ DO YOU KNOW THE WAY TO SAN JOSÉ
DIONNE WARWICK from DIONNE WARWICK SINGS THE BACHARACH & DAVID SONGBOOK
Dionne Warwick – the greatest of all Bacharach/David interpreters – sings this so light it almost floats away on the melody.

❷ CASINO ROYALE HERB ALPERT & THE TIJUANA BRASS from DEFINITIVE HITS
The main hook is built around glorious bright parping stabs of brass, and the maracas midway are sublime.

❸ TRAINS AND BOATS AND PLANES
FOUNTAINS OF WAYNE from OUT OF STATES
The NYC popsters make this track entirely their own, with a cool acoustic treatment. It never made sense before, but here it is a miniature classic.

❹ I SAY A LITTLE PRAYER ARETHA FRANKLIN from RESPECT
Aretha made this hers, positively smouldering with soul over a cool Motown-style vibe.

❺ THE LOOK OF LOVE DUSTY SPRINGFIELD from AT HER VERY BEST
Delivered in a smoky, jazz-bar style, Dusty really sounds smitten, and her crystalline vocals contrast beautifully with the understated sax solo.

❻ (THE MAN WHO SHOT) LIBERTY VALANCE GENE PITNEY from THE PLATINUM COLLECTION
Romance, heroism and a deadly Wild West showdown – this concise melodrama has it all.

❼ (THEY LONG TO BE) CLOSE TO YOU THE CARPENTERS
Just why do birds suddenly appear? The Carpenters' immaculate explanation is so sweet it could make your teeth fall out. Dionne Warwick did it more elegantly, perhaps, but this remains definitive.

❽ TWENTY FOUR HOURS FROM TULSA
GENE PITNEY from THE PLATINUM COLLECTION
Not the most obviously recognizable Bacharach & David number, but Pitney was perfect for this bitter tale of infidelity set to a mariachi-style arrangement.

❾ WALK ON BY DIONNE WARWICK from DIONNE WARWICK SINGS THE BACHARACH & DAVID SONGBOOK
Another classic tale of heartbreak, this is arguably Dionne's finest song: pure emotion, with its message of fragile defiance perfectly set against the smooth piano and trumpet hooks.

❿ WHAT'S NEW PUSSYCAT? TOM JONES from THE PLATINUM EDITIION
The swaggering bar-room piano is genius and Jones's fruity, love-addled bellow one of the iconic pop performances of the 1960s.

Essi Berelian

Bad men

If you believe Flannery O'Connor, a good man is hard to find. But if you're looking for a bad man? Just turn on your stereo.

❶ YOU'RE NO GOOD LINDA RONSTADT from HEART LIKE A WHEEL
Ronstadt doesn't exactly go for specifics when she skewers the subject of this song, but maybe that isn't a requirement. Hear that catch in her voice? Feel the set of her jaw? The lady knows what she's talking about, and she knows how to interpret a song.

❷ YOU'RE SO VAIN CARLY SIMON from NO SECRETS
You want specifics? Carly Simon's got specifics, right down to the apricot scarf on her *cad du jour*. In a jilted, knowing alto, she paints her portrait of a bad man. Vanity is one of the seven deadly sins, after all. Plus, he cheats.

❸ HEY JOE JIMI HENDRIX from ARE YOU EXPERIENCED?
There are bad men and then there are bad men. Jimi Hendrix sings low and mysterious over the psychedelic tones of his one-of-a-kind guitar. Where is Joe going with that gun in his hand? It's probably meant as a rhetorical question but Joe answers it, and then some.

b

❹ 32-20 BLUES ROBERT JOHNSON from ROBERT JOHNSON: THE COMPLETE RECORDINGS
Just to show "Hey Joe" was not without precedent. The legendary Robert Johnson keeps his woman in line with a pistol on his chest and a guitar by his side.

❺ BAD, BAD LEROY BROWN JIM CROCE from PHOTOGRAPHS AND MEMORIES: HIS GREATEST HITS
He was a soft-peddler in the 1970s, see "Time In A Bottle" but in "Leroy Brown," Jim Croce created an edgy character. Bad? You bet. But by the end of the song, Leroy is road kill. Is there a moral? Perhaps. Do "old King Kong" and "junkyard dog" rhyme? Not quite.

❻ 6 'N THE MORNIN' ICE-T from RHYME PAYS
Like much bad-boy street music, Ice T's gangsta rap is highly nuanced, a mix of gallows humour with on-the-street realities: drinking, stealing, pimping and (self-justified) killing. A song with a body count. Is there a moral? Perhaps. Do "dough" and "hoe" rhyme? Yes!

❼ MAMA HE TREATS YOUR DAUGHTER MEAN RUTH BROWN from THE ESSENTIALS: RUTH BROWN
Ruth Brown's lovely, brass vocals front a toe-tappin' blues about a no-good husband who's ready for the boot. Lazy, crazy and mean, he's a bad man.

❽ GOODBYE EARL THE DIXIE CHICKS from FLY
The Dixie Chick's Earl treats his woman mean, too, but when things gets physical, the song's victim and her best friend commit a (self-justified) murder by way of poisoned black-eyed peas. The Chicks bury him in a chorus of harmony and sass.

❾ PROBLEM CHILD AC/DC from DIRTY DEEDS DONE DIRT CHEAP
This is exactly the type of song you would expect to hear from a grown man in a school uniform. AC/DC guitarist Angus Young bangs out the beat for every parent's nightmare; Bon Scott lion-roars the lyrics. Stealing, drinking, fighting and (not justified) killing.

❿ SYMPATHY FOR THE DEVIL THE ROLLING STONES from BEGGARS BANQUET
The ultimate bad man as personified by Mick Jagger, who apparently made a deal with the guy. This Stones classic gives the devil his due, with just the right amounts of swagger and sin.

Madelyn Rosenberg

Badly Drawn Boy

Singer-songwriter Damon Gough, aka Badly Drawn Boy, is both bouncy and bittersweet –

an inspired choice to provide the soundtrack to the movie of Nick Hornby's *About A Boy*.

❶ THE SHINING
from THE HOUR OF BEWILDERBEAST
The horns portray the rising sun mentioned in the lyrics and the strings are persuasive. One of the great album openers.

❷ A PEAK YOU REACH from ABOUT A BOY
Energetic keyboards and percussion – all the sounds you need when driving.

❸ SOMETHING TO TALK ABOUT
from ABOUT A BOY
A beautifully constructed song that manages to swing along tightly.

❹ SILENT SIGH from ABOUT A BOY
A tune driven by a piano riff and a solid beat that is crying out for football montage.

❺ HAVE YOU FED THE FISH?
from HAVE YOU FED THE FISH?
The chorus/title line finally makes sense, before the bounciest of riffs kicks in.

❻ YOU WERE RIGHT from HAVE YOU FED THE FISH?
BDB at his storytelling best, observing that songs are only "the soundtrack to a life".

❼ ANOTHER DEVIL DIES
from ONE PLUS ONE IS ONE
After the quiet piano opening, the passion is over-whelming and almost out of control.

❽ THE WAY THINGS USED TO BE
from BORN IN THE U.K.
Simple, dreamy and almost Dylan-esque, the album's odd-track-out flows effortlessly. Back to his best.

Daniel Crewe

Chet Baker

Chet wasn't the nicest man, by all accounts, but was there ever a cooler while jazz horn player or jazz crooner?

❶ MY FUNNY VALENTINE from THE COMPLETE GERRY MULLIGAN QUARTET WITH CHET BAKER
Achingly lonely version of the Rodgers and Hart classic, which established Baker as the most popular trumpeter of his generation.

Robyn Hitchcock's
The Band

Psychedelic songsmith ROBYN HITCHCOCK (see his own playlist) has been called the human jukebox for his ability to play any song, any style. For this book, he sent in an entry for The Band: "In Levon Helm, Richard Manuel and Rick Danko, Robbie Robertson had three great character actors to sing his songs. Garth Hudson was the alchemist who found melodies on keyboards and horn that hadn't ever been found before. Though Levon contends that the songs were not Robertson's as much as Robbie claims, no one could accuse Robbie of overplaying."

❶ CALEDONIA MISSION
from MUSIC FROM BIG PINK
A meandering, autumnal verse leads into a funky chorus that is peppered with Richard's gleeful piano, scurrying around like a squirrel.

❷ UP ON CRIPPLE CREEK from THE BAND
Levon sang the libido tracks, mostly, and here he puffs up like an Arkansas toad in anticipation of Bessie down in Lake Charles, Louisiana.

❸ WHISPERING PINES from THE BAND
Richard's eerie, lonesome melody foreshadows his own suicide in a motel in 1983. Robbie's lyrics evoke a very desolate coast.

❹ W.S. WALCOTT MEDICINE SHOW
from STAGE FRIGHT
By contrast, Levon leads the boys through a leering carnival groove with no regrets at all. Garth's

saxophone is so buoyant, everything a horn break should be and usually isn't.

❺ CHEST FEVER from MUSIC FROM BIG PINK
A murky song about some Scandinavians getting excited in a dairy that was preceded live by Garth's keyboard opus "The Genetic Method".

❻ KING HARVEST from THE BAND
Ray Bradbury meets Flannery O'Connor under a big orange moon while the weather holds its breath. "My horse Jethro, well he went mad," sings Rick, and you know it did.

❼ IT MAKES NO DIFFERENCE from SOUTHERN CROSS
Rick was the goofiest but also the most poignant of The Band's three vocalists. A requiem for a still-bleeding relationship, Rick sings this in straight pain – no accusation, all hurt.

❽ THE SHAPE I'M IN from STAGE FRIGHT
Richard leads the band through a fun catalogue of woe. Garth's shapes on the keyboard are a good example of how you hear only the sound he makes, not the instrument that he's playing.

❾ DON'T DO IT from THE LAST WALTZ
Not written by The Band, but the last thing played by them at "The Last Waltz", it's punctuated by Robbie's terse, flaming guitar and is one of their most rockin' recordings.

❿ ALL LA GLORY from STAGE FRIGHT
Levon sings this lullaby so sweet and unsentimental, all honey and no sacharine, falling leaves at bedtime and a painkiller tomorrow. Another masterful solo from Garth on some unfathomable instrument.

❷ WALKIN' SHOES from THE COMPLETE GERRY MULLIGAN QUARTET WITH CHET BAKER
Archetypical West Coast wizardry from the trend-setting piano-less Mulligan Quartet, with Gerry and Chet weaving contrapuntal magic.

❸ MAID IN MEXICO from CHET BAKER QUARTET WITH RUSS FREEMAN
Enchanting Latin ditty that changes gear to steaming 4/4, from the 1953 quartet, featuring pianist Freeman.

❹ BUT NOT FOR ME from CHET BAKER SINGS
The first cut on Chet's famous 1954 10-inch album, revealing his unique vocal gifts: soft, smooth and pretty as a lady.

❺ SAD WALK from CHET BAKER IN PARIS
An alluring Bob Zieff mood piece featuring Chet's short-lived 1955 quartet which included pianist Dick Twardzik who died of an overdose days after this session.

6 I'VE NEVER BEEN IN LOVE BEFORE
from CHET BAKER SINGS

A highlight of Chet's second all-vocal session from 1956, this *Guys And Dolls* ballad has never sounded so wistful and innocent, and Baker's trumpet solo is heartbreaking.

7 DO IT THE HARD WAY from CHET BAKER SINGS IT COULD HAPPEN TO YOU

An obscure Rodgers and Hart throwaway is subjected to Chet's polite and immaculate scat.

8 E.S.P. from ONCE UPON A SUMMERTIME

A surprisingly muscular and inventive approach to Wayne Shorter's elliptical tune, from an excellent 1977 album.

9 I WAITED FOR YOU
from THE TOUCH OF YOUR LIPS

From the scores of European albums made in his last decade, the 1979 trio with Niels-Henning Ørsted Pedersen (bass) and Doug Raney (guitar) in Denmark stands out for sheer beauty and musicality.

10 ALMOST BLUE from LET'S GET LOST

Written with Baker in mind by fan Elvis Costello, Chet unsurprisingly manages to make perfect sense of this peculiar, brooding song in 1982.

Chris Ingham

Banned songs

Ever since people have been making music, other people have been trying to suppress it. Many of the sex, drugs and violence bans are comic, although Thomas Mapfumo reminds us of the more serious ramifications of censorship. Here are ten favourites they didn't want you to hear, with a special prize for Link Wray, who managed to get an instrumental banned…

1 RELAX FRANKIE GOES TO HOLLYWOOD from WELCOME TO THE PLEASURE DOME

Responding to the urging of DJ Mike Read, the BBC banned "Relax" on grounds of obscenity ("Relax, Don't do it, When you wanna come"). It promptly went to #1 in the UK in 1984, selling two million copies.

2 SMACK MY BITCH UP THE PRODIGY from FAT OF THE LAND

The "Firestarter" video had already been banned. Then along came this sonic thunderstorm of electro-thrash.

In the UK the BBC insisted that they weren't banning the song, merely that its airplay had been "limited". In America, Wal-Mart and K-Mart both refused to stock the parent album – and it still went to #1 .

3 JE T'AIME … MOI NON PLUS SERGE GAINSBOURG AND JANE BIRKIN from JANE BIRKIN & SERGE GAINSBOURG

The first ever UK #1 to be banned, but if you've ever tried translating the French lyric you'll know it's more hilarious than erotic ("I come between your kidneys"!).

4 GOD SAVE THE QUEEN THE SEX PISTOLS from NEVER MIND THE BOLLOCKS, HERE'S THE SEX PISTOLS

"God save the Queen, the fascist regime, they made you a moron, a potential H-bomb" – banned by the BBC and by high street retailers, with the Pistols themselves arrested when they played it from a boat on the River Thames. Those were the days…

5 STORMY MONDAY T-BONE WALKER from BLUES MASTERS: THE VERY BEST OF T-BONE WALKER

Not quite a banned record as such, but when Pat Boone covered it his record company demanded he change the lyric "drinkin' wine" to "drinking Coca-Cola".

6 LOVE FOR SALE BILLIE HOLIDAY from THE VERY BEST OF BILLIE HOLIDAY

ABC network banned Lady Day's version of the Cole Porter song because it was about prostitution.

7 RUMBLE LINK WRAY from THE BEST OF LINK WRAY

Some achievement this – American radio banned this instrumental for its incitement to violence.

8 NDOYA MARASHA (I'M MAD AS HELL) THOMAS MAPFUMO from RISE UP

Mapfumo was censored by Zimbabwean president Robert Mugabe – just as he once had been by Rhodesian Prime Minister, Ian Smith.

9 LET'S SPEND THE NIGHT TOGETHER THE ROLLING STONES from 40 LICKS

The Ed Sullivan show insisted the lyric was changed to "let's spend some time together" and, rather tamely, Mick Jagger agreed.

10 THE LEDGE THE REPLACEMENTS from PLEASED TO MEET ME

Banned by MTV as likely to encourage teen suicide.

Nigel Williamson

Syd Barrett

Original lead singer, lead guitarist and principal songwriter of Pink Floyd, Syd's deviously playful acid visions remain pinnacles of psychedelic rock, even if the ragged drug casualty solo work that followed his 1968 exit from the Floyd wasn't quite all the stuff of legend.

❶ SEE EMILY PLAY PINK FLOYD from RELICS
Swooping slide guitar, exotic organ and a definitive lyrical portrait of a flower child.

❷ ARNOLD LAYNE PINK FLOYD from RELICS
Pink Floyd's debut 45 was this whimsically unsettling tale of a suburban pervert: "Arnold Layne, don't do it ay-gayne!"

❸ ASTRONOMY DOMINE PINK FLOYD from PIPER AT THE GATES OF DAWN
Pink Floyd's journey to the heart of the sun starts with this pulsating space rocker, the scat vocals descending like asteroids hurtling through the cosmos.

❹ LUCIFER SAM PINK FLOYD from PIPER AT THE GATES OF DAWN
Early Barrett/Floyd at their most devilish, propelled by surf-music-from-hell guitar twang, edgy intimations of the occult and maybe Syd's own oncoming madness.

❺ FLAMING PINK FLOYD from PIPER AT THE GATES OF DAWN
Barrett's Floyd at their most ingratiatingly childish, making interstellar travel sound easy.

❻ MATILDA MOTHER PINK FLOYD from PIPER AT THE GATES OF DAWN
Another catchy, otherworldly Barrett fairytale – or is it, with that evil mother leaving the singer/child eternally waiting for the story's end?

❼ BIKE PINK FLOYD from PIPER AT THE GATES OF DAWN
A Lewis Carroll-like dive into childhood fantasies, utterly subverted by the frightening climax of discordant crashes and incessantly clacking ducks.

❽ GOLDEN HAIR from THE MADCAP LAUGHS
Enchanting adaptation of James Joyce's poem, its lingering, almost lethargic sensuality evoking a temptation whose fulfilment lies permanently just out of reach.

❾ MILKY WAY from OPEL
Solo Syd was at his bounciest and most haphazardly likable on this street-busker-as-space-cowboy outtake.

❿ WOULDN'T YOU MISS ME (DARK GLOBE) from OPEL
A plaintive folky dirge on the surface, a moving bemoaning of loss of identity underneath.

Richie Unterberger

The Beach Boys

The Beach Boys produced the most perfectly sung, melodically sophisticated 1960s California Dream pop, before the dream turned to nightmare with the crash of leader Brian Wilson's psyche.

❶ I GET AROUND from ALL SUMMER LONG
Dizzying vocal harmonies, chugging guitar and organ, and an unabashed celebration of the 1960s Southern Californian teenage lifestyle.

❷ GOOD VIBRATIONS from SMILEY SMILE
An early zenith of psychedelic pop, with an ebullient love song of great sexy tenderness under its unworldly theremin chords and exquisitely layered production.

❸ DON'T WORRY BABY from SHUT DOWN VOL 2
Some of the finest lead falsetto/group harmony blends in all of rock'n'roll, and one of the first hints of Brian Wilson's depthless vulnerability.

❹ GOD ONLY KNOWS from PET SOUNDS
A love song that becomes a hymn to the deity of Love itself, courtesy of its heavenly orchestral production.

❺ SURFIN' U.S.A. from SURFIN' U.S.A.
Chuck Berry gets dressed in multi-part harmony and heads to the beach on the greatest vocal surf hit of all.

❻ THE WARMTH OF THE SUN from SHUT DOWN VOL 2
An overlooked early ballad with one of the group's most supremely seductive melodies, blurring together melancholy and golden optimism as one.

❼ CAROLINE, NO from PET SOUNDS
Yes, it's an ode to lost innocence (and lost long hair) – but has heartbreak ever been so pretty?

❽ DON'T TALK PUT YOUR HEAD ON MY SHOULDER from PET SOUNDS
The spookiest piece of rock-cum-chamber music from Pet Sounds, the simulated heartbeats echoing like an oncoming visitation from Kingdom Come.

❾ SURFER GIRL from SURFER GIRL
Later Beach Boys love songs might have got more sophisticated in both production and lyric, but few were as suffused with lovely longing.

Brian Wilson's
Tributes

The two great geniuses of 1960s American pop music were Beach Boys' mastermind BRIAN WILSON and Phil Spector – and here the former pays generous tribute to the latter with no fewer than five of his "wall-of-sound" productions in his all-time Top 10.

❶ BE MY BABY THE RONETTES from BEST OF

❷ YOU'VE LOST THAT LOVIN' FEELIN' THE RIGHTEOUS BROTHERS from BEST OF

❸ RIVER DEEP MOUNTAIN HIGH IKE & TINA TURNER from RIVER DEEP MOUNTAIN HIGH

❹ DA DOO RON RON THE CRYSTALS from BEST OF

❺ WALKING IN THE RAIN THE RONETTES from BEST OF

❻ (I CAN'T GET NO) SATISFACTION THE ROLLING STONES from BIG HITS (HIGH TIDE...)

❼ HEY JUDE THE BEATLES from MAGICAL MYSTERY TOUR

❽ THE LONG AND WINDING ROAD THE BEATLES from LET IT BE

❾ WHAT A FOOL BELIEVES THE DOOBIE BROTHERS from MINUTE BY MINUTE

❿ REALLY WANNA KNOW YOU GARY WRIGHT from THE RIGHT PLACE

---

❿ YOU STILL BELIEVE IN ME from PET SOUNDS
Like a choirboy ensemble grown adult, the Boys offer a beautifully harmonized sermon that beams with optimism and redemption.

Richie Unterberger

The Beastie Boys

From thrashy teen punks to 1980s bad boys to style-magazine statesmen, the Beastie path has been a chequered one. But they've always been extremely good at shouting over the drums.

❶ EGG RAID ON MOJO from SOME OLD BULLSHIT
The embryonic Beasties (with a token Beastie Girl on bass) sound just like any other bunch of kids who like Minor Threat and Black Flag: Beasties punk rock at its most authentic.

❷ FIGHT FOR YOUR RIGHT TO PARTY from LICENSE TO ILL
Spoilt rich kids have rarely sounded so feral as on this snotty, spotty pyschodrama: a *Lord Of The Flies* for 1980s American teenagers.

❸ POSSE IN EFFECT from LICENSE TO ILL
Ridiculously incoherent boasting over impassive drum machines that sound like fridge-freezers being slammed together incessantly.

❹ BRASS MONKEY from LICENSE TO ILL
A cheerleading chant, with empty liquor bottles instead of pom-poms, champions the boys' favourite tipple.

❺ EGG MAN from PAUL'S BOUTIQUE
The Beasties at their most poetic and political: a celebration of the humanist levelling of having egg on your face. A rework of an early punk track, it's an unlikely paean to "eggalitarianism".

❻ PASS THE MIC from CHECK YOUR HEAD
Contains the laziest rhyme in rap history ("rehearsal" rhymed with "rehearsal"), but its titanic drums, excoriating scratching and looped guitar feedback seize the day.

❼ ILL COMMUNICATION from ILL COMMUNICATION
A seasick electronic tone provides the bassline, nudging a jazz piano off-kilter, while guest rapper Q-Tip and the boys talk about nothing in particular with quirky finesse.

❽ BODY MOVING from HELLO NASTY
Cacophonously messy steel drums and Mix Master Mike's octopoid cuts make for an ear-catching Beasties party invitation.

⑨ ELECTRIFY from HELLO NASTY
Throbbing cables of electro psychedelia pullulate virally. Positively radioactive.

⑩ THE BROUHAHA from TO THE FIVE BOROUGHS
A concise synth loop that's as cute as a riff by Yellow Magic Orchestra daintily supports the now (marginally) more mature trio, determined to grow old disgracefully.

Matt Milton

Chris Ingham on
The Beatles

Ten tracks for The Beatles? You're having a laugh. Chris Ingham, author of *The Rough Guide to The Beatles*, refused point blank. But he did agree to do three lists with a twist, picking the best Lennon/McCartney collaborations, and the top tunes creates by just one or other of the duo.

Lennon/McCartney

The Lennon/McCartney songbook is the greatest achievement in pop history. But not every song for which Paul and John share the credits was a genuine collaboration. Here are ten that were.

❶ I SAW HER STANDING THERE from PLEASE PLEASE ME
Composed in 1963 in the front room of the McCartney family home in Forthlin Road, Liverpool – and with a bassline nabbed from Chuck Berry's "Talkin' 'Bout You" – this was The Beatles at their Cavern-rocking best.

❷ I WANT TO HOLD YOUR HAND from PAST MASTERS 1
Like "From Me To You" and "She Loves You" before it, this – The Beatles' first US #1 and the very essence of their apparently innocent charm – was written by John and Paul together in a hotel room on tour.

❸ I'LL GET YOU from PAST MASTERS 1
Slight but winning B-side of "She Loves You", knocked out to a 1963 formula. McCartney was particularly pleased with the "faggy" way the boys sing "oh yeah, oh yeah".

❹ THIS BOY from PAST MASTERS 1
Delicious three-part harmony feature on the B-side of "I Want To Hold Your Hand".

❺ EIGHT DAYS A WEEK from BEATLES FOR SALE
On the way to a 1964 writing session with John, Paul heard his driver use this phrase about his own work schedule, whereupon the Lennon/McCartney song factory turned it into one more love ditty.

❻ DRIVE MY CAR from RUBBER SOUL
After a slow writing session in 1965, Paul and John eventually got onto such a roll with this tongue-in-cheek faux soul song, they even thought "beep-beep, beep-beep, yeah" a good idea. It was.

❼ WITH A LITTLE HELP FROM MY FRIENDS from SGT PEPPER'S LONELY HEARTS CLUB BAND
A little something for Ringo to sing – one of the lesser tracks on their 1967 magnum opus album, but with ground-breaking Greek chorus questions in the backing vocals and notably resourceful basswork.

❽ A DAY IN THE LIFE from SGT PEPPER'S LONELY HEARTS CLUB BAND
After hitting on the idea of inserting a song of Paul's into the middle of one of John's, they finished their magnificently stoned masterwork together.

❾ YOU KNOW MY NAME (LOOK UP THE NUMBER) from PAST MASTERS 2
The B-side of "Let It Be", this Goons-esque collage of daft voices and jazzy pastiche was hardly The Beatles' finest hour, but in a period when John and Paul were barely talking, at least they could still have a little fun.

❿ I'VE GOT A FEELING from LET IT BE
In which a Lennon half-song ("Everybody Had A Good Year") is bolted onto a McCartney half-song ("I've Got A Feeling"), making little sense but a good vehicle for a fabulous Apple rooftop performance in January 1969.

Beatle John

Ten "Lennon/McCartney" compositions that were actually penned by John...

❶ I SHOULD HAVE KNOWN BETTER from A HARD DAY'S NIGHT
A chiming, harmonica-driven rocker from the 1964 album (dominated by Lennon), memorably performed in the *Hard Day's Night* movie in the luggage compartment of a train.

❷ YOU'VE GOT TO HIDE YOUR LOVE AWAY from HELP!
Lennon goes Dylan in 1965, complete with cap, trucilently strummed acoustic guitar and this enchantingly opaque folk-waltz.

❸ NOWHERE MAN from RUBBER SOUL

Banks of vocal harmonies, Harrison's glistening Rickenbacker chords and the retrospectively unmistakeable sound of an unhappily married Beatle.

❹ TOMORROW NEVER KNOWS from REVOLVER

Inspired by *The Tibetan Book Of The Dead*, as quoted by acid guru Timothy Leary, this 1966 melange of drones, backward tapes and thunderous drumming is a virtual psychedelic revolution.

❺ SHE SAID SHE SAID from REVOLVER

A scything, splashing acid-rock peak for the band, with Lennon stumbling onto death and childhood amid resplendent guitars and dizzying beat shifts.

❻ STRAWBERRY FIELDS FOREVER
from BEATLES 1967–1970

Two entirely different versions of Lennon's deliciously hallucinatory reminiscence spliced together by producer George Martin into one glorious, multi-hued slab of Beatle music.

❼ ALL YOU NEED IS LOVE
from BEATLES 1967–1970

Though casually elliptical in the verses, the timelessly uplifting chorus ensures this 1967 hippy anthem will endure for years to come.

❽ I AM THE WALRUS
from MAGICAL MYSTERY TOUR

Somewhere between Lennon at his sly, free-association best and a writhing pit of nasty nonsense, "Walrus" is stunning psychedelia.

❾ JULIA from THE BEATLES "WHITE" ALBUM

A delicate, ruminative, finger-picking ballad in which Lennon blends a paean to his mother Julia with a reverie for new love Yoko.

❿ COME TOGETHER from ABBEY ROAD

Leary, Dylan and Chuck Berry influences can be detected, but this beautifully performed swamp-rock is Beatle music of the ultra-Lennon variety.

Beatle Paul

...and another ten Fabs classics written by Macca.

❶ ALL MY LOVING from WITH THE BEATLES

With furious triplets under a sunnily ascending scale of a melody, McCartney's pop classic was the first tune The Beatles played on their *Ed Sullivan Show* debut in February 1964.

❷ CAN'T BUY ME LOVE from A HARD DAY'S NIGHT

Paul injected a little blues into this song, written in the George V Hotel in Paris in January 1964, and nabbed the A-side of The Beatles' next single, to Lennon's chagrin.

❸ EVERY LITTLE THING from BEATLES FOR SALE

Written in Paul's bedroom at 57 Wimpole St, where he lived with the family of his girlfriend Jane Asher, this melodic attempt at a single ended up being a 1964 album track sung by John, a rare instance for The Beatles of the composer relinquishing lead vocal duties.

❹ I'M DOWN from PAST MASTERS 1

In an effort to supplant "Long Tall Sally" as his Little Richard-style live feature, McCartney fashioned this throat-tearing rocker, the climax of the Beatles' 1965 Shea Stadium set.

❺ YESTERDAY from HELP!

This mature and elegant ballad apparently arrived fully formed as McCartney awoke one morning in 1965. Following the Paul-plus-string-quartet "Beatles" recording it went on to be one of the most covered songs in pop history.

❻ YOU WON'T SEE ME from RUBBER SOUL

Another Wimpole Street missive, petulantly composed after a row with Jane Asher, this is a great album track – never performed live by The Beatles or McCartney.

❼ FOR NO ONE from REVOLVER

A chilly, blank-eyed vignette about a once-intimate couple drifting apart, which perhaps betrays more about McCartney's inner life in 1966 than his work is usually credited with.

❽ WHEN I'M SIXTY-FOUR from SGT PEPPER'S LONELY HEARTS CLUB BAND

Paul was 16 when he came up with the tune in Liverpool and 24 when he revived it for Sgt Pepper, turning it – with George Martin's help – into archetypal rootie-tootie Macca.

❾ FOOL ON THE HILL from MAGICAL MYSTERY TOUR

Mysterious meditation on an inscrutable spiritual leader of the same general size and build as the Maharishi. Also features one of the great recorder solos in pop.

❿ HEY JUDE from BEATLES 1967–1970

A special blend of personal encouragement and universal celebration, Hey Jude was written for Lennon's son Julian, though John thought it was a message to him and Yoko, while McCartney realized later it was about himself and Linda.

Beatles covers

The Fabs' best songs didn't always make for great cover versions (sit down please, The Massed Band of the Grenadier Guards…) but just occasionally it all came together.

❶ A DAY IN THE LIFE EUGENE CHADBOURNE from DOWNTOWN DOES THE BEATLES: LIVE AT THE KNITTING FACTORY

The iconoclastic guitarist/singer troubadour lets fragments of "For No One" and "I'll Follow The Sun" bleed into his skewed version of "A Day In The Life", in which he sings about "10,000 holes in Margaret Thatcher".

❷ WITH A LITTLE HELP FROM MY FRIENDS JOE COCKER from WITH A LITTLE HELP FROM MY FRIENDS

A remarkable reinvention, as Ringo's bouncy mum's-and-dad's pop turns into heavy 6/8 rock with gospel overtones. With justice, this is the track, sung at Woodstock, that made Cocker's career.

❸ RAIN THE LONDON JAZZ FOUR from TAKE A NEW LOOK AT THE BEATLES

The B-side of the 1966 single "Paperback Writer" is coolly reharmonized by the obscure MJQ-soundalike combo led by pianist Mike McNaught in 1967, from one of the best Beatle covers albums ever.

❹ DAY TRIPPER OTIS REDDING from THE OTIS REDDING DICTIONARY OF SOUL

A stomping, relentless 1966 reimagining of the Fabs' 1965 single with soul screamer Redding on searing form.

❺ I WANT YOU (SHE'S SO HEAVY) BOOKER T AND THE MGS from MCLEMORE AVENUE

Lennon's cry of sexual dependency is given the cool-hot Stax treatment, with guitarist Steve Cropper really chewing on the blues licks and Booker T lashing out some sharp organ work.

❻ DRIVE MY CAR BOBBY MCFERRIN from SIMPLE PLEASURES

Elastic-voiced McFerrin manages to sing bassline, melody, lyric and percussion parts in one vocal pass. Has to be heard to be believed.

❼ REVOLUTION GRANDADDY from I AM SAM

This Sean Penn movie had a neat hook: a character obsessed by Beatles songs. Cue the soundtrack album, whose delights include Rufus Wainwright doing "Across The Universe" and this very cool take from California band Grandaddy.

❽ ONE AFTER 909 LAIBACH from LET IT BE

Growling, industrial reading of the Quarrymen-era rocker by a provocative Slovenian collective, taken from their 1988 album in which they mangle the whole of The Beatles' *Let It Be* to fascinating effect.

❾ ELEANOR RIGBY STANLEY JORDAN from MAGIC TOUCH

"All the lonely people" get an impressive seven-minute workout from innovative fret-tapping jazz guitarist Jordan in 1984.

❿ BLUE JAY WAY BUDDHA PEST from DOWNTOWN DOES THE BEATLES: LIVE AT THE KNITTING FACTORY

Covers connoisseurs must hear this: a whispered vocal, a cello carrying the tune, thrash punk interludes and a free jazz attitude make for a startling Fabs-inspired experience.

Chris Ingham

Bebop classics

In the mid-1940s, a new breed of jazz virtuosi emerged – a fleet-of-finger crew with a penchant for substitute chords and intricate melodies. Put your hands together for the Beboppers.

❶ HOT HOUSE DIZZY GILLESPIE from THE DIZZY GILLESPIE STORY

A slippery Tadd Dameron theme based on the chords of Cole Porter's "What Is This Thing Called Love?" is given its inaugural outing by Dizzy's All-Stars (including Charlie Parker) in 1945.

❷ KOKO CHARLIE PARKER from THE COMPLETE CHARLIE PARKER ON SAVOY

The theme of Ray Noble's "Cherokee" is dropped, Bird cuts loose over the chords and creates an improvised classic in 1945.

❸ INDIANA BUD POWELL from TEMPUS FUGUE-IT

The king of bop piano at his clear-thinking best, a sparkling trio performance of the 1917 warhorse from 1947.

❹ OW! DIZZY GILLESPIE AND HIS ORCHESTRA from THE DIZZY GILLESPIE STORY

Dizzy's bebop big band didn't last long but produced some classic cuts like this "I Got Rhythm" variation in 1947.

❺ MILESTONES MILES DAVIS from EARLY MILES

A cool alternative to Gillespie's fiery trumpet style on this thoughtful, measured performance by Miles Davis in 1947, making his first appearance as leader.

❻ DONNA LEE CLAUDE THORNHILL from BEBOP SPOKEN HERE

Excellent big-band realization of Miles Davis's labyrinthine bop theme, set to the chords of Indiana and a clear forerunner to Miles's *Birth Of The Cool* nonet sessions of 1948–49.

❼ NOSTALGIA FATS NAVARRO from THE FATS NAVARRO STORY

The trumpeting stylistic bridge between Gillespie and Clifford Brown, Fats is faultless and incisive on his 1947 variation on the changes to the 1931 standard Out Of Nowhere.

❽ BONE-O-LOGY J.J. JOHNSON from BEBOP SPOKEN HERE

The first trombone virtuoso of bebop on his original variation of Sir Charles Thompson's "Robbin's Nest" in 1947, J. J. makes his double time, 16th-note runs sound as easy as turning on a tap.

❾ EPISTROPHY THELONIOUS MONK from THE COMPLETE THELONIOUS MONK ON BLUE NOTE

From a unique pianist/composer, this is extraordinarily original music from 1949 with its roots in bop harmony, but with an eccentric swing all of it own.

❿ TWISTED WARDELL GRAY from THE WARDELL GRAY STORY

A vivid 1949 blues from the ill-fated tenor saxophonist, with a riffy, weaving solo sufficiently melodic for singer Annie Ross to put lyrics to in her famous vocalese.

Chris Ingham

Beck

Lurching onto the scene with a beat-up guitar, a tote bag full of songs, two turntables and a microphone, Beck Hansen singlehandedly gave focus to the term "Slacker" as applied to his generation of peers and that particularly American musical genre. He made it cool for indie kids to dance, for Anglo kids to pick up some Hispanic groove and came up with the line, "MTV makes me want to smoke crack". Love the Beck.

❶ LOSER from MELLOW GOLD

Mixing up a meaty stew of Delta blues, the kind of Spanish you never find in textbooks, hip-hop and psychedelia, this is the track with the refrain "I'm a loser, baby, so why don't you kill me" that a million unfairly treated teenagers have retired to their rooms to play.

❷ NITEMARE HIPPY GIRL from MELLOW GOLD

Anybody who has spent a deal of time on the underground side of things will know this woman. Her male counterpart, it must be said, is equally irritating, but Beck didn't write a song about him.

❸ DEVIL'S HAIRCUT from ODELAY

Equal parts rap and sub-Dylan nonsense-rambling, giving the man a chance to concentrate on his dance moves. Beck sure can get down!

❹ NEW POLLUTION from ODELAY

Beck's most confidently weird surefire chart success, this blends trippy keyboard and guitar lines with a rock-hard precision-tooled set of beats that will drag your funky bones out to the dancefloor.

❺ NOBODY'S FAULT BUT MY OWN from MUTATIONS

Mid-period Beck moved away from the relentless beats of his hip-hop roots and focused instead on his folkie, country influences, while he grew up a little and sorted out his soul in the wake of a broken romance. Tragic, but totally irresistible.

❻ WE LIVE AGAIN from MUTATIONS

Sorrowful, thoughtful and with every word weighed in advance, Beck dives deep into the universal soul.

❼ SEXX LAWS from MIDNITE VULTURES

Putting the fun and the funk back into his music can't have been that easy, but he makes it appear a cinch. Performing this track in the full heat of a Glastonbury summer afternoon, wearing a tweed suit and smoking a briar pipe, Beck bumped and ground his way across stage, winning swathes of the audience with every swivel of his hips.

❽ DEBRA from MIDNITE VULTURES

The whole *Midnite Vultures* album, looked at in the right light, can be seen as a tribute to Prince in his sex-elf majesty. Debra is not only magnificently Beck, it's superbly Prince at the same time.

❾ E-PRO from GUERO

Back in the studio with his old sparring team The Dust Brothers at the production desk, Beck put together *Guero*, a stunning 21st-century creation, with "E-Pro" one of its standout cuts.

❿ BLACK TAMBOURINE from GUERO

Layering different sounds, and instrumentation with a gentle touch, Beck whips up a frothy piece of patisserie, just to show he can. Sounds blend seamlessly, from strings to keyboards to slide guitar.

Al Spicer

Bee Gees

Chipmunk voices, big hair, tight trousers, prickly Thatcher enthusiasts – the UK-born, Australian-raised brothers Gibb committed every kind of faux pas possible and still managed to sell over one hundred million records.

❶ NEW YORK MINING DISASTER 1941 from BEE GEES GOLD VOL 1
Debut 1967 hit employs a Beatleish refrain as the bros get maudlin about a mining tragedy.

❷ TO LOVE SOMEBODY from BEE GEES GOLD VOL 1
A minor hit in 1967 that went on to become a standard with the likes of Janis Joplin and Gram Parsons covering it.

❸ HOW CAN YOU MEND A BROKEN HEART from BEE GEES GOLD VOL 1
In The Bee Gees hands this sounds trite but when Al Green got hold of it a few years later it became an epic soul ballad. Obviously, the songs were good but the singing ...

❹ JIVE TALKIN' from MAIN COURSE
With producer Arif Mardin at the controls The Bee Gees became the world's most unlikely urban American act. This cracking disco shuffle took them to the top of the US charts.

❺ NIGHTS ON BROADWAY from MAIN COURSE
A propulsive celebration of living and partying in the heart of the city. Get those polyester flares and gold chains on and boogie!

❻ YOU SHOULD BE DANCING from CHILDREN OF THE WORLD
An anthem from the heart of the disco era. The voices rise, strings swell and the rhythm rips.

❼ STAYING ALIVE from SATURDAY NIGHT FEVER
Remember the opening scene of *Saturday Night Fever* with John Travolta strutting down the street as Staying Alive blasts across the cinema? Has being young and urban ever appeared more exciting?

❽ NIGHT FEVER from SATURDAY NIGHT FEVER
Worldwide #1 from 1978 when the planet did indeed appear to have Bee Gee disco fever.

❾ HOW DEEP IS YOUR LOVE from SATURDAY NIGHT FEVER
Lush, lush ballad effectively employed to track some fabulous dancing in *Saturday Night Fever*.

❿ SHADOW DANCING from BEST OF
And let's not forget doomed kid brother Andy Gibb. Penned by Barry this slice of disco bubblegum gave 19-year-old Andy a US #1 in 1978. A decade later he would be a genuine shadow dancer after a blizzard of cocaine burned him out.

Garth Cartwright

Belle & Sebastian

Scots popsters with peculiar staying power: nobody does melancholy quite as well.

❶ THE STATE I'M IN from TIGERMILK
Mattter-of-fact melancholia: "I was happy for a day in 1975", channelling The Monkees'"Daydream Believer".

❷ GET ME AWAY FROM HERE, I'M DYING from IF YOU'RE FEELING SINISTER
Bleak lyrics, surrounded by an impossibly bouncy track. A B&S classic in every respect.

❸ THE STARS OF TRACK AND FIELD from IF YOU'RE FEELING SINISTER
One of the definitive lost love songs of its era

❹ I'M WAKING UP TO US from PUSH BARMAN TO OPEN OLD WOUNDS
A fine song that Stuart Murdoch swears is *not* about his break-up with Isobel Campbell.

❺ I LOVE MY CAR from PUSH BARMAN TO OPEN OLD WOUNDS
"I love my Carl, I love my Brian, Dennis, and my Al, I can even find it in my heart to love Mike Love… wish I could say the same for you…" Not bitter or anything, then?

❻ WRAPPED UP IN BOOKS from DEAR CATASTROPHE WAITRESS
Farfisa organ + twelve-string electric = pop bliss.

❼ DRESS UP IN YOU from THE LIFE PURSUIT
Their sound grows lusher with each release: this features beautiful background vocals and trumpet.

❽ ANOTHER SUNNY DAY from THE LIFE PURSUIT
"The lovin' is a mess. What happened to all of the feeling?" Lovelorn isolation as seen through the eyes of the keen horticulturalist.

Peter Labella

b

Berns/Ragovoy

Bert Berns and Jerry Ragovoy (a.k.a. Norman Meade), who between them wrote and produced all of these selections, are two of the great white backroom heroes of soul music. The Beatles, the Stones, Janis Joplin and Van Morrison are just a few who have performed their songs.

❶ GET IT WHILE YOU CAN HOWARD TATE from GET IT WHILE YOU CAN

Top track by one of the great lost soul singers, rediscovered in 2001.

❷ STAY WITH ME LORRAINE ELLISON from STAY WITH ME

Definitive, hyper-dramatic deep soul with an almost Spectoresque arrangement, recorded with a full-size orchestra after a Sinatra session was cancelled.

❸ TIME IS ON MY SIDE IRMA THOMAS from TIME IS ON MY SIDE

Originally written for jazz trombonist Kai Winding, later covered by the Rolling Stones, but this remains the version to hear.

❹ ARE YOU LONELY FOR ME FREDDIE SCOTT from THE HEART AND SOUL OF BERT BERNS

Mid-1960s New York soul at its finest, showing Southerners didn't have a monopoly on feeling.

❺ EVERYBODY NEEDS SOMEBODY TO LOVE SOLOMON BURKE from THE HEART AND SOUL OF BERT BERNS

Covered by Wilson Pickett and The Blues Brothers, but Burke's version is the best.

❻ CRY BABY GARNET MIMMS from THE HEART AND SOUL OF BERT BERNS

Incendiary uptown gospel-soul by the sorely under-appreciated Mimms.

❼ PIECE OF MY HEART ERMA FRANKLIN from THE HEART AND SOUL OF BERT BERNS

Everyone knows Janis Joplin's cover, but this is the original by Aretha's sister.

❽ CRY TO ME SOLOMON BURKE from THE HEART AND SOUL OF BERT BERNS

As always with Burke, it's the dramatic expressiveness of his voice that impresses.

❾ TWIST AND SHOUT ISLEY BROTHERS from THE HEART AND SOUL OF BERT BERNS

Before the Beatles, the Isleys infused this dance-craze tune with gospel intensity.

❿ HERE COMES THE NIGHT THEM from THE STORY OF THEM FEATURING VAN MORRISON

One of the Belfast band's best-known songs, with Van Morrison on lead vocals. Berns later produced his pre-Astral Weeks Bang sessions, including "Brown Eyed Girl".

Neil Foxlee

Chuck Berry

Though he's best known as the pioneer of the rock'n'roll guitar riff, Chuck Berry also deserves to be remembered as rock's first great songwriter, thanks to his intricate, deft and often very funny lyrics. All of these tracks feature on several Greatest Hits compilations, as well as such desirable items as *The Chess Box*.

❶ JOHNNY B. GOODE from THE CHESS BOX

The saga of the Louisiana country boy who could play the guitar just like ringing a bell. There are few better songs to teach yourself rock'n'roll.

❷ BROWN EYED HANDSOME MAN from THE CHESS BOX

Some see this song as a searing indictment of racial prejudice; others simply think Chuck's wordplay has never been cleverer.

❸ BACK IN THE USA from THE CHESS BOX

A consummate, idealized vision of what it was like to live in the US in the rock'n'rolling 1950s; the perfect companion piece to The Beatles' Back In The USSR, which it inspired.

❹ ROCK AND ROLL MUSIC from THE CHESS BOX

All the joy and release of the rock'n'roll rebellion, crammed into two and a half minutes.

❺ NO PARTICULAR PLACE TO GO from THE CHESS BOX

From the man for whom automobile was a three-letter word – S-E-X – this is the best car song of the lot. Can you imagine the way that he felt, when he couldn't unfasten his safety belt?

❻ TOO MUCH MONKEY BUSINESS from THE CHESS BOX

An exhilarating outpouring of youthful nihilism, in which Chuck dismisses everything as more bother than it's worth.

❼ MEMPHIS from THE CHESS BOX

Chuck's story-telling may be a little leaden, and the twist might make you wince, but the beat is just too damn catchy for that to matter.

b

❽ YOU NEVER CAN TELL from **THE CHESS BOX**
Perhaps Chuck's loveliest song: a tender, witty, swinging meditation on the passing of time.

❾ PROMISED LAND from **THE CHESS BOX**
Chuck wrote this one in prison with an atlas on his knees; it's hardly surprising that his yearning for freedom, as represented by sunny California, should be so palpable.

❿ SWEET LITTLE SIXTEEN from **THE CHESS BOX**
In which one of the major archetypes of rock'n'roll – the wide-eyed teenage ingenue – springs fully-fledged from Chuck's lascivious imagination.

Greg Ward

The Bevis Frond

For nearly twenty years, Nick Saloman has been crafting some of the best neo-psychedelia around as The Bevis Frond, with the help of such cohorts as Ade Shaw (ex-Hawkwind) and Andy Ward (ex-Camel).

❶ STAIN ON THE SUN from **NEW RIVER HEAD**
This slow, meandering, majestic and unbearably moving tale of a failing relationship climaxes in a weeping guitar solo that leaves us all wondering who put the bullet hole in the Holy Roman flag.

❷ LIGHTS ARE CHANGING from **TRIPTYCH**
Lord knows why this phenomenally catchy psych pop wasn't #1 for weeks. Oh, it was never a single.

❸ LONDON STONE from **LONDON STONE**
Powerful and eloquent lament for the destruction of the environment in Nick's native East London. Enough to simultaneously warm and chill the cockles of any Cockney's heart.

❹ ONCE MORE from **INNER MARSHLAND**
Not many tracks open with Harry H Corbett moaning about Sooty and Sweep and culminate in a Hendrix-style guitar fest via a gentle British folk interlude.

❺ HE'D BE A DIAMOND from **NEW RIVER HEAD**
This strum-along singalong ditty has been covered by Teenage Fanclub as well as Mary Lou Lord. The line "an unpaid analyst who shags" used to crack them up in concert.

❻ SPLENDID ISOLATION from **MIASMA**
Nick Saloman emerged from years of splendid isolation into magnificent obscurity with his debut album,

the highly psychedelic *Miasma*. This song set his power pop benchmark very high.

Nick Edwards

Bhangra/Asian underground

British Asians have created a dynamic music scene that for the most part exists independently of the mainstream. Bhangra has roots in Punjabi folk and Hindi pop, but in its current incarnation, and in Asian underground, owes as much to dance music of all persuasions.

❶ KORI PMC from **DHOL JAGEERO DA**
Gidda track that slows down and speeds up intermittently, sending clubbers into a frenzy.

❷ MERA LAUNG GAWACHA BALLY SAGOO from **STAR CRAZY 1**
Sung by Rama with rap from Cheshire Cat, this bhangramuffin classic translates as "I've lost my nose-ring".

❸ KE HAI BARI SANGEETA PYAR from **FLOWER IN THE WIND**
Sangeeta's biggest song to date, with lyrics by Preet Nihal and music by Kuljit Bhamra. She sings in Hindi instead of the Punjabi customary in bhangra music.

❹ FLIGHT IC 408 STATE OF BENGAL from **ANOKHA – SOUNDZ OF THE ASIAN UNDERGROUND**
Massive drum'n'bass tune with swirling sitars and frenetic tabla beats, themed around a flight from Bangladesh

❺ NEELA TRICKBABY from **HANGIN' AROUND**
Compelling, hypnotic instrumental East–West concoction.

❻ BOR BOR PARTNERS IN RHYME from **REPLAY**
Bouncy bhangra at its best.

❼ FINGERS JOI from **ONE AND ONE IS ONE**
Trancey techno with sitar and a house vibe featuring the voice of Shusheela Raman.

❽ NACHANGEH SARI RAATH TAZ from **SLAVE TO THE FUSION**
Pop-house Hindi number with a Latin American edge.

DJ Ritu

b

Big-band jazz

Ten big-band numbers from the heart of the swing era, 1934–42. You'll find them on countless compilations, as well as the CDs listed below.

❶ STOMPIN' AT THE SAVOY CHICK WEBB'S SAVOY ORCHESTRA from STOMPIN' AT THE SAVOY

The Savoy Orchestra, led by hunchback drummer Webb and featuring the arranging of Edgar Sampson (who co-wrote this swing classic with Benny Goodman), swung as hard as any band of the period.

❷ WALKIN' AND SWINGIN' ANDY KIRK from THE 12 CLOUDS OF JOY

Neat, intricate arranging from band pianist Mary Lou Williams for Andy Kirk's Kansas City heroes in 1936.

❸ ONE O'CLOCK JUMP COUNT BASIE from THE COUNT BASIE STORY

From the same town in the same period, Basie's outfit featured simpler, more straightforwardly swinging arrangements to showcase – on this jazz-blues staple – the two contrasting tenor stars, Herschel Evans and Lester Young.

❹ DON'T BE THAT WAY BENNY GOODMAN from THE CARNEGIE HALL CONCERT, JANUARY 16 1938

This ingenious lick is one of the great anthems of the swing era and one of its biggest hits from its biggest star, the thrilling clarinettist and crowned King Of Swing.

❺ IN THE MOOD GLENN MILLER from IN THE MOOD

The most famous swing theme of all was played by what considered a "sweet" band, but its infectious syncopations and compelling dynamics make the 1939 recording of Andy Razaf and Ed Garland's riff an imperishable classic.

❻ T'AIN'T WHAT YOU DO (IT'S THE WAY THAT YOU DO IT) JIMMIE LUNCEFORD from STRICTLY LUNCEFORD

Lunceford's orchestra is considered by many to be the great band of the era, with its exciting arrangements by Sy Oliver and audience-pleasing swing-pop like this 1939 hit (which was a hit again in 1982 for Fun Boy Three.)

❼ AT THE WOODCHOPPER'S BALL WOODY HERMAN AND HIS ORCHESTRA from WOODY HERMAN'S FINEST HOUR

Herman's outfit was billed as "The Band That Plays The Blues" and this breakthrough 1939 hit proved it; by no means the subtlest record of the era, but replete with raw excitement.

❽ TAKE THE 'A' TRAIN DUKE ELLINGTON from GREATEST HITS

Ellington's compositional prowess set him rather apart from the swing craze, but this memorably dissonant swinger from 1941 – actually composed by Billy Strayhorn – did his popularity no harm at all, and became the Ellington Orchestra theme tune for the rest of its existence.

❾ DRUM BOOGIE GENE KRUPA from THAT DRUMMER'S BAND

A charismatic drumming star with Benny Goodman, Krupa scored a huge hit with his own band in 1941 on this rockin' novelty featuring manic drums, shouts of "boogie" from the band and a fine vocal by Irene Day.

❿ FLYING HOME LIONEL HAMPTON from ALL STAR SESSIONS VOL 1: OPEN HOUSE

Another former star of the Goodman outfit, vibra-phonist Hampton specialized in swing music as roaring exhilaration, like this 1942 hit which builds a delirious momentum.

Chris Ingham

Birdsong

Avian songs that fly.

❶ HIGH-FLYING BIRD JUDY HENSKE from HIGH-FLYING BIRD

❷ BIRD OF PARADISE SNOWY WHITE from WHITE FLAMES

❸ FREEBIRD LYNYRD SKYNYRD from ALL TIME GREATEST HITS

❹ SONGBIRD FLEETWOOD MAC from RUMOURS

❺ YELLOW BIRD HUBERT SMITH from BERMUDA IS ANOTHER WORLD

❻ THE LITTLEST BIRDS (SING THE PRETTIEST SONGS) THE BE-GOOD TANYAS from BLUE HORSE

❼ FLY LIKE AN EAGLE STEVE MILLER BAND from FLY LIKE AN EAGLE

❽ EAGLE ABBA from ABBA THE ALBUM

❾ LES TROIS BEAUX OISEAUX DE PARADIS LINDA THOMPSON from ONE CLEAR MOMENT

❿ THREE LITTLE BIRDS BOB MARLEY from SONGS OF FREEDOM

David Honigmann

Björk

Since her separation from crazed Icelandic indie outfit Sugarcubes, this pint-sized vocal gymnast has gone from strength to strength, consistently roping in top producers for her work and crafting album after album of stunning and ground-breaking music.

❶ VENUS AS A BOY from DEBUT
The lush strings and off-kilter beats gave a few clues of the genius and oddness that would soon follow.

❷ COME TO ME from DEBUT
Björk's larynx doesn't jump through any hoops, but it's still a stunning cut.

❸ PLAY DEAD from DEBUT
With rousing horns and strings, this could almost be a Bond theme – awesome.

❹ MOUTH'S CRADLE from MEDULLA
A deeply elegant arrangement of bleeps, choruses and processed voice samples – dislocated listening not to be missed.

❺ ALL IS FULL OF LOVE from HOMOGENIC
This is angelic music at its best – a cacophony of atmospherics, beats and love.

❻ HYPERBALLAD from TELEGRAM
It was a great song the first time around, but this reworked version features the radical strings of The Brodsky Quartet.

❼ PAGAN POETRY from VESPERTINE
A confusion of denticulated beats and melodies wash and splash around Björk's vocal musings – glorious and euphoric.

❽ IT'S OH SO QUIET from POST
This is pure pop, as Bjork creates a swing number all her own. Quirky, happy, almost silly – more fun than a sack of kittens in a wool factory.

❾ IN THE MUSICALS from SELMA SONGS
A stupendous track with balls (literally). The whole album is great, inspired by the Björk-starring movie *Dancer In The Dark*.

❿ GRATITUDE from DRAWING RESTRAINT 9
This soundtrack album's opening cut is the most accessible of a wonderful, largely instrumental, clutch; it features the vocal twangs of Will Oldham.

Peter Buckley

Black rock

While it's universally accepted that black blues and rock'n'roll musicians (Chuck Berry, Little Richard, Bo Diddley, Fats Domino) created what we now know as rock music it's still rare to find black musicians playing Rock; ya know, the heavy, churning, white boy boogie. Here's ten who turned their guitars up loud.

❶ HEY JOE JIMI HENDRIX from THE BEST OF
Manager Chas Chandler convinced Hendrix to record the garage band standard as his debut 45 so Jimi cut one of the most menacing songs ever.

❷ I WANT TO TAKE YOU HIGHER SLY & THE FAMILY STONE from WOODSTOCK
Sly's fusion of soul, funk and rock reached its apotheosis at Woodstock where he had the great unwashed chanting along with this anthem of psychedelic uplift.

❸ MAGGOT BRAIN FUNKADELIC from MAGGOT BRAIN
George Clinton and co are in Detroit, listening to Hendrix, reading apocalyptic texts and taking too much acid. Eddie Hazel's guitar work slices through ten minutes of the darkest music ever recorded.

❹ SOMEBODY TO LOVE MOTHER'S FINEST from MOTHER'S FINEST LIVE
Georgia hard rock-funk band who were legendary for their incendiary live performance.

❺ BIG TAKEOVER BAD BRAINS from ROCK FOR LIGHT
Talk about epoch busters: Bad Brains involved Washington DC jazz fusion musicians who turned Rasta and played hardcore punk like no one else.

❻ MEMORIES CAN'T WAIT LIVING COLOUR from VIVID
Vernon Reid's black hard rockers reinterpret Talking Heads, matching loud guitars with high IQs.

❼ SWIM FISHBONE from GIVE A MONKEY A BRAIN
Mad LA band that mixed ska, funk and thrash. Swim is a grinding mosh-pit monster.

❽ COP KILLER BODY COUNT from BODY COUNT
Gangsta rapper Ice-T puts a thrash band together with his Compton homies and sings about murdering police officers. Charlton Heston lead the cavalry of outrage leading Warner Brothers to drop the band.

❾ POOR MAN'S RELIEF KINSEY REPORT from EDGE OF THE CITY
Guitarist Donald Kinsey had played in Albert King and Peter Tosh's bands so bought these influences to his

b

family band, meshing blues and reggae with a hard rock attack.

⑩ LET'S GO CRAZY PRINCE from PURPLE RAIN
Stuffed full of power chords and screaming solos, this is Prince performing mock-Hendrix. And you might just say that Lenny Kravitz has based a career on replicating this one song.

Garth Cartwright

Black Sabbath/ Ozzy Osbourne

Monolithically heavy Sabbath were core progenitors of modern metal, and, of course, frontman Ozzy Osbourne has rollicked his way to ever greater stardom.

BLACK SABBATH

❶ BLACK SABBATH from BLACK SABBATH
Thunder rolls, a distant bell tolls and a titanic doom-laden riff grinds into life. Scarily brilliant.

❷ KILLING YOURSELF TO LIVE from SABBATH BLOODY SABBATH
Slickly produced, Sabbath rarely sounded quite so focused. Great solos, terrific drumming and a storming vocal performance.

❸ PARANOID from PARANOID
Written in just a few minutes (as the legend goes), this is one of the most famous and enduring metal tunes ever.

❹ PLANET CARAVAN from PARANOID
Not a distorted guitar within earshot as Sabbath bring it down several notches for this spacey and oddly mellow drift through the cosmos.

❺ SUPERNAUT from VOL 4
A looser, more rock'n'roll feel to Tony Iommi's guitar here, and one hell of a sizzling solo.

❻ SWEET LEAF from MASTER OF REALITY
First a hacking cough, then a sledgehammer riff and Ozzy's voice wreathed in cool herbal smoke. An awesome doper's anthem.

❼ SYMPTOM OF THE UNIVERSE from SABOTAGE
Basic and brutal there's no messing about here – until the crazy, inspired jazz'n'blues acoustic breakdown at the end.

❽ WAR PIGS from PARANOID
The scream of air-raid sirens welcomes you to the hell of war. Ozzy rails against the destruction and madness in this timeless classic.

OZZIE OSBOURNE

❾ MR CROWLEY from BLIZZARD OF OZZ
Just listen to that immense cathedral organ intro. How can you go wrong with a song about arch-Satanist Aleister Crowley?

⑩ SUICIDE SOLUTION from BLIZZARD OF OZZ
In which Ozzy gets serious about the booze as guitarist Randy Rhoads creates a stunning monster riff.

Essi Berelian

Blaxploitation

Cheaply made, nastily violent and gratuitously sexy – the blaxploitation films of the 1970s were, hopefully, all of that. But the back story was one of black pride, which was celebrated with soundtracks that opened up new areas of creativity and personnel to bring the very best out of some of the era's soul-music talent.

❶ PURSUIT OF THE PIMPMOBILE ISAAC HAYES from TRUCK TURNER
Screaming tyres, flying hub caps, scattering pedestrians and acres of crushed velvet…hammering hi-hat, hyperactive wah-wah guitar, assassin squad brass and a sumptuous string section. It's all here in this white-walled '74 Cadillac of a tune.

❷ SLICK WILLIE HUTCH from THE MACK
A relatively small-scale piece of work that keeps the horns at arm's length, but maintains a smoke-and-mirrors-type trickery as paranoid bongos supercharge the basic rhythms.

❸ MAIN THEME BARRY WHITE from TOGETHER BROTHERS
Big sounds from the big man, as a full orchestra slugs it out with a tight funk rhythm section to create a springboard for all manner of musical strutting and showing-off.

❹ ACROSS 110TH STREET BOBBY WOMACK from ACROSS 110TH STREET
A superb balance of menace and desperation, manifesting itself in the plaintiveness of Bobbie Womack's vocals, brilliantly captures the tension that was shot through the film itself, as well as this classic soundtrack.

⑤ SEE THE LIGHT EARTH, WIND & FIRE from
THAT'S THE WAY OF THE WORLD
An expectedly positive offering from EWF, with beautifully harmonizing vocals and bubbling, percussion-laced rhythms, proving it wasn't all doom and gloom in "the hood".

⑥ CAFÉ REGIO'S ISAAC HAYES from SHAFT
Of course, any blaxploitaion film worth its Afro had sex to go with the violence, and this is lazy, Sunday morning, guitar-led, flute-flavoured orchestral smooove of the highest order.

⑦ T PLAYS IT COOL MARVIN GAYE from TROUBLE MAN
With the drums up front in the mix and endlessly layered electric pianos, moogs and ARPs, this is as tough as it is cool and cleverly jazzy. The entirely self-written and produced soundtrack was always Gaye's favourite among his own albums.

⑧ THE BOSS JAMES BROWN from BLACK CAESAR
Tight, taut and totally James Brown, an ascending spiral of funk that escalates from scratch guitar into a JB extravaganza that hovers on the edge of overwhelming.

⑨ FREDDIE'S DEAD CURTIS MAYFIELD from SUPERFLY
Thematically turning the perceived blaxploitation ethic on its head, but doing so with a simmeringly complex exercise in orchestral funk that keeps the latter firmly in control.

⑩ TIME IS TIGHT BOOKER T & THE MGS from UPTIGHT
Blaxploitation before the word was invented (1968), this elegant funk is timeless and probably the most unrelenting interplay between a Hammond organ and a bass guitar ever to grace a groove.

Lloyd Bradley

Blondie

Blondie was a band, and a damn good one: they blended pure songwriting craft with a fistful of punk attitude, and they had, in Debbie Harry, one of the all-time great front women.

❶ RIP HER TO SHREDS from BLONDIE
Their first calling card: catchy, nasty and wrapped up in a sharp-and-shiny package. The song made for a great advert, too

❷ NO IMAGINATION from PLASTIC LETTERS
The gems on Blondie's second album are hidden away. This one is sass on legs.

❸ HANGING ON THE TELEPHONE from PARALLEL LINES
A ringing tone – and then Harry slams in, daring the band to keep up. Has any album started better?

❹ SUNDAY GIRL from PARALLEL LINES
One of the best Blondie homages to Brill-Building Girl-Group pop. Also in French.

❺ FADE AWAY AND RADIATE from PARALLEL LINES
Spooky guitar lines, loads of shimmering reverb, an air of unspecified and impossibly cool threat.

❻ ATOMIC from EAT TO THE BEAT
Futuristic and classic at the same time: the riff is unforgettable, and when the band come back in after the break, it just keeps growing.

❼ CALL ME (FULL VERSION) from AMERICAN GIGOLO SOUNDTRACK
For this smash-hit Giorgio Moroder collaboration, you want the full eight-minutes-and-then-some heavy-breathing version. Anything shorter would be premature foreclosure.

❽ RAPTURE from AUTOAMERICAN
A pure distillation of New York, 1980, with its proto-rap and references to Fab Five Freddy.

❾ ISLAND OF LOST SOULS from THE HUNTER
Blondie's take on The Paragons'"The Tide Is High" may have outworn its welcome, but this second stab at Caribbean summer fun still sounds like a good time.

❿ MARIA from NO EXIT
As if they had never been away.

David Honigmann

Blue (kind of)

The colour of the sky, of the sea, of the night, of sadness, of covetable footwear… it even has a whole genre named after it.

❶ BLUE SKIES ELLA FITZGERALD from THE JOHNNY MERCER SONGBOOK

❷ BLUE MOON THE COWBOY JUNKIES from THE TRINITY SESSIONS

❸ TANGLED UP IN BLUE BOB DYLAN from BLOOD ON THE TRACKS

❹ BLUE JONI MITCHELL from BLUE

❺ SKY BLUE PETER GABRIEL from UP

⑥ BLUE NILE ALICE COLTRANE from PTAH, THE EL DAOUD

⑦ AFRICAN SKY BLUE JULUKA from AFRICAN LITANY

⑧ COOL BLUE EURYTHMICS from TOUCH

⑨ BLUE SUEDE SHOES ELVIS PRESLEY from ELVIS '56

⑩ BLUE VELVET BOBBY VINTON from GREATEST HITS

David Honigmann

Bluegrass

While mainstream country music was embracing trends like honky-tonk, Bill Monroe & His Blue Grass Boys steadfastly clung to the "high lonesome" sound of old-time Appalachian string bands. Modernizing it with lightning-speed picking, the group gave birth to bluegrass.

❶ BLUE MOON OF KENTUCKY BILL MONROE & HIS BLUE GRASS BOYS from THE ESSENTIAL, 1945–1949
The song that started it all, Monroe's big hit inspired Elvis (though you can't waltz to the King's version).

❷ THE WHITE DOVE THE STANLEY BROTHERS from THE COMPLETE COLUMBIA STANLEY BROTHERS
The epitome of "high lonesome".

❸ FOGGY MOUNTAIN BREAKDOWN LESTER FLATT, EARL SCRUGGS & THE FOGGY MOUNTAIN BOYS from 'TIS SWEET TO BE REMEMBERED
A breakdown so fast and furious that even city slickers will break out their rebel yells.

❹ YOU DON'T KNOW MY MIND JIMMY MARTIN from YOU DON'T KNOW MY MIND 1956–66
The self-styled "King of Bluegrass" mixes in some honky-tonk.

❺ I WONDER HOW THE OLD FOLKS ARE AT HOME MAC WISEMAN from 'TIS SWEET TO BE REMEMBERED
A model lesson in how the banjo and fiddle elevate nostalgia above greeting-card sentimentality.

❻ RANK STRANGER THE STANLEY BROTHERS from RIDIN' THAT MIDNIGHT TRAIN
The definitive bluegrass hymn, and indeed sung at Bill Monroe's funeral. It has the perfect mingling of Carter's emotional lead and Ralph's ethereal tenor.

❼ LONG BLACK VEIL HAZEL DICKENS & ALICE GERRARD from WHO'S THAT KNOCKIN'
The first ladies of bluegrass deliver what may be the finest interpretation of this classic of American song.

❽ GET DOWN ON YOUR KNEES AND PRAY THE DEL MCCOURY BAND from THE FAMILY
On this goose-bump-raising track there are no instruments, only voices that climb and twist and bend, with McCoury's high tenor reaching forever skyward.

❾ WILL THE CIRCLE BE UNBROKEN NITTY GRITTY DIRT BAND from WILL THE CIRCLE BE UNBROKEN
Maybelle Carter, Jimmy Martin, Roy Acuff, Merle Travis and other old school country and bluegrass artists reach out to the unwashed hippies from California.

❿ DUELING BANJOS ERIC WEISSBERG & STEVE MANDELL from DELIVERANCE ORIGINAL SOUNDTRACK
Even if it wasn't in *Deliverance*, this would have been an instant classic.

Peter Shapiro/Madelyn Rosenberg

Blue Öyster Cult

Too clever by half to be heavy-metallers (though not too clever to deploy a Heavy Metal umlaut), the Cult's list of listenable songs goes nowhere near eleven. But these ones are the biz, at their best on the live albums.

❶ DON'T FEAR THE REAPER from AGENTS OF FORTUNE
The one Öyster Cult song everyone can hum: call-and-response comic death cutlery with a circular riff that won't let go.

❷ VETERAN OF THE PSYCHIC WARS from EXTRATERRESTRIAL LIVE
This Michael Moorcock-penned tale of Forever War ends in a lengthy inferno of guitar soloing, after which you too will feel like the veteran of a thousand wars.

❸ TAKE ME AWAY from THE REVOLUTION BY NIGHT
A relatively late and little regarded song, but tight and hard and heavy as they come. It is, of course, about UFO abductions.

❹ ASTRONOMY from SOME ENCHANTED EVENING
In the studio, the opening is underpowered and meandering; live, it achieves real menace.

❺ GODZILLA from SPECTRES
Fabulously rhymes "There goes Tokyo" with "Oh no".

❻ BLACK BLADE from EXTRATERRESTRIAL LIVE
More Moorcock: the Elric of Melnibone saga handily condensed.

David Honigmann

b

Nigel Williamson on
The Blues

You could fill a *Playlists* book with blues lists. Indeed, **NIGEL WILLIAMSON** has done just that, and some, with his *The Rough Guide to Blues*. We cut him a bit of slack and allowed two core lists – one acoustic and one electric.

He says: "As will be evident from the two lists below, my love of the blues was born in the late 1960s and came via rock covers of classic songs from the Delta and Chicago. I then traced the music back to its roots, a process that in those pre-CD and pre-Amazon days was rather like a treasure hunt. I've never stopped listening and learning about this music."

Acoustic blues

❶ NOBODY'S FAULT BUT MINE BLIND WILLIE JOHNSON from THE COMPLETE BLIND WILLIE JOHNSON
Found the song on the first *Better Days* album in 1973 and thought it was magnificent. Checked out the original and discovered that while Paul Butterfield was pretty good, Blind Willie was a blues genius.

❷ CANDY MAN MISSISSIPPI JOHN HURT from THE BEST OF MISSISSIPPI JOHN HURT
So many of these songs were originally heard in other versions – this one first encountered on a Donovan album.

❸ ATLANTA STRUT BLIND WILLIE MCTELL from ATLANTA STRUT: 20 LEGENDARY RECORDINGS
I bought a twelve-string guitar after hearing McTell – although McGuinn probably had something to do with it, too – and I actually learned to play this song extremely badly.

❹ I'M A MIGHTY TIGHT WOMAN SIPPIE WALLACE from COMPLETE RECORDED WORKS VOL 2
Once again, thanks to Bonnie Raitt's 1971 debut for the discovery of this song and the wonderful world of Sippie Wallace.

❺ CROSSROAD BLUES ROBERT JOHNSON from KING OF THE DELTA BLUES SINGERS
The very first blues album I ever bought in 1968. After I'd heard this, I sold my Cream albums to a schoolfriend.

❻ GALLIS POLE LEADBELLY from THE LEGEND OF LEADBELLY
Heard someone sing this in a folk club in Orpington when I was 15 years old in 1969 and asked them who did the original. Whoever you were, thanks for pointing me in the right direction…

❼ STEALIN' STEALIN' MEMPHIS JUG BAND from THE BEST OF THE MEMPHIS JUG BAND
Sometimes known as "Circle Round The Sun", the best rock version of this was by Clover, which once again led me all the way back to Memphis circa 1928.

❽ THAT'S NO WAY TO GET ALONG ROBERT WILKINS from ROBERT WILKINS: PRODIGAL SON
Covered by the Rolling Stones in 1968 as "Prodigal Son" on the *Beggar's Banquet* album, it took me years to find the original.

❾ BROWN SKIN WOMAN SNOOKS EAGLIN from NEW ORLEANS STREET SINGER
In 1973, a friend called Mick Linton took off back-packing around the world and left me his collection of blues LPs for safe-keeping. This was on one of them and I never gave it back.

❿ DELIA BOB DYLAN from WORLD GONE WRONG
For the impossibly heartbreaking way he sings "all the friends I ever had are gone" alone – plus a hundred other reasons. Nobody sings the blues like Bob Dylan. Which doesn't make him the best – just unique.

Electric blues

❶ DUST MY BROOM ELMORE JAMES from THE SKY IS CRYING: THE HISTORY OF ELMORE JAMES
Arguably the best blues guitar riff ever, first heard on Fleetwood Mac's version in 1968 and then traced back in time-honoured fashion to its source.

❷ MANNISH BOY MUDDY WATERS from HIS BEST
The first Muddy Waters album I heard was his 1969 psychedelic experiment *Electric Mud* on which he covered "Let's Spend The Night Together". Not the best introduction, but I worked back from there and found it got better and better until I landed in Chicago, circa 1955.

❸ LITTLE RED ROOSTER HOWLIN' WOLF from HIS BEST
I couldn't believe Chester Burnett had not only written this for the Rolling Stones but had also penned songs for Cream and The Doors. Then I discovered he'd recorded them himself as Howlin' Wolf – and the power of the originals made the covers sound insipid by comparison.

b

Charlie Musselwhite's
Blues harp tunes

Mississippi born, Memphis raised, Charlie Musselwhite was the original Blues Brother – the movie's characters really were modelled on him. He is one of the great blues men, a master harmonica player who chose ten blues tunes graced by some of the most soulful blues harp ever cut. "To me the harmonica is special for it's unique voice like qualities," says Musselwhite. "It can sound happy or sad – it can wail and scream or whisper low. It's the only instrument that you can't see how it is played and it's also the only instrument that you breathe in and out of – all of which go to make it a very personal instrument with a very personal sound."

❶ **KEY TO THE HIGHWAY** LITTLE WALTER from HIS BEST

❷ **TELEPHONE BLUES** GEORGE SMITH from HARMONICA ACE

❸ **DECORATION DAY** JOHN LEE "SONNY BOY" WILLIAMSON from THE ESSENTIAL RECORDINGS

❹ **MIGHTY LONG TIME** RICE "SONNY BOY WILLIAMSON" MILLER from COOL COOL BLUES: HIS CLASSIC 1951–56 SIDES

❺ **WHEN THE SAINTS COME MARCHING IN** PAPA LIGHTFOOT from NATCHEZ TRACE

❻ **TOUGH ME LIGHT** MAMA BULLET WILLIAMS from ALABAMA HARMONICA KINGS

❼ **BEDROOM STOMP** RHYTHM WILLIE from HARPS, JUGS, WASHBOARDS AND KAZOOS

❽ **KANSAS CITY BLUES** WILL SHADE AND THE MEMPHIS JUG BAND from MEMPHIS JUG BAND

❾ **BOOGIE IN THE DARK** JIMMY REED from I'M JIMMY REED

❿ **EAGLE ROCK** JUNIOR WELLS from BLUES HIT BIG TOWN

❹ **DON'T START ME TO TALKIN'** SONNY BOY WILLIAMSON II from HIS BEST
Sharing a surname made it easy and so he became my second blues discovery after Robert Johnson. For a while in the fifth form at Chislehurst & Sidcup Grammar, I insisted on being called Sonny Boy III.

❺ **THE THRILL IS GONE** B.B. KING from THE BEST OF B.B. KING
Oddly enough, I think I heard Freddie King and Albert King before I heard B.B. and Lucille. But when this came out in 1969, the thrill was just beginning…

❻ **IF LOVING YOU IS WRONG I DON'T WANT TO BE RIGHT** BOBBY 'BLUE' BLAND from HIS CALIFORNIA ALBUM
After discovering him via The Grateful Dead's cover of "Turn On Your Love Light", I bought this when the album was released in 1973 and found myself in blues-soul heaven.

❼ **RED HOUSE** JIMI HENDRIX from ARE YOU EXPERIENCED?
From his 1967 debut album, bought at the time of its release. If anyone reckons being a psychedelic warlord meant he couldn't also be a bluesman, check out not only this, which rivals any of Clapton's electric blues of the period, but also his magnificent acoustic version of "Hear My Train A'Comin".

❽ **NEED YOUR LOVE SO BAD** FLEETWOOD MAC from THE BEST OF PETER GREEN'S FLEETWOOD MAC
Peter Green's finest hour with the best string arrangement I've ever heard on a blues record. A rare instance where I think the cover actually exceeds Little Willie John's 1956 original.

❾ **NEW WALKIN' BLUES** PAUL BUTTERFIELD'S BETTER DAYS from BETTER DAYS
Like many, I became terribly snobbish about white blues once I'd discovered the original Delta sources. But I've always loved this from what I've long regarded as Butterfield's best album – although I've never found anyone who agreed with me.

❿ **PLEASE SEND ME SOMEONE TO LOVE** PERCY MAYFIELD from THE VERY BEST OF PERCY MAYFIELD
I was in my 30s before I really discovered Percy Mayfield – then wondered how I'd missed out on one of the great lyric poets of the blues for so long.

Nigel Williamson

Blues ain't dead

In fact, here are ten tracks that show the blues ain't even endangered.

❶ DEATH LETTER I JOHNNY FARMER WITH ORGANIZED NOIZE from NEW BEATS FROM THE DELTA
A dance beat with samples, it's been done again since, but never with as much feeling for the original.

❷ MISSISSIPPI KKKROSSROADS CHRIS THOMAS KING from DIRTY SOUTH HIP-HOP BLUES
A new version of the crossroads myth, with a redneck lawman in the role of the devil.

❸ BLUESMAN ON THE RUN NUBLUES from DREAMS OF A BLUES MAN
The spirit of the wandering wronged musician oozes from this track.

❹ WHO DO YOU LOVE? THE JESUS AND MARY CHAIN from BARBED WIRE KISSES
An odd choice at first glance, but a cover that has all the swagger and menace left out of other versions.

❺ REVELATIONS CHRIS THOMAS KING from DIRTY SOUTH HIP-HOP BLUES
Mixing Son House's "John The Revelator" with Robert Johnson's "If I had Possession Over Judgement Day" to fine apocalyptic effect.

❻ RIDE ON (FIGHT ON) LITTLE AXE from THE WOLF THAT HOUSE BUILT
The magnificent Skip Mcdonald mixes dub textures with blues guitar on this slice of history.

❼ IT'S BAD YOU KNOW R.L. BURNSIDE from COME ON IN
Contemporary blues on the Fat Possum label, this is the excellent Burnside with remixed beats behind him.

❽ DARK AS THE NIGHT, COLD AS THE GROUND LITTLE AXE from HARD GRIND
An old tune remade in the Little Axe manner.

❾ ST. JAMES SNAKEFARM from SONGS FROM MY FUNERAL
An eerie and moving version of an old standard, the very sparse arrangement adding to the mood of the piece.

❿ DEATH LETTER II JOHNNY FARMER AND ORGANIZED NOIZE WITH PREECHER from NEW BEATS FROM THE DELTA
A rerun of the first track, but now with a rap about death and vengeance that shows how the old blues and new rap worlds are linked.

Steve Birt

Blur

"There's No Other Way" or "Chemical World"? "Beetlebum" or "Tender"? This playlist favours the material leading up to the golden era of Britpop.

❶ I KNOW (EXTENDED) from SHE'S SO HIGH SINGLE
Before they were famous: this bouncy psychedelic classic was the B-side of Blur's first single and could – should? – have been a hit.

❷ SING from LEISURE
An early sign of the band's depth, with a pounding drum and persuasive riff that leaves space to do some of the work yourself.

❸ THERE'S NO OTHER WAY from LEISURE
After Sing come four of the best opening bars in indie history. Awesome, classic guitar-pop, and their first Top 10 hit.

❹ FOR TOMORROW from MODERN LIFE IS RUBBISH
A darker piece that opens their great but hard-to-make second album with strings, London life and perhaps Blur's finest Kinksy la-la-las.

❺ STARSHAPED from MODERN LIFE IS RUBBISH
Worth playing just for the angelic call-and-response vocals. Great oboe too.

❻ TO THE END from PARKLIFE
A hit romantic ballad, made with Laetitia Sadier from Stereolab, which is in a different class – in many ways – from the rest of the album. The *version française* B-side is even better.

❼ CLOVER OVER DOVER from PARKLIFE
OK, so the title's not up to much, but listen to the opening bars and drum fill and you'll be swept into its atmosphere.

❽ THIS IS A LOW from PARKLIFE
Blur's best downbeat song: beautifully constructed, with wailing guitars.

❾ THE UNIVERSAL from THE GREAT ESCAPE
The highlight of a disappointing album, with the "it really, really, really could happen" line, warning that future life might be rubbish, still making it potentially inspirational.

❿ BEETLEBUM from BLUR
A gentle love song that shows the influence of American indie rock.

Daniel Crewe

The name's Bond...

The world's most famous spy also has some of the world's best theme tunes. A life in espionage never sounded so good.

❶ A VIEW TO A KILL DURAN DURAN from DECADE
The lyrics are nonsensical but the collision of Duran Duran's poppy funk and more traditional Bond-esque orchestra make this far superior to the film.

❷ DIAMONDS ARE FOREVER SHIRLEY BASSEY from 20 OF THE BEST
Second only to her own performance on *Goldfinger*, Shirley Bassey's voice drips ice-cold avarice with every note.

❸ FROM RUSSIA WITH LOVE MATT MUNRO from THE VERY BEST OF...
Super smooth crooner Matt Munro brings a touch of romance to this deadly Cold War thriller.

❹ GOLDFINGER SHIRLEY BASSEY from 20 OF THE BEST
Sensual, chilling and passionate all at once, our Shirl's golden tonsils make this possibly the most famous Bond theme ever.

❺ JAMES BOND THEME MONTY NORMAN from COMPLETING THE CIRCLE
Monty Norman's twangy and suspenseful original is a modern classic, recognized as the soundtrack to espionage, mayhem and romance the world over.

❻ LIVE AND LET DIE PAUL MCCARTNEY & WINGS from WINGS GREATEST
Macca with unusual attitude, sounding positively mean. One of the rockiest Bond themes in the canon so far.

❼ MR KISS KISS BANG BANG SHIRLEY BASSEY from THE BEST OF JAMES BOND 30TH ANNIVERSARY EDITION
Almost the theme to what eventually became *Thunderball*, Dionne Warwick recorded a version but Shirley just pips her on this.

❽ ON HER MAJESTY'S SECRET SERVICE THE PROPELLERHEADS from SHAKEN AND STIRRED
John Barry's moody instrumental original is a classic but this beefy, funky version is a seriously groovy mini epic in its own right.

❾ THE MAN WITH THE GOLDEN GUN LULU from THE MAN WHO SOLD THE WORLD
A mediocre Roger Moore effort with a brilliant theme. How Lulu kept a straight face delivering the cheeky double entendres we'll never know.

❿ YOU ONLY LIVE TWICE NANCY SINATRA from THE ESSENTIAL NANCY SINATRA
Achingly beautiful strings and a subtle Oriental atmosphere provide Nancy Sinatra's smoky vocals with an irresistible backdrop.

Essi Berelian

Boogie-woogie

From the whorehouses of New Orleans to the lumber camps of Alabama and from the honky tonks of Texas to the juke joints of Mississippi, the piano has always been at the core of the blues. In latter years, it perhaps lost pride of place in many jazz and blues combos to the ubiquitous Hammond organ. But these ten blues and boogie-woogie piano tracks have all left an indelible stamp on musical history...

❶ PINE TOP'S BOOGIE WOOGIE PINE TOP SMITH from MARTIN SCORSESE PRESENTS THE BLUES: A MUSICAL JOURNEY
The first boogie-woogie piano hit, recorded in Chicago in Dec 1928. Tragically, Smith was murdered before its release.

❷ HONKY TONK TRAIN BLUES MEADE LUX LEWIS from BOOGIE WOOGIE STOMP: SHAKIN' THAT THING
More classic early boogie-woogie, cut in Chicago in 1927, but not released until after Pine Trop's Boogie Woogie. Intriguingly, the two shared an apartment, together with a third boogie-woogie pioneer, Albert Ammons.

❸ HOW LONG HOW LONG BLUES LEROY CARR from WHISKEY IS MY HABIT, WOMEN IS ALL I CRAVE
Intimate and sophisticated piano blues from1928 on Carr's greatest composition, accompanied by Scrapper Blackwell on guitar.

❹ DIRTY MOTHER FOR YOU DON'T YOU KNOW ROOSEVELT SYKES from ROOSEVELT SYKES VOL 4 1934-36
Known as "the Honeydripper", Sykes' ribald 1936 recording evokes the piano blues of the lumber camps, whorehouses and gambling dens where he cut his musical teeth.

❺ ROLL 'EM PETE PETE JOHNSON WITH JOE TURNER from BOOGIE WOOGIE STOMP: SHAKIN' THAT THING
Flawless boogie-woogie, recorded following Turner's specatacular appearance at the "Spirituals to Swing" concert at Carnegie Hall in Dec 1938. Joe Turner's vocal completes the masterpiece.

❻ WORRIED LIFE BLUES BIG MACEO from COMPLETE RECORDED WORKS VOL 1 1941–45
A shuffling classic recorded in Chicago in 1941 with Tampa red on guitar from one of the architects of modern blues piano.

❼ HONEYDRIPPER JOE LIGGINS from JOE LIGGINS AND THE HONEYDRIPPERS
Infectious piano swing from 1944 with some equally irresistible sax from Little Willie Jackson and James "Ham" Jackson.

❽ DRIFTIN' BLUES CHARLES BROWN from DRIFTIN' BLUES: THE BEST OF CHARLES BROWN
Elegant West Coast piano blues betrays Brown's classical training on this 1945 classic released under the name "Johnny Moore's Three Blazers", accompanied by his own smooth-as-velvet voice.

❾ MOTHER EARTH MEMPHIS SLIM from MOTHER EARTH
Sweet sophistication and an immaculate arrangement on Slim's signature tune, recorded in Chicago in 1950.

❿ GOOD MORNING MR BLUES OTIS SPANN from PIANO BLUES
Stark but magisterial solo piano blues recorded in Denmark in the early 1960s after a decade spent playing on some of Chess's greatest recordings by Muddy Waters and others.

Nigel Williamson

Book I read

Do rockers read books? Indie ones obviously do, and write about 'em, too.

❶ READ IT IN BOOKS ECHO AND THE BUNNYMEN from CROCODILES
"I've seen in your eyes/I've read it in books/Who wants love/Without the looks."

❷ BOOK I READ TALKING HEADS from TALKING HEADS '77
"I'm embarrassed to admit it hit the soft spot in my heart /When I found out you wrote the book I read."

❸ BOOKS ABOUT UFOS HUSKER DÜ from NEW DAY RISING
"Walking down a sunny street to the library/ Checking out the latest books on outer space."

❹ ADULT BOOKS X from WILD GIFT
"Like Adult books/I don't understand/ Jackie Susann meant it that way."

❺ WRAPPED UP IN BOOKS BELLE AND SEBASTIAN from DEAR CATASTROPHE WAITRESS
"Our aspirations are wrapped up in books/ Our inclinations are hidden in looks".

❻ EVERYDAY I WRITE THE BOOK ELVIS COSTELLO from PUNCH THE CLOCK
"You said you'd stand by me in the middle of chapter three/But you were up to your old tricks in chapters four, five and six."

❼ THE DANGLING CONVERSATION SIMON AND GARFUNKEL from PARSLEY, SAGE, ROSEMARY AND THYME
"And you read your Emily Dickinson/ And I my Robert Frost."

❽ PAPERBACK WRITER THE BEATLES from REVOLVER
"Dear Sir or Madam, will you read my book?/ It took me years to write, will you take a look?"

❾ I AM THE SUB LIBRARIAN PIANO MAGIC from LOW BIRTH WEIGHT
"A steady diet of Brautigan, 'Tapestry' on the walkman/ Paranormal ill-health from dusting off the top shelf."

Butch Lazorchak

Bootsy

Always more than just George Clinton's sideman, William "Bootsy" Collins, his bass guitar and his ludicrous alter-egos put a spin on P Funk that won him a cartoon audience following and made the lay-deeez melt. He could sing a bit too.

❶ AHH … THE NAME IS BOOTSY, BABY from AHH … THE NAME IS BOOTSY, BABY!
Elastic bass riffs stride across pin point horns, chicken scratch guitars and chants of "We want Bootsy"… Funk is, indeed, its own reward.

❷ STRETCHIN' OUT (IN A RUBBER BAND) from STRETCHIN' OUT IN BOOTSY'S RUBBER BAND
This is really little more than fooling about, from Bootsy and the band, and the result is a breezy, casual obviously-enjoying-themselves funkiness.

❸ YOU GOT ME WIDE OPEN/BOOTSY & BERNIE WORRELL from THE FRIDAY SOUNDTRACK
Bernie's clavinet, Bootsy's bass and something akin to a straight soul ballad But not without a serious sprinkling of "P".

❹ MUNCHIES FOR YOUR LOVE from AHH ... THE NAME IS BOOTSY, BABY!

Ballad that builds slowly and spectacularly, with Bootsy's bass dripping off it to form warm velvety puddles all over your floor.

❺ BE MY BEACH/FUNKADELIC from LET'S TAKE IT TO THE STAGE

A truly tender moment in a double album of acid paranoia, Funkadelic's guitars and stacked vocals were an ideal framework for P Funk's newest recruit.

❻ IF 6 WERE 9/AXIOM FUNK from FUNCRONOMICS

Bootsy and Bill Laswell combining in a trancey, ambient, dubwise style to put an achingly beautiful spin on the Hendrix classic.

❼ NO FLY ZONE/ZILLATRON from LORDS OF THE HARVEST

Fabulously throwaway love song of the type that can only be achieved by days of groove-tightening rehearsal.

❽ I'M LEAVIN' U (GOTTA GO GOTTA GO) from FRESH OUTTA "P" UNIVEERSITY

MC Lyte sparring with Bootsy over an ultra laidback bass riff for the e-e-e-easiest action hip hop ballad.

❾ J.R (JUST RIGHT) INSTRUMENTAL/BOOTSY'S NEW RUBBER BAND from BLASTERS OF THE UNIVERSE (DISC ONE)

Perfectly pointless deeply funky five minutes of fooling about. Perfectly perfect, I guess.

❿ HOLLYWOOD SQUARES "FUNK ATTACK" from PLAYER OF THE YEAR

Rubberized, nursery rhyme funk in which Boosty celebrates everything ... everything Bootsy, and it's impossible not get swept up in the proceedings.

Lloyd Bradley

Cool bossa

Bossa nova will always mean lift music to some, but to its fans the genre has produced some of the most laid-back, melting small-hours music ever made – sweet moments of serenity in a noisy world. Some of the very coolest...

❶ LIGIA JOÃO GILBERTO & STAN GETZ from THE BEST OF TWO WORLDS

Singer and guitarist Gilberto – bossa nova's originator – in a 1976 reunion with the master saxophonist, on one of Antonio Carlos Jobim's most achingly gentle songs.

❷ BOM SINAL CELSO FONSECA from NATURAL

It can still be done. Fonseca glides through a modern bossa without a hair out of place.

❸ ELA E CARIOCA VINICIUS CANTUARIA from VINICIUS

A contemporary, left-field take on Jobim's classic paean to a Rio beauty.

❹ MARIA/LINDA FLOR MARIA BETHÂNIA & JOÃO GILBERTO from 25 ANOS

A pair of old-school Brazilian ballads, caressed into life by two masters of the style.

❺ SAMBA DO AVAIO LEILA PINHEIRO from THE STORY OF BOSSA NOVA

Another Jobim warhorse, about looking at Rio from a plane, given a treatment as soft and lush as a club-class seat.

❻ CORAÇÃO VAGABUNDO JOÃO GILBERTO from JOÃO: VOZ E VIOLÃO

Singing and playing as if he's trying not to wake the baby next door, Gilberto gives a great reading of Caetano's lament for the waywardness of the heart.

❼ APARECIDA IVAN LINS & TERENCE BLANCHARD from THE HEART SPEAKS

Blanchard's muted jazz trumpet tiptoes through one of Lins's greatest compositions.

❽ MALAGA JOÃO GILBERTO from JOÃO

Forsaking Portuguese for Italian – but with an accent so thick the difference is almost academic – Gilberto's vocal is cushioned by wonderful, swooning strings.

❾ COISA MAIS LINDA CAETANO VELOSO from CAETANO, THE DEFINITIVE COLLECTION

Caetano sings this tender declaration of love as if he's whispering in her ear.

❿ CORCOVADO JOÃO GILBERTO from O AMOR, O SORRISO E A FLOR

Well, this Jobim song had to be in – though this is the first version, without the lisping Astrud Gilberto. At 1'58", a perfect miniature, arguably never bettered in Gilberto's career.

Alex Webb

David Bowie

Approaching the end of four decades in the music business, the Dame of Rock has a back catalogue of classic tunes to live and die for – and maybe it's time to forget that he also recorded The Laughing Gnome. Here's a scattering of the classics; if life had any justice, it should really be twice the length.

❶ CHANGES from HUNKY DORY
Swinging from *The Golden Bough* and quaking with futureshock, Bowie moves from doubt and disappointment through to a joyous yell of defiance as he sees the children growing strong and marching to save us all.

❷ LIFE ON MARS from HUNKY DORY
Orchestral flourishes, trilling strings and a thoughtful, well-paced guitar solo make a beautiful accompaniment to Bowie's celebration of the ravishing power of cinema (when you're young, misunderstood and have just had a row with your parents).

❸ STARMAN from THE RISE AND FALL OF ZIGGY STARDUST & THE SPIDERS FROM MARS
Ziggy's eleven songs were all but perfect, with Bowie and Mick Ronson hanging happily off one another's shoulders, singing and grinning at the musical and emotional harmony they'd found. Starman itself is patent nonsense, but who ever said classic pop had to make sense?

❹ REBEL REBEL from THE RISE AND FALL OF ZIGGY STARDUST & THE SPIDERS FROM MARS
Quintessential Ziggy. "You've got your mother in a whirl, She's not sure if you're a boy or a girl" ticks the gender-confusion box and "You can't get enough, but enough ain't the test" covers the obscurity, while Mick and the band take care of the headbanging pop.

❺ JOHN, I'M ONLY DANCING from BEST OF
One of the man's great singles, but never part of an "official" album, this is purest 1970s pop, set to a monumental guitar riff.

❻ GOLDEN YEARS from STATION TO STATION
After *The Man Who Fell To Earth*, Bowie reverts to full-on diva mode with blood-chilling, heartwarming and passionate results.

❼ TVC15 from STATION TO STATION
In what seems a bizarre prequel to recent horror flick *The Ring*, our protagonist's boy/girlfriend crawls from the living room into the TV, never to be seen again. Though the lyrics are mad as a badger, this is clearly one of the all-time great dance tunes.

❽ HEROES from "HEROES"
Take Fripp's epic guitar, add Bowie's gently burning vocal and you get a piece that swells so big that they couldn't film it even in wide-screen. The greatest song he's ever written.

❾ BREAKING GLASS from LOW
Drug-induced madness, paranoia, shame, defiance and regret, and there are only four lines of lyrics! Deep dark beats and downright menacing guitar turn this into an episode from the darker side of glam rock.

❿ LET'S DANCE from LET'S DANCE
Bowie's 666th reinvention was prompted by a new label, vastly improved financial arrangements, decent management and 1980s star-treatment. Match an artist of Bowie's quality with a producer like Nile Rogers's and you can sit back and watch the magic happen.

Al Spicer

Boy George/ Culture Club

Flamboyant, camp, witty and blessed with a gorgeous voice, Boy George cut some sublime pop with Culture Club before an intermittently successful solo career.

CULTURE CLUB

❶ DO YOU REALLY WANT TO HURT ME from KISSING TO BE CLEVER
This loping, reggae-inflected tune topped the UK charts and made the Boy a thrillingly unlikely household name.

❷ TIME (CLOCK OF MY HEART) from KISSING TO BE CLEVER
A heart-stopping vocal from George as he waxes soulfully on CC's second huge hit.

❸ CHURCH OF THE POISON MIND from KISSING TO BE CLEVER
Faux Motown with wailing gospel-flavoured backing vocals. Where's the church, George?

❹ I'LL TUMBLE 4 YA from KISSING TO BE CLEVER
Infectious, uptempo playground pop – who would have thought that a cross-dresser would become a kids favourite?

❺ KARMA CHAMELEON from COLOUR BY NUMBERS
#1 on both sides of the Atlantic and much else of the world – this is CC at the peak of their pop powers.

❻ MISS ME BLIND from COLOUR BY NUMBERS
Funky dancefloor workout number with George warning an estranged boyfriend that he's gonna miss him.

❼ THE WAR SONG from FROM LUXURY TO HEARTACHE
"War is stupid and people are stupid", sings George on perhaps the silliest protest song ever. Catchy though.

BOY GEORGE

❽ EVERYTHING I OWN from GREATEST MOMENTS
George goes solo and repents for heroin addiction with a lilting reggae take (via Ken Boothe) on the David Gates ballad.

❾ THE CRYING GAME from GREATEST MOMENTS
The Dave Berry tune became the theme tune for Neil Jordan's film. When George sings "I know all there is to know about the crying game", you believe him.

❿ EVIL IS SO CIVILISED from CHEAPNESS AND BEAUTY
George rages against homophobic murders, backed by a cracking glam-rock band.

Garth Cartwright

Billy Bragg

A career of mixing pop and politics makes Billy Bragg easy to caricature. But his Barking manner hides a keen ear for cant and a punning lyrical gift easily the equal of Costello or Ray Davies.

❶ A NEW ENGLAND from LIFE'S A RIOT WITH SPY VERSUS SPY
This was Bragg's debut, with the acoustic wallop of a busker echoing off a tiled underpass. Everything he does well is wrapped up here: despite the insistence that he isn't looking for a New England, just another girl, he clearly wants both.

❷ BETWEEN THE WARS from BETWEEN THE WARS
What comes on like 1930s nostalgia turns out to be 1980s foreboding. Now as dated as a nineteenth-century union ballad, its plea for moderation as the heart of the nation remains sweetly affecting.

❸ WORLD TURNED UPSIDE DOWN from BETWEEN THE WARS
Leon Rosselson's tribute to Gerald Winstanley and the Diggers (and, obliquely, to the Marxist historian Christopher Hill), and their occupation of St George's Hill in Weybridge, Surrey, in 1649.

❹ A13 TRUNK ROAD TO THE SEA from PEEL SESSIONS
As a musical parodist, Bragg is a rarity, inasmuch as he writes parodies that can be listened to more than once. This Essex take on "Route 66" makes the end of the road in Southend (via Grays, Thurrock, Basildon and Leigh-on-Sea) sound almost tempting.

❺ LEVI STUBBS' TEARS from TALKING WITH THE TAXMAN ABOUT POETRY
A tiny domestic drama: the central character's only comfort is her Four Tops tape. And just before the end, over Bragg's percussive guitar, Dave Woodhead's flugelhorn floats as fragile as an angel.

❻ WAITING FOR THE GREAT LEAP FORWARDS from WORKERS' PLAYTIME
Rueful political songs are few and far between, and this is one of the finest. In the wake of Labour's third election defeat of 1987, Bragg looks back on a career of mixing pop and politics and wonders what the use is, before rousing himself and his audience through a singalong chorus of slogans, half-ridiculous and half-defiant.

❼ RUMOURS OF WAR from DON'T TRY THIS AT HOME
By the early 1990s there was a New World Order, and Cold War certainties dissolved into turbulence in the Balkans and the Gulf. Rumours of War deals subtly with domestic denial of clouds on foreign horizons. June Tabor, uncharacteristically, later murdered it with over-emotion; Bragg lets it speak for itself.

❽ A PICT SONG from WILLIAM BLOKE
Bragg became increasingly obsessed with notions of Englishness, and how it can be rescued from nationalism. And so, inevitably, he comes up against Rudyard Kipling, another populist with an uneasy relationship with Empire. Bragg sets Kipling's verse to abrasive guitar that harks back to his earliest work.

❾ ALL YOU FASCISTS BOUND TO LOSE from MERMAID AVENUE TOUR OFFICIAL BOOTLEG
None too subtle, this lyric of Woody Guthrie's: Bragg and the Blokes give it a rousing chorus that falls just the right side of embarrassing.

❿ ENGLAND HALF ENGLISH from ENGLAND HALF ENGLISH
Still celebrating the new England, one that mingles and mixes cultures as it has done throughout the centuries. The musical mixing is in the hands of a band directed by the great ex-Mustapha, Ben Mandelson.

David Honigmann

Billy Bragg's
Busking tunes

" I did a bit of busking in London in the early 1980s, sometimes earning as much as fifteen quid a day. Of the many songs I busked, these were my favourites. Occasionally I play one or two during my soundcheck, just to keep my hand in…"

❶ ME AND BOBBY MCGEE KRIS KRISTOFFERSON from THE BEST OF KRIS KRISTOFFERSON
Any busker worth their salt should be able to play this, a classic of the genre. Contains the frequently mis-heard lyric "Somewhere miscellaneous Lord, I let her slip away…"

❷ BRING IT ON HOME TO ME SAM COOKE from THE BEST OF SAM COOKE
I always found a little Sam Cooke helped things along, be it "Wonderful World", "A Change is Gonna Come" or this beauty.

❸ LOVE HAS NO PRIDE BONNIE RAITT from GIVE IT UP
Complex chord changes, but they really wring the heartbreak out of a lyric that must rank among the greatest sad songs ever sung.

❹ CATCH THE WIND DONOVAN from WHAT'S BIN DID AND WHAT'S BIN HID
A song that just rolls gently along, drawing the listener in so that by the time they get to where you are playing their hand is already in their pocket…

❺ EARLY MORNING RAIN GORDON LIGHTFOOT from LIGHTFOOT!
Easy to play, great to sing. Buskers should always do a couple of rambling songs, to give passers-by the impression that they are travelling round the world with nothing but their musical talent to support them, even if they are just travelling in from Acton Town where they live with their Mum and Dad.

❻ THE MOUNTAINS OF MOURNE DON MCLEAN from PLAYIN' FAVOURITES
It's always good to have an unashamedly sentimental song in your repertoire. This was mine, written in 1896 by Percy French, an Irishman who also wrote "Abdul Abulbul Amir".

❼ THAT'S ENTERTAINMENT THE JAM from DIG THE NEW BREED
This was my nod to contemporary taste – the only Jam song you can play convincingly on an acoustic guitar.

❽ SPANISH IS THE LOVING TONGUE BOB DYLAN from DYLAN
Dylan wrote quite a few busker's standards, but not this one, which is based on a poem by a guy named Badger Clarke.

❾ YOU DON'T MISS YOUR WATER OTIS REDDING from OTIS BLUE
The definitive William Bell classic…

❿ CAN'T HELP FALLING IN LOVE ELVIS PRESLEY from THE HOLLYWOOD HITS
"Wise men say only fools rush in…" There was something about Elvis ballads that just kept the small change coming, and this one was my *pièce de résistance*. Sung full-throated on my favourite pitch, the long subway that runs from South Kensington tube station to the Science Museum, I found the tiled walls of the tunnel greatly assisted my attempts to summon up some of its overwrought grandeur.

Brazil classics

The country covering half of South America produces more than its fair share of music, which is almost always instantly recognizable as Brazilian. After all, this is the culture which gave the world both samba and bossa nova.

See also BOSSA NOVA and SAMBA playlists.

❶ ADEUS BATUCADA CARMEN MIRANDA from IMPERATRIZ DO SAMBA
Though best known for wearing a fruit headdress during her Hollywood career of the 1940s, this 1935 hit shows why Miranda was the original "Empress of Samba".

❷ DESAFINADO JOÃO GILBERTO from JOÃO VOZ E VIOLÃO
Originally recorded by Gilberto in 1957 – when it was hailed as the first bossa nova – this remake from 2000 shows him still to be a master of timing.

❸ THE GIRL FROM IPANEMA ASTRUD GILBERTO from THE GENIUS OF ASTRUD GILBERTO

By singing slightly off key, the daughter of João Gilberto (also on this 1963 recording) ensured enduring listenability; as millions made subconscious corrections, she made millions.

❹ MAS QUE NADA JORGE BEN JOR from THE DEFINITIVE COLLECTION

A worldwide hit that many will know (even if they don't know its name) for its unforgettable chorus. Also a hit for Sergio Mendes, though this is the superior original.

❺ CRICKETS SING FOR ANA MARIA MARCOS VALLE from BRAZILICA (VARIOUS ARTISTS)

A jumpy little English-language samba-pop number from 1968, by a singer-songwriter who is still making good records.

❻ CHICLETE COM BANANA GILBERTO GIL from THE EARLY YEARS

A defiant musical manifesto from this pioneer of the tropicalia movement, now culture minister for Brazil's socialist government.

❼ LONDON, LONDON CAETANO VELOSO from THE DEFINITIVE COLLECTION

Another tropicalista, Veloso penned one of his most memorable tunes while in exile from Brazil's military government. Depictions of homesickness don't come much more soulful.

❽ ROMARIA ELIS REGINA from LITTLE PEPPER: THE DEFINITIVE COLLECTION

The late lamented diva lived fast and died young, leaving behind a trail of wonderful interpretations. This intensely spiritual 1977 recording lives up to its title ("Pilgrimage").

❾ MARIA, MARIA MILTON NASCIMENTO from CLUBE DA ESQUINA 2

This exhilarating love song from Nascimento's seminal late 1970s masterpiece always gets the crowds going at his gigs.

❿ RITMO NUMBER ONE PAULINHO DA COSTA from BATUCADA THE SOUND OF THE FAVELAS

Absolutely everything you can do with percussion instruments in eight and a half minutes of glorious, driving samba. Who needs melody?

Jon Lusk

Jacques Brel

The work of the Flemish songwriter and poet is familiar through a host of cover versions; here is a choice selection.

❶ MATHILDE SCOTT WALKER from SINGS JACQUES BREL

Scott Walker's interpretations are the standard by which others are judged, and this rip-snorting romp sees him getting fantastically carried away.

❷ IF YOU GO AWAY DUSTY SPRINGFIELD from NEXT: A TRIBUTE TO JACQUES BREL

An aptly deadpan version of the heartbreaking "Ne Me Quitte Pas" over sublime orchestral backing.

❸ AMSTERDAM DAVID BOWIE from NEXT: A TRIBUTE TO JACQUES BREL

Bowie pays tribute over a minimal acoustic guitar backing, slowly building to a thrashing climax and much impassioned shrieking.

❹ THE BULLS MARC AND THE MAMBAS from TORMENT AND TOREROS

Almond covered this tale of matadors again on a later solo album, but this stripped-back Mambas version drips with withering sarcasm.

❺ IF WE ONLY HAVE LOVE DIONNE WARWICK from NEXT: A TRIBUTE TO JACQUES BREL

Better known for her Bacharach interpretations, Warwick's version of "Quand on n'a que l'amour" is, nevertheless, an unfailing showstopper.

❻ MY DEATH SCOTT WALKER from SINGS JACQUES BREL

There's room for two Scott Walker selections in this list, and this sombre, moving performance is a definite highlight.

❼ SEASONS IN THE SUN TERRY JACKS from NEXT: A TRIBUTE TO JACQUES BREL

Jacks prepares his friend, his dad and his girlfriend for his imminent death. The royalties paid for a new roof for Jacks' house, apparently.

❽ NEXT GAVIN FRIDAY from NEXT: A TRIBUTE TO JACQUES BREL

An already grim tune is turned into a gruesome nightmare by a savage, spitting Friday and his off-kilter backing troupe.

❾ THE DESPERATE ONES NINA SIMONE from NEXT: A TRIBUTE TO JACQUES BREL

A wonderfully intimate, personal version featuring Simone's beautifully erratic voice and extravagantly improvised piano.

JACKY MARC ALMOND from TENEMENT SYMPHONY
This galloping version of Brels' autobiographical opus ripped up the original score, and rewrote it in synth format.

Rhodri Marsden

Brill Building

Situated at 1619 Broadway, New York City, the Brill Building was a nexus of popular music in the post-war world. At its peak, some 165 music businesses had offices in the building. They included record companies, agents and managers, and, famously, music publishers who employed teams of salaried songwriters to churn out teen anthems and other hits by the hour.

1 STUPID CUPID CONNIE FRANCIS from THE BEST OF CONNIE FRANCIS
The first hit penned by a 19-year-old Neil Sedaka and his lyricist Howard Greenfield. They'd begun writing together in 1952 when Sedaka was 13.

2 TEENAGER IN LOVE DION from THE BEST OF DION AND THE BELMONTS
Doc Pomus had a track record in blues and R&B, writing for Big Joe Turner and Ray Charles. Then he teamed up with Mort Shuman in a Brill Building cubicle and started turning out hits for Fabian, Bobby Darin – and this unforgettable cry of youthful angst for Italian-American doo-wop singer Dion Di Mucci.

3 TAKE GOOD CARE OF MY BABY BOBBY VEE from THE VERY BEST OF . . .
An American #1 from the pens of husband and wife team Gerry Goffin and Carole King for the clean-cut boy from Fargo, North Dakota, who had hits with a string of Brill Building teen anthems.

4 WILL YOU STILL LOVE ME TOMORROW THE SHIRELLES from THE VERY BEST OF...
Perhaps the most famous of the early Goffin/King hits, due to King's own plaintive reinvention of the song almost a decade later on her platinum *Tapestry* album.

5 THE LOCOMOTION LITTLE EVA from THE BEST OF...
Another winner from the Goffin/King team and a hit all over again many years later for Kylie Minogue.

6 I WANNA LOVE HIM SO BAD THE JELLY BEANS from JELLY BEANS
Sometimes the Brill Building was more like a marriage bureau than a songwriting factory. Jeff Barry and

Ellie Greenwich met there, married and then wrote a stream of hits for Phil Spector as well as this wonderful piece of 1960s pop innocence.

7 UPTOWN THE CRYSTALS from UPTOWN
Evocative urban romanticism 1962-style on a Phil Spctor production of a song written by another of the Brill's married couples, Barry Mann and Cynthia Weill.

8 OH CAROL NEIL SEDAKA from THE VERY BEST OF...
A 1959 lament for Sedaka's former girlfriend, Carole King. Life could get very incestuous around the Brill. She replied with a song called "Oh Neil"...

9 CHERRY CHERRY NEIL DIAMOND from THE ULTIMATE COLLECTION
Discovered by Jeff Barry and Ellie Greenwich singing in a Greenwich Village coffee house, Diamond became a Brill staffer who wrote hits for everyone from Bobby Vinton to the Monkees. This Barry/Greenwich production gave him his own first chart hit in 1966.

10 WHY DO LOVERS BREAK EACH OTHER'S HEARTS? BOB B. SOXX AND THE BLUE JEANS from ZIP-A-DEE-DOO-DAH
Before she met and married Barry Mann, Ellie Greenwich worked briefly with Tony Powers, coming up with this classic teen anthem for one of Phil Spector's many manufactured groups.

Nigel Williamson

Brit-blues

By the mid-1960s, most of the great American blues performers couldn't get arrested in their homeland. But they found an enthusiastic young audience in Britain where the blues enjoyed a boom and inspired the likes of Eric Clapton, Jimmy Page and The Rolling Stones. Quite what qualified middle-class white boys from the English suburbs to play the music of sharecroppers from the Mississippi Delta has never been fully explained. But there's no doubt that they played it with a genuine conviction and passion.

1 I'D RATHER GO BLIND CHICKEN SHACK from CHICKEN SHACK: THE COLLECTION
Singer Christine Perfect (later McVie) lived up to her then name on the Etta James song.

2 I'M GOING HOME TEN YEARS AFTER from WOODSTOCK
A highlight of the Woodstock festival, movie and soundtrack album which saw Alvin Lee crowned the fastest guitarist in the West.

❸ NEED YOUR LOVE SO BAD FLEETWOOD MAC from THE BEST OF FLEETWOOD MAC

Peter Green's guitar plus strings equals blues heaven. on this Little Willie John song

❹ SPOONFUL CREAM from FRESH CREAM

Willie Dixon gets the power trio treatment, copped by Clapton from Buddy Guy's band.

❺ RAMBLIN' ON MY MIND JOHN MAYALL'S BLUESBREAKERS (WITH ERIC CLAPTON) from BLUESBREAKERS

Robert Johnson cover from the only album "God" ever made with the Godfather.

❻ TRAIN TO NOWHERE SAVOY BROWN from BLUE MATTER

A train to nowhere arguably carrying coals to Newcastle from the one British blues band to enjoy more success in America than at home.

❼ GOIN' DOWN SLOW FREE from TONS OF SOBS

They were alright then, back in the days when their debut album made them the toughest British blues combo of them all.

❽ MESSIN' WITH THE KID RORY GALLAGHER from LIVE IN EUROPE/STAGE STRUCK

Not really British, as he came from across the Irish Sea, but he sure had those white boy blues.

❾ BOYFRIEND BLUES JO-ANN KELLY from BLUES AND GOSPEL

The British Bonnie Raitt, who turned down the chance to sing with both Canned Heat and Johnny Winter.

❿ DEAR JILL BLODWYN PIG from A HEAD RINGS OUT

Perhaps the best British slide guitar solo ever, from ex-Jethro Tull guitarist Mick Abrahams.

Nigel Williamson

Britpop

When Blur, Oasis et al. arrived in the early 1990s, British pop music became a national obsession. For a time it seemed that even the attentions of Prime Minister (and student rock-singer) Tony Blair couldn't kill it. Nowadays it seems very much like history, but these ten numbers, released from 1993 to 1995, remain live and kicking.

❶ PARKLIFE BLUR from PARKLIFE

The Colchester group's third album provided a quintessentially English snapshot, with this jaunty Phil Daniels-enhanced song.

❷ LIVE FOREVER OASIS from DEFNITELY MAYBE

The first Oasis song to break the UK, this displayed the burgeoning songcraft of Noel Gallagher. Brother Liam's unrefined vocals neatly counterpoint the gentle melody, and there's a triumphant guitar solo.

❸ CONNECTION ELASTICA from ELASTICA

A moody three-quarters-female band with a sharp attitude and a sound that wore its influences on its sleeve. Debts to The Stranglers, Wire and Blondie were obvious, but this is still a pop-punk gem.

❹ ALRIGHT SUPERGRASS from I SHOULD COCO

A summertime singalong anthem that thrust the hairy Oxford trio into the big league, the song throbs with teenage exuberance and shows a keen ear for melody.

❺ I CAN'T IMAGINE THE WORLD WITHOUT ME ECHOBELLY from EVERYBODY'S GOT ONE

A tad Morrissey-inclined, but Echobelly made their own impression through provocative lyrics, chunky tunes and Sonya Madan's distinctive intonation.

❻ COMMON PEOPLE PULP from DIFFERENT CLASS

Jarvis Cocker's Sheffield smoothies had been making music for years before their popularity rocketed in the Britpop era. A bouncy ode to class pretension, Common People matched sharp, witty lyrics with disco-friendliness.

❼ INBETWEENER SLEEPER from SMART

Buoyant, husky vocals were Louise Wener's speciality, coupled with a sassy, cynical take on suburbia. Bright, chiming guitars and a shout-out chorus, too.

❽ FOR THE DEAD GENE from OLYMPIAN

A spoonful of The Jam and a wink to The Faces enhanced the Morrissey-like intonation of singer Martin Rossiter on the Watford band's debut single. Graceful and sophisticated, it was a welcome antidote to the boorish rivalries of their contemporary Britpoppers.

❾ SO YOUNG SUEDE from SUEDE

Bowie-esque glamour, Bernard Butler's exhilarating guitar and Anderson's trademark wailing captivated an army of devotees. So Young covers the themes that would come to be known as Suede's stock-in-trade: sex, drugs and alienated youth.

❿ SPEAKEASY SHED SEVEN from CHANGE GIVER

These next-big-things from York enjoyed moderate success at home and were great live performers, led by the rubber-limbed Rick Witter. Top-notch riffs and strident but smooth vocals show off the Sheddies' best qualities.

Ed Wright

b

Britpop (again!)

Britpop returned around 2004, as home-grown acts again dominated the UK airwaves and set off to dent the US, loading credible songs with bold influences, youthful energy and teasing wit.

❶ CAN'T STAND ME NOW THE LIBERTINES from THE LIBERTINES
Frontmen Carl Barat and Pete Doherty serialized their turbulent friendship through emotionally charged songwriting. Few Libertines tracks surpass the impact of this poppy yet poignant cat-and-mouse duet.

❷ I BET YOU LOOK GOOD ON THE DANCEFLOOR ARCTIC MONKEYS from (WHATEVER PEOPLE SAY I AM, THAT'S WHAT I'M NOT)
The Sheffield young guns pound their way through three minutes of hot-blooded nightclub ogling, amid incessant guitars, drums and yelps. But it was the scattergun wordplay and couplets that really set them apart, with this take on grimy, after-hours Britain.

❸ NAÏVE THE KOOKS from INSIDE IN INSIDE OUT
A tightly-wrought ingot of radio-friendly indie pop that splices twangy, exuberant guitars with a soft, conversational lyric, the latter seemingly at odds with the Brighton quartet's shaggy, leather-jacketed rockstar guise.

❹ DO YOU WANT TO? FRANZ FERDINAND from YOU COULD HAVE IT SO MUCH BETTER
This explosive pop stompathon from the Glasgow rockers' second album invites you boogie on down to their artschool party. Alex Kapranos's arch delivery of his cocksure lyrics leaves you in no doubt it's an evening not to miss.

❺ THE PRAYER BLOC PARTY from A WEEKEND IN THE CITY
The East End indie kids inject a crunking dancefloor vibe to their spiky sonic template. Pounding drum loops, swirling synths and gnawing guitars rise up in this hymn to clubbing excess.

❻ RUBY KAISER CHIEFS from YOUR'S TRULY ANGRY MOB
From the top of the Leeds quintet's second album, Ruby's confident, foot-stomping formula renews the band's vows to dispatch catchy, riffing tunes to the masses with an unshakeable chorus.

❼ MADE-UP LOVE SONG #43 GUILLEMOTS from THROUGH THE WINDOWPANE)
Fyfe Dangerfield's eccentric ornithologists soar through the airwaves with this shimmering slice of orchestral whimsy. Disarmingly haphazard lyrics bathed in

---

Carl Barat's
Libertine raves

The Libertines, the London-based band CARL BARAT formed with Pete Doherty, achieved notoriety for their in-fighting and drug abuse. Yet the intoxicating, grimy anthems of their self-titled debut album proved it was more than hype and that they were one of the most exciting new bands in many a year. Then it all went horribly wrong as the band split amid lurid tabloid headlines. Still, here's what Barat himself rates.

❶ OH YOU PRETTY THINGS DAVID BOWIE from HUNKY DORY

❷ HURRICANE BOB DYLAN from DESIRE

❸ PERSONALITY CRISIS NEW YORK DOLLS from NEW YORK DOLLS

❹ REMOTE CONTROL THE CLASH from THE CLASH

❺ ETON RIFLES THE JAM from SETTING SONS

❻ NO MORE HEROES THE STRANGLERS from NO MORE HEROES

❼ TOO MUCH TOO YOUNG THE SPECIALS from THE SPECIALS

❽ BIG MOUTH STRIKES AGAIN THE SMITHS from BIG MOUTH STRIKES AGAIN

❾ SORTED FOR E'S AND WIZZ PULP from DIFFERENT CLASS

❿ FIT BUT YOU KNOW IT THE STREETS from A GRAND DON'T COME FOR FREE

mellifluous instrumentation deliver three-and-a-half minutes of heart-melting magic.

❽ SMOKERS OUTSIDE THE HOSPITAL DOORS EDITORS from AN END HAS A START

This lesson in majestic melancholy sees Birmingham's moody art-rockers embellish the urgent Interpol-informed sound of their first outing with lush guitarwork and choral flourishes as Tom Smith's rich, velvety baritone draws comparison with Ians Curtis & McCulloch.

❾ EITHER WAY THE TWANG from LOVE IT WHEN I FEEL LIKE THIS)

Another Birmingham band, this time fusing Madchester era guitar licks to Phil Etheridge's raw vocals, and drawing on weekend pubbing, clubbing and lovin' with savvy swagger.

❿ OUR VELOCITY MAXÏMO PARK from OUR EARTHLY PLEASURES

Lurching between melodies and rhythms like spinning musical plates, this frenetic pinball of a track from the spirited Geordie rockers whizzes along breathlessly, true to form. Paul Smith cranks up his vocals to match the breakneck guitar-and-drums ricochets (or is it the other way round?)

Ed Wright

Brit-reggae

British reggae never quite managed to sound "authentically" Jamaican – and was all the better for it. The musical environment West Indians experienced growing up in the UK meant these acts were much more aware of a pop mainstream, imported US soul and rock. Hence lovers' rock (covered also in a separate list), interesting instrumentation and Steel Pulse.

❶ WARRIOR CHARGE ASWAD from SHOWCASE

A militant roots reggae track like no other, which could only have been made in Britain and succeeds in sounding positive, obnoxious, celebratory and scary all at the same time.

❷ HARD TIMES PABLO GAD from DON'T CALL US IMMIGRANTS (VARIOUS ARTISTS)

When this double-time hi-stepping rocker came out in 1979, nobody guessed it was British, but then we were having too much fun singing along with the chorus: "When I was a yout', I used to burn collie weed in a Rizla/Now I am a man, I jus' a burn collie weed in a chalwa..."

❸ SIX ONE PENNY MISTY IN ROOTS from DON'T CALL US IMMIGRANTS (VARIOUS ARTISTS)

Gently rocking roots that sums up UK reggae in its clever approach to pop-friendly sounds and easy-access melodies, but with a bass-and-drum balance that leaves you no doubt what it is.

❹ MUSIC IN THE AIR MATUMBI from EMPIRE ROAD: THE BEST OF MATUMBI

Matumbi were always the cleverest, most musically literate and stylistically open of the British reggae bands, and this is them at their cool, creeping best.

❺ NATTY ROCKERS TRADITION from TRADITION IN DUB

The dub of their big hit "Moving On", this is pretty basic bass, drum, spinning echo and a few rising piano chords, but their tricky, cascading approach to the mix gives it real class.

❻ SOME GUYS HAVE ALL THE LUCK MAXI PRIEST from BEST OF ME

British reggae taken to its logical conclusion, as Maxi manages to be totally TOTP-friendly, but retains all the deep roots feeling he needs to keep it on the right side of the riddim police.

❼ LOVE MARCUS BLACK HARMONY single

A cruelly under-appreciated reggae band who were usually rocking dancefloors with their smoooove lovers rock, but here they apply the same easy-rocking action to deep roots lyrics.

❽ SILLY GAMES JANET KAY from I'M IN THE MOOD FOR LOVE

This best-known, best-loved lovers' rock tune has all its pop-reggae ducks in a row: slow-skanking beat, pop-oriented melody, strong bassline and a teenage girl singing about the problems of her love life.

❾ HIGHER RANKING DENNIS BOVELL AND 4th STREET ORCHESTRA from SCIENTIFIC HIHER RANKING DUB

Circular, escalating dub track, by Matumbi under an assumed name, that manages to turn in on itself two or three times and still come out sounding upful.

❿ HANDSWORTH REVOLUTION STEEL PULSE from HANDSWORTH REVOLUTION

Shimmering, superbly crafted, intricate song that would be a standout track in any genre from rock to pop to soul, but it's reggae and it raised the bar for anybody who came after...

Lloyd Bradley

Mykaell S Riley's
Brit-reggae roots

MYKAELL S RILEY was a founder member of Steel Pulse, and co-wrote their definitive *Handsworth Revolution* album. Today, based in London, he runs The Reggae Philarmonic Orchestra, lectures in music at the University of Westminster and composes TV and film music.

❶ HANGING ON A STRING LOOSE ENDS from THE BEST OF LOOSE ENDS
Great 1980s British R&B that we have not seen the likes of since.

❷ HANDSWORTH REVOLUTION STEEL PULSE from HANDSWORTH REVOLUTION
The revolution has taken place but little has changed.

❸ THE TIDE IS HIGH THE PARAGONS from THE TREASURE ISLE STORY
Demonstrates the resilience of a great song: Blondie… Atomic Kitten… as the lyric says, it's number one.

❹ GHOST TOWN THE SPECIALS from THE SPECIALS SINGLES
Great social commentary from the Midlands.

❺ MOVE ON UP CURTIS MAYFIELD from MOVE ON UP
Classic 1970s soul, and for the world's black population the message remains the same.

❻ WALK ON BY ISAAC HAYES from HOT BUTTERED SOUL
Powerfully mellow version of a timeless classic, by the original walrus of love.

❼ SKIN DEEP DUKE ELLINGTON from SKIN DEEP
An exciting expression of individual feeling and musicianship – especially if you like drum solos.

❽ COCONUT ROCK THE SKATALITES from STUDIO ONE SCORCHER INSTRUMENTALS
Ska meets jazz in a big band Jamaican swing style.

❾ LONG TALL SALLY SALLY LITTLE RICHARD from LONG TALL SALLY
Rock'n'roll comes in many forms but not much better than this.

❿ THERE'S NOTHING LIKE THIS OMAR from THERE'S NOTHING LIKE THIS
Classic British soul, which demonstrates we can deliver – if only in small doses.

Broken-hearted

Breaking-up is by a long chalk the most written about subject in popular music. Let's hear it for dark nights of the soul.

❶ MOST OF THE TIME BOB DYLAN from OH MERCY
He made the greatest break-up album of all time with *Blood On The Tracks*. But this song combines emotional desolation with a wonderfully knowing self-delusion: "I can survive, I can endure and I don't even think about her…most of the time."

❷ YOU'VE LOST THAT LOVIN' FEELIN' RIGHTEOUS BROTHERS from YOU'VE LOST THAT LOVIN' FEELING
That heart-stopping moment when you're still head-over-heels and it suddenly dawns that the object of adoration no longer feels quite the same way…

❸ HERE COME THOSE TEARS AGAIN JACKSON BROWNE from THE PRETENDER
Just when you thought you were getting over the betrayal, she walks back in as if nothing had ever happened. Do you slam the door in her face or lick her all over like a grateful puppy?

❹ IT'S TOO LATE CAROLE KING from TAPESTRY
"Stayed in bed all morning just to pass the time…" Stop moping and pull yourself together, woman.

❺ STOP! IN THE NAME OF LOVE THE SUPREMES from GREATEST HITS
At Motown's peak Holland, Dozier and Holland seemed to turn out classic teenage tear-jerkers every week. For the Supremes alone, they penned "Where Did Our Love Go", "My World Is Empty Without You" and "You Keep Me Hangin' On", among others. But perhaps best of all was this 1965 pleading, needing piece of pop perfection.

❻ NOTHING COMPARES 2 U SINEAD O'CONNOR from I DO NOT WANT WHAT I HAVEN'T GOT

Prince wrote it, but it was Sinead who recorded the most heartbreaking version, accompanied by a marvellous video with a tear rolling down her cheek that she insists to this day was real.

❼ YESTERDAY THE BEATLES from HELP!

The most covered song of all time, although it loses some of its emotional resonance when you remember that before he came up with the finished lyric, McCartney's guide vocal for the tune was built around the phrase "scrambled eggs".

❽ OH LONESOME ME NEIL YOUNG from AFTER THE GOLDRUSH

Written by Don Gibson, but Neil's version tops the original for squeezing every last ounce of self-pity out of the morose lyric.

❾ AIN'T NO SUNSHINE BILL WITHERS from JUST AS I AM

A song whose end-of-the-world heartache even survived being covered by the 13-year-old Michael Jackson.

❿ LINGER THE CRANBERRIES from EVERYBODY ELSE IS DOING IT SO WHY CAN'T WE?

Seldom has the sound of a broken heart sounded so lovely.

Nigel Williamson

James Brown

The mighty main man with the master plan, the way-cool boss with the real hot sauce, Mr Dynamite... the late, lamented James Brown had more nicknames and honorifics than any other musician. Here are the ten records that made him the one true Godfather of Soul.

❶ PLEASE PLEASE PLEASE from STAR TIME

Before rewriting every rule about the role of rhythm in Western music, Brown laid waste to the standard notion of a ballad singer – a feat perhaps even more important than his mutations of rhythm.

❷ I'LL GO CRAZY from LIVE AT THE APOLLO, 1962

One of the most brilliant performances of his incandescent career.

❸ PAPA'S GOT A BRAND NEW BAG from FOUNDATION OF FUNK: A BRAND NEW BAG 1964–1969

Reducing the gospel vocal tradition to falsetto shrieks and guttural roars and positing the bottom end as the be-all and end-all of music, this is Brown's most revolutionary record.

❹ I GOT YOU (I FEEL GOOD) from FOUNDATION OF FUNK: A BRAND NEW BAG 1964–1969

"I feeeeeeeeel nice…": one of the most glorious moments in pop history.

❺ IT'S A MAN'S MAN'S MAN'S WORLD from STAR TIME

Preposterous, grotesque, over-the-top: pure James Brown. One of the all-time great intros.

❻ COLD SWEAT from FOUNDATION OF FUNK: A BRAND NEW BAG 1964–1969

Brown uses his own voice like he uses the rest of the band – as a percussion instrument.

❼ GET UP (I FEEL LIKE BEING A) SEX MACHINE from STAR TIME

With almost nothing else but Jabo Starks' drums for company, the tension built up by Bootsy Collins' liquid bass and Catfish Collins' rawboned guitar is staggering.

❽ HOT PANTS (SHE'S GOTTA USE WHAT SHE'S GOT TO GET WHAT SHE WANTS) from HOT PANTS

Relishes the fact that it goes nowhere fast – it hits the groove from the get-go and stays there for nine minutes.

❾ THE PAYBACK from THE PAYBACK

A Tantric cut exploring the deepest regions of mantric wah-wah funk.

❿ GET UP OFFA THAT THING (RELEASE THE PRESSURE) from STAR TIME

Brown's last fast-and-furious record before The Original Disco Man was eclipsed by the genre he helped to create.

Peter Shapiro

These are the JBs

Every so often James Brown let his sidepersons out from under his shadow, and they never failed to make the most of such opportunities to prove they could funk without supervision.

❶ SAME BEAT PARTS 1, 2 & 3 FRED WESLEY & THE JBS from DAMN RIGHT I AM SOMEBODY

A totally anchored, easy action backbeat is laced with horn riffs and provides the ideal platform for the guys to take turns showing off.

❷ MAMA FEELGOOD LYN COLLINS from BLACK CAESAR
She was known as The Female Preacher and this
barrelling, gospelly stomper leaves you in no doubt
as to why.

❸ SOUL POWER '74 MACEO from US
So funky it's only Maceo's supremely soaring saxophone that stops this collapsing in on itself. Remains a
club classic over thirty years later.

❹ GIMME SOME MORE THE JBS from PASS THE PEAS
If you looked up "groove" in the dictionary, there'd be
a picture of this song. Circular, escalating and with no
purpose beyond making you move.

❺ BREAKIN' BREAD FRED & THE NEW JBS from BREAKIN'
BREAD
The joys of down home eating, set off to the joys of
Fred Wesley's funky trombone.

**❻ IT'S MY THING YOU CAN'T TELL ME WHO TO
SOCK IT TO** MARVA WHITNEY from JAMES BROWN'S FUNKY
PEOPLE VOL 3
Marva never really got given her due, and this sassy,
funky feminist anthem makes that even more bewil-
dering.

❼ I KNOW YOU GOT SOUL BOBBY BYRD from JAMES
BROWN'S FUNKY PEOPLE VOL 2
As a longstanding Revue member and big time James
Brown songwriter, Byrd had a better understanding
of "funky" than most. This song more than proves that
point.

❽ PARRTY MACEO from US
Funky proof that less really is more, as this tune never
seems to be doing too much, but it never stops moving. Neither will you.

**❾ YOU CAN HAVE YOUR WATERGATE JUST GIMME
SOME BUCKS AND I'LL BE STRAIGHT** THE JBS from
DOING IT TO DEATH
This unambiguous comment on the inner city
irrelevance of governmental scandal had such a
buoyant groove it became one of the ultimate
bumping songs.

❿ PICKING UP THE PIECES ONE BY ONE THE ABOVE
AVERAGE BLACK BAND from JAMES BROWN'S FUNKY PEOPLE
VOL 3
It was James Brown's incognito (at the time) reaction
to The Average White Band having a hit on black radio,
and it just about out-funked the Scotsmen.

Lloyd Bradley

Bubblegum

**There has been manufactured teen-pop in every
postwar decade. But bubblegum's golden era was
launched by the invention of The Monkees (who
soon transcended it) and reached its cartoonish
peak in the late 1960s before shading into glam-
rock and Eurovision-pop in the early 1970s. Here
are five of the stickiest – yet chewable – songs
from the period; as disposable pop singles, no
album sources are listed.**

❶ LAST TRAIN TO CLARKSVILLE THE MONKEES
They were the ultimate, manufactured pop group, but
Tommy Boyce and Bobby Hart provided them with
this uplifting song for their first hit, which effortlessly
swept aside the limitations of the genre.

❷ SUGAR SUGAR THE ARCHIES
The Archies, like The Monkees, were a Don Kirshner
creation. But there was no chance of this bunch of
cartoon characters turning serious on him.

❸ SIMON SAYS 1910 FRUITGUM COMPANY
An in-house creation from the "Super K" production
team of Jerry Kasenetz and Jeff Katz – and what could
be more perfect for a bubblegum hit than adding a
dance beat to a children's nursery rhyme?

❹ LOVE GROWS (WHERE MY ROSEMARY GOES)
EDISON LIGHTHOUSE
Essentially a vehicle for session singer Tony Burrows,
who went on to further bubblegum crimes with White
Plains, Brotherhood Of Man and The Pipkins.

❺ GREEN TAMBOURINE LEMON PIPERS
The New York quartet added a psychedelic swirl to
their bubblegum on this 1968 hit.

Nigel Williamson

Jeff Buckley

**Buckley Jnr was the ultimate morbid romantic,
the most yearning and wistful of singers. His early
death sealed it all in intangible aura.**

❶ LOVER, YOU SHOULD HAVE COME OVER from GRACE
Buckley's best finds him in typically romantic/morbid
mood: funereal harmonium, rainy acoustic guitar and
steadily building yearning.

❷ LAST GOODBYE from GRACE
Another heartbreaker – as the guitars, vocals and strings pile up, that climactic sound is Buckley's sink being unplumbed.

❸ EVERYBODY HERE WANTS YOU from (SKETCHES FOR) MY SWEETHEART THE DRUNK
Simpler now, leaner, with a soulful groove: a flood of intense images building up to the moment his guitar appears to swoon at 3:14.

❹ MOJO PIN from GRACE
Opening *Grace* with a whimper which builds to a colossal bang: wave upon wave of guitar builds beneath an increasingly tortured vocal.

❺ MORNING THEFT from SKETCHES FOR MY SWEETHEART THE DRUNK
Lovely, stark, minor-key ballad hymning Jeff's brief romance with Cocteau Twin Liz Frazer.

❻ HALLELUJAH from GRACE
John Cale's rewrite of Leonard Cohen's Hallelujah is taken places neither could conceive via Buckley's elegy and eulogy.

❼ GRACE from GRACE
With emotions as convoluted as Gary Lucas's guitar part, there's plenty for those in search of portents: "I am not afraid to die" etc.

❽ FORGET HER from GRACE (LEGACY EDITION)
Replaced at the last minute by So Real, this is a power ballad effective enough to have interested Aerosmith.

❾ YARD OF BLONDE GIRLS from (SKETCHES FOR) MY SWEETHEART THE DRUNK
Buckley at his most direct, a chugging rocker that evokes summer, lazy sensuality and almost innocent sexuality.

❿ SHE IS FREE from SONGS FOR NO ONE (JEFF BUCKLEY AND GARY LUCAS)
Recently unearthed track from Buckley's early days in New York, the posthumous brass section lifts the song's soul elements into sunlit relief.

Toby Manning

Tim Buckley

One of the most expressive voices in popular music, with a range that allegedly swooped and soared across five octaves, Buckley Snr was dead at 28. But he left a series of nine albums that spanned folk, psychedelia, jazz and blue-eyed soul.

❶ ONCE I WAS from GOODBYE & HELLO
The archetypal troubadour love song.

❷ PLEASANT STREET from GOODBYE & HELLO
Folk-rock meets emotional abandon.

❸ MORNING GLORY from GOODBYE & HELLO
Buckley as medieval minstrel…

❹ SONG TO THE SIREN from STARSAILOR
His best-known song, thanks to covers by This Mortal Coil and Robert Plant.

❺ DREAM LETTER from HAPPY SAD
Written about his estranged son – and answered by Jeff a quarter of a century later on with his song "Dream Brother".

❻ BUZZIN' FLY from HAPPY SAD
Tim's voice at its most honeyed, supremely under-pinned by Lee Underwood's guitar and David Friedman's vibraphone.

❼ MONTEREY from STARSAILOR
Demonic wails from his avant-garde masterpiece.

❽ SWEET SURRENDER from GREETINGS FROM LA
From the X-rated, in-your-face album of pure lust that followed the experimental *Starsailor*.

❾ MOVE WITH ME from GREETINGS FROM LA
"She was drinking alone, what a waste of sin…"

❿ DOLPHINS from SEFRONIA
Moody, atmospheric cover of the Fred Neil song.

Nigel Williamson

Lord Buckley

Richard Myrle Buckley was maybe the funniest hip wiseman of them all. He passed away in 1960 but had already influenced everybody from Lenny Bruce to Bob Dylan with his re-interpretations of classic works of history, literature and religion in "hip-semantic". He left a small but legendary legacy of recordings – and a cult following.

❶ JONAH & THE WHALE from HIS ROYAL HIPNESS
The biblical tale: "Jonah, what's that you's smokin' in there?"

❷ WILLIE THE SHAKE from BUCKLEY'S BEST
The Stratford bard's Mark Anthony funeral oration. "Hipsters, flipsters and fingerpoppin' daddies, knock me your lobes…"

❸ THE GASSER from BUCKLEY'S BEST
The true story of Alvar Nuñez Cabeza de Vaca in 1510, incorporating Ferdinand The First of Spain, Vasco Da Gama The Island Bumper and a parrot.

❹ THE NAZZ from BUCKLEY'S BEST
Classic Buckley on J.C. and his miracles. "Nazz and his buddies were goofing off down the boulevard one day when they met this little cat with a bent frame… "

❺ SCROOGE from THE BAD RAPPING OF THE MARQUIS DE SADE
Dickens in hip – the story of the three spooks.

❻ THE BLACK CROSS from LORD BUCKLEY IN CONCERT
Not everything Buckley performed was full of mirth. Witness this stark tale of a Southern lynching.

Ian Anderson

Burning Spear

Winston Rodney, who borrowed the name Burning Spear from Kenyan leader Jomo Kenyatta, has been at the forefront of roots reggae since his first extraordinary recordings for Studio One in the late 1960s. With his hypnotic voice, direct yet deeply spiritual lyrics and uncompromising vision, he's still a compelling live performer.

❶ DOOR PEEPER from SOUNDS FROM THE BURNING SPEAR
The unsurpassable confidence of Burning Spear's 1969 Studio One debut is breathtaking, from its spoken intro onwards.

❷ CREATION REBEL from SOUNDS FROM THE BURNING SPEAR
Another eerily sparse and meditative song from Spear's Studio One days.

❸ MARCUS GARVEY from MARCUS GARVEY
This massive 1975 Jamaican hit became the title track of Spear's breakthrough Island album the following year.

❹ SLAVERY DAYS from MARCUS GARVEY
A big hit in Jamaica, this 1975 song's refrain "Do you remember the days of slavery?" struck a deep chord.

❺ MAN IN THE HILLS from MAN IN THE HILLS
Spear has always blended the personal with the political, as in this 1976 exaltation of the joys of rural living.

❻ SOCIAL LIVING from SOCIAL LIVING
With its simple message that "social living is the best", this represents Spear at his most anthemic.

❼ HAIL H.I.M. from HAIL H.I.M.
The title track of Spear's last truly great album, from 1980, is an uplifting Rasta hymn.

❽ COLUMBUS from HAIL HIM
An irresistible polemic, denouncing Christopher Columbus as a "damn blasted liar" for claiming to have discovered Jamaica.

Greg Ward

Kate Bush

With a supernatural vocal range and a penchant for weird songs and wacky videos, Kate Bush was always one hell of an eccentric talent. And she proved she is still very much out there, returning in 2005 after a twelve-year break from recording.

❶ WUTHERING HEIGHTS from THE KICK INSIDE
This was how Kate Bush emerged into the world, a fully formed talent, in 1978. English literature turned into classic pop, the song is haunting, disturbing and utterly brilliant in its windswept, witchy delivery.

❷ THE MAN WITH THE CHILD IN HIS EYES from THE KICK INSIDE
Even a love song is never straightforward for Kate Bush. One of her earliest songs, this is both romantic and just a little bit creepy.

❸ WOW from LIONHEART
Who else could get so much mileage out of just three letters? One word is stretched out into a hypnotic chorus.

❹ IN THE WARM ROOM from LIONHEART
What carnal delights lie within the warm room? The single piano and intimate vocal are totally enchanting.

❺ ARMY DREAMERS from NEVER FOR EVER
A heartbreaking anti-war tune circling around a delicate mandolin melody. The vocals are almost childlike in their innocence.

❻ VIOLIN from NEVER FOR EVER

Kate goes rock with a completely bonkers vocal that seesaws violently from squeak to shriek. And the amazing scream towards the end is just inhuman.

❼ CLOUDBUSTING from HOUNDS OF LOVE

Built around subtle, layered strings and a strangely martial rhythm, this is one of Kate's finest 1980s moments.

❽ RUNNING UP THAT HILL from HOUNDS OF LOVE

A life-swapping deal with God is on the table, complete with unmistakable honking synths and a terrific drum track.

❾ KING OF THE MOUNTAIN from AERIAL

This was the comeback single, from *Aerial*, and as if she'd never been away from the studio she piles on the styles, drenches the song in electronic doo-dahs and tops it with her own, only part comprehensible lyric. A delight to be savoured.

❿ JOANNI from AERIAL

Bush's music can of course be enjoyed simply for its charm, but there's a bitter kick to her lyric that's just as irresistible. Here, Bush gets to grips with Joan of Arc and meditates on the reaction she drew from the armies that followed her, in a work that drips with a brooding sense of bloodshed yet to come.

Essi Berelian

The Byrds

When The Byrds put a 4/4 beat to a Bob Dylan song, folk-rock was born. Then they embraced space-rock and country-rock. By the end of the 1960s, Roger McGuinn was the only original Byrd remaining and they were grounded soon after. But what a glorious flight it was while it lasted.

❶ MR TAMBOURINE MAN from MR TAMBOURINE MAN

The Byrds recorded more than a dozen further Dylan songs, but this was the jingle-jangle original that invented folk-rock and which they never bettered.

❷ TURN! TURN! TURN! (TO EVERYTHING THERE IS A SEASON) from TURN! TURN! TURN!

The words come from the Bible. But accompanied by McGuinn's twelve-string Rickenbacker and sung in a hipster drawl, you'd never have guessed.

❸ SO YOU WANT TO BE A ROCK'N'ROLL STAR from YOUNGER THAN YESTERDAY

A sardonic commentary on the music industry given added power by Hugh Masekela's trumpet and the addition of real screams from a 1965 Byrds concert in Bournemouth.

❹ EIGHT MILES HIGH from FIFTH DIMENSION

You can believe their claim that it was written about a Transatlantic jet flight, if you like. But to most of us it will always be one of the greatest drug songs ever recorded.

❺ EVERYBODY'S BEEN BURNED from YOUNGER THAN YESTERDAY

David Crosby's increasingly experimental compositions eventually led McGuinn and Chris Hillman to kick him out, but this ravishing song was a landmark in the group's growing sophistication.

❻ WASN'T BORN TO FOLLOW from THE NOTORIOUS BYRD BROTHERS

Carole King briefly replaces Dylan as the group's favourite songwriter.

❼ HICKORY WIND from SWEETHEART OF THE RODEO

Gram Parsons' finest moment on the group's country-rock landmark. When he quit before the album's release, many of his vocals were replaced. Fortunately, this one was left extant.

❽ BALLAD OF EASY RIDER from THE BALLAD OF EASY RIDER

Dylan wrote half the lyric and then gave it to film director Dennis Hopper, saying "McGuinn will know what to do with it."

❾ CHESTNUT MARE from UNTITLED

The line-up in which McGuinn was joined by Clarence White, Skip Battin and Gene Parsons was perhaps the band's best-ever live incarnation. But they proved they could also cut it in the studio with this, co-written by McGuinn and Jacques Levy.

❿ FOR FREE from THE BYRDS

An overlooked gem from the 1973 reunion album by the original line-up, with one of Crosby's finest vocals on Joni Mitchell's song.

Nigel Williamson

David Byrne

David Byrne's combination of cerebral art rock with a dance beat once led *Time* magazine to dub him a renaissance man for our times. The former Talking Head continues to aim at your head and your feet…

❶ THE JEZEBEL SPIRIT WITH BRIAN ENO from MY LIFE IN THE BUSH OF GHOSTS
Electro-funk exorcism from groundbreaking sampling collaboration with Brian Eno.

❷ INDEPENDENCE DAY from REI MOMO
Lurching, off-kilter Tex Mex anthem that opened his Latin-loving masterpiece.

❸ MAKE BELIEVE MAMBO from REI MOMO
Horn-driven salsa power juxtaposed with whimsical Walter Mitty fantasies.

❹ NOW I'M YOUR MOM from UH-OH
Do the sex-change boogie.

❺ CRASH from DAVID BYRNE
"I met my love at a funeral" may just be the most arresting opening line in popular song.

❻ ANGELS from DAVID BYRNE
A strong echo of "Once In A Lifetime" meant Talking Heads fans thought this was his best song in years.

❼ GATES OF PARADISE from FEELINGS
Who else would even think of mixing country-and-western and trip-hop?

❽ U.B. JESUS from LOOK INTO THE EYEBALL
Disturbing and danceable at the same time.

❾ LAZY (WITH X-PRESS 2) SINGLE
Improbable house music collaboration and a British #1 hit single a quarter of a century on from Psycho Killer.

❿ EMPIRE from GROWN BACKWARDS
Mordant post-Iraq commentary complete with a lyrical spoof on "The Times They Are A-Changin'".

Nigel Williamson

C

Cajun & zydeco

Cajun and zydeco are descended from the fiddle and accordion music of Arcadian settlers who landed in Louisiana's bayous after fleeing the English in Nova Scotia.

❶ ALLONS A LAFAYETTE JOSEPH & CLEOMA FALCON from HARRY SMITH'S ANTHOLOGY OF AMERICAN FOLK MUSIC
Tiny, guitar-picking Cleoma and her accordion-playing husband cut this, the first Cajun record, in 1928 and enjoyed an instant regional hit.

❷ A BLUES DE LA PRISON AMEDEE ARDOIN from THE FIRST BLACK ZYDECO RECORDING ARTIST: HIS ORIGINAL RECORDINGS 1928–1938
A pioneering black accordionist, Ardoin was viciously beaten by white racists at a concert (for accepting a white woman's handkerchief to wipe his brow), and died in 1941 in the Louisiana State Institution for the Mentally Ill. It doesn't get much rougher than that.

❸ FAIS PAS ÇA THE HACKBERRY RAMBLERS from EARLY RECORDINGS 1935-1948
The band lay down a good beat and yelp while Lennis Sonnier sings and swings. This legendary Cajun band formed in the 1930s and are still playing today.

❹ GRAND MAMOU HARRY CHOATES from THE FIDDLE KING OF CAJUN SWING
The Cajun Hank Williams: played fast, lived hard, and died at 28.

❺ DYING IN MISERY NATHAN ABSHIRE from A CAJUN LEGEND: THE BEST OF NATHAN ABSHIRE
The greatest of all Cajun accordionists, Abshire helped popularize Cajun music internationally. Here Dewey Balfa lends his plaintive voice.

❻ JOLE BLON THE BALFA BROTHERS from PLAYS TRADITIONAL CAJUN MUSIC VOLS 1 & 2
Dewey, Will and Rodney Balfa were Cajun music's greatest-ever ambassadors, and they perform the Cajun anthem with great zest on their 1965 debut recording.

❼ BON TON ROULET CLIFTON CHENIER from ZYDECO DYNAMITE: THE CLIFTON CHENIER ANTHOLOGY
The King of Zydeco. Gave the music a swinging groove and made many fine recordings between 1955 and 1987, including this swampy stomper. Classic black Creole music.

❽ WADE'S WALTZ MICHAEL DOUCET from BEAU SOLO
Ambassador of Cajun music and culture both solo and with his band Beausoleil. Here he demonstrates deep Cajun fiddle.

❾ HEY NEGRESS QUEEN IDA from CAUGHT IN THE ACT
The first lady of zydeco, Ida sings and plays accordion and takes no prisoners. This traditional ballad is tough Louisiana blues.

❿ BOUGHT A RACOON BUCKWHEAT ZYDECO from BEST OF LOUISIANA ZYDECO
Slick, funky BZ are led by Stanley Dural Jnr, who used to play in Clifton Chenier's band. Downhome humour permeates this good-time number.

Garth Cartwright

John Cale

John Cale is one of rock's more enigmatic characters. A classically trained musician with an interest in minimalism, a Velvet Underground veteran, a songwriter and producer of some of the classic records of the 1970s and 80s, his own work reveals a complex, intelligent and, deep down, romantic soul.

❶ CHICKENSHIT from SABOTAGE
Vicious, loud and terrifying, this is Cale dealing badly with success, stardom and the "godfather of punk" label stuck on him by a lazy music press.

❷ GUN from FEAR
Menacing guitar, evil-spirited drumbeat and a lyric that tells of a night lit up by drunken violence that ends in tears and emergency surgery. Phil Manzanera and Eno add their own strains of distorted electro-nastiness to the mix and we sit transfixed through an eight-minute horrorshow

❸ ROSEGARDEN FUNERAL OF SORES from SABOTAGE
Nobody does long, drawn-out, lugubrious tales of slowly building menace like John Cale, and this shows the man at his best.

4 GUTS from SLOW DAZZLE

A drug-fuelled love/hate quandary. Kevin Ayers and Cale's wife Cindy had misbehaved just before a concert, inspiring the opening lyric: "The bugger in the short sleeves fucked my wife. Did it quick and split."

5 DARLING I NEED YOU from SLOW DAZZLE

Part Two of the debacle. The drugs have worn off and the emotions are a little less raw. Cale's honesty is to be admired, but it's painful to listen to something so close-up and personal.

6 HEARTBREAK HOTEL from JUNE 1, 1974

Elvis might have recorded the best-selling version of this song, but he never sounded even remotely heartbroken when performing it. John Cale, performing on the same stage as the above-mentioned Kevin Ayers, sounds like somebody's pulled his living heart out through his ribs and squeezed it dry in front of him.

7 FEAR IS A MAN'S BEST FRIEND from FEAR

Beautiful piano and twiddly bass from the Welsh bard of rock'n'roll. It begins in "Waiting For My Man" narrative territory and expands into a rousing paranoiac chorus, part chapel-hymn part pub-band boogie.

8 MAN WHO COULDN'T AFFORD TO ORGY from FEAR

A cuddly pop ballad, this song has hooks galore, sweetheart backing vocals and genuinely funny lyrics (complete with a delightful mispronunciation of "orgy" with a hard "g").

9 TWILIGHT ZONE from HOBO SAPIENS

A classic Cale episode from a recording that's notable for its overall optimistic feel. Showcasing his familiar taste for tortured instrumentation moaning in pain behind a melody line of stately elegance, it shows there's a great deal of malice in the old wizard yet.

Al Spicer

Calypso & soca

Calypso has come far since the 1930s when the first calypso tents were raised in Port of Spain, Trinidad, to house contestants for the sharpest commentary on island life or world news. In the 1970s, promiscuous as every Caribbean style, calypso made a formal alliance with soul and disco, to be reborn as soca.

1 LONDON IS THE PLACE FOR ME LORD KITCHENER from LONDON IS THE PLACE FOR ME

Opening to a piano version of Big Ben chimes, this entrancing calypso jazz is led on clarinet and guitar,

behind Kitch's witty observations on "the mother country", which he reached in 1948.

2 FREE UP CHRIS "TAMBU" HERBERT from THE ROUGH GUIDE TO CALYPSO & SOCA

Bright, quintessential soca – brass upfront, electric guitar mimicking steel drum melodies, jigging jumpy rhythms and vocals from Tambu.

3 PHILIP MY DEAR THE MIGHTY SPARROW from THE ROUGH GUIDE TO CALYPSO & SOCA

Calypso's great lyricist-newscaster conjures a raunchy conversation between the Queen and Prince Philip about the intruder in her palace bedroom.

4 VOICES FROM THE GHETTO SINGING SANDRA from THE ROUGH GUIDE TO CALYPSO & SOCA

One of calypso-soca's rare female singers, Sandra documents Trinidadian ghetto life behind the carnival gloss. Backed by sweet guitars and punchy trumpets.

5 MAN PIABA HARRY BELAFONTE from THE BEST OF HARRY BELAFONTE

Belafonte put calypso into the world's pop charts in the 1950s. Here, a poor, confused boy wonders aloud about the birds and bees stories he's offered by adults.

6 LORRAINE EXPLAINER from THIS IS SOCA MUSIC

Huge international hit in 1982; brassy but sweet. Every track on this Charlie Gillett compilation is a treat.

7 BURN DEM BLACK STALIN from THIS IS SOCA

References to Mussolini, the Führer and the KKK accompanied by sweet girls' chorus, salsa brass and merengue saxes. A late 1980s cocktail by one of Trinidad's most radical lyricists.

8 ROUND AND ROUND (PABLO (FLORES) MIX) SPICE AND COMPANY single

Thumping, nostalgic drums, jangling cowbells, shards of brass punctuating the beats, and a Bajan line-dance caller instructing the dancers: mad and irresistible.

9 BILLS, INTERPOLATED AS BUSTED ARROW from SOCA DANCE PARTY

The rule-breaking Arrow constantly redesigned soca, and his un-PC tirade about bills – "gas bill, alimony bill, girlfriend bill, children bill! Bills!" typically breaks the mould with pealing zouk and soukous guitars.

10 BAHIAN GYAL DAVID RUDDER & CHARLIE'S ROOTS from THIS IS SOCA MUSIC 2

Imaginative, inventive, eclectic, Rudder shifts emphasis from Trini to Bahia in Brazil, with this sweet and jumpy samba/soca beaten out on conga drums.

Sue Steward

Glen Campbell

Glen Campbell has been a singer, composer, part-time Beach Boy and country-pop hitmaker as well as an actor, golfer and hell-raiser. Thought of mainly as a MOR favourite, his backlist offers a surprisingly diverse range of styles.

❶ WICHITA LINEMAN from WICHITA LINEMAN
Often praised as the greatest song of all time by fans of Jimmy Webb. Check out the great version by Johnny Cash on *American IV: The Man Comes Around*.

❷ BY THE TIME I GET TO PHOENIX from BY THE TIME I GET TO PHOENIX
This was a huge hit, thanks to its bittersweet lyrics and lush orchestration. Famously covered by both Nick Cave and Frank Sinatra.

❸ GALVESTON from GALVESTON
A thinly disguised anti-war epic, this was written in the Vietnam era.

❹ GUESS I'M DUMB from THE CAPITOL YEARS 1965–77
Beach Boy Brian Wilson wrote this one for Glen as a thank you for standing in for him while he was ill.

❺ GENTLE ON MY MIND from GENTLE ON MY MIND
An oft-covered John Hartford song, this became Glen's first hit single.

❻ RHINESTONE COWBOY from RHINESTONE COWBOY
After several years in the wilderness for Glen this track became a US #1 single. It's great.

❼ ALL I HAVE TO DO IS DREAM from THE CAPITAL YEARS 1965–77
Glen recorded plenty of duets with Bobbie Gentry on TV shows and albums. All are worth checking out, but this one's a cracker.

❽ SOUTHERN NIGHTS from SOUTHERN NIGHTS
Glen's last proper hit single was funkier than almost all his other material, and mighty fine to boot.

Dave Atkinson

Can

At the tail end of the 1960s, the European response to the experimentalism of The Velvet Underground included an entire generation of German musicians making *kosmische Rock*. Can were the consummate Krautrockers, and their music is as entrancing now as when it was first released. It is both delightfully weird and unexpectedly beautiful.

❶ YOO DOO RIGHT from MONSTER MOVIE
A 20-minute masterwork, this was Can's response to the Velvet's epic-length "Sister Ray". Its lyrics were loosely based on the intimate contents of a love letter. A monstrous jam of infinite variety, it features a short section when all the amps break down – through which singer Malcolm Mooney and the drumbeat press on oblivious.

❷ MOTHER UPDUFF from UNLIMITED EDITION
Far funnier than any of the Velvet's story-length outings, Upduff is a jazzy, rocky roller-coaster ride with lyrics about a couple who take granny on holiday.

❸ BLUE BAG from UNLIMITED EDITION
A deeply introspective, stoned exploration of what is of course the vital factor of a bag of salt'n'shake crisps, this track boasts pops, bangs and whistles, and is psychedelia at its fun-loving best.

❹ FATHER CANNOT YELL from MONSTER MOVIE
Mooney yelps and barks a bad-trip story of childbirth gone wrong over the classic "motorik" beat of Jaki Liebezeit. It has an old-school groove from Holger Czukay, appropriately scary guitar attacks from Michael Karoli and a stomach-churning, low-end keyboard wobble from Irmin Schmidt.

❺ UPHILL from DELAY
This is Can at full power: a breathless Malcolm Mooney helms the space-rock jam that Hawkwind never quite achieved.

❻ MUSHROOM from TAGO MAGO
Jaki Liebezeit's drum patterns are insanely great and have been endlessly sampled since. Damo Suzuki's vocal is pretty great, too – whatever it is he is singing about.

❼ GOMORRHA from UNLIMITED EDITION
This is the most beautiful, theatrical space-rock ever, pierced by a meandering solo from Karoli.

❽ SHE BRINGS THE RAIN from SOUNDTRACKS
A lovely and, for Can, oddly conventional blues. Mooney delivers a simple poetic invocation: "she brings the rain, it feels like spring".

❾ DIZZY DIZZY from SOON OVER BABALUMA
Damo Suzuki had left, and Czukay took over vocals for this trancey, dubby opener, which bounces along like a kind of Germanic ska.

⑩ PERSIAN LOVE from HOLGER CZUKAY'S MOVIES
Czukay played the radio as an instrument in the latter days of Can, switching the dials on stage. He developed this idea in his solo work, most memorably on this Iranian love song, embroidered upon with a gorgeous loop of guitar.

Al Spicer/Mark Ellingham

Secretly Canadian

Did you know some of the biggest names in American music actually came from north of the 49th parallel?

① HELPLESS NEIL YOUNG from DEJA VU (C, S, N & Y)
"There is a town in north Ontario/With dream comfort memory to spare/And in my mind I still need a place to go/All my changes were there."

② A CASE OF YOU JONI MITCHELL from BLUE
"On the back of a cartoon coaster in the blue TV screen light/I drew a map of Canada…"

③ DEMOCRACY LEONARD COHEN from THE FUTURE
"Democracy is coming to the USA", sings Cohen – an expat Canadian's prayer.

④ IF YOU COULD READ MY MIND GORDON LIGHTFOOT from IF YOU COULD READ MY MIND
He tried the American dream for a while, writing TV jingles in Hollywood, and hated it so much he fled back across the border to write songs like this instead.

⑤ YOU OUGHTA KNOW ALANIS MORISSETTE from JAGGED LITTLE PILL
The line "Is she perverted like me?" appeared to confirm what many Americans had always suspected about their northern neighbours.

⑥ HALLELUJAH RUFUS WAINWRIGHT from SHREK SOUNDTRACK
A double bill: half-Canadian Rufus delivers the perfect version of Cohen's song – and for a CGI ogre, to boot.

⑦ UNIVERSAL SOLDIER BUFFY SAINTE-MARIE from THE BEST OF
During the Lyndon Johnson years her name appeared on a White House list of those whose music "deserved to be suppressed" after she penned this peace movement anthem.

⑧ CONSTANT CRAVING KD LANG from INGENUÉ
And she even made a covers album of songs by other Canadian writers called *Hymns Of The 49th Parallel*.

⑨ THE NIGHT THEY DROVE OLD DIXIE DOWN THE BAND from THE BAND
It took a bunch of good ol' Canuck boys to really understand the American Civil War.

⑩ SUMMER OF '69 BRYAN ADAMS from SO FAR SO GOOD
Whatever the song says, at the time Bryan was actually a nine-year-old boy growing up in Kingston, Ontario.

Nigel Williamson

Cape Verde

This arid, volcanic archipelago west of Senegal produces some of the most seductive music on the planet. Cesaria Evora – the "Barefoot Diva" – is by far the country's best-known export, but her work is just one strand of an exceptionally rich musical culture.

① PETIT PAYS CESARIA EVORA from ANTHOLOGY
On this yearning *morna*, Cesaria fondly lists the good things about her island home, backed by the gentle sway of her excellent acoustic band. Mesmerizing stuff.

② BOAS FESTAS LUIS MORAIS from THE SOUL OF CAPE VERDE
A sweetly soulful instrumental cut by the late saxophonist and composer, who was a revered and much loved figure of Cape Verdean music.

③ TERRA LONGE BONGA from A VOZ DE OURO
The grand old man of Cape Verdean song interprets this B. Leza classic with enormous pathos, shadowed throughout by a sinuous clarinet solo.

④ NOTE DE MINDELO TITINA from BETWEEN SEA AND SKY: A DREAM VOYAGE TO THE SOUL OF THE ISLES
A stark and tremulous performance of this *morna* (also written by the great B. Leza) about the magic of the night on the island of Mindelo. Goosepimples guaranteed.

⑤ DANÇA MA MI CRIOLA TITO PARIS from DANÇA MA MI CRIOLA
A very danceable *coladeira* by this well-respected singer, who runs the famed B. Leza club in Lisbon. A cool horn arrangement, fine gravelly vocals and a memorable tune.

⑥ FALSO TESTEMUNHO MARIA ALICE from D'ZEMCONTRE
It's been on so many compilations it might as well be here: by far the most famous track by this Lisbon-based singer.

❼ CHICO MALANDRO ANA FIRMINO WITH TITO PARIS from PUTUMAYO PRESENTS CAPE VERDE

A slinky love song with strummed acoustic *cavaquinho* – a typical instrument of Cape Verdea – which became the ukulele when Portuguese sailors took it to Hawaii.

❽ FUNDO BAXO GRUPO FERRO GAITA from THE ROUGH GUIDE TO CAPE VERDE

Ferro Gaita are a powerful live experience. Their speciality is the hard dance style called *fundá* – an accordion and percussion-based groove. This is a typical example.

❾ FLADU FA SIMENTERA from TR'ADICTIONAL

Lead singer Tété Alhinho gives an amazingly sensual performance and the arrangement is to die for. This one speeds up into a carnival blur of sound.

❿ VELOCIDADE CESARIA EVORA from VOZ D'AMOR

Another Luis Morais song, this time one of his upbeat, bouncy *coladeiras*.

Jon Lusk

Captain Beefheart

Mixing deep Delta blues and free jazz with surreal, often punning lyrics sung in the most extraordinary voice you've ever heard, Captain Beefheart – a.k.a. Don Van Vliet – constructed an entire new musical universe. Like Jimi Hendrix, he took his art to such limits that there was literally nowhere left to go. In 1982 he retired to the Mojave Desert to paint, leaving behind these weird and wonderful creations.

❶ SURE NUFF 'N YES I DO from SAFE AS MILK

The opening track from the debut album: the first an astonished world heard of Don's magnificently mutant blues and his psychedelically warped band.

❷ ELECTRICITY from SAFE AS MILK

Buzzing theramin, the mighty Ry Cooder on slide guitar and the Captain's best feral bellow.

❸ AH FEEL LIKE AHCID from STRICTLY PERSONAL

Psychedelic blues at its most unsettling … you might want to think twice before tripping out to this scary soundtrack.

❹ ELLA GURU from TROUT MASK REPLICA

Almost a pop tune, then the guitars fracture, the sonic hurricane blows and Don delivers a bestial vocal – one of the best moments from his peerless masterpiece.

❺ MY HUMAN GETS ME BLUES from TROUT MASK REPLICA

Discordant, abrasive guitars, crazed time signatures and a rollercoaster ride of surrealist abandon – business as usual for the Captain, then.

❻ DACHAU BLUES from TROUT MASK REPLICA

Dark, convoluted visions of the atrocities of war with a vocal so intense you barely notice the music.

❼ NEON MEATE DREAM OF A OCTAFISH from TROUT MASK REPLICA

Neo-Beat poetry meets folk myth against a backing of mind-boggling musical complexity as the Captain gasps the sexual lyric with asthmatic excitement.

❽ I LOVE YOU, YOU BIG DUMMY from LICK MY DECALS OFF, BABY

A more orthodox rock tune for once. But this is Beefheart, of course, so such descriptions are relative.

❾ BIG EYED BEANS FROM VENUS from CLEAR SPOT

"Mr Zoot Horn Rollo, hit that long lunar note and let it float…" – an insight into the Beefheartian school of musical direction.

Nigel Williamson

Carter Family

Asked to name a song by country pioneers the Carter Family, many would scratch their heads. Yet they popularized over three hundred songs that have entered the collective consciousness of the US, and further afield. Tracks are available on various Carter Family compilations, the best being the single CD *An Introduction To The Carter Family* and the five-CD box set *The Carter Family: 1927–1934*.

❶ WILL THE CIRCLE BE UNBROKEN

Theirs was the definitive version of the song that gave its name to the splendid biopic about the Carters made for American PBS television.

❷ WABASH CANNONBALL

One of the first recordings of the folk standard, made in Atlanta in 1929, later covered by Roy Acuff and countless others.

❸ WILDWOOD FLOWER

A nineteenth-century North American parlour song popularized by the Carters after they recorded it in 1928.

❹ KEEP ON THE SUNNY SIDE
The theme song of their popular 1930s radio show.

❺ LITTLE DARLING PAL OF MINE
Maybelle Carter shines here on her self-converted steel guitar.

❻ THE FOGGY MOUNTAIN TOP
This has been covered by everyone from bluegrass kings Flatt & Scruggs to Irish soulman Van Morrison.

❼ NO DEPRESSION IN HEAVEN
The song that gave its name to the movement that became alt.country.

❽ WORRIED MAN BLUES
Recorded in Memphis in 1930, with thrilling trio harmonies from Maybelle, Sara and A.P.

❾ LONESOME VALLEY
More magnificent three-part harmonies from the same session that produced "Worried Man Blues".

❿ I'M THINKING TONIGHT OF MY BLUE EYES
If you wondered where Roy Acuff's Great Speckled Bird and Hank Thompson's "The Wild Side Of Life" came from, look no further than this 1929 recording.

Nigel Williamson

Johnny Cash

A rich and resonant baritone and an outlaw heart? It must be country music's one and only Man In Black…

❶ A BOY NAMED SUE from AT SAN QUENTIN
A novelty song with a lopsided grin on its face. Who else could sing about losing a piece of his ear and make it sound both angry and funny?

❷ FOLSOM PRISON BLUES from AT FOLSOM PRISON
He shot a man in Memphis just to watch him die. A tale of murder and regret recorded in front of a real crowd of inmates. Simply electrifying.

❸ GOING TO MEMPHIS from MURDER
That chain gang sounds mighty mean, even with the twangy guitar and honky-tonk piano. You can almost taste the parched dust and misery.

❹ I WALK THE LINE from LOVE
A plain old-fashioned love song with a measured guitar refrain and Cash's charming leathery drawl centre stage. Unbeatable.

❺ JOE BEAN from EVERYBODY LOVES A NUT
The shadow of the gallows falls long and grim in this brief melodrama. Retribution doesn't come more ironic than this.

❻ SAN QUENTIN from AT SAN QUENTIN
You want pure rage? Just listen to Cash's venomous attack against the infamous prison in this definitive live performance.

❼ FIELD OF DIAMONDS from AMERICAN III: SOLITARY MAN
Brimming with romantic longing, this simple and deeply poetic song features June Carter Cash and Sheryl Crow along for the ride.

❽ RING OF FIRE from RING OF FIRE
Those melodic stabs of Mexican brass and understated backing vocals are pure genius. Another passionate classic straight from the heart.

❾ THE MAN COMES AROUND from AMERICAN IV: THE MAN COMES AROUND
The man in black's last recording comprised mostly cover versions, selected to frame the myth and history of Johnny Cash. In the self-written opener and title track, Cash sings as if he stared cold hard death right in the eye across the mike stand in the studio. Johnny's guitarman hands and passion-drenched vocals give an echo of eerie spirituality fresh from the fire and brimstone preaching school of apocalyptic backwoods Christianity.

❿ HURT from AMERICAN IV: THE MAN COMES AROUND
Nobody ever imagined he'd create such a moving performance from a song penned by raucous noise mongers Nine Inch Nails. Cash looked way back into his misspent past and returned with this obviously heartfelt and poignant confessional.

Essi Berelian

Cat Power

Cat Power is the creative guise of Chan Marshall, whose voice is at times gentle, at times brutal and bluesy. From indie trooper, she has emerged as one of America's best 21st-century songwriters.

❶ ICE WATER from MYRA LEE
Cat Power, the band, fall in line behind Chan as she sings with power and presence over lolloping guitar picking and distant drums.

❷ AMERICAN FLAG from MOON PIX
It's the reversed shuffle of a drum machine and oozing electric guitar that make this cut – seductive and strange.

❸ SAY from MOON PIX
Stormclouds (and guitars) gather around an uplifting lyric of hope and confession.

❹ CROSS BONES STYLE from MOON PIX
The hypnotic guitar line plaits itself around a gallop of drums, while Chan sings a deep meandering harmony. Glorious.

❺ (I CAN'T GET NO) SATISFACTON from THE COVERS ALBUM
An intimate yet lazily-spun cover of the Stones classic. Chan makes it all her own.

❻ NUDE AS THE NEWS from WHAT WOULD THE COMMUNITY THINK
A rousing indie rocker with swathes of guitar and vocals that swell and crash like rolling waves.

❼ GOOD WOMAN from YOU ARE FREE
A song for when you know it's over. Chan's deep velvet voice is grazed by violin, a choir of children and, um, Eddie Vedder.

❽ WEREWOLF from YOU ARE FREE
The string arrangement is sublime and haunting, but not half as chilling as the vocals.

❾ WILLIE DEADWILDER
from SPEAKING FOR TREES
It's eighteen minutes long, and wonderful, with Chan sounding at her most relaxed and silky as she sings "even if it is too long, I don't care, I love to share".

❿ THE GREATEST from THE GREATEST
The standout cut of an album that premiered a far richer, soulful Cat Power purr.

Peter Buckley

Nick Cave

Australia's greatest songwriter – simple as that. Styles come and go but Old Nick remains true to his art.

❶ THE MERCY SEAT from TENDER PREY
The intense thoughts of a man facing his imminent demise on the electric chair. Notably covered by Johnny Cash.

❷ THE WEEPING SONG from THE GOOD SON
A slow, heavy and very powerful duet between Nick and guitarist Blixa Bargeld.

❸ WHERE THE WILD ROSES GROW from MURDER BALLADS
A murder ballad gave Nick his only chart hit (with a little help from compatriot Kylie). Strange, but oddly romantic.

❹ IN THE GHETTO from FROM HER TO ETERNITY
A cover of Elvis's hit – gloomy and dramatic, but what more could you hope for when Nick meets Elvis?

❺ STRAIGHT TO YOU from HENRY'S DREAM
A beautiful love song and, boy, can he write a beautiful love song…

❻ DO YOU LOVE ME? from LET LOVE IN
A huge rock number and a live favourite. Yes Nick, of course we all love you.

❼ INTO MY ARMS from THE BOATMAN'S CALL
The album from whence it came marked a turning point in style, demonstrated perfectly by its introspection and hope.

❽ THERE SHE GOES MY BEAUTIFUL WORLD from ABATTOIR BLUES/LYRE OF ORPHEUS
A gospel-infused rocker from what is perhaps his best album ever.

❾ BREATHLESS from ABATTOIR BLUES/LYRE OF ORPHEUS
Fabulous poetry and one of the stand-out tracks from an amazing double album.

❿ NO PUSSY BLUES GRINDERMAN from GRINDERMAN
The Cave monster's most recent gang of ne'er do well henchmen sound just as you'd expect from a band so named. Nick gets down and dirty from the get go, moaning about his lack of success in the world of love.

Dave Atkinson

Central Asia

The art of fine, virtuosic singing is integral to the music of central Asia, in which bards are still important and venerated.

❶ KELMADY MUNADJAT YULCHIEVA & ENSEMBLE SHAVKAT MIRZAEV from A HAUNTING VOICE
Munadjat unveils her beautiful voice slowly and subtly, building up from a tranquil melancholy to culminate in a vibrant, expressive mood.

❷ EY ENCALAR ALIM QASIMOV & FERGANAH QASIMOVA from
LOVE'S DEEP OCEAN

An energetic homage to Nusrat Fateh Ali Khan by
Azerbaijan's foremost exponent of vocal art, and his
skilful daughter. "Today is the day my soul parts from
my body. Tears flow from my eyes like rain."

❸ DEVONAH SHAW DAVLATMAND from MUSIQUES
SAVANTES ET POPULAIRES

This spiritual song uses a lovely swaying rhythm
played on the setar, a long-necked lute. Davlatmand,
from Tajikistan, is as profoundly rooted in the Sufi
tradition as Munadjat Yulchieva.

❹ KÖGMEN SABIJLAR from THE SILK ROAD – A MUSICAL
CARAVAN

Khakas throat singing accompanied by horse-head
fiddle, taken from a must-have anthology. Sabijlar
revive the traditional music.

❺ PENJIGAH MUQAM OF ILI THE UYGHUR MUSICIANS
FROM XINJIANG from MUSIC FROM THE OASIS TOWNS OF
CENTRAL ASIA

Music affirms the Uyghur identity, which is under
permanent threat. A compact version of a *mugham*
(suite), featuring fine singing and interaction from a
large ensemble: "Let the dawn breeze carry my greet-
ing to that girl who is slim like the poplar."

❻ GUL-I-ZARIM TURGUN ALIMATOV from OUZBEKISTAN:
TURGUN ALIMATOV

He is the don on the plucked dutar and tanbur and the
bowed tanbur or sato. On this one he delivers a highly
dramatic duet with his son and pupil.

❼ GRANADINA YENGI YOL from DE SEVILLE À BOUKHARA

The project of Emmanuel Hossein During, son of
the foremost connoisseur and researcher of Central
Asian music, Jean During: young traditional musicians
merge Spanish guitar with local music. They are definitely exploring new paths.

❽ AN TUWRALI EL'MIYRA ZANABERGENOV from MUSIC from
ALMATY

"Listeners, I wish to present you a tune. I don't shake
my head simply because I sing a song. It is also quite
embarrassing to open the mouth wide while singing."
A song about the art of singing by a great female
singer coming from the semi-classical tradition in
Kazakhstan.

❾ BAYATY ASHKABAD from CITY OF LOVE

What a wonderful name for a city and for a band, too.
These musicians merge regional traditions and instruments with the modern to find a new tone, a contemporary urban folklore.

❿ YOR-YOR SEVARA NAZARKHAN from YOL BOLSIN

Hector Zazou's Western electronics combine remarkably well the Uzbek instruments and singing of an
ensemble led by singer Sevara Nazarkhan.

Jean Trouillet

Manu Chao

**Manu Chao is a superstar in Europe, and just
about the only "world music" figure who has got
albums that are largely not sung in English across
to a wide audience of English speakers. But
language is irrelevant here: Manu mixes reggae,
African music and Spanish and French roots to
create an addictive party cocktail. And he spread
fairy dust across the wonderful, bluesy Malian
duo, Amadou & Mariam, producing and
collaborating on their topselling album.**

MANU CHAO

❶ LUNA Y SOL from CLANDESTINO

After disbanding Mano Negra, the Franco–Spanish
punk band, Manu went travelling in South America
and the Caribbean: the two-million-selling *Clandestino*
was the result. A seductive mix of samples and influences: here it's the turn of Mexican horns. Wild and
fun.

❷ BONGO BONG from CLANDESTINO

Ping-ping go the guitars, and Manu rolls the nonsense
(in English) about being "King of the Bongo Bong".

❸ MINHA GALERA from CLANDESTINO

The sweetest, catchiest, most contemporary bossa
nova. He could play this with a comb and toilet paper
and bring the house down. Which he kinda does.

❹ WELCOME TO TIJUANA from CLANDESTINO

"Tekila, sexo y marihuana" – a daft, dubby assemblage
of Latin sounds that goes down a storm in Manu's live
shows.

❺ ME GUSTA TU from PROXIMA ESTACION ESPERANZA

A song that chugs along as Manu enunciates all he
likes and keeps returning to the object of his affec-
tions: "Me gustas tu."

❻ DENIA from PROXIMA ESTACION ESPERANZA

It's the way he mixes things up: this is a delicate,
upbeat number, sung in Arabic but unlike any Arab
song.

❼ PROMISCUITY from RADIO BEMBA SOUNDS SYSTEM
There is no better festival headliner and this live record shows why: Manu and band embark on a mad whoop of Latin ska.

AMADOU & MARIAM

❽ LA RÉALITÉ from DIMANCHE A BAMAKO
An Amadou & Mariam blues-rocker transformed into a potential stadium-winner, with a slice of Chao rhythm, a recurrent police siren, and audience invocations.

❾ TAXI BAMAKO from DIMANCHE A BAMAKO
Manu is very much at the controls on this gentle lilt of a track, sampling the sounds of a Malian taxi rank and children's song.

❿ SENEGAL FASTFOOD from DIMANCHE A BAMAKO
A Manu track in all but name, as he takes on lead vocals, namechecking all points West African, and joined by Amadou & Mariam for a catchy good-time chorus.

Mark Ellingham

Chapel Hill

For a time in the early 1990s, Chapel Hill, NC, was touted as the "next Seattle" – a designation only slightly less hazardous than a singer-songwriter being tagged the "new Dylan". Chapel Hillians gracefully sidestepped early attempts to pigeonhole the town's sound as fresh-scrubbed indie punk, to create a diverse body of music.

❶ SLACK MOTHERFUCKER SUPERCHUNK from SUPERCHUNK
This widely misinterpreted song about a lazy co-worker became a slacker anthem at the dawn of the 1990s.

❷ ROCK POST ROCK POLVO from SHAPES
Rock Post Rock is one of the highlights of the band's final album, where their angular guitars were finally successfully harnessed to a set of well-developed songs.

❸ WEB IN FRONT ARCHERS OF LOAF from ICKY METTLE
Often characterized as a scruffier version of Pavement, the Archers hit the jackpot the first time around with this bouncy singalong that kicked off their debut album from 1994.

❹ ANYTHING BUT LOVE SQUIRREL NUT ZIPPERS from ROASTED RIGHT
These musical archivists exploring the hot jazz sounds of the 1920s and 30s turned out to be the most financially successful of all the bands from the scene.

❺ ROADSIDE WRECK SOUTHERN CULTURE ON THE SKIDS from TOO MUCH PORK FOR JUST ONE FORK
Roadside Wreck is an example of how the band incorporated the swampy blues of Slim Harpo and the rockabilly energy of Dale Hawkins into an edgy brew that counterbalanced their more lighthearted efforts.

❻ YOU'RE SOAKING IN IT PIPE from 6 DAYS TO BELLUS
Pipe shows were as much about audience participation (beer tossing) as they were about the band's relentless punk-rock assault.

❼ THE TRAIN MOTOCASTER from ACID ROCK
Stadium-sized rock action from a Raleigh power trio who eventually signed to Interscope.

❽ SERVICE ENTRANCE FIASCO SPATULA from MEDIUM PLANERS AND MATCHERS
One of the first tracks to fully incorporate cellist Chris Eubank into their instrumental mix, this track moves fluidly from a scorched-earth guitarscape to a jaunty Eastern European hoedown and back again.

Butch Lazorchak

The Charlatans

You know what you're getting with the Charlies, so if you like it, you'll always be smiling.

❶ WHITE SHIRT from SOME FRIENDLY
Blunt, Burgess and Collins keep it bright, upbeat and simple, with a brief but masterful key-change.

❷ THE ONLY ONE I KNOW from SOME FRIENDLY
You hear the opening to their second single and know you've got eight seconds to get to the dancefloor. One of the all-time indie greats.

❸ I DON'T WANT TO SEE THE SIGHTS from BETWEEN 10TH AND 11TH
The best of the band's ready-to-explode openers solicits with a dancy guitar hook.

❹ COME IN NUMBER 21 from UP TO OUR HIPS
Another album-opening classic, with the instruments seemingly talking, and the "ooh-ooh-ooh"s exploding all over.

Tim Burgess's
Play for today

The singer with the Charlatans, the most enduring group to come out of the late-1980s "Madchester" scene, TIM BURGESS sent us this list from somewhere deep in the the canyons of LA, where he now lives. He marked it with the words "Just for today".

❶ **STRAIGHT TO HELL** THE CLASH from COMBAT ROCK

❷ **DANCE STANCE** DEXY'S MIDNIGHT RUNNERS from THE BEST OF

❸ **MAGIC CORNER** BELITA WOODS from NORTHERN SOUL FEVER VOL 1

❹ **WHO THE CAP FIT** BOB MARLEY & THE WAILERS from RASTAMAN VIBRATION

❺ **THE MOST EXHALTED POTENTATE OF LOVE** THE CRAMPS from SMELL OF FEMALE

❻ **BUTTERBEAN** B52'S from WHAMMY!

❼ **SUNRISE** NEW ORDER from LOW LIFE

❽ **A HARD RAIN'S A-GONNA FALL** BOB DYLAN from FREEWHEELIN' BOB DYLAN

❾ **A SONG FOR YOU** LEON RUSSELL from LEON RUSSELL

❿ **GIMME SHELTER** MERRY CLAYTON from GIMME SHELTER

❺ **I NEVER WANT AN EASY LIFE IF ME AND HE WERE EVER TO GET THERE** from UP TO OUR HIPS
All the ingredients of a classic Charlatans song, as well as a wicked descending bassline and screaming Burgess vocal.

❻ **HOW HIGH** from TELLIN' STORIES
The best of The Charlatans three-minute pop songs (well, 3 mins, 6 secs), and one of their biggest successes. Here it's all in the solid, relentless vocals.

❼ **HAPPEN TO DIE (LONG VERSION)** from SONGS FROM THE OTHER SIDE
On this 1992 B-side to "Tremelo Song" the simple, flowing lyrics take a back seat to the driving force of an awesome bassline.

Daniel Crewe

Ray Charles

One of the founding fathers of soul music, mixing gospel, pop, blues and jazz with that immediately recognizable grainy, yearning voice.

❶ **WHAT'D I SAY** from ULTIMATE HITS COLLECTION
Rock'n'roll as a revival meeting, with that great circular keyboard line and orgiastic call-and-response vocals.

❷ **HIT THE ROAD JACK** from ULTIMATE HITS COLLECTION
Both the anvil-descending melody and brook-no-discussion female backing vocals make it clear this relationship is kaput, though Ray certainly pleads his case with wolfish charm.

❸ **I GOT A WOMAN** from ULTIMATE HITS COLLECTION
By setting a gospel melody to a sexy lyric and music that both swung and cooked, Charles also set the table for soul itself.

❹ **I BELIEVE TO MY SOUL** from THE BIRTH OF SOUL
Seems like Ray's reaching down into the soles of his shoes on this anguished vocal, set to pounding electric piano and one of his trademark minor-keyed melodies.

❺ **UNCHAIN MY HEART** from ULTIMATE HITS COLLECTION
Yet another tune that's at once grim but impossibly catchy, with suave and snazzy horns and female backing vocals.

❻ **I DON'T NEED NO DOCTOR** from ANTHOLOGY
It was only 1966, but this wailing, urgent (and again minor-keyed) rocker was really about his last great moment on record.

❼ **BUSTED** from ULTIMATE HITS COLLECTION
Nothing's going Ray's way on this forceful jazzy number, sung as if he's honoring his misfortune with a bemused mock zest.

❽ ONE MINT JULEP from ULTIMATE HITS COLLECTION
Charles could play jazz too, as he did on this exuberant horn-organ-duel 1961 hit single – instrumental apart from occasional way-hip spoken-shouted asides.

❾ DON'T SET ME FREE from ULTIMATE HITS COLLECTION
Near-enslavement to passion was a common theme for Charles, here expressed with an almost get-it-over-with rush.

❿ STICKS AND STONES from ULTIMATE HITS COLLECTION
Ray and his backup make being abused sound down-right pleasurable, with an electric piano solo almost the equal of "What'd I Say"s.

Richie Unterberger

Cheap Trick

Featuring the wildly talented and sartorially challenged guitarist Rick Nielsen, classy hard rock acts don't come funnier, edgier or more intelligent than this lot.

❶ CALIFORNIA MAN from HEAVEN TONIGHT
A top of the range Roy Wood tune given a transatlantic facelift. You want vintage rock'n'roll swagger? Just crank this one up.

❷ CLOCK STRIKES TEN from IN COLOR
Like Little Richard rocking out with Sweet, this is bubblegum pop packing some serious hard rock heat.

❸ COME ON, COME ON from IN COLOR
Is that Noddy Holder on backing vocals? Another formidably fine tune showcasing the Trick's British glam-rock affinities.

❹ DREAM POLICE from DREAM POLICE
You've gotta love those violin-like keyboards and melodramatic mid-section. Yet another cracking pop rocker from the band that makes it all sound so easy.

❺ ELO KIDDIES from CHEAP TRICK
A reference to The Electric Light Orchestra? With a cursory nod to the Brum sound, the pummelling drums belong to something Gary Glitter might have cooked up.

❻ GONNA RAISE HELL from DREAM POLICE
At over nine minutes, this is the heavy antithesis of the Trick's pop sensibilities. Nevertheless, it contains a great riff and a fist-banging, anthemic chorus.

❼ HE'S A WHORE from CHEAP TRICK
Ironic lyrics married to a melodic Beatlesy sensibility wrapped around a dark-hearted chorus that demands you shout along.

❽ I WANT YOU TO WANT ME from AT BUDOKAN
In the studio this was cute. Live, it sounds like a classic. Lush pop-rock delivered to an audience willing to lap up every lovingly honed note.

❾ SURRENDER from HEAVEN TONIGHT
Clever, cutting lyrics, one of the band's best choruses, and everything underpinned by swirling keyboards and a terrific multilayered climax.

❿ WRONG ALL ALONG from CHEAP TRICK
Kicks off like an AC/DC style shuffle boogie before plunging headlong into a punchy and raucous stompalong.

Essi Berelian

Cheer up, Brian

In which we explore a few songs designed to lift your mood, lighten your step, and stiffen your resolve, in a Chumbawumba-free zone.

❶ GET HAPPY JUDY GARLAND from GET HAPPY
The original cheer-up song from the great tragedienne, who turns a hymn into a hope.

❷ GOOD VIBRATIONS BRIAN WILSON/THE BEACH BOYS from PET SOUNDS BEACH BOYS AND SMILE BRIAN WILSON
Brian Wilson's symphonic rhapsody meets classic Beach Boys surferboy harmonies, given an even more rococo treatment in his later album *Smile*.

❸ FROM HEAD TO TOE ELVIS COSTELLO from IMPERIAL BEDROOM
This is what happens when the archetypal cool guy gets exuberantly toe-tappy and a tad honkytonk on the piano. He actually uses the phrase "go steady with me".

❹ MOVE ON UP CURTIS MAYFIELD from MOVE ON UP
Real soul shows that size does matter when you've got a big horn section.

❺ EVERYTHING REMINDS ME OF MY DOG JANE SIBERRY from BOUND BY THE BEAUTY
Top shelf novelty song from the Canadian quirkster. If you don't smile when you hear it, you're dead, or a cat person.

❻ CELEBRATE KOOL AND THE GANG from THE VERY BEST OF KOOL AND THE GANG
These funky sampling favourites had their own effervescent party-mix smash hit in 1980.

❼ WALKIN' ON SUNSHINE KATRINA AND THE WAVES from GREATEST HITS: WALKING ON SUNSHINE
Diabolical girlie sing-along that cheers everyone up despite themselves.

❽ LOUIE LOUIE THE KINGSMEN from THE VERY BEST OF THE KINGSMEN
Nobody understands the lyrics (despite an FBI investigation) but everybody understands you have to dance.

❾ YOU CAN GET IT IF YOU REALLY WANT JIMMY CLIFF from YOU CAN GET IT IF YOU REALLY WANT
The reggae great has an attractive concept we'd all like to believe is true.

❿ ALWAYS LOOK ON THE BRIGHT SIDE OF LIFE from MONTY PYTHON SINGS
Crucifixion? It calls for something special – and Eric Idle delivers.

Kaz Cooke

1980s cheese

Nothing screams 1980s like a sax solo, supple synth hook, sappy power ballad or film soundtrack from Kenny Loggins. Some things are so bad they're good.

❶ MANEATER DARYL HALL & JOHN OATES from H2O
The lyrics are beyond inane, but that "dum-dum-dum, dum-dum-de-dum" bassline is irresistible.

❷ CAN'T FIGHT THIS FEELING
REO SPEEDWAGON from WHEELS ARE TURNIN'
So many words rhyme with "or"; REO pull out the rhyming dictionary to "fall upon your floor", "crash through your door" and whatever else might fit.

❸ TOTAL ECLIPSE OF THE HEART BONNIE TYLER from FASTER THAN THE SPEED OF NIGHT
Deliciously overdramatic, Tyler gives new meaning to the phrase "belt it out".

❹ AFRICA TOTO from FOUR
"I must do what's right/Sure as Kilimanjaro rises like Olympus above the Serengeti." If this isn't the best slice of pretentious rock poetry ever sung, then it's surely close.

❺ MR ROBOTO STYX from KILROY WAS HERE
Hear a grown man sing "secret, secret, I've got a secret". But wait, is it in fact a robot singing that? The future never sounded less scary.

❻ SISTER CHRISTIAN NIGHT RANGER from MIDNIGHT MADNESS
The transition from tender piano ballad to revved-up, electrified rocker is so phony it makes you want to hear it over and over again.

❼ THE ONE THAT YOU LOVE AIR SUPPLY from THE ONE THAT YOU LOVE
The unabashed kings of schmaltzy love songs scale all sorts of epic heights – not least the chorus's use of the third person – on their most successful ballad.

❽ DON'T STOP BELIEVIN' JOURNEY from ESCAPE
The small town girl, the city boy – this is the kind of archetypal rock'n'roll fable that makes you want to head straight back to high school.

❾ DANGER ZONE KENNY LOGGINS from TOP GUN SOUNDTRACK
Someone so close to the middle of the road deserves a medal for chutzpah in claiming he'll "take you right into the Danger Zone". Still, it sort of rocks.

Andrew Rosenberg

The Chemical Brothers

Outstandingly chunky, heavyweight beats delivered by two of the least likely-looking funkmeisters ever. Ed and Tom Chemical met at university over a shared passion for old-school hip-hop and started out as The Dust Brothers, a name borrowed from a successful US production team. When their own success moved into the same orbit, a name change was in order.

❶ SUNSHINE UNDERGROUND from SURRENDER
Do not listen to this song while driving. It cranks itself up to an unbelievably fearsome pitch of excitement.

❷ IT BEGAN IN AFRICA from COME WITH US
Massive beats pay tribute to the root of all our dance music.

❸ BLOCK ROCKIN' BEATS from DIG YOUR OWN HOLE
Jack your body into the osteopathy clinic with this electro-based blast from the recent past.

❹ FUCK UP BEATS from EXIT PLANET DUST

The track that the radio DJs never announce fully. One of the Chems' first compositions, its title is basically their motto.

❺ MUSIC: RESPONSE from SURRENDER

Robot vocals and a Kraftwerkian steady might lull you into a false sense of security. But halfway through it you'll find yourself on the dancefloor again.

❻ SONG TO THE SIREN (LIVE) from EXIT PLANET DUST

Beats of electro-mechanical passion provide a solid base for enticing, looped female vocals. Then, with no warning, the trance kicks in and we're sailing ever closer to the rocks.

❼ INFLUENCED from SURRENDER

This features a perfect vocal sample from a consummate rock chick, somewhat partied out and perhaps, one dare say, a little under the influence herself.

❽ THE TEST from COME WITH US

Looking back to Ken Kesey and the "Acid tests" he carried out with the Grateful Dead, the beats will carry you away and keep you dancing way past bedtime.

❾ LEFT RIGHT from PUSH THE BUTTON

Righteous, swaggering, hard-edged R&B beats see themselves blended here with a fine guest hip-hop contribution from Anwar Superstar, with the mix poured into a tall glass filled with chunks of keyboard and cubes of guitar.

❿ DO IT AGAIN from WE ARE THE NIGHT

Ali Love offers guest vocals but as usual, the magic comes from the boys' studio skills and knack of finding just the beats for the job.

Al Spicer

Cher

Cherilyn Lapierre started out as a backing singer on Phil Spector sessions then married Spector accomplice Sonny Bono. Ahead lay decades of hit singles, Academy Awards, celebrity partners and more fame than most mortals could stand. Brassy, trashy and unashamedly a pop culture icon, Cher may not do deep but she's a lotta fun.

SONNY & CHER

❶ I GOT YOU BABE from THE BEAT GOES ON

Timeless love duet from the most successful husband and wife in pop history.

❷ BABY DON'T GO from THE BEAT GOES ON

But she did – go solo that is. Initially with Sonny producing. Then she left him. He became a Republican politician while she became the original template for mega-female pop fame.

CHER

❸ ALL I REALLY WANT TO DO from THE GREATEST HITS

Cher sings Dylan and outsells The Byrds (who had covered the same tune at the same time). "They beat you, man!" said a flabbergasted Bob to Roger McGuinn.

❹ BANG BANG from THE GREATEST HITS

Epic pop melodrama, absolutely stupid and enjoyable for this. One of the best songs Sonny Bono ever wrote and Cher delivers it with a panache that hints at the actress inside her.

❺ THE BEAT GOES ON from THE GREATEST HITS

Cher gets slinky on this standard. With her purring away you may well want the beat to go on and on.

❻ GYPSIES, TRAMPS & THIEVES from THE GREATEST HITS

Wild, stomping US #1 celebrating growing up among outsiders so being condemned by the straight suburban masses. Cher's best ever tune?

❼ HALF-BREED from THE WAY OF LOVE

Cher apparently has Native American bloodlines. Here she celebrates them ever so tastefully.

❽ DARK LADY from THE WAY OF LOVE

Another hymn to her fine self. Anyone who's ever witnessed Cher's stage attire will realize she's not the shy, retiring type.

❾ IF I COULD TURN BACK TIME from THE GREATEST HITS

Disco should have suited Cher – she was signed to Casablanca – but she never really scored. However, 1980s power ballads to return her to the charts. One to wave your lighter at.

❿ BELIEVE from THE GREATEST HITS

1998 dancefloor friendly, vocoder powered megahit that topped both US and UK charts so making the then 52-year-old Cher the oldest female yet to dominate the pop charts. The song? Catchy, incessant, forgettable, in a word: classic Cher.

Garth Cartwright

Neneh Cherry

Being Don Cherry's daughter gave Neneh a musical head-start. Moving away from her punk-jazz roots, she became a feisty B-girl in the late-1980s before seating herself down on the comfy trip-hop sofa in the 90s.

❶ TAX SEX RIP, RIG & PANIC from I AM COLD
Chaotic, brittle disco, with Neneh and Andrea Oliver's mischievous taunts giving way to zippy, post-Cecil Taylor piano acrobatics.

❷ STORM THE REALITY ASYLUM RIP, RIG & PANIC from I AM COLD
Taking its title from one of William Burroughs's revolutionary exhortations, this is an anarchic, sloganeering anthem with a touch of the showtune.

❸ THOSE ESKIMO WOMEN SPEAK FRANKLY RIP, RIG & PANIC from GOD
If Public Image Ltd had ever decided to write a playground skipping-rope song, it might have sounded as contrary as this.

❹ THE LONELIEST GIRL FLOAT UP CP from KILL ME IN THE MORNING
Swooning viola, a clicky drumbeat, and slightly reticent funk bass render Neneh's impassioned ballad all the sweeter.

❺ SEXY BUSHES FLOAT UP CP from KILL ME IN THE MORNING
Imagine Kate Bush being harangued by Frank Zappa to the mildewed parping of a horn section that smells of a 1980s squat.

❻ BUFFALO STANCE NENEH CHERRY from RAW LIKE SUSHI
Ms Cherry restyles herself as "urban", via a few feisty put-downs, frothy hip-hop beats and the sort of perky but assertive keyboards that regularly soundtracked 1980s cop show *Miami Vice*.

❼ MANCHILD NENEH CHERRY from RAW LIKE SUSHI
Apparently, it was playing with the "autochord" voicings on a cheap keyboard that led Neneh to one of the most imaginative string arrangements on a pop record since Prince's *Parade* album.

❽ TOGETHER NOW TRICKY from NEARLY GOD
Neneh's vocal verges a little too close to the histrionic, but Tricky's bruised and lolloping blues-guitar riff keeps things grounded.

Matt Milton

Chess R&B

Best-known for its straight blues output (Muddy Waters, Howlin' Wolf etc.), Chicago-based Chess was also responsible for releasing some great R&B, soul and rock'n'roll, most notably Chuck Berry.

❶ HELP ME SONNY BOY WILLIAMSON from THE CHESS BLUES-ROCK SONGBOOK
Is it heresy to suggest this was the basis for Booker T and the MGs' "Green Onions"?

❷ WALKING BY MYSELF JIMMIE ROGERS from CHESS PIECES
Muddy Waters sideman rocks with the help of a superb Big Walter Horton harmonica solo.

❸ ROCKET 88 JACKIE BRENSTON & HIS DELTA KINGS from CHESS PIECES
Brenston got the credit, but it's Ike Turner behind this Sun-recorded candidate for the first rock'n'roll record.

❹ MUMBLIN' GUITAR BO DIDDLEY from THE STORY OF BO DIDDLEY
Bo makes his guitar talk over a typical Diddley beat. Crazily compelling.

❺ HI HEELED SNEAKERS LITTLE TOMMY TUCKER from CHESS PIECES
Oft-covered but never bettered Mod favourite.

❻ AIN'T GOT NO HOME CLARENCE 'FROGMAN' HENRY from CHESS PIECES
Henry sings like a girl then like a frog over a typical New Orleans backbeat.

❼ THE WALK JIMMY MCCRACKLIN from CHESS PIECES
The lyrics refer to long-forgotten dances, but the music still hits the spot.

❽ SUZIE Q DALE HAWKINS from CHESS PIECES
Covered by Creedence Clearwater Revival, the original features some great James Burton guitar work.

❾ RESCUE ME FONTELLA BASS from CHESS PIECES
Classic 1960s bass-driven soul dancer, one of Chess's biggest hits.

❿ DIRTY MAN LAURA LEE from CHESS PIECES
Lee lays into her two-timing partner on this tasty slice of Muscle Shoals soul. Covered by Joss Stone.

Neil Foxlee

Chic Productions

In the late 1970s and early 80s the sound of the Chic production team (guitarist Nile Rodgers and bassist Bernard Edwards) was the sleekest and most stylish in popular music. Some might even say that it was never surpassed.

❶ DANCE, DANCE, DANCE (YOWSAH, YOWSAH, YOWSAH) CHIC from CHIC
The first record that didn't remove sub-bass tones. Get up, dance and feel the bottom end in your bowels.

❷ LE FREAK CHIC from C'EST CHIC
Maybe the archest, most ambiguous dance-craze disc ever.

❸ AT LAST I AM FREE CHIC from C'EST CHIC
Who says a dance band can't move you to tears?

❹ SATURDAY NORMA JEAN from NORMA JEAN
A cult disco classic that features one of Edwards' most outlandish basslines.

❺ LOST IN MUSIC SISTER SLEDGE from WE ARE FAMILY
An ode to the power of music so perfect that it drove Mark E. Smith to cover it with The Fall.

❻ GOOD TIMES CHIC from RISQUÉ
The greatest ever disco record, and one of the most influential records of the last thirty years.

❼ I'M COMING OUT DIANA ROSS from DIANA
Not since The Supremes' heyday has Ross sounded this good – or this coy.

❽ WHY CARLY SIMON from SOUP FOR ONE
Perhaps Chic's greatest feat – making Carly Simon listenable.

❾ LIKE A VIRGIN MADONNA from LIKE A VIRGIN
Rodgers' synthed-up Motown production turned Madonna into the biggest star ever.

❿ NOTORIOUS DURAN DURAN from NOTORIOUS
The boys from Birmingham finally got to work with their idol, who pulls out all the stops.

Peter Shapiro

Chickens & insects

Or should that be "more songs about poultry, insects and arachnids"? Musicologists continue to come to blows over the precise definition of what remains one of music's most enduring genres.

❶ CHICKEN CRAZY JOE TEX from SKINNY LEGS AND ALL
Joe Tex was always one who could conjure a silk purse from a sow's ear; this really is a soul classic about how lots of people like eating chicken.

❷ BEST DRESSED CHICKEN IN TOWN DR ALIMANTADO from BEST DRESSED CHICKEN IN TOWN
Backed by Lee Perry's trademark production squawkings, the good doctor free-associates on a topic dear to his heart, farmyard fowl and their natty attire.

❸ DO THE FUNKY CHICKEN RUFUS THOMAS from FUNKY CHICKEN
Back in 1970, there was a brief period when flapping your elbows and strutting around with your knees bent really did seem pretty funky.

❹ LITTLE RED ROOSTER THE ROLLING STONES from BIG HITS HIGH TIDE AND GREEN GRASS
The Stones stole this one from the mighty Howlin' Wolf, but somehow it's easier to see Mick as a cocky little bantam.

❺ COLD TURKEY JOHN LENNON from SHAVED FISH
Never one to make a molehill when a mountain would do, John bemoans those Boxing Day blues.

❻ HEY THERE LITTLE INSECT JONATHAN RICHMAN AND THE MODERN LOVERS from JONATHAN RICHMAN AND THE MODERN LOVERS
So does Jonathan want the little insect to "calm down" or to "come down"? Either way, it would do best to stay out of his reach rather than let him "fool around".

❼ I GOT ANTS IN MY PANTS JAMES BROWN from MAKE IT FUNKY
In which the Godfather of Soul finally reveals the secret behind those hard-working legs.

❽ BORIS THE SPIDER THE WHO from MY GENERATION, JON "THE OX"
Entwistle turns whimsical, albeit in a ponderous, quite-bass-player kind of a way.

❾ MOSQUITO SONG QUEENS OF THE STONE AGE from SONGS FOR THE DEAF
Just what were the Queens playing at, revealing their hitherto unknown sensitive, acoustic side in this "secret" hidden track?

❿ I MAN A GRASSHOPPER PABLO MOSES from REVOLUTIONARY DREAM
It's a little hard to tell quite what 1970s reggae star

Moses was saying here, but the general gist seems to be that in his propensity for weed he's no more criminal than a little green grass-eater.

Greg Ward

Chickflicks

There's a whole lot more to chick flick songs than "I Will Always Love You" and "Wind Beneath My Wings". Look at these ten for starters: were there ever better movie soundtracks?

❶ DO YOUR THING BASEMENT JAXX from BEND IT LIKE BECKHAM
Impossibly infectious dance tune – with the immortal refrain "And a boom boom boom and a bang bang bang (boom, bang, boom, bang bang)" – from Brixton's finest house music outfit.

❷ MOON RIVER DANNY WILLIAMS from BREAKFAST AT TIFFANY'S
Henry Mancini's small, sweet and perfectly formed song won an Oscar – and though no one knows for sure what it is, a "huckleberry friend" sounds like a delightful thing to have.

❸ ALL BY MYSELF JAMIE O'NEAL from BRIDGET JONES'S DIARY
Who hasn't bellowed along to this one, eyes screwed shut, in a frenzy of self-pity after one glass too many?

❹ RESPECT ARETHA FRANKLIN from BRIDGET JONES'S DIARY
And who hasn't snapped out of it double quick with a feisty rendition of this? (Thelma and Louise do a pretty fine version, too.)

❺ JUST BLEW IN FROM THE WINDY CITY DORIS DAY from CALAMITY JANE
While it was the film's yearning "Secret Love" that won the Best Song Oscar, the rambunctious "Windy City" has Doris giving it more oomph, at her gutsy thigh-slapping best with every throaty "no, sir-eee!".

❻ AS TIME GOES BY DOOLEYWILSON from CASABLANCA
"You must remember this…" – who could ever forget?

❼ KIDS IN AMERICA THE MUFFS from CLUELESS
Kim Wilde's lo-fi 1980s classic gets a mid-1990s makeover and comes over all Californian garage-punk.

❽ THESE ARMS OF MINE OTIS REDDING from DIRTY DANCING
Nobody on earth sings about love like the Love Man himself. Wrap yourself up in his voice and swoon.

❾ UNCHAINED MELODY THE RIGHTEOUS BROTHERS from GHOST
Grand melodrama meets blue-eyed soul. Just try to hit that high note while choking back the lump in your throat.

❿ THE BALLAD OF LUCY JORDAN MARIANNE FAITHFULL from THELMA & LOUISE
For any woman who, at the age of 37, realized she would never drive – to Paris – in a sports car – with the warm wind in her hay-ayr…

Sam Cooke

Chill-out

Or Ambient, as we once used to call it in those distant pre-chill club night…

❶ A HUGE EVER-GROWING PULSATING BRAIN… THE ORB from ADVENTURES BEYOND THE ULTRAWORLD
Ambient music, for many people, started here, when sampled ocean noises and abstracted Minnie Riperton vocals hit the UK charts.

❷ 2/1 BRIAN ENO from AMBIENT 1: MUSIC FOR AIRPORTS
Twelve years before The Orb, in 1978, came this calm piano-cum-electronic-effects tune.

❸ GYMNOPÉDIE NO. 1 ERIK SATIE from SARBAND: DANSE GOTHIQUE
Erik Satie wanted to create *musique d'ameublement*, music which is part of the furniture. Here, one of his best-known piano pieces is played on medieval and Middle Eastern instruments.

❹ KALAVATI REMIXES SUNS OF ARQA from GIVE PEACE A DANCE VOL 2: THE AMBIENT COLLECTION
Indian bansuri flute sets the tone for a tune that lasts forever (well, 23 minutes).

❺ LITTLE FLUFFY CLOUDS THE ORB from THE ORB'S ADVENTURES BEYOND THE ULTRAWORLD
It all starts with the cry of a rooster, over which Rickie Lee Jones tells us: "When I lived in Arizona and the skies always had little fluffy clouds in them and there were lots of stars at night." Ambient made it to the dancefloors.

❻ DREAM TIME IN LAKE JACKSON KLF from CHILL OUT
Central Asian throat singing and synth drones langorously merge.

69

❼ THE THIRD CHAMBER PART 4 LOOP GURU from DUNIYA

It starts with a muezzin, then in comes some gamelan from Indonesia, a sample of Sheila Chandra's singing, birdsong, and electronics. All of which create a serene atmosphere.

❽ SPEEDLEARN (EMPATHYMIX) THE HIGHER INTELLIGENCE AGENCY from COLOURFORM

Masters of the chill-out zones of numerous raves, The Agency really know how to tease a rhythmic progression from the ethereal atmospheres of their samplers.

Jean Trouillet

❺ THE CAT CREPT IN MUD from THE VERY BEST…

Mud still exist, touring for eternity the windswept holiday camps of the UK, condemned to wear the same drapesuits and perform the same dance routine. This is a cheerful enough tune, though, to perform every night…

❻ WIG WAM BAM THE YUMYUMS from SWEET AS CANDY (COLD FRONT; 1997)

The music masters from Østfold in Norway took this away from The Sweet – who recorded the original – and made it into a piece of tuneful, sunny perfection. Powerful pop, sugar coated and pumped with additives.

Al Spicer

Chinn & Chapman

Loathed and despised by "real" rock fans, Nicky Chinn and Mike Chapman were the songwriting team behind a stream of bubblegum hits, from Sweet's "Funny Funny" in 1971 through to Toni Basil's "Mickey" in 1982, on Micky Most's RAK records. Here are six of the best, both originals and oddly cool revisitings.

❶ DEVIL GATE DRIVE SUZI QUATRO from GREATEST HITS

Holding the biggest bass guitar and wearing the tightest leather cat-suit, Suzi's possibly kinky girl-next-door good looks had her teenage-boy target-market sewn up. She fronted a totally professional band and kicked ass in a way that girls in pop didn't do back then.

❷ BALLROOM BLITZ THE DAMNED from MACHINE GUN ETIQUETTE

Never a tune of shrinking virginal innocence, The Sweet's version of this was about a fight kicking off in a discotheque. Then The Damned, featuring the none-more-tasteless stylings of Captain Sensible and Dave Vanian, got their dirty punk rockers' hands on it.

❸ BLOCKBUSTER THE SWEET from THE VERY BEST OF

The Sweet were macho enough under all that make-up to appeal to the young lads, and pretty enough for the girls to plaster their rooms with their photos. They never surpassed this invigorating shriek of glam nonsense.

❹ ROCKET THE WEDDING PRESENT from HIT PARADE

Some reckon that Mud's original extracted the last drop of emotion from this ChinniChap masterpiece, but just give the Weddoes' version a spin for the full juice.

Eric Clapton

The 1960s graffiti called him God – and few other guitarists save old rivals Jeff Beck and Jimmy Page can match his blistering solos when he gets in the mood. What is more often overlooked is Clapton's talent as both a singer and songwriter.

❶ SUNSHINE OF YOUR LOVE CREAM from DISRAELI GEARS

The riff that launched a thousand bands. Heavy, man!

❷ WHITE ROOM CREAM from WHEELS OF FIRE

Who isn't thrilled when that wah-wah kicks in?

❸ CROSSROADS CREAM from WHEELS OF FIRE

A radical reinterpretation of Robert Johnson that redefined how white men play the blues.

❹ BADGE CREAM from GOODBYE CREAM

A whiff of psychedelia about the lyrics (courtesy of George Harrison), and a sound that echoes the Byrds.

❺ AFTER MIDNIGHT from ERIC CLAPTON'

A J.J. Cale song that he has reworked several times in his career, this best exemplifies Clapton's ability to make country rock sound almost funky.

❻ LAYLA DEREK AND THE DOMINOS from LAYLA AND OTHER ASSORTED LOVE SONGS

A lovelorn plea to George Harrison's wife – and a major hit to boot.

❼ WHILE MY GUITAR GENTLY WEEPS from CONCERT FOR BANGLADESH

Clapton played on The Beatles' original and no one makes a guitar weep like he does on this live performance from the 1970 charity gig.

Eric Clapton's
Blues roots

What was it about the blues that struck such a chord with a bunch of white kids growing up in suburban England in the 1950s? "There was something about the solo bluesman and the knowledge that this guy was probably uneducated and on the bottom rung of the social ladder," ERIC CLAPTON recalls. "I grabbed at that and I had a built-in admiration for it but I still don't know why. I'd like to say it was something to do with my upbringing but it would be very hard to find a tangible cause…" Here are ten of those original inspirations.

❶ I LOVE THE WOMAN FREDDIE KING from BLUES GUITAR HERO

❷ KINDHEARTED WOMAN BLUES ROBERT JOHNSON from THE COMPLETE RECORDINGS

❸ HOBO BLUES JOHN LEE HOOKER from THE LEGENDARY MODERN RECORDINGS

❹ HAND IN HAND ELMORE JAMES from THE BEST OF ELMORE JAMES

❺ SPECIAL STREAM LINE BUKKA WHITE from MISSISSIPPI BLUES GIANT

❻ FRANKIE AND ALBERT MISSISSIPPI JOHN HURT from SATISFYING BLUES

❼ CHOCK HOUSE BLUES BLIND LEMON JEFFERSON from BLIND LEMON JEFFERSON

❽ ALABAMA WOMAN BLUES LEROY CARR from THE ESSENTIAL LEROY CARR

❾ STAESBORO BLUES BLIND WILLIE MCTELL from ATLANTA STRUT

❿ STRUTTIN' WITH SOME BARBECUE LOUIS ARMSTRONG AND THE HOT FIVE from THE BEST OF LOUIS ARMSTRONG AND THE HOT FIVE

❽ GO BACK HOME STEPHEN STILLS from STEPHEN STILLS
Clapton has often played his best as a special guest, and he is on fire on this bluesy number from Stephen Stills' first solo effort.

❾ LET IT GROW from 461 OCEAN BOULEVARD
A gentle ballad with an insistent refrain. Effortless emotion for the 1970s party set.

❿ I SHOT THE SHERIFF from CROSSROADS
This spirited live version from 1974 shows that Clapton is able to weave his own guitar magic on the song without smothering it.

Chris Coe

The Clash

One of the seminal punk-rock bands, The Clash wrote the book when it comes to sneering, teeth-bared rebellion. Then they went to America…

❶ LONDON'S BURNING from THE CLASH
This tells you everything you need to know about the boredom, street tension and frustration of late 1970s Britain. Paramilitary beats, combat-strength guitar riffs and Joe's most tongue-flappingly lackadaisical vocals render this track essential.

❷ COMPLETE CONTROL from THE CLASH
The best ever "Fuck the record company!" song, full of artistic outrage and played by guys who are finally getting to grips with their instruments and gelling as a band.

❸ (WHITE MAN) IN HAMMERSMITH PALAIS from THE ESSENTIAL CLASH
A well-intentioned stab at UK pop reggae, a fine reminiscence of a great gig, and a bit of sniping at the boneheads. Marvellous.

❹ LONDON CALLING from LONDON CALLING
The title-track stomp from their most accomplished album. Redolent of its time, with equal parts romance and menace, and as classic a slice of London life as anything by The Kinks.

⑤ THE GUNS OF BRIXTON from LONDON CALLING

Our brave lads throw down the gauntlet on behalf of the capital's dispossessed youth.

⑥ RUDIE CAN'T FAIL from LONDON CALLING

White-boy skanking of the highest order. Strummer's never been in better voice.

⑦ LOST IN THE SUPERMARKET from LONDON CALLING

Mick Jones' most effective vocal outing. He sounds completely knocked sideways by the choice on offer at his local co-op.

⑧ IVAN MEETS G.I. JOE from SANDINISTA!

Electronic noises bleep happily in the background as the guys envisage World War III as a computer game.

Al Spicer

Eddie Cochran

Arguably the originator of the power-chord rock style, Cochran's rockabilly offered some of the most joyous celebrations of teenage fun of the late 1950s. All selections are from *Somethin' Else: The Fine Lookin' Hits Of Eddie Cochran*.

① SUMMERTIME BLUES

The all-time disenfranchised teenage schoolboy anthem, its massively thick riff-chords simmer with bottled-up frustration.

② C'MON EVERYBODY

Party-party-party time on another thickly chorded hit whose uplifting riff is almost as good as the one on "Summertime Blues".

③ SOMETHIN' ELSE

Rockabilly at its most cocksure, Cochran broadcasting the charms of the babe he's got his eye on.

④ NERVOUS BREAKDOWN

Stuttering rockabilly goofiness dominates this relatively unknown gem.

⑤ WEEKEND

Another wholly unselfconscious celebration of good times, from those distant days when the weekend offered the only relief for youth with energy to burn.

⑥ SITTIN' IN THE BALCONY

Eddie's in a smoochier mood than usual on this rocka-ballad, the wholesome scenario dotted by a slight suggestion of naughtiness.

Richie Unterberger

Cocteau Twins

Robin Guthrie and Simon Raymonde and vocalist Liz Fraser – collectively, the Cocteau Twins – have, for the last two decades, cultivated a unique blend of ethereally expressive music, with vocals that have reinvented the map. If an emotion exists, there is a Cocteau Twins moment for it.

① PANDORA from TREASURE

Liz's siren-like higher range blossoms out here, as she dives headlong into verbal abstraction.

② ICEBLINK LUCK from HEAVEN OR LAS VEGAS

Lush, indie-jangly guitars and driving drums heralded a sharper, tighter sound, as reverbs and echoes are stripped back to reveal startlingly clear vocals.

③ SERPENTSKIRT from MILK AND KISSES

Stark, gothic guitars and snares intro a track that waxes and wanes between bleak, whispering voids and swelling multi-vocal rivers. Then, just when you think it's all been said, the Twins shift gear and fire another blissful tangent.

④ WHALES TAILS from VICTORIALAND

Fraser and Guthrie tumble on the Arctic breeze, snowflake-light, wafting between billowy cumulonimbi and shimmering ice floes.

⑤ CICO BUFF from BLUE BELL KNOLL

Elegant piece with Liz leisurely sliding up and down the scales before a sublime guitar solo propels her up and out into bursting choral incandescence.

⑥ THE SPANGLE MAKER from THE PINK OPAQUE

Throbbing bass and great whining feedback arcs, redolent of the Twins' punky debut, smooth out into anthemic grandeur.

⑦ THOSE EYES, THAT MOUTH from LOVE'S EASY TEARS

As with so many of the Cocteau's best tracks there is build and pay-off. The build here centres on pounding 3/4 guitar cycles spiralling round Fraser's full-pelt barks; the pay-off is an achingly tender wall of sound.

⑧ NEED-FIRE from JUDGE DREDD SOUNDTRACK

Liz turns to crushingly vulnerable child in one of the Cocteaus' most vocally spare tracks. Washes of guitar delays are carried along by a warm digital thump.

⑨ MUD AND DARK from EVANGELINE

Listen carefully and before your very ears will unfold the story of Echo and Narcissus, and the dangers of falling for an egotist.

⑩ GREAT SPANGLED FRITILLARY from TINY DYNAMINE/
ECHOES IN A SHALLOW BAY EP

Liz duets her own unearthly yodelling across a morse-code pattern of butterfly names. Undulating bass, kicking in midway, tugs you bodily into the disquieting soundjungle.

Link Hall

Leonard Cohen

Songs of Love and Hate he called his best known album, and the laconic Cohen was for years seen as a byword for gloom. But his star has shone in recent years, with everyone from The Pixies to R.E.M. covering his songs.

❶ FAMOUS BLUE RAINCOAT from GREATEST HITS

A bitter-sweet tale of a triangular love affair in which the cuckold detests then forgives his partner's seducer. Propelled by Paul Buckmaster's strings, this is Cohen's most iconic song, later wonderfully reworked by his backing singer Jennifer Warnes in her album of covers.

❷ THE STRANGER SONG from FIELD COMMANDER COHEN

Compare and contrast with Billy Joel's take on the same personality type (The Stranger). Cohen's conversational depiction is full of self-knowledge, while Joel's feels like a simple-minded pop song.

❸ SEEMS SO LONG AGO, NANCY from LIVE SONGS

Suicide was never far from Cohen's early work and this meditation about a suicide victim, first released on *Songs From A Room*, is even more eerie and chilling live with the likes of Jennifer Warnes wailing in the background.

❹ I CAN'T FORGET from I'M YOUR MAN

A lilting, lyrical, moving number – almost his answer to Kurt Weill's "September Song" – in which Len nostalgically confides "I can't forget… but I can't remember what".

❺ FIRST, WE TAKE MANHATTAN from I'M YOUR MAN

In which the narrator has the energy left for a marvellously sinister laugh and a bid for world domination involving Manhattan and Berlin. Beautifully played, sardonically sung, compellingly daft, this is a minor masterpiece.

❻ HEY THAT'S NO WAY TO SAY GOODBYE from
GREATEST HITS

A rare outing for Cohen as love-struck fool, although even here the tender promise that "our steps will always rhyme" is undermined, as love runs aground.

❼ DRESS REHEARSAL RAG from SONGS OF LOVE AND HATE

After some of the bitterest self-reproach in his songbook, reinforced by an angry, beaten-up, backing, the singer just pulls back from slashing his wrists in a song which, for all the agony, is almost exhilarating.

❽ BIRD ON THE WIRE from SONGS FROM A ROOM

Kris Kristofferson has promised to use the line about struggling to be free "like a drunk in a midnight choir" as his epitaph. Listen to this often covered grandiloquent whimsy and it's easy to understand why.

❾ CHELSEA HOTEL from GREATEST HITS

A wistful, self-lacerating, tuneful account of Cohen's brief fling with Janis Joplin, in which he makes it perfectly clear that the blues chanteuse wasn't that nice to him and that, even dead, she doesn't prey on his mind very much.

⑩ THE FUTURE from THE FUTURE

A hypnotic, low-key, ode in which Cohen reveals that he has seen the future and it's murder. But then we'd expect no less.

Paul Simpson

Coldplay

On first appearance, you might have put money on Coldplay remaining a bit of a cult band, full of quiet songcraft. But with stadium status, celebrity status and PC status all secured, the sky seems not to be the limit for these lads. Here are exemplary cuts from each of their three top-notch albums.

❶ YELLOW from PARACHUTES

Buckland's triumphant descending chords and Chris Martin's voice-just-breaking vocals helped make this the first hit single.

❷ TROUBLE from PARACHUTES

This song's worth goes well beyond its intro being borrowed for a myriad mobile ringtones. The sombre piano and lazy structure typify the band's forte at sweetly describing desperation.

❸ DON'T PANIC from PARACHUTES

The strummed opener ("We live in a beautiful world") sounds doomed, with Martin's vocal counterpointed by some divine guitar-picking.

❹ WARNING SIGN from A RUSH OF BLOOD TO THE HEAD

Soulsearching strings and keyboards enrich the strummed simplicity of the song, and the line "When the truth is, I miss you" is genuine goosepimples territory.

❺ IN MY PLACE from A RUSH OF BLOOD TO THE HEAD
A gentle but piercing guitar riff sets the tone for the singer to lament being lost in his classic pained tunefulness.

❻ THE SCIENTIST from A RUSH OF BLOOD TO THE HEAD
Martin's majestic piano chords and more bleeding heart vocals raise this love song on high before the band weigh in to bring it gradually back to earth.

❼ TALK from X&Y
This plea to overcome alienation rides on a seething magma of bass and synthesizer, while the haunting guitar bursts through like birds flying out of the mist.

❽ THE HARDEST PART from X&Y
Superbly crafted song with a series of sublime hooks to complement the wistful lyrics. Buckland's guitar flows like honey throughout.

❾ WHITE SHADOWS from X&Y
Quirky off-beat drums and sawing guitars almost remind us of Joy Division before Martin's shift into the melodic chorus remind us who we are listening to.

❿ HOW YOU SEE THE WORLD from WARCHILD: HELP!
This new version of an old song was the band's contribution to Warchild, the charity run by their new producer, Brian Eno.

Nick Edwards

Colours

There isn't a colour in the rainbow that hasn't featured in a song title.

❶ RED RED WINE UB40 from LABOUR OF LOVE
White wine just won't do to ease the pain of heartache for these Brummie reggae fans who took a shine to the classic written by Neil Diamond.

❷ ORANGE CRUSH R.E.M. from GREEN
"I've got my spine, I've got my Orange Crush," sings Michael Stipe, in an askance reference to Agent Orange, the deadly nerve gas of the Vietnam war.

❸ YELLOW SUBMARINE THE BEATLES from YELLOW SUBMARINE
Why it was yellow and not some other colour is a mystery. So much so that the French, desperate for a rhyme, changed it to *vert*.

❹ GREEN GREEN GRASS OF HOME TOM JONES from THE BEST OF TOM JONES
From South Wales to New South Wales, farmers the world use far too much fertilizer.

❺ BLUE JONI MITCHELL from BLUE
The title track of the Californian singer/songwriter's most iconic album.

❻ MOOD INDIGO NINA SIMONE from NINA: THE ESSENTIAL NINA SIMONE
What's bluer than blues? Ah, of course.

❼ PURPLE HAZE JIMI HENDRIX from EXPERIENCE HENDRIX: THE BEST OF JIMI HENDRIX
Not quite violet, but close enough. Love is the drug seems to be the basic message.

❽ CRIMSON AND CLOVER TOMMY JAMES & THE SHONDELLS from ANTHOLOGY
Double colours from the Pittsburgh band that brought you the original version of "I Think We're Alone Now".

❾ WHITE LINES GRANDMASTER FLASH & MELLE MEL from GREATEST HITS
The anti-coke hip-hop smash backfired: many saw it as the best ever ad for charlie.

❿ BROWN SUGAR THE ROLLING STONES from STICKY FINGERS
Not one from the rainbow, granted, but it does feature one of pop music's most instantly recognizable riffs. A British band do America better than the Americans.

Jon Lusk

Coltrane on call

John Coltrane's place at the front of the stage in the Great Jazz Club In The Sky is safe, primarily as a result of his extraordinary feats as a bandleader (see list opposite). But every master was once a pupil, and Coltrane was given his first break as a relative unknown when he was picked in place of the great Sonny Rollins to be Miles Davis's tenor player. He was a fast learner, and graduated with honours.

❶ ROUND MIDNIGHT MILES DAVIS from ROUND ABOUT MIDNIGHT
Coltrane shows he can devote himself to a tune as well as improvise on it, supporting Miles's dry trumpet with deep, long notes.

Hugh Hopper picks
John Coltrane

HUGH HOPPER was, with Robert Wyatt, a founder member of the Canterbury group of musicians who went on to form Soft Machine, Gong, Caravan, etc. He continues to record and play in many projects (see *www. hughhopper.com*) and cites Coltrane as his greatest jazz influence. "John Coltrane came to prominence playing with Miles Davis – like so many other great musicians. But it was after he left Miles that he began to forge that totally dedicated music life. Surrounding himself with the energy of drummer Elvin Jones and the hypnotic piano of McCoy Tyner, he transcended jazz as it had been up to that time."

❶ AFRICA from AFRICA/BRASS
Two basses and McCoy Tyner chanting away, Coltrane wailing over Elvin Jones's jungle and Eric Dolphy's whooping brass arrangements.

❷ MR SYMS from COLTRANE PLAYS THE BLUES
A sad yet sweet mood. Coltrane just hints at a solo.

❸ TUNJI from COLTRANE
Absolutely pared-down modalism, as McCoy Tyner's hypnotic piano combines with Elvin Jones's silky cymbals.

❹ SPIRITUAL from LIVE AT THE VILLAGE VANGUARD
The almost dirty sound of Eric Dolphy's bass clarinet alongside the classic Coltrane Quartet.

❺ CHASING THE TRANE from LIVE AT THE VILLAGE VANGUARD
Really a duet between Coltrane and Elvin. Total energy.

❻ SOUL EYES from COLTRANE IN A SOULFUL MOOD
Mal Waldron's ballad. Coltrane plays with deep soul and tenderness.

❼ DAHOMEY DANCE from OLÉ COLTRANE
Bassist Reggie Workman's ostinato octave riff started a whole new jazz feel.

❽ GREENSLEEVES from AFRICA/BRASS
One of the great 3/4-time epics that Coltrane loved to indulge in (alongside "My Favourite Things" and "Inchworm"). The rhythm section would work up a relentless steaming soundscape for Coltrane's sax.

❾ TRANSITION from TRANSITION
Coltrane and Elvin's most extreme blast of pure energy. I can listen to this CD about once a year.

❿ BLUE TRAIN from BLUE TRAIN
A Blue Note classic. Cooler than this you won't find.

❷ SALT PEANUTS MILES DAVIS from STEAMIN' WITH THE MILES DAVIS QUINTET
Coltrane and Davis do their cooler version of Bird'n'Diz with this fast yet spacious track immortalized by the earlier duo.

❸ TRANE'S BLUES MILES DAVIS from WORKIN' WITH THE MILES DAVIS QUINTET
JC's unique style is already well in evidence in these sessions from 1956, and this blues provides an example of his early forays into composition.

❹ TENOR MADNESS SONNY ROLLINS from TENOR MADNESS
A fascinating opportunity to compare the two tenor giants of the day (Rollins being the better established). Much more anger is evident in Coltrane's playing.

❺ BLUES BY FIVE MILES DAVIS from COOKIN' WITH THE MILES DAVIS QUINTET
Coltrane's interpretation of the blues is clearly developing on this track as he seeks a middle way between Davis's "cool" and his own "fire".

❻ TRINKLE TINKLE THELONIOUS MONK from THELONIOUS MONK WITH JOHN COLTRANE
In some ways Coltrane seems more at home with Monk's disjointed and angular compositions than Miles; this track resulted from a short-lived though influential partnership.

❼ ON GREEN DOLPHIN STREET MILES DAVIS from '58 SESSIONS
From the first recordings by the sextet that would make the seminal *A Kind of Blue*, this warm, Bill Evans-inspired

exposition features Coltrane and Cannonball Adderley sparring on saxes.

8 SID'S AHEAD MILES DAVIS from MILESTONES
Another blues, demonstrating the increasing confidence that would lead Coltrane to leave Miles Davis eighteen months later to form his own group.

9 BLUE IN GREEN MILES DAVIS from KIND OF BLUE
One of Coltrane's most beautiful solos, perfectly constructed and demonstrating his ability to mould himself to another's vision.

10 ALL BLUES MILES DAVIS from KIND OF BLUE
On the greatest track on a great album, Coltrane – dark and brooding – and Cannonball – light and melodious – are in total harmony.

Nat Defriend

Conditionals

From hopes for the future (first conditional) to hypothetical situations (second), expressions of regret (third) and crimes against the English language, conditionals can just about say it all. Especially if you're a country singer.

1 IF LOVING YOU IS WRONG, I DON'T WANT TO BE RIGHT LUTHER INGRAM from GREATEST HITS [RIGHT STUFF]
This Southern soul singer was a Stax stalwart in the 1970s. A mixed conditional aptly conveys the mixed-up results of forbidden love. Rod Stewart also covered it.

2 IF WISHES WERE CHANGES NANCI GRIFFITH from THE BEST OF NANCI GRIFFITH
As Nanci observes in this wistfully strummed ballad, "wishing won't change right from wrong". Too right.

3 SOUTH OF CINCINNATI DWIGHT YOAKAM from GUITARS, CADILLACS, ETC ETC.
The finest song on Yoakam's wonderful debut album is one long list of conditionals, the most crucial being: "If you ever get south of Cincinnati, I'll be yours again".

4 IF DRINKIN' DON'T KILL ME HER MEMORY WILL GEORGE JONES from 16 BIGGEST HITS
George Jones' heartfelt rendition of this broken-hearted weepie is a classic. If you listen to this, you'll really feel sorry for him by the end of it!

5 IF YOU'RE NOT THE ONE DANIEL BEDINGFIELD from GOTTA GET THRU THIS
Perhaps Beder's most glucose ballad, but nonetheless a very fine example of mixed conditional.

6 IF I CAN'T HAVE YOU YVONNE ELLIMAN from SATURDAY NIGHT FEVER: THE ORIGINAL MOVIE SOUNDTRACK
Guilt tripping sometimes works if you can't get your way ("If I can't have you/I don't want nobody, baby!") and this passive aggressive disco number certainly did the business.

7 IF I SHOULD FALL FROM GRACE WITH GOD THE POGUES from IF I SHOULD FALL FROM GRACE WITH GOD
"Let me go boys" instructs Shane McGowan on the last great album he made with the Anglo–Irish hell raisers. It's a long way down from the top.

8 IF YOU DON'T KNOW ME BY NOW HAROLD MELVIN & THE BLUE NOTES from IF YOU DON'T KNOW ME BY NOW: THE BEST OF HAROLD MELVIN & THE BLUE NOTES
Silky soul crooner Teddy Pendergrass launched his solo career of the back of his lead vocal on this song, later covered by Simply Red. Domestic angst with a sugar coating.

9 IF THERE'S ANY JUSTICE IN THIS WORLD LEMAR from TIME TO GROW
He really means "If there WAS any justice. . . " but artistic licence has done away with grammatical conventions in the name of a lyric that scans. Lynne Truss would not approve. I blame Fame Academy.

10 TIME IN A BOTTLE JIM CROCE from THE DEFINITIVE COLLECTION
Perhaps the most iconic number by this American singer-songwriter artist who died at just 30 in a plane crash in 1973. Now, if he'd just missed that flight…

Jon Lusk.

Congolese

Congolese music – rumba, soukous, call it what you will – has been the core African dance sound for more than thirty years, influencing just about every other African pop style in existence.

1 COOPERATION FRANCO & SAM MANGWANA from THE ROUGH GUIDE TO CONGOLESE SOUKOUS
From the first bars of the rousing guitar intro to the pure joy of the pair's vocal duelling, this is a bona fide classic.

2 FRANCO & OK JAZZ MABELE from MABELE
A long, slow talking blues written by "le Poète" Simaro Lutumba and sung emotionally by Sam Mangwana.

❸ EL MANICERO BANTOUS DE LA CAPITALE from EL MANICERO

The all-time classic, "Peanut Vendor", reprised here by two of Congo's finest saxophonists and co-founders of this Brazzaville institution.

❹ L'UNION BISSO NA BISSO from RACINES

It's rap, but not as we know it. This melodic and respectful track is a great intro to Passi's Parisian posse.

❺ SENTIMENT AWA ZAIKO LANGA LANGA from SENTIMENT AWA-ESSESSE

Fine melody, great harmonies and wild passion come together shortly before ZLL split acrimoniously.

❻ TWIST WITH THE DOCTEUR RYCO JAZZ from RUMBA'ROUND AFRICA

A Congolese take on 1960s rockabilly that adds humour to the export rumba.

❼ CELIO CHOC STARS from LES MERVEILLES DU PASSÉ, CHOC STARS VOL 3

Sweet and soft, this marks the high spot for a formidable team of soukous crooners.

❽ LUFUA NDONGA KONONO NO1 from CONGOTRONICS

Smash-bang, low-tech urban reinventions of timeless ancestral music.

❾ MALI YA MUNGU MOSE FAN FAN from BAYEKELEYE

Gentle, introspective, semi-acoustic treatment of a typical Kikongo ballad by the one-time hard man of Congo guitar.

❿ SAMBA LITA BEMBO from KITA MATA ABC

Lita goes wild at the mic, while Stukas crank up the excitement level to fever pitch.

Graeme Ewens

Sam Cooke

The soul singer's soul singer, Cooke was the idol of everyone from Otis Redding and Aretha Franklin to Muhammad Ali and Rod Stewart. Selections #3–#10 are all Cooke compositions.

❶ ANY DAY NOW from SAM COOKE WITH THE SOUL STIRRERS

Cooke's consummate artistry and the intimacy of his approach take the listener close to heaven – just listen to how his voice roughens when he sings "sorrow".

❷ WONDERFUL from SAM COOKE WITH THE SOUL STIRRERS

This was the original – it was recut for the pop maket as "Lovable" – but it leaves that version trailing in the dust, confirming Cooke's gospel supremacy.

❸ JESUS, WASH AWAY MY TROUBLES from SAM COOKE WITH THE SOUL STIRRERS

Two minutes of aching, yearning beauty, simultaneously rough and smooth.

❹ NEARER TO THEE from THE GREAT 1955 SHRINE CONCERT

Performing live in front of an ecstatic 6000-strong audience, Cooke and the Soul Stirrers strain every vocal chord in an epic eight-and-a half minute attempt to bring about the Second Coming through song. They nearly succeed.

❺ YOU SEND ME from PORTRAIT OF A LEGEND

Melismatic magic. Cooke's transcendent voice and trademark yodel glide pure and free.

❻ WONDERFUL WORLD from PORTRAIT OF A LEGEND

A pure pop masterpiece, and – perhaps – a coded plea for racial acceptance.

❼ TWISTING THE NIGHT AWAY from PORTRAIT OF A LEGEND

The most memorable of Cooke's dance/party records, back when "gay" and "queen" signified very differently.

❽ THAT'S WHERE IT'S AT from PORTRAIT OF A LEGEND

As gritty and soulful as Sam got on a studio recording.

❾ BRING IT ON HOME TO ME from PORTRAIT OF A LEGEND

Coming straight from the church, the call-and-response of Cooke and Lou Rawls'"yeah" is the icing on the cake of this oft-covered classic.

❿ A CHANGE IS GONNA COME from PORTRAIT OF A LEGEND

Inspired by Dylan's "Blowing In The Wind", Cooke's majestically orchestrated encapsulation of the black experience in pre-civil rights America became his musical epitaph after his shooting.

Neil Foxlee

Julian Cope

Since dismantling The Teardrop Explodes (see list), Cope has gone from psychedelic pop through stadium rock to pagan krautrock oddball. Here's a chronological way in.

❶ KOLLY KIBBER'S BIRTHDAY from WORLD SHUT YOUR MOUTH

Post-Teardrops psychedelia: a frantic drum machine, a Casiotone organ and Cope's nonsensically deep wordplay create an uptight urgency.

❷ LUNATIC AND FIRE PISTOL from WORLD SHUT YOUR MOUTH
Plummy vocals invoke village greens and gentleman soldiers on a breathless organ and oboe ballad.

❸ REYNARD THE FOX from FRIED
Things get weirder – Julian morphs into a hunted fox on this compelling glam-garage epic.

❹ WORLD SHUT YOUR MOUTH from SAINT JULIAN
The self-deification now became unashamedly populist and found Cope in the charts wearing leather strides and riding a killer riff.

❺ EAST EASY RIDER from PEGGY SUICIDE
The best of an entire oeuvre of car songs by this eco-campaigner. Here he has baggy, rocky fun with his own contradictions.

❻ SAFE SURFER from PEGGY SUICIDE
Like Neil Young jamming with the Spiders From Mars, this AIDS warning extracts the max from a one-line lyric and Michael Mooney's fantastically fried guitar.

❼ LAS VEGAS BASEMENT from PEGGY SUICIDE
Built around a cyclical bass riff as cavernous and magical as the basement it hymns.

❽ UPWARDS AT 45° from JEHOVAKILL
The angle is that of the penis on a pagan symbol. Vocally Cope's never sounded so godly as on this folk freakout from his Krautrock period.

❾ TRY TRY TRY from 20 MOTHERS
A return to pop – and the charts – with this jaunty, catchy ode to his mother.

❿ I WILL BE ABSORBED from CITIZEN CAIN'D
Cope at his loosest, a 1970s power trio jam positing death as a reabsorption into nature.

Toby Manning

Elvis Costello

Known for his puns and putdowns, Elvis has never run out of things to say or new sounds to say those things to, as he's taken stabs at R&B, country, jazz and classical. Here's how the career to date stacks up.

❶ (THE ANGELS WANT TO WEAR MY) RED SHOES from MY AIM IS TRUE
The type of clever rockabilly singalong that marked his accomplished and assured debut.

Elvis Costello's
Extreme restraint

An inveterate list-maker, ELVIS COSTELLO once published a list of his all-time five hundred essential albums, with a key track highlighted from each – and even then he complained: "The minute this list goes to press I will think of twenty records that I left out…" Exercising extreme restraint, here he plumps for ten favourite African-American records, drawn from jazz, blues and classic soul.

❶ LET'S DO IT (LET'S FALL IN LOVE) LOUIS ARMSTRONG from BEST OF THE VERVE YEARS

❷ I LOVE THE LIFE I LIVE (I LIVE THE LIFE I LOVE) MUDDY WATERS from THE ESSENTIAL COLLECTION

❸ YESTERDAYS CLIFFORD BROWN from CLIFFORD BROWN'S FINEST HOUR

❹ YOU AIN'T LIVIN' TILL YOU'RE LOVIN' MARVIN GAYE from YOU'RE ALL I NEED [WITH TAMMI TERRELL]

❺ DO RIGHT WOMAN, DO RIGHT MAN ARETHA FRANKLIN from ATLANTIC RHYTHM & BLUES VOL 6, 1965–1967

❻ THE LOVE YOU SAVE (MAY BE YOUR OWN) JOE TEX from THE LOVE YOU SAVE

❼ BRING THE BOYS HOME FREDA PAYNE from BAND OF GOLD: THE BEST OF FREDA PAYNE

❽ HIDDEN CHARMS HOWLIN' WOLF from CHESS 50TH ANNIVERSARY COLLECTION

❾ I'M A RAM AL GREEN from GETS NEXT TO YOU

❿ STEAL AWAY CHARLIE HADEN & HANK JONES from STEAL AWAY

❷ (I DON'T WANT TO GO TO) CHELSEA from THIS YEAR'S MODEL
The thick bass rumble sounds like an invite to a fight, and Elvis's sneered vocals ("Capital punishment, she's last year's model") step up to meet the challenge.

❸ OLIVER'S ARMY from ARMED FORCES
One of his early defining moments – a rollicking mix of pop and politics that counts "Dancing Queen" as a musical cousin, among others.

❹ MOTEL MATCHES from GET HAPPY!
The soulful delivery of this perfect late-night torch song suggest Elvis may have had an alternate career as a modern-day Sinatra – or maybe it just presages some future moves.

❺ MAN OUT OF TIME from IMPERIAL BEDROOM
In between the screeching beginning and end (spliced from a sped-up alternate version) comes a torrent of complex, unforgettable wordplay.

❻ INVISIBLE MAN from PUNCH THE CLOCK
The horn section, blasting away, adds pep and sparkle to this supremely poppy confection, somewhat at odds with its narrator's struggles against a Big Brother-like world gone mad.

❼ AMERICAN WITHOUT TEARS from KING OF AMERICA
Can a country-ish song about identity, emigration and culture shock really sound so stately and transporting? Apparently so. There's an "American Without Tears No. 2", too, a worthy sequel.

❽ I WANT YOU from BLOOD AND CHOCOLATE
Nearly seven minutes of tension, desperation and, ultimately, exhaustion, set to a spare, menacing guitar line.

❾ COULDN'T CALL IT UNEXPECTED NO. 4 from MIGHTY LIKE A ROSE
A sweet, lilting melody that seems to have been rescued from a carnival junkyard; one of the highlights from a neglected 1991 album.

❿ GOD GIVE ME STRENGTH from PAINTED FROM MEMORY
Costello has experimented with collaborators of all walks; his time with Burt Bacharach produced this gorgeous ballad, which features a dramatic vocal performance you may not have known he had in him.

Andrew Rosenberg

Mary Coughlan

The Galway singer Mary Coughlan has done herself no commercial favours by being so hard to categorize: is this folk, or jazz, or blues, or all stations in-between? No matter: she has a voice so compelling that when she sings a song, you forget any other versions you've ever heard.

❶ DOUBLE CROSS from TIRED AND EMOTIONAL
"This is by an old ex-husband of mine", says Coughlan when she sings this live – and what a parting gift!

❷ I WANT TO BE SEDUCED from TIRED AND EMOTIONAL
Almost unaccompanied, Coughlan makes her intentions plain. Even the bass glissandos want in on the act.

❸ MY LAND IS TOO GREEN from UNDER THE INFLUENCE
This lulls you into a false sense of security by sounding like an old Irish ballad. Slowly the meaning creeps up: this is an indictment of easy sentimentality and acquiescence in the face of sectarian violence.

❹ MOTHER'S LITTLE HELPER from UNCERTAIN PLEASURES
When Mick Jagger sang about what a drag it was getting old, he was play-acting. But Mary Coughlan knows all too well.

❺ MAGDALENE LAUNDRY from SENTIMENTAL KILLER
Coughlan's unforgettable, defiant take on this song about the scandal of the Magdalene Laundries, where the fallen women of Ireland were pressed into service as launderers for Mother Church.

❻ DAMN YOUR EYES from LOVE FOR SALE
This smouldering slow-burn blues uses her throaty growl to best effect, running from delicate precision to full-voiced wail.

❼ THAT FACE from AFTER THE FALL
Deceptively quiet piano ballads with a sting in the tail are a speciality in the Coughlan household: this Jimmy McCarthy-penned sleeper is one of her best.

❽ DETOUR AHEAD from LONG HONEYMOON
Greg Cohen buried Coughlan's voice on this album under a morass of scratchy detail. But Detour Ahead escaped free and clear, just piano and trumpet accompanying her down the road.

❾ SENTIMENTAL KILLERS from SENTIMENTAL KILLER
A jaunty jig through a disintegrating marriage, nine parts betrayal and regret to one of redemption.

❿ PULL UP TO THE BUMPER from RED BLUES
Grace Jones made this as a sleek, precision-tooled German vehicle oozing vorsprung and technik; Coughlan's version is more of a beaten-up jalopy.

David Honigmann

Country cheatin'

Love inspires good music, but the best stuff comes from good lovin' gone bad. Here are some country tunes in honor of that seven-year itch.

❶ WE'LL SWEEP OUT THE ASHES IN THE MORNING GRAM PARSONS WITH EMMYLOU HARRIS from GRIEVOUS ANGEL
Parsons' brief but influential career married rock with country, but on this song, country remained a bachelor, and Parsons and Harris blend their voices in bittersweet harmony.

❷ JOLENE DOLLY PARTON from THE ESSENTIAL DOLLY PARTON VOL 2
Desperation, Dolly's way. Her songwriting shines and her usual fresh-linen voice has bite on this track, one of her biggest hits.

❸ YOU AIN'T WOMAN ENOUGH LORETTA LYNN from YOU AIN'T WOMAN ENOUGH
A straight shooting, line-in-the-dirt song from the strong-voiced, strong-willed Lynn.

❹ FOOLIN' AROUND PATSY CLINE from THE PATSY CLINE SHOWCASE WITH THE JORDANAIRES
Cline belts out the part of the self-possessed cuckold in this Buck Owens tune, while the legendary Jordanaires offer the finger-wagging backup.

❺ MOVE IT ON OVER HANK WILLIAMS from GOLD
When Williams moves into the doghouse, he brings a toothbrush. A warm and loose cheating song by the author of "Your Cheatin' Heart", it was his first single to hit the Billboard charts for MGM.

❻ SNAKE IN THE HOUSE DEL McCOURY BAND from COLD HARD FACTS
The licks are hot, and the solos – each instrument gets one – are seamless. Jason Carter's fiddle slides through each verse and McCoury's voice is as high as the moon.

❼ FRANKIE AND JOHNNY JIMMIE ROGERS from MY OLD PAL
Recorded by everyone from Louis Armstrong and Duke Ellington to Elvis Presley and Doc Watson, this traditional ballad tells the tale of a woman who catches her true love in the act and then does him in. Rogers' version contains what others don't: his trademark yodel.

❽ DARK END OF THE STREET LINDA RONSTADT from HEART LIKE A WHEEL
The lyrics of this Don Penn–Spooner Oldham country-soul song provide the time and the place; Ronstadt provides the voice, emotive, complicit and sultry. Just listening to it makes you feel like you're committing adultery.

❾ JACKSON JOHNNY CASH WITH JUNE CARTER from AT FOLSOM PRISON
One of the most upbeat and unapologetic of the cheating songs, perhaps because it's all threat and no follow-through. Or perhaps because Johnny and June were so in love that we only hear the part about being married in a fever, and not the part about messin' around.

❿ DIM LIGHTS, THICK SMOKE (AND LOUD, LOUD MUSIC) MARTY STUART from ONCE UPON A TIME
Marty Stuart and company give a fiery, bluegrass treatment to Joe Maphis's honky-tonk classic about a faithful husband and his straying bride.

Madelyn Rosenberg

Country rock

Country-rock can mean anything today, especially as most Nashville product now is more rock than country. But back in the late 1960s and early 70s the blend was fresh and made for some truly majestic music.

❶ HICKORY WIND THE BYRDS from SWEETHEART OF THE RODEO
With Gene Clark and Chris Hillman in their original lineup there was always going to be a lot of country in The Byrds sound. When Gram Parsons joined and contributed this reflective ballad they single-handedly invented country rock.

❷ SING ME BACK HOME THE EVERLY BROTHERS from ROOTS
Originally modelling themselves on bluegrass acts like The Louvin Brothers before achieving 1950s pop stardom, this 1968 return to roots found Don and Phil showing how Merle Haggard's prison anthem could work as country-rock.

❸ BROTHERS SIN CITY FLYING BURRITO from GILDED PALACE OF SIN
Dressed in drug decorated Nudie suits, The Burritos gave country rock an LA cocaine cowboy chic best served on this apocalyptic anthem.

❹ GARDEN PARTY RICKY NELSON from GARDEN PARTY
Nelson was a 1950s teen star who cut some tasty rockabilly but by 1972 he was writing country rock as good as any. This was his last US Top 10.

⑤ SEVEN BRIDGES ROAD STEVE YOUNG from COUNTRY OUTLAWS

Alabama-born Steve Young is a fine guitarist-singer-songwriter who never achieved fame yet found the likes of Waylon Jennings and The Eagles plundering his songbook. Here he exalts the South of his youth in epic terms.

⑥ LAY LADY LAY BOB DYLAN from NASHVILLE SKYLINE

Late 1960s and Dylan strips back his music until it found him recording in Nashville with Johnny Cash. Here, on one of his most beautiful songs, he croons a hymn to bedroom bliss.

⑦ DALLAS THE FLATLANDERS from MORE A LEGEND THAN A BAND

Formed in Lubbock, Texas, by Joe Ely, Jimmie Dale Gilmore and Butch Hancock, The Flatlanders were longhairs with an almost surreal taste for reinventing country's yearning white soul.

⑧ I CAN'T HELP IT IF I'M STILL IN LOVE WITH YOU LINDA RONSTADT from HEART LIKE A WHEEL

Ronstadt and The Eagles took country rock into the upper reaches of the US pop charts and here, from her finest album, the Californian princess turns a Hank Williams tune into a breathless epic.

⑨ RAMBLIN' MAN THE ALLMAN BROTHERS from BROTHERS & SISTERS

Many a Southern rock band tried to blend some country into their epic guitar strangling but few had the skill of The Allmans to pull it off. They scored a huge 1973 hit with this twangy ode to running free.

⑩ LITTLE JUNIOR GARY STEWART from LITTLE JUNIOR

Stewart came on like Jerry Lee Lewis with added hillbilly swagger and this roaring boast to being a hellraiser "like daddy was" is as tough a tune as anyone cut in the mid-1970s.

Garth Cartwright

Brilliant covers

These interpretations go beyond mere homage, surpassing the originals for their style, innovation or just sheer audacity. See also "Weird covers".

❶ MRS ROBINSON THE LEMONHEADS from IT'S A SHAME ABOUT RAY

Originally part of a UK-only EP, this rockin' version of Art & Paul's folk classic proved to be The Lemonheads' breakout hit.

❷ AT LAST I AM FREE ROBERT WYATT from MID-EIGHTIES

Okay, the Chic version is delightful. But Wyatt takes the song and does something extraordinary, slowing it beyond real, revealing the most poignant of lyrics.

❸ HURT JOHNNY CASH from AMERICAN IV

A hugely affecting rendition of the noisy "Nine Inch Nails" track, on which Cash leaves his vocal stamp, moulded from a lifetime's experience.

❹ NOTHING COMPARES 2 U SINÉAD O'CONNOR from I DO NOT WANT WHAT I HAVEN'T GOT

Written by Prince for The Family (part of his Paisley Park stable), O'Connor's definitive version of his tear-jerking break-up song fully justified its global success.

❺ TAINTED LOVE SOFT CELL from NON STOP EROTIC CABARET

Marc Almond de-funks the 1970s Gloria Jones track, excising the animated horns and the plunking basslines, but fills the void with posturing indignation and electro-histrionics.

❻ MS JACKSON THE VINES from OUTTATHAWAY

The Sydney band threw aside OutKast's R&B funk for acoustic guitar and Craig Nicholls' measured, elegiac delivery to create a moving modern rock ballad.

❼ ALL ALONG THE WATCHTOWER THE JIMI HENDRIX EXPERIENCE from ELECTRIC LADYLAND

Dylan's original tale of revolution featured lyrics more arresting than the accompanying music, but when Hendrix dovetailed the words with equally dramatic instrumentation, the song was reborn as a rallying cry.

❽ SAILING STINA NORDENSTAM from PEOPLE ARE STRANGE

The Sutherland Bros/Rod Stewart schlock is stripped down to a few piano chords in this startling and affecting Stina reinvention.

❾ WONDERWALL RYAN ADAMS from LOVE IS HELL

This pared-down take on the Oasis hit needed only Adams' lilting vocals and an acoustic guitar to elevate it further. Noel Gallagher himself conceded after Adams' performance at a Manchester gig: "You can have that song, man, 'cos we could never quite get it right."

❿ MAD WORLD MICHAEL ANDREWS FEATURING GARY JULES from DONNIE DARKO SOUNDTRACK

Everyone who saw *Donnie Darko* adored the minimalist Tears for Fears cover that closed the movie. Andrews and Jules remodelled the song for a new generation, as far removed as possible from 1980s synth stylings.

Ed Wright

Cowboy fantasies

Throughout the English speaking world, there's a peculiar and particular kind of guy who walks like he's wearing spurs and who stands at the bar like he's fixin' to draw on a mean hombre. Deep inside, he always wanted to be a cowboy. This is the soundtrack to his life.

❶ CHESTNUT MARE THE BYRDS from UNTITLED/ UNISSUED
The guy in this stoned country epic spends the whole of the song chasing after a horse with whom he plans to be friends for life. Whether the lyric "she'll be just like a wife" would get the green light these days is debatable, but the piece conjures up endless vistas.

❷ HORSE WITH NO NAME AMERICA from THE DEFINITIVE AMERICA
Monotone delivery evokes the unbroken scrub and dried out riverbeds crossed by our hero and horse. Nine days they rode out together and they didn't even exchange the most basic of social courtesies?

❸ RIDERS IN THE SKY MARTY ROBBINS from THE BEST OF...
With its lyrics urging the traditionally godless cowpoke to mend his ways or else, this version of the spookiest of all cowboy songs turns on all the atmospheric tricks – echoing vocals, ringing guitar lines and fey backing calls of "Yippee-yi-yay, yippee-yi-yo".

❹ I'M SO LONESOME I COULD CRY COWBOY JUNKIES from THE TRINITY SESSION
The CJs' superlative take on this old Hank Williams classic manages to sound even more broken down and distraught than the original.

❺ WHOOPEE TI YI YO – GET ALONG LITTLE DOGIES WOODY GUTHRIE from THE VERY BEST OF...
One of the wannabe cowboy's greatest singalong items, performed by one of the great folk artists of the twentieth century.

❻ GAMBLER'S GUITAR RUSTY DRAPER from GREATEST HITS OF...
Spend too long in the saddle and, like Rusty here, you'll start talking to your horse, passing wildlife and your six-string buddy. The slightly deranged laughter that he affects between verses underlines the regret.

❼ NO MOTHER OR DAD LESTER FLATT & EARL SCRUGGS from A PROPER INTRODUCTION TO...
A man shouldn't oughta ride the range without a heap of bluegrass a-loaded on his iPod, the more tear-jerking the better. Flatt and Scruggs get down to the eye-watering nitty gritty in this masterful story of orphans all alone.

❽ COWBOYS LIKE US GEORGE STRAIT from LET THERE BE ROCK
Old-style waltz-time number, dripping with fiddles and steel guitar flourishes. And even though they're self-declared outlaws out on the run, George and his pals ride steel horses, probably manufactured by Harley Davidson.

❾ MY RIFLE, MY PONY AND ME DEAN MARTIN from THE VERY BEST OF... VOL 2
Western guitars so clichéd you can hear the varnish peeling off them in embarrassment, and a lyric matched in cheesiness only by Dino's delivery of them, this is one of the all-time great cowboy croon-tunes.

❿ THE LAST COWBOY SONG JOHNNY CASH AND WILLIE NELSON from HIGHWAYMAN
Sad as the death of your favourite horse, prime piece of cattle or even your wife, this is the kind of tune that has grown men complaining that the trail dust is making their eyes water.

Al Spicer

Creedence Clearwater Revival

For a brief moment in the late 1960s/early 70s, Creedence were the biggest band in America, with their choogling, roots-based swamp rock coupled to the magnificent songwriting of John Fogarty (even if he did go on to write Status Quo's theme tune, "Rockin' All Over The World").

❶ SUSIE Q from CREEDENCE CLEARWATER REVIVAL
The 1957 Dale Hawkins hit became the definitive psychedelic, primal Creedence stomp.

❷ PROUD MARY from BAYOU COUNTRY
John Fogarty came from California, but few since Mark Twain have tapped more intuitively into the romantic imagery of the Old South.

❸ BORN ON THE BAYOU from BAYOU COUNTRY
Cajun queens and freight trains to New Orleans on the song that became their signature tune.

❹ BAD MOON RISING from GREEN RIVER
Earthquakes and lightning, hurricanes a-blowing, rivers overflowing, and voices of rage and ruin.

Fogarty conjures up a Biblical curse: concise, raw, rocking perfection.

⑤ DOWN ON THE CORNER from WILLY AND THE POOR BOYS

Perhaps the best song ever written about the sheer, funky joy of playing in a band.

⑥ FORTUNATE SON from WILLY AND THE POOR BOYS

It could have been a Springsteen song, as Fogarty shows who's really the boss when it comes to articulating life on the wrong side of the tracks.

⑦ I HEARD IT THROUGH THE GRAPEVINE from COSMO'S FACTORY

In stark contrast to Fogarty's two-and-a-half minute anthems, here are eleven glorious minutes of Credence's most epic choogling.

⑧ HAVE YOU EVER SEEN THE RAIN? from PENDULUM

That after six albums in two and a half years Fogarty was *still* coming up with songs as strong as this was nothing less than astonishing.

Nigel Williamson

Crosby, Stills, Nash (& Young)

They couldn't live together and they couldn't live apart. But there was something special when C, S, N and occasionally Y stopped bickering for long enough to raise their voices in harmony. Neil Young's prolific solo career is dealt with elsewhere in this book, so most of these ten concentrate on CSN (together and solo), although Old Shakey's Ohio simply couldn't be left out.

① SUITE: JUDY BLUE EYES from CROSBY, STILLS AND NASH

Stephen Stills pours his heart out, after breaking up with Judy Collins, on the opening track of 1969's debut CSN album.

② WOODEN SHIPS from CROSBY, STILLS AND NASH

Crosby's sci-fi tale of the aftermath of a nuclear holocaust ameliorated by some of CSN's sweetest harmonies.

③ MARRAKESH EXPRESS from CROSBY, STILLS AND NASH

Former Hollies-man Nash brings a breath of breezy pop fresh air to CSN's debut album.

④ DÉJÀ VU from DÉJÀ VU

Weird time signatures and dreamy harmonies combine magically on the Crosby-penned title track of the first CSN&Y album

⑤ CARRY ON from DÉJÀ VU

Captain Many Hands (as the multi-talented Stills was dubbed by his colleagues) at his life-affirming best.

⑥ COWBOY MOVIE from IF I COULD ONLY REMEMBER MY NAME

David Crosby's first solo album was a veritable West Coast jam session and included this brilliant Wild West allegory of the complex relationships within CSN&Y.

⑦ PAGE 43 from GRAHAM NASH/DAVID CROSBY

Minus Stills and Young, a hidden gem of hippy philosophy from a 1972 duo album.

⑧ OHIO from SO FAR

Neil Young's angry reaction to the shooting of four protesting students at Kent State University was written the same day, recorded the next and in stores a week later, giving CSNY an American Top 20 hit.

⑨ WOODSTOCK from DEJA VU

Joni Mitchell wrote Woodstock, but as she wasn't actually there, it took CSN&Y (who were) to record the definitive version.

⑩ LOVE THE ONE YOU'RE WITH from STEPHEN STILLS

Not sure that Mrs Stills left waiting back at home would have approved the sentiment, but this was the highlight of Stills' first solo album and also heard to fine effect on the CSN&Y live album *4 Way Street*.

Nigel Williamson

Cuban classics

For close on a century now, Cuba has given the world some of the best popular music going. Here are a few indelible gems from the songbook.

① SON DE LA LOMA TRIO MATAMOROS from CUBA: I AM TIME

Miguel Matamoros has few equals in Cuban song. You can almost hear the sugarcane rustling.

② YIRI YIRI BON BENY MORÉ from BENY MORÉ: LA COLECCIÓN CUBANA

The king of the mambo a.k.a. "El Barbarito Del Ritmo" (the wild man of rhythm), sings this with such chutzpah that it feels like he's right there in front of you.

c

❸ CUANDO SALI DE CUBA GUILLERMO PORTABALES from
EL CARRETERO

So much aching nostalgia, patriotism and longing has seldom been invested in one song: "When I left Cuba, I left my life, my love." He went to live in Puerto Rico and was killed by a passing car after a gig.

❹ BESAME MUCHO OMARA PORTUONDO from OMARA
PORTUONDO: LA COLECCIÓN CUBANA

Cuba's evergreen diva does the business on this cabaret-style arrangement complete with dodgy electric guitar solo.

❺ AL VAIVEN DE MI CARRETA ÑICO SAQUITO from
GOODBYE MR CAT

An unforgettable nagging refrain on this surging *guajira* just burns itself into the brain. Born in 1901, Saquito was one of the most revered Cuban songwriters of the twentieth century.

❻ EL MANICERO (THE PEANUT VENDOR) ALBITA from
SON

One of the most thoroughly covered Cuban songs ever (especially in West Africa) since Moisés Simon penned it in 1931. This Miami-based Cuban singer gives it her best shot.

❼ SANTA BARBARA CELINA GONZÁLEZ
from SANTA BARBARA

This feisty celebration of Chango – the West African god of thunder and lightning – from Cuba's Santería faith is easily the best-known song by this great Cuban icon.

❽ GUAJIRA GUANTANAMIRA VIEJA TROVA
SANTIAGUERA from HOTEL ASTURIAS

The now retired supergroup of veteran soneros from Santiago de Cuba did a highly original and atmospheric take on this infamous number composed by Joseito Fernandez in the 1930s. Everybody knows the tune!

❾ TRES LINDAS CUBANAS RUBÉN GONZÁLEZ from
INTRODUCING...

The late much-loved pianist who gained overdue international fame through his part in *Buena Vista Social Club* is at his best on this elegant and swinging *danzón*. Sublime.

❿ DOS GARDENIAS IBRAHIM FERRER from BUENA VISTA
SOCIAL CLUB

A stellar version of this smoochy bolero, which catapulted the singer out of retirement.

Jon Lusk

Cult icons

Where would music magazines, second-hand record dealers, many an indie musician and label, and overly serious music fans be without cult musical icons? Drug addiction, madness, lack of commercial success and dying young are the order of the day here, for ten cult icons whose appeal never appears to wane.

❶ VEGA-TABLES BRIAN WILSON from SMILE

Serious Wilson devotees tend to skip his earlier Beach Boys hits and dwell on the *Smile* sessions he recorded as he melted down mentally. Thus songs about vegetables.

❷ SEPTEMBER GURLS BIG STAR from 1 RECORD

Memphis's Big Star possessed shimmering songs and in Alex Chilton a quixotic talent. No one bought the albums at the time, co-founder Chris Bell committed suicide and Chilton went on to make ever more erratic records: thus the cult.

❸ TIME HAS TOLD ME NICK DRAKE from 5 LEAVES LEFT

Fragile English folkie almost completely ignored while alive, contributing to mental problems and a fatal overdose of pills. Long venerated and currently inspiring countless singer-songwriters.

❹ SLIP INSIDE THIS HOUSE 13TH FLOOR ELEVATORS from
EASTER EVERYWHERE

Texan psychedelic cowboys who created a great rush of sound until band leader Roky Erickson was subjected to electric shock treatment while institutionalised on drug charges. Roky's fragile mental health since make him a ghostly icon of sorts.

❺ FRANKIE TEARDROP SUICIDE from SUICIDE

New York's pioneering electronic duo's 1977 debut album inspired some and upset many. This song is an overwrought odyssey of murder-suicide featuring Alan Vega's blood curdling screams. Excellent for clearing out unwanted guests.

❻ HEROIN VELVET UNDERGROUND from THE VELVET
UNDERGROUND & NICO

The original cult band with songs about drugs and S&M and arty pretensions and white noise. Lou Reed, John Cale and Nico all went on to carve out solo careers of sorts but this epic ode to putting needles in veins is the reason anyone really cares about them.

❼ A SONG FOR YOU GRAM PARSONS from GP

The original drugstore cowboy helped pioneer country-rock with The Byrds before leading The Flying Burrito Brothers, befriending The Rolling Stones and dying of an overdose aged 26. Here he's at his most winsome and fragile – country music's Nick Drake.

❽ CRIPPLE CREEK SKIP SPENCE from OAR
Having been drummer on the first Jefferson Airplane album and formative in Moby Grape, Skip ended up hospitalized for mental health problems before making *Oar*, one of the oddest albums of the psychedelic era. Nothing else was heard and he died in poverty before *Oar* was reissued to much adulation from the likes of Beck.

❾ GOLDEN HAIR SYD BARRETT from THE MADCAP LAUGHS
Pink Floyd's founding talent was fired from the band when too much LSD ate his mind. His two 1970 solo albums found him making a scratchy, plaintive folk rock before schizophrenia forced his withdrawal.

❿ DREADLOCKS IN MOONLIGHT LEE "SCRATCH" PERRY from ARKOLOGY
Perry's 1960s–70s reggae productions remain amongst reggae's highpoints but it's his eccentricities – planting records, burning down Black Ark studios, Apocalyptic gibberish – that ensure many rockers think Lee is one wild guy.

Garth Cartwright

❺ PRIMARY from FAITH
The guitars chug like locomotives over a driving drum machine, while Smith spits out the words of this great little single from 1981.

❻ AT NIGHT from SEVENTEEN SECONDS
The whole album, from 1980, is unmissable, but this cut's frosty keyboard rumbles add venom to Smith's nocturnal phobias.

❼ A FOREST from SEVENTEEN SECONDS
It had to be here. This is the song that really put The Cure on the map and which became an immortal goth anthem.

❽ PLAY FOR TODAY from SEVENTEEN SECONDS
A great little song. Uncharacteristically chirp for the period.

❾ ONE HUNDRED YEARS from PORNOGRAPHY
This track is a seething monster of dark imagery and densely layered sound – hard work, but worth it.

❿ PORNOGRAPHY from PORNOGRAPHY
Darker still, this album-closer is a majestic piece of music, its turmoil perhaps reflecting the fractured state of the band at the time.

Peter Buckley

The Cure

For almost thirty years Robert Smith and various cohorts have been churning out a unique brand of alternative pop. The band's music has changed a great deal, and though many of Smith's biggest hits came from mid-period albums such as *Head On The Door* and *Kiss Me, Kiss Me, Kiss Me*, the real gems are to be found on sets from the group's early catalogue.

❶ 10.15 SATURDAY NIGHT from THREE IMAGINARY BOYS
A metronomic slice of claustrophobic punk – minimal and moody – and a great lyric.

❷ THREE IMAGINARY BOYS from THREE IMAGINARY BOYS
The Cure frequently closed their sets with a blinding, epic, album title-track and this is one of their best.

❸ KILLING AN ARAB from BOYS DON'T CRY
An early hit for the band, this nihilistic recontextualization of a scene from Albert Camus's *The Stranger* is an undisputed classic.

❹ FAITH from FAITH
One of their many stunning album epilogues, this time finding Smith at his most gloriously gloomy.

Cypress Hill

The multiracial LA hip-hop trio pioneered rapping in Spanglish and championed marijuana. DJ Muggs's blunted, dubby groove proved hugely influential on hip-hop and trip-hop. Sure, by the mid-1990s they had descended into self-parody yet their early work remains among the genre's best.

❶ HOW I COULD JUST KILL A MAN from CYPRESS HILL
Urban horror-show featuring lumpy drum machine beat, screeching feedback, fairground melodies and a rush of Latino voices boasting that violent death is certain to those who cross them.

❷ HAND ON THE PUMP from CYPRESS HILL
Doo wop classic "Duke Of Earl" gets looped to awesome effect as B-Real and Sen Dog swap rhymes about *la vida loco*. This one builds and builds.

❸ TRES EQUIS from CYPRESS HILL
Bilingual rappers B-Real and Sen Dog share a Cuban mother so let loose a flurry of Spanglish rhymes over twangy guitar and organ loop.

❹ STONED IS THE WAY OF THE WALK from CYPRESS HILL

B-Real rhymes about the difficulties of getting good Buddha when you're broke.

❺ I WANNA GET HIGH from BLACK SUNDAY

Eerie, effective mantra that finds B-Real's nasal whine intoning "I Wannnnnna Gettttt Hiiiiiigh" over a brooding dub soundscape.

❻ INSANE IN THE BRAIN from BLACK SUNDAY

Alt-rock favourite: all together now, "insane in the membrane, yeah!"

❼ A TO THE K from BLACK SUNDAY

Tribal drum patterns, bleached guitars, squirrelly alarm noises all blend to make extremely menacing music while Sen and B celebrate coming of age in the 'hood via gun crime.

❽ THROW YOUR SET IN THE AIR from TEMPLES OF BOOM

Fame and copious THC consumption only made Cypress Hill more uneasy. Thus even crowd pleasers like this sound as unnerving as their murder raps.

❾ KILLA HILL NIGGAS from TEMPLES OF BOOM

Joined by Wu Tang Clan's RZA for a paranoiac meeting of West and East Coast rap masterminds.

❿ EVERYBODY MUST GET STONED from TEMPLES OF BOOM

Playing on Dylan's "Rainy Day Woman" chorus, B-Real promotes life as lived through red eyes.

Garth Cartwright

board riffs before the confidence-mashing vocal sets you to dance or die.

❽ INSOMNIA FAITHLESS from REVERENCE
A hands-aloft, blow-your-whistle, wide-eyed mood-elevator of a track, sweetly reminiscent of those nights when we were all just too excited to sleep.

❾ I'M ALIVE STRETCH'N'VERN from I'M ALIVE EP
Cheesier than a double cheeseburger supreme with extra cheese, served on a cheesy bun, this is still a floorfiller and will still 100% mess with your head.

❿ FRENCH KISS LIL LOUIS & THE WORLD from LIVING BEAT HOUSE CLASSICS (VARIOUS)
One last rich slice of classic house for the big finish to get your funky self hot, sweaty and ready to pick up pneumonia as you wait in the taxi queue.

Al Spicer

Dance anthems

Taking you back to the old skool. This set of mood elevators will have you waving your arms in the air like you just don't care! Top one, Smiley T-shirts in da house! Sorted! Choooooooooooooooooon!

❶ SWEET HARMONY (SAINTS & SINNERS MIX) LIQUID from SWEET HARMONY EP
Saints & Sinners mix of this heavenly soulful tune lays on even more maxi-diva vocals without taking anything from the dancing piano.

❷ GO SINGLE MOBY from GO: THE VERY BEST OF MOBY
Straight-edge 1994 dancefloor classic from a time when advertising deals were just a dream. This is a pure, head-clearing rush of a track.

❸ PROMISED LAND JOE SMOOTH from PROMISED LAND
Any mix of Joe Smooth's clubland triumph will do the trick. It's uplifting enough to get the straightest male strutting like a podium queen.

❹ BREAK 4 LOVE RAZE from BREAK 4 LOVE EP
Classic loved-up groove with soulful vocals and a melody that dances down from your fingertips to your knees, tickling all the way.

❺ PROFESSIONAL WIDOW TORI AMOS (ARMAND VAN HELDEN MIX) from BOYS FOR PELE
Armand's magic touch made Tori Amos, amazingly, a one-hit dancefloor wonder.

❻ (AMERICA) WHAT TIME IS LOVE THE KLF from THE WHITE ROOM
Pre-millennial techno revision of their top hit throws everything in the mix – Volga Boatmen choruses, chants of "muu-muu" and more.

❼ DON'T YOU WANT ME FELIX from DON'T YOU WANT ME EP
Delicious shivers of love-fear and paranoia turn into deep spine-massaging beats and skin-tingling key-

Dance crazy

In those far-off days before The Beatles, young America loved to dance. Formation dancing, pumping R&B, snappy rock'n'roll: crazes came and went as fast as the artists who championed the new moves. Here are ten that moved the crowd.

❶ THE TWIST HANK BALLARD & THE MIDNIGHTERS from LAND OF 1000 DANCES VOL 2
Chubby Checker's version may have cracked the pop charts and got Jackie Kennedy twisting but this is the hip shakin', floor stompin' original.

❷ LAND OF 1000 DANCES WILSON PICKETT from WILSON PICKETT'S GREATEST HITS
Twice an R&B hit before producer Jerry Wexler matched leather lunged Pickett with Booker T & The MGs and together they taught the world about the na-nanana-na land.

❸ PAPA'S GOT A BRAND NEW BAG JAMES BROWN from THE GODFATHER
James Brown had more dance hits than any other artist in history and this 1965 tune is JB at his most radical. "You do the monkey, the mashed potato", he commands as he leads the new breed onto the floor.

❹ MICKEY'S MONKEY THE MIRACLES from THE MIRACLES – GREATEST HITS
Remember that scene in *Mean Streets* when DeNiro dances around Harvey Keitel's Cadillac to Mickey's Monkey? Proto-funk from the Motor City.

❺ BACON FAT ANDRE WILLIAMS from **LAND OF 1000 DANCES VOL 2**

Sleazy, funny stuff from one of R&B's most enigmatic pioneers celebrating a dance the cotton pickers "are doing down south".

❻ DANCING IN THE STREET MARTHA & THE VANDELLA from **MOTOWN CHARTBUSTERS VOL 3**

One of the great dance anthems. Back in the day when revolution appeared to be in the air, militants used DITS as a call to arms.

❼ THE CRUSHER THE NOVAS from **LAND OF 1000 DANCES VOL 2**

Gloriously distorted novelty dance tune that celebrates Reggie "The Crusher" Lisowski, a famous Mid-Western wrestler. C'mon now, "do the hammer-lock!"

❽ SHAKE A TAIL-FEATHER THE FIVE DU-TONES from **LAND OF A THOUSAND DANCES VOL 2**

Another Andre Williams classic, this one encouraging dancers to get that ass moving. Made very famous by The Blues Brothers.

❾ BABY, DO THE PHILLY DOG THE OLYMPICS from **LAND OF A THOUSAND DANCES FUNK & SOUL EDITION**

You mean you can't do the Philly dog? Shame shame shame (as Shirley & Co sang on another great dance tune)!

❿ LET A MAN COME IN AND DO THE POPCORN JAMES BROWN from **LAND OF A THOUSAND DANCES FUNK & SOUL EDITION**

JB's got ants in his pants and can't stop moving. Here he is demonstrating how to dance the popcorn. Yeh!

Garth Cartwright

Dancehall reggae

Practically all reggae gets played in a dancehall, but this, post-roots, late-1970s onwards material was made specifically for that purpose. There was never going to be too much to sit down and listen to and contemplate, and the subject matter was deliberately less spiritually charged, buthe best ranks as the most exciting Jamaican music ever.

❶ RING THE ALARM TENOR SAW from **ORIGINAL STALAG 17–19**

An urgent, pleading ode to the decline of sound systems due to police pressure and, by implication, the impending doom of the Jamaican music industry. But actually it's a pretty bouncy beat.

❷ UNDER MI SLENG TENG WAYNE SMITH from **SLENG TENG/PRINCE JAMMY'S COMPUTERIZED DUB**

The first reggae track not to bother with a bassline, instead building itself up on a tiny Casio keyboard. It doesn't suffer in the slightest.

❸ MR LOVER MAN SHABBA RANKS & MAXI PRIEST from **MR MAXIMUM**

The combination of the gruff-voiced Shabba and the sweetly crooning Maxi Priest fitting round a suitably springy rhythm is a textbook example of what dancehall was about.

❹ GUNMAN MICHAEL PROPHET from **GUNMAN**

Jaunty condemnation of ghetto gunmen that owes a great deal to roots reggae's traditional dub techniques, but does so with a deftly computerized punch.

❺ HOW THE WEST WAS WON RANKING TOYAN from **HOW THE WEST WAS WON**

Real early dancehall, setting a righteous toast on top of a slowly rocking rhythm so sparse you could drive a tractor around the gaps.

❻ DISEASES MICHIGAN & SMILEY from **DOWNPRESSION**

Given that the subject matter concerns Jah smiting the wicked with all manner of dreadful, deforming diseases, this is one of the most cheerful rhythms to come out of early dancehall.

❼ ALMS HOUSE CAPLETON from **THE BEST OF**

Back to basics with a super-sparse backing track, but there's a lightness to Capleton's toasting that propels this track forward.

❽ PRETTY LOOKS ISN'T ALL SANCHEZ from **I CAN'T WAIT**

Original dancehall had quite a tradition of updating classic rock steady rhythms, but Sanchez and later crooners updated whole songs. It works because his voice smoothes out the backing track's sharp edges.

❾ IT'S GROWING GARNETT SILK from **GOLD**

One of modern Jamaican music's sweetest voices, which brought an increasingly longed-for tunefulness back into the dancehall, but kept the excitement.

❿ DUPPY OR GUNMAN YELLOWMAN from **DUPPY OR GUNMAN**

You can't have a dancehall playlist without King Yellow in there somewhere, and, showing there was so much more to him than slackness, it's his playful sense of humour that drives this dubwise skit.

Lloyd Bradley

The Darkness

The Darkness, led by cartoon-like singer Justin Hawkins, and backed by a group of metalhead neanderthals, exploded onto a somewhat jaded UK music scene in 2003. But before anyone could work out if they were for real, the firework of their career had flown, showered everyone in sparks and disappeared into the night.

❶ GET YOUR HANDS OFF MY WOMAN FROM PERMISSION TO LAND

This first hit single was responsible for thousands of ill-advised attempts to singalong with Justin's falsetto; it brought back the skintight jumpsuit as streetwear for skinny rock singers; and returned the epic guitar solo to its rightful plinth. Fun.

❷ LOVE IS ONLY A FEELING from PERMISSION TO LAND

One of their biggest hits, and with good reason. Great acoustic verses, an immense, hookladen riff and chorus, plus a guitar hero solo.

❸ I BELIEVE IN A THING CALLED LOVE from PERMISSION TO LAND

Evidently beginning to believe their own mythology, Justin and the lads pull out all the stops, crank up all the knobs, plug themselves in for a jolt of electricity and let rip. Riffs cascade, drums gambol, Justin bellows, it's just perfect, and sounds like it was recorded thirty odd years ago.

❹ ONE WAY TICKET from ONE WAY TICKET TO HELL … AND BACK

Their most over-the-top track so far, complete with pan pipes, sitar solos and a massive chorus celebrating the ol' Bolivian marching powder.

❺ BALD from ONE WAY TICKET TO HELL … AND BACK

Nice and heavy, a skull-pounding ode to slipping gradually towards slap-headedness. This features one hell of a follicle-stimulating riff.

❻ DINNER LADY ARMS from ONE WAY TICKET TO HELL … AND BACK

A genuinely touching, misty-eyed love song delivered in that trademark Darkness tongue-in-cheek style. Subtle and hugely infectious all at once.

❼ ENGLISH COUNTRY GARDEN from ONE WAY TICKET TO HELL … AND BACK

A Queen-tastic homage if ever there was one, featuring a fabulous, hammering piano riff and Justin Hawkins getting his rocks off among the petunias.

Essi Berelian

Miles Davis

Miles – the coolest jazz musician of them all – clearly needs more than one list. So here's the core work from at least two mind-blowing careers.

Acoustic

It's taking nothing away from the "electric years" of Miles Davis to say that, for most of us fans, it's the acoustic albums we return to again and again. There's an intimacy in this work which never fails to reach across the decades.

❶ BOPLICITY from BIRTH OF THE COOL

The most charming of all the gems from these 1949 sessions – Miles, at just 22, leading the nine-piece ensemble with his buttery trumpet, and announcing a new, "cool" aesthetic.

❷ ROUND ABOUT MIDNIGHT from TALLEST TREES

Is this the greatest version of Thelonius Monk's much-recorded tune? Miles whispers eerily through the melody, setting up John Coltrane's menacing tenor for one of his classic solos.

❸ I COULD WRITE A BOOK from RELAXIN'

Written on the same day (in 1956) as the track above, this is a candidate for the most perfect jazz track ever: Miles' muted trumpet sketches a superbly poised solo before Philly Joe Jones' drums propel Coltrane into overdrive.

❹ CHEZ LE PHOTOGRAPHE DU MOTEL from L'ASCENSEUR POUR L'ÉCHAFAUD

The soundtrack to Louis Malle's thriller was recorded in one session while Miles and his group watched it on screen. It produced some of his most abstract and beautiful music.

❺ SOMETHIN' ELSE from SOMETHIN' ELSE

Miles's last date (1958) as sideman, to the great altoist Cannonball Adderley, and he pulls out one of his greatest and fiercest blues solos.

❻ MILESTONES from MILESTONES

Childishly simple, and a modern jazz classic – one which, for the first time, eschewed continual chord changes in favour of looser "modes". Sidemen Adderley, Coltrane and pianist Red Garland all rise to the challenge.

⑦ GONE from PORGY AND BESS
So many collaborations with arranger Gil Evans could make this list; this fast minor blues that Evans added to the Gershwin score shows Miles fusing melancholy and momentum.

⑧ BLUE IN GREEN from KIND OF BLUE
All five tracks of this 1959 album are classics, but this ballad is the most affecting of all – never did Miles sound so lonely, nor pianist Bill Evans so rhapsodic.

⑨ SOMEDAY MY PRINCE WILL COME from SOMEDAY MY PRINCE WILL COME
Miles transmutes a Disney song into a mature lament, with great supporting solos from tenorists Hank Mobley and Coltrane.

⑩ ALL OF YOU from MILES LIVE IN EUROPE
The 1963 live debut of the great quintet, with Herbie Hancock (23) and drummer Tony Williams (just 17), produced an uncompromising album, with this Cole Porter classic barely recognizable in Miles' inspired recomposition.

Alex Webb

Electric

Even more radical a break with tradition than Bob Dylan going electric, Miles Davis plugging in and embracing the studio as a compositional tool was complete heresy to jazz orthodoxy. It produced some of the most breathtaking and challenging music in recorded history.

① IN A SILENT WAY/IT'S ABOUT THAT TIME from IN A SILENT WAY
Constructed in the studio from vamps and grooves and solos, this is the record that launched jazz fusion in 1969.

② BITCHES BREW from BITCHES BREW
Distorted harmonics, huge blocky keyboards and a deep funk bottom make this 1970 track one of the most influential jazz recordings ever.

③ FUNKY TONK from LIVE-EVIL
Davis' most fiery, most pulsating rhythmic experiment.

④ RIGHT OFF from A TRIBUTE TO JACK JOHNSON
Davis, Herbie Hancock, guitarist John McLaughlin and bassist Michael Henderson channel Sly Stone into an unholy funk groove.

⑤ ON THE CORNER from ON THE CORNER
McLaughlin is absolutely ferocious on this wah-wah monster, from 1972.

⑥ PRELUDE from AGHARTA
With axe-slingers Reggie Lucas and Pete Cosey in tow, this 1976 combo may have been the greatest guitar band ever.

Peter Shapiro

De La Soul

De La Soul rewrote all the rules with their debut album, adding psychedelic colour to a stentorian hip-hop world.

① THE MAGIC NUMBER from 3 FEET HIGH AND RISING
Its distinctive opening riff quickly ushers in spritely, messy drums that seem to be so excited to be there they trip over themselves.

② TREAD WATER from 3 FEET HIGH AND RISING
The 1960s backyard R&B sound that De La specialized in back then soundtracks the adventures of our three heroes as they swap lifestyle tips with Mr Squirrel, Mr Fish and Mr Monkey.

③ PLUG TUNIN' from 3 FEET HIGH AND RISING
A honkin' horn riff, slowed down to an amenable sloth's pace, keeps a rendezvous with a naive chorus of falsetto humming: the whole thing has a very cute, dayglo nostalgic vibe about it.

④ OODLES OF OS from DE LA SOUL IS DEAD
A rubbery double-bass descends repeatedly with a take-it-or-leave-it languor. "We're selling O's y'all", the trio inform us.

⑤ PEASE PORRIDGE from DE LA SOUL IS DEAD
A quirky, rattling tea-dance beat and explicit exhortations to tap-dance rub uneasily up against impatient, tetchy lyrics.

⑥ ITSOWEEZEE from STAKES IS HIGH
"I guess a diamond's just a rock with a name" muses Trugoy, pondering a failed love affair. A laidback electric piano shrugs. Eezee come, eezee go.

⑦ OOH from ART OFFICIAL INTELLIGENCE: MOSAIC THUMP
Listen past the squelchy moogs and you'll hear the same old see-saw rifferama that characterized De La's debut. The chorus has all the foolproof immediacy of an anthem and the drums are satisfyingly crunchy.

⑧ U CAN DO (LIFE) from ART OFFICIAL INTELLIGENCE: MOSAIC THUMP

Those synth sounds may be plain and unassuming, but they conceal a surprisingly subtle melody hiding down there in the low-end.

⑨ BIG BROTHER BEAT from STAKES IS HIGH

A gorgeous, murky bass riff is sprinkled with clipped techno bleeps: a welcoming carpet for guest rapper Mos Def. "We remain on your mind like skulls, not a golem", claim De La.

⑩ PATTI DUKE FROM BUHLOONE MINDSTATE

Knitting-needle jazz drums skipped along and, aided by a flute and a Gang Starr sample, De La convincingly tripped into the jazz-rap era.

Matt Milton

Death metal

Growling cookie-monster vocals and thrashy gore. What's not to like?

① BLACK SEEDS OF VENGEANCE NILE from BLACK SEEDS OF VENGEANCE

Death metal ancient-Egyptian-style. Ornate lyrics recount tales of terror from antiquity.

② BLINDED BY FEAR AT THE GATES from SLAUGHTER OF THE SOUL

A furious cut with flashes of tunefulness lurking beneath the aural violence.

③ CADAVERIC INCUBATOR OF ENDOPARASITES CARCASS from SYMPHONIES OF SICKNESS

Medical dictionaries and sick bags at the ready? A veritable soundtrack to an autopsy.

④ CURSE THE FLESH MORBID ANGEL from HERETIC

One from Deadly Time Changes 'R' Us. A headspinning amalgam of ultra-heavy mid-paced chuggery and lightning-fast kick-drum mayhem.

⑤ LIKE THIS WITH THE DEVIL ENTOMBED from DCLXVI: TO RIDE, SHOOT STRAIGHT AND SPEAK THE TRUTH

Grade A death'n'roll from the masters themselves. Deadly thrash metal collides head(bang)-on with Motörhead.

⑥ PAIN THE BERZERKER from THE BERZERKER

Your worst nightmare turned into skin-flaying noise. Industrial strength percussion pushes the bpm meter well beyond meltdown.

⑦ SCORN IN FLAMES from COLONY

Essential melodic death-a-go-go. A gargantuan production sound coupled with complex riff harmonics and terrific widdling guitars.

⑧ ZOMBIE RITUAL ZOMBIE RITUAL from SCREAM BLOODY GORE BY DEATH

The clue is in the name. One of the most celebrated and influential extreme metal bands with a thrashy horror classic.

Essi Berelian

Deep Purple

With supernaturally talented Ritchie Blackmore on guitar, Purple were purveyors of classy, ear-bleeding heavy rock. Even without him, they cooked.

① CHILD IN TIME from MADE IN JAPAN

A lengthy, hyper-indulgent version of a classic. It starts mellow enough, but Gillan's awesome scream will send shivers through your soul.

② DEMON'S EYE from FIREBALL

An ominous throbbing amplifier leads into a terrific heavy blues riff, and Jon Lord delivers a cracking little keyboard solo.

③ HIGHWAY STAR from MACHINE HEAD

What an intro! That scream, those chugging riffs. This simply oozes rock'n'roll attitude and is, funnily enough, perfect for burning rubber.

④ SMOKE ON THE WATER from MACHINE HEAD

Inspiration to generations of rockers. A legend, pure and simple, featuring one of the best-known riffs ever.

⑤ SPEED KING from IN ROCK

You'll swear you've blown your amp at the start 'cos it sure sounds like Blackmore's blown his. The definition of heavy rock.

⑥ STRANGE KIND OF WOMAN from MADE IN JAPAN

Is Gillan laughing halfway through? A great big swaggering rocker turned into a live epic with some wonderful instrumental excesses.

⑦ KNOCKING AT YOUR BACK DOOR from PERFECT STRANGERS

The 1980s yielded some great material, not least this pumping effort with Gillan indulging in some typically smirk-inducing innuendo.

❽ TED THE MECHANIC from PURPENDICULAR
Steve Morse replaced Blackmore years ago and Purple still rock very hard. Great, fret-shredding solos, and Gillan never sounded better.

Essi Berelian

Depeche Mode

Quite simply, one of the great synth bands in the history of pop. They dominated the singles charts during the 1980s and early 90s and are still going strong.

❶ BLASPHEMOUS RUMOURS from SOME GREAT REWARD
You want dark? How about midnight at the bottom of a mineshaft? Religion, attempted suicide and a car accident make for a bleak classic.

❷ EVERYTHING COUNTS from CONSTRUCTION TIME AGAIN
It's a competitive world, indeed. The Mode boys clinically dissect the politics of greed helped by what sounds like a snake charmer.

❸ HOME from ULTRA
Some sumptuously arranged strings almost take this (bizarrely) into Bond theme territory. Plush and soulful vocals from David Gahan too.

❹ IT'S NO GOOD from ULTRA
This could have come from the soundtrack of a psycho-stalker thriller. Sounds like a love song until the lyrics sink in like a slow-acting poison.

❺ MASTER AND SERVANT from 101
Less clinical than the studio version, the crowd here really sound like they're more than game for a little computerized domination and submission.

❻ NEW LIFE from SPEAK & SPELL
Kraftwerk a-go-go! Sounds wonderfully naive and youthful, with loads of plinky-plonky synth noodling and a suitably robotic chorus.

❼ PEOPLE ARE PEOPLE from SOME GREAT REWARD
Great, clattering, metallic percussion, a wonderful synth bassline, and an instant chorus.

❽ PERSONAL JESUS from VIOLATOR
Reach out and touch faith! Everything is great about this provocative gem, the intimate lyrics, the twangy riff and especially the bouncy rhythm track.

❾ STRIPPED from 101
Sounds like the band were performing live in a steel foundry. Some seriously heavy clanging percussion give this a powerful industrial edge.

❿ SWEETEST PERFECTION from VIOLATOR
This one will slither and creep up on you. The lyrics edge towards tormented obsession and the over-loaded climax is beautifully orchestrated.

Essi Berelian

Just desserts

It's a common misconception that musicians are too busy thinking about sex to be interested in food. In fact, bluesmen would do almost anything for a nice bit of jelly, while fruit of all kinds, especially when baked in a pie, remains beloved by rock'n'rollers young and old.

❶ BANANA IN YOUR FRUIT BASKET BO CARTER from BANANA IN YOUR FRUIT BASKET
Ever game for a double entendre, the impish Bo begged in 1931 to "let me put my banana in your fruit basket" before it spoils.

❷ GOOD JELLY BIG BILL BROONZY from WHEN THE BLUES BEGAN
Back in 1934, Big Bill recounted a fruitless search in New Orleans for a woman who had "good jelly".

❸ IT MUST BE JELLY GLENN MILLER from MAJOR GLENN MILLER AND THE ARMY AIRFORCE BAND
A masterpiece of culinary deduction from 1943 – "it must be jelly, 'cos jam don't shake like that".

❹ I LIKE MY BABY'S PUDDING WYNONIE HARRIS from RISQUÉ BLUES VOL 1
Baffled by the world's preference for chicken and rice, Wynonie plumps for a simple pudding.

❺ WATERMELON MAN HERBIE HANCOCK from THE SOUND OF THE CITY: CHICAGO
When you're about to embark on a ground-breaking instrumental groove like this, a little watermelon is just what the doctor ordered.

❻ SUGAR DUMPLING SAM COOKE from PORTRAIT OF A LEGEND
Smooth-voiced soul pioneer Sam Cooke is the man to persuade us that sugar dumpling really is "the sweetest thing in the world".

❼ HONEY PIE THE BEATLES from THE BEATLES WHITE ALBUM
Late-period Beatles had a knack for these music-hall ditties, hymning the pie that drove them crazy.

8 COUNTRY PIE BOB DYLAN from NASHVILLE SKYLINE

During his laid-back country phase, Dylan convincingly eulogized that old country pie; "Little Jack Horner got nothing on me" indeed.

9 BROWN SUGAR THE ROLLING STONES from STICKY FINGERS

Turn it off quick, if you'd rather not listen to that nasty Mick slurping the juice off his sticky fingers.

10 ICE CREAM MAN JONATHAN RICHMAN AND THE MODERN LOVERS from ROCK'N'ROLL WITH THE MODERN LOVERS

To tell the truth, it's the ice-cream man's chimes that Jonathan finds especially neat, but you just know he'll end up licking a lolly or two.

Greg Ward

Detroit rockers

Maybe it's the noise of industry around them, or all the fuel-injected cars, or the mighty shadow of Motown, but rockers from the Motor City always turn out full-throttle, pedal-to-the-metal music.

1 JENNY TAKE A RIDE MITCH RYDER & THE DETROIT WHEELS from TAKE A RIDE

Rave-up mash-up of Chuck Willis's "CC Rider" and Little Richard's "Jenny Jenny" that was the birth of the Motor City's high-energy rock tradition.

2 STORY OF MY LIFE UNRELATED SEGMENTS from WHERE YA GONNA GO

Some forty years later this remains the best garage record to be produced in Detroit.

3 I NEED YOU THE RATIONALS from THE RATIONALS

The link between the garage and The Stooges.

4 UP ALL NIGHT SRC from MILESTONES

An Ann Arbor classic that sounds like The Nazz, only a thousand times harder.

5 KICK OUT THE JAMS MC5 from KICK OUT THE JAMS

An unholy marriage of hippy and punk.

6 SUPER STUPID FUNKADELIC from MAGGOT BRAIN

George Clinton's troupe of merry pranksters bring it harder and faster than nearly anyone.

7 I GOT A RIGHT THE STOOGES from I GOT A RIGHT

They may have made more important records, but none as fearsome as this.

8 CITY SLANG SONIC'S RENDEZVOUS BAND from CITY SLANG

High-energy fury from veterans from the MC5, The Stooges and The Rationals.

9 WHAT I LIKE ABOUT YOU THE ROMANTICS from THE ROMANTICS

A great, great garage/power-pop blast that would have sounded just as good in 1966 as it did in 1980.

10 FELL IN LOVE WITH A GIRL WHITE STRIPES from WHITE BLOOD CELLS

In which Jack White channels Iggy Pop for 1:48.

Peter Shapiro

Devil's work

Did the Dark Lord get all the best tunes? Take a ride on the Highway to Hell and let's consider the proposition.

1 RUNNING WITH THE DEVIL VAN HALEN from VAN HALEN.

Something of a mission statement from the band, or at least Diamond Dave, propelled by stomping drums and bass. You know they mean business from the first ominous note.

2 DON'T SHAKE ME LUCIFER ROKY ERICKSON from I THINK OF DEMONS

Crazed, rocking and oddly touching, like much of Erikson's music; Roky always seems to singing just over the shoulder of his demons. This undoubtedly has the best pronunciation of the word "compromising" on wax.

3 THE NUMBER OF THE BEAST IRON MAIDEN from THE NUMBER OF THE BEAST

Singer Dickinson's fire-and-brimstone wail seems like it could summon the devil himself.

4 SYMPATHY FOR THE DEVIL ROLLING STONES from BEGGARS BANQUET.

The most famous underworld celebration of all, heralded by one of the most famous opening lines in rock; the guitar in the last couple of minutes just scorches.

5 THE DEVIL IN ME JOHN WESLEY HARDING from HERE COMES THE GROOM

A kind of twenty-year update on "Sympathy for the Devil"– adding acid rain and pollution to JFK and Jesus – but good power pop from an underrated songwriter.

d

6 FRIEND OF THE DEVIL GRATEFUL DEAD
from AMERICAN BEAUTY
A gentle little bluegrass ditty with a lovely melody; Jerry stays a step ahead of the hellhounds on his trail, but doesn't seem in any hurry to keep it that way.

7 WHERE THE DEVIL DON'T STAY DRIVE BY TRUCKERS
from THE BEAUTIFUL SOUTH
Greasy, backwoods southern rock; how bad does a place have to be to be unfit for ol' Scratch?

8 UP THERE from SOUTH PARK, BIGGER, LONGER AND UNCUT: MUSIC FROM AND INSPIRED BY THE MOTION PICTURE
The view of the world from a different kind of aspirational Satan – a hilarious take on a swelling, heartfelt Broadway-style number.

9 SATAN, YOUR KINGDOM MUST COME DOWN
UNCLE TUPELO from MARCH 16–20
Acoustic gloom and doom from the alt.-country heroes.

10 THE DEVIL'S COACHMAN ROBYN HITCHCOCK
from QUEEN ELVIS
This lilting, off-kilter tune is like a staggered nursery rhyme gone bad. What do you do when you see the devil in the nude? In a mood? In your food? Play with him, of course!

Andrew Rosenberg

Dexys Midnight Runners

Passionate, intense, physically fit, disciplined and the tightest white soul band in decades, Dexys were marshalled by front man Kevin Rowland into shunning the very stimulants from which they took their name.

1 GENO from SEARCHING FOR THE YOUNG SOUL REBELS
Check the lyrics: Kevin Rowland is a difficult man to impress even if you're Geno Washington. Then check the music – Dexys playing it just as hard, tight, fast and funky as The Ram Jam Band.

2 THE CELTIC SOUL BROTHERS (MORE PLEASE THANK YOU) from TOO-RYE-AY
Exploding onto the stage of their pure passion soul-revue show, Kevin and the gang flash all the floodlights and set off all the pyrotechnics.

3 COME ON EILEEN from TOO-RYE-AY
The best sexual frustration song since the golden age of rock'n'roll. It stops dead, crawls back into slow life and pumps muscle up to a stomping climactic finish.

4 JACKIE WILSON SAID (I'M IN HEAVEN WHEN YOU SMILE) from TOO-RYE-AY
One of the few men brave enough to attempt a Van Morrison cover, Kevin never quite succeeds in over-shadowing the masterful soul musicians backing him up. Still good though.

5 THERE THERE MY DEAR from SEARCHING FOR THE YOUNG SOUL REBELS
Sarcastic, bitchy, generally fantastic upbeat number with too many words crammed into the poor suffering musical spaces available.

6 UNTIL I BELIEVE IN MY SOUL from TOO-RYE-AY
Soulful, melodramatic, shimmering, beautiful. With some fantastic horn work and the whole band at their pristine best, Kevin lets rip with his yodelling passionate spirit on display.

7 MY NATIONAL PRIDE (FORMERLY KNOWLEDGE OF BEAUTY) from DON'T STAND ME DOWN
With Kevin at his uncompromising, ranting best and yet another total change of image, *Don't Stand Me Down* was destined to become a great lost album. A heart-wrenching tune, too cruelly overlooked.

8 I LOVE YOU (LISTEN TO THIS) from DON'T STAND ME DOWN
An absolute treat of a song. This is a desperate epic, sobbing and ebbing away with every throb of that vein at Kevin Rowland's temple.

Al Spicer

Dion

The Wanderer himself: Dion di Mucci. Or, in the words of Lou Reed, inducting him into The Rock'n'Roll Hall Of Fame in 1989: "Who could be hipper than Dion?" Not a question, a statement.

1 THE WANDERER from DION & THE BELMONTS, LIVE AT THE MADISON SQUARE GARDEN 1972
A classic Bronx–Brooklyn singalong, when Dion and pals came back to perform their 1961 hit.

2 PURPLE HAZE from DION
"We're going to the same place, different expression" – was Jimi's response to this folksy version of his classic.

❸ THE TRUTH WILL SET YOU FREE from INSIDE JOB
Dion crossing over from Bronx junkie to Catholic survivor, swapping junk for God in 1968.

❹ BORN TO BE WITH YOU from DION: KING OF NEW YORK STREETS
A perfect 1976 wall-of-sound-production by fellow New Yorker Phil Spector.

❺ NO ONE KNOWS from PRESENTING DION & THE BELMONTS
A teenage angst classic, telling of some heartbreakers he doowooped with the guys from Belmont Avenue. You can just see a young Brian Wilson humming along.

❻ BOOK OF DREAMS from DEJA NU
Dion cover of the Springsteen song. And he has the right: in one concert his backing singers included Lou Reed, Bruce Springsteen, Paul Simon and Billy Joel.

❼ TURN ME LOOSE from A TRIBUTE TO DOC POMUS
Pomus wrote the song originally for Elvis, but then Fabian wrecked it. Dion did the song justice.

❽ YOU MOVE ME from LITTLE KINGS: LIVE IN NEW YORK
"I love a good rock'n'roll song, you know, cars, girls, music," was Dion's comment on this recording. "There is a beauty in simplicity".

Werner Pieper

Peter Shapiro's
Disco

PETER SHAPIRO is author of the acclaimed *Turn The Beat Around: The Secret History Of Disco* (Faber, 2005). The book is, in his words, a trawl through the roots, development and excesses of "the music that taste forgot". It's an amazing story. Shapiro asserts that "although disco may be the most maligned genre in human history, these are ten records no one should be ashamed of owning."

❶ LAW OF THE LAND THE TEMPTATIONS from MASTERPIECE
The relentless 4/4 beat marks this as most likely the first disco record.

❷ TEN PERCENT DOUBLE EXPOSURE from TEN PERCENT
The very first commercially available 12" single is also one of the very best, thanks to a decadent mix by the great Walter Gibbons.

❸ DON'T LEAVE ME THIS WAY THELMA HOUSTON from ANY WAY YOU LIKE IT
Contains nearly every element of classic disco: the skipping hi-hats, the popping bassline, the slicing strings and the erotic, over-the-top, gospel-charged vocals.

❹ YOU MAKE ME FEEL (MIGHTY REAL) SYLVESTER from STEP II
With its synth licks, mechanized bassline and drum-machine beats, this was the genesis of the disco sub-genre known as Hi-NRG, and one of the most glorious, uplifting records in the disco canon.

❺ WEEKEND PHREEK from DISCO CONNECTION (AUTHENTIC CLASSIC DISCO 1976–81)
A surging, percolating record that is all about dancefloor exorcism.

❻ I FEEL LOVE DONNA SUMMER from I REMEMBER YESTERDAY
The cocaine chill of the "Me Decade" in a nutshell.

❼ I WILL SURVIVE GLORIA GAYNOR from LOVE TRACKS
Moan and groan if you want, but ten million hen parties haven't managed to ruin what is the best disco record not made by Chic (who were so great they have their own playlist).

❽ DISCO CIRCUS MARTIN CIRCUS from MARTIN CIRCUS
Proof that daft European novelty records aren't necessarily the scourge of the earth.

❾ VERTIGO/RELIGHT MY FIRE DAN HARTMAN from RELIGHT MY FIRE
A record so good, not even Take That could mess it up.

❿ GO BANG #5 DINOSAUR L from 24>24 MUSIC
Crafted by the great disco maverick Arthur Russell, this is seven minutes of inspired dancefloor lunacy.

21st-century divas

Headstrong and, some might say, image-led, there's a new breed of diva in town. Fond of a drink on occasion, partial to cigarrettes and other bad habits, these kids have taken to the rock'n'roll lifestyle like Keef's adopted granddaughters.

❶ REHAB AMY WINEHOUSE from BACK TO BLACK
The song which won her the nickname "Amy Housewine"is both a celebration of life on the large side and a mind-blowing tribute to the great R&B and soul sounds of the 1960s.

❷ SMILE LILY ALLEN from ALRIGHT, STILL
Lily Allen's patented "ball gowns and trainers" look and UK tabloid fame have tended to distract from the sheer quality of her voice and the talented song-writing behind it. "Smile", above all, bursts with feel-good, no regrets, gutsy attitude.

❸ WHAT'S A GIRL TO DO BAT FOR LASHES from FUR AND GOLD
A drum riff, closely related to that which opens the Ronettes'"Be My Baby", kicks once before giving way to a spine-tingling harpsichord riff and whispered ghost vocals. Neo-goth anyone?

❹ TRAIN GOLDFRAPP from BLACK CHERRY
Adding lush production to the sexed-up persona Alison adopted for her second album was a smart move. "Train" broods and bristles, hinting at heaving passions somewhere down below.

❺ FLUSHED CHEST JOAN AS POLICEWOMAN from REAL LIFE
Slow-paced and cool as a Texas deputy in an air-con cruiser, "Flushed Chest" is the standout track on the album that took young Joan from New York scene collaborator (Rufus Wainwright, Antony and the Johnsons) to front of stage.

❻ BUCKY DONE GUN M.I.A. from ARULAR
Genre-shattering second single (after the amazing "Galang") from Sri Lankan Tamil-born rapper Maya Arulpragasam (MIA).

❼ ONLY SKIN JOANNA NEWSOM from YS
Joanna's vocal-harp epic stretches effortlessly to fill almost twenty minutes aided and abetted by engineer Steve Albini – and with grunted vocal contributions from Bill Callahan (of Smog).

❽ CAROLINE'S A VICTIM KATE NASH download single
This is far more than simply irritatingly catchy; it slips under the skin and itches like crazy.

❾ FIDELITY REGINA SPEKTOR from BEGIN TO HOPE
Don't let her precise diction fool you, Regina's on the brink. She hears voices in her head, and one day they'll tell her "Stop with the music already – time to take out the meat cleavers and carve some revenge."

❿ EARTH INTRUDERS BJÖRK from VOLTA
Iceland's best-known export is famous both for her achingly passionate music and for her "mad as tits" elfin persona. Bringing both to the fore for this recent single, Björk shows the new girls who's daddy.

Al Spicer

Divine Comedy

Neil Hannon's delicious and mischievous mix of big arrangements, gentle satire and Scott Walkerish crooning is utterly unique.

❶ SOMETHING FOR THE WEEKEND from CASANOVA
The sleazy side of life, with a wonderfully dirty middle-aged chortle to get it going.

❷ NATIONAL EXPRESS from FIN DE SIÈCLE
Poking fun at cosily out-of-date UK institutions is one of Neil Hannon's favourite pastimes – and his delivery here, with its fantastically anachronistic backing vocals and characteristic croon, is perfectly judged.

❸ GENERATION SEX from FIN DE SIÈCLE
Jaunty satireof the sex-and-celebrity obsessed generation.

❹ SOMEONE from A SHORT ALBUM ABOUT LOVE
Brooding, big orchestration and Hannon's achingly emotional delivery make this the most dramatic song in the parade of dramatic songs that make up *A Short Album About Love*.

❺ EVERYBODY KNOWS (EXCEPT YOU) from A SHORT ALBUM ABOUT LOVE
Neil Hannon at his most gentle on this straightforward love song. The words, arrangement and backing vocals are glorious kitsch.

❻ IN PURSUIT OF HAPPINESS from A SHORT ALBUM ABOUT LOVE
A great, lush album opener, which also, bizarrely, did time as a theme for BBC TV's *Tomorrow's World*.

❼ COMMUTER LOVE from FIN DE SIÈCLE
Touching number about unrequited love on the morning train.

❽ BECOMING MORE LIKE ALFIE from CASANOVA

Harking back to the risqué 1960s Michael Caine movie somehow perfectly encapsulates The Divine Comedy: saucy slap-and-tickle with a deeply serious underbelly.

❾ LADY OF A CERTAIN AGE from VICTORY FOR THE COMIC MUSE

Never short of a piercing lyric to open up a hidden history, Hannon here explores the lack of love experienced at the other end of life's weary path. A subject of much delicacy, treated with maturity and respect.

❿ ARTHUR C CLARKE'S MYSTERIOUS WORLD from VICTORY FOR THE COMIC MUSE

Standout track on an album with many moments of bliss. Hannon lets himself go on a sci-fi inspired exploration of the differences between us boys and girls.

Martin Dunford

Willie Dixon Songbook

Willie Dixon wrote the electric blues songbook with savage wit and monster hooks. Chuck Berry, Bob Dylan and Tom Waits all learned from his songcraft and he provided The Stones–Cream–Zeppelin with their raison d'etre. Not bad for the seventh son of Mississippi sharecroppers who hoboed to Chicago, worked as Joe Louis' sparring partner and was jailed for refusing to fight in World War II. "Why should I fight to defend someone intent on killing me and my people?" he reasoned.

❶ HOOCHIE COOCHIE MAN MUDDY WATERS from THE CHESS STORY 1947–1975

Muddy starts muttering how he's got "a black cat bone" and "a mojo hand" so bringing Southern voodoo lore into the music scene. Black Sabbath and all their dum-dum disciples owe a debt to this tune.

❷ BACK DOOR MAN HOWLING WOLF from THE GENUINE ARTICLE

"I eat more chicken than any man seen" boasts the Wolf in this ominous celebration of a serial shagger who begins to sound very, very dangerous.

❸ MY BABE LITTLE WALTER from THE CHESS STORY 1947-1975

The fiery tempered harmonica-blowing maestro enjoyed a #1 R&B hit with this infectious tune.

❹ YOU CAN'T JUDGE A BOOK BY ITS COVER BO DIDDLEY from BO DIDDLEY'S GREATEST HITS

Artists like Chuck Berry and Bo Diddley built rock'n'roll

out of Dixon's blues(print) so no surprise this funky homily was a Willie tune that hit for Bo.

❺ WANG DANG DOODLE KOKO TAYLOR from THE CHESS STORY 1947–1975

Based on a legendary lesbian ball, this is a wild American narrative. Koko sang with the required raucous groove and Buddy Guy smokes on guitar. Sign of the times: WDD was Chess Records' last major blues hit.

❻ INSANE ASYLUM KOKO TAYLOR from WHAT IT TAKES: THE CHESS YEARS.

Not so much a standard as an exception with Willie singing about losing his baby to the infirmary while Koko screams the chorus like a woman possessed. One of the craziest (literally) songs ever cut!

❼ I JUST WANT TO MAKE LOVE TO YOU MUDDY WATERS from THE CHESS BOX 1947–1975

Brooding blues that makes no attempt to hide the singer's sexual intentions. Muddy delivers the sermon while Little Walter blows blues harp that matches John Coltrane for sheets of sound.

❽ I CAN'T QUIT YOU BABE OTIS RUSH from THE COBRA SESSIONS

Chess turned down Rush so Dixon quit the company and set up Cobra, scoring a huge R&B hit with this ferocious tune. Listen to Otis shred and shriek!

❾ LITTLE RED ROOSTER THE ROLLING STONES from ROLLED GOLD

Originally a Howling Wolf hit, this finds the Stones savouring deep Chicago blues. Brian Jones lays down weeping slide guitar so justifying his brief, blighted existence.

❿ SPOONFUL CREAM from LIVE CREAM

Clapton and Co dig deep into this Howling Wolf song so sparking a wild rock rave-up on this most elemental of Dixon songs. Cream and the Stones credited Dixon while Led Zeppelin stole outright his tunes – "Whole Lotta Love" is his "You Need Love" – so leading him to suing them (successfully). Willie Dixon – ass kicker!

Garth Cartwright

Dizzee Rascal

Maintaining an air of amused astonishment at the little outrages of modern life while still managing serious comment on the major issues is a neat trick that Dylan Mills carries out perfectly. As Dizzee Rascal, one of modern urban Britain's most socially conscious voices, he runs a wildly

entertaining live show, blending hip-hop, UK garage and his own secret mix of herbs into a particularly potent grime sound of his own.

❶ FIX UP LOOK SHARP from BOY IN DA CORNER
Just 18 years old when he stormed the hipper radio shows with this screaming challenge to himself and the world around him, Dizzee's first single is still an absolute blinder.

❷ ROUND WE GO (AIN'T NO LOVE) from BOY IN DA CORNER
After opening like a dance track, the wavering lyric tells an involved tale of street love gone wrong (again) that's too interesting to jig about to.

❸ JUS' A RASCAL from BOY IN DA CORNER
One from the old school of "This is my music and this is my name" tunes, this comes equipped with enough bass to blow the windows out of your car, possibly even your house. The mad high-pitched backing vox send a cold shiver down the spine at the same time as they shoot a giggle up the funny bone.

❹ I LUV U from BOY IN DA CORNER
That sweet as syrup sample which opens the track soon descends into a mildly menacing robotic cyber love chant. Then the bass loses all sense of self-respect and squidges all over the four walls of Dizzee's padded cell. Great boy v. girl rap.

❺ STOP DAT from BOY IN DA CORNER
Downbeat plea aimed at all the city gangs to quit wounding and killing one another. On a Friday night the emergency rooms of London's hospitals look like Rambo's been in the area.

❻ EVERYWHERE from SHOWTIME
Unsurprisingly inward looking and at times claustrophobic, *Showtime* was recorded in the aftermath of the notorious incident in which Dizzee was stabbed in the chest on the Cypriot resort of of Ayia Napa. "Everywhere" yells with pain, rage and defiance.

❼ OFF II WORK from OFF II WORK
Kicking off with beautifully half-hearted whistling, this is an irresistibly asthmatic off-key skank, with wheezing synth percussion and messy dub reggae snares. The most effervescent and carefree Dizzee's ever sounded (and on a song about work, too).

❽ KNOCK KNOCK from SHOWTIME
Dizzee turns the "Knock, knock" joke into a series of threats, while the music sounds as if the collected synths and drum machines of Jan Hammer, Ryuichi Sakamoto and Tangerine Dream are playing an aleatory string of their most tumescent noises.

❾ WORLD OUTSIDE from MATHS & ENGLISH
Just how scary is this? The "beats" on this track are sampled from a martial arts film and comprise knives, axes and cleavers being sharpened up for battle. Like something Wu-Tang would shy away from, this is life on the mean streets of Bow boiled down to a single chilling clash of metal on metal.

❿ SIRENS from MATHS & ENGLISH
Intense and genuinely exciting, this first track from the older, wiser Dizzee's third album shows him still out there, mashing things up with a wry grin, on the furthest edge of the British scene.

Al Spicer

Dr Dre

From practically inventing West Coast electro-funk with World Class Wreckin' Cru, to creating the blueprint for gangsta rap with NWA, to birthing G-Funk as a solo artist, Dr Dre has started more mini-epochs in popular music than anyone this side of James Brown.

❶ CABBAGE PATCH WORLD CLASS WRECKIN' CRU from TURN OFF THE LIGHTS (BEFORE THE ATTITUDE)
For his first trick, Dre kick-starts the Cabbage Patch dance craze.

❷ HOUSE CALLS WORLD CLASS WRECKIN' CRU from TURN OFF THE LIGHTS (BEFORE THE ATTITUDE)
Proto-techno electro-funk from Dr Dre, "not your average gigolo".

❸ STRAIGHT OUTTA COMPTON NWA from STRAIGHT OUTTA COMPTON
Dre's drum machines knock you in the solar plexus.

❹ FUCK THE POLICE NWA from STRAIGHT OUTTA COMPTON
Dre is as unflinching as the rappers as they stare down the devil.

❺ ALWAYZ INTO SOMETHIN' NWA from EFIL4ZAGGIN
With its whining synth lick and rolling rhythm, this is the blueprint for G-Funk.

❻ DEEP COVER DR DRE from DEEP COVER
A beat more menacing and askew than anything trip-hop would come up with in five years of ripping it off.

❼ NUTHIN' BUT A G THANG DR DRE from THE CHRONIC
So effortlessly funky – the ultimate G-Funk anthem.

⑧ CALIFORNIA LOVE 2PAC from ALL EYEZ ON ME

Bringing in Zapp's Roger Troutman to rock the Vocoder may have been the most inspired move of Dre's illustrious career.

⑨ MY NAME IS EMINEM from THE SLIM SHADY LP

The kiddie-park calliope keyboard and sing-song bassline helped propel Eminem towards superstardom.

⑩ LET ME BLOW YA MIND EVE from SCORPION

The catchiest record Dre has made.

Peter Shapiro

Dr John

Mac Rebennack – aka Dr John – has played everything from R&B through psychedelic voodoo-rock to funk, jazz and swing, yet the spirit of everything he has done has remained rooted in the rich musical heritage of New Orleans.

① GRIS GRIS GUMBO YA-YA from GRIS GRIS

"They call me Dr John, known as the Night Tripper, got my bottle of gris gris in my hand…" Has rock'n'roll ever sounded more spooked?

② WALK ON GILDED SPLINTERS from GRIS GRIS

Forget Paul Weller's version. This is the real voodoo.

③ RIGHT PLACE, WRONG TIME from IN THE RIGHT PLACE

Backed by The Meters and produced by Allen Toussaint, N'Awlins fonk at its rocking best.

④ SUCH A NIGHT THE BAND from THE LAST WALTZ

The original was on the *In The Right Place* album, but try this joyous live version backed by The Band at their farewell concert.

⑤ JUNKO PARTNER from GUMBO

A tribute to the music of New Orleans, the entire *Gumbo* album is a roots masterpiece, but this syncopated take on a tune made famous by James Booker is a standout.

⑥ WHAT COMES AROUND (GOES AROUND) from DESITIVELY BONAROO

With Toussaint and The Meters back on board, this cut is even funkier – if that's possible – than anything on *Right Place, Wrong Time*.

⑦ GOIN' BACK TO NEW ORLEANS from GOIN' BACK TO NEW ORLEANS

A swinging, trumpet-driven tribute to the Crescent City, featuring the Neville Brothers on a tune written by Joe "Honeydripper" Liggins.

⑧ MAKIN' WHOOPEE from IN A SENTIMENTAL MOOD

A wonderfully brassy duet with Rickie Lee Jones that won a Grammy for best jazz vocal performance.

Dr John's
Big Easy

DR JOHN has been a New Orleans legend for half a century, so it's hardly surprising that more than half of his list comes from the Crescent City.

① PLEASE SEND ME SOMEONE TO LOVE PERCY MAYFIELD from THE BEST OF PERCY MAYFIELD

② IN THE NIGHT PROFESSOR LONGHAIR from FESS: THE PROFESSOR LONGHAIR ANTHOLOGY

③ SOPHISTICATED CISSY THE METERS from BEST OF THE METERS

④ WILL THE CIRCLE BE UNBROKEN THE STAPLE SINGERS from WILL THE CIRCLE BE UNBROKEN

⑤ WHEN MY DREAMBOAT COMES HOME FATS DOMINO from MY BLUE HEAVEN: THE BEST OF

⑥ SWEET LITTLE ANGEL BB KING from BEST OF BB KING

⑦ SEVEN SPANISH ANGELS WILLIE NELSON & RAY CHARLES from FRIENDSHIP

⑧ TOUGH LOVER ETTA JAMES from HICKORY DICKORY DOCK

⑨ I WONDER LOUIS ARMSTRONG from THE COMPLETE RCA VICTOR RECORDINGS

⑩ MEET DE BOYS ON THE BATTLEFRONT WILD TCHOUPITOULAS from WILD TCHOUPITOULAS

❾ PARTY HELLFIRE from IN ANUTHA ZONE
In 1997 Parlophone decided to reinvent the good doctor by teaming him with the Britpop hordes. Against all the odds, the result was a great album that included this classic, featuring Paul Weller and Ocean Colour Scene.

❿ I'M GONNA GO FISHIN' from DUKE ELEGANT
In the twilight of his career, Mac paid tribute to Ellington with an album of funk-fried versions of the Duke's tunes that showcased his own keyboard skills.

Nigel Williamson

Dog's life

Man's best friend has inspired its fair share of songs, providing metaphors for all kinds of situations – oddly, few any of them actually concerning dogs.

❶ ATOMIC DOG GEORGE CLINTON from THE BEST OF GEORGE CLINTON
A hilarious song about, err, chasing cats by the P-Funk inventor. George said he was in an"enhanced state" while writing it and the lyrics support that claim.

❷ DOGGY DOG WORLD SNOOP DOGGY DOG from DOGGYSTYLE
Snoop's lazily grinding "G-Funk" drew heavily on P-Funk, both stylistically and thematically, as this cut shows. Backing vocals from Tha Dogg Pound.

❸ CAN YOUR PUSSY DO THE DOG? THE CRAMPS from A DATE WITH ELVIS
This storming slice of psychobilly is another not exactly subtle song about cat–dog interaction. Singer Lux Interior does his best deranged Elvis impression.

❹ HOUND DOG ELVIS PRESLEY from ELVIS 56
The best-known version of this splendidly absurd Leiber & Stoller number ("…you ain't never caught a rabbit And you ain't no friend of mine!") first covered by Big Mama Thornton.

❺ BLACK DOG LED ZEPPELIN from LED ZEPPELIN 4
One of the Zep's most successful blues rip-offs, and another song about having sex, though the title was inspired by a black dog that was wandering around the studio where they recorded it.

❻ I WANNA BE YOUR DOG THE STOOGES from THE STOOGES
Same subject matter, different singer. Iggy Pop's lusty, howling anthem anticipated punk rock by several

years and ensured immortality among dog fanciers the world over.

❼ I'M THE WOLF HOWLIN' WOLF from THE GENUINE ARTICLE – THE BEST OF HOWLIN' WOLF
A suitably lupine twelve-bar blues groove by the only artist properly qualified to sing it.

❽ WHO LET THE DOGS OUT? BAHA MEN from WHO LET THE DOGS OUT?
With their memorable canine refrain ("woof, woof – woof, woof"), these Bahamian one-hit wonders were soon dogged by imitators.

❾ THE HOUNDS OF LOVE KATE BUSH from THE HOUNDS OF LOVE
The title track from Kate's unlikely mid-1980s smash. Complete with poochy chorus vocals, it's an extended metaphor for the fearfulness of giving in to love.

❿ I WON'T BE YOUR DOG ANYMORE PAUL KELLY from IN CONCERT
Oz folk minstrel resolves to leave the dog's life he's been leading behind on this stark acoustic ballad with just guitar and harmonica as accompaniment.

Jon Lusk

Fats Domino

One of the saddest moments in the 2005 New Orleans flood tragedy came when it was reported that Fats Domino was dead. Fortunately, it turned out the news was incorrect and Fats wasn't goin' home just yet. At the time of writing he's still walkin' and still playin' at the grand old age of 78, So, let's hear it for the Fat Man…

❶ BLUEBERRY HILL from THE FATS DOMINO JUKEBOX
Fats' signature and a #1 hit in 1956. Surprisingly, it was one of the few hits not co-written by Fats and Dave Bartholomew, but by Larry Stock.

❷ BLUE MONDAY from THE FATS DOMINO JUKEBOX
First recorded by Smiley Lewis in 1953, Fats' version was a top-five hit four years later after its inclusion in the film *The Girl Can't Help It*.

❸ I'M WALKIN' from THE FATS DOMINO JUKEBOX
A classic New Orleans shuffle beat set up by Earl Palmer's walking bass introduction.

❹ THE FAT MAN from THE FATS DOMINO JUKEBOX
Fats' first R&B hit from 1950, based on Champion Jack Dupree's "Junker's Blues".

❺ GOIN' HOME from THE FATS DOMINO JUKEBOX
Fats' first crossover pop hit from 1952 after it caught the American public's "Bring our boys home!" disquiet over the Korean war.

❻ AIN'T THAT A SHAME from THE FATS DOMINO JUKEBOX
Pat Boone covered this in 1955 and took his anodyne version to #1, meaning Fats' original only made #10. But half a century on this is the only version that anyone wants to hear.

❼ ALL BY MYSELF from THE FATS DOMINO JUKEBOX
Chuck Berry had just released "Maybelline" and you can hear rock'n'roll beginning to influence Fats' R&B sound.

❽ I'M IN LOVE AGAIN from THE FATS DOMINO JUKEBOX
His first rock'n'roll hit and a #3 in the pop charts in 1956. Listen out for Lee Allen's magnificent sax.

❾ MY GIRL JOSEPHINE from THE FATS DOMINO JUKEBOX
A huge hit in 1960, featuring superb guitar by Roy Montrill with an almost Caribbean feel.

❿ WALKING TO NEW ORLEANS from THE FATS DOMINO JUKEBOX
Written by Bobby Charles ("See You Later Alligator"/ "But I Do"), this is lush Fats with strings courtesy of the New Orleans Symphony Orchestra.

Nigel Williamson

Doo wop

With its incessant nonsense syllables, dreamy harmonies, and solid R&B base, doo wop gave birth to some of the quaintest, most frivolous and fun rock'n'roll classics. Romantic, too.

❶ COME GO WITH ME THE DEL-VIKINGS FROM THE BEST OF DOO WOP UPTEMPO
The opening "dum dum be-dooby-be-dum"s are as unforgettably catchy as any doo wop line devised on this swinging, rocking smash from 1957.

❷ GET A JOB THE SILHOUETTES from THE BEST OF DOO WOP UPTEMPO
Not far behind are the "yip yip yip"s and other assorted infectious goofball phrases swirling around "Get a Job", an unusually socially conscious early rock'n'roll hit.

❸ DUKE OF EARL GENE CHANDLER from THE DOO WOP BOX VOL 2
The drooping low backup intonations of the title on this 1962 chart-topper sparked one of the last great doo wop classics.

❹ SINCE I DON'T HAVE YOU THE SKYLINERS from THE BEST OF DOO WOP BALLADS
A sumptuously orchestrated ballad with dreamy male–female harmonies and violins that both glide and pluck, the female part ascending above the heavens on the super-high finish.

❺ IN THE STILL OF THE NIGHT THE FIVE SATINS from THE BEST OF DOO WOP BALLADS
The most mystical of all doo wop hits, with a hushed atmosphere made to order for the dead-of-night lyrics, gently pushed along by sublime "shoo-be-doo"s.

❻ HUSHABYE THE MYSTICS from THE BEST OF DOO WOP UPTEMPO
The Beach Boys learned a lot from both the doo wop harmonies and melodic construction of hits like "Hushabye", which they covered in the mid-1960s.

❼ WHY DO FOOLS FALL IN LOVE FRANKIE LYMON & THE TEENAGERS from THE BEST OF DOO WOP UPTEMPO
An irresistibly jiving intro sets the pace for this bubbly bopper, whose high-pitched singer's chirp echoed all the way down to the young Michael Jackson.

❽ AT MY FRONT DOOR (CRAZY LITTLE MAMA) THE EL DORADOS from THE BEST OF DOO WOP UPTEMPO
Doo wop is just one step removed from jump blues and jazz on this mid-1950s rouser, a brilliant nonstop series of compulsive riffs and vocal tradeoffs.

❾ BLUE MOON THE MARCELS from THE BEST OF DOO WOP UPTEMPO
A pop standard gets stood on its head right from its irrepressible intro, which jams several dozen nonsense syllables into no more than a half dozen seconds.

❿ GEE THE CROWS from THE BEST OF DOO WOP UPTEMPO
One of the first doo wop hits to cross from the R&B charts to the pop radio stations, "Gee" epitomizes early rock'n'roll at its most charmingly naive and innocent.

Garth Cartwright

The Doors

A psychedelic supernova of rock, blues, jazz, classical and Jim Morrison's transcendental poetry, The Doors are a genuine musical legend.

❶ LIGHT MY FIRE from THE DOORS
An obvious starter, but no other psychedelic rocker is as hypnotic as this 1967 American chart-topper, best heard in this extended LP version.

❷ RIDERS ON THE STORM from L.A. WOMAN
The hitchhiker's guide to hell, the hushed-and-damned atmosphere heightened by Jim Morrison overdubbing a whispered vocal on top of his singing.

❸ THE CRYSTAL SHIP from THE DOORS
A mesmerizing ballad of dream images melting in and out of focus, guided by Ray Manzarek's spellbinding blend of organ and piano.

❹ BREAK ON THROUGH (TO THE OTHER SIDE) from THE DOORS
A perfectly concise summary of Morrison's obsessions with breaking the barriers of ordinary experience, set to an explosive "bossa nova meets Ray Charles" arrangement.

❺ L.A. WOMAN from L.A. WOMAN
Los Angeles's unofficial highway-cruising anthem, under which lies a cinéma-vérité-like blues of the city's darker side.

❻ THE UNKNOWN SOLDIER from WAITING FOR THE SUN
The horrors of war, brought to life in the creepy bitter-sweetness of the verse, brutally killed in the mock-execution of the "instrumental" break.

❼ TAKE IT AS IT COMES from THE DOORS
Serene existentialism that soars like an arrow until the surprise dropout of everything save bass and drum near the end.

❽ HELLO, I LOVE YOU from WAITING FOR THE SUN
If it's a rip-off of the Kinks' "All Day And All Of The Night", at least it's a hell of a riff to rip off.

❾ PEOPLE ARE STRANGE from STRANGE DAYS
Bouncy dark carnival-saloon music strut, given an entirely different and disquieting dimension by the sober alienation of Morrison's words and voice.

❿ YOU'RE LOST LITTLE GIRL from STRANGE DAYS
Sex that's simultaneously dangerously threatening and irresistible: the supremely haunting, winding melody worthy of a horror flick.

Richie Unterberger

Nick Drake

The ultimate cult singer-songwriter, Nick Drake's idiosyncratic brand of reserved British folk-rock melancholy went virtually unheard in his brief lifetime – but that cult just grows and grows.

❶ HAZEY JANE II from BRYTER LATER
The surface prettiness of the motorway-cruising, brassy rock arrangement can't bury the uncertain doubt oozing from every pore of the lyrics and vocal.

❷ POOR BOY from BRYTER LATER
When the female backing singers on this languid soul-folk beauty croon "Oh poor boy, so sorry for himself", it's as close as Drake came to sly, self-deprecating wit.

❸ CELLO SONG from FIVE LEAVES LEFT
Marvellous fingerpicking guitar, haunting cello and congas on an unclassifiable slice of autumnal brooding.

❹ AT THE CHIME OF A CITY CLOCK from BRYTER LATER
Great, graceful string orchestration on this muted but chilling paean to urban loneliness. But is Drake reviling it or revelling in it?

❺ SUNDAY from BRYTER LATER
Mixing folk-rock and baroque classical orchestration, *Bryter Later*'s closing instrumental says as much about fleeting hope and crushing disappointment as any of Drake's lyrics.

❻ WAY TO BLUE from FIVE LEAVES LEFT
Not so much folk-rock as chamber folk, Drake's lilting regret accompanied only by Robert Kirby's sadness-soaked string arrangement.

❼ I WAS MADE TO LOVE MAGIC from TIME OF NO REPLY
The finest delicately enunciated airy-fairy folk-rock song this side of Donovan, who, incidentally, was probably more of an influence on Drake than many acknowledge.

❽ STRANGE MEETING II from TIME OF NO REPLY
More Donovan influence on this posthumously released outtake, which boasts as captivating a minor-keyed melody as any of Drake's more renowned pieces.

❾ ONE OF THESE THINGS FIRST from BRYTER LATER
He'd only just entered his 20s, but Drake was already singing as though his life was a litany of missed opportunities.

❿ NORTHERN SKY from BRYTER LATER
Amid the repressed despair, a golden ray of hope strains toward the heavens on this effervescent, effortlessly engaging jazzy ballad.

Richie Unterberger

Hey Bartender! Drinking songs

You may not remember the words in the morning, but you can't beat a good drinking song last thing at night.

❶ WHAT'S THE USE OF GETTING SOBER WHEN YOU GONNA GET DRUNK AGAIN? LOUIS JORDAN from THE BEST OF LOUIS JORDAN
There's nothing like a cataclysmic world war to prompt a hard-bitten drinking song, like this 1943 gem.

❷ DRINKIN' WINE, SPO-DEE-O-DEE STICKS MCGHEE from ATLANTIC RHYTHM & BLUES 1947–1974
In which bluesman Brownie McGhee's lesser-known brother recalls a memorable 1949 night out in New Orleans.

❸ ONE SCOTCH, ONE BOURBON, ONE BEER AMOS MILBURN from ORIGINAL JAMAICAN SOUND SYSTEM STYLE
John Lee Hooker cut a magnificently slurry version of this late-night anthem, but Milburn's 1953 original still has the edge.

❹ HEY BARTENDER FLOYD DIXON & HIS BAND from BLUES MASTERS VOL 14
Also from 1953, but Floyd Dixon went one better than Milburn by ordering four beers at a time.

❺ ALABAMA SONG WHISKEY BAR THE DOORS from THE DOORS
Even if you're immune to the charms of Jim Morrison's own poetry, you can't help but drink along to this 1967 rendition of Kurt Weill's boozers' charter, from the opera *The Rise and Fall of the City of Mahogany*.

❻ DRUNKARD PSALM PRINCE BUSTER from THE PROPHET 1967
"Rum is their shepherd, they live in want; It maketh them to lie down in the gutter on an empty stomach, and vomit up some green things they did not eat."

❼ DOWN WHERE THE DRUNKARDS ROLL RICHARD & LINDA THOMPSON from THE BEST OF ...
Linda carries the lovely melody, but it's Richard's lugubrious, stop-motion, down-in-the depths harmonizing that really tells the story.

❽ DELIRIUM TREMENS CHRISTY MOORE from ORDINARY MAN
Irish minstrel Christy Moore recorded this splendid vision of Ireland through the bottom of a beer-glass in 1985.

❾ WHISKEY IN THE JAR THE POGUES & THE DUBLINERS from WHISKEY IN THE JAR
Few were the eyebrows raised in shock that when the Pogues found themselves in the studio with the Dubliners in 1989, their collective minds turned to drink.

❿ TOO DRUNK TO FUCK NOUVELLE VAGUE from NOUVELLE VAGUE
Postmodern Gallic popsters reinterpret a punk classic in 2004.

Greg Ward

Drivetime

Songs in cars make a different kind of sense as your vehicle becomes a combination of walkman-on-wheels and leather-seated bedroom. But where you are makes a big difference. Drivetime in America summons up the intoxicating personal and sexual freedom of the open road. In the UK and Europe, it's about traffic jams, dodgy motors and the ever-present risk of colliding with a ten-ton truck. Hence an extended list, split in two by continent.

ACROSS THE US

❶ NO PARTICULAR PLACE TO GO CHUCK BERRY from CHESS MASTERS
Riding around in his automobile, his baby beside him, Berry finds himself frustrated at his inability to unfasten her safety belt.

❷ PROMISED LAND JOHNNIE ALLAN from ANOTHER SATURDAY NIGHT
Johnnie Allan forgets one whole verse of Chuck Berry's classic, and you can hear his band members falling about behind him, but it's just perfect.

❸ CAR WHEELS ON A GRAVEL ROAD LUCINDA WILLIAMS from CAR WHEELS ON A GRAVEL ROAD
The female Keith Richards hears the scrunch of tyres on gravel as both promise and threat.

❹ FREEWAY OF LOVE ARETHA FRANKLIN from WHO'S ZOOMIN' WHO
Sharp and shiny pop-funk, as 1980s as a pillar-box-red G-reg Golf GTI.

❺ WILLIN' LITTLE FEAT from LITTLE FEAT
Balladeering trucker takes the back roads so he won't get weighed.

❻ PASSENGER IGGY POP from LUST FOR LIFE
Given how colossally stoned Iggy sounds, just be glad he isn't driving.

AND AROUND EUROPE

❶ DRIVING AWAY FROM HOME IT'S IMMATERIAL from LIFE'S HARD AND THEN YOU DIE
Northwestern one-hit wonders hymn the M62. If they're feeling ambitious, they might even make it to Glasgow.

❷ CARS AND GIRLS PREFAB SPROUT from FROM LANGLEY PARK TO MEMPHIS
A direct rebuke to Bruce Springsteen: some things, insist the fey rockers, mean much more than cars and girls.

❸ DRIVING IN MY CAR MADNESS from COMPLETE MADNESS
Nutty Boys buy a clunker from a north London Brazilian expat.

❹ STOLEN CAR BETH ORTON from CENTRAL RESERVATION
Folky electronica queen Beth Orton goes joyriding.

❺ AUTOBAHN KRAFTWERK from AUTOBAHN
The Düsseldorf robot-lovers at their most minimalist.

❻ THERE IS A LIGHT THAT NEVER GOES OUT
THE SMITHS from THE QUEEN IS DEAD
Morrissey pleads with an unspecified lover to go out driving and to perish in a fiery collision; the way he puts it, it sounds not unattractive.

David Honigmann

Drug songs

"There's a hole in Daddy's arm where all the money goes." If only there was enough left over for the occasional CD, then we might have learned to avoid all this misery.

❶ WHITE LIGHT/WHITE HEAT VELVET UNDERGROUND from WHITE LIGHT/WHITE HEAT
The world's best song in praise of the world's best drugs; our old friends, the central nervous-system stimulants. All the fun of a seven-day weekend without having to deal with those awful dealers.

❷ MR PHARMACIST THE FALL from 458489 A SIDES
Following the punk-rock belief of singing what you know about, Mark E Smith and The Fall carried out years of chemical research, one way and another, to

prepare them spiritually and mentally for their own manic take on The Other Half's psychedelic garage-rock triumph.

❸ TOO MUCH TO DREAM LAST NIGHT STIV BATORS from DISCONNECTED
Strangely poignant and fairly faithful version of the Electric Prunes' original from the sadly missed Stiv (ex-Dead Boys), a man who genuinely did have too much last night every night.

❹ CHINESE ROCKS THE HEARTBREAKERS from L.A.M.F.
Penned by Dee Dee Ramone but initially turned down by his band, this song was credited to The Heartbreakers when they released it as a single. Although the royalties and hostility were eventually sorted out, there no beating the sense of "been there, done that, stole the T-shirt" in The Heartbreakers' definitive version.

❺ EBENEEZER GOODE THE SHAMEN from EBENEEZER GOODE
Deliriously "naughty naughty naughty", this is a chant'n'beats, barely disguised tribute to the delights of an MDMA-assisted chemical smile. The accompanying video looked as if it was sponsored by the Ecstasy Marketing Board.

❻ I DON'T LIKE THE DRUGS (BUT THE DRUGS LIKE ME) MARILYN MANSON from MECHANICAL ANIMALS
Sexy tune – in a robotic, numb-from-the-brain-down kind of way – from Marilyn and the crew. But it sounds depressingly like the track was just one more damn thing to get out of the way before everyone could get back to powdering their noses in front of the mirror.

❼ PILLS THE NEW YORK DOLLS from THE NEW YORK DOLLS
"Taking this junk against my will"? Yeah, right. Any complaint about having to take drugs involuntarily is gonna sound a tad fake coming from the Big Apple's greatest ever set of fuck-ups. Still, a superb take on Bo Diddley's song.

❽ COMFORTABLY NUMB SCISSOR SISTERS – TIGA REMIX from THE REMIX! EP
Taking nothing from the sensitive Pink Floyd original but the lyrics, New York's Scissor Sisters updated this for the frantic pace and mind-boggling cocktails of today's music scene.

❾ COLD TURKEY PLASTIC ONO BAND from LIVE PEACE IN TORONTO
This live take of Lennon's withdrawal classic is rendered even more harrowing by the contribution of Yoko Ono (shut up in a bag on stage at the time).

⑩ THE NEEDLE AND THE DAMAGE DONE NEIL YOUNG from LIVE RUST

On a good night, Neil can hush a stadium with this track, his own intensely personal contribution to the anti-heroin campaign. Then some pinhead yells "yeeeeeeeaaaahhh!" and the spell evaporates.

Al Spicer

Singing drummers

They don't just hit things, you know.

① BACK OFF BOOGALOO RINGO STARR from BLAST FROM YOUR PAST

Ringo's rather groovy second solo single from 1971, on which he gets to moo about three notes with startling enthusiasm.

② HOTEL CALIFORNIA DON HENLEY from HOTEL CALIFORNIA

Henley's poignant vocal on The Eagles' 1976 epic of pessimistic LA soft rock helped the album become one of the biggest in history.

③ THE NIGHT THEY DROVE OLD DIXIE DOWN LEVON HELM from THE LAST WALTZ

He had sung it on The Band's second album *The Band* in 1969, but Helm – vocalizing from behind his kit – performed Robbie Robertson's resonant tale of the US Civil War at the group's farewell concert in 1976 as though his life depended on it.

④ SQUONK PHIL COLLINS from TRICK OF THE TAIL

With Genesis having trouble finding a replacement for Peter Gabriel, drummer Collins had a little go at this thunderous track and produced a soaring vocal; his fate was sealed.

⑤ SILENCE IS GOLDEN DAVE MUNDEN from CHIP, DAVE, ALAN AND RICK

Just one of the lead vocalists in the harmony-laden Tremeloes, but distinctive enough to take many a lead line on their various hits in the late 1960s and early 70s.

⑥ I'M NOT YOUR STEPPING STONE MICKEY DOLENZ from MORE OF THE MONKEES

He probably didn't play the galloping tom-tom part on the record, but he played it in later live performances, and the sinister lead vocal on Tommy Boyce's manufactured garage-classic is all Dolenz.

⑦ WE'VE ONLY JUST BEGUN KAREN CARPENTER from CLOSE TO YOU

One of the great expressive pop voices of all time

could also keep tidy time behind a kit, but after initial studio sessions, she usually left it to someone else.

⑧ MOULDY OLD DOUGH NIGEL FLETCHER from THE BEST OF LIEUTENANT PIGEON

Not only was Fletcher responsible for co-writing the Lieutenant Pigeon 1972 novelty smash hit and the militaristic snare patter that drove the catchy beggar, he also got to growl "mouldy old dough" in the chorus at the same time.

Chris Ingham

Drum'n'bass

Drum'n'bass is too easily derided for being heavy metal's ugly, dance-music cousin. These ten tracks show that there's loads of jazz, funk and pop sensibility lurking within the breaks. Dancefloor classics, one and all. They're all singles but available on compilations.

① INNER CITY LIFE GOLDIE/METALHEADZ

Metalheadz label-owner and twisted graffiti-artist applies visualization to the art of beat sculpture with engineer Rob Playford to create a soaring epic of sound and scope previously unheard in the genre.

② CIRCLES ADAM F

A clubland anthem that grew to a chart hit, still fresh whenever played. The art of sample had became skilful surgery in the hands of the producers by this time, and here the 1970s funk influence spins dizzying harmonies over synthetic beats to create futurejazz.

③ PULP FICTION ALEX REECE

Simple yet lethally effective, Pulp Fiction's warping bassline and minimalist structure were like nothing before or since, shifting away from chopped breakbeats into two-step patterns.

④ BROWN PAPER BAG RONI SIZE/REPRAZENT

Drum'n'bass shifted out of purely clubland mode into the live arena with the creation of Roni Size and his Full Cycle cohorts' Reprazent project. This track was a big part of it.

⑤ SHAKE YOUR BODY SHY FX & T POWER

King of the party sound, Shy FX has a history of relatively few releases, but every one of them is essential. After a string of anthems, he hits his pinnacle (so far) with this, one of the most energetic singles ever to grace the UK Top 10.

6 SUPER SHARP SHOOTER GANJA CREW

This is where it started for DJ Zinc, a prolific shapeshifter of an artist with a killer instinct for melody. The track kicks off at half-speed hip-hop tempo, before morphing into twisted drum'n'bass/jungle.

7 MUSIC (I NEED YOU) LTJ BUKEM

The pioneer of melodic style drum & bass, Bukem opened the eyes of the Hardcore audience with this pivotal track.

8 BODY ROCK SHIMON & ANDY C

Andy C, the biggest DJ in the drum'n'bass world, teams up with Shimon to rewrite the rules once again with this new take on the rhythmic DNA of the music's structure: a ludicrously springy bassline and triplet-pattern beats that won anthem status in the clubs.

9 MUTANT REVISITED T POWER/DJ TRACE

Starting life as Horny Mutant Jazz, a slower-tempoed Scorsese-esque mindscape laden with lazy brass and scene-setting vocal samples, T Power had his masterpiece twisted beyond recognition by DJ Trace – a pioneer of the Techstep subgenre. A classic to this day.

10 LK DJ MARKY & XRS

Taking the drum'n'bass world by storm on his arrival in the UK from his native Brazil, DJ Marky and XRS created a sublime slice of music that brought a true breath of fresh air with its Latin guitar and skittering percussion.

Gavin McNamara/Paul Laidlaw

Dub

Popularized in Jamaica, dub is the technique of stretching, extending and remixing a record by dropping parts of the rhythm in and out of the mix, using EQ effects and altering the feel of the record with echo, delay and reverb. It is one of the most intoxicating sounds in music.

1 SENSEMILLA KAYA DUB THE UPSETTERS from BLACKBOARD JUNGLE DUB

A union of titans: Lee Perry and King Tubby dub the heck out of the riddim of Bob Marley's Kaya.

2 WATERGATE ROCK LARRY MARSHALL from I ADMIRE YOU IN DUB

King Tubby again remaking the track "with a flick of his musical wrist".

3 RIVER NILE VERSION HERMAN CHIN LOY from AQUARIUS ROCK

A quirky, offbeat version of Augustus Pablo's legendary "East Of The River Nile".

4 SATIA KEITH HUDSON from PICK A DUB

Militant version of The Abyssinians' classic "Satta Massa Gana".

5 DUB FI GWAN KING TUBBY from DUB GONE CRAZY

Tubby takes a ride on Bunny Lee's fabled "flying cymbals".

6 KING TUBBY'S MEETS ROCKERS UPTOWN KING TUBBY/AUGUSTUS PABLO from KING TUBBY'S MEETS ROCKERS UPTOWN

Leagues deep, foggy, spacey – perhaps the pinnacle of dub.

7 DREAD LION LEE "SCRATCH" PERRY & THE UPSETTERS from SUPER APE

Perry ditches the raw drum'n'bass sound in favour of layer upon layer of sound and effects.

8 SATURDAY NIGHT STYLE MIKEY DREAD from AFRICAN ANTHEM

Derided by many purists as simple gimmickry, this is nevertheless a stunning sonic tour de force.

9 CHAPTER THREE JOE GIBBS from AFRICAN DUB ALL MIGHTY CHAPTER THREE

Another dub dominated by sound effects rather than low-end exploration, but one that had a profound effect on the dancefloor.

10 DOIN' THE BEST THAT I CAN BETTY LAVETTE from WEST END STORY VOL 2

Disco remix maestro Walter Gibbons shows what dub techniques can do for dance music.

Peter Shapiro

Dubstar

If popular music were a family, the underrated, underachieving Dubstar would probably be younger siblings to New Order, Pulp and Pet Shop Boys, with The Smiths their cousins. Their lyrics are funny, dark and tender, Steve Hillier's melodies are beautiful, and Sarah Blackwood has one of the purest voices in British pop. And a northern accent, which can't be bad.

❶ BOW WOW NOW from STARS
The silly name belies a heartwrenching description of saying goodbye forever to your best friend.

❷ GHOST from GOODBYE
Daily routine can't mask a constant yearning for lost love. Again, Blackwood shows emotion can be expressed without soulless vocal gymnastics.

❸ POLESTAR from GOODBYE
Beautiful piano ballad. Newcastle has never sounded so poetic.

❹ SAY THE WORST THING FIRST from GOODBYE
Ugly truths are fearlessly confronted with sharp words, and producer Stephen Hague works his magic.

❺ STARS from DISGRACEFUL
The song that started it all off, with sliding bass, sparkling synths and Blackwood's melancholy voice on top form.

❻ WHEN THE WORLD KNOWS YOUR NAME from MAKE IT BETTER
This heartbreaker is probably Dubstar's greatest track. It's hard to stay composed when "the jukebox says our moment has arrived" and the chord change kicks in.

Robert Evers

Duets

Apart from opera and Broadway musicals, there aren't as many duets out there as you might imagine in the world of popular music. But these make you wish for more.

❶ I GOT U BABE SONNY & CHER from LOOK AT US
Romantic, bohemian and carefree, what pair of young lovers has not imagined this was written just for them?

❷ UNFORGETTABLE NAT KING COLE AND NATALIE COLE from UNFORGETTABLE
Some thought her duetting with her old man from beyond the grave was in bad taste. The five million who bought the album disagreed.

❸ FAIRY TALE OF NEW YORK KIRSTY MacCOLL AND SHANE MacGOWAN from IF I SHOULD FALL FROM GRACE WITH GOD
Possibly the only cool Christmas song ever.

❹ GIRL FROM THE NORTH COUNTRY BOB DYLAN AND JOHNNY CASH from NASHVILLE SKYLINE
The only track officially released from sessions for

what remains one of the great lost albums of our time.

❺ THIS ONE'S FROM THE HEART TOM WAITS AND CRYSTAL GAYLE from ONE FROM THE HEART
Beauty and the beast – an improbable but inspired pairing.

❻ ALL KINDS OF EVERYTHING SINEAD O'CONNOR AND TERRY HALL from COLLABORATIONS
You take a naff old Eurovision hit by Dana, an unhinged Irish diva and a grumpy bloke from The Specials and the result is genius.

❼ HENRY LEE PJ HARVEY AND NICK CAVE from MURDER BALLADS
They both shared a dark side, which is what drew them together – and forced them apart.

❽ JACKSON JOHNNY CASH AND JUNE CARTER CASH from JACKSON
George Jones and Tammy Wynette were the king and queen of country duets, but it's arguable whether they ever bettered this classic.

❾ LOVE HURTS GRAM PARSONS AND EMMYLOU HARRIS from GRIEVOUS ANGEL
They were born to sing together and more than thirty years after his death, Emmylou is still the keeper of his flame.

❿ AIN'T NO MOUNTAIN HIGH ENOUGH MARVIN GAYE & TAMMI TERRELL from UNITED
One of the most smouldering soul duets of all time.

Nigel Williamson

Duran Duran

Which one did you fancy? Two-tone wedge-cut bassist John Taylor or singer Simon Le Bon? New Romantic froth rarely came better. The 1993 reunion was fun, too.

❶ THE REFLEX from SEVEN AND THE RAGGED TIGER
The stuttering vocal intro lodges instantly in the brain on this polished, stadium-sized funk-pop piece .

❷ THE CHAUFFEUR from RIO
A masterpiece of mood and atmosphere, charged with detached, voyeuristic sexual tension. Sing blue silver, indeed.

❸ ORDINARY WORLD from THE WEDDING ALBUM
Mature songwriting ruled on this revivalist 1993 hit – Old Romanticism, if you will.

④ RIO from RIO

Ah, that video, the yacht, the supermodels, all that dayglo paint splashing around. A great Andy Taylor riff topped off with a suitably sultry sax solo. Effortless and chic.

⑤ GIRLS ON FILM from DURAN DURAN

Another great video, especially the X-rated late night version, and another pop classic. This is a perfect and preening hymn to a world of hedonistic decadence.

⑥ PLANET EARTH from DURAN DURAN

The epitome of New Romantic disco. The bouncing bassline demands you make a fool of yourself on the dancefloor.

⑦ ELECTRIC BARBARELLA from MEDAZZALAND

The 1997 album wasn't up to much, but this single was terrific: a tale of fetishistic robot-love that's creepy and addictive.

⑧ NEW MOON ON MONDAY from SEVEN AND THE RAGGED TIGER

Rhodes' keyboard flourishes really make this track, with what can only be described as a sonic firework display in the middle.

⑨ LONELY IN YOUR NIGHTMARE from RIO

It sounds almost as if John Taylor is making his bass talk on this number, understated compared with the exuberant excesses of the band's big hits, and all the better for it.

⑩ MY OWN WAY (SINGLE VERSION) from RIO

A brisk and sparkling funk gem decorated with splashy stabs of Technicolor disco strings missing from the album mix.

Essi Berelian

Ian Dury

Ian Dury's lyrics were poignant, confrontational and very funny. Combined with the Blockheads' funky music-hall style the result was a legend in British pop.

① HIT ME WITH YOUR RHYTHM STICK from SEX & DRUGS & ROCK & ROLL – THE BEST OF

Dury's having real fun with the lyrics and the joyously smooth disco vibes are simply terrific. Great sax and guitar solos too.

② MASH IT UP HARRY from MR LOVE PANTS

A brilliant latter-day slice of Blockheads bravura with a cheeky, witty set of lyrics and a sublime swing to proceedings.

③ MISCHIEF from DO IT YOURSELF

This sounds like an anarchist's manifesto set to a groovy rock track. Dury's soft, almost understated delivery makes it all the funnier.

④ REASONS TO BE CHEERFUL PART 3 from SEX & DRUGS & ROCK & ROLL – THE BEST OF

The NME dissed this as just a shopping list – but it's without doubt one of the best in pop history. Fantastic sax solo.

⑤ SEX AND DRUGS AND ROCK AND ROLL from SEX & DRUGS & ROCK & ROLL – THE BEST OF

What else is there really? Dury talks complete sense here. Slinky ivory tinkling midway through, plus cool animal noises at the end.

⑥ SPASTICUS AUTISTICUS from LORD UPMINSTER

Banned by the BBC, the frank and ironic lyrics will challenge your sensibilities, but the relentlessly funky rhythms command you to dance.

⑦ SWEET GENE VINCENT from NEW BOOTS AND PANTIES!!

Do you want to hear Dury doing sensitive instead of sweary? A wistful and nostalgic ballad opening leads to some good old fashioned rock'n'roll.

⑧ THERE AIN'T HALF BEEN SOME CLEVER BASTARDS from SEX & DRUGS & ROCK & ROLL – THE BEST OF

Dury proves that swearing is big and clever. Where else would you find Noël Coward, Einstein and Van Gogh rubbing shoulders? Clever bastards one and all.

⑨ UNEASY SUNNY DAY, HOTSY TOTSY from DO IT YOURSELF

Shut your gob! Up your bum! Dury's on a roll with this brisk trot of a political tune – if it doesn't make you laugh, something's wrong.

⑩ WAKE UP AND MAKE LOVE WITH ME from NEW BOOTS AND PANTIES!!

Great bassline, some fabulous Moog magic and some of Dury's most intimate, affectionate and funny lyrics.

Essi Berelian

Nigel Williamson on
Bob Dylan

There really is no one to touch Dylan in terms of essential catalogue: early acoustic, electric rebel, genius of rock's greatest album, *Blood On The Tracks*, and then the erratic deliverer on the Never-Ending Tour. NIGEL WILLIAMSON is a contributing editor to this book and author of *The Rough Guide To Bob Dylan*. At his bidding, we have given Bob a mighty four-part überlist.

The protest years

When he arrived in Greenwich Village in early 1961, Dylan was a scruffy Woody Guthrie wannabe singing other people's songs. Within little more than a year, he'd become the foremost songwriter of his generation. Two years later he was ready to leave folk and protest behind and sail into new and uncharted waters. The times they were a-changin' and Bob was in one helluva hurry to stay ahead of them.

❶ BLOWING IN THE WIND from
THE FREEWHEELIN' BOB DYLAN
How could you not start with this anthem? Yet oddly it was never a hit for Dylan, with Peter, Paul and Mary getting all the chart action.

❷ A HARD RAIN'S A GONNA FALL from
THE FREEWHEELIN' BOB DYLAN
Inspired by the Cuban missile crisis, almost every line could have made a song in itself. Dylan said at the time he put them together because he didn't know if there would be enough time left to write them all.

❸ DON'T THINK TWICE, IT'S ALL RIGHT from THE
FREEWHEELIN' BOB DYLAN
He could write tender love songs, too, when he wasn't too busy putting the world to rights.

❹ MASTERS OF WAR from THE FREEWHEELIN' BOB DYLAN
The angriest, most potent protest song he ever wrote – and as relevant today as it was forty-something years ago.

❺ MIXED UP CONFUSION from BIOGRAPH
An early rocker recorded at the time of the *Freewheelin'* sessions that pointed the way to what was to happen when he went electric.

❻ THE TIMES THEY ARE A-CHANGIN' from
NO DIRECTION HOME: THE SOUNDTRACK
Not the familiar studio version, but a jaw-dropping 1963 live performance featured in Martin Scorsese's splendid documentary.

❼ THE LONESOME DEATH OF HATTIE CARROLL from
THE TIMES THEY ARE A CHANGIN'
Stunning storytelling on one of Bob's most effective protest songs. As objective as a newspaper report but with an emotional punch so strong it required no rhetorical flourishes.

❽ CHIMES OF FREEDOM from ANOTHER SIDE OF BOB DYLAN
For the countless, "accused, misused … the abandoned and forsaked" – Dylan at his most humane and universal. Critic Paul Williams reckoned it Bob's "Sermon On The Mount".

❾ TO RAMONA from ANOTHER SIDE OF BOB DYLAN
The best of the several songs inspired by the end of Dylan's relationship with Suze Rotolo. That was her on the cover of *Freewheelin',* and when she turned up in Scorsese's 2005 biopic, she still looked like an angel.

❿ IT AIN'T ME BABE from ANOTHER SIDE OF BOB DYLAN
A farewell message to the folkies on his last all-acoustic album for almost thirty years.

Electric Messiah

Between 1965 and 1966, Dylan released the most audacious trilogy of rock albums ever made, a white-hot creative onslaught of breathtaking power and inventiveness. The folkies felt betrayed and booed him when he plugged in at Newport, backed by members of Paul Butterfield's blues band. Bloody but unbowed, his response was to recruit The Hawks (soon to become The Band) and launch a world tour.

❶ LIKE A ROLLING STONE from LIVE 1966
The infamous live version preceded by the shout of "Judas!". "I don't believe you. You're a liar", Dylan responds before turning to The Hawks and telling them to "Play fuckin' loud!" One of the most electrifying moments in rock'n'roll history.

❷ SUBTERRANEAN HOMESICK BLUES from BRINGING
IT ALL BACK HOME
Chuck Berry meets Woody Guthrie.

❸ BALLAD OF A THIN MAN from HIGHWAY 61 REVISITED
Even Dylan has never sneered better than on this classic put-down.

❹ DESOLATION ROW from HIGHWAY 61 REVISITED
He may have gone rock'n'roll, but the poetry remained peerless and he could still namecheck Ezra Pound *and* T.S. Eliot.

❺ VISIONS OF JOHANNA from BLONDE ON BLONDE
"Ain't it just like the night/To play tricks when you're trying to be so quiet." Perhaps his finest epic of all.

❻ SAD EYED LADY OF THE LOWLANDS from BLONDE ON BLONDE
The masterpiece that took up all of side four of Bob's 1966 double album.

❼ ONE OF US MUST KNOW (SOONER OR LATER) from BLONDE ON BLONDE
With Al Kooper's swirling organ, the epitome of what Dylan called "that wild mercury sound" and the first track recorded for *Blonde On Blonde*.

❽ POSITIVELY FOURTH STREET from BIOGRAPH
"You've got a lot of nerve to say you are my friend." Possibly the nastiest song ever written.

❾ CAN YOU PLEASE CRAWL OUT YOUR WINDOW from BIOGRAPH
Bob's third hit single in six months after "Rolling Stone" and "Positively 4th Street".

❿ TELL ME, MOMMA from LIVE 1966
A brilliant song which Dylan tried recording for *Blonde On Blonde*. It officially saw the light of day on the live album from his 1966 tour, eventually released in 1998.

After the crash

After a motorcycle crash in the autumn of 1966, Dylan retreated to Woodstock. When he re-emerged with *John Wesley Harding* he sounded very different. His output over the next eight years was decidedly patchy. Yet it contained some fine songs, even before the release of 1975's *Blood On The Tracks*, one of his absolute masterpieces.

❶ THIS WHEEL'S ON FIRE from THE BASEMENT TAPES
A rare co-write with The Band's Rick Danko. The words may or may not refer to that famous motorcycle crash.

❷ I SHALL BE RELEASED from THE BASEMENT TAPES
Revenge, faith and acceptance – and a chorus that delivers salvation more convincingly than anything from his "born again" phase.

❸ ALL ALONG THE WATCHTOWER from JOHN WESLEY HARDING
Hendrix made the song his own, and in concert Dylan follows the guitarist's super-charged arrangement. But the original has a stark and sombre beauty of its own.

❹ LAY LADY LAY from NASHVILLE SKYLINE
Believe it or not, the biggest hit single of his entire career…

❺ IF NOT FOR YOU from NEW MORNING
One of Dylan's simplest and most honest love songs, written for his wife Sara before it all went wrong (see #9, below).

❻ KNOCKING ON HEAVEN'S DOOR from PAT GARRETT & BILLY THE KID
It sounds like a hymn, and it lifted the soundtrack of Sam Peckinpah's film to another level.

❼ FOREVER YOUNG from PLANET WAVES
Written for his youngest son Jakob, the only one of Dylan's children to follow him into the rock'n'roll life.

❽ TANGLED UP IN BLUE from BLOOD ON THE TRACKS
The opening track of the greatest break-up album ever written.

❾ IDIOT WIND from BLOOD ON THE TRACKS
"Peace and quiet's been avoiding me so long, It seems like living hell". After ten years of marriage it was a very long way from "without your love I'd be nowhere at all" (see #5, above).

❿ SIMPLE TWIST OF FATE from BLOOD ON THE TRACKS
The softer side of the break-up – mournful, romantic and still hoping another twist might throw them back together again.

Bob ain't dead

You thought it was all over after *Blood On The Tracks*? Well it's not dark yet. In fact, it's not even getting there. Here are ten songs you need, from *Desire* onwards.

❶ HURRICANE from DESIRE
Hard on the heels of *Blood On The Tracks*, *Desire* got few plaudits. But for many it's an overlooked masterpiece and this song, with Dylan's voice counterpointed by Scarlet Rivera's violin, is one of his greatest.

Bob Dylan's
Bible theme time

In 2006, Dylan launched into a new career as a DJ and playlist compiler, with a "Theme Time Radio Show", on XM radio (www.xmradio.com). He has, to date, recorded more than fifty shows, each based on a theme, ranging through "Radio" to "Drink" to "Spring Cleaning" to 'The Bible'. Here's how the man introduced his Biblical selections: "For the next hour we're gonna be playin' music about Genesis, Exodus, Leviticus and Numbers, Deuteronomy, Joshua, Judges, The Wisdom of Solomon, First Maccabees and Second Maccabees, First Samuel and Second Samuel, First Kings, Second Kings. We're gonna be playing stuff that comes out of the Psalms and the Proverbs. You know all of these. Jonah and Malachi – how come nobody's named Malachi any more? We're gonna be playing music that has something to do with Nehemia, Esther, Job, Matthew, Mark, Luke and John. And of course, The Book of Revelations. So gather the family around the radio and hear the good news. Seek and you shall find."

❶ BOTTLE AND A BIBLE THE YAYHOOS from FEAR NOT THE OBVIOUS

❷ SAMSON AND DELILAH REV. GARY DAVIS from HARLEM STREET SINGER

❸ HE WILL SET YOUR FIELDS ON FIRE KITTY WELLS from QUEEN OF COUNTRY MUSIC 1949–1958

❹ ADAM COME AND GET YOUR RIB WYNONIE HARRIS from BIG HIT

❺ THE OLD ARKS A-MOVING A.A. GRAY & SEVEN FOOT DILLY from DOWN IN THE BASEMENT: JOE BUSSARD'S TREASURE TROVE OF VINTAGE 78'S: 1926–1937

❻ DENOMINATION BLUES PART 1 WASHINGTON PHILLIPS from STOREFRONT AND STREETCORNER GOSPEL (VARIOUS ARTISTS)

❼ I'M USING MY BIBLE FOR A ROADMAP RENO & SMILEY from DON REMO, RED SMILEY & THE TENNESSEE CUT-UP'S TALK OF THE TOWN

❽ I'M USING MY BIBLE FOR A ROADMAP THE FOUR INTERNS from BEST OF KING GOSPEL (VARIOUS ARTISTS)

❾ ELIJAH ROCK OLLABELLE FEATURING AMY HELM from OLLABELLE

❿ BY THE RIVERS OF BABYLON THE MELODIANS from YOUNG GIFTED AND BLACK

⓫ JOHN THE REVELATOR BLIND WILLIE JOHNSON from SWEETER AS THE YEARS GO BY

⓬ BOOGIE WOOGIE PREACHIN' MAN JESS WILLARD from HONKY TONK HARDWOOD FLOOR

⓭ OH MARY, DON'T YOU WEEP THE SWAN SILVERTONES from WONDERFUL MEMORIES FROM THE FAMILY PRAYERBOOK: (VARIOUS ARTISTS)

⓮ THAT'S WHAT THE GOOD BOOK SAYS THE ROBINS from MELLOW CATS N KITTENS: HOT R&B AND COOL BLUES 1946–52 (VARIOUS ARTISTS)

❷ CHANGING OF THE GUARDS from STREET LEGAL
A storming, anger-charged, momentum-laden anti-anthem. Like many of Bob's most rewarding songs, the precise meaning is wide open to interpretation.

❸ PRECIOUS ANGEL from SLOW TRAIN COMING
The most tender song from the first and best of the gospel albums (1979). Try those high notes yourself – they are not easy, nor meant to be.

❹ BLIND WILLIE MCTELL from THE BOOTLEG SERIES VOL 3
A Deep South song from 1983 that would feel at home

in any Dylan decade. Sin, the blues and one of Bob's most haunting tunes, in honour of the legendary bluesman.

❺ JOKERMAN from INFIDELS
Lyrically a kind of Mr Tambourine Man for the 1980s; musically, just a nice cool breeze.

❻ BROWNSVILLE GIRL from KNOCKED OUT LOADED
Dylan goes to the movies in 1985. He's in the front row with soaring girlie chorus watching Gregory Peck. Or is it Gregory Peck?

⑦ TWEETER AND THE MONKEY MAN from TRAVELLING WILBURYS VOL 1

A New Jersey crime thriller yarn with the poser: who is the monkey man? The vocalist – on *Blonde On Blonde*-style form – is easier to suss on this 1988 outing.

⑧ CAN'T WAIT from TIME OUT OF MIND

Dylan twanging and impatient – full of a taut energy rare in an otherwise magnificently resigned must-have album from 1997.

⑨ NOT DARK YET from TIME OUT OF MIND

Dylan seems to foresee his death: "It's not dark yet, but it's getting there." Emmylou Harris reckoned it "the greatest song ever about growing old… it brings up things we didn't even know we were capable of feeling".

⑩ THINGS HAVE CHANGED from THE BEST OF BOB DYLAN VOL 2

Dylan for the couldn't-care-less generation, used in the 1999 movie, *Wonder Boys*. Almost bouncy. The times had a-changed again.

Nigel Williamson/Andrew Lockett

Dylan covers

They didn't necessarily *improve* on the originals, but all these interpretations added something fresh and new.

① MR TAMBOURINE MAN THE BYRDS from MR TAMBOURINE MAN

The rhythm was changed from 3/4 to 4/4, McGuinn added his jangling electric twelve-string, and folk-rock was born.

② WHEN I PAINT MY MASTERPIECE THE BAND from CAHOOTS

They'd backed him when he was being booed and they let him record *The Basement Tapes* at their house, so it was no surprise that they covered him better than most.

③ THIS WHEEL'S ON FIRE JULIE DRISCOLL, BRIAN AUGER & THE TRINITY from A KIND OF LOVE-IN

The spookiest version ever of one of Dylan's spookiest songs – later adopted as the theme of TV comedy *Absolutely Fabulous*.

④ PERCY'S SONG FAIRPORT CONVENTION from UNHALFBRICKING

A heartbreaking vocal from the late Sandy Denny on a song Dylan himself didn't officially release until sixteen years later.

⑤ IT AIN'T ME BABE JOHNNY CASH from THE ESSENTIAL JOHNNY CASH

Well, he could sing anything and make it sound his own (even a Nine Inch Nails song).

⑥ ALL ALONG THE WATCHTOWER THE JIMI HENDRIX EXPERIENCE from ELECTRIC LADYLAND

After this, the song was never the same again, and even Dylan copied Hendrix's arrangement in concert.

⑦ LIKE A ROLLING STONE SPIRIT from SPIRIT OF '76

The hardest jewel in the Dylan crown to cover, Randy California's band managed it by shrouding the song in a shimmering, ethereal beauty.

⑧ CHIMES OF FREEDOM YOUSSOU N'DOUR from WOMMAT (THE GUIDE)

A protest anthem given an entirely new meaning in an African context.

⑨ EVERY GRAIN OF SAND EMMYLOU HARRIS from WRECKING BALL

An almost spiritual version of one of Dylan's later masterpieces.

⑩ MAGGIE'S FARM THE SPECIALS from THE SINGLES COLLECTION

It's 1981 and Thatcherism is in full cry, so you can guess which Maggie they didn't want to work for.

Nigel Williamson

Eagles & Doobies

LA country-flavoured rock dominated the US through the 1970s – and The Eagles' *Greatest Hits* is still the biggest-selling album of all time.

❶ HOTEL CALIFORNIA THE EAGLES from HOTEL CALIFORNIA
Perhaps the most paranoid track about being a crazy rock star ever written. Should be declared California's state anthem.

❷ DESPERADO THE EAGLES from DESPERADO
Guaranteed to moisten eyes in biker bars across the US.

❸ TAKE IT EASY THE EAGLES from THE EAGLES
Co-written by Jackson Browne, this power ballad defined LA as the place for laidback dudes who, while getting high and rich, philosophized about life.

❹ TAKE IT TO THE LIMIT THE EAGLES from ONE OF THESE NIGHTS
Fine harmony vocals caress a very LA lyric, helping to build this slice of country rock into a man's-gotta-do-what-he's-gotta-do epic.

❺ LIFE IN THE FAST LANE THE EAGLES from HOTEL CALIFORNIA
Joe Walsh is snarling on guitar and the boys are telling how tough you gotta be to cope with all the women, drugs and fame. A record so macho it'll put hairs on your chest.

❻ BLACK WATER THE DOOBIE BROTHERS from WHAT WERE ONCE VICES ARE NOW HABITS
Country rock never had a tighter groove than this US #1 hit from 1974. As the chorus bubbles up you can't help being hooked.

❼ JESUS IS JUST ALRIGHT THE DOOBIE BROTHERS from TOULOUSE STREET
This snappy, gospel-flavoured hit is a cool tribute to J Christ, man o' the people.

❽ TAKIN' IT TO THE STREETS THE DOOBIE BROTHERS from TAKIN' IT TO THE STREETS
For white boys, The Doobies were pretty funky, especially on this track, to which ex-Steely Dan vocalist Michael McDonald brings an R&B flavour.

❾ LISTEN TO THE MUSIC THE DOOBIE BROTHERS from TOULOUSE STREET
An annoyingly infectious early 1970s tune. Lots of "whoo whoos" that today go down well in karaoke clubs.

❿ WHAT A FOOL BELIEVES THE DOOBIE BROTHERS from MINUTE BY MINUTE
Classic slice of blue-eyed soul that topped charts internationally.

Garth Cartwright

Steve Earle

Drugs, divorce, jail – Steve Earle's motto seems to be that you can't sing about it if you haven't lived it. Here are ten of his most uncompromising statements.

❶ GUITAR TOWN from GUITAR TOWN
Not so much an anthem as a manifesto: "Gotta keep rockin' while I still can/I gotta two-pack habit and a motel tan/But when my boots hit the boards I'm a brand new man/With my back to the riser, I make my stand."

❷ COPPERHEAD ROAD from COPPERHEAD ROAD
Magnificent twang-infested hard-rock on a knock-'em-dead tale of hillbilly bootleggers turned 'Nam vet drug-runners.

❸ THE DEVIL'S RIGHT HAND from COPPERHEAD ROAD
The original country outlaw Waylon Jennings covered it – but this is still the definitive renegade version.

❹ JOHNNY COME LATELY from COPPERHEAD ROAD
Backed by The Pogues with predictably rowdy and rousing results.

❺ GOODBYE from TRAIN A-COMIN'
One of Earle's tenderest lost-love songs, written for his first album after his release from jail (and then brilliantly covered by Emmylou Harris).

❻ CHRISTMAS IN WASHINGTON from EL CORAZON
"Come back Woody Guthrie, come back to us now…" If he did, he'd probably be Steve Earle.

❼ ELLIS UNIT ONE from DEAD MAN WALKING SOUNDTRACK

Written for Tim Robbins' death-row movie – "even Jesus couldn't save me, though I know he did his best…"

❽ THE MOUNTAIN from THE MOUNTAIN

The best track from an album recorded with the Del McCoury Band. Bluegrass hadn't sounded this *edgy* in decades.

❾ OVER YONDER (JONATHAN'S SONG) from TRANSCENDENTAL BLUES

An even more unflinching treatment of the same subject as Ellis Unit One, made more personal by being about Jonathan Wayne Nobles, whom Earle befriended and then watched die in the electric chair.

❿ JOHN WALKER'S BLUES from JERUSALEM

Who else would or could write a song from the point of the view of an incarcerated American Taliban fighter, other than the Woody Guthrie of his times?

Nigel Williamson

Earth, Wind & Fire

Levitating bass players, all-seeing pyramids, metaphysical mumbo jumbo … what tended to get lost was that underneath all of that was a truly brilliant big band funk outfit.

❶ THAT'S THE WAY OF THE WORLD from THAT'S THE WAY OF THE WORLD

Shows off all the band can do – intricate harmonies, layered instrumentation, clever percussion, while they're not yet quite mad enough to be scaling the cosmic pyramid.

❷ SUN GODDESS RAMSEY LEWIS FEATURING EARTH WIND & FIRE from SUN GODDESS

Maurice White used to be Ramsey Lewis's drummer, hence the connection, but this semi-instrumental of dazzlingly mellow jazz funk beauty is much more about EWF.

❸ SERPENTINE FIRE from ALL 'N ALL

That EWF could be straight up funky was never in doubt but seldom exhibited. This is one of those wonderfully uncomplicated occasions.

❹ FANTASY from ALL 'N ALL

When most people think of Earth, Wind & Fire, they're probably thinking of this tune. Possibly the most uplifting, stupidly optimistic anthem you'll ever hear.

❺ LET'S GROOVE from RAISE!

Taut, swinging and surprisingly straightforward – ie more concerned with pleasures of the flesh than anything quasi-spiritual. It can still rock a dancefloor.

❻ SHINING STAR from THAT'S THE WAY OF THE WORLD

More about the singing than the playing, and shows that even without the mega productions of later years they had the power to entrance and surprise.

❼ AFTER THE LOVE IS GONE from I AM

What ought to be a straight ahead pop song is so much more thanks to an arrangement that puts a 1970s funk take a classic soul revue style.

❽ I'LL WRITE A SONG FOR YOU from ALL 'N ALL

By EWF standards this is virtually a cappella, a masterpiece of crisp, restrained vocal soul.

❾ RUNNIN'/BRAZILIAN RHYME INTERLUDE FROM All 'N All

Samba style funk driven by brass and topped off with some of the breeziest vocals this side of Sugarloaf Mountain.

❿ BOOGIE WONDERLAND EARTH, WIND & FIRE FEATURING THE EMOTIONS from I AM

The Emotions' vocals sparring with the group's elevate what could be generic into a soaring, rousing funk soul classic that at five minutes is frustratingly short.

Lloyd Bradley

Easy Rider

Whip out those mirror shades…

❶ MOTORBIKIN' DEE DEE RAMONE from GREATEST & LATEST

The original lacks the guts of Dee Dee's version, to which Chris Spedding (who wrote the song and took it to the charts back in 1977) chips in guitar skills and studio expertise.

❷ BORN TO BE WILD THE CULT from ELECTRIC

Ian Astbury gets back to his hard-rockin' roots in this superior reworking of the old Steppenwolf number. Rick Rubin's masterful production adds a hard and sharp 1980s edge.

❸ WHITE LINE FEVER MERLE HAGGARD from OKIE FROM MUSKOGEE

Your bike might be fast, but Merle reminds you that no matter what you do, "the years keep flying by like the highline poles" and that all those miles will just put wrinkles on your forehead.

❹ THE ROAD'S MY MIDDLE NAME BONNIE RAITT from NICK OF TIME
She's wild and free, and she lives for the thrill of a motorcycle ride. Sadly, she doesn't exist – except in songs like this gem from Bonnie.

❺ MOTORBIKE BEAT THE REVILLOS from TOTALLY ALIVE IN LONDON
A cylinder-cracking piece of rock'n'roll, complete with engine effect and the echoing vocals of Ms Fay Fife.

❻ ROLL ON DOWN THE HIGHWAY BACHMAN-TURNER OVERDRIVE from THE COLLECTION
The big, bearded fellers from Canada tell it like it is in this slice of motorcycle outlaw life. Will make you yearn for the smell of petrol.

❼ TWO-LANE BLACKTOP ROB ZOMBIE from PAST, PRESENT AND FUTURE
Hard-grinding road song that revs and throttles like an overloaded Bonneville pushing on a bad stretch of hill.

❽ TAKE THE HIGHWAY THE MARSHALL TUCKER BAND from ANTHOLOGY: THE FIRST 30 YEARS
A country-coloured tale of farewell in which the pull of the endless trail wins out over the desire to remain with the one you love.

Al Spicer

Eels

Eels – Mark Everett – have been turning out weird, crafted, Copland-esque pop for a decade.

❶ OVERTURE from OH, WHAT A BEAUTIFUL MORNING
From the live album, this Eels primer blends bits of all the band's hits into a theatrical, over-the-top overture.

❷ NOVOCAINE FOR THE SOUL from BEAUTIFUL FREAK
Eels' big break in the mid-1990s, much weirder than most radio hits, and still sounding fresh.

❸ LAST STOP: THIS TOWN from ELECTRO-SHOCK BLUES
Bizarre baroque pop song, with an infectious rhythm track, shout-along chorus and guitar-freakout bridge.

❹ CLIMBING TO THE MOON from ELECTRO-SHOCK BLUES
Heartbreaking centrepiece of E's best record, perhaps written from the perspective of his late, mentally ill sister.

❺ GRACE KELLY BLUES from DAISIES OF THE GALAXY
The forlorn, pedal-steel-adorned first track from E's "happy" album, with joyful lyrics like "I think, you

know, I'll be okay".

❻ MR E'S BEAUTIFUL BLUES from DAISIES OF THE GALAXY
One of E's catchiest pop gems, and typical of his foul-mouthed enthusiasm for life: "Goddamn right it's a beautiful day".

❼ SOULJACKER, PART 1 from SOULJACKER
The standout from Everett's "hard" album, a grungey, tribal, fuzzed-out rave-up about a serial killer called "Souljacker".

❽ RAILROAD MAN from BLINKING LIGHTS AND OTHER REVELATIONS
E heads out on the rails in this foot-tappin', countryfied ramblin' song from his return-to-form album.

❾ THINGS THE GRANDCHILDREN SHOULD KNOW from BLINKING LIGHTS AND OTHER REVELATIONS
E's last will and testament, where the enigmatic songwriter declares: "If I had to do it all over again, it's something I'd like to do".

❿ P.S. YOU ROCK MY WORLD from ELECTRO-SHOCK BLUES
Electro-Shock Blues, which grew out of the death of E's mother and sister, ends with this tragic yet oddly life-affirming masterpiece.

Hunter Slaton

Electric Light Orchestra

Starting off as a Move offshoot project featuring Roy Wood and Jeff Lynne, ELO took their Beatles-influenced, string-laden rock to the tops of the charts around the globe.

❶ 10538 OVERTURE from THE ELECTRIC LIGHT ORCHESTRA
This is where it all started. Originally an idea for a Move track by Jeff Lynne, it was beefed up with Roy Wood sawing away madly on the cello. Still sounds scintillating.

❷ ALL SHE WANTED from ZOOM
From a solo LP in all but name, Jeff Lynne handles almost everything on this honky-tonk style rocker, save some cool slide guitar from George Harrison.

❸ MISSION A WORLD RECORD from A NEW WORLD RECORD
Sci-fi rock'n'roll from the 1970s. The denizens of a

visiting space craft cast a critical eye over this curiously beautiful planet. Features some very cool funky keyboards.

❹ MR BLUE SKY from OUT OF THE BLUE
Another instant classic. A very tasteful guitar solo decorates the mid section, but the clever and breathy vocal harmonies are the obvious highlight.

❺ ROCKARIA from A NEW WORLD RECORD
You can really hear the makings of "Out Of The Blue" on this string-heavy homage to classic rock 'n' roll. Features superb operatic vocals and some gritty guitar riffing.

❻ ROLL OVER BEETHOVEN from ELO2
Plenty of ivory tinkling and some dramatic string section action as the Chuck Berry standard gets the overblown orchestral treatment.

❼ STANDIN' IN THE RAIN from OUT OF THE BLUE
The kick-off to "Concerto For A Rainy Day" is a lush and complex affair, packed with phased vocals and seductive string arrangements.

❽ SWEET TALKIN' WOMAN from OUT OF THE BLUE
An unmistakeable intro; faux classical violins merge with phased vocals before the main acoustic riff lifts off. Sheer Beatlesy genius.

❾ THE DIARY OF HORACE WIMP from DISCOVERY
How poor old timid Horace landed himself a wife. Among the usual slinky strings this features a great voice-of-God type chorus telling our hero what to do.

❿ TURN TO STONE from OUT OF THE BLUE
The intro fades in like a 747 zooming overhead. One of Jeff Lynne's finest compositions, the vocal harmonies almost kiss your ears they're so awesome.

Essi Berelian

Duke Ellington

When it comes to jazz nobility, no one holds a higher position than the Duke, one of the greatest composers – and certainly the greatest bandleader – in twentieth-century music. His recorded legacy was immense, so the following selection only highlights the tip of an enormous iceberg.

❶ BLACK AND TAN FANTASY from MASTERPIECES
A 1927 minor blues designed to show off the extraordinary plunger mute work of co-writer Bubber Miley.

❷ SINGLE PETAL OF A ROSE from THE QUEEN'S SUITE
From a 1959 suite privately recorded, pressed on a single disc and delivered to Queen Elizabeth at Buckingham Palace, this lovely arpeggiated piano piece shows Ellington at his most sumptuous.

❸ THE MOOCHE from MASTERPIECES
A prowling, haunting 1928 theme for wailing clarinets, named after the shuffling dance craze of the late 1920s, but performed by Duke's orchestra into the 60s.

❹ ROCKIN' IN RHYTHM from MASTERPIECES
Tightly arranged for the saxophone section, this intricate 1931 melody pointed the way for the big-band swing era and became one of Ellington's most enduring instrumentals.

❺ REMINISCING IN TEMPO from MASTERPIECES
After flirting with longer forms (notably on "Creole Rhapsody") Ellington expressed his grief following his mother's death in 1935 with this dense and beautiful thirteen-minute composition.

❻ CARAVAN from MASTERPIECES
An early attempt to import musical textures from foreign lands, this 1937 piece of Eastern exotica featured the Latin-tinged trombone of co-composer Juan Tizol.

❼ KO-KO from MASTERPIECES
Dark and mysterious, this 1940 composition is a series of increasingly intense blues choruses, with star soloists Tizol and Jimmy Blanton (bass) contributing to the sultry heat.

❽ CONCERTO FOR COOTIE from MASTERPIECES
A subtly arranged 1940 showcase for trumpeter Cootie Williams, who delivers three distinct themes on mute, growl plunger and open horn.

❾ MADNESS IN GREAT ONES from SUCH SWEET THUNDER
From Duke's 1957 Shakespearean Suite, an imaginative portrait of Hamlet's unbalanced state, with high-note specialist "Cat" Anderson providing suitably frantic musical hysteria.

❿ ISFAHAN from FAR EAST SUITE
Co-composed with Billy Strayhorn in 1965, this lusciously harmonized piece was a perfect showcase for Johnny Hodges' liquid alto sax.

Chris Ingham

Eminem

More than just another white guy selling black music to middle-class kids so they can scare their parents, Eminem has brought a healthy dose of humour and self-doubt into a scene crippled by machismo and bragging.

❶ MY NAME IS from THE SLIM SHADY LP
Eminem exploded onto the scene with this, one of the great "this is me, who tha fuck are you?" songs. Stylistically, Snoop Dogg is never far away.

❷ '97 BONNIE & CLYDE from THE SLIM SHADY LP
Chilling little fairytale of spouse murder couched in terms of a daddy taking his li'l daughter to the beach with mom's corpse in the trunk.

❸ JUST DON'T GIVE A FUCK from THE SLIM SHADY LP
You're a teenager, you're alienated, you just got ordered to clean your room. You need this song, whose beats are heavy enough to cover up your stomping compliance.

❹ STAN from THE MARSHALL MATHERS LP
OK, it unleashed a tide of Dido on a world that deserved better, but as a response/coda to "'97 Bonnie And Clyde", it can't be beat.

❺ THE WAY I AM from THE MARSHALL MATHERS LP
Our man Marshall muses on the price of fame.

❻ THE REAL SLIM SHADY from THE MARSHALL MATHERS LP
Kinda ironic, coming from a guy who dresses like a clone from the zone, but this ditty of imitation is one of his funniest tunes.

❼ WHITE AMERICA from THE EMINEM SHOW
Eminem roars his defiance (again) with some masterful use of the English language.

❽ WITHOUT ME from THE EMINEM SHOW
A consummate piece of white hip-hop. Committed, erudite even, our hero explains his stand and why he's still essential to the rap scene.

❾ LOSE YOURSELF from 8 MILE SOUNDTRACK
From Eminem's movie debut, this ode to stage-fright, overcoming it and the rush that follows encapsulates the feeling that turns every performer into an addict.

❿ LIKE TOY SOLDIERS from ENCORE
The sweetness of the ultra-corny sample (from Martika's "Toy Soldiers") threatens to overwhelm the evident sincerity of Eminem's regretful reminiscences but never succeeds, with the resulting single turning

out successful, catchy and with a bit of luck influential in increasing the peace.

Al Spicer

English eccentrics

Quirky or cool, the eccentrics of English pop are a genuine national treasure.

❶ TRAMS OF OLD LONDON ROBYN HITCHCOCK from I OFTEN DREAM OF TRAINS
A lovely evocation of some of the city's most charming street names and districts, marred only by the unforgivable couplet "Oh, it seems like ancient myth/They once ran to Hammersmith".

❷ GOOD BOY KEVIN COYNE from MARJORY RAZORBLADE
Viciously patronizing compliments from some unspecified authority blended with hostility from ill-defined peers and accompanied by the most angry acoustic guitar you've ever heard.

❸ SUNSHINE SUPERMAN DONOVAN from SUNSHINE SUPERMAN
Once he stumbled out of Dylan's shadow, Donovan created some great psychedelia, such as this splendid little number, which struts like a hippy grooving up Portobello Road.

❹ KING'S LEAD HAT BRIAN ENO from BEFORE AND AFTER SCIENCE
Gleefully intense, happily pointless and guaranteed to pack experimental disco dancefloors, this is Eno at his pre-ambient best, all feathers, flounces and random synth settings.

❺ AT LAST I AM FREE ROBERT WYATT from HIS GREATEST MISSES
Wyatt couldn't have picked a more poignant tune to cover, and couldn't have treated it with greater respect.

❻ EFFERVESCING ELEPHANT SYD BARRETT from BARRETT/THE MADCAP LAUGHS
Before the Pink Floyd founder plunged into seclusion, he recorded a brace of solo albums that show him still welling over with creativity and stoned stories for kids, like this charming tale of life in the jungle.

❼ CRACKS ARE SHOWING VIV STANSHALL from TEDDY BOYS DON'T KNIT
After the Bonzo Dog Band, Viv made it to the studio on several occasions, letting a hint of his madness and misery slip through into tracks such as this.

❽ SAFESURFER JULIAN COPE from PEGGY SUICIDE
Close lyrical analysis reveals this song to have some connection with love in a time of plague, prophylaxis and seduction. But forget the details – check out that guitar solo!

❾ WUTHERING HEIGHTS KATE BUSH from THE WHOLE STORY
Kate's master musicianship is often neglected in the rush to describe her eccentricities, but this catchy, complex track – with precise, coloratura vocals – still has the power to stun.

❿ CHILD OF MY KINGDOM ARTHUR BROWN from THE CRAZY WORLD OF ARTHUR BROWN
A stoned soul picnic. Arthur contributes mystic folde-rol and viola; his merry men bring along music-hall stylings and some ripe, cheesy jazz.

Al Spicer

21st-century English folk

Most of the great "source" artists of English traditional music are long gone, the giants of the 1960s folk revival are now whiskery oldsters, and Irish and Scottish music has held the limelight in the UK for several decades. But in the 21st century there has been a rebirth of passion for English traditional folk song and dance music, with a new generation of artists injecting new life into old forms.

❶ PRETTY PLOUGHBOY ELIZA CARTHY from ANGLICANA
Singer, fiddler, bandleader, writer – this talented scion of the Waterson/Carthy dynasty takes no prisoners.

❷ MONKEY COKEY JOHN SPIERS & JON BODEN from TUNES
As a melodeon, fiddle and vocal duo or fronting their eleven-piece big-band Bellowhead, "Squeezy & Stompy" have even inspired crowd surfing at recent festivals.

❸ LORD BATEMAN CHRIS WOOD from THE LARK DESCENDING
An entrancing singer and fiddler, and a peerless arranger and writer, Chris Wood shines on this tradi-tional number.

❹ THE WEDDING/BECAUSE HE WAS A BONNY LAD KATHRYN TICKELL from DEBATABLE LANDS
Tickell's take on this slice of the Northumbrian tradi-tion shows the trailblazing piper (who was a role model for the new wave of performers in the 1980s) at her best.

❺ GYPSIES JIM MORAY from SWEET ENGLAND
Controversial, original and questing, Jim Moray was the man who dared take a laptop to folk gigs. Here he adds crisp electric guitar to a well-worn number.

❻ THE LYKE WAKE DIRGE ALASDAIR ROBERTS from NO EARTHLY MAN
Roberts came from an indie-rock background to become one of the most intriguing writers of songs in the traditional style – and then a performer of the old ones, such as this great lyric ballad.

❼ DOWNHILL DREAM HEKETY from FURZE CAT
A great piece of "e-ceilidh", the new wave of country dancing that's proving to be one of the fastest-grow-ing strands of English folk.

❽ POLLY OLIVER EMILY PORTMAN & LAUREN MCCORMICK from SONG LINKS 2
A fine showcase for two stunning young singers – both of them graduates of Newcastle University's recently inaugurated folk-music course.

❾ THE CREEL THE DEMON BARBER ROADSHOW from WAXED
All English folk life is here – a core folk/rock band fronted by Damien Barber and Bryony Griffith, plus fast-moving rappers, and morris and mini-skirted clog dancers. Spectacular!

❿ BARHAM DOWN/ THE YELLOW JOAK THE GLOWORMS from BEAM
Impressive hornpipes from the English country dance trio headed up by dynamo fiddler and folk advocate Laurel Swift.

Ian Anderson

Brian Eno

Eno doesn't have a TV, so he has more time than other people. Or that's his story. But to leaf through his credits, since forming and leaving Roxy Music thirty years ago, is quite awesome. He invented ambient as a genre decades before its time; has produced outstanding work from Bowie, U2, John Cale and Talking Heads; and his own songs are quiet masterpieces. He declined to contribute a playlist to this book by the way: he doesn't approve of "list culture".

❶ BABY'S ON FIRE from HERE COME THE WARM JETS
It's 1973 and Eno is not long out of Roxy, citing musical differences. But this great funk number would have been a huge Roxy hit. Instead, it got treated to a fabulous Fripp guitar solo.

❷ ON SOME FARAWAY BEACH from HERE COME THE WARM JETS
Simplicity itself: two notes that gradually build to a swirl of orchestral voices and guitar before, almost as an afterthought, a song drifts in.

❸ I'LL COME RUNNING (TO TIE YOUR SHOE) from ANOTHER GREEN WORLD
You don't think of Eno as a lyricist, but this is a witty, affecting song. What a great title – and the treated guitar is splendid, too.

❹ ANOTHER GREEN WORLD from ANOTHER GREEN WORLD
A slice of artful wistfulness that most Brits can actually hum (due to years of use as the theme tune for BBC arts documentary series *Arena*).

❺ SLOW WATER from MUSIC FOR FILMS
Music For Films is a wonderful album, including some pieces that sound like they *should* be used in movies, and others that really are, such as this delicate wonder, which graced Derek Jarman's *Jubilee*.

❻ WARSZAWA DAVID BOWIE from LOW
Summoned to Berlin by Bowie, Eno propelled him in a new direction that spawned his last great song, "Heroes", and this wordless wonder.

❼ HERE HE COMES from BEFORE AND AFTER SCIENCE
Catchy as they come: a great tune, set to a glimmer of guitars. Eno picked it to kick off his own Desert Island selection of his work.

❽ 1/1 from MUSIC FOR AIRPORTS
More ambient than a cloud of helium, this is a sumptuous cut from Eno's most influential instrumental set.

❾ DEEP BLUE DAY from APOLLO
Originally written to accompany footage of the Apollo space missions, these tones were more recently heard on the soundtrack of *Trainspotting*.

❿ AND THEN SO CLEAR from ANOTHER DAY ON EARTH
Just when you thought Eno had forsaken songs, back

he comes with an album full of them, including this marvel of Vocodered voice.

Mark Ellingham

E.S.T.

Since their first release in 1993, the Esbjörn Svensson Trio has been tirelessly re-inventing the traditional jazz trio format of piano, bass and drums. There's no other pianist like Svensson, and his is a jazz trio that rocks!

❶ WHEN GOD CREATED THE COFFEE BREAK from STRANGE PLACE FOR SNOW
Esbjörn and bassist Dan Berglund put together one of the most savage bass patterns in modern jazz. Not to be played while driving.

❷ GOOD MORNING SUSIE SOHO from GOOD MORNING SUSIE SOHO
The title-track from E.S.T.'s third album, this has become the band's signature piece.

❸ BEMSHA SWING from ESBJÖRN SVENSSON TRIO PLAYS MONK
A top cut from the only E.S.T. album where the material is not original. Monk would be proud.

❹ SERENADE FOR THE RENEGADE from STRANGE PLACE FOR SNOW
Subtle electronics and piano "treatments" (such as the placing of a steel pipe on the instrument's strings) give way to a wonderfully haunting, lilting melody.

❺ MINGLE IN THE MINCING-MACHINE from SEVEN DAYS OF FALLING
Dan Berglund's fuzzed-out double-bass solo is like nothing else in jazz-trio history.

❻ SEVEN DAYS OF FALLING from SEVEN DAYS OF FALLING
What E.S.T. does best. Sit back, close your eyes and be transported.

❼ LOVE IS REAL VIKTORIA TOLSTOY from SHINING ON YOU BY
This cover of E.S.T.'s Believe, Beleft, Below is 100% true to the original, but Tolstoy has a far better voice than Svensson. One of the most beautiful jazz ballad recordings ever made.

Geoff Colquitt

Ian Anderson's
European roots

IAN ANDERSON has edited *fRoots* – the pioneering folk/world music magazine formerly known as *Folk Roots* – for the past twenty-odd years. He has championed the idea of listening to the music of other countries and cultures – and in particular the many roots-based styles found across Europe. But he puts it all much better himself: "You may think, when you turn on your radio in any European capital – London no exception – that globalized American pop has obliterated most traces of regional individuality. But down at the roots you can increasingly find joyful new noises as local cultures fight back in a myriad of inventive ways. The new music starts here."

❶ LA FIESTA AMPARANOIA from SOMOS VIENTO
Leading Spain's mestizo scene, Amparo Sanchez's party band mix roots from Mexico to the Balkans with songs and a voice to die for.

❷ LO GABIAN MOUSSU T E LEI JOVENTS from MADEMOISELLE MARSEILLE
This spin-off group from ragamuffins Massillia Sound System creatively fire up the cultural blender that is Marseille.

❸ MOJIMIR NOVAKOVIC I KRIES KOLENDE from IVO I MARA
Croatian folklore looking outwards: big vocals, bagpipes, lijericas and beatboxes.

❹ AIRE DE RIEN JAUNE TOUJOURS from BARRICADE
Like their Belgian compatriots Think Of One, Jaune Toujours have a high-energy mix of roots musics from across Europe with brass, rock and politics.

❺ O TURCO NISTANIMERA from CHORÉ
From the deep south of Italy, where there's still a Greek-speaking minority and North Africa is closer than most of Europe.

❻ LO PRUMIER DE MAI LA TALVERA from POBLE MON POBLE
Occitan folk music from southern France, collected at source and given a 21st-century spin.

❼ RAMBLING SAILOR BELLOWHEAD from E.P.ONYMOUS
England erupts in a blaze of brass, strings and squeezebox: Benjamin Britten meets Kool & The Gang.

❽ CLOSE MY EYES KRISTI STASSINOPOULOU from THE SECRET OF THE ROCKS
Out of the Athens rock underground, adapting electronica and world music to Greek island traditions and inspirations.

❾ MAKEDÓN BESH O DROM from CYI!
Futuristic hi-energy Hungarian wedding band: Balkan Gypsy meets jazz and a scratching DJ.

❿ GRIMBORG GJALLARHORN from GRIMBORG
Nordic folk musicians do cool and moodily atmospheric as second nature: this Swedish quartet do it with a special energy.

Eurovision

Inexplicably taken seriously by audiences across continental Europe, despite the screaming histrionics, lyrical inanities and vaguely scary dance routines, the Eurovision Song Contest is viewed in the UK as a piece of camp heaven. Here's a selection of cheese that the French Agricultural Commission would be proud of.

❶ NEL BLU DI PINTO DI BLU ("VOLARE") DOMENICO MODUGNO from THE STORY OF EUROVISION
A 1958 corker straight outta *La Dolce Vita* and responsible in part for the world's romantic adoration of *la bellissima Italia*.

❷ POUPÉE DE CIRE POUPÉE DE SON FRANCE GALL from THE STORY OF EUROVISION
Strangely, this engaging 1965 ditty failed to do the same for the Luxembourg tourist industry.

❸ **CONGRATULATIONS** CLIFF RICHARD from EUROVISION VOL 2

Shredding the little credibility he'd carried into the era of free love, Cliff was first inflicted on the wider European audience with this 1968 entry – a piece of irrepressible singalong dross.

❹ **WATERLOO** ABBA from EUROVISION VOL 2

ABBA turn the bloody carnage of 1815 into a jaunty metaphor for total submission in love.

❺ **SAVE YOUR KISSES FOR ME** BROTHERHOOD OF MAN from EUROVISION 1956–1999

Known to a generation of school kids as "Kippers For Tea", this 1976 entry launched BoM into a career in cruise-ship entertainment and northern British caba-ret clubs. Justice is done.

❻ **NE PARTEZ PAS SANS MOI** CÉLINE DION from EUROVISION VOL 2

Born in Quebec, previously unrecognized as an outpost of the Swiss empire, Dion was nonetheless chosen to warble this uninspired material to the top of the Eurovision chart.

❼ **DIVA** DANA INTERNATIONAL from EUROVISION VOL 2

This victorious 1998 entry from Israel (part of the Eurovision TV distribution network) captures the ideals of the contest better than any.

❽ **MY NUMBER ONE** HELENA PAPARIZOU from MY NUMBER ONE

In 21st-century entries such as this (Greece, 2005) the "la la la" is replaced by a synthesized "boom boom boom". But, as ever, the music is corny, the outfits outrageous and the presenters hilariously sincere. Long live Eurovision!

Al Spicer

Eurythmics

The finest of the his'n'hers synth'n'diva duos. Their solo careers have never quite matched up.

❶ **TAKE ME TO YOUR HEART** from IN THE GARDEN

Though airbrushed out of history, Eurythmics's Conny Plank-produced debut album contains a couple of excellent songs. On this one Ann Lennox (as she was then) sings unshowily and directly.

❷ **NEVER GOING TO CRY AGAIN** from IN THE GARDEN

Tim Wheater's flute nails down the obsessive chorus here, and there's a fleeting appearance from Can's Holger Czukay on French horn.

❸ **SWEET DREAMS ARE MADE OF THIS** from SWEET DREAMS

Lennox in all her gender-bending dominatrix glory. It's hard to believe this triumphant symphonic torrent was made on an eight-track.

❹ **HERE COMES THE RAIN AGAIN** from TOUCH

The apogee of the electronic singles, with Lennox floating melismatically over swooning strings and trickling keyboards.

❺ **WOULD I LIE TO YOU** from BE YOURSELF TONIGHT

Suddenly they started rocking out: a mean female chorus responds to Lennox's calls while Stewart exploits his electric guitar.

❻ **BALL AND CHAIN** from BE YOURSELF TONIGHT

An insistent circular rhythm, played slightly too fast for its own good, subverts this bright and shiny 1980s production.

❼ **THERE MUST BE AN ANGEL** from BE YOURSELF TONIGHT

The harmonica just pours out of Stevie Wonder while Lennox flutters up and down the octaves.

❽ **MISSIONARY MAN** from REVENGE

An in-your-face classic. Get this version (rather than the single on *Greatest Hits*) for its moody intro.

David Honigmann

Bill Evans

The most influential jazz pianist of his generation, Evans was universally admired for the lyricism of his playing, his harmonic inventiveness and sheer musicality. His cocaine-induced death robbed the jazz world of one of its finest.

❶ **SO WHAT** MILES DAVIS from KIND OF BLUE

Though supporting Davis, Evans is a cornerstone in this, one of jazz's greatest tracks. Subtlety, sophistica-tion – Evans in his early prime.

❷ **I LOVES YOU PORGY** from AT THE MONTREUX JAZZ FESTIVAL

A tender yet passionate solo rendering of this wistful Gershwin song. The live atmosphere seems to create real urgency in Evans's playing.

❸ **WALTZ FOR DEBBIE** from NEW JAZZ CONCEPTIONS

One of Evans' few compositions, written for his 3-year-old niece. A beautiful song without words (until Tony Bennett got his voice round it).

❹ MY FOOLISH HEART from THE TONY BENNETT/BILL EVANS ALBUM

Evans brings out the best of Bennett in this intimate and inspired collaboration. With just piano accompaniment, Bennett's voice is exposed but richly expressive.

❺ OUR LOVE IS HERE TO STAY from AT SHELLY'S MANNE-HOLE

A jaunty, melodic right hand soars above daringly chromatic harmonic sequences. Fabulous trio playing with Chuck Israels (drums) and Larry Bunker (bass).

❻ PEACE PIECE from EVERYBODY DIGS BILL EVANS

Six and a half minutes of haunting and absorbing impressionistic improvisation. Satie, Debussy, Evans…

❼ BLUE IN GREEN from PORTRAIT IN JAZZ

A pensive Evans composition (which Miles Davis tried to claim as his own) played with Scott LeFaro (bass) and Paul Motian (drums) – arguably the greatest jazz trio of all time.

❽ ALICE IN WONDERLAND from SUNDAY AT THE VILLAGE VANGUARD

A joyous example of how 3/4 time lent itself to Evans' floating right hand and complex harmonies. Weeks later, bassist LeFaro was dead.

❾ THE WASHINGTON TWIST from EMPATHY

Evans is in perfect syncopation with Shelly Manne's exciting drums in this edgy twelve-bar blues. Parts of your anatomy will move uncontrollably.

❿ JUST YOU, JUST ME from CONVERSATIONS WITH MYSELF

A unique insight into Evans' musical psyche. His brilliant, idea was to make an album of three over-dubbed piano tracks – all his own. Almost too much to take in.

Alastair Rolfe

Evil women

If a man's singing about a woman being evil, you can rest assured his motive has something to do with sex. And if a woman's doing the singing? More than likely it's the same deal.

❶ IF THAT'S YOUR BOYFRIEND HE WASN'T LAST NIGHT MESHELL NDEGEOCELLO from PLANTATION LULLABIES

Not-so-sweet and low, Meshell Ndegeocello flicks a fake fingernail and a fine beat in her subject's face during this unapologetic taunt. Pure bitch.

❷ CELL BLOCK TANGO HE HAD IT COMIN' QUEEN LATIFAH, LIL' KIM AND MACY GRAY from CHICAGO

This rap made the soundtrack, but not the movie musical. Here Queen Latifah and company testify about their (self-justified) murder with calculated glee and not a trace of Broadway.

❸ TURTLE BLUES BIG BROTHER AND THE HOLDING COMPANY from CHEAP THRILLS

Some rollicking piano here, but it is Janis Joplin's from-the-gut vocals that firebrand this tune about a jaded woman with the devil in her veins.

❹ CHRISTINE'S TUNE FLYING BURRITO BROTHERS from THE GILDED PALACE OF SIN

Gram Parson's wood-warm voice makes the Burrito Brothers' Christine appear lovable, even if the lyrics make her out to be the devil in disguise.

❺ YOU'RE THE DEVIL IN DISGUISE ELVIS PRESLEY from PRESLEY: ALL TIME GREATEST HITS

Different year, different tune. Here Elvis and the boys play tennis with the tempo while the king emotes about a woman who isn't what she seems.

❻ MEAN LITTLE MAMA ROY ORBISON from THE LEGENDARY ROY ORBISON

Roy Orbison's shredding guitar and electric voice bring home this rocker about a woman who withholds sex.

❼ I WANNA BE EVIL EARTHA KITT from IN PERSON AT THE PLAZA

Eartha Kitt purrs and hisses her way through a song that teaches us how to be evil in easy-to-follow steps.

❽ EVIL WOMAN ELECTRIC LIGHT ORCHESTRA from FACE THE MUSIC

A catchy beat, deft lyrics (there's a hole in my head where the rain comes in) and Richard Tandy's thumping keyboard give "Evil Woman" undeniable appeal.

❾ EVIL WOMAN BLACK SABBATH from BLACK SABBATH IMPORT

An odd, Beatlesque intro gives way to the Sabs' usual thunderstorm of guitar and throbbing bass.

❿ SHE TOOK AN AXE FLOTSAM AND JETSAM from DOOMSDAY FOR THE DECEIVER

Because nothing says evil quite like a good hatchet murder. Flotsam and Jetsam thrash their way through the story of Lizzie Borden, who was acquitted of murdering her father and stepmother. Eric (A.K.) Knutson's wailing vocals make clear that the group sides with the rest of the state of Massachusetts: they don't believe her.

Madelyn Rosenberg

⑨ OOH LA LA from OOH LA LA
Rod didn't want to sing this, because he didn't think it, was good enough, so Ronnie Wood took over. (He likes it now.)

⑩ YOU CAN MAKE ME DANCE, SING OR ANYTHING (EVEN TAKE THE DOG FOR A WALK) from GOOD BOYS WHEN THEY'RE ASLEEP
The band's swansong – and a fantastic single, too.

Dave Atkinson

The Faces

The original good-time, straightforward rock'n'roll party band of the early 1970s, The Faces even had a bar on stage with them. Hugely influential and a great springboard for Rod Stewart's solo career.

❶ THREE BUTTON HAND ME DOWN from FIRST STEP (A.K.A. "SMALL FACES")
Organ, slide guitar, four-to-the-floor rhythms and a terrific tune (pinched from "Can't Get Next To You"). The shape of things to come.

❷ MAYBE I'M AMAZED from LONG PLAYER
A magnificent version of a great Paul McCartney tune.

❸ RICHMOND from LONG PLAYER
Folky song from Ronnie Lane, sounding very similar to Slim Chance, his next group.

❹ YOU'RE MY GIRL (I DON'T WANT TO DISCUSS IT) from FIVE GUYS WALK INTO A BAR
From a BBC session, the only Faces version of this brilliant tune, previously recorded by Amen Corner.

❺ HAD ME A REAL GOOD TIME from LONG PLAYER
Back to their raving best – a full-on, loud and groovy live favourite.

❻ STAY WITH ME from A NOD IS AS GOOD AS A WINK... TO A BLIND HORSE
Lyrically this could be regarded as a little misogynistic, but it shows the band doing what they did best – heads-down rock'n'roll.

❼ CINDY INCIDENTALLY from OOH LA LA
Top Rod lyric – and he's nice to the lady this time.

❽ POOL HALL RICHARD from OOH LA LA
Ode to a wayward lad. What was Rod thinking?

Factory Records

Founded in 1978 by Granada Television presenter Tony Wilson, Factory started life as a club night and grew into a record company that became synonymous with the music emanating from Britain's second city of Manchester, much of it centred on the legendary Hacienda Club. The story was rather brilliantly told in the 2002 film *24 Hour Party People*.

❶ JOY DIVISION LOVE WILL TEAR US APART from PERMANENT: THE BEST OF JOY DIVISION
Six weeks before the release of this haunting single in June 1980, singer Ian Curtis put a rope around his neck and hung himself.

❷ BLUE MONDAY NEW ORDER from THE BEST OF NEW ORDER
Out of Joy Division arose New Order to release this best-selling twelve-inch single of all time.

❸ ALL NIGHT PARTY A CERTAIN RATIO from EARLY
Hilarious, post-punk dance cover of Banbarra's anti-marriage song that became a cult track in New York dance clubs and made the Billboard R&B chart.

❹ BAADER MEINHOF CABARET VOLTAIRE from BEST OF 78–82
Fascist-baiting debut single from 1978 with a white noise industrial sound as Germanic as the title, before they went on to make their definitive statement on Rough Trade with "Red Mecca".

❺ WITHOUT MERCY 1 THE DURUTTI COLUMN from WITHOUT MERCY
Half a dozen years earlier he'd been in Ed Banger & The Nosebleeds. By 1984, Vini Reilly was composing side-long pieces of modern chamber music like this, somewhere between Mike Oldfield and Philip Glass.

❻ WROTE FOR LUCK HAPPY MONDAYS from BUMMED
A classic slice of Madchester dancefloor rock-funk produced by Martin Hannett and remixed by Erasure's Vince Clarke.

⑦ HYMN FROM A VILLAGE JAMES from BEST OF JAMES

An astonishingly literate and intelligent song that sounds like it might have been written by Morrissey but came from the pen of the band's idiosyncratic frontman, Tim Booth.

⑧ ELECTRICITY ORCHESTRAL MANOEUVRES IN THE DARK from THE BEST OF OMD

Cheerful, catchy, lightweight early synth-pop. With the benefit of hindsight, you can hear how the band's Andy McCluskey ended up writing hits for Atomic Kitten.

⑨ GET THE MESSAGE ELECTRONIC from ELECTRONIC

Sublime, lush pop from a Mancunian super-group of Johnny Marr (The Smiths) and Bernard Sumner (Joy Division/New Order) with help from pet Shop Boy Neil Tennant.

⑩ SECTION FOUR STEVE MARTLAND from THE FACTORY CLASSICAL SAMPLER

Who remembers that in 1989 Factory launched a classical imprint, which released works by Benjamin Britten, Shostakovich, Tippett and Ligeti? They also signed iconoclastic contemporary Liverpool-born composer Martland.

Nigel Williamson

Fado

The new millennium has seen a major revival of this bittersweet and quintessentially Portuguese music, spearheaded by a new generation of artists. While adding their own new twists, they are of course indebted to their forebears. Here are some choice cuts from both.

① FADO INÚTIL AMÁLIA RODRIGUES from FADO, THE SOUL OF PORTUGAL

The undisputed queen of fado is at the peak of her extraordinary powers in this 1951 recording. Talk about transcending the genre…

② ADEUS MOURARIA CARLOS RAMOS from BIOGRAFIAS DO FADO: CARLOS RAMOS

This 1957 recording is a fond farewell to the streets of Mouraria – the *bairro* (neighbourhood) of Lisbon most commonly namechecked in fado lyrics.

③ BAIRROS DE LISBOA ALFREDO MARCENEIRO WITH FERNANDA MARIA from BIOGRAFIAS DO FADO: ALFREDO MARCENEIRO

A good example of the now rare *desgarrada* form

of improvised duet, with one of the godfathers of 20th-century fado and a less familiar but rather feisty partner.

④ FADO ZÉ ANTÓNIO MARIA TERESA DE NORONHA from FADO PORTUGUÊS VOL 1

Restrained passion was the trademark of this fine singer, who enjoyed a brief international career in the 1960s.

⑤ TROVA DO VENTO QUE PASSA ANTÓNIO BERNADINO from THE ROUGH GUIDE TO FADO

The best-known singer from Coimbra (the second city of fado, after Lisbon) performing a song which became an anthem of hope in the dark days of Portugal's dictatorship.

⑥ MEMÓRIAS DE UM CHAPÉU CAMANÉ from ESTA COISA DA ALMA

Despite not having really capitalized outside Portugal on the recent fado revival, Camané is still the leading male voice of the "new school" at home. This is a singer who really uses his nose.

⑦ TRAGO ALENTEJO NA VOZ ANTÓNIO ZAMBUJO from O MESMO FADO

A popular tune celebrating this promising young singer's home in the Alentejo region. His voice brims with emotion and is very highly rated in Lisbon, his adopted home.

⑧ SOU DO FADO, SOU FADISTA ANA MOURA from GUARDA-ME A NA MÃO

A great version of a song by writer/producer Jorge Fernando. Moura's is a natural fado voice that we should be hearing a lot more from.

⑨ O QUE FOR HÁ-DE SER KATIA GUERREIRO from NAS MÃOS DO FADO

A magnificent reworking of Dulce Pontes' song Ciranda. This may not strictly be fado, but Guerreiro is a fado fundamentalist and really gives it the treatment.

⑩ HÁ UMA MÚSICA DO POVO MARIZA from TRANSPARENTE

Backed by Jaques Morelenbaum's subtle orchestral arrangements, the leading contemporary female fadista kicks off her third album with new-found maturity and restraint.

Jon Lusk

Mariza's
Voices

"I could have made a list of great fado singers," says Portuguese fadista MARIZA, who has become one of the biggest names in world music in recent years. "But I love great voices whether they're singing jazz, classical or pop and that's mostly what I went for in this list."

❶ ERA NÃO ERA DO TAMANHO DE UM PARDAL GAITEROS DE LISBOA from MACAREU

❷ UPA NEGUINHO ELIS REGINA from ELIS REGINA LIVE IN MONTREUX

❸ WHAT'S GOING ON MARVIN GAYE from WHAT'S GOING ON

❹ BLUE MOON BILLIE HOLIDAY from BILLIE'S BLUES

❺ DO NOTHIN' TILL YOU HEAR FROM ME NINA SIMONE from SINGS ELLINGTON

❻ O SUAVE FACIULLA MARIA CALLAS from ROMANTIC CALLAS

❼ CANÇÃO VERDES ANOS CARLOS PAREDES from O MELHOR DE CARLOS PAREDES

❽ DONGO WALDEMAR BASTOS from RENASCENCE

❾ DINDI FRANK SINATRA & ANTONIO CARLOS JOBIM from FRANCIS ALBERT SINATRA & ANTONIO CARLOS JOBIM

❿ NEW YORK STATE OF MIND TONY BENNETT from PLAYIN' WITH MY FRIENDS

Fairport Convention

The original electric folk band are still going, and that longevity means their origins as Britain's answer to Jefferson Airplane often gets overlooked. Not here.

❶ A SAILOR'S LIFE from UNHALFBRICKING
The song that invented electric folk is spiky and spooky, like The Velvet Underground playing trad. Sandy Denny's singing is luminous.

❷ WHO KNOWS WHERE THE TIME GOES from UNHALFBRICKING
Given extra poignancy by Sandy Denny's early death, this ballad succeeds in slowing down the time whose speed it mourns.

❸ SLOTH from FULL HOUSE
Guitarist Richard Thompson and fiddler Dave Swarbrick do battle on this anti-war dirge.

❹ TAM LIN from LIEGE AND LIEF
Electric folk at its best: a tricky tempo and a slashing riff giving meat to an off-with-the-fairies tale of, well, fairies and fair maidens.

❺ FOTHERINGAY from WHAT WE DID ON OUR HOLIDAYS
Denny's evocation of Mary Queen of Scots' sequestering floats on a wash of acoustic guitars and voices.

❻ I'LL KEEP IT WITH MINE from WHAT WE DID ON OUR HOLIDAYS
Pre-trad Fairport were top Dylan interpreters. Here's a stunning version of an obscure gem.

❼ MATTY GROVES from LIEGE AND LIEF
A romp of adultery, tell-tale servants and murder which the Fairports attack full throttle, finishing up in a rollickingly inappropriate reel.

❽ THE LOBSTER from FAIRPORT CONVENTION
Neglected pre-Denny Fairport: a precursor of their VU folk sound. Oddball, creepy but captivating.

❾ ROSIE from ROSIE
Utterly uncharacteristic – almost poppy – mature Fairport. Charming.

❿ MEET ON THE LEDGE from WHAT WE DID ON OUR HOLIDAYS
The enduring Fairport theme song, a roustabout hymn to friendship past and present.

Toby Manning

Marianne Faithfull's
Icons

An icon in her own right, and a role model for generations of female singers, from Chrissie Hynde to PJ Harvey, MARIANNE FAITHFULL picks tracks from ten of the most iconic artists of the twentieth century.

❶ **ONE MORE CUP OF COFFEE** BOB DYLAN from DESIRE

❷ **PAIN IN MY HEART** OTIS REDDING from PAIN IN MY HEART

❸ **REDEMPTION SONG** BOB MARLEY from UPRISING

❹ **CHAIN OF FOOLS** ARETHA FRANKLIN from LADY SOUL

❺ **FINE & MELLOW** BILLIE HOLIDAY from THE SOUND OF JAZZ

❻ **LUST FOR LIFE** IGGY POP from LUST FOR LIFE

❼ **MOTHER** JOHN LENNON from PLASTIC ONO BAND

❽ **FIRST WE TAKE MANHATTAN** LEONARD COHEN from I'M YOUR MAN

❾ **THAT'S ALL RIGHT** ELVIS PRESLEY from THE SUN SESSIONS

❿ **DELIA'S GONE** JOHNNY CASH from AMERICAN RECORDINGS

Marianne Faithfull

From the innocent convent girl of "As Tears Go By" to the raging harpie of "Why D'Ya Do It", Marianne Faithfull's career has zigzagged unconventionally from triumph to disaster – and then back again.

❶ **AS TEARS GO BY** from MARIANNE FAITHFULL
The first song Mick Jagger and Keith Richards ever wrote.

❷ **IS THIS WHAT I GET FROM LOVING YOU?** from THE VERY BEST OF MARIANNE FAITHFULL
A Goffin/King number that deserved to chart much higher in 1967 than the modest #43 it achieved.

❸ **SISTER MORPHINE** from THE VERY BEST OF MARIANNE FAITHFULL
It took Mick Jagger twenty years to admit that Marianne had helped write the words and to add her name to the credits on The Stones' version.

❹ **THE BALLAD OF LUCY JORDAN** from BROKEN ENGLISH
A magnificently warm rendition of the Shel Silverstein song from the1979 album that redefined her career.

❺ **WHY D'YA DO IT?** from BROKEN ENGLISH
Based on a poem by Heathcote Williams, this is a raging, X-rated rant, the like of which we'd never heard from a woman in rock before.

❻ **BALLAD OF THE SOLDIER'S WIFE** from LOST IN THE STARS: THE MUSIC OF KURT WEILL
Away from her pop career, Marianne has become a compelling interpreters of the Brecht/Weill songbook.

❼ **THE MYSTERY OF LOVE** from BEFORE THE POISON
The best of the five tracks written and produced by PJ Harvey for MF's 2004 album.

Nigel Williamson

The Fall

The Fall's cranky, shambling, Mancunian incomprehensibility generates instant love or loathing. Here are some reminders for those who have forgotten – and tasters for those who have yet to catch the bug.

❶ **VARIOUS TIMES** from EARLY SINGLES
Creepy keyboards, spooky guitar and our man Mark E. Smith rambling on about witch trials, Nazi camp guards and weak beer.

❷ **NO XMAS FOR JOHN QUAYS** from TOTALE'S TURNS
Barely keeping the lid on, this is a band playing their hearts out.

❸ SPECTRE VS RECTOR from DRAGNET
The best of The Fall's early epics, and a tale scarier than *The Exorcist*.

❹ NEW FACE IN HELL from GROTESQUE
Government-induced paranoia, a guitar riff strong enough to build bridges from, and a whole bunch of throwaway one-liners.

❺ HIP PRIEST from HEX ENDUCTION HOUR
Making the most of that double drummer line-up.

❻ HIT THE NORTH from THE FRENZ EXPERIMENT
Celebrating the glorious countryside around Greater Manchester and urban Lancashire, The Fall do their bit for regional tourism.

❼ KURIOUS ORANJ from I AM KURIOUS, ORANJ
A strange tie-in to a ballet suite performed by Michael Clark's dance troupe, and a searing indictment of the Oranges.

❽ BIRMINGHAM SCHOOL OF BUSINESS SCHOOL from CODE: SELFISH
Dreamy, laid-back MES sounds like a Mancunian Sly Stone as he drools a lyric of the purest contempt and the band circle endlessly through one of their best riffs.

❾ HEY! STUDENT from MIDDLE CLASS REVOLT
This used to be called Hey! Fascist, but after swapping it to a rant against the complacency of the educated elite, it works just as well.

❿ STRYCHNINE from THE COMPLETE PEEL SESSIONS 1978–2004
Recorded in 1993 after a good few years in the business, Mark and the band proudly demonstrate no musical progress whatsoever.

Al Spicer

We are family

In pre-TV days, music was something many families indulged in for an evening's entertainment. Some were really quite talented…

❶ FAMILY AFFAIR SLY & THE FAMILY STONE from THERE'S A RIOT GOING ON
Sly, brother Freddie, sister Rose, cousin Cynthia and buddies Larry, Jerry and Greg were the brightest flowering of San Francisco psychedelia. "Family Affair", recorded in a cocaine haze in LA, suggests how family and band relations were disintegrating.

❷ WE ARE FAMILY SISTER SLEDGE from WE ARE FAMILY
Sisters Kathy, Debra, Joni and Kim were disco's brightest lights when produced by Chic. "We Are Family" is one of those celebratory tunes guaranteed to get people dancing at weddings, funerals, everything.

❸ WILL THE CIRCLE BE UNBROKEN THE CARTER FAMILY from THE CARTER FAMILY
With Sara's voice, Maybelle's guitar playing and A.P.'s song catching writing skills, The Carter Family offered up primal American music, stuff rooted in hillbilly culture yet capable of laying many of the foundations of country music.

❹ I WANT YOU BACK THE JACKSON 5 from DIANA ROSS PRESENTS THE JACKSON 5
Drilled by dictatorial father Joe, The Jacksons were working Mid West black clubs while still children. Their debut single IWYB was a perfect slice of pop-funk and went on to be the fastest selling 45 in Motown's history. Lead singer Michael would never again sound quite as alive as on this cut.

❺ STRAWBERRY LETTER 23 THE BROTHERS JOHNSON from BLAST!
Hard funk brothers George and Louis Johnson were Quincy Jones' protégés and scored several memorable hits in the late 1970s.

❻ I'LL TAKE YOU THERE THE STAPLE SINGERS from RESPECT YOURSELF: THE BEST OF THE STAPLE SINGERS
Gospel outfit lead by guitar playing dad Pops Staples and featuring his three throaty daughters, Cleotha, Yvonne and the awesome Mavis. Signed to Stax in 1968 so shifted to secular if moral material and had a US #1 with this hugely uplifting tune in 1972.

❼ WHIPPING POST THE ALLMAN BROTHERS from LIVE AT THE FILMORE
Duane Allman was a guitar playing prodigy who sizzled on Southern soul albums but became a legend when he formed The Allman Brothers with kid brother Greg. Their tough blues-rock fusion was at its most powerful on this 1971 live track.

❽ RANK STRANGER THE STANLEY BROTHERS from 16 GREATEST GOSPEL HITS
Ralph and Carter Stanley came out of Virginia playing mountain music – pure bluegrass gospel unadorned by flashy technique. On this haunting ballad a prodigal son returns home to find all his family and friends deceased.

❾ DRUNKARD'S SORROW WALTZ THE BALFA BROTHERS from THE BALFA BROTHERS PLAY TRADITIONAL CAJUN MUSIC
Fiddle-playing Louisiana native Dewey Balfa leads his

four brothers in cutting ancient music with French roots. Music to hunt alligators by.

🔟 MOCKINGBIRD INEZ & CHARLIE FOXX from GREATEST HITS

Inez and Charlie, the brother and sister duo from North Carolina, cut gutsy soul across the 1960s and were loved by London's mods. "Mockingbird", which Charlie worked up from a childhood nursery rhyme, is the sound of a smile set to music.

Garth Cartwright

Brenda Fassie

Africa's top diva, Brenda was blessed with a voice that could stop anyone in their tracks. Until her untimely death in 2004 she blasted out some of the continent's finest pop tunes.

❶ VUL'NDLELA from MEMEZA

Brenda's biggest-ever hit – a rousing wedding song set to a stomping *mbaqanga* beat – this later became an ANC campaign anthem.

❷ WEEKEND SPECIAL from GREATEST HITS

Her first hit, from 1983, features Brenda in the role of weekend lover of a married man. It became an instant and deserving disco classic.

❸ GOOD BLACK WOMAN from TOO LATE FOR MAMA

Recorded in the nightmarish late 1980s, this is full of strength and pain.

❹ TOO LATE FOR MAMA from TOO LATE FOR MAMA

Silly lyrics but who cares? A bubblegum classic.

❺ NTSWARE-NDIBAMBE from MALI

One of her last recordings, with Brenda almost growling at times, the voice laced with compelling menace.

❻ NGOHLALA NGI NJE from MINA NAWE

Builds beautifully from quavering solo to rousing anthem in inimitable Brenda fashion.

❼ BAXAKEKILE OXAM' from MYEKELENI

A great mix of jazz and Xhosa traditional rhythms, with Brenda's voice soaring and swirling above them.

❽ SUM' BULALA from MEMEZA

A gentle, beautiful ballad, with Brenda's voice the epitome of understated power.

Gregory Salter

Fatboy Slim

Norman Cook's most successful alterego first appeared in 1996 with the *Better Living Through Chemistry* album, a slab of keyboard and computer trickery and dubious legality welded together by a man possessed of the spirit of funk and the Big Beat. Since then he's gone on to become a superstar artist, producer and DJ who these days clears the rights to samples before using them on his records.

❶ GOING OUT OF MY HEAD from BETTER LIVING THROUGH CHEMISTRY

Starting from Yvonne Elliman's cover of the Who's "I Can't Explain" and layering on the effects like a chef sprinkling sugar, Norman whips up a cotton-candy tribute to getting out of your head.

❷ EVERYBODY NEEDS A 303 from BETTER LIVING THROUGH CHEMISTRY

Norm's ode to man's best friend – the Roland TB303 bassline generator.

❸ THE ROCKAFELLER SKANK from YOU'VE COME A LONG WAY, BABY

Norman's greatest hit so far – as catchy as the black plague. (But why didn't he just call it "Right About Now, The Funk Soul Brother"?)

❹ PRAISE YOU from YOU'VE COME A LONG WAY, BABY

Takes you to a beautiful place where scratch-happy MCs, gospel divas and twangy axe-players shake their asses in unison.

❺ STAR 69 from HALFWAY BETWEEN THE GUTTER AND THE STARS

Hip-hop in a Brighton stylie: enormous waves of electronic beats, merciless basslines and naughty lyrics ideal for shouting out en masse.

❻ WEAPON OF CHOICE from HALFWAY BETWEEN THE GUTTER AND THE STARS

If Bootsy Collins joins your team, anything you do will be 100% funky. Convince Christopher Walken to donate some menace to the video and the result is a trip to Planet Silly, where the fun never stops.

Al Spicer

Female fire

While men just like to shout and break things, female anger is a many splendoured thing.

❶ CAUGHT OUT THERE KELIS from KALEIDOSCOPE
There are plenty of lines full of fire in this epic, but nothing sums up the song better than those post-chorus "AAAARGH!" That, or the sound of a handgun pumping.

❷ YOU OUGHTTA KNOW ALANIS MORISSETTE from JAGGED LITTLE PILL
While her later career choices may have dented Alanis' reputation, there's no softening the blow of this hate-filled missive to an ex who moved on a little too smoothly.

❸ SEE SAW ARETHA FRANKLIN from THE VERY BEST OF ARETHA FRANKLIN
Some would choose "Think" for a playlist like this, but it's hard to ignore La Franklin when she howls at the hapless hot-and-cold subject of this song, "It ain't right, it ain't, it ain't RIGHT!"

❹ SUCK MY LEFT ONE BIKINI KILL from THE CD VERSION OF THE FIRST TWO RECORDS
Growling riot grrrl firebrand Kathleen Hanna's message here is pretty clear, isn't it?

❺ DEAR MR PRESIDENT PINK from NOT DEAD YET
It might not be her brashest song, but "Dear Mr President" is Alecia Moore's most striking moment of passion and candour – when she howls "Minimum wage with a baby on the way", Mr President would have to be dead not to sit up and listen.

❻ BUT JULIAN, I'M A LITTLE BIT OLDER THAN YOU COURTNEY LOVE from AMERICA'S SWEETHEART
Hole – and Courtney Love – may have had louder moments, but this overlooked gem from Love's solo debut seethes with misplaced libido, fury and confusion. Oh yeah, there's the "I know where you live" bit, too.

❼ SHE WORKS HARD FOR THE MONEY DONNA SUMMER from SHE WORKS HARD FOR THE MONEY
Who'da thought disco queen Donna Summer could whip up such a forceful anthem for female empowerment? The implied lyric following "you better treat her right" was certainly "OR ELSE!"

❽ IT'S ON THE ROCKS THE DONNAS from SPEND THE NIGHT
It's simple, really: you mess with The Donnas, prepare for doom (including having your Mercedes destroyed). Like, whatever.

❾ WOULD I LIE TO YOU EURYTHMICS from BE YOURSELF TONIGHT
Annie Lennox unleashes a rain of terror on a hapless male with typical verve on this brass heavy rant; the revving motorcycle engines could very well be being powered by her uncompromising vocal.

❿ SURVIVOR DESTINY'S CHILD from SURVIVOR
How to get back at bitchin', dissin', good-for-nothin' ex-band members? Write a song about how much better you're doing without them, and then make it a mega-selling hit. Revenge has never been so tuneful.

Clem Bastow

Finger-pickin' guitar

In most hands the folk guitar provides little more than a simple strummed accompaniment. But during the 1960s folk and acoustic blues revival, a number of virtuoso performers (most of them Brits but some Americans too) took plucking and picking to a completely new level – with dazzling results.

❶ BLACKWATERSIDE BERT JANSCH from JACK ORION
A tune so good that Jimmy Page borrowed and recorded it with Led Zeppelin as "Black Mountain Side" – and cheekily claimed the writing credit for his own.

❷ SWEET POTATO JOHN RENBOURN from SIR JOHN ALOT OF MERRIE ENGLAND
Renbourn's guitar duets with Jansch were heard to brilliant effect in Pentangle, and he was equally adept playing folk-blues or in the ornate style he called "mock Tudor".

❸ ANJI DAVY GRAHAM from GUITAR PLAYER PLUS
Graham was just 21 when he recorded this stunning instrumental, later covered by both Jansch and Paul Simon.

❹ SCARBOROUGH FAIR MARTIN CARTHY from MARTIN CARTHY
Controversially nicked by Paul Simon, who failed to credit Carthy's arrangement, resulting in the two men not speaking for thirty years.

❺ BLUES RUN THE GAME JACKSON C FRANK from BLUES RUN THE GAME
An American who came to London in the mid-1960s

to become Sandy Denny's boyfriend and bequeath this much-covered tune.

❻ RANDOM JIG RICHARD THOMPSON from STRICT TEMPO!
Thompson's songwriting and electric-guitar work often overshadowed the fact that he was a genius acoustic picker, as he proved on his 1981 album of jigs, reels, hornpipes and polkas.

❼ DAZZLING STRANGER WIZZ JONES from THE LEGENDARY ME
"Wizz was *the* guy to listen to in the early days", John Renbourn says. "But he didn't actually have any gigs 'cos he had such long hair and bare feet that he wasn't allowed into most of the folk clubs."

❽ THE DRIVING OF THE YEAR NAIL LEO KOTTKE from SIX AND TWELVE STRING GUITAR
The American-born Kottke drew on the blues as well as the folk tradition, but this instrumental displays his dazzling dexterity to awesome effect.

❾ ON THE SUNNY SIDE OF THE OCEAN
JOHN FAHEY from THE TRANSFIGURATION OF BLIND JOE DEATH
Fahey was a cult figure with a style as idiosyncratic as it was complex. This track is beautiful and impressionistic, yet slightly bluesy and dissonant. It displays the man's technical genius and his weird and wonderful musical vision.

❿ MAPLE LEAF RAG STEFAN GROSSMAN from YAZOO BASIN BOOGIE
Another American folk-blues legend with an astonishing pickin' technique, Grossman is heard to brilliant effect on his guitar transcription of the Scott Joplin classic.

Nigel Williamson

Ella Fitzgerald

The First Lady of jazz song, and a genius of scat, Ella possessed one of the most dazzling voices of the 20th century – pure, polished and powerful, with a massive three-octave range. She put it to use during a prolific four-decade recording career, of which the following only scrapes the surface.

❶ IT'S ONLY A PAPER MOON from ELLA AND HER FELLAS
Ella's easy-swinging 1945 version of this Harold Arlen and Yip Harburg standard. The Delta Rhythm Boys provide creamy harmony.

❷ HOW HIGH THE MOON from BEBOP SPOKEN HERE
Ella announced her musical allegiance with the modern jazz movement on this brilliant 1947 scat reading of one of bop's great anthems.

Bert Jansch
Under the influence

The doyen of English acoustic folk guitarists, BERT JANSCH is revered as an influence by the likes of Jimmy Page and Neil Young. His own musical tastes run to jazz, blues, rock and soul, all of which are reflected in his rather eclectic playlist.

❶ BLUES RUN THE GAME JACKSON C. FRANK from BLUES RUN THE GAME

❷ BLACKWATERSIDE ANNE BRIGGS from A COLLECTION

❸ KEY TO THE HIGHWAY BIG BILL BROONZY from TROUBLE IN MIND

❹ PROUD MAISRIE DAVEY GRAHAM AND SHIRLEY COLLINS from FOLK ROOTS, NEW ROUTES

❺ OH LORD, DON'T LET THEM DROP THAT ATOMIC BOMB ON ME CHARLES MINGUS from OH YEAH

❻ (I'M YOUR) HOOCHIE-COOCHIE MAN MUDDY WATERS from THE BEST OF MUDDY WATERS 1947–55

❼ BYKER HILL MARTIN CARTHY WITH DAVE SWARBRICK from BYKER HILL

❽ THE FROG GALLIARD JOHN DOWLAND from JULIAN BREAM VOL 7: FANTASIES, AYRES & DANCES

❾ CHARLOTTE HOPE SANDOVAL AND THE WARM INVENTIONS from BAVARIAN FRUIT BREAD

❿ GREEN ONIONS BOOKER T & THE MGs from THE VERY BEST OF BOOKER T & THE MGS

❸ MY ONE AND ONLY LOVE from ELLA AND ELLIS
This soaring tune is just one highlight from the immaculate 1950 album recorded with pianist Ellis Larkins.

❹ EV'RY TIME WE SAY GOODBYE from THE COLE PORTER SONGBOOK
From her first songbook album, this famous, touching 1956 recording ensured the hitherto underexposed Cole Porter tune a place in the pantheon of all-time standards.

❺ A SHIP WITHOUT A SAIL from THE RODGERS AND HART SONGBOOK
One of the more obscure Rodgers and Hart songs from Ella's second songbook and a plaintive gem from the 1930 show *Heads Up*.

❻ DAYDREAM from THE DUKE ELLINGTON SONGBOOK
Part of the magnificent album recorded with Duke's orchestra in 1956, this is a truly shimmering version of the Strayhorn/Ellington ballad.

❼ STOMPIN' AT THE SAVOY from ELLA AND LOUIS AGAIN
The Ella and Louis albums made with the Oscar Peterson Trio in 1956–57 were full of magic. From the rematch, spurred on by producer Norman Granz, this hits an extraordinary level of excitement and spontaneity.

❽ THERE'S A LULL IN MY LIFE from LIKE SOMEONE IN LOVE
Arranged by Frank De Vol in 1957, this gorgeous Harry Revel song suited Ella's sweetly sad ballad style perfectly and makes for one of her most divine performances.

❾ BLUE SKIES from THE IRVING BERLIN SONGBOOK
The remarkable scat feature from the otherwise restrained and respectful *Berlin Songbook*, recorded with Paul Weston in 1958.

❿ JUST YOU, JUST ME from ELLA SWINGS LIGHTLY
Ella is typically virtuosic over Marty Paich's *Birth Of The Cool*-style arrangement.

Chris Ingham

Flamenco

One of the great musical forms of Europe, flamenco has a history and repertoire that few traditional or folk cultures can match. Today it thrives both in its "pure" form and in countless new flavours borrowing influences from all over the world.

❶ ENTRE SABANAS DE HOLANDA LA NIÑA DE LOS PEINES from LA NIÑA DE LOS PEINES VOZ DE ESTAÑO FUNDIDO
A key voice of the 20th century sings a glorious folk piece.

❷ LA VOZ DEL TIEMPO TOMATITO & EL CAMARÓN DE LA ISLA from TOMATITO
Underpinned by an upbeat chorus and the guitar of Tomatito, this track confirms the late El Camarón to be "the voice of the time".

❸ MOGUER ESTRELLA MORENTE from MY SONGS AND A POEM
A poem by Juan Ramón Jiménez (exiled during the Franco regime) set to music by this young star's illustrious father, Enrique Morente.

❹ LA VIDA SALE JOSE MERCÉ from AIRE
The rough-edged chorus, blasts of trumpet, vamping piano, percussion and above all, the rusty, yearning voice of Mercé make this an unbelievably sexy number.

❺ JARABI KETAMA WITH TOUMANI DIABATÉ from KETAMA
A fine example of the passion and energy of 1980s New Flamenco, this is a beautiful encounter between the Ketama ensemble, Malian kora player Toumani Diabaté and bassist Danny Thompson.

❻ DAME TU BOCA JAVIER RUIBAL from SAHARA
Pure musical seduction from this flamenco-influenced singer-songwriter.

❼ EL YEDDI HAG ENNAS RADIO TARIFA from FIEBRE
An unbeatable live version of this compelling song, with a wild sax solo to boot.

❽ CORAZÓN LOCO BEBO Y CIGALA from LÁGRIMAS NEGRAS
A sublime flamenco telling of a classic Latin tale – a man torn between wife and lover.

❾ TIEMPO DE SOLEA OJOS DE BRUJO from BARI
A superb *solea* from this cutting-edge Barcelona collective.

❿ COGE LA ONDA EL LEBRIJANO CON LA ORQUESTA ARÁBIGO ANDALUZA from CASABLANCA
Consummate Arabic–Spanish fusion partnering the earthy voice of Juan Peña with Hassan Jebelhbibi and Arabic chorus.

Jan Fairley

Flaming Lips

Fronted by oddball genius Wayne Coyne, still cooking twenty years into their career, the Lips are surely the cult band de nos jours.

❶ SHE DON'T USE JELLY from TRANSMISSIONS FROM THE SATELLITE HEART
This 1993 track was played on Beavis and Butthead and suddenly the Lips had an American top-ten single.

❷ WHEN YOU SMILE from CLOUDS TASTE METALLIC
Cosmic orgasms that looked forward to their later dreamy experiments on *The Soft Bulletin* album.

❸ ENTHUSIASM FOR LIFE DEFEATS EXISTENTIAL FEAR from 20 YEARS OF WEIRD: FLAMING LIPS 1986–2006
Washes of antique lo-fi synths and a languidly plucked banjo made for one of their best tracks, originally given out free at the SxSW festival.

❹ SUDDENLY EVERYTHING HAS CHANGED from THE SOFT BULLETIN
A standout track from the 1999 album in which Wayne Coyne assumed the mantle of a new Brian Wilson.

❺ THE GASH from THE SOFT BULLETIN
…and when he wasn't being Brian Wilson, he was busy playing at Phil Spector.

❻ RACE FOR THE PRIZE (SACRIFICE OF THE NEW SCIENTISTS) from THE SOFT BULLETIN
Waves of mellotron and off-beat electronica create celestial pop at its most heavenly.

❼ ONE MORE ROBOT (3000-21) from YOSHIMI BATTLES THE PINK ROBOTS
Coyne the visionary, as weird and wonderful as you could wish.

❽ DO YOU REALISE? from YOSHIMI BATTLES THE PINK ROBOTS
Hypnotic, modern psychedelia that makes you wish for a constitution to take all those hallucinogens.

❾ THE YEAH YEAH YEAH SONG from AT WAR WITH THE MYSTICS
Acid bubblegum on the opening track of their third successive masterpiece.

❿ POMPEII AM GOTTERDAMMERUNG from AT WAR WITH THE MYSTICS
Who needs a Pink Floyd reunion when we've got the Flaming Lips?

Nigel Williamson

Fleetwood Mac

Around the eternal nucleus of Mick Fleetwood (drums) and John McVie (bass), Fleetwood Mac have battled through since 1967. Their story has been described as the ultimate rock soap opera, but even the most imaginative scriptwriter would struggle to dream up such a litany of success, failure, love, hate, alcoholism, disappearance, sex and drugs. And that was just 1971.

❶ ALBATROSS from ENGLISH ROSE
Atypically gentle, this windswept instrumental was a #1 hit in Britain.

❷ BLACK MAGIC WOMAN from ENGLISH ROSE
Better known in the classic version by Santana, Fleetwood Mac's original has a stronger undercurrent of mystery and dread.

❸ OH WELL from THEN PLAY ON
One of the most astonishing cuts of the late 1960s: a blistering rock track segues into a dramatic instrumental with classical overtones.

❹ GREEN MANALISHI (WITH THE TWO-PRONGED CROWN) from 25 YEARS: THE CHAIN
Later covered by Judas Priest, this aggressively menacing song was one of the last that vocalist/guitarist Peter Green wrote for the band.

❺ HYPNOTIZED from MYSTERY TO ME
One of the highlights of the Bob Welch era: a breezy tune with just the right hint of mystery, and a precursor to the combination of moods that would make the band wildly successful in the late 1970s.

❻ RHIANNON from FLEETWOOD MAC
The first of the great Stevie Nicks songs – and the one that came to define her public persona.

❼ GO YOUR OWN WAY from RUMOURS
Lindsay Buckingham's chiming rhythm and scorching lead guitars frame the song that summed up the band's internal personal tangle.

❽ YOU MAKE LOVING FUN from RUMOURS
The fourth and final single from *Rumours* was one of the best songs on the radio in 1977.

❾ SISTERS OF THE MOON from TUSK
A moody work reflecting Stevie Nicks's fascination with nocturnal imagery and mysterious female characters.

🔟 BROWN EYES from TUSK

A rare Christine McVie track displaying some of the dark undercurrents found in Nicks' best work. It's said to include uncredited guitar work from Peter Green.

Butch Lazorchak

Flying Nun

Famously feted by the late John Peel as a model independent record label, Flying Nun took punk's DIY ethic (also a defining feature of New Zealand culture) and nurtured the "pop primitive" sound that defined Kiwi music from the early 1980s.

❶ NOTHING'S GOING TO HAPPEN TALL DWARFS from HELLO CRUEL WORLD

Quite untrue: this lo-fi but poetic and adventurous debut single by the maverick duo augured well for the future. Plenty did happen.

❷ POINT THAT THING SOMEWERE ELSE THE CLEAN from ANTHOLOGY

The ghost of The Velvet Underground hovers heavy over this driving early tune. David Kilgour's distinctive narcoleptic vocal mumbles through the mix. God knows what it's about.

❸ PINK FROST THE CHILLS from HEAVENLY POP HITS: THE BEST OF THE CHILLS

An early 7" by this Dunedin band, which has a wonderfully dark but luminous quality to it. Somehow The Chills' albums never quite sustained the giddy rush of such pop thrills.

❹ DEATH AND THE MAIDEN THE VERLAINES from YOU'RE JUST TOO OBSCURE FOR ME

This stop-start strummer transcends its literary pretensions. Another band that inspired the "Dunedin Sound" tag, which a lot of Flying Nun material was saddled with.

❺ RANDOLPH'S GOING HOME SHANE CARTER & PETER JEFFRIES from THE FLYING NUN RETROSPECTIVE COMPILATION: GETTING OLDER 1981–91

A suspenseful, melancholic one-off single that's become a collector's item in its original 7" format. Shane Carter went on to form Straightjacket Fits and Dimmer.

❻ THE MAN WITH NO DESIRE EXPENDABLES from TUATARA

Jay Clarkson's haunting jazz-tinged voice hints at possibilities that were never quite realized in a career that showed lots of early promise.

❼ DADDY'S HIGHWAY THE BATS from DADDY'S HIGHWAY

Skirling guitars suggest the influence of Scotland, where this band were well received. Prolific songwriter Robert Scott's inability to sing in tune only adds to their charm.

❽ NOT GIVEN LIGHTLY CHRIS KNOX from MEAT

Honest-to-goodness lurve song (very unusual!) by the godfather of Kiwi punk (The Enemy, Toy Love, Tall Dwarfs), which remains by far his biggest hit.

❾ NUDE STAR GARAGELAND from LAST EXIT TO GARAGELAND

Musings on the fame that pretty well eluded them outside New Zealand. For a time they were the label's big hope of the 1990s, but they broke up after three albums.

🔟 PIRATE LOVE THE D4 from 6TWENTY

The best song on their 2001 debut is actually a cover of a Johnny Thunders song – fitting in a way, since this Auckland foursome's pop punk isn't exactly typical Nun fare.

Jon Lusk

Folk-rock (1): English & Irish

English folk-rock peaked early: Fairport Convention's 1970 release *Liege And Lief* fused trad ballads and rock rhythms so perfectly that the form had really nowhere left to go. Its Irish cousin proved to have longer legs, largely thanks to the disorderly behaviour of the Pogues.

❶ A SAILOR'S LIFE FAIRPORT CONVENTION from UNHALFBRICKING

Liege And Lief was their landmark , but it was this track a year earlier that created the template for that album and unleashed the remarkable interplay between Richard Thompson's guitar and Dave Swarbrick's violin.

❷ THOMAS THE RHYMER STEELEYE SPAN from NOW WE ARE SIX

Produced by Jethro Tull's Ian Anderson and the highlight of an album, featuring, of all people, David Bowie on saxophone.

❸ WHISKEY IN THE JAR THIN LIZZY from VAGABONDS OF THE WESTERN WORLD

Basically a hard-rock act, Phil Lynott's band

nevertheless achieved folk-rock immortality with this brilliantly reworked Irish trad ballad.

❹ MORRIS CALL ALBION BAND from MORRIS ON
The opening track from the classic 1972 album by Ashley Hutchings' all-star folk-rock super-group – if that's not an oxymoron.

❺ THE HANGED MAN MR FOX from GYPSY
Volatile, classic early-1970s English folk-rock from the soon-to-be-divorced Bob and Carole Pegg.

❻ ENGLISH MEDLEY ROBIN AND BARRY DRANSFIELD from ROUT OF THE BLUES
The Yorkshire brothers actually turned down an invitation to join Steeleye. This track from their seminal 1970 debut shows why.

❼ TRIBUTE TO PAEDAR O'DONNELL
MOVING HEARTS from THE STORM
Synthesizers and bodhrans from the band that legends Christy Moore and Donal Lunny formed after leaving Planxty.

❽ HAL-AN-TOW OYSTERBAND from STEP OUTSIDE
These days they call it "English roots" rather than folk-rock, but this explosive version of the trad standard from Oysterband's landmark 1986 album helped to keep the flame alive.

❾ DIRTY OLD TOWN THE POGUES from RUM, SODOMY AND THE LASH
The Clash meet The Dubliners in a combustible cocktail of amphetamine sulphate and Guinness.
Nigel Williamson

Folk-rock 2: 1960s America

Combining the best of both worlds, American folk-rock started when The Byrds put Bob Dylan to a Beatles beat, setting the scene for some of the most enduring musical statements of the 1960s.

❶ MR TAMBOURINE MAN THE BYRDS from MR TAMBOURINE MAN
The Transatlantic #1 hit that started it all in 1965, combining Bob Dylan's poetry, Roger McGuinn's jingle-jangle electric twelve-string and the Byrds' skyscraping harmonies.

❷ TURN! TURN! TURN THE BYRDS from TURN! TURN! TURN!
What The Byrds did for Dylan they also did for Pete Seeger, turning a folk dirge into an anthem of peace and tolerance.

❸ LIKE A ROLLING STONE BOB DYLAN from HIGHWAY 61 REVISITED
Cathedral-filling organ, hard blues-rock guitar and sneering, spiteful vocal coalesce on the hit that delivered Dylan to a rock audience.

❹ FOR WHAT IT'S WORTH BUFFALO SPRINGFIELD from BUFFALO SPRINGFIELD
An on-the-ground report of unrest on Sunset Strip, with an indelible chorus and Neil Young's ringing guitar notes acting as the hooks.

❺ THE SOUND OF SILENCE SIMON & GARFUNKEL from SOUNDS OF SILENCE
It might be an allusion to modern alienation, but it was so beatifically harmonized that it had no trouble making the duo into superstars.

❻ CALIFORNIA DREAMIN' THE MAMAS & THE PAPAS from IF YOU CAN BELIEVE YOUR EYES AND EARS
Deftly woven male–female harmonies and an absurdly catchy melody transform California into Utopia.

❼ GET TOGETHER THE YOUNGBLOODS from THE YOUNGBLOODS
A Utopian vision for not just California but all of humankind, steered clear of sappiness by Jesse Colin Young's gentle yet soulful vocals.

❽ DO YOU BELIEVE IN MAGIC THE LOVIN' SPOONFUL from DO YOU BELIEVE IN MAGIC
The Beatles-meets-Motown melody and an uplifting chorus cement this declaration of the healing powers of rock'n'roll. Folk-rock at its sunniest.

❾ BOTH SIDES NOW JUDY COLLINS from WILDFLOWERS
Joni Mitchell's classic taking-stock folk song, turned into a glittering folk-rock hit with a multi-hued orchestral arrangement and Collins' pristine singing.

❿ TODAY JEFFERSON AIRPLANE from SURREALISTIC PILLOW
A heartbreakingly pretty, largely acoustic ballad of cup-runneth-over hippy love that could have been a big hit, saved from schmaltziness by thundering Spectorian percussion.
Richie Unterberger

Folk-rock (3): Folktronica?

Folk Britannica gets rediscovered every few years and the current revival is being led by the likes of Kate Rusby and Eliza Carthy, Dubbed by the media as "acid-folk" , "psych-folk" or "folktronica", many of them take their inspiration from the late-1960s sounds of the likes of Fairport Convention, the Incredible String Band and Pentangle.

❶ CHINESE CHILDREN DEVENDRA BANHART from CRIPPLE CROW
OK – he is actually American, but Banhart has become a kind of neo-hippie totem of the new movement, revered as a modern-day Nick Drake.

❷ HIGHEST TREE 18TH DAY OF MAY from 18TH DAY OF MAY
Flutes, dulcimers, autoharps and mandolin from the London-based collective whose American singer Allison Brice recalls the great Sandy Denny.

❸ MOTHER'S DAUGHTER TUUNG from THIS IS TUNNG
Wicker Man-influenced pagan folk meets futuristic electronic bloops and bleeps.

❹ FAREWELL MY LOVE SETH LAKEMAN from KITTY JAY
Like the best work of Richard Thompson, a song that sounds like it could have been written 200 years ago.

❺ BARBARA ALLEN JIM MORAY from JIM MORAY
A familiar song – but performed like you've never heard it before.

❻ THE OUTLANDISH KNIGHT JAMES RAYNARD from STRANGE HISTORIES
Raynard's take on a Trad song learned from his mentor Martin Carthy, from a superb debut album that found him hailed as "the new Jim Moray".

❼ ISABELLA SOFT HEARTED SCIENTISTS from UNCANNY TALES FROM THE EVERYDAY UNDERGROWTH
Otherworldly strangeness from the trippy Welsh trio who evoke the spirit of the Incredible String Band.

❽ LOCKED TOGETHER KING CREOSOTE from KC RULES OK
An improbably gorgeous song about a shopping trip to *Safeways* from Kenny Anderson, Scotland's new monarch of the glen.

❾ RINGING IN MY EAR ADEM from HOMESONGS
Folk and electronica blend seamlessly on a track recorded in his Stoke Newington, north London, flat by moonlighting bass player from Fridge.

❿ EACH MOMENT NEW LOU RHODES from BELOVED ONE
Quiet and gentle beauty from the debut solo album by former female singer with electro-dance duo Lamb.

Nigel Williamson

Foo Fighters

Foo Fighters have made life after Nirvana worth persevering with. And main man Dave Grohl has proved to be something of an ace songwriter to boot.

❶ ALL MY LIFE from ONE BY ONE
This track hinges on a cool stuttering riff which swings psychotically between loud and soft and lets Grohl indulge in some of his finest screaming to date.

❷ AURORA from THERE IS NOTHING LEFT TO LOSE
There's no hiding the sense of aching loss and bitter-sweet memories in this teasingly enigmatic, delicate yet powerful number.

❸ BIG ME from FOO FIGHTERS
Short but very sweet, this gentle strumalong is a welcome antidote to Grohl's imposing guitar violence.

❹ LEARN TO FLY from THERE IS NOTHING LEFT TO LOSE
Textbook songwriting, with shimmering guitars, soaring vocals and a killer chorus. Grohl makes it all sound outrageously simple.

❺ MONKEY WRENCH from THE COLOUR AND THE SHAPE
An intensely melodic punk tune with one hell of a memorable hook.

❻ TIMES LIKE THESE from ONE BY ONE
Even if there were no vocals on this you'd be humming it for days after hearing it just once.

Essi Berelian

George Formby

Still no sign of him on iTunes, but the Brylcreemed, ukelele-bashing, Wigan-born singer/actor was once Britain's highest-paid entertainer. You'll find the following tracks on any number of greatest hits compilations, all of which will take you to a lost world of seaside fancies and triple entendres.

❶ THE EMPEROR OF LANCASHIRE from ENGLAND'S FAMED CLOWN PRINCE OF SONG

George the Cotton King returns home to throw a big tripe party for everyone. Oddly moving, and a great little dance tune.

❷ WHY DON'T WOMEN LIKE ME? from ENGLAND'S FAMED CLOWN PRINCE OF SONG

The Smiths used to play this one. The chorus goes: "If women like them like men like those, why don't women like me?"

❸ YOU DON'T NEED A LICENCE FOR THAT from ENGLAND'S FAMED CLOWN PRINCE OF SONG

Such is the bureaucracy of post-War Britain that the only thing George doesn't need a licence for is "two bob's worth of dark" (a snog in the cinema).

❹ CHINESE LAUNDRY BLUES from ENGLAND'S FAMED CLOWN PRINCE OF SONG

Mr Wu, knickers and other classic Formbyisms.

❺ WITH MY LITTLE STICK OF BLACKPOOL ROCK from ENGLAND'S FAMED CLOWN PRINCE OF SONG

"It may be sticky but I never complain/It's nice to have a nibble at it now and again."

❻ OUR FANNY'S GONE ALL YANKEE from ENGLAND'S FAMED CLOWN PRINCE OF SONG

The perils of GI infiltration into northwest England. Woodbines replaced by Camels, and "ee bah gum" replaced by "okay big boy".

Simon Garfield

Aretha Franklin

Under Jerry Wexler's supervision at Atlantic, the arrangements, choice of material and musicians all came together to create the perfect setting for Aretha's voice, which soared as it had never done before (and never has since).

❶ I NEVER LOVED A MAN (THE WAY I LOVE YOU) from I NEVER LOVED A MAN THE WAY I LOVE YOU

One of just two tracks Aretha laid down at Muscle Shoals for her Atlantic debut – and what a debut! Outside gospel, had anyone heard a woman express emotion like this on record before?

❷ DO RIGHT WOMAN – DO RIGHT MAN from I NEVER LOVED A MAN THE WAY I LOVE YOU

The other Muscle Shoals track. Written by top country-soul songwriters Dan Penn and Chips Moman, this – incredibly – was the B-side of "I Never Loved A

Man". A restrained but heartfelt plea for equality and respect, which brings us to…

❸ RESPECT from I NEVER LOVED A MAN THE WAY I LOVE YOU

More an answer record than a cover of Otis Redding's original, it still sounds every bit as anthemic as the day it was recorded.

❹ DR FEELGOOD (LOVE IS A SERIOUS BUSINESS) from I NEVER LOVED A MAN THE WAY I LOVE YOU

Originally the B-side of "Respect", making Aretha's second Atlantic single another strong contender for the best 45 ever. Unrestrained passion.

❺ (YOU MAKE ME FEEL LIKE) A NATURAL WOMAN from LADY SOUL

Aretha turns this Goffin/King/Wexler composition into a hymn to the redemptive power of human love.

❻ I SAY A LITTLE PRAYER from ARETHA NOW

Written by Bacharach and David for Dionne Warwick, but the sheer expressiveness and dynamic range of Aretha's voice make this the definitive version.

❼ THINK from ARETHA NOW

Another clarion call for respect (and freedom), immortalized on film in *The Blues Brothers*.

❽ LET IT BE from THIS GIRL'S IN LOVE WITH YOU

Paul McCartney is said to have written this with Aretha in mind, and you can see why: once again, she takes the song onto a higher plane.

❾ BRIDGE OVER TROUBLED WATER from RESPECT

Paul Simon took his inspiration from a gospel song, and Aretha takes it back where it belongs. A transformation.

❿ NEVER GROW OLD from AMAZING GRACE

And she never will, on these recordings at least. Aretha, the preacher's daughter, back home in church.

Neil Foxlee

Franz Ferdinand

These shamelessly arty Glaswegian bohemians have become renowned for rejuvenating New Wave and 1980s indie boy rock with their wonderfully angular, spiky song writing.

❶ AUF ACHSE from FRANZ FERDINAND

There are touches of Joy Division here with the stark, lonely synth and hypnotically memorable melody line. Strangely claustrophobic and romantic all at once.

❷ COME ON HOME from FRANZ FERDINAND
Rhythmically tight and crisp. The way the guitars and drums mesh together will send shivers up your spine. Great New Wavey synth too.

❸ DARTS OF PLEASURE from FRANZ FERDINAND
Great lyrics all about, well, the power of words. Includes an absolutely genius ending refrain – delivered in best O-level German.

❹ DO YOU WANT TO from YOU COULD HAVE IT SO MUCH BETTER
It's virtually impossible not to join in with the infectious "Do ya, do ya wanna's!" The kind of song you hear once and remember forever.

❺ ELEANOR PUT YOUR BOOTS ON from YOU COULD HAVE IT SO MUCH BETTER
Starts like a piano recital before the acoustic guitars kick in and the smooth vocal harmonies recall the pristine pop of the Fab Four.

❻ FADE TOGETHER from YOU COULD HAVE IT SO MUCH BETTER
Whimsical and touching, Alex Kapranos' wistful vocals are heavy with the passing years and melt effortlessly into the gentle piano refrain.

❼ JACQUELINE from FRANZ FERDINAND
The slow-building and low-key opening verse leads into a pumping bass line and a colourful eruption of life-affirming noise.

❽ THE DARK OF THE MATINEE from FRANZ FERDINAND
A clever and funny ode to those lost afternoons bunking off school to the local flea pit. The essential sound of a misspent youth.

❾ THE FALLEN from YOU COULD HAVE IT SO MUCH BETTER
Great lyrics, a gloriously catchy melody and one of those ballsy, brisk marching rhythms that Franz Ferdinand do so well.

❿ YOU COULD HAVE IT SO MUCH BETTER from YOU COULD HAVE IT SO MUCH BETTER
Packed with so much gutsy energy this is verging on punk rock. An attitude-filled musical call to arms it's tough to resist.

Essi Berelian

Free
Featuring Paul Rodgers' warm vocals and Paul Kossoff's ace guitar talents, these legendary

bluesy youngsters possessed soul and maturity way beyond their years.

❶ ALL RIGHT NOW from FIRE AND WATER
A hooky stop-start riff, Rodger's sexy yelp and some seriously funky bass and percussion make this a feel-good classic.

❷ FIRE AND WATER from FIRE AND WATER
Paul Rodgers is hurtin' bad, mama, and he's just gotta get it off his (very hairy) chest. Kossoff makes his guitar cry like a true pro.

❸ HEAVY LOAD from FIRE AND WATER
How can a piano sound so world-weary? A beautifully wrought slice of misery with guitars relegated to the searing climax.

❹ LYING IN THE SUNSHINE from FREE
Summer heat turned into a liquid guitar refrain and complemented by Rodgers' languid vocals – he almost sounds like he's melting.

❺ MOUTHFUL OF GRASS from FREE
The sense of peace and space conjured up by this blissful instrumental is almost celestial. Less is definitely more.

❻ OH I WEPT from FIRE AND WATER
A gentle and lilting effort – Rodgers' voice almost cracks from the emotional struggle. Another economical but profound classic.

❼ SOLDIER BOY from FREE AT LAST
Martial drum rolls lead you into battle. Dark and troubled in tone, the song features some simple yet powerful guitar work.

❽ THE HUNTER from TONS OF SOBS
Just listen to Kossoff's guitar wail on this ferocious makeover of an R&B classic. Amazing to think the band were just teenagers at this time.

❾ THE STEALER from HIGHWAY
Andy Fraser's slippery, almost squelchy bass gives this track – which edges more towards rock – a fine and funky groove.

❿ WISHING WELL from HEARTBREAKER
A lot heavier and darker than their early stuff, with a stonking riff that makes this an early heavy-rock masterpiece.

Essi Berelian

French chansons

OK, our French friends do not do *le rock*, but when it comes to songs – well, they are the masters. We could, maybe should, have done a whole list for many of the figures below, especially Charles Trenet (he of Boum!), who graced half the classic French movies of the postwar years. Oh well, next edition...

❶ LA MER CHARLES TRENET from LA MER
Bobby Darin reworked this as "Beyond The Sea" but Trenet's haunting original is the one to play as you cruise the Croisette in your 2CV.

❷ LA VIE EN ROSE EDITH PIAF from SONGS OF A SPARROW
The Little Sparrow's best-known song may be "Je Ne Regrette Rien" but this swirling accordeon-backed ballad is her finest work as both performer and lyricist.

❸ ET MAINTENANT GILBERT BÉCAUD from L'ESSENTIEL
Becaud was the epitome of a singing French heartthrob – his "Et Maintenant" became Shirley Bassey's "What Now, My Love". Becaud gives his original the famous sex-charged 100,000 volts.

❹ SOUS LE CIEL DE PARIS JULIETTE GRÉCO from THE BEST
You can almost smell the Gauloises and taste the Ricard in this classic rendering of a song that conjures up 1960s Paris, when Greco was the proto-hippy-chick icon of the Left Bank.

❺ LA CHANSON DE JACKY JACQUES BREL from INFINIMENT
Belgian-born Brel inspired a generation of songwriters, from David Bowie to Marc Almond and Scott Walker, who had a hit with this track in English. Insist on the original.

❻ COMME D'HABITUDE CLAUDE FRANÇOIS from COMME D'HABITUDE
Paul Anka took this gentle reflection on unrequited love and turned it into Sinatra's balls-out "My Way". Again, enjoy the more thoughtful and melancholic original.

❼ LE GORILLE GEORGE BRASSENS from LE GORILLE
Brassens remains an iconic French figure who composed thoughtful, witty songs. This one's about a well-endowed gorilla who escapes captivity and sodomizes a judge.

❽ JE T'AIME ... MOI NON PLUS SERGE GAINSBOURG & JANE BIRKIN from JANE BIRKIN & SERGE GAINSBOURG
English actress Birkin took over the singing role originally intended for Brigitte Bardot in this orgasmic romp, censured by the Vatican.

❾ VOUS QUI PASSEZ SANS ME VOIR JEAN SABLON from C'EST SI BON
Sablon's song was a big hit in France in 1937, when he rivalled Maurice Chevalier on the world stage. To be taken with a glass of cognac in the wee small hours.

❿ J'ATTENDRAI TINO ROSSI from J'ATTENDRAI
Corsican-born Rossi was a great prewar pin-up who produced a string of hits, and none better than this lush, atmospheric ballad.

Frank Barrett

French roots

The French roots music scene is big and vital and the country has numerous and strong regional strands. But the most fun to be had is in the South, so that is the emphasis here.

❶ JOHNNY BRATSCH from RIEN DANS LES POCHES
Bratsch are the foremost band in France, having played together for thirty years now. Here these mad instrumentalists join forces with Hungarian Gypsy musicians Ando Drom on a song made famous by Edith Piaf.

❷ A L'ARENE DES AUDACIEUX LO JO from AU CABARET SAUVAGE
Lo Jo is a wildly eclectic musical collective from Angers. With an imaginative array of instruments, and fronted by two North African sisters, they kick like hell on this.

❸ PAS DE CI FABULOUS TROUBADORS from ERA PAS DE FAIRE
A professor of linguistics and a B-boy fuse the troubadours, Brazilian *nordestina* and reggae. Inspired lyrics (in French and Occitan) are the icing on the cake.

❹ PAGHJELLA DONNISULANA from PER AGATA
Donnisulana were revolutionaries in Corsican traditional music. Until they came on the scene, women were allowed only to sing to their babies and mourn the dead.

❺ LOS GOJATS COMPAGNIE LUBAT DÉ GASCONHA from SCATRAP JAZZCOGNE
Four free-jazz musicians relocate to the small southern town of Uzeste to create a mindblowing mix of jazz, rap, reggae and roots.

⑥ VOLI PAS MAI MOLZER LAS VACAS LA TALVERA from PAMPALIGOSSA

An outstanding combination of Southern French traditionals and dub-infused reggae.

⑦ ONDA LES NOUVELLES POLYPHONIES CORSES from LES NOUVELLES POLYPHONIES CORSES WITH HECTOR ZAZOU

An almost ambient rendering of traditional polyphonic singing with electronics, Ryuichy Sakamoto's piano and the clarinet of Ivo Papasov from Bulgaria.

⑧ MIRLIN TURKI ERIC MARCHAND ET LE TARAF DE CARABENSEBES from +DOR

Breton Eric Marchand combines with a gypsy band from Romania on this outing, which gives a new jazzy feel to both musics.

⑨ FACE À LA MER LES NÉGRESSES VERTES from 10 REMIXES 87–93

The Négresses did a fantastic fusion of rock with roots. Here Massive Attack reconstructed their song about a cemetery by the beach.

⑩ CAMINA DUPAIN from CAMINA

A Provençal song from this Marseille band, set to plaintive trumpet, hurdy gurdy and vocals. Ancient roots but 100% contemporary.

Jean Trouillet

Dodgy French

Somehow, putting a few French *mots* in an otherwise *anglais* song pretty much guarantees *sérieux* kitsch. Blondie manage to get away with it; way down at the other end of the scale, there's Bill Wyman.

① DENIS BLONDIE from PLASTIC LETTERS

The lyrics are equally indecipherable in either French or English. But in general, Denis-dippy-doo, it's safe to assume that Blondie is in love with you-ah-oo. (In fact, she loves you so much she wants "a giant, everlasting fuck", to translate the last line.)

② LE FREAK CHIC from C'EST CHIC

"Young and old are doing it, I'm told." Aaaaaah freak off.

③ HIT ME WITH YOUR RHYTHM STICK IAN DURY AND THE BLOCKHEADS from SEX & DRUGS & ROCK & ROLL

"Das ist gut, c'est fantastique" – not just French, but German too! Hit me! Hit me! Hit me!

④ I'M NOT SCARED EIGHTH WONDER from FEARLESS

The Pet Shop Boys' Neil Tennant asks us to "débarasse-moi de ces chiens/Avant qu'ils mordent". Yes, please get these dogs away from him before they bite.

⑤ JE NE SAIS PAS POURQUOI KYLIE from KYLIE

Sadly, we don't know why either. Maybe Kylie should have thought about it first?

⑥ JOE LE TAXI VANESSA PARADIS from M&J

OK, so she's French, but the lyrics are so bizarrely awful that her only excuse should have been being English.

⑦ LADY MARMALADE LABELLE from NIGHTBIRDS

Voulez-vous coucher avec moi? If you put it like that, then yes. A cover of a 1974 song about New Orleans prostitutes by The Eleventh Hour. Much covered since – by All Saints, and the lethal combination of Christina Aguilera, Lil' Kim, Mya & Pink (who you'd think were more likely to insist).

⑧ MICHELLE THE BEATLES from RUBBER SOUL

"… ma belle/These are words which go together well." Or perhaps not.

⑨ PSYCHO KILLER TALKING HEADS from TALKING HEADS '77

"Qu'est-ce que c'est/Fa fa fa fa fa fa fa fa fa fa/Far better". As David Byrne admits, "you're talkin' a lot, but you're not sayin' anything".

⑩ SI SI JE SUIS UN ROCK STAR BILL WYMAN from BILL WYMAN

Bill habite dans le south of France. Voulez-vous partir wiv' 'im? Unforgettable (unfortunately). Actually, the English lyrics are better still: "We can take a hovercraft/Across the water/They'll think I'm your dad/And you're my daughter." Umm…

James McConnachie

Street-funk

As the 1960s gave way to the 1970s and soul osmosed into funk, the more in-your-face end of things was street-funk. Gloriously confident, deceptively three dimensional, totally infectious and often brought to us by our fellow teenagers.

① WHO IS HE, WHAT IS HE TO YOU? CREATIVE SOURCE from CREATIVE SOURCE

Written by label-mate Bill Withers, this orchestral monster of streetfunk paranoia was probably the finest Norman Whitfield never produced.

❷ STOMP & BUCK DANCE THE CRUSADERS from SOUTHERN COMFORT

A bit of an surprise back in 1974 when this churning, honking, totally irresistible sax-led stomper popped up out of a double album of mostly mellow jazz funk.

❸ HERE COMES THE EXPRESS BT EXPRESS from DO IT 'TIL YOU'RE SATISFIED

This band only had two big hits, but when one of them was as relentlessly-looping and window-rattlingly self-celebratory as this, you don't need any more.

❹ SO MUCH TROUBLE IN MY MIND SIR JOE QUARTERMAIN & FREE SOUL from SIR JOE QUARTERMAIN & FREE SOUL

The merciless groove is go-go ten years before the term was invented, while Sir Joe's catalogue of his everyday woes makes for a very 1970s take on the blues.

❺ SLIPPING INTO DARKNESS WAR from ALL DAY MUSIC

War were always more like a gang than a group and their lowriding, Latino-tinged funk was never as worryingly edgy as this.

❻ PAPA DON'T TAKE NO MESS JAMES BROWN from HELL

Everything James Brown and the JBs did from "Sex Machine" onwards led up to this quarter of an hour of rumbling, creeping, spiralling groove.

❼ TROPICAL AFRICAN MUSIC MACHINE from BLACKWATER GOLD

Horn-tastic, tempo switching while groove maintaining instrumental is a brilliant example of street funk's intrinsic musicality.

❽ GUT LEVEL THE BLACKBYRDS from THE BLACKBYRDS

If only all records were this accurately titled.

❾ FENCEWALK MANDRILL from THE COMPOSITE TRUTH

Guitar'n'brass madness with more capacity to surprise than any five minutes of music has any right to.

❿ NIJA WALK STREET WALK THE FATBACK BAND from PEOPLE MUSIC

Skin tight guitar, barrel-chested bassline, apparently random horn riffs and hollered vocals about having no car – classic Fatback-party-in-the-studio.

Lloyd Bradley

Jazz-funk

A 1970s/early 1980s phenomenon marrying deep funk grooves to jazz's melodic sensibilities, jazz-funk allowed jazzers of all stripes to reach the dancefloor.

❶ EXPANSIONS LONNIE LISTON SMITH from EXPANSIONS

The much-sampled bassline will be familiar to many, while the relationship between the rhythm and the soloing set a template for so much of the genre.

❷ ROLLER JUBILEE AL DIMIOLA from SPLENDIDO HOTEL

Very South American, very uptempo, very lightweight in linen shirt and panama hat kinda way. A club classic and exactly the sort of thing that got jazz-funk such bad press in the punk-obsessed music papers of the day!

❸ WHISTLE BUMP DEODATO from LOVE ISLAND

Staying, just, on the acceptable side of disco, Brazilian arranger/composer weaves layers over a driving beat to build up a truly towering dancefloor anthem.

❹ WESTCHESTER LADY BOB JAMES from BOB JAMES THREE

It was skittering complicated rhythms that made jazz-funk so compelling, but this is so on edge there must be a 1970s espionage thriller out there wants its theme tune back.

❺ THEME FROM MASH ROY AYERS UBIQUITY from CHANGE UP THE GROOVE

Vibraphonic delicacy and a solid funk rhythm section ensure of the original movie's vocal version's melancholy, but with no danger of anybody opening a vein.

❻ LASANA'S PRIESTESS DONALD BYRD from STREET LADY

The best track on Byrd's most exciting album – 1973's *Street Lady*. The trumpeter and his arranger Larry Mizell are clearly having huge fun exploring just how far they can take this jazz-funk thing.

❼ UNICORN DIZZY GILLESPIE AND LALO SCHIFRIN 12" SINGLE

Dizz recruited Lalo in Argentina, this is South American-flavoured bop in a thoroughly contemporary (in 1977) setting.

❽ GROVER WASHINGTON MISTER MAGIC from MISTER MAGIC

Grover was the sax player Kenny G must've wanted to be, and this shows why. Total understanding of what makes funk, smoothed over with an oozing sax.

❾ COME TOGETHER GEORGE BENSON from THE OTHER SIDE OF ABBEY ROAD

What with all the dodgy vocals and the Jehovah's Witnessing, people often forget Benson was a damn good guitarist. Here, a particularly gruff take on the Beatles' riff provides a perfect funk platform for it.

⑩ CHAMELEON HERBIE HANCOCK from HEAD HUNTERS
Fifteen-minute-long slinky, tricky wholly absorbing adventure in time, exploring just about every corner of these new-fangled keyboard thingies.

Lloyd Bradley

P-funk

It's safe to say that nobody has traversed the mind-booty divide more audaciously than George Clinton, with his Parliafunkadelicment Thang. Here are ten records that prove that funk "can not only move, but remove, ya dig?"

❶ (I WANNA) TESTIFY THE PARLIAMENTS from I WANNA TESTIFY
One of the very first records to blend guitar psychedelia with vocal-group harmonizing.

❷ MAGGOT BRAIN FUNKADELIC from MAGGOT BRAIN
Ten minutes of devastatingly emotive post-Hendrix guitar; the result of Clinton directing Eddie Hazel to play like his "mother had just died".

❸ UP FOR THE DOWN STROKE PARLIAMENT from UP FOR THE DOWN STROKE
Preposterously funky monolithic groove.

❹ COSMIC SLOP FUNKADELIC from COSMIC SLOP
A remarkable tale of a mother turning tricks to feed her kids.

❺ CHOCOLATE CITY PARLIAMENT from CHOCOLATE CITY
White stereotypes of insatiable black hypersexuality, turned into a black power fantasy to keep George Wallace and Enoch Powell awake at night.

❻ GIVE UP THE FUNK (TEAR THE ROOF OFF THE SUCKER) PARLIAMENT from MOTHERSHIP CONNECTION
One of Clinton's most outlandish sci-fi funk fantasies.

❼ VANISH IN OUR SLEEP BOOTSY'S RUBBER BAND from STRETCHIN' OUT IN BOOTSY'S RUBBER BAND
A scary/funny, acid-soaked conflation of Eros and Thanatos.

❽ FLASH LIGHT PARLIAMENT from FUNKENTELECHY VS. THE PLACEBO SYNDROME
The collective's greatest groove was one of the first records truly to appreciate the synth's abilities as a rhythm machine.

❾ ONE NATION UNDER A GROOVE FUNKADELIC from ONE NATION UNDER A GROOVE
Clinton's most unabashedly anthemic record.

⑩ ATOMIC DOG GEORGE CLINTON from COMPUTER GAMES
The synth stomp that launched a thousand G-funk rap records.

Peter Shapiro

Funkadelic

Funkadelic were to many the essence of P-funk, born out of screaming guitars, mountains of acid and intricate vocal arrangements that owed themselves to a competition-winning barbershop quintet.

❶ COSMIC SLOP LIVE from HARDCORE JOLLIES
Recorded in aircraft hangar, this is Funkadelic in rehearsal and it still blows most bands concerts away. Importantly though, introduces teenage guitar pyro Mike Hampton.

❷ ONE NATION UNDER A GROOVE INSTRUMENTAL from THE WHOLE FUNK & NOTHING BUT THE FUNK
It sort of sounds less like a Parliament track with Mike Hampton's guitar taking over from the lead vocals.

❸ ELECTRIC SPANKING OF WAR BABIES from THE ELECTRIC SPANKING OF WAR BABIES
The group was in dispute with the record company, so delivered an album that was "one for the fans" and as far removed from the previous offering (Uncle Jam) as possible. Good for them.

❹ BECAUSE/LAST TIME ZONE from HOW LATE DO U HAVE 2BB4UR ABSENT?
Acoustic madness. Nuff said.

❺ LET'S TAKE IT TO THE STAGE from LET'S TAKE IT TO THE STAGE
Off the cuff self-celebratory bravado as Funkadelic fool about over the tightest of guitar riffs.

❻ NO COMPUTE from COSMIC SLOP
There's a countrified air about this as the guitars duel in the background of this jaunty tale of everyday life inn the 'hood.

❼ UNDISCO KIDD from TALES OF KIDD FUNKADELIC
Bernie Worrell, Bootsy and Mike Hampton chase each other around relentless rhythm.

8 (NOT JUST) KNEE DEEP from UNCLE JAM NEEDS YOU
Possibly the only Funkadelic tune that manages to
sound straightforward and freaky at the same time.

**9 IF YOU DON'T LIKE THE EFFECTS, DON'T
PRODUCE THE CAUSE** from AMERICA EATS IT YOUNG
An anti-protest protest song – now just how
Funkadelic is that?

10 MAGGOTBRAIN from LIVE MEADOWBROOK, ROCHESTER
Fourteen minutes of vintage Funkadelic fronted by
Eddie Hazel and dark and unsettling enough to reveal
the essence of the group at that time (1971).

Lloyd Bradley

Sons of The P

No P-funk, very little gangsta rap. Indeed such
was early 1990s hip-hop's debt to George Clinton's
crew, part of it even dubbed itself G-funk. These
are some of the more high profile borrowings. Oh
–and yes, it has to be filed under "F".

1 WHO AM I WHAT'S MY NAME? SNOOP DOGG from
DOGGYSTYLE
Contains a sample of "Give Up The Funk" from
Mothership Connection.

2 BOP GUN ONE NATION ICE CUBE from LETHAL
INJECTION
Contains a sample of "One Nation Under A Groove"
and features George Clinton on the track.

3 GET UP EVERYBODY GET UP SALT-N-PEPA from A SALT
WITH A DEADLY PEPA
Contains a sample of "Up For The Down Stroke" and

"All Your Goodies Are Gone", both from *Up For The
Down Stroke*.

4 LET ME RIDE DR DRE from THE CHRONIC
Built on a sample of "Swing Low Sweet Chariot" from
Parliament Live: P Funk Earth Tour and also features a
sample from "Mothership Connection".

5 ME MYSELF AND I DE LA SOUL from 3 FEET HIGH AND
RISING
Built on the main riff from "(Not Just) Knee Deep" from
Uncle Jam Wants You.

6 NIGGAZ4LIFE NWA from EFIL4ZAGGIN
Contains a sample from "Sir Nose D'Voidoffunk" from
Funkentelechy vs The Placebo Syndrome.

7 LYRICS OF FURY ERIC B & RAKIM from FOLLOW THE
LEADER
Contains a sample from "No Head No Backstage Pass"
from *Let's Take It To The Stage*.

8 HOLLER IF YOU HEAR ME 2PAC from RESURRECTION
Contains a sample of "Atomic Dog" from *Computer
Games*.

9 NIGHT TRAIN PUBLIC ENEMY from APOCALYPSE 91 ...
THE ENEMY STRIKES BLACK
Barely recognizable, but it's built on a snatch of
"Flashlight" from *Funkentelechy vs The Placebo
Syndrome*.

10 THE HUMPTY DANCE DIGITAL UNDERGROUND from
SEX PACKETS
Built on a deconstructed riff from "Bop Gun" from
Funkentelechy vs The Placebo Syndrome.

Lloyd Bradley

G

Gabber

Gabber is harder, faster and nastier than any other genre of dance music. Look beyond the (occasionally puerile) shock tactics, though, and you might just discover some gems among these brutalist anthems. Play LOUD.

❶ WE HAVE ARRIVED MESCALINUM UNITED from INDUSTRIAL FUCKING STRENGTH
Made in 1989, "We Have Arrived" is much slower and more restrained than what was to come, but is widely acknowledged as being the first ever gabber record.

❷ I WANNA BE A HIPPY (REMIX) THE SPEEDFREAK from I WANNA BE A HIPPY
Technohead's radio-friendly cut of this pop-gabba tune reached the UK Top 40. Who knows what the Smash Hits kids made of The Speedfreak's friskier version on the flip side.

❸ FUCKING HOSTILE '96 DJ SKINHEAD from INDUSTRIAL FUCKING STRENGTH
A bouncy, stomping number. The characteristically direct Pantera-sampling lyric is punctuated by a screaming 303 and doomy synth stabs.

❹ 6,000,000 WAYS TO DIE TURBULENCE & TERRORIST from ROTTERDAM MOST WANTED HARDCORE
Stripped down to the brutal kick drum, this is gabber at its purest and nastiest.

❺ 666 I'M SIX O'SICK OMAR SANTANA from MASTERS OF HARDCORE CHAPTER XIV – THE EVILUTION OF ABANDONED SOULS
Santana's immaculate production gives this definitive rave track a raw, physical punch.

❻ CANNIBAL HOLOCAUST FACE HOOVER from FRUIT OF THE DOOM CHAPTER II
If you like your rave music to come with a healthy side-order of fear, emptiness and claustrophobia, then listen to this doom-laden stomper.

❼ UNLEASH THE BRUTALITY DISCIPLES OF ANNHILATION from INDUSTRIAL FUCKING STRENGTH VOL 2: UNLEASH THE BRUTALITY
Possibly the scariest five minutes of music you will ever hear.

❽ ULTRAVIOLENCE HELLFISH from BASTARD SONZ OF RAVE
Insanely chopped-up breaks add another dimension to the scything attack of the pitched kick drum.

❾ CUNTFACE NASENBLÜTEN from 100% NO SOUL GUARANTEED
Light, if extremely offensive, relief from Australia.

❿ EXTREME HARDCORE SHIT EXTREMENT from 12" SINGLE
A short, sharp, sweet blast of speedcore, only ever released on a double A-sided 12" that Extrement shared with the equally hardcore, and fantastically named, Geordie Gabba Mafia. You can't have my copy.

Dan May

Peter Gabriel

After six albums with Genesis, Peter Gabriel walked, reinventing himself as a sound collagist – more landscape gardener, you might say, than rock god.

❶ SOLSBURY HILL from PETER GABRIEL 1
A deceptively simple acoustic guitar riff runs through-out this celebration of artistic freedom and the pleasures of rural Wiltshire.

❷ HERE COMES THE FLOOD ROBERT FRIPP from EXPOSURE
On Peter Gabriel 1 this song was operatic. Here, on a Robert Fripp solo album, it emerges sparsely from dripping electronica and is all the more effective for it.

❸ GAMES WITHOUT FRONTIERS (MASSIVE/DB REMIX) from STEAM
A West Country trip-hop remix freshens up this war-horse and restores its playfulness.

❹ ACROSS THE RIVER from THE SECRET WORLD LIVE
Drums crash and Gabriel wails in an early example of his interest in world music. It first appeared on an album to pay off the debts incurred by the first WOMAD festival.

❺ WALLFLOWER from PETER GABRIEL 4
Unlike his song "Biko" (which he gave initially to Robert Wyatt), this human rights anthem has an anonymous

hero facing interrogation from "clean white coats", Fairlight synthesizer samples rising from the shadows.

6 MERCY STREET from SO
A rippling melody, one notch above ambient, drives this song about the poet Anne Sexton.

7 SLEDGEHAMMER from SO
A song that inspires genuine affection even from non-fans – and one of the few occasions where Gabriel's love of steam-driven Motown-tinged funk pays off.

8 BLOOD OF EDEN from US
A second cousin to Gabriel's duet with Kate Bush, "Don't Give Up", this sees him teaming up with Sinead O'Connor, as brilliant and berserk as ever. The mix is loose and supple, with a keening duduk refrain.

9 WHILE THE EARTH SLEEPS from THE STRANGE DAYS SOUNDTRACK
A collaboration with Belgian sonic colonialists Deep Forest sets Gabriel against Congolese pygmies for a mesmeric dance-workout.

10 DOWNSIDE UP from OVO
The Gabriel-soundtracked theatrical circus show was the one redeeming feature of the Millennium Dome: his music celebrated multicultural Britain and stood up in its own right.

David Honigmann

Galaxyquest

Space, the final musical frontier. Meet the songwriters who have boldly gone where no songwriters had gone before, exploring the universe's vast potential for cosmic metaphor.

1 LIFE ON MARS? DAVID BOWIE from HUNKY DORY
Describing a young girl's escapism through cinema, this is prime Bowie, building from simple piano to a towering orchestral finale.

2 SATURN STEVIE WONDER from SONGS IN THE KEY OF LIFE
Paradise is nowhere to be found on Earth, according to a world-weary Stevie. Above futuristic synth effects, he's "going back to Saturn where the people smile".

3 PLANET CLAIRE B52s from THE B52s
A perfect introduction to this band of cosmic crazies, Planet Claire is a wonderfully nonsensical cut of kitsch post-punk pop. Peter Gunn-esque strains and Fred Schneider's raving about aliens make for a surefire party-starter.

4 PLANET EARTH DURAN DURAN from DURAN DURAN
The Brummie pin-ups' blistering debut single. In between the catchy "bop-b'dop"s, Simon Le Bon alludes to impending global disaster.

5 APOLLO 9 ADAM ANT from VIVE LE ROCK
Prince Charming waxes philosophical about a female who's escaped his attentions by hopping a passing star. Not that it seems to dampen his spirits.

6 SATURN 5 INSPIRAL CARPETS from DEVIL HOPPING
A nostalgic jaunt through the heyday of space exploration, courtesy of Oldham's bowl-cut-wearing baggies. Clint Boon's childhood fascination with the 1960s moon landings is complemented by the band's cheerful energy and telltale organ tinkling.

7 FLY ME TO THE MOON FRANK SINATRA from SINATRA AT THE SANDS
Ol' Blue Eyes gave us the definitive version of this popular song, which namechecks a few other celestial bodies for good measure. This 1966 live recording showcases Sinatra and Count Basie at their best.

8 ROCKET MAN ELTON JOHN from HONKY CHATEAU 1972
Bernie Taupin's lyrics explore the isolation of an astronaut (a topical theme for the period), while Elt provides his inimitable flourish.

9 GIRL FROM MARS ASH from 1977
Wistful memories of the eponymous sweetheart are moulded into an energetic speed ballad by the then-teenage Tim Wheeler and co.

10 SATURN RETURN R.E.M. from REVEAL
Rich, electronic background music is kept in check, ceding centre-stage to Michael Stipe's reflective, confessional tone. A simple, but effective example of understated elegance.

Ed Wright

Garage rock

Decades before garage rock was synonymous with fake brother-and-sister bands or boarding-school alumni, the term meant nondescript American teens and college kids desperately trying to imitate the Stones. It was everything rock'n'roll was supposed to be.

1 LOUIE LOUIE THE KINGSMEN from THE KINGSMEN IN PERSON
The Rosetta Stone of rock'n'roll.

g

❷ WOOLY BULLY SAM THE SHAM & THE PHARAOHS from WOOLY BULLY
Strip-joint R&B taken out into the stratosphere by a guy wearing a turban. There's a long-running debate on what the words are, or mean. "Got a cold haddock" is a possible for the opening line.

❸ PSYCHO THE SONICS from HERE ARE THE SONICS
Drunken frat boys try to sing soul with gloriously sloppy results.

❹ DIRTY WATER THE STANDELLS from DIRTY WATER
As close as the Yanks got to the snarl and strut of The Rolling Stones.

❺ YOU'RE GONNA MISS ME THE 13TH FLOOR ELEVATORS from THE PSYCHEDELIC SOUNDS OF THE 13TH FLOOR ELEVATORS
Surf guitar + crazy electric jug + the punkiest vocals before Iggy Pop came along = perhaps the most intense garage record.

❻ 96 TEARS ? & THE MYSTERIANS from 96 TEARS
The record that definitively proved how much power one single note can have.

❼ HEY JOE THE LEAVES from HEY JOE
Byrds jingle-jangle meets lysergic feedback freakout.

❽ LAST TIME AROUND THE DEL-VETTS from OH YEAH! THE BEST OF DUNWICH RECORDS VOL 1
Total Yardbirds rip-off, but when the results are this fuzzy and wild, who cares?

❾ PSYCHOTIC REACTION COUNT FIVE from PSYCHOTIC REACTION
Even groovier than the group's stage apparel, which was no mean feat, as the Five all wore Dracula capes.

❿ ACTION WOMAN THE LITTER from DISTORTIONS
The venom of The Stones gets teleported "out there" by one of the great guitar wig-outs of the 1960s.
Peter Shapiro

Jan Garbarek

The cathedral-toned Norwegian saxophonist Jan Garbarek defined the "ECM sound" – sepulchral northern European jazz. He moves seamlessly through Norwegian folk, Indian idioms, medieval polyphony, even electronica.

❶ BEAST OF KOMMODO from AFRIC PEPPERBIRD
Terje Rypdal on electric guitar, Arild Andersen on bass and Jon Christensen on percussion provide an exotic

rhythmic ground, over which Garbarek howls and growls on tenor and flute: a far cry from his later reverent stillness.

❷ VIDDENE from DIS
Ralph Towner's backdrop of twelve-string guitar and wind-harp throbs and breathes as Garbarek declaims on soprano. A couple of minutes in, the mood turns almost Spanish.

❸ LILLEKORT from EVENTYR
Nana Vasconcelos's talking drums ripple underneath a duet between Garbarek and John Abercrombie's mandolin.

❹ SAGA from RAGAS AND SAGAS
Pakistani musicians joined Garbarek for four ragas and one saga. On the former, Garbarek keeps a respectful distance; the saga is a fuller collaboration, Garbarek's sax bouncing off Ustad Fateh Ali Khan's singing.

❺ BROTHER WIND SONG from TWELVE MOONS
After a couple of minutes of fragmented chaos, a determined melody starts, which swells into a march. Towards the end, Rainer Bruninghaus takes a perfect, trickling piano solo.

❻ PARCE MIHI DOMINE from OFFICIUM
The Hilliard Ensemble and Garbarek play a mass for the dead. Garbarek's chorister-like soprano responds and rises up in praise.

❼ O LORD IN THEE IS ALL MY TRUST from MNEMOSYNE
A return to the monastery: in this case, it is Thomas Tallis's anthem over which Garbarek swoops, rising nearer God with each verse.

❽ IN PRAISE OF DREAMS from IN PRAISE OF DREAMS
Garbarek and viola player Kim Kashkashian slip in and out of time with each other to increasingly fractured and unsettling effect.

❾ MOLDE CANTICLE from I TOOK UP THE RUNES
Over the space of half an hour, Garbarek repeats essentially the same soprano phrase, while the band crash mountainously around him. Amazingly, it sustains interest for the whole time

❿ TWELVE MOONS from TWELVE MOONS
Garbarek provides a delicate prickle of synthesizers while Manu Katche drums up a clattering blizzard.
David Honigmann

145

Judy Garland

Child star, adult diva, showbiz legend and the Mistress of POW!

❶ YOU MADE ME LOVE YOU from BROADWAY MELODY OF 1938
Aged 15 but sounding 30, in the movie Judy delivers this emotional version of the 1913 warhorse while gazing at a photograph of movie star Clark Gable.

❷ OVER THE RAINBOW from THE WIZARD OF OZ
Rescued from being cut during previews, the definitive version of the yearning Arlen/Harburg song appeared in the 1939 classic. It made Judy a star.

❸ THE TROLLEY SONG from MEET ME IN ST LOUIS
Best of a string of great Blaine/Martin songs ("Have Yourself A Merry Little Christmas", "The Boy Next Door") in the movie. Garland's rhythmic fizz and energy are irresistible.

❹ A COUPLE OF SWELLS from EASTER PARADE
A genuinely funny duet number with Fred Astaire from the 1948 movie Easter Parade, for which Judy and Fred portray tramps.

❺ FOR ME AND MY GAL from LIVE AT THE PALACE
Judy was reinvented by husband Sid Luft as a concert performer after MGM sacked her and this version of an old Garland movie song is from her 1951–52 residency in New York. Her charisma shines through the lo-fi recording.

❻ THE MAN THAT GOT AWAY from A STAR IS BORN
From the 1954 movie that (briefly) re-launched her film career after an unstable period, a devastating, single-take tour de force of the Arlen/Gershwin song.

❼ ZING WENT THE STRINGS OF MY HEART from JUDY IN LOVE
A Garland favourite first heard in the 1938 movie Listen, Darling, Nelson Riddle recasts it as a hard swinger on her 1958 album for Capitol, and Judy comes out guns blazing.

❽ WHEN YOU'RE SMILING from JUDY AT CARNEGIE HALL
It was in concert that mature Judy made sense; from her legendary 1961 live album, her opening number sets the tone: sentimental, funny, powerful and utterly unforgettable.

❾ MEDLEY from JUDY, FRANK AND DEAN
After some amiable fun with guests Sinatra and Martin, Judy steals her own 1962 TV special with a final mesmerizing selection of vaudeville and movie oldies.

❿ BY MYSELF from I COULD GO ON SINGING
From her final movie in 1963 in which Judy virtually played herself, a heartstopping version of the Deitz/Schwartz ballad.

Chris Ingham

Marvin Gaye

From his early solo hits and duets with Tammi Terrell and others, to his later, more political and more confessional work, Marvin Gaye was the most diverse and original soul artist of all time.

❶ WHAT'S GOING ON? from WHAT'S GOING ON?
Motown soul music gets political. This initiated Gaye's ground-breaking song-cycle of religion, poverty and the modern world.

❷ LET'S GET IT ON from LET'S GET IT ON
The steamy opener on Gaye's remarkable and unprecedented album of sex and relationships grooves.

❸ MERCY MERCY ME from WHAT'S GOING ON?
Not only was this song's subject-matter – the environment – unusual for its time, especially for a soul artist, but the stark arrangement, gently repetitive rhythm, gutsy sax and stagey ending make it a piece of pure innovation.

❹ JUST TO KEEP YOU SATISFIED from LET'S GET IT ON
Gaye's voice is never better than on this soaring, painfully explicit valediction to his wife and failed marriage. Perhaps the most poignant piece of music he ever produced.

❺ WHEN DID YOU STOP LOVING ME; WHEN DID I STOP LOVING YOU? from HERE MY DEAR
Gaye's attack on his ex-wife Anna Gordy, from the album whose royalties he was ordered to pay to her as alimony, is a rambling affair, but this track is as passionate as anything he recorded.

❻ SEXUAL HEALING from MIDNIGHT LOVE
The comeback song, with Gaye returning to form – and sobriety – in Belgium, where he wrote this solid sexy groove in twenty minutes.

❼ TOO BUSY THINKING ABOUT MY BABY from MPG
Not the obvious solo Marvin track from this era, but

displaying all the right Motown credentials – great song, great arrangement, and inch-perfect delivery.

❽ HOW SWEET IT IS (TO BE LOVED BY YOU) from HOW SWEET IT IS (TO BE LOVED BY YOU)
Marvin at the zenith of his solo pop career – his biggest seller before Grapevine.

❾ YOU'RE ALL I NEED TO GET BY MARVIN GAYE & TAMMI TERRELL from THE COMPLETE DUETS
This symbiotic duet represents the pinnacle of Marvin's time with probably his greatest partner, Tammi Terrell, before she died tragically young. They were perhaps the ultimate singing duo.

❿ MAIN THEME FROM TROUBLE MAN from TROUBLE MAN
Marvin wrote every note of this Blaxploitation soundtrack, and it is an overlooked gem: cool, spare and not unlike *What's Going On* in mood. One of Gaye's own favourites.

Martin Dunford

Genesis

With their widdly diddly keyboards and crazy concept albums, the original Genesis were synonymous with prog rock until Phil Collins led them into the world of 1980s pop. Here's a selection from both camps.

GABRIEL DAYS

❶ THE FOUNTAIN OF SALMACIS from NURSERY CRYME
Greek gods and nymphs meet in this odd little prog drama. Sun-dappled waters and isolated glades never sounded more enchanting.

❷ SUPPER'S READY from FOXTROT
At nearly 23 minutes this is an early defining epic. Surreal, blackly humorous and cryptic, you'll hear something new every time.

❸ I KNOW WHAT I LIKE (IN YOUR WARDROBE) from SELLING ENGLAND BY THE POUND
The band's first proper hit. Typically wacky lyrics about sentient lawnmowers (or something) from Gabriel and some great whirring effects.

❹ THE LAMB LIES DOWN ON BROADWAY from THE LAMB LIES DOWN ON BROADWAY
Concept albums ahoy! A majestic opening to a classic album, Gabriel's loopy lyrics joyously defy logic.

❺ IN THE CAGE from THE LAMB LIES DOWN ON BROADWAY
Beware weird time-signatures. Gabriel seems to manifest multiple personalities and Banks' twiddly synths run rings around your brain.

❻ THE CARPET CRAWLERS from THE LAMB LIES DOWN ON BROADWAY
This could have been a pop song if it wasn't just so damn weird. The melody and lush, layered vocals almost hypnotize through their beautiful simplicity.

PHIL TAKES THE MIKE

❼ ROBBERY, ASSAULT AND BATTERY from A TRICK OF THE TAIL
A jolly and ironic little tale of crime and punishment.

❽ ALL IN A MOUSE'S NIGHT from WIND AND WUTHERING
Gorgeously arranged, this proggy Tom and Jerry cartoon set to swirling synths must rank among the more eccentrically humorous post-Gabriel efforts.

❾ FOLLOW YOU, FOLLOW ME from ...AND THEN THERE WERE THREE...
Light and commercial without being too sugary. Tony Banks' light keyboards give the song a pop feel while harking back to their prog past.

❿ MAMA from GENESIS
Sweat drips down the walls and a dim light flickers in the corner – Collins sounds improbably sinister in this steamy, slow-building epic.

Essi Berelian

Dizzy Gillespie

The beret-sporting, goateed figurehead of the modern jazz revolution, a stunning trumpeter and as dizzy as a fox.

❶ WOODY 'N' YOU from THE DIZZY GILLESPIE STORY
It was Coleman Hawkins' date in 1944, but this carefully cascading chord sequence (apparently arrived at during the session itself and hurriedly recorded) is the unmistakable work of the far-thinking young trumpeter.

❷ BE BOP from THE DIZZY GILLESPIE STORY
Tenor saxophonist Don Byas does well with this uptempo 1945 exercise in minor-chord improvisation, but Dizzy's blistering, bubbling solo is a virtuosic revelation.

❸ GROOVIN' HIGH from THE DIZZY GILLESPIE STORY
Fashioned ingeniously from the extended chords of old chestnut, Whispering, it's an intricately arranged 1945 chart that perfectly sets up Diz's midway grandstanding four-bar break before a lovely half-time coda.

❹ SALT PEANUTS from THE DIZZY GILLESPIE STORY
The offbeat humour of the minimalist theme and daft vocal barely distract from the dazzling instrumental skill of Parker and Gillespie on this sizzling 1945 "I Got Rhythm" variation.

❺ THINGS TO COME from THE DIZZY GILLESPIE STORY
A jaw-dropping Gill Fuller/Gillespie theme extending the minor theme of Bebop to ludicrously intricate levels in 1946 proving that a big band could handle the new music.

❻ A NIGHT IN TUNISIA from THE DIZZY GILLESPIE STORY
He'd recorded his exotic classic with Bird at a 1945 studio session, but this extended 1947 Carnegie Hall rendition – again with Parker – has five full minutes of mature bop genius.

❼ MANTECA from THE DIZZY GILLESPIE STORY
A mighty 1947 example of Dizzy's blending of latin rhythms, big band textures and bebop language to create an exciting hybrid genre, later dubbed "Cubop".

❽ OOL-YA-KOO from THE DIZZY GILLESPIE STORY
One of Dizzy's occasional scat novelties (see also Oo-Bop-Sh'Bam and Oo-Pop-A-Da). As usual the tonsil-twisting on this 1947 bop blues contains a wealth of musical detail.

❾ CON ALMA from AFRO
Based on chords inspired by Bach, this bewitching piece dates back from his first big band, but was revisited by Dizzy throughout his career, including this effectively Latinized 1954 version.

❿ THE ETERNAL TRIANGLE from SONNY SIDE UP
Dizzy acts as wise old ringmaster in the 1957 cutting contest between Sonny Stitt and Sonny Rollins, and gets in some sparkling stuff of his own on this fiendish Stitt theme taken at breakneck speed.

Chris Ingham

Classic girl groups
The finest professional pop songwriters of the early to mid 1960s, layered production packed with imagination, the catchiest tunes on the hit parade, and young women who believed what they sang – that was the classic girl-group sound.

❶ BE MY BABY THE RONETTES from THE BEST OF
Drums boom like the hearts of the most infatuated young lovers on Phil Spector's grandest production. Ronnie Spector delivers a bewitching invitation that's impossible to refuse.

❷ LEADER OF THE PACK THE SHANGRI-LAS from THE BEST OF
Rock's most excessive and most effective mini-melodrama, garnished with violent motorcycle crash effects and a hammering, tragedy-foretelling piano.

❸ HE'S SO FINE THE CHIFFONS from THE BEST OF
It's a simple upward-climbing riff, but it's among pop's most magical hooks. The plain-spoken devotion of the lyric is amplified by the Chiffons' lilting "doo-lang, doo-lang"s.

❹ HE'S A REBEL THE CRYSTALS from THE BEST OF
Adolescent rebellion often lurked behind the good-hearted curtain of the girl group sound, as in this proud idolization of a misfit hero.

❺ SALLY GO ROUND THE ROSES THE JAYNETTES from THE BEST OF THE GIRL GROUPS, VOL 1
One of the most memorable one-hit wonder smashes of all time, its elliptical piano riff and enigmatic lyric saturated with foggy mystery.

❻ WILL YOU STILL LOVE ME TOMORROW THE SHIRELLES from 25 ALL-TIME GREATEST HITS
"Yes!" is the no-brainer answer to this winsome plea dusted with dancing strings and an immensely likable Gerry Goffin/Carole King-penned melody.

❼ TELL HIM THE EXCITERS from THE BEST OF THE GIRL GROUPS VOL 2
Staccato strings that jab like a doctor's needle, the stern, proud admonitions of the verse giving way to a chorus of bullfight-cheering strength.

❽ ONE FINE DAY THE CHIFFONS from THE BEST OF
Insanely raucous piano catapults this into overdrive and keeps it there, buoyed by another outstanding Goffin-King tune and waves of "shoo-be-do-be-do-be-do-be-bo-bop-bop"s.

❾ MY ONE AND ONLY, JIMMY BOY THE GIRLFRIENDS from EARLY GIRLS VOL 3
Perhaps the finest imitation Phil Spector production of all, its combination of defiantly grinning vocal and pummelling rhythm is the equal of any Crystals hit.

⑩ REMEMBER (WALKIN' IN THE SAND)

THE SHANGRI-LAS from THE BEST OF

Shaky rehearsal hall-quality piano, a Moonlight Sonata-like melody, mournful vocals and chattering seagull effects add up to a downbeat girl-group classic.

Richie Unterberger

Girly kick-arse anthems

The real test of a kick-arse girly anthem is that all the women in the pub know the words and after a couple of drinks they don't just hum – they belt it out, then go home and refuse to sleep with their boyfriend.

❶ RESPECT ARETHA FRANKLIN from THE VERY BEST OF ARETHA FRANKLIN

The original, breathtaking R&B classic that still puts a little steel in the spine of every woman who hears it.

❷ I WILL SURVIVE GLORIA GAYNOR from I WILL SURVIVE, THE ANTHOLOGY

Just when you think it's gone forever a DJ will play it again, and suddenly everyone's on the dancefloor waving their underpants in a circle above their heads.

❸ SINCE U BEEN GONE KELLY CLARKSON from BREAKAWAY

The first *American Idol* winner gives great break-up song, from a whisper to a full-throated rage.

❹ I FEEL LIKE A WOMAN SHANIA TWAIN from COME ON OVER

This country rock hit struck a chord: even burly truck-drivers with large sideburns sang along.

❺ GIRLS JUST WANNA HAVE FUN CYNDI LAUPER from SHE'S SO UNUSUAL

Cyndi's punk-lite tulle confections and squinty sincerity came along at just the right 1980s moment to mobilize the girls for…we forget. Is there any chocolate?

❻ SISTERS ARE DOIN' IT EURYTHMICS from BE YOURSELF TONIGHT

Aretha Franklin and Annie Lennox belt out a feminist anthem. Somebody had to.

❼ STRONG ENOUGH CHER from BELIEVE

You must be strong enough Cher, you look like you're made of industrial-strength bakelite. A dancefloor fave.

❽ DON'T COME THE COWBOY WITH ME SONNY JIM

KIRSTY MCCOLL from KITE

A lovely, lilting reminder to a chap that she has his number.

❾ STUPID GIRLS PINK from I'M NOT DEAD

Miss Pink scorns talentless blonde starlets with tiny dogs who try to make stupidity and lack of accomplishment into a virtue. Who could she possibly mean?

⑩ I COULD WIPE THE FLOOR WITH YOU LISA MILLER from AS FAR AS LIFE GOES

You can just tell this sweet-voiced Aussie could make good on her deliciously languid threats.

Kaz Cooke

Glam rock

For a brief but rather wonderful spell in the early to mid 1970s, pop music in the UK resolutely refused to take itself seriously. Grown men – and sometimes even a few women – put stars on their foreheads, glitter under their eyes and platform soles on their big shiny boots.

❶ ALL THE YOUNG DUDES MOTT THE HOOPLE from ALL THE YOUNG DUDES

A little Bowie magic went a long way for this otherwise rather dull band. He sang backing vocals, did handclaps, and wrote and produced what would turn out to be one of their classic songs.

❷ VIRGINIA PLAIN ROXY MUSIC from THE BEST OF ROXY MUSIC

Though Roxy soon became something both more suave and more strange, glam rock seemed like a fitting pigeonhole for early work such as their dazzling first single. It's hard to imagine them minding much, given their collective dress sense.

❸ GUDBUY T'JANE from GET YER BOOTS ON: THE BEST OF SLADE

Is it the red-hot riff, Noddy Holder's lusty, bellowed vocal, the insistent maracas or the stoopid spelling of the title that made this the best single of the 1970s? Discuss…

❹ ZIGGY STARDUST DAVID BOWIE from THE RISE AND FALL OF ZIGGY STARDUST…

A theatrical masterpiece. The hilarious lyrics squirm with febrile rock'n'roll imagery and epic myth-making, such as: "He took it all too far/But boy could he play guitar!"

❺ SOLID GOLD EASY ACTION T REX from 20TH CENTURY
BOY: THE ULTIMATE COLLECTION

In 1973, I asked my dad to buy me this single. "You'll
be sick of it in a week!" he declared, before relent-
ing. He still likes it. Marc Bolan at his most gloriously
juvenile.

❻ HELLO! HELLO! I'M BACK AGAIN GARY GLITTER from
32 GLAM HITS

Five words you're unlikely to ever hear again from the
exiled-in-disgrace Leader Of The Gang.

❼ SEE MY BABY JIVE WIZZARD from SINGLES As & Bs

The most hummable hit from this OTT band fronted
by ex-ELO member Roy Wood, whose excessive make-
up emphasized a pair of wildly staring eyes.

❽ 48 CRASH SUZI QUATRO from GREATEST HITS

This leather-clad, bass-toting singer was a role model
for a whole generation of female rockers and more
besides. Suzi always gave a good chorus, as this rousing rocker shows.

❾ BALLROOM BLITZ SWEET from THE BEST OF SWEET

Fantastic energy and an unforgettable vocal by the
late Brian Connolly. With the help of the brilliant songwriting duo Chinn and Chapman, Sweet had a string
of hits at the height of glam.

❿ PERSONALITY CRISIS THE NEW YORK DOLLS from THE
NEW YORK DOLLS

The leading Stateside exponents of glam rock were a
bunch of hard-rockin' cross-dressing New York
substance-abusers, whose raucous output anticipated
punk.

Jon Lusk

Dexter Gordon

**With his cavernous tone and impeccable phrasing,
Gordon's name and sound are synonymous with
the smoky clubs of jazz cliché. However, despite
his preference for popular tunes, he was one of
jazz's great interpreters, with an unparalleled
ability to communicate through simplicity.**

❶ DON'T EXPLAIN from A SWINGIN' AFFAIR

Dexter Gordon doing what he does better than anyone else: telling a love story in the early hours.

❷ ERNIE'S TUNE from DEXTER CALLING

Another towering ballad from the master, his sax
sound more human than ever.

❸ I GUESS I'LL HANG MY TEARS OUT TO DRY from GO

The title's clumsy but the playing is gorgeous.

❹ LOVE FOR SALE from GO

A jumpy rendition of the Cole Porter classic. Gordon's
line is clipped and accurate.

❺ SCRAPPLE FROM THE APPLE from OUR MAN IN PARIS

Gordon harks back to his hard-bop roots with this fluid
version of Charlie Parker's tune.

❻ A NIGHT IN TUNISIA from OUR MAN IN PARIS

Dizzy gets the Dexter treatment: a muscular version of
the trumpeter's best-known composition.

❼ DOXY from BOTH SIDES OF MIDNIGHT

Gordon is at his bluesy, breezy best in this imperious
take on a Sonny Rollins number.

❽ FRIED BANANAS from MORE POWER!

A swinging example of the perfection of the saxophonist's tone and phrasing.

Nat Defriend

Gorillaz

**Damon Albarn and pals – Jamie Hewlitt and Dan
"The Automator" Nakamura – created the world's
first "virtual band" in 1999 and proceeded to issue
set of exquisitely tuned videos.**

❶ CLINT EASTWOOD from GORILLAZ

The band's first single matched Damon's drooled
bluesy vocals to a chewy blend of harmonica and
vintage hip-hop beats, and proved that even without
the videos, Gorillaz music could stand up.

❷ 19-2000 (SOULCHILD REMIX) from GORILLAZ

Deliciously infectious mix of silly rap lyrics and
fantastic funky bass.

❸ ROCK THE HOUSE from GORILLAZ

Leaning heavily on a sweet brass riff and masterful
sampler work, "Rock The House" showcases Del's
chilled out rap style.

❹ TOMORROW COMES TODAY from GORILLAZ

A slow dub rhythm and a harmonica riff that sticks like
egg yolk to a blanket: Gorillaz do gloom.

❺ LIL' DUB CHEFIN' (SPACEMONKEYZ REMIX) from
LAIKA COME HOME

A tribute to the golden age of Jamaican skanking, this
is an old-style "version" remix – complete with that

vintage "space echo" effect on the vocals – of Gorillaz's track "M1 – A1".

❻ FEEL GOOD INC. (FEATURING DE LA SOUL) from DEMON DAYS
A few years down the line and the Gorillaz, jaded through excess, embittered by life on the road, returned to the public eye with this li'l dance number. Damon's 2D seems infested with the spirit of Beck.

❼ DARE from DEMON DAYS
Inviting British rock's most notorious loose cannon to contribute vocals must have seemed a risky idea at first; Shaun Ryder (ex-Happy Mondays) spent days messing up "It's there" before the band gave in and changed the title to "Dare" to match. Joyous stuff.

❽ DIRTY HARRY from DEMON DAYS
Bootsie Collins does the bass, there's a gorgeous cymbal riff going on from start to finish and even the dubious inclusion of a kids' choir can't detract from the full on funkiness.

❾ EL MAÑANA from DEMON DAYS
Mournful, downbeat vocals of regret over a military funeral's drumbeats. The very definition of "wistful".

❿ GHOST TRAIN from G-SIDES
Remix and rarities albums are rarely worth the outlay but hey, with an animated band, anything's possible. This is as sweet & sour as anything the band produced.

Al Spicer

American gospel

Religion aside, gospel is the bedrock of just about all Anglo-American popular music. Sinners, freethinkers and fence-sitters one and all will appreciate this lot.

❶ HONEY IN THE ROCK BLIND MAMIE FOREHAND from AMERICAN PRIMITIVE VOL 1
The ideal accompaniment to a dark night of the soul.

❷ MOTHER'S CHILDREN HAVE A HARD TIME BLIND WILLIE JOHNSON from THE COMPLETE BLIND WILLIE JOHNSON
The spelling may be flawed (it should read "mother-less"), but it's hard to imagine a more perfect record.

❸ I'LL BE RESTED (WHEN THE ROLL IS CALLED) BLIND ROOSEVELT GRAVES & BROTHER from AMERICAN PRIMITIVE VOL 1
Guitarist John Fahey called this the hottest religious record ever made – it's hard to disagree.

❹ GOSPEL TRAIN GOLDEN GATE JUBILEE QUARTET from THE GOLDEN GATE QUARTET VOL 1
This swings like nobody's business.

❺ MOVE ON UP A LITTLE HIGHER MAHALIA JACKSON from HOW I GOT OVER: THE APOLLO SESSIONS
There surely has never been a performance captured on record as physically powerful.

❻ MILKY WHITE WAY THE TRUMPETEERS from JUBILATION! GREAT GOSPEL PERFORMANCES VOL. 1
One of the best selling gospel records ever, and for good reason.

❼ BY AND BY THE SOUL STIRRERS from SHINE ON ME
Long before Sam Cooke joined the group, they were the best of the male gospel groups. This shows why.

❽ MARY DON'T YOU WEEP THE SWAN SILVERTONES from THE SWAN SILVERTONES
Gospel at its most acrobatic and intense.

❾ OLD LANDMARK ARETHA FRANKLIN from AMAZING GRACE
Gospel, or any other music, doesn't get any more fiery than this.

❿ MARION WILLIAMS GO DOWN MOSES from THE GREAT GOSPEL WOMEN VOL 2
Archaic sounding but nevertheless shows why many critics call Williams the greatest singer ever.

Peter Shapiro

South African gospel

It doesn't come much more stirring than South African gospel, and these tracks range from solo divas to massed choirs.

❶ NGIYEKELENI REBECCA MALOPE from NGIYEKELENI
Perhaps the greatest track from the pint-sized but full-voiced queen of SA gospel.

❷ NOH! NOH! SEBEHLALA BEJABULA JABU HLONGWANE from JOYOUS CELEBRATION 3
Massive choral sound, assuring listeners that we will always be happy in heaven. If it sounds anything like this up there, it must be true.

❸ AVULEKILE AMASANGO ISHMAEL from GOSPEL GROOVES
"The gates of heaven are opening", sings Ishmael in this heartstring-tugging classic.

❹ **IMVUSELELO YASE NATALI** IZIGI from IZIGI

Superbly rousing choral number. The lyric's claim – "I can feel the stamping" – says it all.

❺ **VUYO MOKOENA PURE MAGIC** NJALO from NJALO

Smooth singing Vuyo is the Barry White of SA gospel and this is his finest song.

❻ **DIPHALA DI RAPEDISA MOPORESIDENTE THABO MBEKI** SOLLY MOHOLO from MOTLHANG KE KOLOBETSWA "DIE POPPE SAL DANS"

The best of the Zionist gospel singers, Moholo wishes the President well in this stirring epic.

❼ **VUMA** BRENDA FASSIE from MINA NAWE

"Allow Him in", advises Brenda, "and you'll be saved." Agree or not, this is a beautifully moving gospel song.

❽ **MBULALI WAMI** MARIA LE MARIA from MARIA LE MARIA

A moving ode to a murderer from his victim, singing "we'll meet in heaven…"

❾ **JERUSALEMA** MANDOZA from GOSPEL GROOVES

Mandoza's best known for his stomp-rock kwaito, but he's a fine gospel artist, too, as this rasping hymn to Jerusalem amply proves.

❿ **EKUSEN' EMATHUNENI** LADYSMITH BLACK MAMBAZO from LIPH' IQINISO

The still sadness of the morning after the crucifixion is the subject of this Joseph Shabalala poem, immaculately arranged, and beautifully delivered by the celebrated LBM.

Gregory Salter

Goth

Acres and acres of black and a fear of bright lights. Be afraid. Be very afraid.

❶ **DESIRE** GENE LOVES JEZEBEL from DISCOVER

Driven and achingly melodic, its ethereal guitar lines ricochet all over the shop.

❷ **I WALK THE LINE** ALIEN SEX FIEND from ALL OUR YESTERDAYS

Surf rock in midnight black: Nik Fiend walks the line between good and evil in this twangy, grim and grandiose goth gem.

❸ **LOVE ME TO DEATH** THE MISSION from GOD'S OWN MEDICINE

Jangly, romantically doomed guitar heaven. Poor Wayne Hussey sounds like he's got it bad.

❹ **LUCRETIA (MY REFLECTION)** THE SISTERS OF MERCY from FLOODLAND

A strident, pumping bass and drum machine (named Doktor Avalanche) hammer this beautifully bleak track right into the dancefloor.

❺ **PREACHER MAN** FIELDS OF THE NEPHILIM from DAWNRAZOR

An Ennio Morricone homage launches this dusty, spaghetti-western-inspired drama. McCoy's deep voice sounding as parched as the Mexican desert.

❻ **SEBASTIANE** SEX GANG CHILDREN from FALL: THE COMPLETE SINGLES

This is way out there. A heaving bassline, screeching violins and Andi Sexgang's barking mad vocals.

❼ **SPELLBOUND** SIOUXSIE AND THE BANSHEES from JUJU

Hypnotically enchanting and starkly violent, the spiralling melody meshing with Siouxsie's possessed vocals.

❽ **SPIRIT WALKER** THE CULT from DREAMTIME

The seeds of stadium rock are present but the chiming guitars and Ian Astbury's wolf-child howl ensure the track remains shrouded in the cloak of Goth.

❾ **THE PASSION OF LOVERS** BAUHAUS from MASK

A tense and turbulent masterpiece with a twisting rhythm hooked on a hyperactive bassline. Peter Murphy's vocals sound gloriously aloof throughout.

❿ **WALK INTO THE SUN** THE MARCH VIOLETS from THE BOTANIC VERSES

Goths and sunlight? Surely some mistake? This is a bouncy, manic little tune complete with a bright and sprightly little sax solo in the middle.

Essi Berelian

Grateful Dead

From spaced-out acid rock to mellow Americana, Grateful Dead covered the whole musical waterfront until the untimely death of their leader Jerry Garcia in 1995.

❶ **DARK STAR** from LIVE DEAD

All these years on, this twenty-minute intergalactic jam recorded live in 1969 still represents the high tide of West Coast acid rock.

❷ **TURN ON YOUR LOVELIGHT** from LIVE DEAD

A showcase for the talents of Pigpen, the blues-and-whisky drenched singer who was the first of three keyboardists to die on the band over the years.

❸ UNCLE JOHN'S BAND from WORKINGMAN'S DEAD
The joyous opening track from the album on which they swapped extended acid jams for tightly constructed country-rock songs.

❹ TRUCKIN' from AMERICAN BEAUTY
Autobiographical anthem of the band's busts and a stirring manifesto of defiance.

❺ RIPPLE from AMERICAN BEAUTY
Exquisite tune from Garcia with Zen-like lyrics by Robert Hunter.

❻ SUGAR MAGNOLIA from AMERICAN BEAUTY
Another classic from their most flawless album, this time written and sung by Bobby Weir.

❼ PLAYING IN THE BAND from GRATEFUL DEAD
Brilliant exposition of the communal Deadhead philosophy from the 1971 live album affectionately known to fans as "Skullfuck".

❽ JACK STRAW from EUROPE 1972
By the early 1970s the Dead were so prolific that many of their best songs never found their way onto a studio album. This cowboy-song gem only ever appeared on a triple live set in 1972.

❾ UNBROKEN CHAIN from FROM THE MARS HOTEL
Classically trained bassist Phil Lesh wrote only a handful of songs for the band over the years. This complex, jazzy 1974 offering was his finest moment.

❿ TOUCH OF GREY from IN THE DARK
After seven years away from the studio, they returned in triumph in 1987 with an album that included Touch of Grey, their only American top-ten single.

Nigel Williamson

Grebo gurus

For a short period during the late 1980s and early 90s the gloriously grubby Midlands/Stourbridge grebo scene was where it was at.

❶ CAN U DIG IT? POP WILL EAT ITSELF from THIS IS THE DAY, THIS IS THE HOUR, THIS IS THIS!
"Riffs? Yeah! Can U dig it?" Absolutely. from Alan Moore to Dirty Harry, a list of cooler pop culture influences it would be hard to find.

❷ DEF.CON.ONE POP WILL EAT ITSELF from THIS IS THE DAY, THIS IS THE HOUR, THIS IS THIS!
This must set some sort of PWEI samples record, featuring snippets of everything from the Osmonds to the Beasties. An awesome track.

❸ GIVE, GIVE, GIVE ME MORE, MORE, MORE THE WONDER STUFF from THE EIGHT LEGGED GROOVE MACHINE
Miles Hunt excels himself with some of his best poetically poisonous lyrics. This is wantonly greedy and ludicrously catchy.

David Gray's
Lost songs

DAVID GRAY has sold more albums in the 21st century than any British artist except Dido. Needless to say, his playlist is heavily dominated by singer-songwriters – with one or two surprises.

❶ IT'S ALRIGHT MA (I'M ONLY BLEEDING) BOB DYLAN from BRINGING IT ALL BACK HOME

❷ PARASITE NICK DRAKE from PINK MOON

❸ MANSION ON THE HILL BRUCE SPRINGSTEEN from NEBRASKA

❹ BALLERINA VAN MORRISON from ASTRAL WEEKS

❺ MERCY MERCY ME MARVIN GAYE from WHAT'S GOING ON

❻ REFUGE OF THE ROADS JONI MITCHELL from HEJIRA

❼ DREAM GERRARD TRAFFIC from WHEN THE EAGLE FLIES

❽ DESIRE TALK TALK from THE VERY BEST OF

❾ JUST LIKE TOM THUMB'S BLUES NINA SIMONE from TO LOVE SOMEBODY

❿ QUIET NIGHT OF QUIET STARS FRANK SINATRA & ANTONIO CARLOS JOBIM from FRANCIS ALBERT SINATRA & ANTONIO CARLOS JOBIM

❹ INFO FREAKO JESUS JONES from LIQUIDIZER

OK, so this lot were from London, but for subversive grebo action this has got everything: great beats and squealing samples, plus plenty of fuzzy guitar.

❺ KILL YOUR TELEVISION NED'S ATOMIC DUSTBIN from GOD FODDER

One of the Ned's top tunes, boasting two bass players, edgy stop-start rhythms and a terrific melody.

❻ NIGHTMARE AT 20,000 FT POP WILL EAT ITSELF from CURE FOR SANITY

That rumbling, pumping bass line feels like low end air turbulence. Tense and eminently danceable.

❼ NOSEDIVE KARMA GAYE BYKERS ON ACID from THE NOSEDIVE EP

One of the Bykers' earliest and best – they sound like they're learning to play as they go along. The riffs and solos are way off the Richter scale.

❽ TEN TRENCHES DEEP LIVE THE WONDER STUFF from LOVE BITES AND BRUISES

No Stuffies concert is complete without this magnificently mad set closer. Martin Gilks' on-the-button drumming is a joy to behold.

❾ UNBEARABLE THE WONDER STUFF from THE EIGHT LEGGED GROOVE MACHINE

Angry, funny, and hateful this is the archetypal Stuffies single, brilliantly bouncy and dripping with bile.

❿ WHAT GIVES YOU THE IDEA THAT YOUR'RE SO AMAZING, BABY? CRAZYHEAD from DESERT ORCHID

Straight outta Leicester, the 'Head were grebo through and through. The distinct 1960s garage vibe and insistent, spiralling hook make this essential.

Essi Berelian

Al Green

No one sings soul quite like Al Green. Even though he has been minister at his own Memphis church for the last 25 years, you only have to see him in concert to realize that the tortured sensuality that infused his 1970s classics still resounds from every note he sings.

❶ TIRED OF BEING ALONE from AL GREEN GETS NEXT TO YOU

Green's first hit, in 1971, saw him very definitely on the lookout for love.

❷ LET'S STAY TOGETHER from LET'S STAY TOGETHER

Al himself didn't like his biggest hit when he first recorded it in 1971; it made him a star regardless.

❸ LOVE AND HAPPINESS from I'M STILL IN LOVE WITH YOU

A strangely compelling saga of love and jealousy, like eavesdropping on someone else's confidences.

Al Green
Plays

One of the greatest soul singers of our age, AL GREEN's playlist recognizes the influences of such classic voices as Sam Cooke and Otis Redding on his own style, but also reveals tastes that range from jazz to hip-hop.

❶ JUST FOR THE LOVE JOHN COLTRANE from LEGENDS OF JAZZ

❷ MOON DREAMS MILES DAVIS from BIRTH OF THE COOL

❸ YOU SEND ME SAM COOKE from GREATEST HITS

❹ THE WIND CRIES MARY JIMI HENDRIX from ARE YOU EXPERIENCED

❺ TRY A LITTLE TENDERNESS OTIS REDDING from COMPLETE AND UNBELIEVABLE: THE OTIS REDDING DICTIONARY OF SOUL

❻ HIGHER GROUND STEVIE WONDER from INNER VISIONS

❼ WHERE DO WE GO FROM HERE CHICAGO from CHICAGO II

❽ SIMPLY BEAUTIFUL QUEEN LATIFAH from THE DANA OWENS ALBUM

❾ IF I AIN'T GOT YOU ALICIA KEYS from THE DIARY OF ALICIA KEYS

❿ THE FACT IS (I NEED YOU) JILL SCOTT from BEAUTIFULLY HUMAN: WORDS AND SOUNDS, VOL 2

g

❹ I'M GLAD YOU'RE MINE from I'M STILL IN LOVE WITH YOU

From its supremely funky drum break onwards – courtesy of Al Jackson – a truly irresistible love song.

❺ SIMPLY BEAUTIFUL from I'M STILL IN LOVE WITH YOU

Another perfect love song, imbued with overwhelming tenderness.

❻ FUNNY HOW TIME SLIPS AWAY from CALL ME

The rueful longing in Green's voice makes this Willie Nelson song his own. One of his many attempts to out-do Elvis.

❼ JESUS IS WAITING from CALL ME

A sublime, almost private meditation from 1973, in which Green duets beautifully with his own multi-tracked self.

❽ TAKE ME TO THE RIVER from AL GREEN EXPLORES YOUR MIND

By 1974, as Green moved back towards the church, the gospel elements were dominating his secular work.

❾ PEOPLE GET READY from GREATEST GOSPEL HITS

A spell-binding rendition of Curtis Mayfield's gospel anthem.

❿ STRAIGHTEN OUT YOUR LIFE from GREATEST GOSPEL HITS

This impassioned 1983 summons to the righteous life marked Green's finest moment in gospel.

Greg Ward

Green Day

World-beating punk-pop and then some. Since breaking through with the hit album *Dookie*, singer/guitarist Billie Joe and Co. have developed well beyond mere three-chord thrashes.

❶ AT THE LIBRARY from 39/SMOOTH

It ain't slickly produced, but it is charming in a simple but affecting boy-lusts-after-girl-who-doesn't-know-he-exists kind of way.

❷ BLOOD, SEX AND BOOZE from WARNING

A jolly little S&M ditty which bounces along like a Rottweiler on a spacehopper.

❸ DON'T LEAVE ME from 39/SMOOTH

Our hero's got the girl, but not for much longer by the sounds of it. A concise and speedy number with acres of great pop harmonies.

❹ GOOD RIDDANCE (TIME OF YOUR LIFE) from NIMROD

Drenched in nostalgia, this acoustic number is simple but effective – only a few well-placed strings underline the melancholy tone.

❺ HITCHIN' A RIDE from NIMROD

Size ten boots and knuckledusters await the unwary in this cautionary tale, which gives you a good going-over right from the opening bars.

❻ JESUS OF SUBURBIA from AMERICAN IDIOT

A punk-rock concept suite? Surely some mistake? Nope, here's a nine-minutes-plus epic flowing from one rambunctious section to the next.

❼ MISERY from WARNING

Fancy a change of pace? Try this bizarre polka punk'n'folk effort complete with accordion, violins and mandolin.

❽ WAKE ME UP WHEN SEPTEMBER ENDS from AMERICAN IDIOT

Gently strummed acoustic guitars and delicate chimes build to a crashing chorus.

Essi Berelian

Grime

Grime is the UK's hip-hop – raw, spontaneous and with very little difference between performers and their audience. Like hip-hop was before MTV discovered it. Grime, however, remains a supremely confident, totally self-sufficient expression of Britain's urban youth.

❶ WOT DO U CALL IT? WILEY from TREDDING ON THIN ICE

Pioneering single from the "godfather of grime", putting distance between his music and the UK Garage scene, while and introducing the world to his distinctive "Eski" sound.

❷ BOYS LUV GIRLS KANO from ROLL DEEP PRESENTS GRIMEY VOL 1

With a strong fan base through pirate radio shows, Kano's breakthrough single cemented his status as underground royalty.

❸ RESPECT ME DIZZEE RASCAL from SHOWTIME

One of Raskit's darker moments as he flows candidly about copycat MCs, getting stabbed and attention from the police over some seriously cold production from underground legend Wonder.

④ MURKLE MAN JAMMER single

One of the hottest producers in the underground scene, Jammer – aka Murkle Man – steps out from behind the board to show everyone what he can do on the mic.

⑤ GET ME BRUZA single

The defining moment in Bruza's music career, as "Get Me" turned an everyday slang phrase into an underground classic.

⑥ JME SERIOUS (RUN THE ROAD REMIX) from RUN THE ROAD

JME kick down doors with this boisterous and self-confident assessment of the grime scene.

⑦ XTRA RUFF SQWAD from GUNS&ROSES VOL2

The first release from the collective's highly anticipated second mixtape signals a rennaisance in a flagging grime scene.

⑧ ADIDAS HOODIE REMIX MIZZ BEATS FT LADY SOVEREIGN, SKEPTA, JME, EARZ, JAMMER & BABY BLUE single

Six of the freshest artists in the scene pay homage to the sportswear giant Adidas, over production from rising star Mizz Beats, on this remix of Lady Sovereign's track. Does it exactly what it says on the label.

⑨ POW FORWARD RIDDIM LETHAL B & GUESTS

Pumping bass line, rowdy chorus and some of the most hype verses you ever heard Lethal B and his Fire Camp marked a return to the underground music scene in serious style on the biggest tune of 2004.

⑩ DESTRUCTION VIP JAMMER FT WILEY, D DOUBLE E, KANO & DURRTY GOODZ from RUN THE ROAD

Staying behind the boards, Jammer's "Destruction VIP" is like a meeting of underground superheroes. Blending his increasingly distinctive sound with such assembled talents, the "Murkle Man" is on course for another underground anthem.

George Bradley

Grunge

The early 1990s sound of Seattle that burst forth onto an unsuspecting audience, fusing the core elements of rock'n'roll, metal and punk in a reaction to the growth of the over-commercialized music mainstream. Thus was born a new post-punk genre, striking raw, imperfect chords, first with disaffected teenagers, then dollar-tinged ones with ad execs.

① ABOUT A GIRL NIRVANA from BLEACH

Grunge's most celebrated break away from the screeching guitars and percussive thuds as an undulating melody and laid-back strumming allow Cobain's voice alone to provide the emotional intensity.

② TOUCH ME I'M SICK MUDHONEY from SUPERFUZZ BIGMUFF

The grunge pioneers combine distorted guitars, pulverizing drums and blood-curdling vocals to create down'n'dirty rock music. Poetic it's not, but for break-neck, bluesy, bar-room-brawl beats, it can't be topped.

③ JESUS CHRIST POSE SOUNDGARDEN from BADMOTORFINGER

Straddling heavy metal and punk, Soundgarden's hard-rock beats fell snugly into the grunge pot. This six-minute opus is an energetic barrage of riffs, feedback and lung-bursting singing.

④ JEREMY PEARL JAM from TEN

An MTV favourite, this hit from the band's debut album showcases their signature classic rock melodies and Eddie Vedder's stentorian vocals, combined with disturbing, provocative subject-matter.

⑤ WOULD? ALICE IN CHAINS from DIRT

Formed in 1987, AIN went on to incorporate the bleak, introspective and self-destructive sensibilities of their grungier Seattle peers. Here, Layne Staley and Jerry Cantrell nail druggy musings onto the latter's beguiling guitar playing.

Ed Wright

Guitar breaks

"Heads down, meet you at the end" guitar riffs have their own list elsewhere in this book (filed under R). But then there's the guitar break, where the singer has to shake a tambourine while the man with the axe seriously gets to show off.

① RED HOUSE JIMI HENDRIX from ARE YOU EXPERIENCED?

On which he teases and twists a standard twelve-bar blues into places it had never been before.

② SHOULDN'T HAVE TOOK MORE THAN YOU GAVE ERIC CLAPTON from DAVE MASON'S ALONE TOGETHER

The best example of wah-wah guitar God – or anyone else – ever recorded.

③ ALIVE MIKE McCREADY from PEARL JAM'S TEN

McCready modestly admitted he'd copped the lick from Kiss's Ace Frehley.

g

④ SILVER AND GOLD BARRY MELTON from COUNTRY JOE AND THE FISH'S C J FISH

If an alien landed and demanded to know what West Coast guitar was all about, this is what you'd play them.

⑤ REELIN' IN THE YEARS ELLIOTT RANDALL from STEELY DAN'S CAN'T BUY A THRILL

Elliott who? But it only takes one classic solo to achieve rock'n'roll immortality.

⑥ STAIRWAY TO HEAVEN JIMMY PAGE from LED ZEPPELIN IV

Yes, the song's pretty daft. But when Robert Plant has finished warbling, Page cuts loose on one of his most lyrical solos – which thousands have tried to copy since.

⑦ SAMBA PA TI CARLOS SANTANA from ABRAXAS

Proving that guitar virtuosity doesn't have to be about how fast you can play.

⑧ LIKE A HURRICANE NEIL YOUNG from STARS AND BARS

Neil's solos were always built around the minimal number of notes, but therein lies his effectiveness.

⑨ DARK STAR JERRY GARCIA from THE GRATEFUL DEAD'S LIVE DEAD

Intergalactic guitar explorations from the man they called "Captain Trips".

⑩ LOAN ME A DIME DUANE ALLMAN from BOZ SCAGGS

Like Clapton, some of brother Duane's best playing was kept for other people's records.

Nigel Williamson

Guns N' Roses

The most dangerous rock band in the world? Probably not. Though when they actually bothered to release albums they were among the very best.

❶ CIVIL WAR from USE YOUR ILLUSION II

A snippet from the movie *Cool Hand Luke* launches into a stunningly heartfelt lyric about the nature of conflict. Who'd have thought the Gunners had it in them?

❷ ESTRANGED from USE YOUR ILLUSION II

One of the finest tunes the Gunners ever recorded. Expertly arranged, the aching guitar refrain frames Axl's emotionally tormented vocals perfectly.

❸ MR BROWNSTONE from APPETITE FOR DESTRUCTION

You want drug songs? This paean to getting wrecked is an addictively succinct effort riding high on a superbly sleazy riff. A real jewel from the gutter.

❹ PARADISE CITY from APPETITE FOR DESTRUCTION

The masterful riff owes a major debt to Aerosmith, while the anthemic chorus gets entire stadiums singing along.

❺ PERFECT CRIME from USE YOUR ILLUSION I

A fast and frenetic rocker, when GN'R are in the groove they're unstoppable. Slash's solo is a ripper and Axl unleashes venomous expletives like a true pro.

❻ RECKLESS LIFE from GN'R LIES

Originally from the band's debut EP, this live track positively reeks of the band's nothing-to-lose attitude. It's fast, tacky and stinks of cheap booze and drugs.

❼ SWEET CHILD O' MINE from APPETITE FOR DESTRUCTION

Could this be Slash's best solo ever? A major hit, this gorgeously arranged love song reveals Axl's sensitive side without a hint of schmaltz.

❽ WELCOME TO THE JUNGLE from APPETITE FOR DESTRUCTION

This is one hell of a way to kick off your debut album: violent, nasty and completely brilliant.

Essi Berelian

Woody Guthrie

With Woody it is as much the idea and the romantic notion of a better, less mean world as it is the music. The music, though, is the clear forerunner to Dylan and then The Clash. So this is a selection of songs with typical hard-hitting content.

❶ I AIN'T GOT NO HOME from DUSTBOWL BALLADS

Quintessential Guthrie, the song of a man for whom a singing, preaching life was the only one he could live.

❷ BIGGEST THING THAT MAN HAS EVER DONE from COLUMBIA RIVER COLLECTION

Fighting Fascists was Woody's mission, and this one is a rallying call for freedom.

❸ THIS LAND IS YOUR LAND from ASCH RECORDINGS VOL 1

The People's National Anthem. Forget G.W. Bush hijacking it, this song was written for everybody: "This land belongs to you and me."

157

❹ JESUS CHRIST from ASCH RECORDINGS VOL 1

The truest vision of radical Christian Socialism: Woody saw Jesus as a martyr put to death by the Boss Classes.

❺ DANVILLE GIRL from ASCH RECORDINGS VOL 2

A love song about a girl spotted on a station platform, who "wore her hat on the back of her head, like high-born people all do". Perfect.

❻ JOHN HENRY WOODY GUTHRIE AND CISCO HOUSTON from WOODY GUTHRIE AND CISCO HOUSTON

Great example of the beautiful close harmonies the duo perfected, and another great working man's song.

❼ HARD TRAVELIN' from ASCH RECORDINGS VOL 3

Again, telling it like it is, the life of a hard working man, "busted, disgusted, not to be trusted".

❽ PRETTY BOY FLOYD from ASCH RECORDINGS VOL 4

The Dustbowl folk romanticized robbers and rebels, and this one is about Pretty Boy, who would leave $50 bills with people who helped him hide from the cops.

❾ TOM JOAD from DUSTBOWL BALLADS

Steinbeck's character from *The Grapes of Wrath* is the template for all Woody's characters, a man for whom the struggle is everything, and camaraderie comes first.

❿ CAR SONG from ASCH RECORDINGS 1

And just to prove Woody could delight three-year-olds, too, a song based around "Brrm Brrm". Delightful.

Richard Baker

Gypsy music

The Romany – commonly known as gypsies – trace their nomadic origins to India and feature strongly in the music-making of many nations.

❶ DZELEM, DZELEM ESMA REDZEPOVA from GYPSY QUEENS

The Romany anthem, as sung by Macedonia's Gypsy Queen.

❷ EDERLEZI AVELA KOCANI ORKESTAR from L'ORIENT EST ROUGE

Tough, dense brass music from eastern Macedonia that celebrates Ederlezi (the Romany holy day).

❸ BALADA CONDUCATOROLUI TARAF DE HAIDOUKS from MUSIQUE DES TZIGANES DE ROUMANIE

Violin and cymbalom weave a weird, dissonant ballad that celebrates the fall of Romanian dictator Nicolae Ceausescu.

❹ SOY GITANO CAMARON DE LA ISLA from SOY GITANO

The greatest flamenco singer of the past fifty years toasts his roots. Paco De Lucia adds fluid flamenco guitar.

❺ BAMBOLEO GIPSY KINGS from GIPSY KINGS

Hoarse vocals, rumba rhythms, flamenco melodies... it can only be the Gipsy Kings.

❻ PELNO ME SAM SABAN BAJRAMOVIC from A GYPSY LEGEND

The golden voiced Serbian wildman sings the gypsy blues.

❼ CINE ARE FATA MARE DONA DUMITRU SIMINICA from CINE ARE FATA MARE

Eerie, haunted music that suggests a darker Transylvania than even Bram Stoker ever dared imagine.

❽ BASAL FERUS FERUS MUSTAFOV from KING FERUS

Bright Balkan dance tune named in honour of the little Macedonian sax and clarinet giant who plays it.

❾ IAG BARI FANFARE CIOCARLIA from IAG BARI

The fastest, funkiest brass band on the planet bust a collective gut and truly go for it.

❿ OTPISANI BOBAN MARKOVIC ORKESTAR from LIVE IN BELGRADE

Horns blazing and sweat pouring, Boban leads a full-on Balkan brass experience.

Garth Cartwright

Hall & Oates

This Philadelphia duo were probably as surprised as anyone when upcoming indie guitar bands recently started namechecking them. But their huge body of work contains some absolute corkers. Just look beyond the moustache...

❶ SHE'S GONE from ABANDONED LUNCHEONETTE
It may take 60 seconds to get going, but their debut single is the quintessential smooth Hall & Oates sound, and, for many, remains the best thing they ever did.

❷ SCREAMING THROUGH DECEMBER from WAR BABIES
How best to follow up a perfect blue-eyed soul album? How about a terrifying prog-rock-spectacular featuring the words "quasar" and "Faustus"? Bizarre.

❸ SARA SMILE from DARYL HALL & JOHN OATES
Written about Hall's then-girlfriend, Sara Allen, this low-key ballad gave the duo their first top-ten hit in the US, and prhaps gave Ms Allen something of an ego boost.

❹ DO WHAT YOU WANT, BE WHAT YOU ARE from BIGGER THAN BOTH OF US
By now mining a rich seam of Philly soul, Hall starts to let loose on the vocal improvisation, while Oates impassively provides the choppy offbeat guitar.

❺ RICH GIRL from BIGGER THAN BOTH OF US
This bite-sized clap-along went straight to #1 in the USA, and impressively rhymed the words "rich girl" with "bitch, girl". Ham-fisted, but undeniably effective.

❻ I DON'T WANNA LOSE YOU from ALONG THE RED LEDGE
Pure Temptations, this one – sweeping violins and an unforgettable chorus.

❼ WAIT FOR ME from X-STATIC
The expansive 1980s production values are creeping into their sound, and this wonderfully laid-back, multi-layered effort had "hit" written all over it. It wasn't.

❽ KISS ON MY LIST from VOICES
A tinny Casio keyboard opens this piano-driven air-puncher. And no, it's not "Lips", it's "List", thus securing a place in the pantheon of misheard lyrics.

❾ I CAN'T GO FOR THAT NO CAN DO from PRIVATE EYES
Their biggest UK hit was rarely off the radio in 1982, and remains one of the most sampled songs by hip-hop and R&B artists over the last 25 years.

❿ OUT OF TOUCH from BIG BAM BOOM
This track was lifted wholesale by United Nations, a dance music-obsessed policeman from Strathclyde, and then reworked into a top-ten hit across Europe in 2005. Don't write off the dynamic duo just yet...

Rhodri Marsden

Hammond Heroes

Invented by Lawrence Hammond to replace the church organ, the Hammond Organ became the favourite instrument of black American churches. Jazz and R&B musicians went on to reinvent the instrument as a seminal tool in 1960s jazz and soul.

❶ THE SERMON JIMMY SMITH from THE SERMON
Smith pioneered the Hammond in jazz and invented soul-jazz. Hugely influential both on the US jazz-soul scene and the UK beat boom, this late-1950s jam finds Smith stretching in a manner his 60s hit circumscribed.

❷ SMOOTH SAILING "BROTHER" JACK MCDUFF from TUFF 'DUFF
Funky and soulful, McDuff was capable of dragging amazing melodies out of his Hammond while pumping fat grooves. He proved a formidable inspiration behind London's Acid Jazz movement.

❸ ALL ABOUT MY GIRL JIMMY MCGRIFF from GREATEST HITS
The Prince of soul jazz to Jimmy Smith's King, McGriff's intense, piercing tone was a huge influence on the UK's Brian Auger and Georgie Fame.

❹ WADE IN THE WATER RAMSAY LEWIS from FINEST HOUR
Lewis was the most consistent hit maker of any of the Hammond's soul-jazz stars and with this instrumental interpretation of the great gospel standard he took black Southern Baptist church into the charts.

❺ MEDITATION BOOKER T & THE MGS from GREATEST HITS
Booker T Jones was the foremost Hammond player in 1960s soul and on this dreamy instrumental he conjures up little bubbles of bliss.

⑥ JUST IN TIME SHIRLEY SCOTT from QUEEN OF THE ORGAN
One of the few female musicians to succeed in the 1950s, Scott pushed the Hammond into bebop so widening its possibilities.

⑦ STEVIE'S GROOVE SPENSER DAVIS GROUP from HAMMOND ORGAN HEROES
Teen prodigy Stevie Winwood took the instrument to the UK's finger-popping masses on such hits as "I'm A Man" and "Gimme Some Lovin'". Here he cooks up a mess of sound for the pure pleasure of the groove.

⑧ WHEN A MAN LOVES A WOMAN PERCY SLEDGE from PERCY SLEDGE'S GREATEST HITS
The teenage Spooner Oldham made his mark by drenching Percy Sledge's debut hit in ghostly church organ. A brilliant session musician, Oldham's organ is present on several of the deepest soul tunes ever cut.

⑨ DARKER SHADE OF BLACK JACKIE MITTOO from CHAMPION IN THE ARENA 1976–1977
Founder member of The Skatalites, easy listening star in Canada and undoubtedly Jamaica's greatest ever Hammond player, Mittoo bought a lilting Caribbean flavour to the Hammond.

⑩ SLIPPIN' INTO DARKNESS WAR from THE BEST OF WAR AND MORE
Lonnie Jordan sets up a moody Hammond vamp for one of the key songs about inner city despair. War were one of the great American bands and Jordan's Hammond playing always anchored the ensemble.

Garth Cartwright

④ CANTALOUPE ISLAND from EMPYREAN ISLES
US3 hip-hopped this into "Cantaloop Island" but they couldn't improve on the musical chassis of the original, with Freddie Hubbard's trumpet over Hancock's repeated piano arc.

⑤ RIOT from SPEAK LIKE A CHILD
Starts slow for a riot but descends into flurrying whirlpools of piano.

⑥ CHAMELEON from HEADHUNTERS
Jazz-funk starts here, with a quintessentially squelchy synth pattern woven contrapuntally with percussion and sax lines.

⑦ WATERMELON MAN from HEADHUNTERS
A revisit for Watermelon Man in *Headhunters* style: the pygmy noises are made by percussionist Bill Summers blowing into a beer bottle.

⑧ PALM GREASE from THRUST
A ride into deep space, with synthesizers like a murmured dispute between two alien species.

⑨ JIMBASING HERBIE HANCOCK AND FODAY MUSA SUSO from JAZZ AFRICA
Hancock collaborating with the Gambian kora player and his dynamic band.

⑩ ROCKIT from FUTURE SHOCK
An early and influential hip-hop track, extravagantly scratched, showed Hancock was still ahead of the curve.

David Honigmann

Herbie Hancock

Herbie Hancock: a bit of a legend. His 1960s Blue Note work is impeccable, he was a bedrock of Miles Davis's quintet, and he invented jazz-funk fusion in the 70s. Great sideman, too.

① WATERMELON MAN from TAKIN' OFF
Hancock's first hit, originally in a version by Mongo Santamaria. On Hancock's own take, Freddie Hubbard and Dexter Gordon punch out the huge Latin brass riffs.

② MAIDEN VOYAGE from MAIDEN VOYAGE
George Coleman's tenor sax drifts over Hancock's rhythmic piano.

③ DOLPHIN DANCE from MAIDEN VOYAGE
One of Hancock's loveliest compositions: hear also the version by the Jazz Jamaica All-Stars.

Happy Mondays

Proof that, given enough drugs, a bunch of unskilled scallywags from the bleak wreckage of England's industrial North could cook up some decent funk.

① STEP ON from PILLS 'N' THRILLS AND BELLYACHES
Owing more than a little to the John Kongos classic "He's Gonna Step On You Again", the Mondays' masterpiece shambles along like it's been sniffing glue all afternoon. Couldn't stomp if they tried to.

② WROTE FOR LUCK (WFL) from LIVE
Forget about having your melons twisted, this one'll mess your head right up. The band's all-time-best closing number, recorded on a night of pharmaceutical euphoria.

❸ KINKY AFRO from PILLS 'N' THRILLS AND BELLYACHES
Laid-back easy-funk confessions from a man old
enough to know better.

❹ HALLELUJAH (CLUB MIX) from GREATEST HITS
Monkish chanting, soul-girl screams and a big baggy
stomping beat that'll pull even the desperately
mashed-up out of their seats.

❺ RAVE ON from THE HALLELUJAH SINGLE
Finest acid squelches, stolen basslines, purloined lyrics
and a dangerously medicated-sounding Shaun take
the listener way back to nights spent in muddy fields
on dodgy pills.

❻ LOOSE FIT (PERFECTO MIX) from GREATEST HITS
The coolest groove ever to leave Lancashire for a
cheeky week in Ibiza.

❼ BOB'S YER UNCLE from PILLS 'N' THRILLS AND
BELLYACHES
Shaun Ryder never sounded sleazier, the band groove
on like they're playing on stage in a Latin bordello.
Harks back to "Why Did You Do It" by Stretch, and no
bad thing either.

❽ COUNTRY SONG from BUMMED
The Mondays were so urban they had tarmac up their
spines, so why this attempt at country and north
western? I blame the drugs…

Al Spicer

Hardcore USA

Punk rock may have been invented in New York,
but it was in California and Washington DC – as
hardcore – that it received its most extreme
expression in the God-fearing United States.

❶ I LOVE LIVIN' IN THE CITY FEAR from THE RECORD
Not quite light speed yet, but as raw as you can bear.

❷ WE MUST BLEED THE GERMS from GI
One of the first American punk records to ratchet up
the speed to masturbatory bleat.

❸ PAY TO CUM BAD BRAINS from BAD BRAINS
Zero to Mach 1 in one minute and thirty seconds.

❹ HOLIDAY IN CAMBODIA DEAD KENNEDYS from FRESH
FRUIT FOR ROTTING VEGETABLES
A brutal parody of the condescension and contradic-
tions of white liberalism.

❺ IN MY EYES MINOR THREAT from MINOR THREAT
Where American punk broke from Britain and turned
intense and earnest.

❻ RISE ABOVE BLACK FLAG from DAMAGED
The high point of Henry Rollins' career.

❼ JOHN WAYNE WAS A NAZI THE STAINS (AKA MDC) from
MILLIONS OF DEAD COPS
Classic right-wing baiting.

❽ I'M NOT A LOSER DESCENDENTS from MILO GOES TO
COLLEGE
Everyone from Green Day to Good Charlotte owes
their careers to this record.

❾ MY OLD MAN'S A FATSO ANGRY SAMOANS from BACK
FROM SAMOA
Self-conscious and satirical, and nails one of hardcore's
central conundrums: "My old man's a fatso, but you
know he owns this house."

❿ BASKET CASE GREEN DAY from DOOKIE
Nostalgic Descendents tune with more hooks.

Peter Shapiro

Roy Harper

England's premier –only? – fried prog-folk poet,
a hero of Floyd, Zeppelin and Kate Bush, and still
going strong in his 1960s.

❶ ONE OF THESE DAYS IN ENGLAND from
BULLINAMINGVASE
The nearest Harper ever came to a hit, this very English
epic is, typically, both angry and pastorally pretty. The
McCartneys sing back-up.

❷ WHEN AN OLD CRICKETER LEAVES THE CREASE
from HQ
Harper's favourite, and another of his greatest paeans
to Englishness. Delicate, nostalgic and borne aloft by
the Grimethorpe Colliery brass band.

❸ ME AND MY WOMAN from STORMCOCK
Harper's sentiments – culminating aptly in some com-
ments on cuckoos – are matched excess for excess by
David Bedford's extravagant orchestration. Prog folk
at its finest.

❹ ANOTHER DAY from FLAT BAROQUE AND BERSERK
A touching song of never-consummated romance. The
modal melody, quavery vocal and first use of strings
audibly inspired an 1980s cover by This Mortal Coil.

⑤ I HATE THE WHITE MAN from FLAT, BAROQUE AND BERSERK

Skip the waffling hippy intro if you must, and you'll witness the best of Harper's acoustic phase: ostensibly Dylan-esque, its angry, poetic intensity is wholly Harper.

⑥ HORS D'OEUVRES from STORMCOCK

The overture to Harper's best album, all tart lyrics, meandering melody and one-man falsetto chorale.

⑦ SAME OLD ROCK from STORMCOCK

Epic anti-religious rant given additional gravitas by the sterling presence of pal Jimmy Page on lead guitar.

⑧ THE LORD'S PRAYER from LIFEMASK

Daunting but rewarding, a brush with death brought on this sidelong suite, shifting from poem to acid incantation. Again featuring Page on guitar.

⑨ HALLUCINATING LIGHT from HQ

From Harper's most rock-oriented album comes this beautiful electric ballad, with an aching vocal.

⑩ YOU from THE UNKNOWN SOLDIER

The last gasp of the classic era, this angular, rocky number finds Harper doing battle with the wailing of Kate Bush and David Gilmour's guitar.

Toby Manning

Emmylou Harris

An early protégée of Gram Parsons, the great Emmylou Harris should be queen of the country establishment. Yet she has somehow managed to maintain "outsider" status, continuing to take risks throughout a long and stellar career.

① LOVE HURTS WITH GRAM PARSONS from DUETS

Recorded with the late lamented country-rock pioneer a year before Emmylou's debut, when she was still carving out her reputation as a harmony vocalist with a rare empathy.

② TILL I GAIN CONTROL AGAIN from ELITE HOTEL

From the second of two albums she released in 1975, this Rodney Crowell song seems made for Emmylou's soulful wail.

③ PONCHO & LEFTY from LUXURY LINER

A wonderful rendering of Townes Van Zandt's signature tune. Emmylou really inhabits the sad poetic storyline, helped by great backing vocals from Rodney Crowell and Albert Lee.

④ MY FATHER'S HOUSE from THIRTEEN

An austere reading of this powerfully cinematic Bruce Springsteen song, from what Emmylou erroneously considers to be her thirteenth solo album; she disowned her true debut.

Emmylou Harris's
Roots 9

The queen of alt.country, EMMYLOU HARRIS has duetted with everyone from Gram Parsons and Bob Dylan to Neil Young and Ryan Adams. As you might have expected, her playlist has a strong American roots flavour, but with an interesting detour to Eastern Europe.

① DREAMING MY DREAMS WITH YOU WAYLON JENNINGS from THIS TIME, THE RAMBLIN' MAN

② UNCLOUDY DAY STAPLE SINGERS from UNCLOUDY DAY

③ UP ON CRIPPLE CREEK THE BAND from THE BAND

④ TALK TO ME OF MENDOCINO KATE AND ANNA McGARRIGLE from KATE & ANNA McGARRIGLE

⑤ THE EMPEROR OF WYOMING NEIL YOUNG from NEIL YOUNG

⑥ MANSION ON THE HILL BRUCE SPRINGSTEEN from NEBRASKA

⑦ THE MAKER DANIEL LANOIS from ACADIE

⑧ POLEGNALA E TODORA (THEODORA IS DOZING) ENSEMBLE OF THE BULGARIAN REPUBLIC CONDUCTED BY PHILIP KOUTEV from MUSIC OF BULGARIA

⑨ NOT DARK YET BOB DYLAN from TIME OUT OF MIND

h

❺ IF YOU WERE A BLUEBIRD from BLUEBIRD
A suspenseful shimmer of mandolin introduces this gorgeous Butch Hancock ballad, which hinges a series of country-spun conditionals.

❻ ROLLIN' AND RAMBLIN' (THE DEATH OF HANK WILLIAMS) from BRAND NEW DANCE
A heartfelt tribute to the honky-tonk hero, powered by rootsy fiddle and accordion.

❼ CRESCENT CITY from COWGIRL'S PRAYER
Vibrant Cajun-flavoured cover of a Lucinda Williams number from this excellent 1994 album, the quality of which hinted at what was on the horizon.

❽ WHERE WILL I BE from WRECKING BALL
The dazzling opener from Emmylou's 1995 reinvention album, which made a daring break with previous work in the choice of rock material and Daniel Lanois' sgrainy production.

❾ BANG THE DRUM SLOWLY from RED DIRT GIRL
Co-written with Guy Clark, this ghostly, bittersweet recollection of her father is deeply auto-biographical.

❿ LITTLE BIRD from STUMBLE INTO GRACE
Canadian sisters Kate and Anna McGarrigle have long been influential on Emmylou, and this pretty and delicate co-write has their magic stamped all over it.

Jon Lusk

George Harrison
Some highlights of the solo output of the dark horse of The Beatles.

❶ I'D HAVE YOU ANYTIME from ALL THINGS MUST PASS
The opening track of George's post-Beatles 1970 masterpiece, a marvellous, surprising collision of Harrison's luscious major seventh chords and Bob Dylan's lusty chorus.

❷ MY SWEET LORD from "ALL THINGS MUST PASS"
The second track, uncomfortably similar to the Chiffons' "He's So Fine" (an "unconscious plagiarism" for which George coughed up £600,000 in 1976), is nevertheless a remarkably rousing, inspirational record.

❸ GIVE ME LOVE (GIVE ME PEACE ON EARTH) from LIVING IN THE MATERIAL WORLD
The single from his 1973 album and its hopeful highlight.

❹ YOU from EXTRA TEXTURE
His albums had become semi-inspired ragbags by the mid-1970s, but this 1975 Springsteen-esque single had some fire in it, courtesy of Jim Horn's saxophone.

❺ BLOW AWAY from GEORGE HARRISON
From 1979, one of Hari's most delightful choruses, an infectious featherweight celebration of the optimism that love can inspire.

❻ ALL THOSE YEARS AGO from SOMEWHERE IN ENGLAND
A 1981 tribute to the recently assassinated Lennon, featuring contributions from Paul and Ringo, boogie-some and big of heart.

❼ THAT'S THE WAY IT GOES from GONE TROPPO
A marvellously judged blend of fatalistic humility and spiritual wisdom in an unfussy strum-along setting, typical early 1980s Harrison.

❽ WHEN WE WAS FAB from CLOUD NINE
An ingenious and affectionate Jeff Lynne-produced Beatles pastiche from George's excellent 1987 "come-back" album.

❾ NEVER GET OVER YOU from BRAINWASHED
Brainwashed, released a year after George's death in 2001, was an alluring mix of lyrical density and musical modesty. This romantic ballad is one of the highlights.

Chris Ingham

PJ Harvey
Practically a grand dame of indie-rock these days, PJ Harvey's career performs a regular swerve from cult to mainstream and back again. Here's a chronological tour.

❶ DRESS from DRY
The debut single: typically uncompromising, railing against conventional femininity, over choppy cello and her own scratchy violin.

❷ O MY LOVER from DRY
Dripping with accusatory irony, this harmonium-laced ballad boasts one of the best and most dismissively despairing grunts in rock.

❸ RID OF ME from 4 TRACK DEMOS
Even more intense than the album version, this solo version absolutely howls outraged rejection, voices and guitars hacking like blunt, bloodied machetes.

163

❹ MISSED from RID OF ME

The two Marys at Jesus's grave isn't an ordinary rock topic, but so extraordinary is this tortured, thudding ballad that it's practically a religious experience.

❺ TECLO from TO BRING YOU MY LOVE

Tracks like this lush spaghetti-western ballad with literal bells on took PJ Harvey right away from her hardcore harridan image. The hot pink jumpsuits helped, too.

❻ SEND HIS LOVE TO ME from TO BRING YOU MY LOVE

The aggression of this acoustic midpacer summarizes Harvey's agony/ecstasy contradictions.

❼ THE DANCER from TO BRING YOU MY LOVE

Another tune that combines the spiritual and the carnal: aptly organ-heavy and featuring a supremely orgasmic vocal.

❽ IS THAT ALL THERE IS? from DANCE HALL AT LOUSE POINT (WITH JOHN PARISH)

This wry version of an old Peggy Lee tune is rare evidence of Harvey's sense of humour. Black humour, naturally.

❾ LOVE TOO SOON from PASCAL COMELADE'S L'ARGOT DU BRUIT

This little-known collaboration with an eccentric Catlan highlights the showtune diva that Harvey only hints at in her own work.

❿ WE FLOAT from STORIES FROM THE CITY, STORIES FROM THE SEA

Swooningly seductive addition to Harvey's subgenre of water songs puts a confident full-stop to her biggest-selling album so far.

Toby Manning

The hat acts

The rise of the music video and CMT – the country equivalent of MTV – helped to create a new kind of male country star. Well scrubbed and usually clean shaven, they looked like football players, except that they dressed in cowboy boots and outsize hats. Musically they tended to be neo-traditionalists, but with a strong pop sensibility, prime for chart action. Star player was Garth Brooks, who by the early 1990s was challenging Michael Jackson as the biggest star in America.

❶ AIN'T GOING DOWN ('TIL THE SUN COMES UP) GARTH BROOKS from IN PIECES

He had a degree in marketing from a business university and became Nashville's biggest commodity in Nashville in the 1990s.

❷ BOOT SCOOTIN' BOOGIE BROOKS & DUNN from BRAND NEW MAN

Two hats for the price of one from Kix and Ronnie, who invented a particularly dopey line dance with this song and now rival Simon & Garfunkel and Hall & Oates as the best-selling duo in musical history.

❸ NEVER KNEW LONELY VINCE GILL from WHEN I CALL YOUR NAME

Former bluegrass musician turned country crooner who has also become familiar as the super-smooth presenter of Nashville's annual Country Music Awards.

❹ ALL MY EXS LIVE IN TEXAS GEORGE STRAIT from OCEAN FRONT PROPERTY

The original 1980s cowboy-in-a-hat, Strait was a major influence on the likes of Garth Brooks and Alan Jackson.

❺ ACHY BREAKY HEART BILLY RAY CYRUS from SOME GAVE ALL

Love him or hate him, you couldn't ignore this line-dancing favourite – or the extraordinary mullet he revealed when he took off his hat.

❻ DON'T GET ANY COUNTRIER THAN THIS TIM MCGRAW from NOT A MOMENT TOO SOON

"I'm a redneck and I admit it", this platinum-selling son of a baseball hero asserted.

❼ A THOUSAND MILES FROM NOWHERE DWIGHT YOAKAM from THIS TIME

The closest any of the hat acts has ever got to rock'n'roll credibility and the only one to get on MTV, he once even covered a Clash song.

❽ TOO GONE TOO LONG RANDY TRAVIS from ALWAYS AND FOREVER

For a while he seemed to be the heir to George Jones's honky-tonk crown, although his star has waned in recent years.

❾ WHERE WERE YOU (WHEN THE WORLD STOPPED TURNING) ALAN JACKSON from DRIVE

Country music demanded an immediate reaction to 9/11 and Jackson obliged with this simple but effective commentary…

⑩ COURTESY OF THE RED, WHITE AND BLUE TOBY KEITH from UNLEASHED
…but Oklahoma's Toby Keith offered a far uglier response on this song that threatened to "put a boot in your ass" if you mess with the US of A.

Nigel Williamson

Hawaiian music

For a spell in the 1920s and 1930s, Hawaii provided the world's favourite pop sounds. It has to be said that much of the early stuff now sounds like novelty songs, but the best maintain real charm. Meantime, in contemporary Hawaii, there's a vibrant roots-based scene, spearheaded by guitarist Gabby Pahinui: more serious fare, but with the trademark steel-guitar lilt still as evocative of paradise as ever. The ten tracks here are a trawl through both ancient and modern.

① OUA OUA KANUI & LULA from HAWAII'S POPULAR SONGS
Strange but true: this irresistible 1929 slice of ukulele–backed doggerel was a #1 hit in Austria in 2001.

② LEPE ULAULA SAM ALAMA & HIS HAWAIIANS from HAWAII'S POPULAR SONGS
A lovely early classic, this time from 1936.

③ HI'ILAWE GABBY PAHINUI from LEGENDS OF FALSETTO
The first major recording by the father of contemporary Hawaiian music, from 1947.

④ ALIKA GENOA KEAWE from THE ROUGH GUIDE TO HAWAII
Infectiously enjoyable 1974 performance by one of Hawaii's greatest falsetto singers.

⑤ KA ULUWEHI O KE KAI HAPA from HAPA
This Maui band revitalized the Hawaiian scene with their debut 1992 album.

⑥ HAWAII 78 ISRAEL KAMAKAWIWO'OLE from FACING FUTURE
The sadly-missed Iz, who died in 1997, included this Hawaiian sovereignty anthem on his seminal 1993 album, *Facing Future*.

⑦ KAWAIPUNAHELE KEALI'I REICHEL from KAWAIPUNAHELE
Since this first 1994 hit, Maui-based hula teacher Reichel has released a succession of beautiful albums.

⑧ ALOHA KA MANINI ISRAEL KAMAKAWIWO'OLE from E ALA E
Iz really deserves his own playlist; this is a sublime rendition of a Hawaiian standard.

⑨ HANAIALI'I NUI LA EA AMY HANAI'ALI'I GILLIOM from HAWAIIAN TRADITION
The leading modern exponent of the falsetto tradition, on fine form in 1997.

⑩ KU'U LEI CYRIL PAHINUI AND BOB BROZMAN from FOUR HANDS SWEET & HOT
Gabby's son Cyril and roving musician Bob Brozman released this gorgeous slack-key guitar duet in 1999.

Greg Ward

Isaac Hayes

Starting out as a house writer for Stax Records in Memphis, Isaac Hayes went on to invent symphonic soul and become a multi-platinum-selling artist – as well as a film and TV star. Now he's the voice of Chef in *South Park* and the world's funkiest scientologist.

① BY THE TIME I GET TO PHOENIX from HOT BUTTERED SOUL
Isaac takes the Jimmy Webb tune on an eighteen-minute journey. Little happens musically but the Voice grabs you and refuses to let go.

② THEME FROM SHAFT from SHAFT
"Who's the black private dick that drives all the chicks crazy?" asks Isaac, not so much about the film's stud cop but about, uh-hum, himself.

③ WALK ON BY from HOT BUTTERED SOUL
The Dionne Warwick song gets stretched. "Walk on!" scream the gospel chorus. Fuzz guitar bleeds. Ike sighs. Listen and melt.

④ NEVER CAN SAY GOODBYE from BLACK MOSES
Another classic extended work-out.

⑤ IKE'S MOOD from INSTRUMENTALS
Hugely atmospheric mood music. Much sampled by trip and hip-hoppers.

⑥ IKE'S RAP 1 from TO BE CONTINUED
Ike's talking over minimal piano-drum backing, telling his woman that Uncle Sam's called him up, but, stay to true 'cos he'll be back. A soul sermon of sorts.

❼ SOULSVILLE from SHAFT
"Some are trying to ditch reality with a $50 high/Only to find out you can never touch the sky." Ike was deep, no doubt.

❽ JOY from JOY
Isaac in rare, uptempo form and laying the seduction on thick: "Sweetness is the name for you, sugar."

❾ IKE'S RAP 4/A BRAND NEW ME from BLACK MOSES
Twenty-minute epic anchored by a gorgeous descending bassline that Tricky built a career on.

❿ NO NAME BAR from SHAFT
An instrumental that conjures up a-bad-place-to-be. Huge horn riffs, thick organ, dizzy flute, brassy sax: this is the sound of the 1970s.

Garth Cartwright

Jimi Hendrix

Modern guitar heroics start here. Six-string abuse doesn't come wilder or more passionate than Jimi in full flight.

❶ ALL ALONG THE WATCHTOWER from ELECTRIC LADYLAND
Jimi takes Bob Dylan's tune and creates what many feel is the timeless and magical definitive version. Simply awesome.

❷ BURNING OF THE MIDNIGHT LAMP from ELECTRIC LADYLAND
Almost a Wall Of Sound-style production, with celestial backing vox, harpsichord and some terrific guitar, building to a huge layered climax.

❸ DOLLY DAGGER from FIRST RAYS OF THE NEW RISING SUN
She drinks her blood from a jagged edge, don'tcha know? A terrifically funky number with a cracking closing solo.

❹ LITTLE WING from AXIS: BOLD AS LOVE
A deceptively simple and lyrically gorgeous little song. The closing solo relies more on soulful flow than flashy histrionics.

❺ MACHINE GUN from LIVE AT THE FILLMORE EAST
War? What is it good for? Drums rattle and Jimi puts his guitar almost literally through the emotional grinder on this awesome political thriller.

❻ PURPLE HAZE from ARE YOU EXPERIENCED
'Scuse me while I kiss the freakin' sky, baby! From the famously choppy intro to the psych overload climax, a stone-cold classic.

❼ SPANISH CASTLE MAGIC from THE JIMI HENDRIX EXPERIENCE
Fancy a trip on a dragonfly? A nice long version here, so hold tight for a great rolling riff and some fantastic soloing.

❽ STAR SPANGLED BANNER from LIVE AT WOODSTOCK
The guitar god lays waste to the national anthem in a historic performance. A shrieking, howling, life-affirming noise.

❾ THIRD STONE FROM THE SUN from ARE YOU EXPERIENCED
A simply wild interstellar trip with a beautifully flowing bassline and Hendrix in weird free-form poetry mode.

❿ VOODOO CHILD (SLIGHT RETURN) from ELECTRIC LADYLAND
Another famous intro, those wacka-wacka licks erupt into an incendiary frenzy and Jimi starts felling mountains with the edge of his hand.

Essi Berelian

Herb superb

Some people might say that ganja and reggae music are somehow inseparable, but, to be honest officer, I couldn't possibly comment. Less open to interpretation, though, is the fact that there are an inordinate number of reggae songs written in veneration of the so-called herb superb. This is a selection from a list so long it would take up your entire MP3 player. Now there's a thought – never mind U2, what about a special edition iPod that's useless before midday and plays the same dodgy old tune over and over again at three o'clock in the morning?

❶ LEGALIZE IT PETER TOSH from LEGALIZE IT
The daddy of all weed songs, that has Tosh as Marketing Director as, over the choppiest of beats, he stacks up the reasons for a change in the law.

❷ SENSEMILLA BLACK UHURU from 20 GREATEST HITS
Percolating, popping, disco-esque rhythm from Sly & Robbie, while the militant vocals make the case against the forces of Babylon and their hardline approach to the weed.

❸ **UNDER MI SLENG TENG** WAYNE SMITH from SLENG TENG EXTRAVAGANZA

Smith exposes the joys of being off his face on this nagging buzzsaw of a tune, the first to use a digital rhythm.

❹ **HERBMAN HUSTLING** SUGAR MINOTT from HERBMAN HUSTLING

An escalating selection of drumbeats are all Minott needs to bolster up his salesman's tale, in a superb example of how, on planet reggae, digital didn't have to mean dismal.

❺ **GANJA SMUGGLING** EEK-A-MOUSE from WA-DO-DEM

The Mouse "skeddebeng"s and "diddidung"s his way through a concise explanation of the economics of the collie trade and how Kingston life can revolve around it.

❻ **I LOVE MARIJUANA** LINVAL THOMPSON from I LOVE MARIJUANA

No-nonsense roots music, with a hymn to the herb as unequivocal as the title. It "keeps the natty dreadlocks singing", apparently.

❼ **KAYA (LEE PERRY PRODUCTION)** THE WAILERS from THE ESSENTIAL BOB MARLEY

Lee Perry's inherent understanding of how a circular reggae beat can be taken to a place beyond merely insistent creates a flawless framework for The Wailers' slow, drawn-out harmonizing and Bob's very stoned lead.

❽ **NATURAL COLLIE** FREDDIE MCGREGOR from THE ANTHOLOGY

A pleading, soulful love song offering up collie weed as an escape route from the tribulations of Jamaican poverty.

❾ **CHALICE IN THE PLACE** U-ROY from DREAD IN A BABYLON

Over the classic rocksteady of The Techniques' "Queen Majesty", U-Roy toasts a truly absurd tale of licking the chalice in Buckingham Palace that blurs into a dancehall love song. Fabulous stuff.

❿ **PASS THE KOUTCHIE** THE MIGHTY DIAMONDS from CHANGES

Laidback in the extreme, multi-layered for a comforting cushion of a rhythm, soothingly harmonized, this record drifts about like a big cloud of particularly pungent smoke. Musical Youth later took a smoke-free version to the top of the UK charts.

Lloyd Bradley

Highlife

An early African music phenomenon, highlife had long golden years from the 1950s to the 70s. Ghana was the epicentre of this easygoing good-time music, though Nigeria and several nearby countries produced their own variants.

❶ **ALL FOR YOU** E.T. MENSAH from ALL FOR YOU

An early 1950s highlight from the undisputed king of highlife, whose career spanned an incredible six decades.

❷ **THE QUEEN'S VISIT** KING BRUCE from GOLDEN HIGHLIFE CLASSICS

This genteel number anticipates Queen Elizabeth II's 1959 visit to Ghana. After all that, HRH did a no-show! Contains the immortal line: "This is the day five million Ghanaians will go gay." How times have changed.

❸ **BONE BIARA SO WO AKATUA** NANA AMPADU & THE AFRICAN BROTHERS from THE ROUGH GUIDE TO HIGHLIFE

Poor recording-quality can't stifle this phenomenal groove. With their "Afrohili" brand of guitar-band highlife, Nana Ampadu and his band were at the top of their game through much of the 1960s and 70s.

❹ **KYENKYEN BI ADI M'AWU** K. FRIMPONG AND HIS CUBANO FIESTAS from AFRO-ROCK VOL 1

This evergreen minor-key highlife from 1976 has been sampled by several contemporary "hiplife" artists.

❺ **MATUTU MIRIKA** ERIC AGYEMAN from HIGHLIFE SAFARI

Infectiously danceable party fave by this modernizer of Kumasi's "sikyi" style. The simple, insistent horn motif would be a ring tone if they'd had mobile phones in Ghana in 1978.

❻ **THE LORD'S PRAYER** SUPER SWEET TALKS from THE LORD'S PRAYER

They say the devil has all the best tunes, but this proves that's a lie. A.B. Crentsil's late-1970s masterpiece is enough to make godless souls shout "Amen!"

❼ **OYOLIMA** CHIEF STEPHEN OSITA OSADEBE from THE ROUGH GUIDE TO NIGERIA AND GHANA

A slinky, laid-back number with muted trumpet, understated guitar, atmospheric percussion and the honeyed vocals of Nigeria's master of Igbo highlife.

❽ **NULAKE KPLE FUWO** BLIND DZIMSON AND HIS MORKPOLAWO GROUP from THE GUITAR AND GUN

Hawaiian guitar adds sweetness and an exotic touch to this wonderful chugging tune, recorded in 1983 at John Collins' legendary Bokoor Studios in Accra.

⑨ FRIENDS TODAY, ENEMIES TOMORROW THE BEACH SCORPIONS from ELECTRIC HIGHLIFE

An epic 1989 song in pidgin English, which floats in the air for nearly ten minutes.

⑩ MAFE WO ALEX KONADU from THE HIGHLIFE ALLSTARS/SANKOFA

Known as "One Man Thousand" for his forceful stage presence, Kumasi-based Konadu was a major figure in 1970s highlife. He made this gloriously retro recording in 2001.

Jon Lusk

Lauryn Hill/ The Fugees

By age 23, Hill had had two smash hit albums with The Fugees and a solo effort that recalled the ambition of 1970s Stevie Wonder. Then, bar an acoustic MTV album, she disappeared. Here's why we miss her.

FUGEES

① RUMBLE IN THE JUNGLE from WHEN WE WERE KINGS

Her intricate, complex, conscious rhymes wipe the floor with such legends as Q-Tip and Busta Rhymes, as well as prefiguring the conscious soul hip-hop she would make her own with *Miseducation*.

② FU-GEE-LA from THE SCORE

The album version, with higher-mixed keyboards, and the Haitians' breakthrough hit. Wyclef and Pras live up to Hill's standard.

③ KILLING ME SOFTLY from THE SCORE

Too close to the original perhaps, but Hill doesn't so much recall Roberta Flack as out-sing her, note for note in her unique baritone.

④ READY OR NOT from THE SCORE

Hill covers this Delfonics song supremely, asserting the hook with absolute authority before showing off her considerable rap skills. Did she really need The Fugees?

LAURYN HILL

⑤ EX FACTOR from THE MISEDUCATION OF LAURYN HILL

Apparently an account of her tortuous relationship with fellow Fugee Wyclef Jean this features an embarrassment of choruses, while its massed harmonies lift it to heartbroken euphoria.

⑥ DOO WOP (THAT THING) from THE MISEDUCATION OF LAURYN HILL

Doo-wop, sprightly, poppy – Hill at her most charming. And there's wit in the sexual sententiousness.

⑦ I GOTTA FIND PEACE OF MIND from MTV UNPLUGGED

From the otherwise patchy Unplugged, this showcases Hill's deft acoustic guitar technique and way with words, before the devastating moment when she begins to cry mid-song.

⑧ TO ZION from THE MISEDUCATION OF LAURYN HILL

Self-deifying though it is ("and then an angel came to me" etc.), there's still something very moving about Hill's epiphanal paean to her baby son.

⑨ THE MISEDUCATION OF LAURYN HILL from THE MISEDUCATION OF LAURYN HILL

Perfect summation of that extraordinary debut, Hill sounding like Roberta Flack and Stevie Wonder's love child, the piano evoking 70s conscious soul, the vinyl crackles a lifetime love of hip-hop.

⑩ TELL HIM from THE MISEDUCATION OF LAURYN HILL

Tucked away as a bonus track at the end of the UK version of the album, this is actually a highlight: a delightfully simple acoustic hip-hop ballad, with one of Hill's most heartfelt vocals.

Toby Manning

Hip-hop classics

Hip-hop has a real history: 25 years of stylistic and technological developments, as well as countless changes in direction and perception. But for this list of classics, completely unscientifically, I've narrowed the territory down to genre-defining tunes from those half a dozen years (late 1980s/early 90s) in between old-skool and gangsta, when it was still naive enough to be musically open-minded, was just beginning to visualize its own long-term future, and had yet to define itself by MTV-oriented guidelines.

① SOLILOQUY OF CHAOS GANG STARR from DAILY OPERATION

A restless, computerized string-section loop moves this spooky rhythm around what sounds like a glockenspiel and a nagging drumbeat, while Guru's rapping is of a gig that turned into a riot.

❷ IT'S TRICKY RUN-DMC from GREATEST HITS
Proving they didn't need to share a stage with
Aerosmith to craft raucous heavy-metal-embracing
hip-hop, the twosome swap rhymes with considerable
aplomb and a good humour seldom associated with
Run-DMC.

❸ I CAN'T LIVE WITHOUT MY RADIO LL COOL J from
RADIO
If one single track summed up what hip-hop was
originally about, this is it. A big, belligerent teenager
playing his ghetto blaster too loud. No wonder it took
so long to go mainstream.

❹ PUSH IT SALT'N'PEPA from HOT, COOL & VICIOUS
B-girls with more front than Selfridges, this noisy,
crisply cut-up stomper proves it's entirely possible to
take rap pop without giving an inch of attitude.

❺ PAID IN FULL (ORIGINAL MIX) ERIC B & RAKIM from
PAID IN FULL
This is what lay underneath a seemingly endless
number of remixes, and being only semi-vocal, it
showcases Eric B's phenomenal turntable skills as well
as the rapper's verbal dexterity.

❻ LADIES FIRST QUEEN LATIFAH from ALL HAIL THE QUEEN
Built on an almost breezy horn sample, this feminist
diatribe is powered by so charming a tune that it
comes across as engaging and never hectoring.

❼ DOOWUTCHALIKE DIGITAL UNDERGROUND from
PLAYWUTCHALIKE
Far from a diatribe of any description, this record is
a rap frat-house party anthem. If anybody remakes
Animal House in a hip-hop stylee, this will be its Louie
Louie.

❽ WELCOME TO THE TERRORDOME PUBLIC ENEMY from
FEAR OF A BLACK PLANET
Public Enemy at their most overwhelming: the samples are sliced up and stacked four or five deep as
the beat's carried by a buzz saw, seemingly random
phrases are thrown in, Chuck isn't going to let anybody off lightly and Flav works hard to counterpoint
the finely focused fury.

❾ BASSLINE MANTRONIX from MANTRONIX
Always at the cutting edge of sound science and
sampling experimentation, this is the point at which
electro osmosed into straight-ahead hip-hop,
setting up some wonderfully involved beat
arrangements.

❿ PEOPLE EVERYDAY ARRESTED DEVELOPMENT from
GREATEST HITS
Gentler, thoughtful, tuneful rap, built around Sly

Stone's Everyday People, from the group that put
"hippy" into hip-hop.

Lloyd Bradley

Global hip-hop

**Hip-hop has conquered the world, and in Africa
it is now the dominant music. Away from the US,
however, attitudes come very different, and (like
reggae before it) hip-hop is more often a vehicle
for sharp political and social comment than for
chat about guns and 'hoes.**

❶ 537 C.U.B.A. ORISHAS from A LO CUBANO
European-based Cuban rappers who cheekily sampled
Buena Vista Social Club's "Chan Chan" on this track
from their debut album.

❷ BOOMERANG DAARA J from BOOMERANG
Wolof rhymes, West African melodies and hip-hop
beats as they celebrate the music's homecoming
– "born in Africa, brought up in America, rap has come
full circle".

❸ ANGELA SAIAN SUPA CREW from KLR
Global hip-hop in the truest sense, as rap, R&B, raga
and zouk all collide on a track that gave this Parisian
street crew the biggest-selling French-language single
of 2000.

❹ BOUGE DE LÀ MC SOLAAR from QUI SÈME LE VENT
RÉCOLTE LE TEMPO
The 1990 debut single from the biggest hip-hop star
in France, the world's biggest hip-hop market outside
America. It translates as "move along" (as a cop would
say).

❺ MEEN ERHABE DAM from ARABRAP (COMPILATION)
Palestinian rappers telling it like it is in the Occupied
Territories. The title means "who is a terrorist" and
the rap includes such lines as "I'm not against peace
– peace is against me."

❻ DIVIDE AND CONQUER SUBLIMINAL from
THE LIGHT AND THE SHADOW
But rap can give out many messages, as right-wing
Israeli rapper and self-confessed Zionist Subliminal
proves here as he sneers at the Middle Eastern peace
accords and those who support the creation of a
Palestinian state.

❼ BLAW POSITIVE BLACK SOUL from
NEW YORK/PARIS/DAKAR
The first and longest-established Senegalese hip-hop

group and the best-known – at least until Daara J came along.

❽ RETURN OF THE TRES DELINQUENT HABITS from MERRY GO ROUND
Tequila-injected hip-hop with a mariachi twist.

❾ BEYROUTH ÉCOEURÉE CLOTAIRE K from LEBANESE
Arabic instruments and programmed beats on a track about the war that tore the heart out of Beirut.

❿ WHAT'S HARDCORE? K'NAAN from THE DUSTY FOOT PHILOSOPHER
Incendiary tales of guns and gangs growing up on the war-torn streets of Mogadishu, from the young Somalian-born rapper.

Nigel Williamson

Robyn Hitchcock

The surreal lyrics about fish, fowl, and flesh – or, as a recent documentary put it, "sex, food, death and insects" – sometimes obscure Hitchcock's deft guitar-work and melodic gifts, but he's as much the progeny of the Beatles, Dylan as Syd Barrett. Or indeed The Band, on whom he contributed a playlist to this book.

❶ AIRSCAPE from ELEMENT OF LIGHT
Over a ringing Byrds-like riff, a ruminative elegy of man's place in the universe . . . or something like that.

❷ BRENDA'S IRON SLEDGE from BLACK SNAKE, DIAMOND RÖLE
Robyn at his manic and just-this-side-of-silly best; the jet-propelled riff practically begs you to hop aboard for the ride.

❸ FILTHY BIRD from MOSS ELIXIR
The sliding guitar chords hypnotize, the decon-structed bridge evokes Sergent Pepper and, somehow, a message about modern society and nature is subtly delivered into your skull.

❹ EGYPTIAN CREAM from FEGMANIA!
Bizarre sexual identity issues surround this keen pop melody, powered by the lush, upbeat instrumentation of his new-old backing band.

❺ LINCTUS HOUSE from EYE
Lovely, dexterous acoustic guitar work supports alternately amusing and heartrending lines on a faded relationship.

❻ UNDERWATER MOONLIGHT from UNDERWATER MOONLIGHT (SOFT BOYS)
Some unbelievably catchy hooks and harmonies make you question why this immaculate slice of psychedelia wasn't a hit. Perhaps because it was about two statues heading off for an evening dip.

❼ CREEPED OUT from SPOOKED
Refreshingly organic, this simple stomp highlights an unusual collaboration with bluegrass neo-traditionalists Gillian Welch and David Rawlings.

❽ YIP SONG from RESPECT
It's a fine line between absurd and touching; the latter somehow wins out while you marvel at how many times he can repeat the word "yip" during a eulogy to his father – and without taking a breath.

❾ ONE LONG PAIR OF EYES from QUEEN ELVIS
A shimmering prism of a melody, perfect for a song referencing light, colour, vision and changing perspectives.

❿ THE AUTHORITY BOX from OLE TARANTULA!
Robyn and his new bandmates rock with anger and authority; you've never had as much fun shouting along to the words "Fuck me, baby – I'm a trolley bus!" Of course you've probably never had the chance before.

Andrew Rosenberg

Billie Holiday

Billie Holiday invested jazz song with the emotional immediacy of the blues. Her voice, with its subtle tremolo and hint of rasp, was as irresistible as her effortlessly liquid, behind-the-beat phrasing. Billie's life was full of tragedy and there's a fragility even to her swinging cuts from the 1930s; in the later years, almost everything she sang was imbued with a profound melancholia – a sense of total acquiescence to some eternal sadness.

❶ THE MAN I LOVE from LADY DAY
Billie's never found the knight in shining amour of Gershwin's song. The closest she came was saxophon-ist Lester Young, whose velvety solo grounds this performance.

❷ BODY & SOUL from LADY DAY
As this classic take shows, with Billie there's always a fine line between sorrow and seduction.

❸ ON THE SUNNY SIDE OF THE STREET from THE COMMODORE MASTER TAKES

Proof that Billie wasn't all pain and tears, this take of the Louis Armstrong favourite is brimming over with infectious joy.

❹ IN MY SOLITUDE from LADY DAY

"In my sar-li-tude…". There's an almost crystalline delicacy to Billie's account of this Ellington number.

❺ GOD BLESS THE CHILD from LADY DAY

There are eighteen recordings of this Billie signature tune, co-written with Arthur Herzog. This 1941 take shows Billie's voice at its technical peak.

❻ STRANGE FRUIT from LADY IN AUTUMN

Written for Holiday, Lewis Allan's anti-lynching song was hugely potent for American audiences of the 1940s, as the hushed atmosphere on this intense live version demonstrates.

❼ I LOVE YOU PORGY from THE LEGEND OF BILLIE HOLIDAY

Billie brings an unmatched tenderness to this high-light from Gershwin's "folk opera". When the rhythm section quietly drops in for the second verse, the tears start rolling.

❽ LOVE FOR SALE from LOVE FOR SALE

Billie's forlorn account of this Cole Porter tune is powerful enough on its own terms. Once you learn that she was a prostitute in her teenage years, her delivery cuts like a blade.

❾ YESTERDAYS from LADY IN AUTUMN

No one was better suited than Billie to this wistful Jerome Kern number, and in this 1953 version her poised vocal is closely miked, with Oscar Peterson's spacey Hammond providing extra bite.

❿ FINE & MELLOW from THE LEGENDARY SOUND OF JAZZ TELECAST

Recorded for TV, this extended version of Billie's self-penned blues saw her reunited with old sideman and dear friend Lester Young – just two years before both would be dead.

Duncan Clark

Holland-Dozier-Holland

Quite simply, Eddie Holland, Lamont Dozier and Brian Holland were the greatest song-writing and production team in the history of popular music. Here's why.

❶ CAN I GET A WITNESS MARVIN GAYE from ANTHOLOGY

H-D-H inject Motown's finest singer with rocking and rolling holy-roller fervour.

❷ LEAVING HERE EDDIE HOLLAND from HEAVEN MUST HAVE SENT YOU: THE H-D-H STORY

A rollicking number that has since become something of a standard for groups like Motor City punkers The Rationals and Motörhead.

❸ WHERE DID OUR LOVE GO THE SUPREMES from THE ULTIMATE COLLECTION

The H-D-H formula in a nutshell: simple, singsong melody surrounded by pure dynamism.

❹ LOVE IS LIKE AN ITCHING IN MY HEART THE SUPREMES from THE ULTIMATE COLLECTION

Some of the most electric music in Motown's super-charged catalogue.

❺ NOWHERE TO RUN MARTHA & THE VANDELLAS from LIVE WIRE!

The Vandellas shadow Martha Reeves' vocals like they're stalking her, while Funk Brother James Jamerson's bassline and that insistent tambourine pro-pel the music to almost unbearable levels of intensity.

❻ REACH OUT I'LL BE THERE THE FOUR TOPS from ANTHOLOGY

Forget Phil Spector – this is the real "wall of sound".

❼ TAKE ME IN YOUR ARMS (ROCK ME A LITTLE WHILE) KIM WESTON from HEAVEN MUST HAVE SENT YOU…

A pulsating plea for love and affection that's been covered numerous times by rockers.

❽ HEAVEN MUST HAVE SENT YOU THE ELGINS from HEAVEN MUST HAVE SENT YOU…

Perhaps the sexiest and most beautiful ballad in the H-D-H songbook.

❾ GIVE ME JUST A LITTLE MORE TIME CHAIRMEN OF THE BOARD from HEAVEN MUST HAVE SENT YOU…

One of the records that created the blueprint for the pop–easy-listening–soul crossover.

⑩ GOING BACK TO MY ROOTS LAMONT DOZIER from HEAVEN MUST HAVE SENT YOU...

A stirring, truly moving record about alienation – and proof that you can go back home again.

Peter Shapiro

Honky tonk heroes

In post-World War II America the honky tonk was the hang out of choice for white Southerners. These skull orchards always had a jukebox, often a live band, and wanted singers in the vein of Hank Williams, men that sung rough, tough tunes about booze and broads. Here are ten who made the grade.

❶ LONG BLACK VEIL LEFTY FRIZZELL from LOOK WHAT THOUGHTS WILL DO

This gothic murder ballad, since recorded by everyone from The Band to Nick Cave, was originally cut by Lefty, the greatest honky tonk singer ever to walk the earth.

❷ WALKING THE FLOOR OVER YOU ERNEST TUBB from COUNTRY MUSIC HALL OF FAME

Tubb was sponsored early on by Jimmie Rodgers widow and he kept the primal honky tonk faith – best caught in this anxious tune - across the decades.

❸ THERE STANDS THE GLASS WEBB PIERCE from KING OF HONKY TONK

Classic ode to the pleasures and pain of alcohol. Many a hungover redneck must have reflected on its stoic philosophy.

❹ CRAZY ARMS RAY PRICE from GREATEST HITS

Huge ballad soaked in despair from one of the great singers in country music.

❺ HONKY TONK MAN JOHNNY HORTON from HONKY TONK MAN

Awesome celebration of the honky tonk life by a singer cut down in his prime by a drunk driver (probably returning from a honky tonk). Dwight Yoakam covered it on his debut so letting you know where he was coming from.

❻ WHAT MADE MILWAUKEE FAMOUS JERRY LEE LEWIS from KILLER COUNTRY

Lewis, having lost his rock'n'roll audience, reinvented himself as a honky tonk singer, problems with women, alcohol, pills and the law being second nature to Jerry Lee.

❼ HANK AND LEFTY RAISED MY COUNTRY SOUL STONEY EDWARDS from POOR FOLKS GOT TO STICK TOGETHER

Fabulous ode about listening to Hank and Lefty on the radio from a black country singer who grew up running a whiskey still.

❽ YOUR PLACE OR MINE GARY STEWART from GREATEST HITS

Wild celebration of one night stands from the most ferocious honky tonk singer of the 1970s.

❾ YOU'VE GOT THE LONGEST LEAVING ACT IN TOWN JOHN ANDERSON from JOHN ANDERSON

Gorgeous 'tear-in-your-beer' ballad from the greatest honky tonk singer of the 1980s.

❿ JUKE JOINT JUMPING WAYNE HANCOCK from THUNDERSTORMS AND NEON SIGNS

Honky tonks and their singers may be vanishing from the US landscape but Wayne "The Train" Hancock refuses to admit defeat.

Garth Cartwright

John Lee Hooker

Miles Davis called John Lee Hooker "the funkiest man alive" – and who's to argue? The man created a mesmeric stomping boogie sound, and the staggering scale of his output across six decades puts him in pole position for the most individually compelling bluesman of them all.

❶ BOOGIE CHILLEN from THE LEGENDARY MODERN RECORDINGS

Hooker unleashed his trademark boogie in his very first recording, from Detroit in 1948.

❷ CRAWLIN' KING SNAKE from THE VERY BEST OF

The first version of a theme to which Hooker was to return again and again, as delivered in 1949.

❸ HUCKLE UP BABY from THE VERY BEST OF

A stunning free-form re-interpretation of Paul Williams' signature tune, from 1950.

❹ I'M IN THE MOOD from THE VERY BEST OF

Though supposedly inspired by Glenn Miller's In The Mood, this early Hooker gem is much more boogie than brass.

❺ DIMPLES from THE VERY BEST OF

This 1956 hit was the most musically straightforward of all Hooker's songs, which is probably why it inspired so many white rock bands.

⑥ BOOM BOOM from THE VERY BEST OF
This odd but successful blues-pop hybrid, cut with the Motown house band in 1962, gave Hooker a rare hit single.

⑦ YOU KNOW, I KNOW from THE VERY BEST OF
A hypnotically compelling Chess single from 1966.

⑧ BURNING HELL from THE VERY BEST OF
This tour de force was recorded with Canned Heat in 1970.

⑨ THIS IS HIP from MR LUCKY
A rumbustious romp from 1991.

⑩ STRIPPED ME NAKED from MR LUCKY
Octogenarian rap from 1991; Hooker rants about the judge who handled his divorce, atop a jazz-tinged accompaniment from Carlos Santana.

Greg Ward

Trevor Horn

"Less is more" is a phrase often bandied about in recording studios But not by Trevor Horn, whose absurdly overblown productions have proved on at least ten occasions that, well, more is more.

① RELAX FRANKIE GOES TO HOLLYWOOD from WELCOME TO THE PLEASUREDOME
The simulated sound of throbbing sexual organs and explosive ejaculate probably took weeks to construct in the studio, and succeeded marvellously in upsetting a prudish BBC. One of the great banned songs.

② SLAVE TO THE RHYTHM GRACE JONES from ISLAND LIFE
Here's Grace! A perfect example of Trev's ability to transform a low-key song into an epic: sweeping strings, soaring horns and several thousand tracks of percussion.

③ A TIME FOR FEAR ART OF NOISE from WHO'S AFRAID OF THE ART OF NOISE
In 1983, a Fairlight computer cost £20,000 and could, if pushed to the limit, replicate the noise of a car starting. Thus The Art Of Noise were born, and this cut shows them at their most thunderous.

④ THE LOOK OF LOVE ABC from THE LEXICON OF LOVE
A downbeat, maudlin lyric has its socks pulled up by a whizz-bang production job – slick, radio-friendly and dripping with 1980s faux-sophistication.

⑤ BUFFALO GALS MALCOLM MCLAREN from DUCK ROCK
A startling and timeless collision of streetwise New York hiphop, African vocal harmonies and a half-hearted Hertfordshire barn dance.

⑥ LEFT TO MY OWN DEVICES PET SHOP BOYS from INTROSPECTIVE
It was already a perfect pop tune, but the 12" mix extended it in flamboyant fashion, throwing in the kitchen sink, deluxe toaster and slimline dishwasher.

⑦ VIDEO KILLED THE RADIO STAR BUGGLES from THE AGE OF PLASTIC
Mr Horn may not have much of a voice, but this track by his band gave Island Records its very first #1 in the UK, and launched his career as a producer.

⑧ THE DAYS OF PEARLY SPENCER MARC ALMOND from TENEMENT SYMPHONY
Horn and Almond's treatment of this cult record by Irish singer-songwriter David McWilliams finally gave it the hit status it deserved, 25 years after it was written.

⑨ CRAZY SEAL from SEAL
Again, nothing was left to chance in the construction of this Christmas hit, which has oozed unctuously out of car stereos ever since.

⑩ DR MABUSE PROPAGANDA from A SECRET WISH
Horn may not have been able to iron out the po-faced Teutonic narration, but the music was synthesized and sculpted into an impressive and slightly sinister goth club smash.

Rhodri Marsden

(Schlock) horror

Horror pop culture has a natural affinity with rock'n'roll and when it comes to pure schlock there's no end of bands willing to combine blood, guts and guitars.

① B-MOVIE SCREAM QUEEN MURDERDOLLS from BEYOND THE VALLEY OF THE MURDERDOLLS
Featuring Slipknot drummer Joey Jordison, the Murderdolls aren't shy with their influences. They rock like a goth-punk Mötley Crüe armed with chainsaws.

② BARK AT THE MOON OZZY OSBOURNE from BARK AT THE MOON
Ozzy dressed up as a slavering werewolf for this blood-thirsty tale of revenge from beyond the grave. Great guitars from Jake E. Lee.

Nick Hornby's
12 great songs you might not know

Author **NICK HORNBY** proved himself a master of lists with his debut, *Fever Pitch*, and took the form to a new art in *High Fidelity*, and his collection of music writing, *31 Songs*. He says, about this list, "Of course, I have no idea what you know and don't know. But I have managed to introduce these songs even to people who listen to a lot of music; maybe you have somehow managed to have missed them."

❶ **WATCH YOUR STEP** BOBBY PARKER from BENT OUT OF SHAPE
❷ **CAN I CHANGE MY MIND?** TYRONE DAVIS from ATLANTIC RHYTHM & BLUES: VOL 7
Two 1960s R&B songs, one slightly menacing, the other exuberant, both of them absolutely irresistible.

❸ **FORMULA, COLA, DOLLAR DRAFT** MARAH from LET'S CUT THE CRAP...
The first three stages of man, neatly encapsulated in four minutes and what seems like a million urgent words, with a beautiful and unusual banjo outro. It rocks, twangs and uplifts.

❹ **I CAN'T BE ME** EDDIE HINTON from HARD LUCK GUY
A writer whose songs were covered by Aretha Franklin and Percy Sledge, Hinton the singer was described by Jerry Wexler as a white Otis Redding. "I Can't Be Me" was recorded just before he died in 1995, and he'd just about perfected blue-eyed soul by then.

❺ **A LONG WAY BACK AGAIN** PETER WOLF from FOOL'S PARADE
More white R&B – the former singer with J Geils is

growing older with dignity and, on this evidence, just the right amount of regret and melancholy.

❻ **GOIN' BACK TO CALI** LL COOL J from ALL WORLD-GREATEST HITS
❼ **BRIDGING THE GAP** NAS from STREET'S DISCIPLE
Hip-hop for people who don't think they'll like hip-hop. Blues riffs, trumpets and the same kind of excitement you'd find in any great rock'n'roll.

❽ **PIECE OF CLAY** MARVIN GAYE from THE MASTER
❾ **STRANGER IN MY OWN TOWN** ELVIS PRESLEY from THE MEMPHIS RECORD
You may think you know all you need to know about these two. But Gaye's "Piece of Clay" is a haunting, mournful ballad released after his death (and, given the circumstances of his death, the first line is pretty chilling); "Stranger In My Own Town" is from the fantastic Memphis sessions, when Elvis briefly twitched back into glorious life after his long, slow 1960s death, like one of the characters in *Awakenings*. Colonel Parker soon put a stop to his fun.

❿ **I WANT TO KNOW WHAT LOVE IS** NEW JERSEY MASS CHOIR from BEGINNER'S GUIDE TO GOSPEL
⓫ **WALK OF LIFE** CHARLES MANN from THE ESSENTIAL COLLECTION
Yes, the Foreigner song and, yes, the Dire Straits song. One is done gospel, the other Cajun, and both make you doubt every aesthetic judgement about songs you've ever made.

⓬ **ME JUST PURELY** BRENDAN BENSON from ONE MISSISSIPPI
A heartbreaking, simple ballad, possibly about giving up drugs. I don't know. I never know what songs are about.

❸ **THE CREATURE FROM THE BLACK LEATHER LAGOON** THE CRAMPS from STAY SICK!
For twisted rockabilly noise look no further than this trashy little B-movie-meets-S&M number.

❹ **DEAD BEAT DANCE** THE DAMNED from THE RETURN OF THE LIVING DEAD OST
A little known Damned horror tune and a bit of a

rarity, this features some nice ghoulish laughter at the kick off and plenty of buzzsaw guitars.

❺ **DEVIL'S FOOD** ALICE COOPER THE BLACK WIDOW from WELCOME TO MY NIGHTMARE
A one-two punch from Alice's superbly camp concept. Vincent Price hams it up mercilessly as the mad scientist engineering the rise of an eight-legged empire.

❻ I WALKED WITH A ZOMBIE WEDNESDAY 13 from TRANSYLVANIA 90210
The living dead rise once more in this Murderdolls off-shoot project. This is crude, brutal and very catchy.

❼ NIGHT OF THE LIVING DEAD MISFITS from WALK AMONG US
The daddies of the horror punk genre, Misfits were masters of gory terror tunes and original vocalist Glenn Danzig is in his fiendish element on this.

❽ NOW IT'S DARK ANTHRAX from STATE OF EUPHORIA
One of the better cuts on an average album. David Lynch's disturbing suburban nightmare Blue Velvet gets a good thrashing.

❾ SUPERBEAST ROB ZOMBIE from HELLBILLY DELUXE
Rob Zombie is a modern one-man spookshow and this sleek, chugging monster is just a taster from a career specializing in cartoonish nastiness.

❿ THEM MISFITS from FAMOUS MONSTERS
Giant radioactive ants created in the wake of desert nuclear testing lay waste in this hair-raising slice of latter day Misfits action.

Essi Berelian

House

"House is an uncontrollable desire to jack your body and as I told you before this is our house and our house music…"

❶ ACID TRAX PHUTURE from TRAX RECORDS: ACID CLASSICS
Original 303 acid house from Chicago.

❷ JACK YOUR BODY STEVE HURLEY from BEST OF HOUSE
For a demonstration of the art of "jacking", just watch a room full of people moving to this.

❸ FRENCH KISS LIL LOUIS from FRENCH KISSES-COMPLETE MIX COLLECTION E.P.
The woman in the breakdown definitely likes this slightly embarrassing house classic.

❹ FOLLOW ME ALY-US single
If you don't get this uplifting end-of-the-night anthem, then you don't get house music.

❺ YOU CAN'T HIDE FROM YOUR BUD DJ SNEAK single
Impeccably filtered disco house: a one-bar loop that twists and winds like a funky snake.

❻ COLOSSUS THOMAS BANGALTER from TRAX ON DA ROCKS VOL 2
Most famous for his poppier Daft Punk tunes, Bangalter can also put together unstoppable underground house tracks like this.

❼ DOUBLE DOUBLE DUTCH DOPE SMUGGLAZ from DOUBLE DOUBLE DUTCH
Put this house version of Malcolm McLaren's "Double Dutch" on at a party and watch it erupt into carnival bacchanalia.

❽ EMOTIONS ELECTRIC A GUY CALLED GERALD from THE CHILLOUT SESSION IBIZA SUNSETS
Warm, breathy synths, spacious production, and a wailing diva vocal made this a rush-inducing staple of "Summer of Love" raves.

❾ GOOD LOVE (REESE DEEPER MIX) INNER CITY single
A relatively recent release from Kevin Saunderson's seminal house outfit, which aptly updates the Good Time vocal sound.

❿ STRINGS OF LIFE RHYTHIM IS RHYTHIM single
Derrick May presents a sparse, mechanical version of house that still retains the crucial funk.

Dan May

Howlin' Wolf

Howlin' Wolf always seemed more of an elemental force than a flesh-and-blood human being. Crammed into his mighty frame were all the essential ingredients of the blues, the rage and passion of the Mississippi Delta, and the electric thunder and urgency of Chicago.

❶ HOW MANY MORE YEARS from MOANIN' IN THE MOONLIGHT
The Wolf's earliest great howl, recorded at Memphis Sun Studios in 1951 by Sam Phillips, who always considered Wolf a greater discovery even than Elvis.

❷ EVIL from MOANIN' IN THE MOONLIGHT
Bellowing with pain, bristling with menace, Wolf is at his scariest in this 1954 recording.

❸ FORTY-FOUR from MOANIN' IN THE MOONLIGHT
You wouldn't want to cross the Wolf in this mood, prowling with his loaded pistol.

❹ SMOKESTACK LIGHTNIN' from MOANIN' IN THE MOONLIGHT

Probably the Wolf's finest hour, from 1956; he's howling partly with longing and partly in emulation of the train on which he's leaving.

❺ I ASKED FOR WATER (SHE GAVE ME GASOLINE) from MOANIN' IN THE MOONLIGHT

Early mentor Tommy Johnson taught Wolf this one back in Mississippi; he electrified it in Chicago in 1956.

❻ WANG DANG DOODLE from MOANIN' IN THE MOONLIGHT

Wolf is said to have loathed Willie Dixon, who he famously called "that fat fuck"; Dixon's songs nonetheless suited him down to the ground.

❼ BACK DOOR MAN from MOANIN' IN THE MOONLIGHT

Another Dixon tour de force, also from 1960. "The men don't know, but the little girls understand."

❽ SPOONFUL from MOANIN' IN THE MOONLIGHT

And Dixon too was responsible for converting this song by Wolf's boyhood mentor Charlie Patton into an electric blues hit in 1960.

❾ THE RED ROOSTER from MOANIN' IN THE MOONLIGHT

The Rolling Stones championed Howlin' Wolf during their earliest American tours, and had a hit single covering this 1961 song.

❿ DON'T LAUGH AT ME from HIS BEST VOL 2

An intriguing self-penned masterpiece from 1965, in which Wolf lays his vulnerabilities bare.

Greg Ward

The Human League

From a minimal electronic outfit with bad haircuts to dancy 1980s chart regulars: let's hear it for Phil Oakey and the glamorous Susanne Sulley and Joanne Catherall.

❶ ALMOST MEDIEVAL from REPRODUCTION

Harsh and almost discordant, the squishy synths and pounding rhythms turn this into a paranoid yet utterly compelling nightmare.

❷ ARE YOU EVER COMING BACK? from CRASH

Another relationship on the rocks makes for an underrated, smooth and catchy mid-1980s electro-pop gem. Should have been a hit.

❸ BEING BOILED from TRAVELOGUE

Not the minimal original but a turbocharged reworking with a throbbing rhythm and decorated with weird, distorted handclaps.

❹ BLIND YOUTH from REPRODUCTION

There is room for optimism in the big bad city after all. The futuristic vibe is brisk, positive and most importantly, highly danceable.

❺ DON'T YOU WANT ME from DARE

With that classic boy–girl vocal split, no 1980s disco is complete without at least one spin of this. Guaranteed to get people singing.

❻ (KEEP FEELING) FASCINATION from THE VERY BEST OF

A super rubbery bassline to this one, with Phil sounding particularly suave, so why didn't this great song end up on 1984's *Hysteria*?

❼ THE LEBANON from HYSTERIA

Just get a load of those corking Big Country-meets-U2-style guitars. Stadium rock meets the spirit of the dancefloor.

❽ LOVE ACTION (I BELIEVE IN LOVE) from DARE

This is Phil talking, kids! The chant-along mid section is (unintentionally) cheesily brilliant and the tink-a-tink rhythm track is terrific, too.

❾ THE SOUND OF THE CROWD from DARE

A mesmerizing beauty, this. You've just got to love the pumping bassline, and the escalating gunshot-style drums are ace, too.

❿ SOUNDTRACK TO A GENERATION from ROMANTIC?

Oh wow! Holy cow! The girls' exclamations are so bright and upbeat you just have to laugh. A great hear-it-once-sing-it-forever chorus, too.

Essi Berelian

Hüsker Dü

Bob Mould, Grant Hart and Greg Norton made hardcore you could thrash, groove or occasionally cry to; and the tension only added to the mix.

❶ I APOLOGIZE from NEW DAY RISING

For a change, Mould's vocals are way up in the mix out in front of the sheets of noise; after some tuneful warming up, he pulverizes as much as apologizes.

❷ EIGHT MILES HIGH from SINGLE

A blistering appropriation of the psychedelic folk

classic, keyed by Mould's raw vocals, which make the loneliness of the lyrics sound about eight miles deep.

❸ MAKES NO SENSE AT ALL from FLIP YOUR WIG

Mould starts to turn some of the longtime fans off and showcases his keen pop sensibilities in this should-have-been-a-hit single.

❹ DIANE from METAL CIRCUS

The Hüskers had that whole Pixies-like guitar squall down half a decade early; on the standout track from their early hardcore albums they wrap it in a lyric from the mind of a psychopath and send it home to meet – or worse – your family.

❺ SORRY SOMEHOW from CANDY APPLE GREY

Whether at Mould or at some former lover, this song points fingers, in as disdainful and tuneful a manner as possible.

❻ I'M NEVER TALKING TO YOU AGAIN from ZEN ARCADE

In the context of their towering concept album, the most plain-spoken declaration of protest, almost nervously set against acoustic guitar.

❼ CELEBRATED SUMMER from NEW DAY RISING

The midway acoustic break from the fury obliquely recalls the Mary Tyler Moore theme song ("Love Is All Around"), which they used to cover; the opening line perhaps intentially perverts that sentiment ("Love and hate was in the air").

❽ FRIEND YOU'VE GOT TO FALL from WAREHOUSE: SONGS AND STORIES

Their last album is almost like a tug of war between Mould and Hart with the former a slight winner; this Bob song is as catchy as any, with a lyric that stares daggers – then throws them.

❾ WHAT'S GOING ON from ZEN ARCADE

Dig the manically pounded piano in the last verse, an almost (and literal) over-the-top addition to this ferocious hailstorm.

❿ HATE PAPER DOLL from FLIP YOUR WIG

You'll either be driven crazy by this pop confection or have it bouncing around in your head all day. The latter is more likely.

Andrew Rosenberg

Iceland rocks

It's not just Björk. Despite a tiny population, Iceland and its capital Reykjavik boast a thriving rock scene noted for its left-field approach.

❶ BIRTHDAY SUGARCUBES from LIFE'S TOO GOOD
The first the world heard of the extraordinary voice of Björk Gudmundsdottir: her band's debut single back in 1988.

❷ ARMY OF ME BJÖRK from POST
It's impossible to represent her solo career with a single track, but this menacing, sinister-sounding iceberg of a song made waves when it was used in the film *Tank Girl*.

❸ AGAETIS BYRJUN SIGUR ROS from AGAETIS BYRJUN
The Icelandic My Bloody Valentine, with added glacial soundscapes – the aural equivalent of an Icelandic postcard.

❹ THE SPELL LEAVES from ANGELA TEST
Whereas this lot, with a lead vocalist who was once an opera singer, have been called the Icelandic Coldplay.

❺ CALM WATER EINAR ORN from GHOSTIGITAL
Once in The Sugarcubes with Björk, Orn was signed up by Damon Albarn to make a weird and wonderful solo album for his Honest Jon's label. It included this piece of dark oddness.

❻ MODERN HAIRCUTS MINUS from JESUS CHRIST BOBBY
Iceland's noisiest and nastiest heavy metal champions. This song also features Einar Orn.

❼ THE LAND BETWEEN SOLAR SYSTEMS MÚM from FINALLY WE ARE NO ONE
An epic, gurgling lullaby sung by twin sisters – two Björks for the price of one.

❽ WEDNESDAY'S CHILD EMILIANA TORRINI from LOVE IN THE TIME OF SCIENCE
It was her voice you heard singing the haunting "Gollum's Song" over the closing credits of *Lord Of The Rings: The Two Towers*, but this equally eerie track comes from her 2000 debut solo album.

❾ AM I REALLY LIVIN'? TRUBROT from LIFUN
Contrary to popular opinion, Icelandic rock did not begin with The Sugarcubes. Trubrot were the country's leading hippy band of the early 1970s, whose finest hour came on the prog concept album *Lifun*, which chronicled "the trip we all take from birth to death", no less.

❿ HIROSHIMA UTANGARDSMENN from GEISLAVIRKIR
Briefly Iceland's biggest band around the time of the punk explosion, they once supported their idols The Clash in Reykjavik.This was their biggest hit. Sample lyric: "You will all, you will all, you will all… DIE!"

Nigel Williamson

Idlewild

This Edinburgh quartet have developed from latter-day punk frenzy into a mature and thought-provoking band. Vocalist Roddy Woomble leads the ship with cool assurance.

❶ THESE WOODEN IDEAS from 100 BROKEN WINDOWS
The sudden jangled intro is overtaken by a hypnotic keyboard motif that underpins the excitement of the guitar-driven chorus. For post-modernists everywhere.

❷ TELL ME TEN WORDS from THE REMOTE PART
The surprising banjo-picked intro soon gives way to the more accustomed crash of crisp guitar and symbols and more great melodies.

❸ LET ME SLEEP (NEXT TO THE MIRROR) from 100 BROKEN WINDOWS
The piercing guitar intro preludes a magnificent verse-hook-chorus that is bound to tickle the hairs on the back of your neck.

❹ PAINT NOTHING from HOPE IS IMPORTANT
This early number points the way towards later glories.

❺ QUIET CROWN from 100 BROKEN WINDOWS
The gentle, almost folky intro is laden with harmonies and harmonics that pave the way for another killer chorus.

Nick Edwards

Mark Ellen picks
The Incredible String Band

MARK ELLEN edits *Word* magazine, the lastest in a string of music magazines he has created, including *Smash Hits*, *Q* and *Mojo*. Ellen has a longstanding passion for ISB. He explains: "The Incredible String Band were a pair of wildly adventurous psychedelic folk gypsies who, at their peak in the late 1960s, were a major influence on John Lennon, George Harrison and Led Zeppelin (among others). A lot of their material is impossibly dated now but these songs still sound immortal."

❶ THREE IS A GREEN CROWN from THE HANGMAN'S BEAUTIFUL DAUGHTER
Indian raga masterpiece knocked out after genius multi-instrumentalist Robin Williamson had "followed the Tarot to Fez" and returned with an oud, assorted flutes, ethnic drums and a bowed gimbri.

❷ NO SLEEP BLUES from 5000 SPIRITS OR THE LAYERS OF THE ONION
Naive psychedelic whimsy in a daft folk shuffle.

❸ KOEEOADDI THERE from THE HANGMAN'S BEAUTIFUL DAUGHTER
A miniature song-cycle on the theme of creation, awash with cosmic riddles and including a section seen from the eyes of a small child. Nothing like this has ever been attempted before or since.

❹ WITCHES HAT from THE HANGMAN'S BEAUTIFUL DAUGHTER
Bizarre slice of atmosphere that sounds like it fell through a wormhole in time from the sixteenth century.

❺ COLD FEBRUARY from HARD ROPE AND SILKEN TWINE
The title of their pinnacle album, *The Hangman's Beautiful Daughter*, was an image of British recovery after World War II (both Williamson and Mike Heron were born in wartime). This late-period live recording was a reflection on the war that preceded it.

❻ OCTOBER SONG from THE INCREDIBLE STRING BAND
Homage to the English and Gaelic folk tradition that Dylan mined just as successfully in the early 1960s.

❼ WALTZ OF THE NEW MOON from THE HANGMAN'S BEAUTIFUL DAUGHTER
Robert Plant once told me that Led Zeppelin had bought a copy of *The Hangman's Beautiful Daughter* "and simply followed the instructions". This, he thought, was the most thrilling and mysterious opening line to a song he'd ever heard in his life – "I hear that The Emperor Of China used to wear iron shoes with ease."

❽ SWIFT AS THE WIND from THE HANGMAN'S BEAUTIFUL DAUGHTER
Heron's dark, faintly Victorian account of a terrified child waking from a nightmare. Wood blocks clack disturbingly in the background. Absolute genius.

❾ DEAR OLD BATTLEFIELD from LIQUID ACROBAT AS REGARDS THE AIR
Lost gem buried in the mire of their ill-advised "folk-rock" interlude.

❿ FIRST GIRL I LOVED from THE 5000 SPIRITS OR THE LAYERS OF THE ONION
Williamson's touching recollection of a love affair when he was 17. Everyone hearing this smiles knowingly to suggest that they, too, once had a similarly deep relationship.

Industrial

With a brutal aesthetic inspired by blighted, noise-polluted cityscapes, "industrial" music came of age in the 1980s and early 1990s, though purists reserve the tag for the mid-1970s output of the Industrial Records label. Trademarks include intoxicating sampling, with savage shouting and provocative imagery – preferably all three.

❶ UNITED THROBBING GRISTLE from GREATEST HITS
Sparse electronica with the bleakest of vocals from the pioneering London experimentalists who consciously chose to play unattractive music.

❷ 13 LOECHER (LEBEN IST ILLEGAL) EINSTÜRZENDE NEUBAUTEN from KALTE STERNE
Groundbreaking musical subversion from "Collapsing New Buildings", the ultimate demolition mob when it comes to razing such niceties as harmony and melody,

and constructing new foundations from the raw soundscapes of electric drills and girders.

❸ ASSIMILATE SKINNY PUPPY from BITES

Most accessible entry-point for the Vancouver band who specialize in otherworldly growls and agonized cries. Closing with a chant of "death, death, death", it creeps through your mind like the wounding excesses of an earthbound hellzone.

❹ HEADHUNTER FRONT 242 from FRONT

Relentlessly pounding stomper that shunned the dissonance of earlier industrial and gave rise to the term "electro body-music" to encapsulate this new dance-friendly direction. Quite possibly the best industrial track of the 1980s.

❺ THIEVES MINISTRY from THE MIND IS A TERRIBLE THING TO TASTE

Al Jourgensen leads his seminal Chicago outfit at a churning grind, crashing into a terrifyingly thrashy chorus as he seethes with venom and contempt for a society bleeding with thieves, liars and hypocrites.

❻ BEERS, STEERS AND QUEERS REVOLTING COCKS from BEERS, STEERS AND QUEERS

Affectionately called Revco, this Ministry offshoot supplied, according to Jourgensen, "disco for psychopaths". This cut is a godless hoedown, complete with crazed "yee-haws".

❼ HEAD LIKE A HOLE NINE INCH NAILS from PRETTY HATE MACHINE

A pulsating industrial dance anthem, written and played entirely by Trent Reznor, an individual so steeped in the macabre that he once lived at 10050 Cielo Drive, the house where Charles Manson murdered Sharon Tate.

❽ I GIVE TO YOU NITZER EBB from EBBHEAD

Orchestral beats and tortured lyrics collide in this outpouring from Essex electronic trio Bon Harris, David Gooday and Douglas McCarthy. Produced by Alan Wilder, it's like early Depeche Mode, only harder.

❾ SKINFLOWERS YOUNG GODS from TV SKY

This track from Scandinavian noisenik Franz Treichler builds to a quirky, Swiss-inflected bellow, while synth-phasers and electro guitar riffs burst through the thunderous, dominating drum machine.

❿ SAVED DOUBTING THOMAS from THE INFIDEL

Cevin Key and Duane Goettel of Skinny Puppy showcase their masterful programming techniques with this dark slice of instrumental electronica. An intricate industrial masterpiece.

Claire Fogg

Instrumental cool

Who needs lyrics? From million sellers to little known gems, this selection proves that instrumentals are way cool.

❶ PEACHES EN REGALIA FRANK ZAPPA from HOT RATS

A scampering number that covers an awful lot of ground. The saturated sound colours are as Day-Glo as they get, from an almost entirely instrumental album that was among Zappa's very best.

❷ GREEN ONIONS BOOKER T. & THE MGs from THE VERY BEST OF BOOKER T. & THE MGs

Grooving interplay between organ and guitar over a cool boogie-inspired bass line. A monster hit for the "best backing group in the history of soul music".

❸ ALBATROSS FLEETWOOD MAC from THE BEST OF PETER GREEN'S FLEETWOOD MAC

An alabatross of the highest quality, from well before the arrival of Lindsay Buckingham and Stevie Nicks, this iconic, brooding soundscape has survived being used on innumerable TV ads and soundtracks.

❹ RUMBLE LINK WRAY from RUMBLE! THE BEST OF LINK WRAY

The best-known tune by the king of surf guitar is a street stompin' treat, which – impressively – was banned in 1959 because of its graphic evocation of brawling hoodlums.

❺ CECILIA ANN PIXIES from BOSSANOVA

Their debt to Mr. Wray and numerous other surf music artists is obvious on the opening cut from what was arguably this Boston alt. rock combo's finest album.

❻ RETURN OF DJANGO THE UPSETTERS from REGGAE CHARTBUSTERS VOL 2

A massively skanking number with rude-sounding horn by Val Bennett. A huge hit in 1969, this was a Lee Perry production from before his space cadet phase.

❼ WALTZ FOR LUMUMBA SPENCER DAVIS GROUP from THE BEST OF THE SPENCER DAVIS GROUP

Not really a waltz at all, this astonishingly African-sounding workout by the pioneer British R&B group includes the precocious talents of Steve Winwood on organ.

❽ SIDE O' THE ROAD CREEDENCE CLEARWATER REVIVAL from WILLIE AND THE POOR BOYS

A sinister feeling pervades this pacing New Orleans-flavoured interlude with coruscating guitar riffs from their mightiest album.

9 SPIRIT OF E9 WILLIE NELSON from SPIRIT

This gorgeously old-fashioned waltz features solos by Willie's sister Bobbie on honky-tonk piano, Johnny Gimble on fiddle and, of course, Willie's unmistakable gut-string guitar.

10 GEORGIA BUCK PRECIOUS BRYANT from FOOL ME GOOD

A delightfully upbeat little tune by the "daughter of the blues" – one of the last living exponents of the southwest Georgia blues tradition. You'll want to hear it "one more time".

Jon Lusk

Irish roots

Accordionist Brendan Begley called Irish traditional music "the only acceptable form of madness". Maybe so. Irish music has survived the exigencies of poverty, famine and emigration as a fully living form, regenerated by generations of younger musicians keen to explore the past and expand the frontiers.

1 ROSE IN THE GAP JOHN MCSHERRY, DÓNAL O'CONNOR from TRIPSWITCH

A thrilling combination of uilleann pipes and fiddle from two of Ireland's finest musicians, driven by throbbing guitar and bouzouki.

2 BEAN PHÁIDÍN LASAIRFHÍONA NÍ CHONAOLA from AN RAICÍN ÁLAINN

An old Connemara comic love song, reinvigorated to gorgeous effect by this young Aran Islands singer, accompanied by hypnotic bodhrán backing.

3 MURPHY'S/THE FAIR HAIRED GIRL ANGELINA CARBERRY & MARTIN QUINN from ANGELINA CARBERRY & MARTIN QUINN

Angelina (on banjo) comes from a famous piping familiy, while Martin (on melodeon) is one of the country's most in demand musicians. This set of a hornpipe and a reel provides clear evidence of their symbiotic skills.

4 THE PINCH OF SNUFF CIARÁN Ó MAONAIGH AND DERMOT MCLAUGHLIN from CEOL A'GHLEANNA

The old-style form of duet fiddling is still enjoyed in Donegal and here given a new lease of life by the nephew of Altan's Mairéad Ní Mhaonaigh and the highly regarded Derry-born fiddler.

5 PASTURES OF PLENTY SOLAS from REUNION

A highlight of the Irish–American band's stupendous live ten-year anniversary album, this sees original vocalist Karan Casey returning on dazzling form and incorporates all the group's renowned instrumental twists and turns.

6 TAIMSE IM' CHODLADH IARLA Ó LIONÁIRD from INVISIBLE FIELDS

The some-time Afro Celts singer's solo album is a spine-tingling affair and nowhere more so than on this ravishing rendition of one of the "big" songs in the Irish tradition, enhanced by a gripping arrangement featuring electronic drones and hammer dulcimer.

7 ASTURIAN WAY FLOOK from HAVEN

Though only half-Irish in terms of personnel, Flook incorporate a thrilling blend of flutes and whistles backed by powerful guitar and bodhrán, no better exemplified than on this energetic set of reels.

8 MY DARLING'S ASLEEP/AN BUACHAILL DREOITE/DOWN THE BACK LANE MARTIN MC CORMACK from UILLEANN PIPES AND WHISTLES

The young Monaghan uilleann piper proves he's among Ireland's finest on this stirring trio of jigs.

9 COLONEL MCBAIN/PADDY KILLORAN'S REEL DRAÍOCHT from LAND'S END

Not a band but a duo, featuring Sligo's June Mc Cormack whose flute whirls and whoops through this set of reels to splendidly appropriate accompaniment from Monaghan harper Michael Rooney.

10 THE WEE WEAVER HELEN ROCHE from SHAKE THE BLOSSOM EARLY

A standout from the Liverpool–Irish singer's debut album of love songs from the (largely Northern) Irish tradition, this unaccompanied song is a tour de force, enhanced by the sheer warmth of Helen's voice.

Geoff Wallis

Iron Maiden

Having rode in on the late-1970s' so-called New Wave Of British Heavy Metal, Maiden are a rock phenomenon still able to sell out stadiums worldwide with supreme ease.

1 12 MINUTES TO MIDNIGHT from POWERSLAVE

A countdown to the apocalypse, featuring great lyrics, a classy galloping bassline and some ace soloing.

2 DIE WITH YOUR BOOTS ON from LIVE AFTER DEATH

This is a real fist-pumping, crowd-pleasing do-or-die anthem with a cracking singalong chorus.

❸ DREAM OF MIRRORS
from BRAVE NEW WORLD

A deeply troubled set of lyrics, exploring second sight and the power of dreams, married to a huge and memorable chorus.

❹ IRON MAIDEN from IRON MAIDEN

Almost punky in its speed, this gritty effort stuffs loads of ideas into just three and a half minutes of spitfire energy.

❺ PASCHENDALE from DANCE OF DEATH

The stench of violent death is almost palpable in this intelligent epic dramatizing one of the World War I's bloodiest battles. Complex, mature and emotional stuff.

❻ PHANTOM OF THE OPERA from IRON MAIDEN

A tune bursting with youthful zeal; the arrangement hints at the proggy influences Maiden would explore more fully later in their career.

❼ RUN TO THE HILLS from NUMBER OF THE BEAST

This cowboys'n'injuns corker features a thumping Steve Harris bassline and one of the most famous intros in metaldom.

❽ RUNNING FREE from IRON MAIDEN

Thundering war drums and Paul DiAnno's rough'n'ready vocals give this a neat street-level punch.

❾ THE NUMBER OF THE BEAST
from NUMBER OF THE BEAST

Hammer horror meets the best of British metal. A terrific creepy intro and one of Bruce Dickinson's best ear-shattering screams. Be afraid, be very afraid.

❿ THE TROOPER
from PIECE OF MIND

The flash of steel, the crack of muskets, the clamour of war – a stunning Maiden battle tune complete with a classic duelling riff.

Essi Berelian

Isley Brothers

Beginning as a gospel group in 1955, the Isleys have moved on through doo-wop, R&B, Motown, psychedelic soul, disco and just about every other form of black American popular music, and are still going strong half a century on...

❶ SHOUT from SHOUT

An early two-part single from 1959, and five years later a big hit for the 15-year-old Lulu.

❷ TWIST AND SHOUT from TWIST AND SHOUT

Another song that led to a rather famous cover by a group from Liverpool.

❸ TESTIFY from IT'S OUR THING

Featuring the guitar of a then obscure member of their backing band named Hendrix.

❹ THIS OLD HEART OF MINE from THIS OLD HEART OF MINE

Their first single for Tamla Motown, penned by the ubiquitous Holland, Dozier and Holland team.

❺ I GUESS I'LL ALWAYS LOVE YOU from THIS OLD HEART OF MINE

The Motown hit factory does its stuff again.

❻ SUMMER BREEZE from 3+3

Written by naff folk duo Seals and Crofts but transformed by the brothers' mighty soul voices.

❼ THAT LADY from 3+3

Almost six minutes long on the album, this sold more than a million copies in 1973, after they split it in two on the single.

❽ HARVEST FOR THE WORLD from HARVEST FOR THE WORLD

Heavily influenced by the sentiments of Marvin Gaye's "Mercy Mercy Me (The Ecology)", this protest song made the UK Top 10 in 1976.

Nigel Williamson

The Jackson 5

The Jackson 5? Who are we kidding? From the moment that pre-pubescent performer launched into "I Want You Back", it was only Michael & Four Taller Blokes. That said, The Jackson 5 canon remains a fabulous record of Wacko's early years.

❶ THE LOVE YOU SAVE from ABC
Mike's clearly been on the orange squash, so this song is much more exciting than anything else on which he was forced to share vocals with Jermaine.

❷ DANCING MACHINE from GET IT TOGETHER
The taut rhythm pumps it all up, and thanks to clever holes in the instrumentation, Michael discovers the freedom to be found within a song.

❸ BLAME IT ON THE BOOGIE from DESTINY
The J5 get funky with a thumping disco beat, popping bass and harmonizing that has Mike sounding like part of a quintet instead of a singer and his backing vocalists.

❹ LOOKING THROUGH THE WINDOWS from LOOKING THROUGH THE WINDOWS
Great big orchestrations that push the vocals to the point at which they turn around and triumphantly kick some over-arranged arse.

❺ NEVER CAN SAY GOODBYE from MAYBE TOMORROW
The brothers opt for a dead straight, finger-snappin', old-school-type backing while 13-year-old Michael soars to the rafters.

❻ I'LL BE THERE from THIRD ALBUM
Mike's heart-wrenching, unreserved and fragile enough to be rescued by Jermaine as his voice gets to the very edge of cracking.

❼ I BET YOU from ABC
Brooding low-key funk with everybody except Marlon taking a turn on lead. George Clinton co-wrote this when he was a Motown staffer.

❽ SHOW YOU THE WAY TO GO from THE JACKSONS
Tight, sophisto-funk Gamble & Huff orchestrations give the J5 the space they need to stretch out in their first post-Motown hit.

❾ SANTA CLAUS IS COMING TO TOWN
from THE JACKSON FIVE CHRISTMAS ALBUM
It's done with great gusto and is as corny as hell, but that's the whole point.

❿ I WANT YOU BACK from DIANA ROSS PRESENTS THE JACKSON FIVE
They never quite recaptured this rush – a cascading piano introduced the world's youngest superstar and the J5 spun off each other like apprentice Temptations.

Lloyd Bradley

Michael Jackson

It wasn't until Michael left the brothers behind that he – well, left the brothers behind and began to show what he was truly capable of.

❶ OFF THE WALL from OFF THE WALL
Mike's watershed song, in which you can hear him, gloriously, sounding like he's surprising himself as much as everybody else.

❷ ROCKIN' ROBIN from GOT TO BE THERE
Funky, frantic and loadsa fun, yet, in the best possible way, this is never more than half an inch away from being completely cheesy.

❸ THE WAY YOU MAKE ME FEEL from BAD
With the chugging background stripped down for so much of the song (well, stripped down in comparison with other MJ records), this gives his voice's natural swing a chance to be heard.

❹ WHY YOU WANNA TRIP ON ME from DANGEROUS
Teddy Riley-produced swingbeat that stirs in an electric guitar and creates a taut, tough tune that was always woefully underrated.

❺ AIN'T NO SUNSHINE from GOT TO BE THERE
Big strings and a chugging rhythm provide a goose-down duvet of an arrangement for Michael to wrap himself up in and croon this evergreen tale of loss.

❻ PEOPLE MAKE THE WORLD GO ROUND from BEN
A Bell/Creed composition, with a delightfully brassy, almost easy-listening, Gene Page arrangement; it's Michael's contribution to the post-"What's Going On" ecology debate.

❼ I WANNA BE WHERE YOU ARE from GOT TO BE THERE
Though an overly fussy orchestration takes up too much of the mix, Michael works incredibly hard and pulls off a fantastic performance.

❽ BILLIE JEAN from THRILLER
Divorce this track from the video and you've got possibly the best example of jumping, pumping pop/funk that it'll ever be your privilege to dance to.

❾ WE'RE ALMOST THERE from FOREVER MICHAEL
A cool hustle of a beat and an orchestration that manages not to overwhelm the funk.

❿ ROCK WITH YOU from OFF THE WALL
Probably the greatest Jackson solo track. Over a gently rocking beat, the arrangements are deceptively smooth but the singer's evident excitement injects a soulful exuberance.

Lloyd Bradley

Jailhouse Pod

As a rule, they do not allow iPods in county jails. If they did, these are the songs that would be on there.

❶ FOLSOM PRISON BLUES JOHNNY CASH from JOHNNY CASH AT FOLSOM PRISON
The quintessential prison song: you get murder, guns, trains and longing. It's all backed by the steady chug of an old guitar and the apocalyptic voice of the man in black.

❷ IN THE JAILHOUSE NOW JIMMIE RODGERS from FIRST SESSIONS, 1927–1928
A cheerful lament about the penalties for playing with cards, dice and loose women.

❸ STACKOLEE DOC WATSON from TROUBLE IN MIND
A fast blues tune recorded by everyone from Roy Bookbinder to Dave Von Ronk. Watson's version shows off his trademark, intricate guitar-picking.

❹ JAILHOUSE ROCK ELVIS PRESLEY from THE BLUE SUEDE SHOES COLLECTION
An obvious choice. You can't help singing along, even as you ponder what exactly he means when he sings "If you can't find a partner use a wooden chair."

❺ BLACKJACK COUNTY CHAINS DEL MCCOURY BAND from COLD HARD FACTS
A haunting cover of a Willie Nelson tune. Del's voice is extra high here, and extra lonesome.

❻ WISE COUNTY JAIL DOCK BOGGS from HIS FOLKWAYS YEARS: 1963–1968
A performer of some note in the 1920s, coal miner Dock Boggs put away his banjo until the 60s, when Mike Seeger called him out of hiding.

❼ WOMEN'S PRISON LORETTA LYNN from VAN LEAR ROSE
There's not much cheer in this track from Lynn's 2004 comeback album, but there is something uplifting in the grind of Jack White's electric guitar.

❽ STONE WALLS AND STEEL BARS RALPH STANLEY & JUNIOR BROWN from CLINCH MOUNTAIN COUNTRY
High lonesome meets low lonesome in a traditional duet about cheating, killing, doing time and the end of the line.

❾ MAMA TRIED MERLE HAGGARD from MAMA TRIED
Another upbeat lament, this classic is one in a slew of prison songs penned from the pages of Haggard's life in juvenile detention halls and San Quentin. Outlaw country at its finest.

❿ MOTORCYCLE MAMA NEIL YOUNG from COMES A TIME
Because what's a prison set without some hope of breaking free?

Madelyn Rosenberg

The Jam

Three angry young men in sharp suits who stormed out of the suburbs and over the frenzy of punk to become one of the biggest bands in the UK.

❶ IN THE CITY from AT THE BBC
This is suburban soul mod-style, delivered in the language of purest punk-rock. Even more raw and urgent in this no-frills BBC production.

❷ MODERN WORLD from THIS IS THE MODERN WORLD
Claimed by both the punks and resurgent mod movement at the time of release, this is still the greatest song The Who never wrote.

❸ DAVID WATTS from ALL MOD CONS
Cover version of The Kinks' number that stomps all over the original – more bitter, more twisted, more venom.

❹ A BOMB IN WARDOUR STREET from ALL MOD CONS
A sketched slice of punk life as the London scene disintegrated into warring factions.

⑤ STRANGE TOWN from VERY BEST OF

One of the best "small town boy in the big bad city" songs ever written. Weller's pithy summaries of cockney-fashioned brush-offs sound depressingly accurate.

⑥ ETON RIFLES from SETTING SONS

With Weller settling comfortably into his role as chronicler of the peculiarities of British society, this is one of his lyrical high points and one of the Jam's true greatest hits.

⑦ GOING UNDERGROUND from VERY BEST OF

Precision-guided lyrical attacks on the bunkers of establishment orthodoxy delivered through intercontinental ballistic soul music.

⑧ START! from SOUND AFFECTS

Mindless, nameless, soulless sex might not be that satisfying, but it's a start. Great to dance to – just ignore the detumescent lyrics.

⑨ THAT'S ENTERTAINMENT from SOUND AFFECTS

As the Jam's main man started looking around for something a little more challenging, his growing disgust with the scene became increasingly apparent, as this lyric indicates.

⑩ BEAT SURRENDER from VERY BEST OF

This, one of the band's farewell songs, shows them leaving the stage with the crowd still begging for more.

Al Spicer

Jamaican vocal trios

The sublime harmonies of Jamaica's all-male vocal trios have been responsible for creating many of ska, rocksteady and reggae's enduring classics.

❶ SATTA MASSA GANA THE ABYSSINIANS
from THREE OF SATTA

The definitive rasta anthem, from 1969.

❷ TWO SEVENS CLASH CULTURE from TWO SEVENS CLASH

Produced by Joe Gibbs, this 1976 piece of prophesying rocketed Culture to worldwide acclaim.

❸ TRAIN TO SKAVILLE THE ETHIOPIANS
from EVERYTHING CRASH: THE BEST OF

Despite its title, a rock steady classic from 1967.

❹ HELLO CAROL THE GLADIATORS
from DREADLOCKS THE TIME IS NOW

During the 1970s, before they lost their way imitating The Wailers, The Gladiators produced a string of classic hits like this recut of their Studio One gem.

❺ WHY WORRY? ISRAEL VIBRATION from THE SAME SONG

Utterly magnificent music from 1976.

❻ ARK OF THE COVENANT THE CONGOS from HEART OF THE CONGOS

Under Lee Perry's direction in 1977, The Congos produced the greatest reggae vocal album of all time.

❼ COOL RASTA THE HEPTONES from THE MEANING OF LIFE: BEST OF

A laid-back jewel from 1976.

❽ I NEED A ROOF THE MIGHTY DIAMONDS from THE RIGHT TIME

Exquisite 1976 harmonies from the dependable Diamonds.

❾ WATCH THIS SOUND THE UNIQUES
from TIGHTEN UP VOL 1

The words may be garbled, but this is a deliciously soulful reinterpretation of Buffalo Springfield's "For What It's Worth" original, from 1969.

❿ JAH JAH GIVE US LIFE WAILING SOULS
from PUTUMAYO PRESENTS THE BEST OF REGGAE

The Wailing Souls delivered the best work of their glittering career at Channel One in 1978.

Greg Ward

Etta James

Through a career that's taken her from R&B through torch ballads, soul, blues and beyond, James has remained one of the greatest but consistently under-appreciated voices of black America. And she's still belting it out in her 60s.

❶ TOUGH LOVER from HICKORY DICKORY DOCK

Etta takes on Little Richard at his own game, with the help of his New Orleans studio band. It's hard to imagine any other female singer of the time keeping up.

❷ I JUST WANT TO MAKE LOVE WITH YOU from AT LAST

Likewise, Etta matches Muddy Waters on this Willie Dixon standard.

❸ AT LAST from AT LAST

Perfect phrasing on this brilliantly orchestrated ballad (originally by Glenn Miller, of all people) from Etta's best early studio album. Immaculate.

❹ SOMETHING'S GOTTA HOLD ON ME from ETTA JAMES ROCKS THE HOUSE

The driving opener from her great 1963 live album, recorded in Nashville.

❺ IN THE BASEMENT from THE CHESS BOX

Funky duet with Sugar Pie De Santo, epitomizing 1960s club soul.

❻ TELL MAMA from TELL MAMA

Etta reinvents herself again as a sock-it-to-me Southern Soul singer on this Clarence Carter number. Complemented perfectly by…

❼ I'D RATHER GO BLIND from TELL MAMA

Chicken Shack's cover was the UK hit, but it's a pale shadow of Etta's original.

❽ I WORSHIP THE GROUND YOU WALK ON from THE CHESS BOX

Rare chance to hear a little-known Dan Penn-Spooner Oldham gem.

❾ GOD'S SONG (THAT'S WHY I LOVE MANKIND) from THE CHESS BOX

One of Etta's remarkable reinterpretations of Randy Newman songs. Gives a whole new meaning to the old "I've seen God – and she's black" joke.

❿ FEELING UNEASY from THE CHESS BOX

Recorded on her first day out of rehab: nearly three minutes' worth of almost wordless but darkly expressive moaning over a moody, low-key backing.

Neil Foxlee

Keith Jarrett

From the free and ecstatic to the honed and romantic to the deeply introspective, the expressive range of one of jazz's great communicators is as wide as it is deep.

❶ GYPSY MOTH from EL JUICIO (THE JUDGEMENT)

A contagious, rolling piece of gospel-flavoured jamming from the American Quartet (featuring Dewey Redman, Charlie Haden and Paul Motian) in 1971.

❷ THERE IS A ROAD (GOD'S RIVER) from EXPECTATIONS

The climax of his ambitious 1972 double album for Columbia, a joyous melange of pumping piano, rock guitar and celestial strings.

❸ THE WINDUP from BELONGING

Stupidly tricksy and utterly compelling, the European Quartet (featuring Jan Garbarek, Palle Danielsson and Jon Christensen) make light work of Jarrett's asymmetrical theme in 1974 before the pianist takes flight.

❹ PART 1 from THE KÖLN CONCERT

Of the scores of Jarrett's solo improvisations available, the extraordinary opening half-hour of his famed and best-selling Köln concert from 1975 is as approachable and rewarding as any.

❺ MY SONG from MY SONG

Simple harmonies, a lyrical, almost childish tune and soaring quasi-pop saxophone from Garbarek; Jarrett's other extreme, from 1978.

❻ SPIRITS 20 from SPIRITS

Featuring his own overdubbed sax, flute, percussion and recorder, this meditative, faintly ethnic music from 1985 has few adherents in the jazz world, though some may detect a mysterious healing quality.

❼ BOOK OF WAYS 18 from BOOK OF WAYS

Beautiful Bach-like ruminations, on solo clavichord, from 1986.

Chris Ingham

Jazz ballads

Classics from the intimate side of the improvisational art… nice.

❶ BODY AND SOUL
COLEMAN HAWKINS from THE SWING ERA

Not written by a jazzer, but presented in 1939 with such imagination by tenor saxophone titan Hawkins that it was almost a gauntlet for the hundreds of versions which followed.

❷ PRELUDE TO A KISS DUKE ELLINGTON from BRAGGIN' IN BRASS

Later turned into a song, this chromatic melody works best as an Ellington instrumental, with fulsome harmony and the tune handled by the sensual alto sax of Johnny Hodges.

❸ ROUND ABOUT MIDNIGHT THELONIOUS MONK from
THE COMPLETE THELONIOUS MONK ON BLUE NOTE
This Thelonious Monk ballad was turned into the song
"Round Midnight", which attracted countless vocal
interpretations.

❹ IF YOU COULD SEE ME NOW SARAH VAUGHAN from
YOUNG SASSY
A bebop ballad composed by Tadd Dameron and
based on the famous coda to Dizzy Gillespie's "Groovin'
High"; this was its definitive reading.

❺ MISTY ERROLL GARNER from THE ORIGINAL MISTY
Composed in the head of the pianist on a plane on
the way to a Chicago recording session, this inaugural
1954 recording of this most covered of romantic melodies was reportedly the first time he ever played it.

❻ CHELSEA BRIDGE DUKE ELLINGTON from MASTERPIECES
Composed by Billy Strayhorn, this is an extraordinarily
evocative piece of jazz impressionism.

❼ GOODBYE PORK PIE HAT CHARLES MINGUS from
MINGUS AH UM
A serpentine melody over an altered blues sequence
forms this rich 1959 tribute by the mighty bassist/
composer to the recently deceased and much-loved
tenor saxophonist Lester Young.

❽ BLUE IN GREEN MILES DAVIS from KIND OF BLUE
Based on the chords of pianist Bill Evans, this
wounded, sensuous theme from 1959 hypnotizes like
an Escher staircase.

❾ CHILD IS BORN HANK JONES from LIVE AT MAYBECK
RECITAL HALL
Master pianist Hank Jones examines his brother Thad's
classic jazz waltz in 1991 and produces elegance and
invention.

❿ DOLPHIN DANCE HERBIE HANCOCK
from MAIDEN VOYAGE
From Hancock's 1965 cerebral classic of modal jazz, a
piece that perfectly exemplifies a modern ballad: rich,
intense and moving.

Chris Ingham

Blue Note jazz

**The label that, to many, is synonymous with jazz.
Its iconic artwork and staggering music defined
a zeitgeist.**

❶ HAT AND BEARD ERIC DOLPHY from OUT TO LUNCH
Angular modernism at its most alarming.

❷ FRANKENSTEIN JACKIE MCCLEAN from ONE STEP
BEYOND
A hunchbacked waltz, its revenant choruses lumber
woozily with all their limbs in the wrong places.

❸ TWO PIECES OF ONE: RED TONY WILLIAMS from
SPRING
Icy and sparse, a chilly fanfare and forensic percussion
heralds nothing less than Blue Note's very own "Rite
Of Spring".

❹ GHETTO LIGHTS BOBBY HUTCHERSON from DIALOGUE
Freddie Hubbard's sly muted trumpet and Hutch's
conspiratorial vibraphone conjure a snide, abstracted
blues.

❺ DEDICATION ANDREW HILL from POINT OF DEPARTURE
Eric Dolphy's mournful lowing and dizzying cascades
sometimes temper, sometimes augment, the lyricism
of Hill's quasi-New Orleans lament.

❻ SPECTRUM ANDREW HILL from POINT OF DEPARTURE
Quizzical, avian, fast-paced debate radically recontex-
tualizes itself halfway through, pulling itself together
to stick out its collective tongue at us.

❼ THE EGG HERBIE HANCOCK from EMPYREAN ISLES
Herbie boldy strides "out there" with an insistent riff,
while Freddie Hubbard essays a cod-Spanish theme.

❽ EVOLUTION GRACHAN MONCUR III from EVOLUTION
Startlingly discordant, precise and doggedly held
chords from the horns render this arguably the most
jarring recording among the Blue Note reels.

❾ CONQUISTADOR CECIL TAYLOR from CONQUISTADOR
Cecil Taylor's scarily dynamic piano playing sounds like
mice in a milk-bottle factory, while the horns of Jimmy
Lyons and Bill Dixon – once they've recovered their
breath – wake up to his *Weltanschauung* sharpish.

Matt Milton

Jazz guitar genius

Ten great spankers of the plank.

❶ NUAGES DJANGO REINHARDT from CLASSICS
A clawed left hand didn't stop the Belgian gypsy
acoustic guitarist being one of the most freewheeling,
witty instrumentalists in jazz.

❷ AIR MAIL SPECIAL CHARLIE CHRISTIAN from THE GENIUS OF THE ELECTRIC GUITAR

In Christian's hands the single-note melodic solo on the electric guitar became as valid a voice as any in jazz.

❸ LET'S COOK BARNEY KESSEL from LET'S COOK

Boppish and bluesy, Kessel was a studio musician for much of his career but remained a thrilling jazz player.

❹ TAKING A CHANCE ON LOVE TAL FARLOW from THE SWINGING JAZZ GUITAR OF TAL FARLOW

His smooth, almost uninflected fluency and bop melodicism mark Farlow as one of the great players. This is from his rich Verve period in the mid 1950s.

❺ CHITLINS CON CARNE KENNY BURRELL from MIDNIGHT BLUE

Restrained, contained and deeply bluesy, Burrell grooves in a medium-hard bop style.

❻ WEST COAST BLUES WES MONTGOMERY from INCREDIBLE JAZZ GUITAR

This original jazz waltz from 1960 captures the essence of Wes's plectrum-free, self-taught style and prodigious melodic imagination.

❼ IF I SHOULD LOSE YOU GRANT GREEN from BORN TO BE BLUE

Green's achievements as Blue Note's house guitarist in the 1960s should not be overshadowed by the dull funk he made in the 70s.

❽ STELLA BY STARLIGHT JOE PASS from VIRTUOSO

In the 1970s, when most jazz guitarists were exploring rockier climbs, Pass was an oasis of straight-ahead virtuosity.

❾ GIANT STEPS PAT METHENY from TRIO 99/00

Often heard in sunny fusion settings, latter-day outings have emphasized Pat's lyrical, unprocessed invention, like this 1999 bossa nova reworking of Coltrane's classic.

❿ DARN THAT DREAM MARTIN TAYLOR from SOLO

Adept in all styles from contemporary to Django-style swing, Taylor excels as a solo performer.

Chris Ingham

Jazz rock

It was Miles Davis's influence which launched rock music's flirtation with jazz in the late 1960s. Quite separate from jazz fusion (essentially jazz musicians moving into crossover territory), jazz rock approached the hybrid from the opposite direction.

❶ SMILING PHASES BLOOD, SWEAT AND TEARS from BLOOD, SWEAT AND TEARS

Astonishingly, Blood, Sweat and Tears were the second-highest-paid act at Woodstock after Jimi Hendrix.

❷ 25 OR 6 TO 4 CHICAGO from CHICAGO II

They later became associated with soft-rock ballads but this 1970 track combined Terry Kath's rock guitar and a full-on horn section in thrilling style.

❸ A LOVE SUPREME CARLOS SANTANA & JOHN McLAUGHLIN from LOVE DEVOTION AND SURRENDER

They shared an Indian guru – and a love of John Coltrane. McLaughlin himself was of course a jazzer – and hence a fusionist – though he set a standard for jazz-rockers with his Mahavishnu Orchestra.

❹ BEWARE THE IDES OF MARCH COLOSSEUM from THOSE ABOUT TO DIE

Classic British progressive jazz-rock from 1969 with the late Dick Heckstall-Smith on sax.

❺ MOON IN JUNE SOFT MACHINE from THIRD

A nineteen-minute suite featuring the conversational vocals of Robert Wyatt. This was the last great song from the Softs, who booted out Wyatt and went over to the jazz side to disastrously dull effect.

❻ O CAROLINE MATCHING MOLE from MATCHING MOLE

After leaving Soft Machine, Wyatt himself formed the esoteric Matching Mole and had a minor hit with this affecting love song.

❼ PEACHES EN REGALIA
FRANK ZAPPA from HOT RATS

Instrumental jazz-rock of astonishing invention from his 1969 solo album.

❽ GOD MUST BE A BOOGIE MAN
JONI MITCHELL from MINGUS

From the album that Joni dedicated to the great man – and which employed the brilliant Jaco Pastorius on bass.

❾ SHINE RY COODER from JAZZ

From his 1978 tribute to Dixieland, with arrangements by Joseph Byrd.

❿ CAT FOOD
KING CRIMSON from IN THE WAKE OF POSEIDON

Proper rock band, featuring a proper jazz guest star – the virtuoso pianist Keith Jarrett.

Nigel Williamson

Jefferson Airplane

Formed in San Francisco in 1965, the Jefferson Airplane helped to create acid rock from a melodic folk-rock sensibility, an artistic desire to explore and a solid grounding in the blues. Oh, and psychedelic drugs. Their best work comes from the period up to 1970.

❶ CHAUFFEUR BLUES from BLUES FROM AN AIRPLANE
The basics: Memphis Minnie's 1930s blues song, belted out by original vocalist Signe Anderson, who left to have a baby.

❷ SOMEBODY TO LOVE from SURREALISTIC PILLOW
Its direct descendant, sung by new vocalist Grace Slick and written by her ex-husband Darby Slick.

❸ WHITE RABBIT from SURREALISTIC PILLOW
This classic of lysergic pop mixes *Alice In Wonderland* with a commanding bolero beat. Still sounds great.

❹ COMING BACK TO ME from SURREALISTIC PILLOW
It's often forgotten that Marty Balin founded the band. His gentle love song of reconciliation illustrates the group's more poetic side.

❺ EMBRYONIC JOURNEY from SURREALISTIC PILLOW
A brief acoustic instrumental from powerful guitarist Jorma Kaukonen and inventive bassist Jack Cassidy (who later returned to rootsier music in "Hot Tuna").

❻ BALLAD OF YOU AND ME AND POONEIL from AFTER BATHING AT BAXTERS
Rhythm guitarist Paul Kanter sings lead on one of the more accessible tracks from the album's disorienting psychedelic experiments and extended "suites".

❼ IF YOU FEEL (LIKE CHINA BREAKING) from CROWN OF CREATION
Driving wah-wah guitars power Balin's exhilarating "if it feels good, do it" rocker, leading the return to more conventional structures.

❽ LATHER from CROWN OF CREATION
Grace Slick is in gentle mood in this compassionate, haunting song about the loss of innocence.

❾ THE OTHER SIDE OF THIS LIFE from BLESS ITS POINTED LITTLE HEAD (LIVE)
The band take the freewheeling sentiment of Fred Neil's (the Neil in Pooneil) folk-blues song and turn it into a rocker.

❿ GOOD SHEPHERD from VOLUNTEERS
The *Volunteers* album, which saw the band turning further towards revolutionary politics and sci-fi, makes more sense as a whole, but Kaukonen's enchanting reworking of this traditional song stands out.

Ian Cranna

The Jesus And Mary Chain

Hailing from East Kilbride, Scotland, the Mary Chain were a band (primarily brothers Jim and William Reid) that harnessed the kind of guitar feedback unheard since the days of The Velvets; for a while they were rulers of the UK indie scene.

❶ UPSIDE DOWN from BARBED WIRE KISSES
Their debut single – three minutes of saturated guitar scree, pounding drums and a perfect-pop melody. A nihilistic classic.

❷ IN A HOLE from PSYCHOCANDY
A standout cut from a standout first album. Again white noise dominates proceedings.

❸ SOME CANDY TALKING from PSYCHOCANDY
At the time of release this junky's lament was boycotted by UK radio DJs, but still made it into the Top 20. It's a blinding song that unashamedly displays the Reid brothers' love of Phil Spector-styled drums and production.

❹ HEAD from BARBED WIRE KISSES
A dark and claustrophobic assault on the ears, Head is one of several early B-sides that growls with defiant experimentation and edgy charm.

❺ DARKLANDS from DARKLANDS
The gentle melody and classic pop "do-do-dos" of this second-album cut surprised many after the thunder of *Psychocandy*.

❻ SIDEWALKING from THE COMPLETE JOHN PEEL SESSIONS
Peel was host to easily the best version of this grinding classic. The drum machine pounds away alongside a killer bassline, while William proceeds to wring unearthly howls from his overdriven guitar.

❼ TEENAGE LUST from HONEY'S DEAD
One of the better cuts from the band's later albums. The bass and drums slide against each other like

pole-dancing lizards, while wah-wahed guitars slice through your speakers.

❽ JUST LIKE HONEY from PSYCHOCANDY
With drums and guitars drenched in top-end and reverb, this album-opener stands as one of the great lost-love songs. It was used to great effect in the film *Lost In Translation*.

Peter Buckley

Jethro Tull

Hoary old folk-blues warriors with a bit of one-legged flute virtuosity thrown in. Leader/ linchpin Ian Anderson is not to be confused with the guitar-wielding editor of *Folk Roots* and contributor to this guide.

❶ FALLEN ON HARD TIMES
from BROADSWORD AND THE BEAST
Broadsword And The Beast saw Jethro Tull turn away from folk-blues towards synthesizer-heavy metallic rock.

❷ THICK AS A BRICK from BURSTING OUT LIVE
The twelve minutes of this song start as a folky strum and build to a rocking roar.

❸ SAID SHE WAS A DANCER
from CREST OF A KNAVE
The guitar work on this has been fed through an industrial-strength Knopflerizer, but the tale of a cautious encounter with an Eastern European femme fatale is pure Anderson.

❹ HUNTING GIRL from SONGS FROM THE WOOD
Ah, the sexual allure of jodhpurs. Even a hunt saboteur would thrill to this.

❺ AQUALUNG from AQUALUNG
Wheezing tramp chic: a shambling blues riff that heralded popular culture's highest-profile asthma sufferer until Darth Vader.

❻ MINSTREL IN THE GALLERY
from MINSTREL IN THE GALLERY
Unashamed folk rock.

❼ FLUTE SOLO IMPROVISATION/GOD REST YE MERRY GENTLEMEN/BOUREE
from BURSTING OUT LIVE
The channelled spirit of Rahsaan Roland Kirk, a Dickensian carol and JS Bach – just to give the band a break between songs.

❽ LIVING IN THE PAST from LIVING IN THE PAST
Uncharacteristic smoothness from this roughest and certainly hairiest of bands.

❾ ORION from STORMWATCH
Guitars crash like thunder and the drums sound like beaten anvils, while the verses provide a brief haven of hush.

❿ WONDERING ALOUD from AQUALUNG
A moment of calm amid the breathy locomotions of *Aqualung*.

David Honigman

Jock Rock

Announcers provide the play-by-play and the crowd provides the screams, but the dude operating the loudspeakers wants more, more, more. The best way to pump up the energy for players and fans alike? A little rock'n'roll. Here's how it plays out in US sports arenas.

❶ HELL'S BELLS AC/DC from BACK IN BLACK
Bells are ringing, and it isn't the ice-cream man. If there's some sort of invisible force that causes heads to bang, AC DC channels it here, in one of rock's darkest and most recognizable riffs.

❷ WE WILL ROCK YOU QUEEN from NEWS OF THE WORLD
More a chant than a song with a solid beat that's an easy mimic for snare drums or clapping fans, this Queen hit was a natural for a sports anthem, especially when followed by the victorious "We Are the Champions." It's fine if dated music, but not such a good lesson in sportsmanship.

❸ IMPERIAL MARCH JOHN WILLIAMS from THE EMPIRE STRIKES BACK: THE ORIGINAL MOTION PICTURE SOUNDTRACK
Better known as "Darth Vader's Theme" and originally recorded by the London Symphony Orchestra, John Williams' composition became the go-to tune for American marching bands. With a stomping melody that destroys everything its path, it has remained a perennial, sporting favorite.

❹ WHO LET THE DOGS OUT THE BAHA MEN from THE BAHA MEN
This panting, island-rap-dance-other hit led The Baha Men to the top of the US charts before the song died and went on to a fulfilling afterlife in the world of sport.

⑤ ROCK AND ROLL, PT. 2 GARY GLITTER from GARY GLITTER'S GREATEST HITS
Glam-rocker Glitter's simple lyrics shouted over driving guitar and percussion made this tune so ubiquitous with US sporting events that many Americans have a hard time believing it got international radio play in the 1970s. These days, Glitter tops those where-are-they-now lists. Answer: you don't want to know.

⑥ ENTER SANDMAN METALLICA from THE BLACK ALBUM
Heavy metal for heavy hitters, James Hetfield's nail-spitting lyrics and grinding guitars made this Metallica tune a major-league favorite, particularly among relief pitchers.

⑦ CENTERFIELD JOHN FOGERTY from CENTERFIELD
Perhaps the most melodic of the jock-rock songs, this tune also finds its audience in the baseball diamond. A solo John Fogerty name-checks the greats over indelible hand-claps and a playful guitar that still has Creedence.

⑧ NA NA HEY HEY KISS HIM GOODBYE STEAM from BILLBOARD TOP ROCK 'N' ROLL HITS: 1968–1972
Another song that's not exactly a lesson in sportsmanship, this one is played at the end of the game, when the losers are headed for the locker room in a cloud of sweat, steam and defeat. The track is on comps for baseball and hockey hits, and the ultimate in American football rock.

⑨ PUMP IT UP ELVIS COSTELLO from THIS YEAR'S MODEL
Though the song suffers from serious over-exposure, the adrenaline in Elvis Costello's guitar and voice is still a surefire way to get people on their feet at both wedding receptions and sporting events. (You'll see no such reaction to his "Shipbuilding," however.)

⑩ SONG 2 BLUR from BLUR
Mostly it's the "whoo-hoo" part that gets played at ballgames, as opposed to the ironic vocal stylings of Blur singer Damon Albarn and a sound that is both an exercise in distortion and a lampoon of grunge.

Madelyn Rosenberg

① TINY DANCER from MADMAN ACROSS THE WATER
On the road in California, with Elt, Bernie and his girlfriend.

② LEVON from MADMAN ACROSS THE WATER
For all those people who hate their parents – and love huge, overblown string arrangements.

③ TAKE ME TO THE PILOT from 17.11.70
Elton rocks, particularly on this live version. But who knows what he's talking about?

④ HONKY CAT from HONKY CHATEAU
Country-ish hocus with great brass and great singing.

⑤ ROCKET MAN from HONKY CHATEAU
Elton's stab at the 1970s space alienation genre.

⑥ BENNIE AND THE JETS from GOODBYE YELLOW BRICK ROAD
Falsetto heaven on this glam classic.

⑦ BURN DOWN THE MISSION from TUMBLEWEED CONNECTION
The slaves are revolting! The climax of Elt and Bernie's Wild West tumbleweed adventure.

⑧ CAPTAIN FANTASTIC AND THE BROWN DIRT COWBOY from CAPTAIN FANTASTIC AND THE BROWN DIRT COWBOY
The story of how it all began.

⑨ DON'T LET THE SUN GO DOWN ON ME from CARIBOU
Lyrics soaked in melodrama, the Beach Boys on backing vocals – what more could anyone want from this live barnstormer.

⑩ FUNERAL FOR A FRIEND/LOVE LIES BLEEDING from GOODBYE YELLOW BRICK ROAD
Pompous 1970s prog-rock instrumental, laden with synthesizers, which segues beautifully into the glorious pop-rock of "Love Lies Bleeding".

Martin Dunford

Elton John

He may be a fat old has-been with dodgy hair, but the 1970s were an extraordinarily creative time for Elton John, who – at least for a while – was a more serious and original singer, songwriter and musician than most people nowadays give him credit for.

Robert Johnson

Even if modern scholars have proved he didn't write all of his songs, Robert Johnson remains the "King of the Delta Blues". Immortalized thanks to two brief recording sessions in 1936 and 1937, he lived the life and died the death (by poisoning) of the archetypal bluesman.

❶ CROSSROAD BLUES
from THE COMPLETE RECORDINGS

The legend that Johnson sold his soul to the Devil at a lonesome Delta crossroads was fuelled by this saga of fear and despair.

❷ SWEET HOME CHICAGO
from THE COMPLETE RECORDINGS

Even if the words may say next to nothing, the boogie behind them went on to change the world.

❸ HELLHOUND ON MY TRAIL
from THE COMPLETE RECORDINGS

Beneath his delicate imagery, Johnson's sense of the hopelessness of trying to outrun his doom is overwhelming.

❹ COME ON IN MY KITCHEN
from THE COMPLETE RECORDINGS

A tender song about love and sex, quite beautiful in its simplicity.

❺ 32-20 BLUES from THE COMPLETE RECORDINGS

Johnson in a less metaphysical mood, threatening to shoot his baby with a revolver.

❻ ME AND THE DEVIL BLUES
from THE COMPLETE RECORDINGS

Perhaps the most chilling of all Johnson's recordings, culminating in the threat that his "evil spirit" would continue to roam the highways after his death.

❼ LOVE IN VAIN
from THE COMPLETE RECORDINGS

A concise poetic narrative of loss and loneliness, as covered by The Rolling Stones.

❽ STOP BREAKIN' DOWN BLUES
from THE COMPLETE RECORDINGS

This song's deadpan arrogance made it too perfect for The Rolling Stones.

❾ WALKING BLUES
from THE COMPLETE RECORDINGS

Johnson borrowed the song from Son House, but made its desolation all his own.

❿ MILKCOW'S CALF BLUES
from THE COMPLETE RECORDINGS

This Kokomo Arnold original was covered by a remarkable triumvirate – Robert Johnson, Elvis Presley and Bob Dylan.

Greg Ward

Elvin Jones

Drummer Elvin Jones achieved prominence with perhaps the greatest jazz group of all time: the Coltrane Quartet of 1961–65. His deep-swinging polyrhythms set a standard for improvisation and with McCoy Tyner and Jimmy Garrison, moved rhythm-section playing from the background to the foreground in a way that had never been done before.

❶ MY FAVORITE THINGS
JOHN COLTRANE from MY FAVOURITE THINGS

A beautiful, lilting and understated performance from Jones over 'Trane's 6/8 rendition of the Rogers & Hammerstein classic.

❷ DAHOMEY DANCE
JOHN COLTRANE from OLÉ

Elvin's impossibly deep swing is high in the mix and pings off the bass duo of Art Davis and Reggie Workman.

❸ SOFTLY AS IN A MORNING SUNRISE
JOHN COLTRANE from THE COMPLETE VILLAGE VANGUARD RECORDINGS

All crisp brushwork and delicate emphasis. Brain therapy from the rhythm master.

❹ MR DAY JOHN COLTRANE
from COLTRANE PLAYS THE BLUES

Jones's increasing telepathy with his fellow band members is evident in this upbeat track from a great album.

❺ OUT OF THIS WORLD JOHN COLTRANE from THE CLASSIC QUARTET – THE COMPLETE IMPULSE RECORDINGS

Popping candy for the ears.

❻ JUJU WAYNE SHORTER from JUJU

Epic and apocalyptic drumming. The only logical explanation for the speed, accuracy and fury is that Jones has cloned himself.

❼ A LOVE SUPREME, PART II – RESOLUTION JOHN COLTRANE from A LOVE SUPREME

The standard is set for group improvisation in Coltrane's groundbreaking masterwork. Jones at his most inventive.

❽ LOVE JOHN COLTRANE from MEDITATIONS

Set free from regular rhythmic structure, Elvin delivers mighty power in this swirling statement of a collective vision.

❾ LIVING SPACE
JOHN COLTRANE from LIVING SPACE
Astonishing drumming. Jones in total, angular synchronicity with bassist Jimmy Garrison and pianist McCoy Tyner.

❿ CONTEMPLATION
McCOY TYNER from THE REAL McCOY
A languid outing compared to the exertions of the last four tracks, this swings right through to your kidneys.

Nat Defriend

George Jones

"George Jones is not just one of country music's master vocalists. He's one of the greatest American song stylists of the 20th century. Care to argue?", asked Kurt Wolff in *The Rough Guide To Country Music*.

❶ BARTENDER'S BLUES
from BARTENDER'S BLUES
James Taylor wrote it. George turned it into his tour de force.

❷ THESE DAYS (I BARELY GET BY)
from THE BEST OF
Co-written by Tammy Wynette, who went and left him two days after he recorded the song.

❸ A GOOD YEAR FOR THE ROSES from BURN
The honky-tonk broken-marriage classic from 1970, later covered by Elvis Costello.

❹ THE GRAND TOUR from THE GRAND TOUR
A number one hit in 1974 at the height of his productive partnership with producer Billy Sherrill.

❺ STILL DOIN' TIME from STILL THE SAME OLE ME
A tale of drunken shame and, like so many of his songs, George had certainly been there…

❻ HE STOPPED LOVING HER TODAY
from I AM WHAT I AM
"He kept some letters by his bed, dated 1962, he had underlined in red every single 'I love you.'" And the today, of course, was the day he died.

❼ IF DRINKING DON'T KILL ME (HER MEMORY WILL) from I AM WHAT I AM
Mostly he sang other people's songs, but this heartfelt lyric was all his own.

❽ SHE THINKS I STILL CARE
from THE GEORGE JONES COLLECTION
At his most pained on this ballad from 1962.

❾ WHITE LIGHTNING
from WHITE LIGHTNING AND OTHER FAVOURITES
His first #1 from 1959, written by J.P. Richardson, better known as the Big Bopper.

❿ I'M RAGGED BUT I'M RIGHT
from COUNTRY SONG HITS
Under the influence of Hank Williams on one of his earliest recordings from 1956, based on a trad song.

Nigel Williamson

Janis Joplin

She shrieked, she screeched, she moaned, she sang the psychedelic-soul-rock blues with the ear-shattering intensity of no other singer before or since.

❶ BALL AND CHAIN BIG BROTHER & THE HOLDING COMPANY from CHEAP THRILLS
An ominous epic of anguished romance, her croon-to-a-scream vocal ideally complemented by Big Brother's wobbly, crazed guitar wails and swoops.

❷ ME AND BOBBY MCGEE from PEARL
Could Janis handle country-folk-blues songs that required sensitivity, not just intensity? Yes she could: this American #1 hit proved it.

❸ PIECE OF MY HEART BIG BROTHER & THE HOLDING COMPANY from CHEAP THRILLS
Joplin made this R&B hit by Erma Franklin (sister of Aretha) her own, particularly on the scarifyingly supplicating chorus.

❹ DOWN ON ME BIG BROTHER & THE HOLDING COMPANY from BIG BROTHER & THE HOLDING COMPANY
Gospel transformed into psychedelic rock, with the combination of desperation and ecstasy heard in many of Joplin's best vocals.

❺ SUMMERTIME BIG BROTHER & THE HOLDING COMPANY from CHEAP THRILLS
The George Gershwin standard never sounded like this, either in Janis's rasp-croon of a vocal or the underrated Big Brother's snaky dirge of an arrangement.

❻ HALF MOON from PEARL
Another indication of Joplin's growing versatility in

her final months, the funk-rock groove dissolving into delectably buttery phrasing in the jazzy chorus.

❼ COO COO BIG BROTHER & THE HOLDING COMPANY from BIG BROTHER & THE HOLDING COMPANY

A thunderous adaptation that stands an overdone folk standard on its head, powered by a maelstrom of raga-rock guitar.

❽ MOVE OVER from PEARL

Joplin's best original composition is an insistent stomper that sounds like a hit single that never was.

❾ TRY (JUST A LITTLE BIT HARDER)
from I GOT DEM OL' KOZMIC BLUES AGAIN MAMA!

The best cut from her underachieving debut solo album, signifying her drift from psychedelia into sexy urgent soul.

❿ GET IT WHILE YOU CAN from PEARL

As the concluding song on her final album, an apt epitaph for a woman who wrenched everything she could from her voice.

Richie Unterberger

Joy Division

There's a dark side to every story of love, and Ian Curtis wrote the music. When he heard Captain and Tenille singing "Love Will Keep Us Together", his response was to write "Love Will Tear Us Apart".

❶ SHE'S LOST CONTROL
from UNKNOWN PLEASURES

Closely observed, almost clinical description of a nervous breakdown in progress. Manic electro drums exquisitely capture the nature of obsession.

❷ ATMOSPHERE from STILL

The world's greatest break-up song: Ian and the band teeter on the very brink of melodrama.

❸ LEADERS OF MEN from SUBSTANCE 1977–1980

Desperate clashes of sheet-steel guitar fence with Ian's equally desperate vocals.

❹ NO LOVE LOST from SUBSTANCE 1977–1980

Piercing insight into the heart of the artist as fickle lover.

❺ HEART AND SOUL from CLOSER

The tragedy of love is that there's never a happy ending to it.

❻ ATROCITY EXHIBITION from CLOSER

Compelling yet repellent, this display of deformity and perverted human imagination scarcely needs Ian Curtis to act as its carnival barker. Great drums, too.

❼ DAY OF THE LORDS from UNKNOWN PLEASURES

Menacing basslines shiver up against guitars frozen beyond all pity and care. The lyrics are no barrel of laughs either.

❽ INTERZONE from UNKNOWN PLEASURES

Based no doubt on some of Manchester's less attractive areas, this combines the fear of a Velvet Underground trip out to score with an urban zone far more menacing than anything dreamed of by William Burroughs

❾ SISTER RAY from STILL

Who would have thought a band from Manchester could make such a totally New York song completely its own?

❿ LOVE WILL TEAR US APART
from UNKNOWN PLEASURES

Ian sounds wretched, like a priest burying his own mother, as he intones the saddest and most honest lyric to emerge from the whole northern English wave of post-punk depression.

Al Spicer

Jungle

Skirting around "coffee-table", "jazzy", and "intelligent" drum'n'bass, this list selects ten of the ruffest, most badboy jungle tunes released. They are all best located on compilations, or downloads, if you're not a 12" single junky.

❶ THE HELICOPTER TUNE DEEP BLUE

An unbelievably funky beat and two chords; nothing else is required. This track still tears up pirate radio stations today, nearly fifteen years after its release.

❷ SUPER SHARP SHOOTER DJ ZINC

The singalong hip-hop vocal ("The S, the U, the P…") made this a hit in student unions as well as with junglists, but a signature Ganja Kru bassline is the real pull.

❸ SHADOW BOXING NASTY HABITS

Proving you don't have to be happy to dance, this cut's doom-laden synth line and chopping beat impact like a karate chop.

❹ PHIZICAL RONI SIZE
From Roni's pre-superstar days, this winning combination of a chunky beat and subtly used sax sample is aimed squarely at the dancefloor.

❺ THE LIGHTER SOUNDS OF THE FUTURE
A true old-skool anthem.

❻ PROTON ED RUSH AND NICO
A monstrously dark hoover bassline and tearing amen beat brought carnage to dancefloors in the mid 1990s.

❼ THE RUCKUS TECHNICAL ITCH
Just as "dark jungle" was looking tired, this 2002 track proved you can always go one step more evil.

❽ CONSCIENCE A HANG DEM DJ C/CAPLETON
Flying the flag for ragga jungle in 2005, DJ C's productions fuse ragga, jungle, gabba and whatever else he can think of.

❾ BAD ASS MICKEY FINN AND APHRODITE
From the kings of the "wobbly bassline", this is a prime example of the Urban Takeover label's speaker-busting jump-up sound.

❿ ORIGINAL NUTTAH SHY FX AND UK APACHE
This infectious slice of ragga jungle made the British pop charts in 1994, but is no sell-out material. It made Shy FX's name.

Dan May

K

Paul Kelly

Arguably Australia's greatest singer-songwriter, Paul Kelly has an extensive catalogue that ranges across places and icons like a guidebook, although often zeroing in on Melbourne.

❶ TO HER DOOR from UNDER THE SUN
A classic "trying to sort things out, will she gives me another chance?" song.

❷ ON A WHITE TRAIN from GOSSIP
We've all got friends who are trouble and this suicidal mate is clearly a big problem.

❸ FROM ST KILDA TO KINGS CROSS from POST
Not only does it link Melbourne and Sydney's sin (and backpacker) centres, it's also the most perfect Sydney put-down song.

❹ FORTY MILES TO SATURDAY NIGHT from UNDER THE SUN
It's the quintessential outback night out: get in the ute and head to the pub – it's only forty miles away.

❺ SYDNEY FROM A 727 from COMEDY
We spend so much time listening to music in planes, it's a wonder there aren't more songs about flying places.

❻ DUMB THINGS from UNDER THE SUN
In a punchy cry from the heart, Kelly regrets just about everything.

❼ FROM LITTLE THINGS BIG THINGS GROW from COMEDY
Occasionally Paul Kelly ranges outside intensely personal song-stories to tell bigger tales, like this moving story of the fight for Aboriginal land rights.

Tony Wheeler

Kids' songs not by purple dinosaurs

Here's a list tested extensively on pre-school kids. Sure, there may be tots who can't get enough of The Itsy Bitsy Spider, or who like the lead singer to dress as a purple dinosaur. But don't underestimate the power of rock'n'roll nonsense.

❶ SURFIN' BIRD
THE RAMONES from ROCKET TO RUSSIA
A rocking cover with vocal effects that sound as if Joey is hiccuping into a toilet bowl.

❷ HELLO GOODBYE
THE BEATLES from MAGICAL MYSTERY TOUR
A layered but gentle introduction to the concept of opposites by a group that lays out the fundamental building blocks of rock'n'roll.

❸ HOUND DOG ELVIS PRESLEY
from ELVIS' GOLDEN RECORDS
Another song chock-full of fundamental building blocks. Plus, kids like songs about dogs.

❹ VEGETABLES THE BEACH BOYS
from SMILEY SMILE/WILD HONEY
Even kids who forgo the green stuff will like this upbeat ode, where the harmonies are blended more smoothly than mashed peas.

❺ MAGIC BUS THE WHO from MAGIC BUS
The percussion – often Keith Moon knocking on a wooden block – gets the bus moving and the Pete Townshend/Roger Daltrey exchange: "I want it, I want it, I want it!"/"You can't have it" hits children where they live.

❻ GOO GOO MUCK THE CRAMPS
from PSYCHEDELIC JUNGLE
A punkabilly monster song in the spirit of those old K-Tel offerings, but with rocking guitar and bass and a creature whose jungle trill evokes old Tarzan movies.

❼ MOLE IN THE GROUND BASCAM LAMAR LUNSFORD
from BALLADS, BANJO TUNES AND SACRED SONGS OF WESTERN NORTH CAROLINA
This old-time tune with a seemingly simple banjo drone is often treated as a children's song, though the verses vary according to when it was recorded and who's doing the singing.

❽ OLD McDONALD HAD A FARM
RUFUS THOMAS from **FUNKY CHICKEN**
There's no telling what kind of impact Old McDonald could have if pre schoolers sang it Thomas' way.

❾ LOOKIN' OUT MY BACK DOOR CREEDENCE
CLEARWATER REVIVAL from **COSMO'S FACTORY**
This tune about elephants and flying spoons has the added advantage of introducing kids to the CCR guitar innovation of "the choogle".

❿ MR. SPACEMAN THE BYRDS
from **FIFTH DIMENSION**
Jangly electric guitars and a small silly factor open up the possibility of a rock'n'roll universe.

Madelyn Rosenberg

Cool kids' music

Okay, okay, by 10 or so, kids have their own taste in music, hopefully entirely at odds with your own. But at 6, 7, 8, they're still very much up for fun tunes and memorable lyrics. Reggae and ska often go down well, as do classic Beatles, Monkees, T Rex and Bowie.

❶ ABOMINABLE SNOWMAN IN THE SUPERMARKET
JONATHAN RICHMAN from **23 GREAT RECORDINGS**
Jonathan Richman can do dark with the best of them, but dozens of his early songs are for or about childhood.

❷ BAGGY TROUSERS MADNESS from DIVINE MADNESS
The daft ska of Madness strikes a chord with most kids, and even more so if you get a DVD with all their very funny pop videos.

❸ KEEP'N IT REAL SHAGGY from HOLES (SOUNDTRACK)
Holes is a cool kids' movie with a top soundtrack, which includes this warm rap-reggae from Shaggy.

❹ JOE LE TAXI SHARLENE BOODRAM
from THE ROUGH GUIDE TO CALYPSO AND SOCA
This has all the ingredients: great tune, fun rap, novelty intro (taxi screeching to a halt) and soca riddim.

❺ YELLOW SUBMARINE
THE BEATLES from **REVOLVER**
Blinding tunes, memorable lyrics: The Beatles hit a chord with kids, from "She Loves You" to "Here Comes the Sun". And does anyone not commit "Yellow Submarine" to memory?

❻ I'M A BELIEVER
THE MONKEES from **THE DEFINITIVE MONKEES**
Hey hey, how can anyone resist The Monkees? And this is a perfect way in, familiar from the Smash Mouth version in *Shrek*.

❼ CHANGES DAVID BOWIE from HUNKY DORY
You wouldn't wish Tin Machine on kids, but 1970s Bowie songs – from "Hunky Dory" and "Ziggy Stardust" – have a singalong magic.

❽ A LITTLE LESS CONVERSATION (JXL REMIX) ELVIS
PRESLEY from 30 #1 HITS
It's remarkable how kids respond to Elvis – the songs and the image – and this fabulous remix is the very best introduction.

❾ GET IT ON T REX from ELECTRIC WARRIOR
The US passed on Marc Bolan, but in Europe he filled the gap for kids left by The Beatles and The Monkees. Start with this spark of genius.

❿ MAKE 'EM LAUGH DONALD O'CONNOR
from SINGIN' IN THE RAIN SOUNDTRACK
Is Julie Andrews getting embarrassing? If so, there's no need to give up on musicals – and this is the funniest number from the greatest of them all.

Mark Ellingham

Kids' TV

Some of the best, most memorable themes belong to kids' shows – but how to track them down? Check out albums by the composers themselves or try some of the *Cult Fiction* compilations from Virgin for instant gratification.

❶ THE BANANA SPLITS THE BANANA SPLITS
The nutty "Tra-la-la-la" song! The kind of insanely sunny theme that would have you bouncing madly around the playground during break. Essential.

❷ DR WHO DELIA DERBYSHIRE
By far the best "Dr Who" is Delia Derbyshire's arrangement of Ron Grainer's immortal classic, promising plenty of hide-behind-the-sofa Tom Baker action.

❸ GRANGE HILL ALAN HAWKSHAW
As soon as this timeless effort kicks off you can just picture the comic-style opening, that fork and the sausage!

❹ HONG KONG PHOOEY SCATMAN CROTHERS
Hanna Barbera's nutty answer to Bruce Lee featured the amazing Scatman Crothers' voice and loads of thwacky-wacky sound effects.

❺ JOE 90 BARRY GRAY
A real gem from Barry Gray, this far-out psychedelic tune sounds more like a strobe-lit 1960s wig-out than a kids TV theme. Groooovy baby!

❻ MAGPIE THE SPENCER DAVIS GROUP
ITV's hipper rival to *Blue Peter* had one hell of a rocking theme from The Spencer Davis Group – check out the lashings of wicked Hammond organ!

❼ ROOBARB & CUSTARD JOHNNY HAWKSWORTH
A green dog, a pink cat plus lots of wobbly animation equals a classic.

❽ THUNDERBIRDS BARRY GRAY
Thunderbirds are GO! Those marching martial drums and blaring trumpet fanfares mean business in this full-on orchestral arrangement from Barry Gray.

❾ TOMORROW PEOPLE DUDLEY SIMPSON
Next to *Dr Who's*, the SF theme most likely to scare the life out of you was this.

❿ WHITE HORSES JACKIE LEE
Jackie Lee had a hit with the theme to *Rupert The Bear* in 1971, but her wistful vocals sound effortless on this Top 10 hit from 1968.

Essi Berelian

BB King

He celebrated his 80th birthday in 2005 and he's been the king of the blues guitar for more than half a century. Everyone from the Stones to U2 has played with him.

❶ EVERY DAY I HAVE THE BLUES from KING OF THE BLUES
Released as a single in 1955, the song that became his signature tune.

❷ SHE'S DYNAMITE from KING OF THE BLUES
Recorded in Memphis in 1951 by Sam Phillips – who three years later would discover Elvis.

❸ THREE O'CLOCK BLUES from KING OF THE BLUES
His first rhythm and blues #1, recorded at the black YMCA in Memphis.

❹ ROCK ME BABY from KING OF THE BLUES
A storming version of a Lowell Fulsom song that hit #1 in the American R&B chart in 1952.

❺ SWEET LITTLE ANGEL from LIVE AT THE REGAL
A classic blues song from one of the all-time classic live albums, recorded in the mid 1960s.

❻ THE THRILL IS GONE from KING OF THE BLUES
"I'd been carrying around that song for six or seven years but it would never come out how I wanted it", BB recalls. Then producer Bill Szymczyk suggested putting strings on it.

❼ LUCILLE from LUCILLE
A tribute to the love of his life – Lucille, the name he gave his gold-plated, pearl-inlaid Gibson 335 guitar.

❽ WHEN LOVE COMES TO TOWN from RATTLE AND HUM
Bono wrote him a song, they recorded it together, stuck it on a U2 album and he suddenly found a whole new audience.

❾ PAYIN' THE COST TO BE THE BOSS from DEUCES WILD
Backed by a combo called The Rolling Stones on his 1997 all-star duets album.

❿ KEY TO THE HIGHWAY from RIDING WITH THE KING
The Big Bill Broonzy tune done acoustically from his 2001 Grammy-winning album with Eric Clapton.

Nigel Williamson

Kings and queens

Long ago, in days untold . . . and more recently, too, people wrote songs about royalty.

❶ KINGS AND QUEENS AEROSMITH from DRAW THE LINE
A molten slow burn that doesn't skimp on the pageantry; the lyrics, too, reach for the sky. On writing it, Steven Tyler avers he was "back with the knights of the round table and that shit".

❷ IN THE COURT OF THE CRIMSON KING KING CRIMSON from IN THE COURT OF THE CRIMSON KING
Moody, stormy prog-rock, which really hits its stride with the flute interlude more than four minutes in. Regal stuff indeed.

❸ QUEEN OF EYES SOFT BOYS from UNDERWATER MOONLIGHT
Chimey whimsy from the master of such stuff; Robyn Hitchcock leads his young neo-psychedelics through a glass, brightly.

❹ RIDING WITH THE KING JOHN HIATT from RIDING WITH THE KING

Honest, old fashioned rock from an honest old-fashioned rocker (with some country and R&B thrown in). And anything that alludes to taking a car ride with Elvis is good with us.

❺ THE QUEEN IS DEAD THE SMITHS from THE QUEEN IS DEAD

Arguably the fiercest rocker in the Smiths illustrious canon, this merciless song aims to bring the monarchy down to its knees or even lower.

❻ KINGS STEELY DAN from CAN'T BUY A THRILL

The exuberant chorus celebrates the passing of the crown; the rest is as smooth as a practised con man.

❼ KING FOR A DAY XTC from ORANGES AND LEMONS

With a pop touch as light as a feather, Colin Moulding argues that it's not always good to be the king.

❽ KING OF PAIN THE POLICE from SYNCHRONICITY

Who knows what Sting was on about; at least the psychobabble usually sounded good, as it does here.

❾ KING OF THE ROAD ROGER MILLER from ALL-TIME GREATEST HITS

You can't hear this song without wondering what it might be like hopping boxcars around the US.

❿ HER MAJESTY THE BEATLES from ABBEY ROAD

If this melodic put-on is good enough to serve as a (very brief) postscript for the towering Abbey Road suite, then it's good enough to finish off this list.

Andrew Rosenberg

Kings of Leon

Growing up on the bench back seat of dad's car while he drove across the southernmost states in the Union, preachin' the word of the Lord, sounds just too American Gothic to be true. But the three Followill boys (Nathan, Caleb and Jared) appear to have survived unscathed – except for their vintage Lynyrd Skynyrd looks.

❶ CALIFORNIA WAITING from HOLY ROLLER NOVOCAINE

Pared back to the raw bone, this lo-fat version of a track later included on *Youth And Young Manhood* pays tribute to the guitar boogie that was the soundtrack to the band's early lives.

❷ WASTED TIME from YOUTH AND YOUNG MANHOOD

KOL nail up their manifesto – beer, girls, good-time boogie and dancing barefoot.

❸ MOLLY'S CHAMBERS from YOUTH AND YOUNG MANHOOD

You want it? She's got it! Blues based guitar rock from the old school. It ain't broke, and these guys don't plan to fix it.

❹ THE BUCKET from AHA SHAKE HEARTBREAK

One of the definitive KOL tracks – impenetrable vocals, beautifully toned guitar twang and a barrage of drums from the garage rock school.

❺ MILK from AHA SHAKE HEARTBREAK

Growling, howling lyrics and swaggering southern fried guitar all in tribute to a girl with an hourglass figure who'll loan you her toothbrush.

❻ TAPER JEAN GIRL from AHA SHAKE HEARTBREAK

Garage rock, taken out of the petrol-scented dark, injected with bull hormones and turned loose. A bed-shaking, headboard-rattling motel room stomp.

❼ CHARMER from BECAUSE OF THE TIMES

Gorgeous dirty guitar and bass, a head-piercing howl every so often and, when you can distinguish the words, some fine sarcastic lyrics

❽ MY PARTY from BECAUSE OF THE TIMES

The Kings make a stab at badass funk with neatly distorted vocals, the traditional hamfisted drumming and chunky guitar work.

❾ CAMARO from BECAUSE OF THE TIMES

West-coast guitar rock meets gutbucket garage blues in a vicious fight with duelling solos, dynamics in the mix and no holds barred. No losers, all winners.

❿ MY PARTY from BECAUSE OF THE TIMES

One thing KOL can't be beaten at is hard rockin' good times music with a hint of mournful in the mix – lonely coyote rock at its best.

Al Spicer

The Kinks

Ray Davies blended pop with nostalgia and a music-hall sensibility, and created something peculiarly English and more than a little eccentric. He's a national treasure, and should be protected by law.

❶ YOU REALLY GOT ME from THE KINKS
The ultimate riff-driven statement of instant lust/ obsession. It's not only dumb-but-great in its own right, but without it we wouldn't have had The Who or The Troggs.

❷ WATERLOO SUNSET from SOMETHING ELSE
Soundtrack for a Swinging London movie: Terry (Stamp) kisses Julie (Christie) on the bridge, and the concrete wilderness of the South Bank turns into paradise.

❸ DAYS from THE VILLAGE GREEN PRESERVATION SOCIETY (BONUS TRACK)
Simple but elegant. A song of celebration and gratitude.

❹ LOLA from KINKS PART 1: LOLA VERSUS POWERMAN AND THE MONEYGOROUND
The song that put transvestism on the map, years before Bowie. Never has pop sexuality been quite so laissez-faire.

❺ DAVID WATTS from SOMETHING ELSE
Fifth-form angst, as Ray idolizes the "pure and noble" paragon who captains both the school and the team.

❻ SUNNY AFTERNOON from FACE TO FACE
Vicious tax demand? Girlfriend left you and taken the car? Ah, well – at least the weather's nice. Mustn't grumble.

❼ THE VILLAGE GREEN PRESERVATION SOCIETY from THE VILLAGE GREEN PRESERVATION SOCIETY
Like Ian Dury, Ray Davies had a talent for compiling lists of things he liked – in this case enshrining all the endangered ingredients of a vanishing England.

❽ DEAD END STREET
from FACE TO FACE (BONUS TRACK)
Poverty, hopelessness, appalling living conditions – and all with no hope of getting out. This was practically a call to armed revolution.

❾ AUTUMN ALMANAC
from SOMETHING ELSE (BONUS TRACK)
Fantastic singalong ode to the joys of autumn – everything from rustling leaves to football and roast beef.

❿ COME DANCING from COME DANCING WITH THE KINKS (COMPILATION)
Rueful regrets about bad town planning, and the lost arts of 1950s romance: i.e. the doorstep snog and the knee-trembler.

Pete Hogan

Kiss

Yes, sometimes the songs sound recycled and have the same puerile subject matter (there's little doubt which of the holy trinity of sex, drugs, and rock'n'roll they're in it for). But nobody betters their outrageous makeup, stage show and killer riffs. Not to mention the length of bassist Gene Simmons' tongue.

❶ STRUTTER from KISS
The music struts as hard as the lady of the title; early Kiss could be as much glam stomp and barroom blues as it is was heavy metal.

❷ ROCK AND ROLL ALL NIGHT from ALIVE!
The party anthem that won't die, and for good reason; it still sounds fresh thirty years later, especially on this hit live version.

❸ PLASTER CASTER from LOVE GUN
Questionable taste as ever – this time about a famous (and real-life) groupie who makes plaster casts of penises – but crackling with energy.

❹ GOD OF THUNDER from DESTROYER
Spinal Tap could have sprung whole from this pounding anthem, the song before which Gene spits blood in concert.

❺ SURE KNOW SOMETHING from DYNASTY
The grooving salvation of their Kiss-does-disco misfire: the bass line sounds vaguely like "One of These Nights", the bridge moves it into rock'n'roll territory.

❻ HEAVEN'S ON FIRE from ANIMALIZE
The boys remove the makeup and gear up for the rise of bands they spawned, like Motley Crue and Poison, with a fiery riff guaranteed to make you pump your fist.

❼ BLACK DIAMOND from KISS
Worth it to hear the Sabbath-like riff that transitions from the tender, ballad-like beginning to the main verse; heck, even the weird ending that sounds like a record being played at the wrong speed is pretty cool.

❽ NEW YORK GROOVE from ACE FREHLEY (SOLO)
It might be too slick for serious headbangers, but it's catchy as hell and Ace shows he can hold a tune, too.

❾ CALLING DR LOVE from ROCK AND ROLL OVER
The awesomest lick Gene ever wrote, with growling lyrics that won't take no for an answer.

⑩ C'MON AND LOVE ME from DRESSED TO KILL

It's unclear how many groupie songs a band can write, but the line, "You're good looking and you're looking like you should be good", is enough to redeem this.

⑪ SHE from DRESSED TO KILL

A heavy rocker whose riff and lyrics scan a bit like a "Foxy Lady" on quaaludes.

⑫ CREATURES OF THE NIGHT from CREATURES OF THE NIGHT

Throbbing heavy metal that came like a breath of fresh air after nearly five years of treading water.

Andrew Rosenberg

Gladys Knight

Gladys led family gospel quartet The Pips to international stardom across the 1960s and 70s with her raw, open throat vocal. Whether on Vee Jay, Motown or Buddha, they were consistent hit makers. These days she's largely confined to the Vegas casino circuit but this doesn't diminish her status as one of soul music's great voices.

❶ EVERY BEAT OF MY HEART from SOUL SURVIVORS: GREATEST HITS

The Pips' first hit from 1961 with the teenage Gladys demonstrating the power and intelligence that now defines her career.

❷ I HEARD IT THROUGH THE GRAPEVINE from THE ULTIMATE COLLECTION

The original recording of this Barrett/Whitfield classic is a wailing gospel number as different from the version Marvin Gaye cut a year later as women are to men.

❸ THE NITTY GRITTY from THE ULTIMATE COLLECTION

Gladys shows she can get down to the nitty gritty on this late 1960s hit.

❹ FRIENDSHIP TRAIN from THE ULTIMATE COLLECTION

Preachy civil rights song sung with real conviction.

❺ IF I WERE YOUR WOMAN from THE ULTIMATE COLLECTION

Few can sing a love song like Gladys and here she brings all her emotion to the boil.

❻ TAKE ME IN YOUR ARMS AND LOVE ME from THE ULTIMATE COLLECTION

Huge 1970 hit that captures Gladys and the Pips smoothing their style to fit Motown's changing sound.

❼ NEITHER ONE OF US WANTS TO BE THE FIRST TO SAY GOODBYE from THE ULTIMATE COLLECTION

Breaking up is hard to do but listening to Gladys and the Pips sure smoothes things.

❽ MIDNIGHT TRAIN TO GEORGIA from IMAGINATION

Huge US and UK hit from 1974 that finds Gladys announcing she's leaving for the rural South as her man's exhausted by the city. The greatest song she's ever tackled and a stone soul classic.

❾ I'VE GOT TO USE MY IMAGINATION from IMAGINATION

Gladys and the Pips take this tough, unsettled soul tune at full throttle.

⑩ LICENSE TO KILL from LICENSE TO KILL SOUNDTRACK

Gladys sings a James Bond theme tune so gets her last major hit. The song's silly but Gladys, being a pro', treats it with serious intent.

Garth Cartwright

Knocked down, but I get up again

Life will occasionally deliver a roundhouse punch to the jaw that sets you spinning on your heels. Here's some music to listen to while the cartoon stars and chirping birdies whirl about your head.

❶ COMPLETE CONTROL THE CLASH from FROM HERE TO ETERNITY-LIVE

Betrayed by evil faceless suits at the record company who put out the wrong album track as the band's second single, The Clash turned their songwriting skills to this tale of defiance.

❷ REBEL MUSIC (3 O'CLOCK.ROADBLOCK) BOB MARLEY AND THE WAILERS from NATTY DREAD

Misbehaving maybe, but doing no harm when you run into a patrol in the middle of the night, then throw out your little 'erb stalk.

❸ I WILL SURVIVE GLORIA GAYNOR from THE BEST OF

Ripped apart by a million drunks, heartbroken and with mascara running figuratively if not literally down their cheeks, this is perhaps the ultimate "end of the affair" song.

❹ TAKE THIS JOB AND SHOVE IT DEAD KENNEDYS from BEDTIME FOR DEMOCRACY

A more vicious, venomous and downright personal version than Johnny Paycheck's original.

❺ MAGGIE'S FARM RAGE AGAINST THE MACHINE from RENEGADES

Bob Dylan wrote this, RATM added the spine, muscle, grit, sweat and anger.

❻ WORKING CLASS HERO MARIANNE FAITHFUL from BROKEN ENGLISH

Ms Faithfull croaks a spine-chilling indictment of traditional life-choices that neither she nor the writer (Lennon) ever had to face.

❼ SIXTEEN TONS THE REDSKINS from NEITHER WASHINGTON NOR MOSCOW

Cold, miserable yet defiant through the darkest days of the 1980s, The Redskins could always be relied on to give the man the finger.

❽ WORKIN' FOR THE MAN ROY ORBISON from ALL TIME GREATEST HITS

Great lyric about putting up with a remarkable amount of bullshit from the boss, while sneakily romancing his daughter.

❾ CAREER OPPORTUNITIES THE CLASH from THE CLASH

Brilliant dose of teenage frustration by a band on the verge of immense success.

❿ TUBTHUMPING CHUMBAWUMBA from TUBTHUMPING

Pure joy from the thoughtful anarchist folkies: a boozed up anthem for the underdog, for all occasions. And masterfully parodied by Homer Simpson: "I take a whiskey drink, I take a chocolate drink, and when I have to pee, I use the kitchen sink!"

Al Spicer

Kool & The Gang

The skill and subtlety of Kool & The Gang's early instrumentations, plus their almost transcendental understanding of how a groove works, are what has given their pop productions such lasting depth. It's no wonder James Brown was moved to describe them as "the second baddest out there".

❶ WILD AND PEACEFUL from WILD AND PEACEFUL

Nine minutes of deeply funky, jungle-influenced jazz, washing over you in waves.

❷ STREET CORNER SYMPHONY from LIGHT OF WORLDS

The bassline's grumbling is, presumably, a reaction to its having to hold up the heaviest horn section that doesn't involve Fred Wesley.

❸ FUNKY STUFF/MORE FUNKY STUFF from WILD AND PEACEFUL

The tune that introduced the whistle as regulation club-going paraphernalia, and so dedicated to the groove that it proves every instrument can be turned into a rhythmic device.

❹ GET DOWN ON IT from SOMETHING SPECIAL

Only a band with their intrinsic understanding of how much work you need to do inside a single riff to stop it getting boring could have taken this one this far.

❺ LADIES NIGHT from LADIES NIGHT

A hen-night classic – with nothing as distracting as lyricism or instrumental twiddliness to get in the way.

❻ OPEN SESAME PTS 1&2 from OPEN SESAME

A pounding up-tempo rhythm is such a solid anchor, even with a bonkers, Ali Baba-ish theme.

❼ NT from LIVE AT PJS

Rubberized bass keeps everything on the bounce; percussion spirals around the mix; and the guitars fall in on themselves.

❽ LET THE MUSIC TAKE YOUR MIND from KOOL AND THE GANG

As teenagers showing off in 1969, they shout, crack jokes, play solos, musically joust but never stray too far from the beat as they build up a track of awesome funk power.

❾ RATED X from GOOD TIMES

A string section, a clavinet and an ARP synthesizer put a perfect cushion between the rhythm section and the brass.

❿ SUMMER MADNESS from LIGHT OF WORLDS

At their most introspective, losing the horns to make a spiritual statement that maintains an astonishing tension.

Lloyd Bradley

Kraftwerk

The showroom dummies from Düsseldorf invented the pop world of pristine shimmering surfaces that we now inhabit. These are the ten cuts that made this brave new world possible.

❶ RUCKZUCK from KRAFTWERK 1

It begins with synth washes before becoming a jam session that has more to do with 1960s avant-garde New York than the future.

❷ KLING KLANG from KRAFTWERK 2
One of their earliest synthscapes, and, despite its name, it's glistening and rather gorgeous.

❸ AUTOBAHN from AUTOBAHN
A pastoral ode to the freeway – one of their greatest and cheekiest records.

❹ RADIOACTIVITY from RADIOACTIVITY
Techno, synth-pop, techno-pop and all other electronic genres start here.

❺ TRANS-EUROPE EXPRESS
from TRANS-EUROPE EXPRESS
The synth washes from "Ruckzuck" return on one of the most influential records of the last thirty years.

❻ METAL ON METAL from TRANS-EUROPE EXPRESS
The rhythmic motif of Trans-Europe Express transposed to tin cans.

❼ NEON LIGHTS from MAN-MACHINE
Yet another of this band's pastorals dedicated to urbanization.

❽ POCKET CALCULATOR from COMPUTER WORLD
By this point (1981) most of the world had caught up with them, but no one else was able to craft such great pop from grating sounds.

❾ NUMBERS from COMPUTER WORLD
Another outlandish exploration of the rhythmic possibilities of the synthesizer.

❿ TOUR DE FRANCE
from TOUR DE FRANCE SOUNDTRACKS
The technology of cycling may be comparatively ancient, but it inspired Kraftwerk's best record.

Peter Shapiro

❷ ARCHANGEL THUNDERBIRD
AMON DÜÜL II from YETI
Gothic, spacy dronerock recast as Teutonic heavy metal.

❸ HALLELUWAH CAN from TAGO MAGO
Guitarist Michael Karoli and keyboardist Irmin Schmidt throw shapes everywhere and sculpt with their battery of effects pedals.

❹ WHY DON'T YOU EAT CARROTS?
FAUST from FAUST
Surreal rock concrète in which Faust lay waste to everything that came before them.

❺ HALLOGALLO NEU! from NEU!
The definitive motorik rhythm loop.

❻ LIGHT: LOOK AT YOUR DARKNESS ASH RA TEMPEL
from SCHWINGUNGEN
A bluesy doom march into the gloomy bowels of psychdom.

❼ LAILA, PART 2 AGITATION FREE from SECOND
Krautrock at its jazziest and most Grateful Dead-like.

❽ HOLLYWOOD CLUSTER from ZUCKERZEIT
Decades ahead of its time, people are still trying to catch up to this record's synth tones and programming sophistication.

❾ CHA CHA 2000 LA DUSSELDORF from VIVA
Twenty minutes of pure kosmische slop.

❿ E2-E4 MANUEL GÖTTSCHING from E2-E4
On paper, a single-track, instrumental concept album about chess is the worst idea ever; in practice, it's a shimmering masterpiece.

Peter Shapiro

Krautrock

A couple of generations' worth of enforced alienation from African-American music caused young Germans in the early 1970s to rethink the role of rhythm in popular music. These are ten of the most startling records that resulted from the experimentation.

❶ THE WITCH THE RATTLES
from RATTLES' GREATEST HITS
Germans try to play a Bo Diddley riff and end up inventing psychedelic glam rock.

Kronos Quartet

Without the Kronos Quartet, the state of contemporary composition would be dramatically poorer. Since violinist David Harrington founded the string quartet in 1973, the ensemble has commissioned some six hundred new works and ranged across musical boundaries to take in tango flavours, East European Gypsy music and Bollywood glitz, as well as promoting the work of avant-garde composers such as Philip Glass and Steve Reich.

David Harrington's
Discoveries

As leader of the Kronos Quartet, **DAVID HARRINGTON** has been in the vanguard of commissioning the best of modern composition, and has pioneered the field of world music/classical crossover. Every day, he puts aside two hours to listen to new music.

❶ FUNERAL CHANT from ANTHOLOGY OF THE MUSIC OF THE AKA PYGMIES

This track features the voices of an entire village lamenting a death. The collective grief heard here is transformed by the community into an awesome beauty.

❷ ARTISTS IN A TIME OF WAR HOWARD ZINN from ALTERNATIVE RADIO, HOSTED BY DAVID BARSAMIAN

As a source of real in-depth thought about world events, *Alternative Radio* is unsurpassed. Howard Zinn's voice and observations give hope for the future.

❸ BACH'S GOLDBERG VARIATIONS played by GLENN GOULD

A testament to the power of the imagination, the *Variations* continue to astonish. In this performance, Gould charted new areas of commitment and virtuosity, setting a standard which is totally off the scale.

❹ LINDA MUSIC BANDA LINDA from CENTRAL AFRICAN REPUBLIC: BANDA POLYPHONY

A recording that features amazing choirs of horns. Each player is responsible for a note and a rhythm. I am always inspired by the raw beauty and interconnectedness this music and these performers have.

❺ STAR-SPANGLED BANNER JIMI HENDRIX from WOODSTOCK

Hendrix's performance transformed our national anthem into a meaningful response to world events – using only sound.

❻ PARI INTERVALLO RITVA KOISTINEN from NEW FINNISH KANTELE

Ritva Koistinen's performance of Arvo Pärt's *Pari Intervallo* sets a new standard of beauty, clarity and holiness. It has its own aura.

❼ DVORAK'S HUMORESQUE from FRITZ KREISLER PLAYS ENCORES

The first note Kreisler plays is the most gentle, beautiful note I've ever heard on a violin: an endless source of inspiration. With his sound, he seems to embody the essence of the violin.

❽ SCHUBERT'S QUINTET IN C MAJOR played by PABLO CASALS ET AL

The depth and generosity of Schubert's imagination is unparallelled, and in this one piece we have available to us a pinnacle of human expression. The performance is a landmark of interpretation, as though each note comes directly from the source of inspiration.

❾ RAGA TODI/RUPAK TAL from RAVI SHANKAR LIVE AT MONTEREY 1967

Ravi Shankar and tabla player Alla Rahka gave a new generation of listeners another way to hear music. This recording captures the exciting moment when these peerless virtuosos are swept up in the thrill of sharing their tradition with a culture far from home.

❿ ST LOUIS BLUES from BESSIE SMITH: THE COLLECTION

Bessie Smith's voice is perfectly counterbalanced by the harmonium and Louis Armstrong's trumpet, and she reveals areas of feeling instrumentalists can only hint at.

❶ BLACK ANGELS from BLACK ANGELS

Groundbreaking electric string quartet composed by George Crumb as an ode to the Vietnam War.

❷ GORECKI'S QUARTET NO. 1: ALREADY IT IS DUSK from HENRYK GORECKI

Alternatively sombre and furious, a fervent prayer for deliverance from the great Polish composer.

❸ TURCEASCA (TURKISH SONG) from CARAVAN

A collaboration with Romania's Taraf de Haidouks as conservatoire training collides with gypsy passion.

❹ ESCALAY FOR TAR & STRING QUARTET: WATERWHEEL from PIECES OF AFRICA

Composed by the Sudanese oud master Hamza El Din for the Quartet's ground-breaking African album.

❺ MORTON FELDMAN'S PIANO AND STRING QUARTET from PIANO QUARTET

Written by the composer for the Kronos in 1987 shortly before his death.

❻ G-SONG, FOR STRING QUARTET & SYNTHESIZER from 25 YEARS: RETROSPECTIVE

The first of several pieces written for the Kronos by composer Terry Riley, based on a sixteen-bar theme of G minor scales played asymetrically over a jazz chord-progression.

❼ MISSA SYLLABICA from 25 YEARS: RETROSPECTIVE

Written by Arvo Pärt for the quartet, who have been consistent champions of the Estonian-born composer.

❽ MEHBOOBA MEHBOOBA from YOU'VE STOLEN MY HEART: SONGS from R.D. BURMAN'S BOLLYWOOD

Indian singer Asha Bhosle joins the Quartet on a song written by her late husband, the film composer R.D. Burman.

❾ FIVE TANGO SENSATIONS FOR BANDONEÓN & STRING QUARTET from FIVE TANGO SENSATIONS

The quartet go tango with Astor Piazzolla on a composition he wrote to play with them.

❿ DIFFERENT TRAINS FOR DOUBLE STRING QUARTET & TAPE from DIFFERENT TRAINS/ELECTRIC COUNTERPOINT

Steve Reich's haunting response to the Holocaust.

Nigel Williamson

Fela Kuti

Fela Anikulapo Kuti was a musician, a politician, a utopian and, above all, a provocateur. In a Nigeria where the authorities responded to provocation with fury, his was a game played for blood. From the 1970s until his death in 1997, he melded elements of Nigerian highlife and American funk into irresistibly jazzy dance music.

❶ LADY from SHAKARA

One of Fela's best-known songs, later covered by Hugh Masekela at a stripped-down five minutes. Ingenious attempts have been made to reclaim this denunciation of uppity women as a feminist anthem, but they are a stretch: Fela's sexual politics were never his strong point.

❷ WATER NO GET ENEMY from EXPENSIVE SHIT

An uncharacteristically lyrical piano line dominates this extended workout.

❸ ZOMBIE from ZOMBIE

A provocation of the army, which had disastrous results: Fela's compound, the self-proclaimed Kalakuta Republic, was raided by soldiers. One of them threw Fela's mother out of a window, causing injuries from which she later died.

❹ NO AGREEMENT from NO AGREEMENT

A rolling, boisterous repeated bass riff, with swirling organ and hammering brass solos.

❺ UNKNOWN SOLDIER from UNKNOWN SOLDIER

An inquiry into the Kalakuta raid blamed an "unknown soldier" – one of the thousand present – for the death of Fela's mother. He was vilified here.

❻ COFFIN FOR HEAD OF STATE from COFFIN FOR HEAD OF STATE

The mass funeral of Fela's mother, herself a leading campaigner for independence and for women's rights, is remembered in this song.

❼ I.T.T. (INTERNATIONAL THIEF THIEF) from I.T.T.

The target here is the multinationals profiting from Africa, and in particular the conglomerate ITT.

❽ ARMY ARRANGEMENT from ARMY ARRANGEMENT

Still baiting the army: Fela hadn't learned.

❾ TEACHER DON'T TEACH ME NONSENSE from TEACHER DON'T TEACH ME NONSENSE

The former colonial nations are cast as teachers telling lies to the African countries and their citizens.

❿ BEASTS OF NO NATION from BEASTS OF NO NATION

The eponymous beasts are Botha, Reagan and Thatcher, slated for their supposed support for apartheid.

David Honigmann

Kwaito killers

South Africa's kwaito (hip-hop) tunes aren't generally built to endure, but rather to fizz and spark until the next hit comes along. Still, here's a selection that have managed to implant themselves as long-lasting dancefloor classics.

❶ NDIHAMBA NAWE MAFIKIZOLO from SIBONGILE
Wonderfully catchy anthem that was a huge hit on release and still always gets the kwaito line-dancers going.

❷ NKALAKATHA MANDOZA from NKALAKATHA
Classic and enjoyable stomp-rock/kwaito tune.

❸ DLALA MAPANTUSLA TKZEE from HALLOWEEN
Laid-back vibes from kwaito maestros TKZee, so sure of themselves they don't mind what you think. As they put it: "Dance if you want to dance, whatever…"

❹ THATH'ISIGUBHU BONGO MAFFIN from CONCERTO
Another line-dancing classic, as Bongo Maffin implore us to "take the drum".

❺ LIFE 'ISKOROKORO BROTHERS OF PEACE from THE D PROJECT
Contemporary house/kwaito tune with a great dub-wise middle section.

❻ UBABA UYAJOLA CHICCO from STREET BASH 2
"Mum's at home while Dad's partying next door", warns Chicco in this retro kwaito masterpiece.

❼ KHAULEZA ARTHUR from YIYO
Arthur crowned himself the king of kwaito – an exaggeration perhaps, but this hit alone made him a strong contender.

❽ DOWN SOUTH REVOLUTION, FEATURING JIMMY DLUDLU from ANOTHER LEVEL
Jazz, house and kwaito all rolled into one from this talented Durban outfit.

❾ MAFIKIZOLO MAFIKIZOLO from SIBONGILE
Superb and evergreen mid-tempo kwaito cut from one of SA's top pop acts.

❿ THE WAY KUNGAKHONA BONGO MAFFIN from BONGOLUTION
Sunny and upbeat, with great vocals from the lovely Thandiswa, who has since gone solo.

Gregory Salter

Kylie

Australia's pop princess has defied all expectations with the longevity of her career and the durability of her hits.

❶ JE NE SAIS PAS POURQUOI from KYLIE MINOGUE
It's those hard Js that make this song so entirely irresistible.

❷ HAND ON YOUR HEART from ENJOY YOURSELF
The first really great Kylie song, with a melody that would stand up in any arrangement, though long-term fans are still waiting for the unplugged version.

❸ BETTER THE DEVIL YOU KNOW from RHYTHM OF LOVE
Whether she was talking about Stock, Aitken or Waterman remains unclear, but sticking with the infamous production/songwriting team for her first four albums did her no harm.

❹ CONFIDE IN ME from KYLIE MINOGUE
One of Kylie's least typical hits, and the best of the Deconstruction wilderness years. Again, lifted by a great video.

❺ WHERE THE WILD ROSES GROW DUET WITH NICK CAVE from MURDER BALLADS
Kylie honestly sounds a bit out of her depth here, though it's kind of appropriate given what happens to her character in the song. The most enduring legacy of her ill-advised "indie" period.

❻ SPINNING AROUND from LIGHT YEARS
"I'm spinning around/Get out of my way." This girl is serious about dancing. And it shows.

❼ ON A NIGHT LIKE THIS from LIGHT YEARS
An admittedly slight addition to the Kylie canon was transformed when she performed it at the Sydney Olympics opening ceremony, ensuring that post-millennial comeback.

❽ BURY ME DEEP IN LOVE DUET WITH JIMMY LITTLE from CORROBORATION
This little-known gem from a 2001 compilation of left-field Aussie acts pairs Kylie with Aboriginal cabaret crooner Jimmy Little on a great Triffids song.

❾ CAN'T GET YOU OUT OF MY HEAD from FEVER
Millions of others couldn't either – Kylie's biggest hit ever even struck gold in the US, which generally hasn't quite "got" Kylie.

❿ SOMEDAY from BODY LANGUAGE
A stroke of genius – Kylie pairs up with the sweet-voiced Green Gartside (Scritti Politti) for a slice of multi-textured pop soul.

Jon Lusk

Lambchop

"Music by which to drift down river, cowboy hat on head, open beer in hand." Actually we didn't write that. We found it, unattributed, on the Internet, but thought it summed up the charm of Kurt Wagner's alt.Nashville collective so perfectly that we couldn't improve on it.

❶ UP WITH PEOPLE from NIXON

Alt.country meets Curtis Mayfield on a track that was also dramatically remixed by Zero 7.

❷ YOUR FUCKING SUNNY DAY from THRILLER

Exquisite country-soul again, this time with a Muscle Shoals influence.

❸ I SUCKED MY BOSS'S DICK from THE EP HANK

OK, it's not Kurt's greatest song. But it's got to be his greatest song title.

❹ THE SATURDAY OPTION
from WHAT ANOTHER MAN SPILLS

A tender but oddly lurid account of bed-time ritual, like Desmond Morris set to music.

❺ I'VE BEEN LONELY FOR SO LONG
from WHAT ANOTHER MAN SPILLS

Kurt's usual baritone drawl turns falsetto on a wonderful cover of Frederick Knight's old hit.

❻ THE NEW COBWEB SUMMER from IS A WOMAN

Whispered, gossamer beauty from the group's most deliciously understated album.

❼ THE BUTCHER BOY from NIXON

An old murder ballad from Harry Smith's *Anthology Of American Folk Music*, but given a new tune by Wagner.

❽ IS A WOMAN from IS A WOMAN

Elegiac, unhurried and intimate – but with a surprising reggae tinge.

❾ NOTHING ADVENTUROUS PLEASE
from AWCMON/YOU CMON

Just to prove that they can rock out when they want to.

❿ NOTHING BUT A BLUR FROM A BULLET TRAIN
from AWCMON/YOU CMON

Gorgeous strings and intimate piano on a masterful minor-key sound poem, with a typically impressionistic Wagnerian lyric that as far as we can tell has nothing to do with Britpop.

Nigel Williamson

Daniel Lanois

The Canadian artist/producer brings a shimmer to his own and others' work. Speciality: rescuing stuck careers, often in collaboration with Eno.

❶ ICE from ACADIE

Acadie is Lanois's finest outing under his own name, a blend of ambient electronica and Francophone folk.

❷ THE MAKER from ACADIE

A slow march with reverberating bass and drums, a trick Lanois would repeat on many of his productions.

❸ FALLEN ANGEL ROBBIE ROBERTSON
from ROBBIE ROBERTSON

A farewell to Robertson's Band-mate Richard Manuel. "Come down Gabriel, blow your horn" implores Robertson, and lo, Peter Gabriel arrives on backing vocals.

❹ YELLOW MOON THE NEVILLE BROTHERS
from YELLOW MOON

Aaron Neville's falsetto is one of Lanois's favourite voices, here used in service of the premier New Orleans funk band.

❺ MAN IN THE LONG BLACK COAT BOB DYLAN from OH MERCY

A spooky nod to the Band's "Long Black Veil".

❻ BLOOD OF EDEN PETER GABRIEL from US

The original version of this, from the film *Until The End Of The World*, is unaccountably stiff: this album version sounds like a lot more fun.

❼ A SORT OF HOMECOMING U2
from THE UNFORGETTABLE FIRE

With chiming guitar and yearning chorus, this set up U2's move from indie energy to stadium mastery.

⑧ WHERE WILL I BE EMMYLOU HARRIS
from WRECKING BALL
A sharp snare drum and an ethereal melody that
sounds like an old Appalachian hymn kick off
Emmylou Harris's best album.

David Honigmann

Latin soul

The blend of Cuban rhythms and jazz was some
twenty years old by the time a new generation
of Puerto Rican immigrants came of age in the
1960s. Instead of looking to the jazz of their
parents' age, they affirmed their Americanness by
blending the sounds of their homeland with the
more aggressive rhythms of soul.

❶ EL SEÑOR EMBAJADOR RICARDO RAY
from SE SOLTO
Perhaps the very first boogaloo, by the man who
would become *el rey del shingaling*.

❷ BANG BANG JOE CUBA
from WANTED DEAD OR ALIVE
Only a complete killjoy can remain unmoved by this
boogaloo classic.

❸ I LIKE IT LIKE THAT PETE RODRIGUEZ
from I LIKE IT LIKE THAT (A MI ME GUSTA ASI)
Boogaloo at its partying best.

❹ ACID RAY BARRETTO from ACID
In which psychedelia and effects entered the vernacu-
lar of Latin music.

❺ HEAT! PUCHO & THE LATIN SOUL BROTHERS from HEAT!
One of the most seamless blends of Latin and soul-jazz
rhythms.

❻ YROCO JIMMY SABATER from EL HIJO DE TERESA
A bewitching combination of hard funk rhythms,
horns, guitars, percussion and chants.

❼ HARLEM RIVER DRIVE (THEME SONG) EDDIE
PALMIERI & HARLEM RIVER DRIVE
from HARLEM RIVER DRIVE
Salsa, soul, jazz – Palmieri fuses them all on this magnificent record.

❽ LATIN STRUT JOE BATAAN from SALSOUL
Monstrous Latin-funk jam that helped clear the way
for disco.

❾ BABALONIA RICARDO MARRERO
from NU YORICA!
Released on Don King's (yes, that Don King) label, this
is an almighty Latin funk jam.

❿ DO IT ANY WAY YOU WANNA LOUIE RAMIREZ from A
DIFFERENT SHADE OF BLACK
Seriously funky, Latin-tinged cover of Peoples' Choice's
disco classic.

Peter Shapiro

Leadbelly

The son of sharecropping parents, Huddie
Ledbetter was not just another Delta blues singer.
He was a repository of American popular music
whose repertoire of five hundred-plus songs
included blues, spirituals, folk ballads, prison
songs, field hollers, Cajun dance tunes and even
cowboy songs. He died virtually penniless in 1949,
but his recordings are widely available and his
songbook has been plundered by rock artists ever
since. Here are ten that he wrote or recorded, and
some of the artists who covered them.

❶ BOURGEOIS BLUES RY COODER: BILLY CHILDISH; ARLO
GUTHRIE; TAJ MAHAL

❷ GALLIS POLE LED ZEPPELIN; ODETTA

❸ IN NEW ORLEANS (HOUSE OF THE RISING SUN)
BOB DYLAN; THE ANIMALS; NINA SIMONE; DOLLY PARTON

❹ GOODNIGHT IRENE FRANK SINATRA; RY COODER; LITTLE
RICHARD; JOHNNY CASH; JIM REEVES; JIMI HENDRIX; JERRY LEE
LEWIS; VAN MORRISON; THE WEAVERS

❺ ROCK ISLAND LINE LONNIE DONEGAN; JOHNNY CASH

❻ COTTONFIELDS THE BEACH BOYS; ELTON JOHN;
CREEDENCE CLEARWATER REVIVAL; THE POGUES

❼ BLACK BETTY RAM JAM; U2

❽ IN THE PINES NIRVANA (AS WHERE DID YOU SLEEP LAST
NIGHT); SMOG

❾ MIDNIGHT SPECIAL CREEDENCE CLEARWATER REVIVAL;
VAN MORRISON; JIMMY SMITH

❿ PICK A BALE OF COTTON ABBA; JOHNNY CASH

Nigel Williamson

Led Zeppelin

The daddies of heavy metal to some, Robert Plant (vocals), Jimmy Page (guitar), John Paul Jones (bass/keyboards) and John Bonham (drums) created some of the most diverse and magnificent rock music ever.

❶ ACHILLES' LAST STAND from PRESENCE
Over ten minutes of manically driven rock built around a thumping rhythm track; the interplay between Bonham and Jones is breathtaking.

❷ DAZED AND CONFUSED from LED ZEPPELIN I
Plant is on top my-woman-done-me-wrong form with this loping, smouldering blues monster.

❸ IMMIGRANT SONG from LED ZEPPELIN III
That supernatural Plantian wail says it all. And it's about Vikings. Really, what more do you need to know? Just succumb to the hammer of the gods.

❹ IN MY TIME OF DYING from PHYSICAL GRAFFITI
A lengthy and turbulent blues-rock work-out. Plant pleads for heavenly salvation and the rest of the band lay waste with a collective sonic sledgehammer.

❺ MISTY MOUNTAIN HOP from LED ZEPPELIN IV
Plant wants to get down with the love generation, but The Man just wants to give them all grief. Bonham's drumming really makes this track what it is.

❻ NO QUARTER from HOUSES OF THE HOLY
Plant sounds like he's singing underwater on this mystical and atmospheric little epic. Jones' keyboard work is nothing short of awesome.

❼ STAIRWAY TO HEAVEN from LED ZEPPELIN IV
Are those recorders at the start? One of the most famous rock songs ever, featuring some of the best lyrics ever, and one of the best solos ever. Not a lot left to say, is there?

❽ THE RAIN SONG from HOUSES OF THE HOLY
The typical Zeppelin bombast is jettisoned in favour of a gorgeously simple guitar melody and some touchingly intimate vocals. An understated, underrated gem.

❾ TRAMPLED UNDERFOOT from PHYSICAL GRAFFITI
Naughty little Robert wants to check your oil pressure with his greasy dipstick, baby. Sex and cars, sex in cars – a timeless rock'n'roll combination.

❿ WHOLE LOTTA LOVE (LIVE) from HOW THE WEST WAS WON
The version on Led Zep II is a classic, but this live concert take exceeds the twenty-minute mark and throws in a bunch of blues standards for good measure.

Essi Berelian

Robert Plant's
Solid gold

With Led Zeppelin he was the golden god. But at heart, ROBERT PLANT remains above all a music fan, as this diverse selection of his faves, old and new, shows.

❶ HOME IN YOUR HEART SOLOMON BURKE from HOME IN YOUR HEART

❷ DOUBLE TROUBLE OTIS RUSH from GOOD'UNS: THE CLASSIC COBRA RECORDINGS

❸ OH DEATH RALPH STANLEY from MAN OF CONSTANT SORROW

❹ SHE'S EVERYTHING RAL DONNER from YOU DON'T KNOW WHAT YOU'VE GOT

❺ FARMER IN THE CITY SCOTT WALKER from FIVE EASY PIECES

❻ MACH SCHAU AND THEY WILL KNOW US BY THE TRAIL OF DEAD from SECRET OF ELENA'S TOMB

❼ SHINE IT ON VERNON GARRETT from KENT'S CELLAR OF SOUL

❽ TOO CLOSE THE STAPLE SINGERS from GLORY! IT'S THE STAPLE SINGERS

❾ MATCH BOX BLUES BLIND LEMON JEFFERSON from CLASSIC BLUES

❿ THE SAME OLD ROCK ROY HARPER from STORMCOCK

Post-Zep solo

Robert Plant has spent much of his solo career denying the Zeppelin legacy and flirting with a variety of musical forms – anything but hard rock, in fact. Jimmy Page, on the other hand, remained an axe hero but failed to match the output of his former band. Until Page & Plant, that was.

❶ SHINE IT ALL AROUND ROBERT PLANT
from MIGHTY RE-ARRANGER
Plant gets just the right mix of Middle Eastern rhythms and dinosaur riffs on this; the various trance remixes are also worth checking out.

❷ SATISFACTION GUARANTEED THE FIRM from
THE FIRM
The combination of Page and ex-Free/Bad Co. singer Paul Rodgers in The Firm should have been a winner, but this gorgeous ballad proved a rare high point.

❸ ROCKIN AT MIDNITE THE HONEYDRIPPERS
from THE HONEYDRIPPERS VOL 1
And rock he (Plant) does, with guests Page, Beck et al. on his superb 50s big-band project.

❹ 50/50 STEPHEN STILLS from RIGHT BY YOU
Jimmy plays a blinder on this salsafied funk offering from Stephen Stills.

❺ WHO'S TO BLAME from DEATHWISH 2 SOUNDTRACK
Neighbour Michael Winner got Page to write him a soundtrack, and this track was the best part of it.

❻ LIFE BEGINS AGAIN ROBERT PLANT WITH AFRO-CELT
SOUNDSYSTEM from 66 TO TIMBUKTU
Tribal drumming, flutes and Plant's inimitable wailing. It could have been a mess, but instead is inspired.

❼ COLOURS OF A SHADE ROBERT PLANT from FATE OF
NATIONS
Plant in full rustic lyricism mode. File under folk-rock.

❽ DARKNESS DARKNESS ROBERT PLANT from
DREAMLAND
A haunting Jesse Colin Young number from Plant's collection of (mostly) 1960s covers.

❾ DON'T LEAVE ME THIS WAY DAVID COVERDALE AND
ROBERT PLANT from COVERDALE/PAGE
A rare return to the blues from this brief, and testoster-one-heavy, collaboration.

❿ ANNIVERSARY ROBERT PLANT from MANIC NIRVANA
Sounds more like the anniversary of a tragedy. Gut-wrenching guitar solo, too.

John Lennon

Poet, peace campaigner, visionary and inspiration to millions, Lennon's reputation currently lurks in the dark, hidden by the many hypocrisies of his life as a rich recluse. These titles from his solo career should help his rehabilitation.

❶ INSTANT KARMA from THE JOHN LENNON COLLECTION
One of the ex-Beatle's earliest solo outings, this shows him to be just as accomplished a master of pop as his erstwhile song-writing partner.

❷ AISUMASEN (I'M SORRY) from MIND GAMES
The best "Sorry, darling" song he ever wrote.

❸ WHATEVER GETS YOU THRU THE NIGHT from WALLS
AND BRIDGES
Upbeat ode to the delights of a chemical smile. This funky tune bounces along in a sunshine of its own making.

❹ NUMBER 9 DREAM from WALLS AND BRIDGES
Lennon explored the hidden crannies of falling and being in love with unique dedication, and continually found new ways to celebrate his emotional attach-ments and dependencies.

❺ MIND GAMES from MIND GAMES
Lennon's worship of Yoko formed the backbone of his solo career. This perceptive and gentle meditation on the peculiar telepathy of sweethearts is applicable to all who are truly in love.

❻ COLD TURKEY from LIVE PEACE IN TORONTO
Credited to the Plastic Ono Band, as Lennon tried to be just one of the guys in the group.

❼ WORKING CLASS HERO from JOHN LENNON/PLASTIC
ONO BAND
Bitter tears on the lyric sheet, blood on the guitar strings. Despite John's upwardly aspirational upbring-ing, he manages to bring a blood-curdling authenticity to this dark moment.

❽ GIMME SOME TRUTH from IMAGINE
With hardened attacks of barbed lyricism such as this to contend with, it's a wonder Nixon endured so long.

❾ I DON'T WANNA BE A SOLDIER from IMAGINE
This is one of his most powerful outings, and forms a major part of his legacy as a lasting campaign song for right-thinking peaceniks.

Chris Coe

❿ JUST LIKE STARTING OVER
from DOUBLE FANTASY
Proof that an honest, sincere love song is never embarrassing.

Al Spicer

The Libertines/ Babyshambles

The Libertines burnt bright as the partnership of Carl Barat and Pete Doherty. But Pete's pharmaceutical decline has produced scant pickings for Babyshambles.

THE LIBERTINES

❶ CAN'T STAND ME NOW from THE LIBERTINES
Remember the sadness of your first unrequited love, the shock of a best friend's betrayal? Three minutes of whining self-pity never sounded so good.

❷ WHAT BECAME OF THE LIKELY LADS
from THE LIBERTINES
If you can ignore that it's one of those "love you man!" songs born of hard drugs and alcohol, this is the best brotherhood song of the decade.

❸ DEATH ON THE STAIRS from UP THE BRACKET
One for all bands that have been knocked back by arrogant pieces of corporate ordure working in A&R.

❹ UP THE BRACKET from UP THE BRACKET
Ammunition for those in search of the next band to take over from The Clash. Fast, tighter than a snake's new skin and just as stylish.

❺ HORRORSHOW from UP THE BRACKET
The best song about using heroin since, well, "Heroin" by the Velvet Underground, with much more to offer than a tired "just say no". Suitably scruffy guitar work.

❻ I GET ALONG from UP THE BRACKET
Carl croons his way through this, slithering over the words like a debauched lizard on warm glass, paying no mind to the road-wreck guitar thrash that's piling up behind him.

❼ DON'T LOOK BACK INTO THE SUN
from THE LIBERTINES
Catchy, one might even say class A and addictive, this is the biggest hit the Libertines had.

❽ SKINT AND MINTED from DON'T LOOK BACK EP
Scrappy production and a less than totally focused performance give this demo a vintage psychedelic garage-rock sound.

PETE DOHERTY/BABYSHAMBLES

❾ FOR LOVERS WOLFMAN AND PETE DOHERTY from FOR LOVERS
Apparently scribbled down after a night of riotous crack-smoking this song is so tender and sweet that the royalties ought to provide a solid pension.

❿ KILLAMANGIRO BABYSHAMBLES from KILLAMANGIRO
This swaggers and sneers head and shoulders above the competition.

Al Spicer

Lighters in the air

The lights go down low and those first sweet'n'slow chords are met by a sea of cigarette lighters held aloft in salute. It's time for the big rawk ballad.

❶ EVERY ROSE HAS ITS THORN POISON
from OPEN UP AND SAY AHH!
If it's good enough to get Bill & Ted into heaven it's good enough for this list. Hair metallers take on the mantle of cowboy troubadours.

❷ HOME SWEET HOME MÖTLEY CRÜE
from THEATRE OF PAIN
Even sleazy glam-rockers get tired of life on the road. Great keyboards plus a massive swaying chorus and widdling guitar solo.

❸ I WANT TO KNOW WHAT LOVE IS FOREIGNER from AGENT PROVOCATEUR
Better fill up that Zippo. Lou Gramm needs a lesson in lurve, baby, and he's got a great big choir to back him up on this super-soft rocker.

❹ IS THIS LOVE WHITESNAKE from 1987
Here we have a pristine vocal and a chorus guaranteed to make the laydeez go weak at the knees.

❺ MORE THAN WORDS EXTREME from PORNOGRAFFITTI
So what if your mum knows all the words? You just can't beat clean vocal harmonies with a lilting acoustic accompaniment.

6 NEVER SAY GOODBYE BON JOVI
from SLIPPERY WHEN WET

Jon gets all misty-eyed and nostalgic. Richie Sambora's insistent and heartstring-tugging guitar refrain is the magic ingredient here.

7 NOTHING ELSE MATTERS METALLICA from METALLICA
Even real men need to get sensitive once in a while.

8 NOVEMBER RAIN GUNS N' ROSES
from USE YOUR ILLUSION I

The Gunners outdo themselves and everyone else. At nearly nine minutes in length, this has piano, violins, and enough guitar solos for at least three songs.

9 STILL LOVING YOU THE SCORPIONS
from LOVE AT FIRST STING

A textbook example of the classic rock-ballad: a slow build-up to a rousing and blisteringly melodic guitar-solo climax.

10 WHEN LOVE AND HATE COLLIDE DEF LEPPARD
from VAULT

Past masters of the smouldering slowie, the Leps pull out all the stops here. Just listen to those sugary strings and ultra-lush vocals.

Essi Berelian

Lit pop

When musicians exhaust the themes of love, hate, sadness and joy, a quick read of a novel or perhaps a slim volume of poetry can unleash the creative juices once more.

1 WUTHERING HEIGHTS KATE BUSH from THE KICK INSIDE

Kate Bush burst onto 1978's punk-dominated scene with this operatic retelling of Emily Brontë's only novel. No Eng Lit slouch, she went on to have a crack at Molly Bloom's soliloquy in *Ulysses* in "The Sensual World".

2 KILLING AN ARAB THE CURE from STANDING ON A BEACH STARING AT THE SEA

The band's 1978 debut single, this drew on a scene in Albert Camus' existentialist novel *L'Etranger*, when the hero commits an act of random murder. Misinterpreted by many poorly read DJs as racist, back then. Might be tricky to release nowadays.

3 NIETZSCHE THE DANDY WARHOLS from THIRTEEN TALES FROM URBAN BOHEMIA

A torpor-inducing wave of slacker psychedelia from Portland, Oregon's boho rockers. Singer and Nietzsche

fan Courtney Taylor-Taylor used a college bathroom graffito as the lyrics for this trippy My Bloody Valentine-esque dreamscape.

4 ALADDIN SANE DAVID BOWIE from ALADDIN SANE

Bowie came home from his first US tour by boat, and read Evelyn Waugh's *Vile Bodies* to keep amused. "Aladdin Sane" updates the "bright young things" with their "Battle cries and champagne just in time for sunrise" to the present day (1973).

5 I AM YOURS/LAYLA DEREK AND THE DOMINOS from LAYLA AND OTHER ASSORTED LOVE SONGS

Here's a top pub quiz question: which twelfth century Azerbaijani poet did Clapton share credits with on "I Am Yours"? The answer is Nizami, whose *The Legend of Layli and Majnun* provides the full text for that song, as well as the title for Derek's most famous number.

6 CALYPSO SUZANNE VEGA from SOLITUDE STANDING

The nymph from Homer's *Odyssey* mourns the departure of her captive of seven years through Vega's sympathetic lyrics and a suitably dreamy arrangement.

7 CEMETERY GATES THE SMITHS from THE QUEEN IS DEAD

The goldmine of literary references that pepper Morrissey's songwriting canon makes choosing a single example of his influences a tricky business. Here though, Wilde, Keats and Yeats sit alongside quotes from *Richard III* and *The Man Who Came To Dinner*. Moz's odd mispronunciation of "plagiarize" only adds to the track's witty tone.

8 SCENTLESS APPRENTICE NIRVANA from IN UTERO

Kurt Cobain's chilling refrain "go away, get away" forms the lasting impression here, inspired by Patrick Süskind's novel *Perfume*, which recounts the life of a Parisian orphan "blessed" with a preternaturally acute sense of smell.

9 LUCY THE DIVINE COMEDY from LIBERATION

Closing an album that mixes feelgood pop with songs inspired by Chekhov and F. Scott Fitzgerald, this abridged setting of Wordsworth's *Lucy Poems* to a lush, baroque arrangement is a perfect showcase for Neil Hannon's superlative musicianship.

10 RATTLESNAKES LLOYD COLE & THE COMMOTIONS from RATTLESNAKES

Dispensing witty, sardonic pop beloved of bedsit-bound students, this album resonates with lovelorn misery and socially perceptive vignettes. The song's narrative draws from two Joan Didion novels, dropping in Eve Marie-Saint and Simone de Beauvoir for good measure.

Ed Wright

Little Feat/Lowell George

Led by Lowell George, Little Feat were among the best American bands of the early 1970s. Commercial pressures, epic egos and drug abuse kicked in and George went solo only to die soon after in 1979.

LITTLE FEAT

❶ WILLIN' from SAILIN' SHOES
Country-flavoured ode to truckers who smuggle people and drugs and survive on "weed, whites and wine". Like Robbie Roberton, George was a gifted chronicler of Americana.

❷ EASY TO SLIP from SAILIN' SHOES
Producer Ted Templeman captures the huge electric rush of Little Feat as the band snort and roar while pulling out all kinds of rhythmic accents.

❸ COLD, COLD, COLD from SAILIN' SHOES
Lowell's slide guitar rips in this mid-tempo stomp that suggests Lowell was already too familiar with certain pharmaceuticals. Raw, dirty rock'n'roll.

❹ TROUBLE from SAILIN' SHOES
Reflective ballad full of everyday surrealism that marked Little Feat as a cut above other blues rockers.

❺ DIXIE CHICKEN from DIXIE CHICKEN
Hot white boy funk. Everyone's invited to the party.

❻ TWO TRAINS from DIXIE CHICKEN
Pulsing rock-soul smothered in layers of slide guitar that finds Lowell demonstrating a lyrical fatalism which now appears prescient.

❼ LONG DISTANCE LOVE from THE LAST RECORD ALBUM
George ranks as one of the best white soul singers and on this ode to the telephone blues he matches Bill Withers in conveying weary, literate R&B.

LOWELL GEORGE

❽ WHAT DO YOU WANT THE GIRL TO DO from THANKS I'LL EAT IT HERE
Swinging rendition of the Allen Toussaint song with Lowell delivering a remarkable vocal, all liquid phrasing and life affirming roars.

❾ EASY MONEY from THANKS I'LL EAT IT HERE
Lowell discovered Rickee Lee Jones when she was still strumming in coffee houses and recorded her great

boho-hipster song as a sparkling celebration of small time hustlers.

❿ FIND A RIVER from THANKS I'LL EAT IT HERE
Reflective ballad, beautifully sung, hints at impending doom and the potential George squandered.

Garth Cartwright

Little Richard

Richard Penniman –aka The Georgia Peach – was the original wildman of rock'n'roll. He cut his most memorable hits in late-1950s New Orleans. Since then he's gone through various religious conversions, employed Jimi Hendrix, influenced everyone from The Beatles to Prince, tried various comebacks and lived to talk and talk and talk about how he is and always was The King.

❶ TUTTI FRUTTI from THE ESSENTIAL LITTLE RICHARD
Richard cut this at his studio session for Specialty Records. Finding the blues too slow Richard started playing around with an obscene novelty song and, hey, a monster was born! Awopbopaloobopawambambam, indeed.

❷ LONG TALL SALLY from THE ESSENTIAL LITTLE RICHARD
Another innuendo laden celebration of a certain Sally who's "built for speed she got everything Uncle John need".

❸ SLIPPIN' AND A SLIDIN' from THE ESSENTIAL LITTLE RICHARD
Wonderful nonsense with a great, trilling "woo!" Listen to the band – Lee Allen and Alvin Tyler on saxophones, the great Earl Palmer on drums – blast!

❹ RIP IT UP from THE ESSENTIAL LITTLE RICHARD
Bob Dylan used to fib that he ran away from home to play piano for Little Richard. Listening to this amphetamine rush of sound one understands the homage.

❺ GOOD GOLLY MISS MOLLY from THE ESSENTIAL LITTLE RICHARD
Wild, slamming rock'n'roll about a certain Molly who "sure knows how to ball". Back in the 1950s most of Richard's audience surely thought this meant simple good times.

❻ LUCILLE from THE ESSENTIAL LITTLE RICHARD
The way Richard slides the syllables around and screams! No one else in popular music tore up language quite so completely.

❼ THE GIRL CAN'T HELP IT from THE ESSENTIAL LITTLE RICHARD

Written as the theme to the greatest 1950s rock movie, this song perfectly captures Jayne Mansfield's outsize and outlandish form.

❽ BAMA LAMA BAMA LOO from THE ESSENTIAL LITTLE RICHARD

Wonderful nonsense from 1964 when Richard was on the comeback trail.

❾ I DON'T KNOW WHAT YOU GOT BUT IT'S GOT ME from VEE JAY: CHICAGO HIT FACTORY

Mid-1960s Richard went to Vee Jay, the African American-owned Chicago soul and blues label and recorded this awesome soul ballad.

❿ GET DOWN WITH IT from THE EXPLOSIVE LITTLE RICHARD

Storming 1967 tune that's become a Northern Soul staple and was the blueprint for Slade's entire career.

Garth Cartwright

Tony Wheeler's
Lonely Planet

TONY WHEELER set up Lonely Planet with his wife Maureen in the early 1970s, fresh off the Southeast Asia hippy trail. They named the company after a (misheard) line from a Joe Cocker song. In a shock transfer to Rough Guides' music division, Tony has also contributed playlists on Paul Kelly, "On The Road" and "Put That Red Dress On". He says: "Lots of businesses seem to have a soundtrack: this is Lonely Planet's, including the song which gave us our name."

❶ WAKE UP SUNSHINE CHICAGO from CHICAGO

In 1971 when Maureen and I lived together in London this was the standard Sunday morning wake-up song; years later we used it on our kids.

❷ ABRAXAS SANTANA from ABRAXAS

When we followed the hippy trail through Afghanistan in 1972, Sigis was the place to eat on Chicken Street in Kabul and Santana's Abraxas was the background music of choice.

❸ EAGLE ROCK DADDY COOL from EAGLE ROCK

At the end of our 1972 Asia overland trip, we landed from a yacht on a west Australian beach and hitch-hiked across to Sydney with this Aussie anthem playing on every truck radio and pub jukebox.

❹ SPACE CAPTAIN JOE COCKER & LEON RUSSELL from MAD DOGS & ENGLISHMEN

In that classic rock-band-on-the-road film from the 1960s, Joe Cocker belts out the line that gave Lonely Planet its name. Except I misheard it.

❺ GOODBYE TIGER RICHARD CLAPTON from GOODBYE TIGER

Australia's pub-rock troubadour of the late 1970s came up with some classic Aussie standards, including this look back to those "dolce vita times".

❻ DR WU STEELY DAN from KATY LIED

During a year in San Francisco in the mid 1980s, Steely Dan was the music of choice, particularly on K-FOG, our favourite radio station.

❼ CONEY ISLAND VAN MORRISON from AVALON SUNSET

Maureen's a Belfast girl, and on a return trip in the early 1990s there was no better guide to Northern Ireland than Van the Man talking his way across the North.

❽ AICHA KHALED from AICHA

In 1996 we lived in Paris for a year and Khaled, the "King of Rai", crooning to "écoutez-moi" to Aicha was clearly the king of the Paris airwaves.

❾ PIU BELLA COSA EROS RAMOZZOTTI from PIU BELLA COSA

After years of Asian and developing-world travel we got back in Europe in the 1990s and one trip was backgrounded by this soaring number.

❿ LOVE IS EVERYTHING KD LANG from HYMNS OF THE 49TH PARALLEL

kd lang positively breaks hearts with this Jane Silbery tearjerker.

London is the place for me

Tourist brochures and picture postcards present a rose-tinted view of life in the big smoke, but songwriters invariably lay bare the bones of the city they call home. These insider snapshots give you a lifetime's worth of London highs and lows, and all in just a few short minutes.

❶ THE GUNS OF BRIXTON THE CLASH
from LONDON CALLING
From a seminal album that embraced rock, punk, ska and reggae, The Clash hammered their right-on politics onto skanking beats for this raw, Jamaican-filtered scowl at authority.

❷ TWENTY-FOUR MINUTES FROM TULSE HILL
CARTER USM from 101 DAMNATIONS
From Carter's debut album, Jim Bob and Fruitbat aim their south-of-the-river bombast at public transport – a whistle-stop tour of the highs and lows of their local train service.

❸ DON'T GO BACK TO DALSTON RAZORLIGHT from
UP ALL NIGHT
If the rumours about its inspiration are true, Londoner Johnny Borrell was just urging a rock-star friend to clean up his life.

❹ WATERLOO SUNSET THE KINKS
from SOMETHING ELSE BY THE KINKS
Like a diary extract, Ray Davies's musings seem almost too personal for public consumption as they describe life viewed from afar, beyond his bedroom window.

❺ PRIMROSE HILL LOUDON WAINWRIGHT III
from LITTLE SHIP
Ever the witty social observer, compassionate folkster Wainwright imagines life as a Tennants-swigging tramp in posh north London.

❻ WEREWOLVES OF LONDON WARREN ZEVON from
EXCITABLE BOY
Zevon's mischievous wordplay elevated his status among American singer-songwriters. If the opening verse doesn't draw you in, the lupine howling will.

❼ A RAINY NIGHT IN SOHO THE POGUES
from THE ULTIMATE COLLECTION
The Irish folk-rockers' main man Shane MacGowan penned a clutch of London songs, but this dreamy ballad is the best of them.

❽ DOWN IN THE TUBE STATION AT MIDNIGHT THE
JAM from ALL MOD CONS
The urgent music is set against tube trains in motion, with the song's tempo changing accordingly, ratcheting the tension further.

❾ MILE END PULP from TRAINSPOTTING
A vital contribution to the sound of *Trainspotting*, this fusion of jangly, upbeat rhythms and tales of bedsit squalor is the ideal song to accompany student life.

❿ PLAISTOW PATRICIA IAN DURY
from NEW BOOTS AND PANTIES
Dury recounts a sad but spirited account of the eponymous junkie and her riotous behaviour. Outrageous, knees-up rocking at its best.

Ed Wright

Love

Achingly pretty folk-rock-psychedelia with a bitter lemon twist, usually though not always from the pen of leader Arthur Lee.

❶ ALONE AGAIN OR from FOREVER CHANGES
Second banana Bryan Maclean's shining moment in Love was also their best track, mixing flamenco, mariachi horns, soaring strings and quavering doubt.

❷ SHE COMES IN COLORS from DA CAPO
Jubilant jazzy folk-rock, its title often rumoured to have been lifted by The Rolling Stones for "She's A Rainbow".

❸ 7 AND 7 IS from DA CAPO
1960s garage rock at its punkiest, powered by nonstop drum rolls, jaws-of-doom guitar chords, and a simulated nuclear explosion.

❹ MY LITTLE RED BOOK from LOVE
Another glorious venting of Love's tougher side – who could believe it was a cover of a Bacharach/David song?

❺ ANDMOREAGAIN from FOREVER CHANGES
Exhibit A in the unsurpassed blend of acoustic guitars, violins and inscrutable lyrics that typified the classic *Forever Changes* album.

❻ THE GOOD HUMOR MAN HE SEES EVERYTHING LIKE THIS from FOREVER CHANGES
Another string-heavy *Forever Changes* ballad that lulls you into bliss.

❼ MAYBE THE PEOPLE WOULD BE THE TIMES OR BETWEEN CLARK AND HILLDALE from FOREVER CHANGES

A kaleidoscopic hot smoggy look down Sunset Boulevard in 1967, set to a psychedelic bossa-nova beat.

❽ STEPHANIE KNOWS WHO from DA CAPO

Wild free jazz meets garage rock, barked out with the ludicrous bravado of a man who knows where he's going even if we don't.

❾ MUSHROOM CLOUDS from LOVE

Devastatingly sad acoustic lament of nuclear holocaust that never makes Love collections.

❿ LIVE AND LET LIVE from LOVE

An amazingly intelligent, probing rock song, considering it begins with the narrator watching snot caking on his pants.

Richie Unterberger

Cheesy love songs

Popular music is designed to excite and please. The last time you fell crazy in love with someone, did you sit around staring out windows at sunsets across a windy moor, or did you dance around like a nong with a stupid grin on your face? Pop songs are like a musical distillation of emotion and mood. Here are ten that cut the mustard, and don't stint on the cheese...

❶ THIS WILL BE (AN EVERLASTING LOVE)
NATALIE COLE from GREATEST HITS VOL 1

That constant "boing" sound is like an aural representation of the lump you get in your throat when you're waiting outside the cinema theatre café for your third date, by which time you suspect that you could very well be onto a good thing.

❷ ALWAYS ON MY MIND THE PET SHOP BOYS from INTROSPECTIVE

Hi-NRG drum machines and synthesized orchestral bursts serve to make this version of "You Are Always On My Mind" more yearning, more desperate. Even without Neil Tennant's heart-string-tuggin' vocal...

❸ COME ON OVER ALL I WANT IS YOU CHRISTINA AGUILERA from CHRISTINA AGUILERA

To paraphrase Bill & Ted's Rufus, this song is excellent for, er, dancing around the bedroom in your underwear spraying perfume on every inch of exposed skin. Can't speak for the boys, of course...

❹ GET USED TO IT ROGER VOUDOURIS from RADIO DREAM

Voudouris' slightly cranky delivery gets you every time; offering crumbs of ecstasy with his clipped vocal, but then – oh! – here comes the middle eight, where he lets himself go, but then corrects himself again – it's pure nervous energy!

❺ WHAT U DO 2 ME BOOMKAT from BOOMKATALOG 1

When Taryn Manning harrumpfs "where are you from?" it perfectly captures that rather unfortunate mating phenomenon where you're trying to be cool but just end up grumpy.

❻ MY CHERIE AMOUR STEVIE WONDER from MY CHERIE AMOUR

You know that slightly seasick feeling you get somewhere between your throat and your stomach in the early stages of an affair? Cue the string section.

❼ LOVIN' EACH DAY RONAN KEATING from 10 YEARS OF HITS

Much like Natalie Cole's "This Will Be" and its swooning djembe, Ronan's "Lovin' Each Day" gets the vote for the thumping bass drum during the bridge and chorus: "I want you right here next to me – BOOM! BOOM! BOOM!" It's like some hyper-tuned heartbeat pumping away, post first kiss.

❽ LOVE IS IN THE AIR (BALLROOM MIX)
JOHN PAUL YOUNG from STRICTLY BALLROOM OST

Kind of like a non-threatening "I Feel Love", John Paul Young's Vanda and Young swansong works its magic by weaving an almost trancelike spell around the listener, with a disco beat mirroring an excited heart-rate before the whole thing explodes in one fabulous climax of gospel choirs, handclaps and orchestral flourishes.

❾ LOVE IS ALL AROUND WET WET WET from FOUR WEDDINGS AND A FUNERAL OST

When you're in love, it is written in the wind and everywhere you go – how many times, during the first throes of love, have you been told to "snap out of it"? All together now: "So if you really love me", – "LOVE ME!!" – "LO-OH-URVE MEH!" – "Come ooooon and let it show!" Of course – you even know the harmonies.

❿ LOVE AT FIRST SIGHT KYLIE MINOGUE from FEVER

If there is a more perfect melding of title, sentiment and sound than this song, I'd like to hear it. "Love At First Sight" is, well, love at first sight, distilled to ten or so notes and a bunch of vocal trills. It's that giddy, dorky, excited feeling, caught on tape. Whee!

Clem Bastow

Love and marriage

There are love songs and cheating songs aplenty. Rarer are the tracks that deal with the state in between. Maybe it's just not rock'n'roll. Still, here are the candidates.

❶ SAGINAW, MICHIGAN LEFTY FRIZELL
from THE BEST OF LEFTY FRIZELL
A disapproving father gets his comeuppance from his street-smart, love-struck son-in-law, sung with a wink by one of country's best crooners.

❷ WOULDN'T IT BE NICE BEACH BOYS from PET SOUNDS
With their high, pitch-perfect harmonies, The Beach Boys wax wistful on the greatest ever album's catchy, layered opening track.

❸ LOVE AND MARRIAGE FRANK SINATRA
from THE VERY BEST OF
Sinatra's songs are such a part of pop culture now that it's hard to think of them just as the well-orchestrated musical pieces they are, replete with big band and that suave, velvet voice.

❹ SOMETHING TO BRAG ABOUT GEORGE JONES & TAMMY WYNETTE from SOMETHING TO BRAG ABOUT
You don't need much if you've got love. Here's Tammy and George in their happier days, before the loving stopped. Jones's voice is young and pliable, his range open and wide; Wynette is a milkshake of sass and grace.

❺ I KNEW THE BRIDE (WHEN SHE USED TO ROCK 'N' ROLL) NICK LOWE from BASHER: THE BEST OF
A great marriage song for realists and rockers, "I Knew The Bride" begins with a churchy intro and then amps it up.

❻ YOU NEVER CAN TELL CHUCK BERRY
from CHUCK BERRY: SAINT LOUIS TO LIVERPOOL
Rollicking piano accents this song, used in a dance scene in the 1994 film *Pulp Fiction*.

❼ TAKE ME BACK TO TULSA BOB WILLS
from TAKE ME BACK TO TULSA
The fiddle has a voice of its own in this upbeat tune about running from the altar. Western swing, sweet and neat.

❽ LET'S GET MARRIED AL GREEN from IMMORTAL SOUL
Punctuated by organ blasts, Green's singing is soulful and smooth. And when he's done belting it out, the Reverend can always perform the nuptials.

❾ BIG BAD BILL (IS SWEET WILLIAM NOW) LEON REDBONE from CHAMPAGNE CHARLIE
Recorded in the late 1970s but evoking a long-ago night club – the kind with "stardust" in the title – Redbone's baritone wraps you up warmer than your grandmother's mink.

❿ TWO SLEEPY PEOPLE FATS WALLER
from THE VERY BEST OF
With a playful, raspy voice that sounds at times like a muted trumpet, Waller sets an intimate mood as he tickles the ivories and sings about being too in love to fall asleep.

Madelyn Rosenberg

Lovers rock

This UK-originated reggae phenomena – lightweight tunes, lyrics about love sung (largely) for teenage girls by teenage girls – was so huge and so deep underground, records regularly sold hundreds of thousands yet rarely troubled the mainstream charts.

❶ SILLY GAMES JANET KAY from REGGAE LOVE SONGS
A UK #2 pop hit and the genre's biggest success story. The teenage Janet had to get time off work to go on *Top of The Pops*.

❷ SLACKS AND SOVEREIGNS VICTOR ROMERO EVANS 12 INCH SINGLE
Janet Kay's husband with a typical boys' song – whereas the ladies sung of heartbreak, the lads' lyrics mostly centred on how cool they were.

❸ CAUGHT YOU IN A LIE LOUISA MARK from LOVERS ROCK SERIOUS SELECTIONS VOL 1
Lousia Mark was 15 when she cut this very early lovers rock tune in 1975 and set the precedent for the genre.

❹ I'M IN LOVE WITH A DREADLOCKS BROWN SUGAR from THE LOVERS ROCK STORY VOL 1
This tale of forbidden love – dreads were the lowest form of life to respectable immigrant families – found huge favour among the lovers rock audience.

❺ AFTER TONIGHT MATUMBI from MUSIC IN THE AIR: ANTHOLOGY
Matumbi"'s front man Dennis Bovell has been credited with inventing lovers rock and his productions for his own band always had an added depth.

6 WIDE AWAKE IN A DREAM BARRY BIGGS from THE
BEST OF BARRY BIGGS

Synth-laden, horn-laced and getting busy with the
echo chamber this was something of a sophistication
bench mark, and fell just short of being a pop hit.

7 I'M SO SORRY CARROLL THOMPSON from
HOPELESSLY IN LOVE

Even as an adolescent Carroll T was musically astute
and golden of voice, hence she was always a step
ahead of her competition and remains the Queen of
Lovers Rock.

8 BLACK SKIN BOY 15, 16, 17 from 7 INCH SINGLE

As an underground black pop style, racial identity
always figured high on the agenda, this became a sound
system classic. The trio's name refers to their ages.

9 IF YOU'RE NOT BACK IN LOVE BY MONDAY
CASSANDRA from THE LOVERS GUIDE TO REGGAE

Although throwaway this tune was an enormous
sound system hit, thanks mostly to Cassandra's
seductive (ie more grown-up sounding) tones.

10 NATTY DREAD A WEH SHE WANT HORACE ANDY from
SKYLARKING: THE BEST OF HORACE ANDY

Horace's featherlight touch made him a lovers rock
natural, and this particular tune always brought a
rousing chorus from the chaps in the dancehall.

Lloyd Bradley

Loretta Lynn

The coal miner's daughter initially knew only
poverty and pregnancy – she had four children
by the age of 18. But her determination to write
and sing saw her become the most original yet
down-home female country star. Recently revived
by Jack White, Lynn's most magical recordings
remain her 1960s and 70s hits.

1 COAL MINER'S DAUGHTER from THE VERY BEST

Autobiographical 1969 hit about growing up in
Depression-era poverty. Yet instead of whining this is
a tale of pride.

**2 DON'T COME HOME A DRINKIN' WITH LOVIN' ON
YOUR MIND** from THE VERY BEST

Lynn provided a straightforward and eloquent
feminism for working class American women. They
responded in kind as this, her first country #1 in 1966,
proves.

3 WOMAN OF THE WORLD LEAVE MY MAN ALONE
from THE VERY BEST

Loretta tells those big city hussies to leave her simple
farm boy alone.

4 THE PILL from THE VERY BEST

A feisty answer record of sorts to Tammy Wynette's
"Stand By Your Man" with Loretta stating that she can
enjoy life now her husband can't keep her barefoot
and pregnant. Banned by many radio stations at
the time.

5 YOUR SQUAW IS ON THE WARPATH from
THE VERY BEST

Raging slice of honky tonk female rage.

6 FIST CITY from THE VERY BEST

Loretta warns a love rival that she will be eating
knuckle sandwiches if she keeps chasing Mr Lynn.

7 AFTER THE FIRE IS GONE WITH CONWAY TWITTY
from THE VERY BEST

Loretta and Conway cut many fine duets; this hymn to
the fag end of a relationship is one of the best.

8 OUT OF MY HEAD AND BACK IN MY BED from THE
VERY BEST

Loretta celebrates sexual pleasure. Only problem, her
husband is out boozing somewhere.

9 YOU'RE LOOKING AT COUNTRY from THE VERY BEST

A defiant statement of roots with Lynn noting that
she'll walk a country mile to find a good ole country
boy.

10 HEY LORETTA from THE VERY BEST

Loretta tells her no-good husband she works her
fingers to the bone yet only gets a little kiss every
week.

Garth Cartwright

⑨ ALLAH ADDU JAM
from MISSING YOU (MI YEEWNII)

Mesmerizing electric hoddu, an extraordinary vocal and some hardcore percussion animate the closing track on this marvellously atmospheric return-to-roots album.

Jon Lusk

Baaba Maal

Always dressed to kill, Baaba Maal possesses the most startling voice. Thanks to his songwriting talent and strong social conscience, he has long been an unofficial ambassador for Senegal, and in particular the Pulaar culture it shares with neighbouring Mauretania.

① MUUDO HORMO from DJAM LEELII
A pulsing, starkly atmospheric piece from the "nearly lost" album Baaba made with friend and long-term collaborator Mansour Seck.

② WANGO ARTI from THE BEST OF THE EARLY YEARS
Seriously cutting cross-rhythms and a restless groove on this poppy electric *mbalax* outing. The title means "Tribal Dance Comeback".

③ BOUYEL from BAAYO
Finger-snapping simplicity and a joyous vibe. This is one of several great songs on Baaba's seriously beautiful 1991 acoustic roots album.

④ DANIIBE from LAM TORO
Despite the language barrier, Baaba's compelling skills as a storyteller are very much in evidence here.

⑤ TABAKALY from N'DER FOUTA TOORO VOL 1
A long, meditative song, with just the tiny banjo-like hoddu for accompaniment.

⑥ AFRICAN WOMAN from FIRIN' IN FOUTA
Latin music is big in Senegal, as this celebration of African womanhood attests.

⑦ MINUIT ERNEST RANGLIN from IN SEARCH OF THE LOST RIDDIM
A gorgeously flowing electro-acoustic treat.

⑧ TROUBLE SLEEP from RED HOT & RIOT
An example of Baaba's AIDS campaigning, recorded for a Fela Kuti tribute album with Antibalas, Taj Mahal and on kora the late Kauding Cissoko.

Kirsty MacColl

One of Britain's best-loved female songsmiths, who collaborated with an extraordinary range of artists before she was killed in a boating accident in 2000. This pick celebrates that variety.

① A NEW ENGLAND from GALORE
Kirsty's take on Billy Bragg's classic gives a poignancy to this tale of a twentysomething's love trysts.

② WALKING DOWN MADISON from ELECTRIC LANDLADY
Gloriously bassy and energetic, this collaboration with former Smiths' frontman Johnny Marr even includes a rap.

③ FREE WORLD from KITE
A bustling, purposeful song that bristles with MacColl's genius. Makes you smile.

④ DAYS from KITE
Covering Ray Davies' saga of life's ups and downs, KIrsty reveals her rich vocal range.

⑤ THEY DON'T KNOW ABOUT US from GALORE
A typically upbeat account of the strifes of love from the early years.

⑥ MY AFFAIR from ELECTRIC LANDLADY
Samba beat, soaring strings, parping brass and Kirsty's mellifluous tones. A divine mix.

⑦ THERE'S A GUY WORKS DOWN THE CHIP SHOP SWEARS HE'S ELVIS from WHAT DO PRETTY GIRLS DO?
Do lyrics get any madder than this? Brings country-music twang to the chippy.

⑧ FAIRYTALE OF NEW YORK from GALORE
Kirsty's lasting legacy will be this Irish-spiced duet with the Pogues' frontman Shane McGowan. Forever Christmas, with rich MacGowan grit and MacColl spring.

Tim Pollard

Madagascar

Not just a location for Hollywood cartoons and habitat for cute furry primates, the huge Indian Ocean island of Madagascar oozes diverse musical cultures and classy performers like few other places on earth.

❶ TSY ZANAKRA MPANARIVO JAOJOBY from MALAGASY
The omnipresent electric music of the northern regions is the driving, skittering 6/8 *salegy*. Its undisputed kings are Jaojoby and his band – one of the world's greatest dance machines.

❷ KOBA TARIKA from SOUL MAKASSAR
Nominated by *Time* magazine as one of the ten best bands in the world, Tarika's high-energy acoustic pop uses most of the island's traditional instruments and inspired harmonies.

❸ ZAZA SOMONDRARA D'GARY from AKATO MESO
Fearsomely talented acoustic guitarist who's up there with anybody that nearby Africa – a continent of guitar heroes – can throw at you.

❹ RAMANJAREO (NY ANY AMINAY) RAKOTOZAFY from VALIHA MALAZA
Late, legendary and influential virtuoso player of the *marovany*, Madagascar's double-sided box zither Rakotozafy has been called the Robert Johnson of Madagascar.

❺ MIERITRERETA RASOA KININIKE from MOLIA RIHA CHERIE
In the deep southwest, the local music is a pumped-up groove called *tsapiky*, full of startling guitars and full-scream, uninhibited arse-rotating singers like the fabulous Rasoa.

❻ FOKAFOKA NY ANTSALY from FOLKLORE DE MADAGASCAR
In the 1950s, this trio led by *valiha* (bamboo-tube zither) master Sylvestre Randafison were the first group to tour extensively abroad.

❼ EKA LAHY REGIS GIZAVO from SAMY OLOMBELO
Regis Gizavo plays a massive button accordeon like it's the simplest instrument on earth. Highly in demand as a session player in France, he is also a sensational live soloist.

❽ TADIDIKO RY ZALAHY MAHALEO from TADIDIKO
An iconic band in the local student upheavals of the 1970s, thirty years on the Beatles of Madagascar are now doctors and parliamentary deputies, but they can still fill stadiums with their anthemic songs.

❾ ERA VAKOKA from INTRODUCING VAKOKA
Not an artist, but a project in which many of the island's current roots musicians workshopped together to produce an inspiringly unified album of the same name.

❿ ZAMAGILA SOLOMIRAL from GASIKARA
This band of brothers call their music *vakojazzana* – a fusion of *vakodrazana* traditional music and jazz.

Ian Anderson

Madness

Rarely out of the UK singles charts or off *Top Of The Pops* during the 1980s, the Nutty Boys were the epitome of ska-tastic pop brilliance.

❶ BAGGY TROUSERS from ABSOLUTELY
Superb lyrics, lashings of bonkers sax and terrific plinky-plonk piano (to use the technical expression) equals a total pop classic.

❷ CARDIAC ARREST from SEVEN
Having the old ticker pack up never sounded quite so enjoyable. The jaunty tune belies the everyday sadness of the lyrics.

❸ DAY ON THE TOWN from SEVEN
Eating chips and fare-dodging with the lads. This features a neat reggae swagger, some cool percussion and an ironic lyrical twist.

❹ HOUSE OF FUN from COMPLETE MADNESS
A fantastic coming-of-age comedy, but a warning lurks beneath the laughs. The swirling fairground-style keyboards are superb.

❺ IN THE MIDDLE OF THE NIGHT from ONE STEP BEYOND
A naughty little tune about a saucy night-time knicker thief. Wonder if he's mates with Pink Floyd's Arnold Lane?

❻ MY GIRL from ONE STEP BEYOND
Hell hath no fury and all that. Written very much in the style of Ian Dury, Suggs plays the poor Everyman suffering woman trouble.

❼ NEW DELHI from THE RISE AND FALL
An unusual tune conjuring up the oppressive heat of India through weird travelogue-style lyrics…or is it all just a feverish delusion?

❽ NIGHT BOAT TO CAIRO from ONE STEP BEYOND
A long instrumental intro and plenty of parping sax. Exactly the kind of insistent Madness tune that demands serious dancefloor action.

❾ OUR HOUSE from THE RISE AND FALL
Shamelessly nostalgic and evocative, this is a fantastic slice-of-life tune, with a great vid too.

❿ YESTERDAY'S MEN from MAD NOT MAD
Madness did melancholy exceedingly well, and the low-key sax and resigned vocals make them sound suitably world-weary.

Essi Berelian

Madonna

The ever-provocative entertainer was never much of an album producer; most of her best songs were singles. But what singles they were – if they don't make you shut up and dance, little will.

❶ BURNING UP from MADONNA
The most worthy relic from her early, bubble-gum dance period, with a funky, percolating bassline and a convincingly uncoy lyric.

❷ OPEN YOUR HEART from TRUE BLUE
An utterly perfect pop confection, built on a joyous, horn-inflected chorus.

❸ LIKE A PRAYER from LIKE A PRAYER
The gospel-choir backing vocals, the spiritual lyrics, the controversial video – Madonna reaches her dance-pop apotheosis.

❹ LIVE TO TELL from TRUE BLUE
Her dramatic chops were put to better use on this powerful ballad than any piece of celluloid she's ever made: a huge leap in vocal maturity.

❺ RAY OF LIGHT from RAY OF LIGHT
On this spirited, swirling track. Madonna successfully catches up to electronica with the help of William Orbit; she hits high notes too.

❻ MATERIAL GIRL from LIKE A VIRGIN
Maybe not her defining musical moment, but ingratiating good fun nonetheless – and who can forget the Marilyn-inspired video?

❼ INTO THE GROOVE from THE IMMACULATE COLLECTION
Quintessential Madonna – a great beat with a lyric basically about enjoying a great beat. It's best to seek out the CD single, which has the uncut version in its full glory.

❽ DON'T TELL ME from MUSIC
An unlikely marriage of sounds and style: lyric borrowed from her brother-in-law Joe Henry (off a vaguely Tom Waits-like song), built over a stuttering, electro-countrified riff.

❾ SECRET from BEDTIME STORIES
As stealthy as its title, this seductively mellow groove wants to worm its way off your headset and into your bedroom.

❿ MUSIC from MUSIC
The kind of celebratory, anthemic sing-along that she just keeps one-upping herself at; Madonna has rarely sounded so sure of her place in the pantheon.

Andrew Rosenberg

Male frailty

A man who lets his sensitive side show is to be admired – but one that sings about it from centre stage? That's to be celebrated! Here are ten great moments when big boys did cry.

❶ MISSING YOU JOHN WAITE from THE COMPLETE JOHN WAITE
Sometime Bad English vocalist Waite almost lets his true feelings show, then attempts to rein it all back in with flashes of stadium rock machismo. It doesn't work; by the end of the song we know very well that he is missing his paramour.

❷ HAND IT OVER CHUCK JACKSON from THE VERY BEST OF CHUCK JACKSON 1961–1967
Not since "Ain't Too Proud To Beg" has a Motown track offered a male vocalist's heart as shamelessly as Chuck Jackson does here; he even needs to ask if his love needs "my arms around you every night."

❸ JEALOUS GUY ROXY MUSIC from STREET LIFE
Recorded in the wake of John Lennon's murder (and with Bryan Ferry presumably still smarting over Jerry Hall leaving him for Mick Jagger in 1977), Ferry's wavering vocal – and, yes, that whistling solo – makes this the definitively heart-rending version.

❹ SO INTO YOU FABOLOUS from SO INTO YOU
Even if he rationalizes his relationship pros for most of this slinky R&B jam, when Fabolous casually asks "How'd you like it If both of our names had Jackson on the end?" you know just how really Into you he is.

❺ WAITING FOR A GIRL LIKE YOU FOREIGNER from DEFINITIVE COLLECTION

The Darkness' Justin Hawkins says Lou Gramm's "A Girl Like You" vocal makes him "weep like a child" – that's if Gramm himself wasn't already sobbing through lines like "This heart of mine has been hurt before…"

❻ SECOND CHOICE ANY TROUBLE from WHERE ARE ALL THE NICE GIRLS?

Any Trouble might've been wondering where the nice girls were in 1980, but it seems the nice boys were happy to just come… second.

❼ IN YOUR EYES PETER GABRIEL from SO

If the line "I get so lost sometimes" doesn't set your heart a-melting, just remember John Cusack in *Say Anything*, using "In Your Eyes" as a last ditch effort to snare Ione Skye – that oughtta do it.

❽ LOVE FOR GRANTED PHOENIX from ALPHABETICAL

The slightly robotic choir of male voices that caress Thomas Mars' lead vocal makes "Love…" a beautifully lonely affair, especially when he begs to "Hang on to a little chance".

❾ SHE IS BEAUTIFUL ANDREW W.K. from I GET WET

He might be shouting, but Andrew Wilkes Krier is really a big softy. All the devils' horns thrown throughout this song are just masking his hand-wringing about how to ask out a particularly beautiful girl.

❿ TELEPHONE LINE ELO from A NEW WORLD RECORD

Imagine that Jeff Lynne is pouring his heart out into an answering machine rather than a sympathetic ear, the sob-rating of "Telephone Line" is increased tenfold.

Clem Bastow

Now that's what I call Mali

Mali has an ancient musical culture, which owes much to its extraordinary Mande Empire, founded eight hundred years ago. Passed down by generations of griots (members of the traditional musicians' caste), it hosts Africa's "classical music" – intricate songs accompanied on the sitar-like kora – and some red-hot rock'n'roll.

❶ MANDJOU AMBASSADEURS INTERNATIONAL WITH SALIF KEITA from THE MANSA OF MALI

An epic, meandering praise song – the most iconic of Salif Keita's early career. This original 1978 recording

was made along with the rest of the album in two hours of stolen studio time. Crime really does pay.

❷ MALIYO SUPER RAIL BAND DU BAMAKO from NEW DIMENSIONS IN RAIL CULTURE

A wonderfully dreamy, meditative cut from their stunning 1982 album, featuring vocals by Lafia Diabaté and the inimitable guitar of Djelimady Tounkara.

❸ SENE ADAMA DIABATÉ from JAKO BAYE

This gorgeous, bouncy track features gutsy griot vocals, sublime *n'goni* playing by husband Makan Tounkara, and spectacular tempo changes.

❹ MOUSSOULOU OUMOU SANGARÉ from MOUSSOULOU

Hair-raising stuff from the groundbreaking 1990 debut by the "Songbird of Wassoulou". The hypnotic, loping rhythm and her soaring voice make for a high goose-pimple rating.

❺ BENIDIAGNAMOGO BOUBACAR TRAORÉ from SAHARA: BLUES OF THE DESERT

Bewitching acoustic guitar and a searing vocal on an intensely melancholic song by one of the country's most celebrated and long-serving artists.

❻ HAWA DOLO ALI FARKA TOURÉ from THE SOURCE

Mali's leading sorcerer of the guitar at his most gentle, playing an acoustic instrument, accompanied only by sympathetic percussion and backing vocals.

❼ SUPER 11 TAKAMBA SUPER ONZE from FESTIVAL IN THE DESERT 2003

Don't even try counting the crossrhythms on this passionate and mesmerizing slice of desert blues! Recorded live, not very far from Timbuktu.

❽ LA RÉALITÉ AMADOU & MARIAM from DIMANCHE À BAMAKO

The blues-rocking duo from Bamako get a fairydust turbo-charge courtesy of Manu Chao on this driving number from their hugely successful collaboration.

❾ NANGA MADY KÉLÉTIGUI DIABATÉ from SANDIYA

Having contributed so much to albums made by other musicians, Mali's most in-demand player of the *balafon* (wooden xylophone) calls in a favour or two on his own – in this case a sparkling performance by guest kora virtuoso Toumani Diabaté.

❿ NAWEYE TORO ALI FARKA TOURÉ AND TOUMANI DIABATÉ from IN THE HEART OF THE MOON

Two geniuses for the price of one on this sublime pulsing duet between kora and guitar. Music to drift down a river to.

Jon Lusk

Manchester: a lot to answer for

There's a well-balanced feel to Manchester bands; buffeted by the weather and by competition from Britain's other great metropolises, they tend to come with a chip on each shoulder. It gives them a fine swaggering attitude – all sneer and "prove it then!".

❶ PSYKICK DANCEHALL THE FALL from DRAGNET
One of the highlights of Salford Council's bus tour celebrating The Fall is visiting the actual Psykick Dancehall of the title. A busy, clanging, glamorous mass of music.

❷ HAND IN GLOVE THE SMITHS from HATFUL OF HOLLOW
With lyrics that include "the sun shines out of our behinds", this Morrissey number could have been born only in Manc.

❸ FRIENDS OF MINE BUZZCOCKS from SPIRAL SCRATCH
Howard Devoto and Pete Shelley emerged from the city's community of art students, documenting some of the peculiarly Manc tastes for excess in this amphetamine grinder.

❹ ROCK 'N' ROLL STAR OASIS from DEFINITELY MAYBE
Rather than pass the traditional torch from one generation to the next, in Manchester the sun sets in one bottom to dawn anew, shining from yet another backside, the next day.

❺ INTERZONE JOY DIVISION from UNKNOWN PLEASURES
An eerie tale lined with hidden menace as our protagonist scoots round the city's meaner streets, on foot and vulnerable.

❻ BYE BYE BADMAN THE STONE ROSES from THE STONE ROSES
Hidden within one of the Roses' finest songs is a lyric of stone-throwing, street-fighting rebellion Every city boasts its crew of such kids, and this is the anthem for the Manc chapter.

❼ GOD'S COP HAPPY MONDAYS from PILLS 'N' THRILLS AND BELLYACHES
Chief Constable Anderton had it coming. He claimed biblical authority for assertions like "gays are swilling around in a cesspool of their own making". They don't make chiefs like that any more, nor these sublime ecstatic grooves.

❽ GETTING AWAY WITH IT JAMES from THE COLLECTION
Scamming the system, working for cash in hand, and spending the dough on messing up your brain are traits perfectly celebrated in Manc music.

❾ BEAST INSIDE INSPIRAL CARPETS from THE BEAST INSIDE
Dark, cold and miserable as a Tuesday night in November, the Carpets waltz gloomily through an elegant little ditty of betrayal and love.

❿ SHADOWS OF SALFORD DOVES from SOME CITIES
To the accompaniment of a rickety pub piano, and an almost angelic chorus of backing vocals, Jimi Goodwin provides the perfect tune for sunset over the post-industrial wasteland.

Al Spicer

Manic Street Preachers

Welsh agit-rockers, provocative punk terrorists, poly-decibel polemicists, call 'em what you will – so long as you realize they're "4 Real" (as legendary missing guitarist Richey Edwards once carved on his arm with a razor).

❶ A DESIGN FOR LIFE from EVERYTHING MUST GO
Personal in content but grand and vast in execution, this is widescreen rock at its best, and the lone drums ending is genius.

❷ FASTER from THE HOLY BIBLE
This song simply rages, vocalist James Dean Bradfield sounding weirdly Dalek-like on the opening lines.

❸ FOUND THAT SOUL from KNOW YOUR ENEMY
On this raw and emotionally driven rocker, a piano is hammered to matchwood beneath the main riff – and the guitar solo is a ripper.

❹ IF YOU TOLERATE THIS YOUR CHILDREN WILL BE NEXT from THIS IS MY TRUTH TELL ME YOURS
Slow but majestic. Throw in lyrics you can actually sing and some seriously swooping strings, and you have a big hit single.

❺ INTRAVENOUS AGNOSTIC from KNOW YOUR ENEMY
The verses sound almost polite before turbulent layers of squalling, thrashing guitars punch you in the gut. A gloriously messy track.

6 THE MASSES AGAINST THE CLASSES from FOREVER DELAYED

Starts off like something by The Monkees before blazing into life with distorted vocals and unleashing a thousand guitars.

7 PCP from THE HOLY BIBLE

A cool post-punk influence pervades this relentless political onslaught. Frantic from first to last.

8 REPEAT (UK) from GENERATION TERRORISTS

A real chant-along sloganeering rocker, absolutely guaranteed to offend readers of the *Daily Mail*, and a cool guitar solo to boot.

9 YOU LOVE US from GENERATION TERRORISTS

The politics of the rock'n'roll spectacle laid bare. A great riff and even greater solos, topped off with a major shift up the gears.

10 YOUR LOVE ALONE IS NOT ENOUGH from SEND AWAY THE TIGERS

With Cardigans singer Nina Persson, the Manics roar back into the stadium-rock arena like they own the place. Blood-engorged vocal cords from the Welsh mob go head to head with the open throated purity of Ms Persson with honour satisfied on both sides.

Essi Berelian

Aimee Mann

The underdog hero of literate pop songwriters everywhere has crafted a signature brand of sharp, tuneful rock following label troubles and the early, flukey success of "Voices Carry".

1 FIFTY YEARS AFTER THE FAIR from WHATEVER

It sounds almost like a throwaway at first, but the swirling guitars and backup vocals mask a touching evocation of lost idealism.

2 DEATHLY from MAGNOLIA SOUNDTRACK

Perhaps her most powerfully rendered and emotionally wrought lyric, this was the lush epic around which PT Anderson built the movie *Magnolia*.

3 GHOST WORLD from BACHELOR NO. 2

Vintage Aimee: character-driven, richly observed, steadily rocking, and once in your head impossible to get out.

4 SAVE ME from MAGNOLIA SOUNDTRACK

So languid and dreamy you probably won't feel any urgency at all to save her from the "ranks of the freaks, who suspect they could never love anyone."

5 RED VINES from BACHELOR NO. 2

From the muted, unassuming intro to the tinkling piano outro, Mann produces something cinematic, in which every added effect – slide guitar here, tambourine shake there – works to perfection.

6 FOURTH OF JULY from WHATEVER

A brittle and vulnerable ballad that turns a big celebratory holiday into a lamentation for what's left once the fireworks have died out.

7 THAT'S JUST WHAT YOU ARE from I'M WITH STUPID

A bouncing, sing-songy kiss-off, with not an extraneous word or note. Nice background harmonies from the Squeeze guys too.

8 CALLING ON MARY from ONE MORE DRIFTER IN THE SNOW

Who says new Christmas standards aren't being written? This is the the finale, and one of a couple of originals, on a surprising – and surprisingly good – holiday album.

9 LITTLE BOMBS from THE FORGOTTEN ARM

The rhythmic strumming gently ticks along, channeling Paul Simon by way of Son Volt; on top of that little bombs explode in the form of fraught, resigned observations ("life just kind of empties out").

10 IT'S NOT SAFE from I'M WITH STUPID

With raucous guitar bursts and rousing harmonies, Aimee gives a vigorous word of warning to those who might cross her path.

Andrew Rosenberg

Marilyn Manson

You want coruscating industrial metal, guaranteed to offend even the most liberal sensibilities? Marilyn Manson are filling just that vital gap in the market.

1 THE BEAUTIFUL PEOPLE from ANTICHRIST SUPERSTAR

The stop-start riff and tribal drumming alone are fabulous. Throw in some cool expletive-driven lyrics and you have a top track.

2 COMA WHITE from MECHANICAL ANIMALS

A coolly observed snapshot of potential suicide. Detached yet perversely beautiful verses drip with hopelessness and despair.

❸ DISPOSABLE TEENS from HOLYWOOD
A fist-bangingly heavy glam-stomp with an irritatingly catchy chorus. Off-the-peg nihilism never sounded quite so attractive.

❹ THE FIGHT SONG from HOLYWOOD
Vicious voice-and-percussion verses boil over into a glamorously violent and electrifyingly provocative chorus. A celebration of defiance.

❺ I DON'T LIKE THE DRUGS (BUT THE DRUGS LIKE ME) from MECHANICAL ANIMALS
Like being invited to an infernal discothèque Manson does strutting industrial cyber-funk complete with great soulful female backing vocals.

❻ LUNCHBOX from THE LAST TOUR ON EARTH
An object lesson in how to work a crowd: great riff, wild synths and Manson teetering on the edge of homicide.

❼ MOBSCENE (SIC)
from THE GOLDEN AGE OF GROTESQUE
One of those great big angry anthems Manson specializes in that makes you want to break things. The cheerleaders are terrific too.

❽ THE REFLECTING GOD from ANTICHRIST SUPERSTAR
There's nothing quite like a slow-building torrent of industrial-strength bile. A great minimal bassline leads to aural apocalypse.

❾ TAINTED LOVE from LEST WE FORGET: THE BEST OF
A song ideally suited to Manson's edgy delivery. The backing vocals are spooky and the distorted guitars build menacingly to the climax.

❿ THIS IS THE NEW SHIT
from THE GOLDEN AGE OF GROTESQUE
Like being trapped in the heart of a very dark machine. Excellent electronic percussion melds perfectly with Manson's stuttering verses.

Essi Berelian

Thomas Mapfumo

Zimbabwe's Thomas Mapfumo is the king of chimurenga: a blend of traditional mbira music and Western instrumentation so rootsy and hypnotic that it might have just welled up from the ground. A furious critic of the despotic regime of President Mugabe – as he was of 1970s white-minority rule – Mapfumo has been the torch-bearer of political resistance for thirty years.

❶ MHONDORO from GWINDINGWI RINE SHUMBA
One of the songs that had the world-music fraternity jumping through hoops in the 1980s, Mhondoro is Mapfumo and the Black Unlimited stripped to the bone.

❷ HOKOYO! from HOKOYO!
"Watch out!" Mapfumo's warning earned him three months in prison in 1979. Rocks with the joy of impending Zimbabwean independence. Ironically, Mapfumo is now exiled by the Mugabe regime.

❹ NYAMUTAMBA NEMOMBE from SINGLES 77–86
Pure, quintessential chimurenga!

❺ KUPERA KWEVANHU from CORRUPTION
You don't have to understand the lyrics to understand the sorrow of war and famine in Mozambique.

❻ JUANITA from MR MUSIC
Heavy on the horns, completely repetitive; your toes will not stop tapping from beginning to end.

❼ MUGARA NDEGA from CHIMURENGA FOR JUSTICE
This collaboration between the Black Unlimited and Misty in Roots must be one of the most mesmerizing slabs of reggae ever produced.

❽ NGOMA YARIRA from TAKE ONE
Phenomenal proto-chimurenga from the Hallelujah Chicken Run Band, featuring Mapfumo and legendary guitarist Joshua Dube.

Tom Bullough

Bob Marley & The Wailers

With Bob virtually beatified, it's worth remembering that Peter Tosh and Bunny Livingstone made the original Wailers a great harmony group. The strength of much of their Island material, on the other hand, was down to the Jamaican practice of successfully "versioning" their best songs from nearly a decade's worth of back catalogue.

❶ ONE LOVE/PEOPLE GET READY (EXTENDED VERSION) from LEGEND
Originally a ska tune for Studio One, then reggae. With lyrics partly borrowed from the Curtis Mayfield/Impressions classic, this inclusive, "let's get together and feel all right" song was an ideal choice for the BBC Song of the Millennium.

❷ I'M STILL WAITING from SONGS OF FREEDOM
Doowop delight – achingly beautiful harmonies from the Wailers in their finest Impressions style.

❸ PUT IT ON from BURNIN'
Originally a defiant rude-boy tune, the Island version is pure pleasure – "feel all right now".

❹ DREAMLAND BUNNY WAILER from BLACKHEART MAN
Based on "My Dream Island" by the El Dorados, this is a gorgeous song with lovely lyrics, beautifully sung by Bunny. The album is a classic.

❺ STIR IT UP from CATCH A FIRE
Johnny Nash made this Marley composition a UK hit in 1972, but Bob's slower five-and-a-half-minute version makes time stand still.

❻ PASS IT ON from BURNIN'
A sublime Marley song, with lead vocals by Bunny Wailer, from the group's best (studio) album.

❼ TRENCHTOWN ROCK from LIVE!
A Jamaican #1, this song was an inspired choice to open the legendary London Lyceum concerts, celebrating both the groups ghetto origins and the power of music itself.

❽ LIVELY UP YOURSELF from LIVE!
Previous incarnations are paradoxically languorous, but the live version is absolutely electrifying – just listen to the audience!

❾ NO WOMAN NO CRY from LIVE!
Although Rita Marley's revelations about her husband's macho misbehaviour make the title seem bitterly ironic, they can't detract from the magic of the music.

❿ REDEMPTION SONG from UPRISING
Marley's musical epitaph. To be compared with Hendrix's acoustic "Hear My Train A Coming".

Neil Foxlee

The Martians are coming!

Mysterious emanations from the Red Planet have exerted a strange influence on the minds of certain songwriters, leading them into flights of fancy and up the paths of whimsy.

❶ HERE COME THE MARTIAN MARTIANS JONATHAN RICHMAN from ROADRUNNER
According to JoJo, when they come, we shouldn't be surprised to see them riding on their Martian bikes.

❷ MARTIAN GIRL THE AQUABATS from FURY OF THE AQUABATS
Cheerful, ska-coloured knees-up with the usual everyday tale of interplanetary attraction gone awry.

❸ LIFE ON MARS FLAMING LIPS from THIS HERE GIRAFFE SINGLE
So wistful and distorted you'd swear Wayne Coyne was pining for his dusty ole home back on the red planet, the Lips' cover of this Bowie classic is more lonesome and much further out there than the original.

❹ I TURNED INTO A MARTIAN THE MISFITS from WALK AMONG US
Coming in at under two minutes, this song gets straight to the point and kicks off with all the reverb, distortion and slam-dance energy that The Misfits have come to represent.

❺ MARTIAN MOMMA KING KURT from ALCOHOLIC RAT
Meaty, blaring horns, a cool guitar-riff and lyrics of purest nonsense combine to make this a must for any interplanetary dance party.

❻ MARTIAN HOP ROCKY SHARPE & THE REPLAYS from ROCK-IT-TO MARS
The original, by The Ran-Dells, was the first track to use "additive synthesis" from a wave generator. This updated version is hooked with high-pitched "space" voices, bouncy guitars and tasty laser-gun effects.

❼ MARTIAN SCREAMING BLUE MESSIAHS from TOTALLY RELIGIOUS
Set the interstellar overdrive to automatic and groove to the red shift as the SBMs take you into warp speed.

❽ MARTIAN SAINTS MARY LOU LORD from MARTIAN SAINTS EP
Spooky Theremin sounds, yes. Usual nonsense lyrics? No way. Ms Lord was scooped up from the Boston subways to blossom into one of the most interesting songwriters to have emerged on the East Coast in years.

❾ BACK FROM MARS AQUA from AQUARIUS
Ultra-cheery pop nonsense on a track that has no more connection to Mars than to any other chocolate bar – but we all need a little Euro-beat in our lives.

⑩ BALLROOMS OF MARS T REX from THE SLIDER

Marc Bolan was at the peak of stardom when *The Slider* was first released; its stately, swanking blues-based progression has lyrics from Planet Rubbish but a guitar solo that'll put you into orbit.

Al Spicer

John Martyn

John Martyn's best work fits into the decade-long gap between the Scottish folkie's discovery of jazz and his discovery of synthesizers. Perfect music for a long hot summer.

❶ SOLID AIR from SOLID AIR

A glorious tribute to troubled pal Nick Drake: lazy acoustic jazz guitar, shimmering organ, Danny Thompson's rumbling bass and Martyn's drunkenly slurred growl.

❷ SMALL HOURS from ONE WORLD

Recorded across a lake at 3am, Small Hours absolutely oozes ambience, Martyn's echo-drenched guitar going places no one previously imagined.

❸ I DON'T WANT TO KNOW from SOLID AIR

Martyn at his most poppy, all righteous testifying, hazy electric pianos and a wall of soulful harmonies. You do want to know.

❹ MAY YOU NEVER from SOLID AIR

As touching a tribute as Solid Air, this breezy acoustic confection seems to belong to some folk memory of perfection (Clapton cover notwithstanding).

❺ SO MUCH IN LOVE WITH YOU from INSIDE OUT

Rarely has passion sounded so strangulated: *Inside Out* was the extreme of Martyn's Echoplex phase: treated, twisted guitar topped by equally gnarled vocals.

❻ BLESS THE WEATHER from BLESS THE WEATHER

This irresistible early appearance of Martyn's snapping acoustic style is just one highlight from a gorgeous album: summery, wistful, woozy.

❼ STORMBRINGER from STORMBRINGER

From the best of his two collaborative albums with wife Beverley: a twinkling, folk-rock wall of sound.

❽ LOOK IN from INSIDE OUT

Martyn's rocky side emerges: a killer distorted four-note riff, explosive drums and one of his roaring best vocals.

❾ JUST NOW from BLESS THE WEATHER

Some of Martyn's most plangently pure singing: an airy piano ballad that's almost unbearably touching.

⑩ SPENCER THE ROVER from ONE WORLD

A late return to the trad style of his youth, now Martyn's voice adds whole worlds of weariness and regret to this tale of a heart-broken wanderer.

Toby Manning

Massive Attack & Bristol-hop

The trip-hop squad and the music they made sauntered out of Bristol puffing on a big spliff, hitched up to London and spent a summer in the spotlight before rambling back home.

❶ UNFINISHED SYMPATHY MASSIVE ATTACK from BLUE LINES

Stately, elegantly paced, delicate and supreme, this is the track that announced Massive Attack to a stunned listening public.

❷ TEARDROP MASSIVE ATTACK from MEZZANINE

Sharp resonant imagery that sits, composed and calm, like a master calligrapher's perfect haiku.

❸ INERTIA CREEPS MASSIVE ATTACK from MEZZANINE

The darkest track on an album steeped in the oppressive reek of too much time in the studio and too many unresolved tour-bus arguments.

❹ PROTECTION MASSIVE ATTACK from PROTECTION

Tracey Thorn's ethereal vocals provide an armour-glass shield of defiance in her duty of care to the one she loves.

❺ RADIATION RULING THE NATION (PROTECTION DUB) MASSIVE ATTACK VS MAD PROFESSOR from NO PROTECTION

The ultimate urban producer from the mean streets of southeast London takes on the dark lords of Bristol under manners.

❻ SPYING GLASS MASSIVE ATTACK from PROTECTION

Massive Attack employed reggae vacolist Horace Andy on their debut album, reviving his career Here they update Andy's original track of paranoia with a sturdy 1990s digital backing.

227

❼ I SPY (SPYING GLASS DUB) MASSIVE ATTACK VS MAD PROFESSOR from NO PROTECTION

Even better suited than Protection to the medicine developed by the Mad Professor, this track is an almighty dub mix strong enough to bend your speaker mounts. Turn it up!

❽ BLACK STEEL TRICKY from MAXINQUAYE

When the most frightening character in Bristol walks into the studio to rasp his way through an updated Public Enemy track, you stand back and let the gentleman do his thing.

❾ HELL IS ROUND THE CORNER TRICKY from MAXINQUAYE

This is darker and far colder than outer space, and comes with an eerie beat sampled perhaps from a wounded human crawling towards the phone.

❿ WANDERING STAR PORTISHEAD from DUMMY

Portishead came and went on a burst of acclaim that would have swamped many a more experienced collective. This was their finest piece, recorded before the attention melted them down.

Al Spicer

New Math

In the 1960s, Tom Lehrer wrote the funny and pointed social critique "New Math". Here's nine (cool number) that have taken heed of their formulas.

❶ LESS THAN ZERO ELVIS COSTELLO from MY AIM IS TRUE

His aim is zeroed in on this crunching anti-fascist diatribe from his debut album. A perfect summation of what politics frequently adds up to.

❷ NOTHING FROM NOTHING BILLY PRESTON from ULTIMATE COLLECTION

One of the most famous session men from the 1960s and 70s steps into the limelight and proffers a simple enough equation: it "means nothing".

❸ 5−4 = UNITY PAVEMENT from CROOKED RAIN, CROOKED RAIN

In reality, just a pleasant little instrumental that melds lots of disparate pieces, including a brief cop of the guitar riff from the Beatles'"I Want You".

❹ LOVE MINUS ZERO/NO LIMIT BOB DYLAN from BRINGING IT ALL BACK HOME

A gentle love song that sounds years past Dylan's age, as did much of his work at this time.

❺ LOVE PLUS ONE HAIRCUT ONE HUNDRED from PELICAN WEST

Immensely enjoyable and utterly meaningless bit of early 1980s new wave, with sax and xylophone helping it bounce frothily along.

❻ ADD IT UP VIOLENT FEMMES from VIOLENT FEMMES

They went after the whole teen angst thing with a cudgel; can't get a kiss, a screw, a fuck (OK, so their imagination was slightly limited). What's a guy to do?

❼ 6.4 = MAKEOUT GARY WILSON from YOU THINK YOU REALLY KNOW ME

Wilson made one of the weirdest of the 1970s; you're not sure whether to laugh or feel a bit queasy from his come-ons.

❽ FROM ONE CUMS ONE FIREHOSE from IF'N

Some great propulsive drumming around which Edfromohio wraps his indignation, at one point shouting "Try and prove this song!" Sorry, can't.

❾ THREE IS A MAGIC NUMBER SCHOOLHOUSE ROCK from MULTIPLICATION ROCK

The whole collection is educational fun with numbers, but this is the most memorable, and was also winningly redone by De la Soul as an affirmation of the power of a musical trio.

Andrew Rosenberg

Curtis Mayfield

Singer-songwriter-producer-guitarist-entrepreneur-social commentator: Curtis was a Chicago genius and soul music's artistic conscience.

❶ GYPSY WOMAN from DEFINITE IMPRESSIONS

The haunting ballad that established The Impressions. A song of timeless beauty.

❷ PEOPLE GET READY from DEFINITE IMPRESSIONS

Biblical civil rights song featuring the finest guitar break in recorded history. The Mount Everest of soul songs.

❸ I'M SO PROUD from DEFINITE IMPRESSIONS

Curtis is proud of his girl, proud to be loved by her, proud to be with her. Listening to him, I'm proud to be human.

❹ CHOICE OF COLORS from THE YOUNG MOD'S FORGOTTEN STORY

"If you had a choice of colors, what would you

choose?" Curtis asked America in 1969. Tough question. Uneasy answers were sure to follow.

❺ IF THERE'S A HELL BELOW WE'RE ALL GONNA GO from CURTIS
Curtis solo espouses hard funk fuelled with dread.

❻ FREDDIE'S DEAD from SUPERFLY
Bad movie gets great soundtrack. Curtis, the soul Buddha, sings a lament for fallen drug-dealer Freddie, bringing the pain and compassion right back home.

❼ PUSHERMAN from SUPERFLY
Rappers sample this as a celebration of dealers. Curtis sang it with harsh irony: "got some dope/want some speed?".

❽ SO IN LOVE from THERE'S NO PLACE LIKE AMERICA TODAY
Lovely laidback groove as Curtis celebrates how fine love is. Gorgeous.

❾ DIRTY LAUNDRY from HONESTY
Overlooked when released, this comment on political and social corruption saw Curtis in exceptional form.

❿ NEW WORLD ORDER from NEW WORLD ORDER
A last whisper of song from the paralysed artist finds Mayfield still searching for human reconciliation.

Garth Cartwright

Mazzy Star

Since forming in LA in 1990, guitarist Dave Roback and vocalist Hope Sandoval have ploughed their very own furrow of melancholic, trance-inducing indie country-rock. Music that is very much at the bleaker end of the psychedelic spectrum.

❶ HARRIET BROWN OPAL from EARLY RECORDINGS
Bohemian story-song from Roback's previous, Syd Barrett-inspired band.

❷ HAPPY NIGHTMARE BABY OPAL from HAPPY NIGHTMARE BABY)
Raw Sex covers Siouxsie Sioux.

❸ RIDE IT ON from SHE HANGS BRIGHTLY
Spare and echoing. As if Nashville's moved to Transylvania.

❹ BEFORE I SLEEP from SHE HANGS BRIGHTLY
Like a lullaby from the end of the world.

❺ FADE INTO YOU from SO TONIGHT THAT I MIGHT SLEEP
Almost lush-sounding piano-led piece.

❻ FIVE STRING SERENADE from SO TONIGHT THAT I MIGHT SLEEP
Sandoval's barely-there drawl gets back-up from five guitar strings and a tambourine.

❼ ALL MY SISTERS from AMONG MY SWAN
Slick psychedelic production. Like falling into a whirlpool.

❽ DROP HOPE HOPE SANDOVAL AND THE WARM INTENTIONS from BAVARIAN FRUIT BREAD
Acoustic cover of the Jesus and Mary Chain B-side.

Rachel Coldicutt

Paul McCartney

OK, Lennon brought out the best in McCartney and when they split there was no concealing the pain. But it wasn't just silly love songs. There's at least a playlist of solo Paul that's Beatles class.

❶ MAYBE I'M AMAZED from MCCARTNEY
A classic from the get-go, this graced Macca's much-derided first solo outing. Affecting lyrics and a naked, powerful vocal.

❷ BACK SEAT OF MY CAR from RAM
Talk about a song with the whole kitchen sink; seems he might have thrown the cabinets and fridge in as well. But it all works to luxuriating effect.

❸ ANOTHER DAY from WINGSPAN: HITS AND HISTORY
His first post-Beatles hit, and it proved that another day was much like most previous days: Paul's penchant for tuneful pop had not passed him by.

❹ MY LOVE from RED ROSE SPEEDWAY
Even if the album wasn't so great, this is a big, big McCartney song: "My love does it good" indeed. Macca does the ballad to perfection.

❺ LET ME ROLL IT from BAND ON THE RUN
Simple, spare and solid as a rock; on an album of songs packed with ideas and flourishes, this one comes more from the gut.

❻ JET from BAND ON THE RUN
A barnstormer in the vein of "Back in the USSR", showing that he hadn't forgotten what a rock band could sound like (even if he probably played most of the instruments himself).

7 LISTEN TO WHAT THE MAN SAID from VENUS AND MARS

He's at the peak of his pop capabilities here; it goes down so easy, you're almost ashamed to ask for more.

8 TAKE IT AWAY from TUG OF WAR

If it's possible to convey a feeling of effortlessness, this lovely, swinging song does it; having Ringo tap away on the drums doesn't hurt one bit.

9 MY BRAVE FACE from FLOWERS IN THE DIRT

Macca sounds rejuvenated with a writing partner his equal in Elvis Costello; have some fun trying to pick who wrote which part.

10 FRIENDS TO GO from CHAOS AND CREATION IN THE BACKYARD

Sounding like a blast from thirty years ago but perhaps a little wrier now, McCartney comes up with a bouncy tribute, style-wise, to late Beatle George.

Andrew Rosenberg

Kate & Anna McGarrigle

While the French–Canadian sisters may now be in danger of becoming better known as mother and aunt, respectively, of Rufus and Martha Wainwright, their folky songwriting has an enduring strength and appeal.

1 HEART LIKE A WHEEL from KATE AND ANNA MCGARRIGLE

A series of similes about the nature of love, famously covered by Linda Ronstadt.

2 SWIMMING SONG from KATE AND ANNA MCGARRIGLE

Written by Kate's ex-husband Loudon Wainwright III (with more subtlety than usual), this could be a metaphor for sexual awakening – or it could just be about swimming.

3 COMPLAINTE POUR STE CATHÉRINE from FRENCH RECORD

French folk-reggae? Oui, s'il vous plaît.

4 MOVE OVER MOON from LOVE OVER AND OVER

Vocoder can't quite hide the honky-tonk roots here.

5 LOVE OVER AND OVER from LOVE OVER AND OVER

Mark Knopfler strolls in for a guitar solo, adding a little FM sheen to a more polished but still quirky album.

6 GOIN' BACK TO HARLAN from MATAPEDIA

Emmylou Harris released this one first, but it is classic McGarrigle work: rustic, allusive, and pretty without being soft.

7 PETITE ANNONCE AMOUREUSE from LA VACHE QUI PLEURE

French folk reggae – and their best song for years.

8 MOTHER MOTHER from HEARTBEATS ACCELERATING

A plaintively-catchy cry for help.

David Honigmann

Blind Willie McTell

As Bob Dylan put it, "nobody sings the blues like Blind Willie McTell". In a career that spanned from the 1920s to the 50s, the itinerant Georgian bluesman produced a legacy of astonishing individuality and power.

1 WRITIN' PAPER BLUES from COMPLETE RECORDED WORKS VOL 1

The very first song McTell ever recorded, in 1927, and already his gifts were fully in place.

2 MAMA, TAIN'T LONG FO' DAY from COMPLETE RECORDED WORKS VOL 1

There's an almost feminine delicacy to the young McTell's voice on this 1927 masterpiece.

3 STATESBORO BLUES from COMPLETE RECORDED WORKS VOL 1

A definitive blues classic, from 1928; McTell's fingerpicking beautifully complements the poignant words.

4 RAZOR BALL from COMPLETE RECORDED WORKS VOL 1

McTell's most infectious dance number, from 1930.

5 SOUTHERN CAN IS MINE from COMPLETE RECORDED WORKS VOL 1

Another piece of entertaining if misogynist hokum, this time from 1931.

6 BROKE DOWN ENGINE BLUES from COMPLETE RECORDED WORKS VOL 1

McTell returned repeatedly to this song throughout his recording career, but it was never more powerful than in this 1931version.

7 SCAREY DAY BLUES from COMPLETE RECORDED WORKS VOL 1

McTell's perfect blending of voice and guitar makes this 1931 recording irresistible.

Danny McNamara's
Influences

"These were the first ten tracks to influence me, listed in chronological order of me discovering them", says DANNY McNAMARA, lead singer with British guitar band Embrace. "The next ten would include The Pixies, Primal Scream, Happy Mondays, Boo Radleys, Pavement, Velvet Underground, Beach Boys, Sly & The Family Stone, P.J.Harvey and Elvis Costello," he adds "But these got there first…"

❶ LOVE ME TENDER ELVIS PRESLEY from JAILHOUSE ROCK/LOVE ME TENDER

❷ KINGS OF THE WILD FRONTIER ADAM AND THE ANTS from KINGS OF THE WILD FRONTIER

❸ TAINTED LOVE SOFT CELL from NON-STOP EROTIC CABARET

❹ BAD U2 from THE UNFORGETTABLE FIRE

❺ DO IT CLEAN ECHO AND THE BUNNYMEN from CROCODILES

❻ HOW SOON IS NOW THE SMITHS from HATFUL OF HOLLOW

❼ LOVE WILL TEAR US APART JOY DIVISION from SUBSTANCE

❽ SO CENTRAL RAIN REM from RECKONING

❾ PERFECT TIME RIDE from WAVES

❿ I AM THE RESURRECTION THE STONE ROSES from THE STONE ROSES

---

❽ LITTLE DELIA from ATLANTA TWELVE STRING
By the time McTell cut a superb batch of songs for the Atlantic label in 1949, his voice was much rougher and gruffer; small wonder Johnny Cash later covered this.

❾ DYING CRAPSHOOTER BLUES from ATLANTA TWELVE STRING
A bravura triumph, this 1949 saga of a dying gambler who asks his friends to "dig my grave with the ace of spades" wouldn't sound out of place on a Dylan album.

❿ MOTHERLESS CHILDREN HAVE A HARD TIME from ATLANTA TWELVE STRING
A lovely demonstration of McTell's instrumental virtuosity, again from 1949.

Greg Ward

Me, Me, Me, Me!

It's no accident that singers warm up by enunciating "Me, me, me, me!" Serious self obsession has produced a genre all its own.

❶ I'M EVERY WOMAN CHAKA KHAN from I'M EVERY WOMAN: THE BEST OF CHAKA KHAN
Covered by Whitney Houston and often misheard as "climb every woman": great fun for karaoke mashers, but best left to the experts.

❷ I'M A MAN/MANNISH BOY MUDDY WATERS from HARD AGAIN OR BO DIDDLEY FROM HIS BEST
They fought over who's version was better, but the blues legends agreed you spell it M…A…N.

❸ I'M A BELIEVER THE MONKEES from THE BEST OF THE MONKEES
Pure joyous pop the original boy band, who had their own TV show AND a tambourine.

❹ I'M FREE ROLLING STONES from STRIPPED
The hippie mantra "love me…but I can do what I want" takes on new meaning from multi-squillionaires.

❺ I'M LIKE A BIRD NELLY FURTADO from WHOA NELLY!
A sublime song that transcends the clichés of soaring and swooping.

❻ I'M NOT LIKE EVERYBODY ELSE THE KINKS from FACE TO FACE.
Ray Davies isn't like everybody else – he tells us so sixteen or so times right here.

❼ I'M COMING OUT DIANA ROSS from DIANA
The Queen of Me hardly raises a sweat on a chirpy anthem ineluctably adopted by gay folk.

❽ I'M TOO SEXY RIGHT SAID FRED from UP
A big hit with the under-10s, even if they're not quite sure what sexy means, and a good thing too.

⑨ I'M STILL STANDING ELTON JOHN from TOO LOW FOR ZERO.

"And if our love was just a circus you'd be a clown by now": lyricist Bernie Taupin resists a juggling trapeze-artist analogy in this easy-listening radio staple.

⑩ I'M WALKIN' FATS DOMINO from THE FATS DOMINO JUKEBOX

The oddly bouncy sing-along classic about being dumped. (Not to be confused with "Walkin' to New Orleans".)

Kaz Cooke

Meat Loaf

Dallas-born singer Marvin Lee Aday aka Meat Loaf got his first break in early 1970s musicals, during which time he met composer Jim Steinman – the rest is million-selling rock history.

① BAT OUT OF HELL from BAT OUT OF HELL

The ultimate in metal-meets-musical soundtracks Screaming Todd Rundgren axes, wild pianos and Mr Loaf laying on the turbo-charged melodrama thick and heavy.

② COULDN'T HAVE SAID IT BETTER from COULDN'T HAVE SAID IT BETTER

Latter day Meat and all the hallmarks are there; duelling vocals with Patti Russo, acres of piano abuse, immense arrangements and a grand chorus.

③ DEAD RINGER FOR LOVE from DEAD RINGER

When those opening guitars rev up you can feel the hairs stand up on your neck. Features some astonishing vocal jousting with Cher.

④ I'D DO ANYTHING FOR LOVE (BUT I WON'T DO THAT) from BAT OUT OF HELL II: BACK INTO HELL

Who'd have thought Marvin could again match the splendour of his debut album? A corking #1 hit on both sides of the Atlantic.

⑤ LIFE IS A LEMON (AND I WANT MY MONEY BACK) from BAT OUT OF HELL II: BACK INTO HELL

Boy, does Meat sound frustrated here It's catharsis time with a nice long list of things that can drive you mad all given the grandiose Jim Steinman treatment.

⑥ MIDNIGHT AT THE LOST AND FOUND from MIDNIGHT AT THE LOST AND FOUND

The album's not so hot but the title track has all you need from a Meat Loaf song: drama, danger, romance and huge production values.

⑦ OUT OF THE FRYING PAN (AND INTO THE FIRE) from BAT OUT OF HELL II: BACK INTO HELL

9 ½ Weeks meets Masterchef, well, kind of. Hot, steamy sex and a dubious cookery metaphor, this must be a Steinman tune, then.

⑧ PARADISE BY THE DASHBOARD LIGHT from BAT OUT OF HELL

Teenage hormones run rampant in this sweaty three-part epic, complete with mid-song baseball commentary. Ellen Foley's glorious vocals are quite stunning.

⑨ READ 'EM AND WEEP from DEAD RINGER

It sounds like Meat is being helped along by a celestial choir of background singers as he reaches for the enormous, seemingly never ending chorus.

⑩ YOU TOOK THE WORDS RIGHT OUT OF MY MOUTH (HOT SUMMER NIGHT) from BAT OUT OF HELL

This is worth it just for the fabulously ripe spoken word intro between the girl and the wolf with the red roses. The rest of the tune is pretty neat, too.

Essi Berelian

Memphis

Named after ancient Egypt's city of kings, Memphis, Tennessee, turned out to be a 20th century city of musical royalty. Until Dr Martin Luther King's assassination in Memphis in 1968 musical magic flowed from the Delta's capital. The city crashed during the 1970s but today musical tourism and gangsta rap are revitalising the Memphis scene.

① JOHN HENRY FURRY LEWIS from SHAKE 'EM ON DOWN

Furry was born in 1893, received his first good guitar from "father of the blues" W.C. Handy, lost a leg while hoboing, made distinctive Memphis blues recordings in the 1920s, swept the city's streets for decades, and was rediscovered by white blues fans in the 1960s – when he enjoyed a second career opening for The Rolling Stones and appearing in Burt Reynolds films.

② WHEN THE LEVEE BREAKS MEMPHIS MINNIE from BLUES CLASSICS

Minnie ran away from her sharecropping parents in 1910, aged 13, to play blues in Memphis, developing into a formidable singer, guitarist and songwriter, one notorious for her hard-partying lifestyle. And, yup, this is the tune Led Zep turned into metal's most celebrated stomp.

❸ NO MORE DOGGIN' ROSCO GORDON from BOOTIN: THE BEST OF THE RPM YEARS

Rosco's boogie woogie piano skills made him an R&B star in the early 1950s and his shuffling rhythm was a huge influence on the emerging Jamaican music.

❹ MYSTERY TRAIN JUNIOR PARKER from JUNIOR'S BLUES

Elvis cut "Mystery Train" as his finest Sun rockabilly tune but the original by Junior Parker, a hugely talented harmonica player and singer, is the stuff of oracles, weird and haunted.

❺ ROCKET 88 JACKIE BRENSTON AND HIS DELTA CATS from THE SOUND OF THE CITY: MEMPHIS

Brenston was singer-saxophonist in Ike Turner's "Delta Cats" and this roaring slice of wild proto-rock boogie was produced by Sam Phillips and hit #1 on the R&B charts in 1950. Just listen to Ike destroy his piano!

❻ GREEN ONIONS BOOKER T & THE MGS from TIME IS TIGHT

Organist Booker T Jones and his Memphis Group cut this sublime instrumental in 1963 for the fledgling Stax label and watched it become an international hit and the city's theme tune. The MGs backed Otis Redding, Sam & Dave and many other awesome soul artists as well as issuing great instrumental albums.

❼ WOOLY BULLY SAM THE SHAM & THE PHARAOHS from THE SOUND OF THE CITY: MEMPHIS

Texan born Chicano Domingo Samudio relocated to Memphis for its thriving music scene and cut this garage rock classic.

❽ SUSPICIOUS MINDS ELVIS PRESLEY from ELVIS IN MEMPHIS

Elvis returned to Memphis in 1968 to make not only his last great recordings but his finest post-Sun album. Hear him wail this epic tale of infidelity and marvel at the potential squandered.

❾ I CAN'T GET NEXT TO YOU AL GREEN from GREATEST HITS

Struggling soul journeyman Green was given a lift from Memphis producer Willie Mitchell. Giving Green The Temptations tune they cut a new Memphis groove that now defines the city's final soul epoch.

❿ IT'S HARD OUT HERE FOR A PIMP THREE 6 MAFIA from HUSTLE & FLOW SOUNDTRACK

The Academy Awards have seen some strange spectacles but little like three Crip gang bangers jumping for joy on winning Best Original Song with this in 2006.

Garth Cartwright

Natalie Merchant & 10,000 Maniacs

The Maniacs were a quintessential college-rock band, yoking good-time party-boy musicians to a solemn singer-songwriter... who finally took off for a solo career.

10,000 MANIACS

❶ HEY JACK KEROUAC from IN MY TRIBE

Only Natalie Merchant could have worried about Jack's relationship with his mother.

❷ DON'T TALK from IN MY TRIBE

Merchant pushes through thickets of guitar to reach a haunting minor-key melody.

❸ LIKE THE WEATHER from IN MY TRIBE

A song about greyness that somehow avoids being grey itself.

❹ EAT FOR TWO from BLIND MAN'S ZOO

A tale of teenage pregnancy, the narrator's folly growing inside her.

❺ THESE ARE DAYS from OUR TIME IN EDEN

A slow march for the end of the band.

❻ TROUBLE ME from MTV UNPLUGGED

A song of solidarity, second cousin to R.E.M.'s "Everybody Hurts".

❼ BECAUSE THE NIGHT from MTV UNPLUGGED

A perfect version of the Patti Smith and Bruce Springsteen anthem, with the solos taken on violin.

NATALIE MERCHANT

❽ CARNIVAL from TIGERLILY

Merchant agonizes about street-level inequality over an intoxicating patter of Brazilian percussion.

❾ THIS HOUSE IS ON FIRE from MOTHERLAND

The strongest of Merchant's solo albums opens with this: Merchant's thick voice, oud and Middle Eastern strings set to a reggae swagger.

❿ WHICH SIDE ARE YOU ON? from THE HOUSE CARPENTER'S DAUGHTER

An oddity, this album: a ragbag of cover versions and old folk songs, including this union ballad from Kentucky miner's wife Florence Reece.

David Honigmann

Mercury Rev

Flaming Lips' only rivals as the most original American band of the last fifteen years. Here are ten tracks that combine whacked-out psychedelic droning, spooked orchestrations and an instinctive empathy with what Greil Marcus once called "the old, weird America…"

❶ VERY SLEEPY RIVERS from YERSELF IS STEAM
Thirteen dizzying minutes of hypnotic, twinkling post-pop genius.

❷ RACING THE TIDE from SEE YOU ON THE OTHER SIDE
Delirious psychedelic joy from their first album, after oddball vocalist David Baker had left.

❸ SUDDEN RAY OF HOPE from SEE YOU ON THE OTHER SIDE
Sure they'd clearly been listening to *Pet Sounds* – but Brian Wilson himself could hardly have synthesized what they heard better.

❹ THE DARK IS RISING from ALL IS DREAM
Cinematic splashes of orchestral colour and Jonathan Donahue's most fragile falsetto.

❺ METH OF A ROCKETTE'S KICK from BOCES
Ten epic minutes of piercing feedback, doo-wop harmonies, guitars, flutes, harps, and brass – and a choir for good measure.

❻ TIDES OF THE MOON from ALL IS DREAM
Unearthly Theremins and ethereal glockenspiels on a typically brooding Rev piece.

❼ CAR WASH HAIR from YERSELF IS STEAM
This sublime Velvet Underground-influenced single was added as a bonus track to the reissue of their 1991 debut album.

❽ DELTA SUN BOTTLENECK STOMP
from DESERTER'S SONGS
Tumultuous slide guitar on one of the band's most audacious sonic experiments.

❾ HOLES from DESERTER'S SONGS
Bowed saws, majestic violins, fluttering flutes and a positively eerie vocal on the sensational opening track of their most acclaimed album.

❿ OPUS 40 from DESERTER'S SONGS
Majestic pocket pop-symphony with The Band's Levon Helm on drums.

Nigel Williamson

Metal classics

You want screaming axes, and amps on eleven? Give your eardrums a serious pounding with these classic metal cuts.

❶ A LIGHT IN THE BLACK RAINBOW from RISING
Everything about this is great: Ritchie Blackmore's bonkers guitar, Cozy Powell's deadly drumming, and Dio's chest-beating vocals.

❷ AM I EVIL? DIAMOND HEAD from LIVING ON BORROWED TIME
Want to know where Metallica got their ideas? Look no further. This song boasts one of the best and heaviest riffs in metaldom.

❸ ANOTHER PIECE OF MEAT THE SCORPIONS from LOVEDRIVE
With Michael Schenker on lead guitar, The Scorpions were truly a force to be reckoned with. This represents them at their aggressive best.

❹ COLD SWEAT THIN LIZZY from THUNDER AND LIGHTNING
One of the heaviest things Phil Lynott wrote – it'll rock you right out of your leather strides. John Sykes' mental soloing is a joy.

❺ ELECTRIC EYE JUDAS PRIEST from SCREAMING FOR VENGEANCE
On this fabulous tune about cyber-surveillance gone mad, singer Rob Halford sounds suitably chilling and dispassionate as the malevolent spy in the sky.

❻ FOREARM SMASH BUDGIE from POWER SUPPLY
A song that does exactly what its title suggests: it brings you down and then jumps up and down on your spine. But in a good way.

❼ HOT FOR TEACHER VAN HALEN from 1984
Thundering tribal drums and a wicked fret-burning run even before the main riff! Singer David Lee Roth never wanted to end up in detention so bad.

❽ SLAVE TO THE GRIND SKID ROW from SLAVE TO THE GRIND
This is so heavy it could easily be mistaken for Metallica. There's nothing fancy going on here, just an honest-to-goodness pummelling and killer chorus.

❾ STILL OF THE NIGHT WHITESNAKE from 1987
A shameless Led Zep rip-off, this may well be, but there's no disguising the sheer metallic splendour of the stuttering stop-start riff and David Coverdale's howling vocals.

⑩ STRONG ARM OF THE LAW SAXON from **STRONG ARM OF THE LAW**
A metal band getting hassled by The Man? Whatever next? A relentless bassline, crunchy riff and tasty solo make this a tried-and-tested live fave.

Essi Berelian

Nu Metal

Taking its aesthetic cues from hip-hop and grunge, nu metal ruled the metal roost in the late 1990s and early noughties, with its wall-to-wall angst and downtuned guitar riffing.

❶ BLIND KORN from **KORN**
"Are you ready?!!" screams vocalist Jonathan Davis, and a genre is born. The first and still the best.

❷ DOWN WITH THE SICKNESS DISTURBED from **THE SICKNESS**
Worth sampling just for the huge drum sound while vocalist David Draiman excels with his infamous animal noises. Very dark and very nasty.

❸ EYE FOR AN EYE SOULFLY from **SOULFLY**
Main man Max Cavalera takes the experimentation of "Roots" era Sepultura to its logical conclusion with one of the heaviest songs ever committed to tape.

❹ FAITH LIMP BIZKIT from **THREE DOLLAR BILL, YALL$**
This incredible mangling of the George Michael hit helped turn Fred Durst into a baggy-shorted, baseball cap-wearing superstar.

❺ FREAK ON A LEASH KORN from **FOLLOW THE LEADER**
Their success seems to be getting to the band on this paranoid little effort. Great bottom end and Davis sounds incredibly nervy.

❻ IN THE END LINKIN PARK from **HYBRID THEORY**
Mike Shinoda's smooth rapping leads into one of Chester Bennington's most impassioned vocal lines. A vast and melodic cut.

❼ LAST RESORT PAPA ROACH from **INFEST**
One of the big hitters from an album that took Papa Roach into the major league. Rap and metal powered by plenty of angst to get the masses moshing.

❽ MY OWN SUMMER SHOVE IT DEFTONES from **AROUND THE FUR**
Front man Chino Moreno unleashes one of his most riveting vocal performances while axe-pert Stephen Carpenter grinds out one hell of a potent riff.

❾ SPIT IT OUT SLIPKNOT from **SLIPKNOT**
Nine boiler-suited blokes in wacky masks making a noise like Satan himself coughing up blood. One of the most extreme cuts from a landmark album.

⑩ SUITE-PEE SYSTEM OF A DOWN from **SYSTEM OF A DOWN**
Check out the fruitcake vocals, the loopy time changes and relentless pace. SOAD are in a league of their own when it comes to invention.

Essi Berelian

Metallica

From cult thrash-fiends to one of the biggest bands in the world, Metallica are stadium-bothering behemoths of metal.

❶ AIN'T MY BITCH from **LOAD**
The success of this bellicose little ditty hinges purely upon James Hetfield repeatedly snarling "Biiii-tch-aaaaaa!", as though he is sneezing violently, throughout the whole thing.

❷ BATTERY from **MASTER OF PUPPETS**
A celebration of Metallica doing what they do best. Don't be fooled by the gentle classical intro.

❸ CREEPING DEATH from **RIDE THE LIGHTNING**
Who'd have thought the Bible could provide such convincing metal fare? The Old Testament recycled into a bludgeoning blood-soaked extravaganza.

❹ DISPOSABLE HEROES from **MASTER OF PUPPETS**
War, what is it good for? Eight-minutes-plus of pure, unrestrained energy, about soldiers bred as cannon fodder.

❺ ENTER SANDMAN from **METALLICA**
The night brings with it wonders and terrors beyond imagining. This features one mother of a riff and a genius pause in the action just before the end.

❻ FUEL from **RELOAD**
Not the first metal tune about the need for speed, but a compact and turbo-charged beauty all the same.

❼ ONE from **...AND JUSTICE FOR ALL**
Based on a Dalton Trumbo anti-war story, the horror of the central character's life takes us from melodic climes to a rampant, violent climax.

❽ RIDE THE LIGHTNING from **RIDE THE LIGHTNING**
You could build a fortress with a riff this big and heavy – a fortress of twisted metal.

⑨ WELCOME HOME (SANITARIUM) from MASTER OF PUPPETS

One of those tunes that sounds as though it's going to be your friend – until it tries to rip your ears off, and climaxes like a runaway juggernaut.

⑩ WHIPLASH from KILL 'EM ALL

A full-on, red-blooded thrasher and then some, on which James Hetfield shrieks like he's trapped his left nut in the top string. Ouch.

Essi Berelian

The Miami sound

Miami Sound Machine's tropical-disco hit "Conga!" gave the city a musical identity to match its unique location – between the US and the Americas – and its exploding Latino population. Today, the city's sound embraces old-school Cubans and young Latino fusionists, Southern Soul, reggaeton and Latin hip-hop – all of which are showcased in its annual carnivals.

① TRES GOTAS DE AGUA BENDITA GLORIA ESTEFAN (WITH CELIA CRUZ) from ALMA CARIBENA

After Miami Sound Machine released Gloria Estefan as a soloist, Grammies flowed. This is a gorgeous duet with Celia Cruz, enhanced by spectacular piano work from Papo Lucca.

② EL CANTOR DEL FONSECA ROBERTO TORRES from LO MEJOR...

Veteran Cuban salsa singer/songwriter Roberto Torres united generations of exiled musicians in scores of renovated classics decades before *Buena Vista*. Here, his sleek tenor leads an exhilaratingly original hybrid of Cuban *charanga* and Colombian *vallenato*.

③ SHAKE YOUR BOOTY K.C. AND THE SUNSHINE BAND from THE BEST OF...

K.C. (H.W. Casey) claims to have invented disco, and built a following with Latinized Southern Soul, full of trumpets, rhythmically repeated choruses and Cuban percussion. Still a booty-shaker after thirty years!

④ MI CLIENTELA WILLIE CHIRINO from ORO SALSERO 10 EXITOS VOL I

Miami superstar Willie Chirino left Cuba as a kid but remained dedicated to the island's salsa. Scores of hits like this reveal a sensitive, distinctive voice, and his productions match the city's heavy heat and proximity to Caribbean musical currents.

⑤ CLEAN-UP WOMAN BETTY WRIGHT from THE VERY BEST OF...

Betty Wright is synonymous with this perennial hit – a fierce, Southern soul gal's warning to girls about men. It's pure 1970s, with the brass making a nod to Philly and Motown, alongside choppy near-reggae guitar.

⑥ WHY CAN'T WE LIVE TOGETHER TIMMY THOMAS from THE VERY BEST OF...

This everlasting song immortalizes one of Miami's great voices. Its hovering, tinny drone-like organ melody adds to the tension behind the questioning title and the drum-machine impression of conga beats is absolutely of the time and place.

⑦ FIESTA LOS FEOS SPAM ALL STARS from FUACATA LIVE

A song by a bunch of young globe-and-genre-trotting musicians who represent Miami's diverse population – among them sensational Cuban flautist, Mercedes Abal, and DJ Le Spam. Barrier-breaking fun-funk.

⑧ FELA SUENALO SOUND SYSTEM from SUENALO SOUND SYSTEM LIVE

Suenalo's coolly fashionable fusion of funk-dub, Colombian cumbia and hip-hop is very Miami. "Fela" is Afro-funk, all bass and brass, but peppered with Latinisms, unexpected wah-wahs and retro electric guitar FX.

⑨ YO QUISIERA ALBITA from ALBITA, HECHO A MANO

The androgynous Cuban singer-guitarist Albita took Miami by storm in the late 1980s, and Emilio Estefan's productions brought her Latin Grammies and fame. This song glories in textures, from Albita's metal-stringed guitar, sharp trumpets and congas, and her unmistakeable voice.

⑩ CROCKETT'S THEME JAN HAMMER from MIAMI VICE II: THE ORIGINAL SOUNDTRACK

A perfect soundtrack album for cruising through Miami with the roof down. Crockett is represented through Hammer's soft funk-fusion with its new shiney electronic drums: big themes for big dangers and heated sexual adventures!

Sue Steward

Michelle Shocked

Michelle Shocked came to prominence when a bootleg tape of a solo acoustic appearance at a folk festival became a surprise hit. For a few years the punk-styled folk-blues-swing-whatever singer could do no wrong; for longer, afterwards, she could seemingly do no right. But her fans remained loyal, and she's back on form.

❶ ANCHORAGE from SHORT SHARP SHOCKED
Shocked's calling card for years, this is the one that casual fans shout out for. The true story of an old friendship reawakened

❷ THE L&N DON'T STOP HERE ANY MORE from SHORT SHARP SHOCKED
Icy, sharp Appalachian ballad by Jean Ritchie about a doomed mining community.

❸ SLEEP KEEPS ME AWAKE from CAPTAIN SWING
When everyone wanted a sequel to *Short Sharp Shocked*, its author took a sudden detour into Western Swing, complete with brass section. This is bluesier than the rest, but retains the same sly charm.

❹ MONA LISA from CAPTAIN SWING
The most seductive song on *Captain Swing*, a melancholy violin lament set to a walking bassline and garlicky puns about robbing the Louvre blind.

❺ PRODIGAL DAUGHTER from ARKANSAS TRAVELER
Arkansas Traveler mingled uneasy meditations on race with the kind of down-home, old-time music, way before *O Brother* made it fashionable. "Prodigal Daughter", a feminist retake on "Cotton-Eyed Joe", stings while it swings.

❻ STILLBORN from KIND-HEARTED WOMAN
The album starts with this stark song about a midwife walking home in the early morning after attending a stillbirth, and gets more depressing from there.

❼ CAN'T TAKE MY JOY from GOOD NEWS
Acapella Pentecostalism in full exuberant flow: this is the music that saw Shocked through dark times.

❽ GOOD NEWS from DEEP NATURAL
A burst of religious fervour (marital heartache saw Shocked turn to God), combining ecstatic joy with fuzzbox guitar.

❾ EARLY MORNING SATURDAY from DON'T ASK DON'T TELL
Don't Ask Don't Tell kisses off Shocked's ex-husband in direct and brutal style, but this, its opener, has a lazy yawning stretch.

❿ MATCH BURNS TWICE from MEXICAN STANDOFF
A song that lopes like mariachi on an album that digs around in the Mexican roots of both Shocked's Texan birthplace and her adopted home in Los Angeles.

David Honigmann

Midnight

Many a fine song has probably been written around the witching hour, and many more have taken it as their inspiration.

❶ MOANIN' AT MIDNIGHT HOWLIN' WOLF from THE BEST OF HOWLIN' WOLF
What else would a wolf do at this time of day? An early hit by the massively influential bluesman.

❷ IN THE MIDNIGHT HOUR WILSON PICKETT from WILSON PICKETT'S GREATEST HITS
The best-known song by this Alabama-born singer is a stompin' soul classic Pickett was aided in no small way by having Booker T and the MGs as his backing band.

❸ MIDNIGHT SPECIAL CREEDENCE CLEARWATER REVIVAL from WILLIE AND THE POOR BOYS
Swinging prison song revived from the Great American Songbook by these good ole boys from California.

❹ I'M A MIDNIGHT MOVER BOBBY WOMACK from MIDNIGHT MOVER THE BOBBY WOMACK STORY
The soul sensation wasn't backwards in coming forward, judging by the way he struts his stuff here.

❺ MIDNIGHT RAMBLER THE ROLLING STONES from LET IT BLEED
Not everybody out and about after dark has good intentions. Mick Jagger sounds suitably demonic on their bluesy 1969 masterpiece.

❻ LADY MIDNIGHT LEONARD COHEN from SONGS FROM A ROOM
An early composition by the Canadian balladeer.

❼ MIDNIGHT LADY MARVIN GAYE from MIDNIGHT LOVE
The upbeat track that opens the tragic singer's final album isn't really typical of what made him so special, but prefigures a lot of what happened in dance music after his death.

❽ HORA ZERO ASTOR PIAZZOLLA from LUNA
This spooky instrumental vividly evokes the midnight wanders around Buenos Aires that Argentina's tango maestro and his musicians used to take between late-night sets.

❾ MIDNIGHT FEAST LAL WATERSON & OLIVER KNIGHT from ONCE IN A BLUE MOON
From a mercurial songwriting talent, perhaps overshadowed by more famous members of her family.

⑩ ROUND MIDNIGHT FRED HERSCH from THELONIOUS

The opening number on the 1997 album subtitled *Fred Hersch Plays Monk* is a spectral treasure – one celebrated pianist putting his own stamp on another's work.

Jon Lusk

Charles Mingus

Once upon a time, Charles Mingus was the bad boy of jazz, his music sneered at by the purists. Today, it sounds less like a tearing up of the rulebook than an intelligent and heartfelt synthesis of all that was great about the bebop, big-band swing, honking R&B and gospel soul of his era.

❶ PITHECANTHROPUS ERECTUS from
PITHECANTHROPUS ERECTUS

A menacing bassline and unreasonable horns render this the aural equivalent of a prelude to a mugging.

❷ SOLO DANCER from THE BLACK SAINT AND SINGER LADY

Archetypal big-band Mingus, his trademark glissandos in the horns smeared all over the two-chord see-saw of the main theme.

❸ VASSARLEAN from MYSTERIOUS BLUES

Recorded by Mingus elsewhere as "Weird Nightmare", this version has all the eldritch benefits of Eric Dolphy's porcine sax snuffling.

❹ HOG CALLIN' BLUES from MINGUS OH YEAH!

A burst of scatted vocalese from Charles cues in some minatory hi-hat and low-end piano; then the insistent riff begins to build up, barked out by threatening horns.

❺ NEW NOW KNOW HOW from MINGUS DYNASTY

Many Mingus tunes are haunted by the ghosts of both his own and the classic jazz songbooks. Here it's "Stars Fell On Alabama", given a zippy Thelonious Monk-like treatment.

❻ FREEDOM (PART ONE) from THE COMPLETE TOWN HALL CONCERT

A rap from Mingus, sloppy handclaps, and a world-weary chorus from his band build up into a hollerin' and testifyin' frenzy.

❼ GUNSLINGING BIRD from MINGUS DYNASTY

Hopping peculiarly, a xylophone punctuates another Monkish melody rapped out by impatient horns, with all the cadres of Mingus' band seemingly one step ahead of each other.

❽ GOODBYE PORK PIE HAT from MINGUS AH UM

A lyrical tribute to the late Lester Young, its spare, breathy sax melody treads carefully, with respect but never reverence.

❾ FABLES OF FAUBUS from MINGUS AH UM

Smoky but sharp, cool but alert, it's Mingus playing things relatively straight – a little like a Henry Mancini soundtrack given a more adventurous, discordant edge.

⑩ THE SHOES OF THE FISHERMAN'S WIFE ARE SOME JIVE ASS SLIPPERS from LET MY CHILDREN HEAR MUSIC

Sustained chords swell upward, like a discordant hymn, into a scrupulous and complex piece of Ellingtonia, with duelling, vamping brass counterpoint that suggests Cubist facets of the old standard "Brazil".

Matt Milton

Ministry

Masterminded by evil genius Al Jourgensen, Ministry are highly influential pioneers of scorching industrial metal, designed to test your pain threshold to its limit. Break out the ear protectors…

❶ ANIMOSITY from ANIMOSITISOMINA

It could be a guitar solo in the middle, then again it could be an angle grinder on an iron girder. A bile-fuelled bullet to the brain.

❷ BAD BLOOD from DARK SIDE OF THE SPOON

A mediocre album, perhaps, but this is a wild-eyed bruiser. It sounds like someone's thwacking sheet steel just before the guitar solo takes your head off.

❸ BREATHE from THE MIND IS A TERRIBLE THING TO TASTE

You want an environmentalist diatribe to end them all? Choking and claustrophobic, the more the screams order you to breathe the harder it becomes.

❹ JESUS BUILT MY HOTROD from PSALM 69

Industrial thrash as the good Lord intended. Butthole Surfers' Gibby Haynes delivers the infamously gibberish vocals to a juiced-up, ass-kicking rhythm track.

❺ THE LAND OF RAPE AND HONEY from THE LAND OF RAPE AND HONEY

An object lesson in the sonic architecture of electrometal. Layer upon layer of samples and instrumentation create a monumental Wall Of Noise.

❻ NO "W" from HOUSES OF THE MOLÉ

Ministry get even more intense and bitter. The ammunition combines industro-metal with screaming hardcore punk, and George Dubya is in the firing line.

❼ N.W.O. from PSALM 69

That's President Bush Snr sampled talking about a New World Order amid the tortured screams and mercilessly pummelling beats. Truly deadly.

❽ WRONG from HOUSES OF THE MOLÉ

Dubya gets it in the neck again. Venomous lyrics, spat with heartfelt conviction, compete with a boiling torrent of industrial punk noise.

Essi Berelian

Minutemen

Short-lived, immensely prolific, and totally committed, the Minutemen churned out brief, pointed jazz-punk-hardcore eruptions that frequently commented on America's shortcomings. Here are ten of the best, though it would take at least twenty to fill a CD.

❶ IF REAGAN PLAYED DISCO from BEAN SPILL EP

Not only would the Prez "sing lame lyrics", but he should know "you can't disco in jack boots". Talk about shredding a man's street cred in 77 seconds.

❷ THE PRICE OF PARADISE from THREE-WAY TIE FOR LAST

A pointed triumphal march for American sacrifices on foreign soil; poignant then, considering D. Boon's death near the album's release, and timely today.

❸ HISTORY LESSON (PART II) from DOUBLE NICKELS ON THE DIME

An earnest but funny and affecting portrait of the band's origins: "Our band could be your life."

❹ TOUR SPIEL from PROJECT MERSH

Sort of like History Lesson Part III, from Watt's perspective – a churning, hypnotic story of life on the road, with chimey breaks for what qualifies as the chorus (and turns spiel into a two syllable word).

❺ BOB DYLAN WROTE PROPAGANDA SONGS from WHAT MAKES A MAN START FIRES

It feels like each syllable is spat out of a machine gun, as George Hurley's drumming powers what seems a backhanded ode to one of their idols.

❻ PARANOID CHANT from PARANOID TIME EP

An early hardcore rant that updates Dylan's "Talking World War III Blues" – things have gotten so bad, our paranoid, preoccupied hero can't even talk to girls!

❼ LITTLE MAN WITH A GUN IN HIS HAND from BUZZ OR HOWL UNDER THE INFLUENCE OF HEAT

What starts as gentle noodling explodes into a frenzy of pulsing drums and loud, staccato guitar; D works himself up into a lather repeating the title.

❽ WORKING MEN ARE PISSED from THE POLITICS OF TIME EP

Sometimes their often-hilarious-yet-dead-serious titles said everything the song needed to say. But when the music it's built around detonates like a livewire, it makes the sentiment all the more powerful.

❾ MAYBE PARTYING WILL HELP from DOUBLE NICKELS ON THE DIME

Somehow, listening to D Boon's intonations, which move from awareness to resignation, you know that it won't – not for the masses nor his lonesome self.

❿ STORM IN MY HOUSE from DOUBLE NICKELS ON THE DIME

Musically one of their catchier and more idiosyncratic songs, with a riff reminiscent of "Don't Fear the Reaper" interpolated on bass, a great guitar break, and Boon wailing about his demons.

Andrew Rosenberg

Mirror mirror

When artists peer into the looking glass, just what *do* they see? Here are ten songs that provide some surprising answers.

❶ MIRROR MIRROR DOLLAR from PRODUCED BY TREVOR HORN

Therese Bazaar and David Van Day jog on the spot, clutching each other tight – it's them against the world! That is until they split, when it seemed like it was every David for himself.

❷ HALL OF MIRRORS KRAFTWERK from TRANS-EUROPE EXPRESS

The eerie electronic nightmare tale of an artist who becomes beguiled by his own reflection.

❸ HALL OF MIRRORS SIOUXSIE AND THE BANSHEES from THROUGH THE LOOKING GLASS

On this more sensual rendering of the Kraftwerk classic, Siouxsie's mesmeric voice wafts round a compelling harp-plucking beat.

❹ I COULD GIVE YOU (A MIRROR) EURYTHMICS from SWEET DREAMS

Annie and Dave rock out in this car-crash ride version of a song that was also heard on the B-side of the "Sweet Dreams" single.

❺ MIRROR MAN HUMAN LEAGUE from GREATEST HITS

Quite a rarified outing from the League here, with the ladies cooing their simple oooohs and aaaahs around Phil, to a quasi-Motown chug.

❻ I'LL BE YOUR MIRROR VELVET UNDERGROUND from VELVET UNDERGROUND & NICO

The Velvets covered all the bases from gorgeously dank to powerfully healing. Here's a prime example of the latter, with Nico's brittle, quivering voice attempting to offer support to a friend in deep existential need.

❼ MIRRORS SALLY OLDFIELD from MIRRORS

Dreamy Hawaiian harmonies lilting through Sally's classic. Here, she's a mirror of the sun, finding it impossible to do anything else but reflect the love that surrounds her.

❽ MAN IN THE MIRROR MICHAEL JACKSON from BAD

Well into his stride, almost a decade after *Off The Wall*, Michael ponders the changes we must make in ourselves if we are to hope to change the world around us.

❾ MIRROR BEAUTIFUL SOUTH from BLUE IS THE COLOUR

Here, musically, the Beautiful South do what they do best: effortless soulful strumming that welcomes you onto its gingham picnic blanket and invites you into its comforting country hamper – although the poignant lyrics might have you looking out for worms in the apples.

❿ MIRROR IN THE BATHROOM THE BEAT from I JUST CAN'T STOP IT

"You can watch yourself while you're eating". Nice idea from the two-tone skankers.

Link Hall

Joni Mitchell

First and foremost a Canadian, whose career in the US has always subtly reflected her roots. Joni Mitchell is a total artist – a painter with words, music and even the images that often grace her album covers. While she was a child of the 1960s, the 70s were her decade, as this selection suggests.

❶ BOTH SIDES NOW from CLOUDS

A much-covered early hit from Joni's second album, which came out in 1969. Only on her third did she really hit her stride.

❷ BIG YELLOW TAXI from LADIES OF THE CANYON

Joni's feeling for rhythm, the environment and pop music are all expertly rolled into this snappy little song.

❸ WOODSTOCK from LADIES OF THE CANYON

The flower-child naivety here still sounds charming, while the odd vocal gymnastics at the end hint at a passion for jazz which would later develop.

❹ CALIFORNIA from BLUE

A strong sense of place is probably the best reason for calling Joni Mitchell's music "folk", and nowhere is that better demonstrated than here.

❺ YOU TURN ME ON I'M A RADIO from FOR THE ROSES

The only hit on this largely forgotten 1972 album, which bridged the stylistic gap between two far more famous efforts.

❻ FREE MAN IN PARIS from COURT AND SPARK

Just one of half a dozen possible representative cuts from an album that masterfully fused jazz, rock and folk.

❼ DON'T INTERRUPT THE SORROW from THE HISSING OF SUMMER LAWNS

Joni really got rhythm on her 1975 album, using the services (long before world music was thought of) of the Drummers of Burundi. This sophisticated, urbane track is a real highlight.

❽ AMELIA from HEJIRA

A cinematic treat with a travelling-through-the-desert vibe. Sounds like it should have been on the soundtrack to Antonioni's *Zabriskie Point*.

❾ PAPRIKA PLAINS from DON JUAN'S RECKLESS DAUGHTER

This epic track filled a whole side of vinyl on its original release in 1977, and inspired bass player Charlie Mingus to approach the artist with a proposal.

❿ THE WOLF THAT LIVES IN LINDSEY from MINGUS

Joni's 1979 album was both a tribute to and a collaboration with jazz-great Mingus. Even some timber wolves got involved in this abstract off-the-wall gem.

Jon Lusk

Moby
Stretches out

From techno to blues via heavy metal and acid house, MOBY's music has touched many bases over his fifteen-year solo career. No surprise, then, that his eclectic playlist stretches from Johnny Cash to Donna Summer.

❶ **I ONLY HAVE EYES FOR YOU** THE FLAMINGOS from THE BEST OF THE FLAMINGOS

❷ **UTOPIA** GOLDFRAPP from FELT MOUNTAIN

❸ **I FEEL LOVE** DONNA SUMMER from THE BEST OF

❹ **NORTHERN SKY** NICK DRAKE from BRYTER LAYTER

❺ **STRINGS OF LIFE** DERRICK MAY from INNOVATOR

❻ **HELPLESS** CROSBY, STILL, NASH & YOUNG from DÉJÀ VU

❼ **OVER THE WALL** ECHO AND THE BUNNYMEN from HEAVEN UP HERE

❽ **THE MERCY SEAT** NICK CAVE from TENDER PREY

❾ **HURT** JOHNNY CASH from AMERICAN IV: THE MAN COMES AROUND

❿ **MEMORIES CAN'T WAIT** TALKING HEADS from FEAR OF MUSIC

Moby

It hasn't always been advert soundtracks from the man with the teashop in Manhattan. In fact, he's done just about everything. Here's the cream.

❶ **GO** from MOBY
The *Twin Peaks*-sampled favourite never tires. Simplicity at its most brilliant.

❷ **MOVE (YOU MAKE ME FEEL SO GOOD)** from MOVE EP
A rave gem with classic piano and anthemic singing. Hands in the air.

❸ **PORCELAIN** from PLAY
Hey, woman. Delicate name, delicate track. *Play*'s finest.

❹ **FIRST COOL HIVE** from EVERYTHING IS WRONG
Surrounded by hyper beats on the album, this sticks out for all the right reasons.

❺ **SICK IN THE SYSTEM** from NATURAL BLUES SINGLE
Strings, piano and beats with an uplifting chord progression – wasted as a B-side.

❻ **FEELING SO REAL** from EVERYTHING IS WRONG
Another rave classic amid the more recent smoother sounds that Moby has made his current trademark. Incredible energy.

❼ **EXTREME WAYS** from 18
Taking the *Play* sound into the 21st century with relative ease. The stand-out track from *18*.

❽ **WHY DOES MY HEART FEEL SO BAD?** from PLAY
Only two tracks from *Play*? Yes, but this sorrowful ditty shines through.

❾ **NEW YORK NEW YORK (ARMAND VAN HELDEN LONG VERSION)** from GO – THE VERY BEST OF MOBY: REMIXED
Nothing's better than a short burst of Moby than a longer burst of Moby – remixed, with increased horsepower and a paintjob de luxe by Armand Van Helden.

❿ **LIFT ME UP** from HOTEL
Beautiful, sweeping string effects and a dancing-dolly disco beat help this stand out as the best track on the otherwise fairly low key Hotel set. The naughty lyric of domestic subversion is just the icing on the cake.

Marten Sealby

Modest Mouse

Longstanding indie troupers from the frozen northwest of the US, Modest Mouse were bank-drainingly underground for years, until "Float On" went global in 2004. And then it all happened for them: US #1 album, signing Johnny Marr...

there clearly is some kind of benevolent Indie god out there, if only it can be roused. Put your hands together for Isaac Brock and the rest of his Washington State pals.

❶ DRAMAMINE from THIS IS A LONG DRIVE FOR SOMEONE WITH NOTHING TO THINK ABOUT

Classy, psychedelic waltz-time divertissement with Isaac bellowing a lyric of vitriol, rage and Dramamine (a pretty good travel sickness remedy). I guess, living in Washington, one gets to know all the good over the counter remedies pretty young.

❷ TALKING SHIT ABOUT A PRETTY SUNSET from THIS IS A LONG DRIVE FOR SOMEONE WITH NOTHING TO THINK ABOUT

Primitive romance skills on display here. Kinda provincial thug meets shop counter princess. A shambolic, messy track, convinced of its own noble soul, and imbued with a strange wistful love.

❸ TINY CITIES MADE OF ASHES from THE MOON AND ANTARCTICA

This is a blast: the chirpiest burst of quirky rhythm on an album otherwise remarkable for its lack of light and empathy for the world at large.

❹ WILD PACKS OF FAMILY DOGS from THE MOON AND ANTARCTICA

OK, you're out on the porch with your guitar, just messin' round a while, and you find yourself singing: "A wild pack of family dogs came running through the yard as my little sister played; the dogs took her away, and I guess she was eaten up." Would you ever be able to look your sister in the eye again?

❺ FLOAT ON from GOOD NEWS FOR PEOPLE WHO LOVE BAD NEWS

Anthemic, irrepressibly cheerful single that refreshes one's belief in pop as the world's best hope of survival.

❻ OCEAN BREATHES SALTY from GOOD NEWS FOR PEOPLE WHO LOVE BAD NEWS

Cymbals wash back and forth over sweeping guitars: a brilliant pop single, gorgeous studio effects, hooks aplenty and lyrics that go in one ear and out the other.

❼ THE GOOD TIMES ARE KILLING ME from WE WERE DEAD BEFORE THE SHIP EVEN SANK

You know your band's on the way when you get offered a Flaming Lips mix for your album. And not a bad job from Wayne and the boys.

❽ DASHBOARD from WE WERE DEAD BEFORE THE SHIP EVEN SANK

Blinking a little in the unaccustomed spotlight,

Modest Mouse duck down behind the wheel of their getaway car and shudder away the fear by dashing off this deceptively simple hit single.

❾ MISSED THE BOAT from WE WERE DEAD BEFORE THE SHIP EVEN SANK

Built over a shaky, cheap rhythm, this is a last-reel singalong tune as sung by a band of good-hearted movieland desperados riding out of town.

❿ LITTLE MOTEL from WE WERE DEAD BEFORE THE SHIP EVEN SANK

MM make a joyful noise to the world through bolting together a mismatched jumble of instruments and influences, and create a thing of beauty.

Al Spicer

Mogwai

Though sometimes labelled "post-rock" or "second-generation shoegazers", Mogwai are a band with a sound all of their own. Here's a handful of their finest glacial slabs.

❶ HELICON 2 from TEN RAPID

A slow and graceful instrumental that perfectly represents the band's ability to capture a fine melody.

❷ ANGELS VERSUS ALIENS from TEN RAPID

Guitars layer and deepen like falling snow, culminating in an explosion of overdrive and stampeding xylophone.

❸ SECRET PINT from ROCK ACTION

The piano line and vocals are beautiful and sad, while the clattering rattle of cymbals sets the tempo.

❹ HUNTED BY A FREAK from HAPPY SONGS FOR HAPPY PEOPLE

A Vocoder-blessed gem of shimmering guitar-chords and strings. Also search out the Peel session version on *Government Commissions*.

❺ LIKE HEROD from GOVERNMENT COMMISSIONS

An eighteen-minute holocaust that first lulls you into a near-slumber and then hurls you into the path of a distortion tornado.

❻ MOGWAI FEAR SATAN (MY BLOODY VALENTINE REMIX) from MOGWAI FEAR SATAN REMIXES EP

Kevin Shields works his magic on a Mogwai original – beats melt into a goo of saturated sounds that'll leave you gasping for air.

Peter Buckley

Money

It truly makes the disc go round. There's a lyric for every aspect, whether it's boasting about having "loadsofit", decrying the evil it makes men and women do, or moaning about having none.

❶ MONEY THAT'S WHAT I WANT! BARRETT STRONG from THE MILLENNIUM COLLECTION: THE BEST OF BARRETT STRONG
A shameless hymn to greed, first recorded by this early Motown artist. The sentiment proved popular; it was covered by The Flying Lizards, John Lee Hooker and The Beatles, who also sang "Can't Buy Me Love". Without a trace of irony.

❷ TAXMAN THE BEATLES from REVOLVER
George Harrison's scathing attack on the Inland Revenue's excessive demands.

❸ MONEY MONEY MONEY ABBA from ABBA GOLD – GREATEST HITS
Hard to believe Sweden's fab four were ever in need of cash, as the title of this collection reminds us, but this lucre-craving classic really captures what it's like to have none.

❹ MONEY PINK FLOYD from THE DARK SIDE OF THE MOON
Complete with percussive proto-sampling of the sound of cash registers and coins, this ambivalent number ironically helped create the Floyd's biggest grossing album.

❺ AINT NOTHIN' GOIN' ON BUT THE RENT GWEN GUTHRIE from THE ULTIMATE COLLECTION
The same cannot be said for this soul diva's lurve manifesto – "No romance without finance".

❻ SHE WORKS HARD FOR THE MONEY DONNA SUMMER from THE JOURNEY: THE VERY BEST OF DONNA SUMMER
The disco diva demands respect for her hard workin' heroine : "She works hard for the money so you'd better treat her right!" The job is not exactly specified.

❼ DO RE MI WOODY GUTHRIE from AMERICA'S FOLK HEROES
America's finest folk troubadour advises dustbowl refugees that arriving in California without a bit of "do re mi" won't be a whole lot of fun.

❽ ONE MORE DOLLAR GILLIAN WELCH from REVIVAL
The hard luck story of a low-paid migrant labourer stranded from a sweetheart by unemployment. The queen of gothic hillbilly alt folk shines on her awesome 1994 debut.

❾ RECESSION BLUES B.B.KING from KING OF THE BLUES
The master bluesman laments hard times and their knock-on effects – he can't afford to keep his baby and has to drink beer and wine rather than "liquor". Everything's relative.

❿ MONEY'S TOO TIGHT TO MENTION THE VALENTINE BROTHERS from FIRST TAKE
For when the going gets really tough… A soulful early 1980s attack on Reaganomics, later reinvented by Simply Red. Credit where credit's due.

Jon Lusk

Thelonious Monk

The most original and iconoclastic of all jazz composers, Monk's music is immediately recognizable. His splintery piano playing is equally individual – simultaneously homely and alien, it's a beautiful law unto itself.

❶ THELONIOUS from GENIUS OF MODERN MUSIC VOL 1
Thumped-out, morse-code piano wakes up an ornery drumkit before everything starts swinging beneath a circular thirteen-note fanfare.

❷ MONK'S MOOD from THELONIOUS HIMSELF
Monk alone at the piano is made all the more affecting by John Coltrane and Wilbur Ware unassumingly (and unexpectedly) joining in towards the very end.

❸ HORNIN' IN from GENIUS OF MODERN MUSIC VOL 2
Trilling and acerbic, this tune is Monk at his nastiest and is as insinuating as a splinter.

❹ FOUR IN ONE from GENIUS OF MODERN MUSIC VOL 2
A generous tangle of a tune, its tricky knots are both challengingly captious and warmly inviting.

❺ PANNONICA from BRILLIANT CORNERS
Monk plays piano with one hand, celeste with the other, adding a delicate clarity to this sidelong lullaby.

❻ BEMSHA SWING from BRILLIANT CORNERS
Max Roach doubles on timpani on a tune that, aided by Sonny Rollins' thick-set but measured tone, manages to sound both muscular and wistful.

❼ OFF MINOR (TAKE FIVE) from MONK'S MUSIC
The dynamic duo of Lester Young and John Coltrane add some stab to Monk's punchy dischords, throwing his minors even further off.

8 SWEET AND LOVELY from MULLIGAN MEETS MONK
Gerry Mulligan's sax tone is as fuzzy as mouldy chocolate, laying back while Monk vamps some of his splayed hammy clusters on a gorgeously discordant ballad.

9 BOO BOO'S BIRTHDAY (TAKE 2) from UNDERGROUND
Dedicated to his daughter, this 1968 tune is quintessential Monk, questing and exploratory but fundamentally tumbling around a single nagging note.

10 INTROSPECTION from SOLO MONK
A gymnastic farrago of sudden twists, turns and reversals; the tune's key changes as abruptly and multifariously as if the tape had been spliced.

Matt Milton

The Monkees

Even if the prefabricated four – Micky Dolenz, Davy Jones, Peter Tork and Mike Nesmith – never had any pretensions to greatness, they were masters of apparently disposable, yet surprisingly durable pop.

1 DAYDREAM BELIEVER from GREATEST HITS
Wondrously wistful, ultra-contagious, and sweetly sung by Davy Jones, this feelgood smash was the best thing to come out of that bizarre late-1960s flowering known as bubblegum pop.

2 I'M A BELIEVER from GREATEST HITS
Covered for the movie *Shrek*, used in an episode of *South Park*, this Neil Diamond composition is a once-heard, frequently hummed timeless shout of joy about the moment when love begins to click.

3 RIO from FROM A RADIO ENGINE TO THE PHOTON WING
Hypnotically indecisive, charmingly melodic solo effort from Mike Nesmith, in which his predicament – should he go to Rio or not? – doesn't seem to matter that much.

4 ALTERNATE TITLE (RANDY SCOUSE GIT) from GREATEST HITS
One of the most inventive pop hits of the 1960s, this is an authentic, angry, freewheeling marvel from the pen of Micky Dolenz.

5 (I'M NOT YOUR) STEPPING STONE from GREATEST HITS
The band's struggles with their own label inspired this bitter diatribe. The furious lyrics, aimed at a feckless lover, could just as easily apply to the Machiavellian figures who run the music industry.

6 WHAT AM I DOIN' HANGING 'ROUND? from THE BEST OF THE MONKEES
A simple slice of corny country pop by Michael Martin Murphey. The Monkees cover, complete with banjo from Doug Dillard, prefigures Nesmith's later move into cult country-rock.

7 PLEASANT VALLEY SUNDAY from GREATEST HITS
Noted, at the time, for its mild social protest, this song is far broader, striking a chord with anyone who's ever endured a pointless Sunday.

8 LAST TRAIN TO CLARKSVILLE from GREATEST HITS
Pop is full of train songs and this one has worn well; possibly because neither The Monkees, nor Boyce and Hart who wrote it, felt obliged to include "choo choo" and "train" in the lyric.

9 VALLERI from GREATEST HITS
Short, unpretentious, lyrics about the girl next door, wailing trumpets, Davy Jones on vocal and none of the other Monkees on it at all.

10 PORPOISE SONG from GREATEST HITS
With sweeping organ, swaying vocals from Dolenz, and cries of encouragement in the chorus from Jones, this theme to the band's movie *Head* is a real fan's favourite.

Paul Simpson

Monster Mash

Bobby "Boris" Pickett's career-defining hit haunts us once a year. But in a world populated by alienated musicians, there are plenty of monster songs to get you through the other 364 days.

1 KING KONG THE KINKS from THE KINKS KRONIKLES
Monsters may be all about allegory, but there's nothing subtle in The Kinks' rocking commentary on the mainstream hunger for power.

2 TWO-HEADED DOG ROKY ERICKSON AND THE ALIENS from THE EVIL ONE PLUS ONE
Battling his own demons for much of his life, Erickson combines a screaming guitar with a soulful shriek to create a fiery masterpiece.

3 SOME KIND OF MONSTER METALLICA from ST ANGER
The Buddha may be in each of us, but so is the monster. The dysfunctional Metallica points this out in a devastating crush of machinery: "The monster lives! We are the monster!"

❹ BIG FOOT THE GROOVIE GHOULIES from MONSTER CLUB

The lighter side of monsterhood. A strong opening riff, fast guitars and flat, nasal vocals set the right tone for the Groovie Ghoulies' punked up tribute to a friendly Big Foot with a hide like a shag carpet.

❺ GODZILLA BLUE OYSTER CULT from SPECTRES

Monster guitar riffs helped lure BOC's "Godzilla" out of the movies and onto the radio. The go-go chorus didn't hurt, either.

❻ CASPER THE FRIENDLY GHOST DANIEL JOHNSTON from YIP/JUMP MUSIC

Percussive cheese organ holds down the melody for outsider artist Daniel Johnston, who, in a childlike voice that is tinged with disdain, sings a tale you won't find in comic books.

❼ HUMAN FLY THE CRAMPS from BAD MUSIC FOR BAD PEOPLE

Swampy guitar and an angry buzz punctuate The Cramps' musical pondering about garbage brains and the complexity of the visual world.

❽ WEREWOLVES OF LONDON WARREN ZEVON from EXCITABLE BOY

The late Warren Zevon always lurked outside the Top 40, but he made it in with this humorous, howling hit, another venture into the lighter side of monsterhood.

❾ VAMPIRE BLUES NEIL YOUNG from ON THE BEACH

The rock 'n' roll lifestyle has produced more than its share of vampires. Here a nimble Neil Young electrifies the traditional blues.

❿ IRON MAN BLACK SABBATH from PARANOID

Long before MTV created an addled monster, Black Sabbath's Ozzy Osbourne keened with clarity about a hunk of misunderstood metal who tried to save the earth and then, when it wasn't appreciated, tried to destroy it. The song remains a training ground for anyone who wants to play electric guitar.

Madelyn Rosenberg

Monty Python

They've been winning awards again with the musical, *Spamalot*. But the Pythons, ably abetted by Neil Innes, always did a nice song. Like the sketches, many sound distinctly dated or dodgy, in the cold light of modern times, but the best remain brilliant.

❶ ALWAYS LOOK ON THE BRIGHT SIDE OF LIFE from MONTY PYTHON SINGS...

Who could resist a toe-tapping crucifixion feel-good number? With a whistling chorus? It just ain't possible What you got to lose? Cheer up you old bugger, give us a grin.

❷ LUMBERJACK SONG from MONTY PYTHON SINGS...

Palin never wanted to be a weather forecaster He wanted to be a lumberjack, and to sing, sing, sing this classic transvestite woodcutters' anthem. He's OK.

❸ ERIC THE HALF A BEE from MONTY PYTHON SINGS...

"ABCDEFG, Eric the half a bee..." Perhaps one of Python's finest philosophical numbers, writ in song.

❹ HEIDEGGER from MONTY PYTHON SINGS...

Were the world's greatest philosophers all piss-heads? It would appear so. Wonderful rhymes and startling logic ("René Descartes was a drunken fart, I drink therefore I am") to a didgeridoo backing.

❺ GALAXY SONG from MONTY PYTHON SINGS...

Python's last film, *The Meaning of Life*, was a stinker, but it spawned this lovely Eric Idle number about the universe: "And pray there's intelligent life somewhere out in space/'Cos there's bugger all down here on earth."

❻ EVERY SPERM IS SACRED from MONTY PYTHON SINGS...

This absurdly ambitious number (also from *The Meaning of Life*) has a cast of hundreds, getting across the immutable Catholic belief: "If a sperm is wasted, God gets quite irate."

Mark Ellingham

Moon songs

There's a good number of rhymes for "moon", a subject long beloved by poets and lyricists.

❶ SHINE ON HARVEST MOON NORA BAYES AND JACK NORWORTH from TOGETHER & ALONE

Vaudeville's Brad and Angelina popularized this famous folk song in the early years of the 20th century.

❷ BLUE MOON OF KENTUCKY BILL MONROE from COUNTRY MUSIC HALL OF FAME

Ripping bluegrass ode to Monroe's Virginia home. Elvis paid homage by cutting it as a rockabilly anthem.

❸ MOONDANCE VAN MORRISON from MOONDANCE

Van at his most joyous and lyrical tells of the magical sway a silver moon can have on young lovers.

❹ BAD MOON RISING CREEDENCE CLEARWATER REVIVAL from GREEN RIVER

Tense, skipping rock'n'roll with John Fogerty employing Biblical metaphor to suggest the US under Pres' Nixon was getting worse.

❺ RIDIN' IN THE MOONLIGHT HOWLIN' WOLF from SINGS THE BLUES

Chester and Co crank it up and let it go as they tear loose on their debut recording. Dig Willie Johnson's wild guitar workout!

❻ YELLOW MOON NEVILLE BROTHERS from YELLOW MOON

Tense, funky ode to the moon above the bayous from New Orleans' first family.

❼ MOONLIGHT ON VERMONT CAPTAIN BEEFHART from TROUT MASK REPLICA

The Captain feels the tug of lunar rays as the Magic Band set about creating a cosmic rush.

❽ PINK MOON NICK DRAKE from PINK MOON

Nick Drake's minimalist final recording suggests a man shutting down. Ironic that this become a posthumous hit after being used in a VW commercial.

❾ WALKING ON THE MOON THE POLICE from GREATEST HITS

Sting sings of the flush feeling when you're falling in love over the fattest reggae bass line he ever rode.

❿ MAN ON THE MOON REM from AUTOMATIC FOR THE PEOPLE

Michael Stipe wonders on the strangeness and alienation of modern life while Peter Buck and Co create a lush acoustic soundscape around him.

Garth Cartwright

Alanis Morissette

Jagged Little Pill may not have been Morissette's debut, but it put her on the map. Inevitably, she's struggled to match its teenage themes of sexual jealousy and confused anger ever since, and half of this list comes from that one album. But we've rounded up a few gems from her later work.

❶ YOU OUGHTA KNOW from JAGGED LITTLE PILL

On which Alanis rivals Marianne Faithfull for the bitterness with which she berates an ex-lover.

❷ ALL I REALLY WANT from JAGGED LITTLE PILL

Brilliant pop production by Glen Ballard.

❸ IRONIC from JAGGED LITTLE PILL

Alanis doesn't quite appear to understand the strict dictionary definition of the word, but a great song, nonetheless.

❹ YOU LEARN from JAGGED LITTLE PILL

Lessons in life from a precocious 19-year-old.

❺ HAND IN POCKET from JAGGED LITTLE PILL

Ballsy but accessible, perfect radio-friendly pop-rock.

❻ THANK U from SUPPOSED FORMER INFATUATION JUNKIE

This was the best song from an otherwise disappointing album. "Thank you India, thank you terror, thank you disillusionment", she sings. What could she be on about?

❼ THAT I WOULD BE GOOD from SUPPOSED FORMER INFATUATION JUNKIE

A chill-out track in which she intriguingly wonders how she would react if she lost all the fame and wealth that *Jagged…* had brought.

❽ 21 THINGS I WANT IN A LOVER from UNDER RUG SWEPT

Tick 'em off and count 'em to see how well you measure up.

❾ KING OF PAIN from ALANIS UNPLUGGED

A surprising cover of the Police song from her 1999 MTV outing.

❿ DOTH I PROTEST TOO MUCH from SO-CALLED CHAOS

The mature Alanis asking a question she would never have contemplated at the time of "You Oughta Know".

Nigel Williamson

Ennio Morricone

Morricone's spaghetti-western sountracks created a whole new genre with their innovative blend of eerie desert sounds, weird abstract vocals and superb orchestration.

❶ THE ECSTASY OF GOLD from THE GOOD, THE BAD AND THE UGLY

A simply gorgeous piece. Understated piano, tolling chimes and oboe motif lead to a slow-building abstract vocal and orchestral arrangement.

② THE GOOD, THE BAD AND THE UGLY from THE GOOD, THE BAD AND THE UGLY

No introduction necessary for this total and utter classic. One of the most famous movie themes (spaghetti western or otherwise) ever written.

③ GUITAR NOCTURNE from DEATH RIDES A HORSE

As the desert sun sets… A mellow and minimal arrangement of hazy voices and percussion floats around a beautiful acoustic guitar solo.

④ INVENZIONE PER JOHN from A FISTFUL OF DYNAMITE

Building upon the vocal and melodic motifs of the main theme, this stunning nine-minute piece moves effortlessly through a variety of emotional moods.

⑤ LA RESA DEI CONTI from FOR A FEW DOLLARS MORE

The fragile chimes of a pocket watch erupt into terrifyingly strident church-organ chords – a moment of stark epiphany.

⑥ MAN WITH A HARMONICA from ONCE UPON A TIME IN THE WEST

Regularly sampled and borrowed, the epic strains of an eerily distant harmonica introduce an arrangement heavily pregnant with brooding violence.

⑦ L'ULTIMA TROMBA from A FIST GOES WEST

A distant cousin to "Man With A Harmonica", on which the haunting tones are leavened by lyrical trumpet and oboe solos, soft voices and soothingly strummed guitars.

⑧ PER QUALCHE DOLLARO IN PIÙ from FOR A FEW DOLLARS MORE

A Jew's harp twangs away in the baking midday heat, and a distant whistled melody ushers in some superb guitar and chanting vocals.

⑨ SE SEI QUALCUNO E' COLPA MIA from MY NAME IS NOBODY

Introduced by a ticking clock, the sense of suspense is epic. Brilliantly distorted electric guitars add to the crucial nail-biting tension.

⑩ THEME FROM A FISTFUL OF DOLLARS from A FISTFUL OF DOLLARS

Stately and sombre in pace; while the vocals play their part, it all hinges around a single mournful trumpet. The sense of emotion is palpable.

Essi Berelian

Morrissey

Bequiffed legend; monarch of miserabilism; aloof eccentric; father of Britpop. Get the picture?

① EVERY DAY IS LIKE SUNDAY from VIVA HATE

An epic song from Mozzer's first solo album, perfectly capturing the drudgery of modern life. Makes Britain's "silent and grey" seaside towns achingly beautiful.

② SUEDEHEAD from VIVA HATE

Morrissey's best solo pop song shares much of its genetic make-up with the finest of The Smiths' back catalogue.

③ I DON'T MIND IF YOU FORGET ME from VIVA HATE

Soaring indie guitar track fizzing with energy and lovers' angst. An outsider's anthem.

④ HAIRDRESSER ON FIRE from BONA DRAG

Proof that Morrissey is strangely addictive: tunes like this touch parts that others just can't reach.

⑤ MUTE WITNESS from KILL UNCLE

Marvellously strange, stuttering from slow piano ballad to pumping guitar rock.

⑥ WE HATE IT WHEN OUR FRIENDS BECOME SUCCESSFUL from YOUR ARSENAL

The arch put-down is a dish best served dripping with Morrissey wit and razor-sharp lyrics.

⑦ TOMORROW from YOUR ARSENAL

Morrissey at his awkward best: impassioned singing about pain and lovelorn loneliness. Trademark yodelling and edgy guitars.

⑧ IRISH BLOOD, ENGLISH HEART from YOU ARE THE QUARRY

Wily musings on the artist's own identity crisis, writ to the catchiest of pop tunes.

⑨ THE FIRST OF THE GANG TO DIE from YOU ARE THE QUARRY

Reinvented, inspired and rejuvenated by his move to the US, Morrissey celebrates the mutual admiration society formed with his most recent and most surprising group of worshippers – the Latino gang members of Los Angeles.

⑩ THE YOUNGEST WAS THE MOST LOVED from RINGLEADER OF THE TORMENTORS

Morrissey's patented wrought delivery works in perfect harmony with the tormented orchestration here to illuminate another mini-tragedy from everyday life.

Tim Pollard

Van Morrison

A professional musician since he was 15, the Belfast bard, uncommon one, and veteran rock-blues-jazz-folk-soul fusionist, has developed into one of the great masters of modern music.

❶ AND THE HEALING HAS BEGUN from INTO THE MUSIC
Momentum-building celebration of love and life with a new-age tinge. Violin and vocals chase each other across the groove.

❷ BROWN EYED GIRL from BLOWIN' YOUR MIND!/THE BEST OF VAN MORRISON
Van's only jukebox perennial and karaoke fixture: "Do you remember when, we used to sing?"

❸ BESIDE YOU from ASTRAL WEEKS
"High" point (in all sorts of ways) of Van's most original, most must-have album. Ecstatic, poetic, with risk-takingly committed vocals.

❹ I FORGOT THAT LOVE EXISTED from POETIC CHAMPIONS COMPOSE
From the darker side of the oeuvre – "heartache after heartache" – one of several smooth and moody tracks from *Champions*.

❺ MOONDANCE from MOONDANCE
A "marvellous night" indeed. Van at his smoothest and lounge-iest.

❻ STREETS OF ARKLOW from VEEDON FLEECE
A fine example of Morrison's Celtic strain, with flute, pastoral lyrics and wandering vocals.

❼ A TOWN CALLED PARADISE from NO GURU, NO METHOD, NO TEACHER
Smooth, saxy redemption song from a beautifully produced fine late album.

❽ SUMMERTIME IN ENGLAND from THE COMMON ONE
Far-out – not just for the lyrics about Wordsworth and Coleridge "smokin' dope in Kendal"– mystic marathon from an underrated album.

❾ WILD NIGHT from TUPELO HONEY
Hit the town and dance. Brisk, breezy, rocky Van-lite.

❿ YOU DON'T PULL NO PUNCHES, BUT YOU DON'T PUSH THE RIVER from VEEDON FLEECE
Go with the flow. Not as trance-inducing as the comparable "Listen to the Lion", but delightfully off-the-wall lyrics and superb musicianship weave a magic spell.

Andrew Lockett

Motörhead

With the legendary Lemmy at the helm, the battle-scarred warhorse that is Motörhead remains the true embodiment of body-slamming rock'n'roll.

❶ ACE OF SPADES from ACE OF SPADES
Brain-rattling drums, *that* riff and Lemmy's rapid-fire bass nailing it all home with snake-eye precision. One of the most famous tunes in metaldom.

❷ BOMBER from NO SLEEP 'TIL HAMMERSMITH
Rawer and dirtier than the studio version, this is delivered with the kind of ferocity that would kill any normal band.

❸ BURNER from BASTARDS
A psychotic cousin to "Ace Of Spades", with a spiky off-kilter chorus that could have your eye out.

❹ DANCING ON YOUR GRAVE from ANOTHER PERFECT DAY
The 'Head went vaguely tuneful for a while thanks to guitarist Brian Robertson – but this underrated effort slays all the same.

❺ LOCOMOTIVE from NO REMORSE
This must contain some of the fastest drumming ever to grace a 'Head tune, and that's really saying something. Casey Jones it ain't.

❻ MOTÖRHEAD from NO SLEEP 'TIL HAMMERSMITH
Yet another gonzoid belter with Lemmy proving his speedfreak credentials. This live version makes the original sound like a nursery rhyme.

❼ ORGASMATRON from ORGASMATRON
Lemmy does cynical evil brilliantly, and nowhere more so than on this grinding, black-hearted epic.

❽ OVERKILL from NO SLEEP 'TIL HAMMERSMITH
This rocket-fuelled live version is faster and more chaotic than in the studio, and still boasts two ace false endings.

❾ R.A.M.O.N.E.S. from 1916
Kindred rock'n'roll spirits with Da Brudders from Noo Yoik, this spot-on tribute number is a blur of bad attitude.

❿ SMILING LIKE A KILLER from INFERNO
Chucklesome and chilling Lemmy is a master of blackly funny lyrics – even your pets aren't safe from the warty one's homicidal instincts.

Essi Berelian

m

Motown

The Detroit-based company was the first successful label to be owned and run by African-Americans. The following are ten finely tuned vehicles from Berry Gordy's Hit Factory, whose style reached perfection in the 1960s and 70s.

❶ **MONEY (THAT'S WHAT I WANT)** BARRETT STRONG from THE BEST OF BARRETT STRONG
It was bigger for The Beatles, but this gritty piece of soul put Motown on the map.

❷ **(LOVE IS LIKE A) HEATWAVE** MARTHA AND THE VANDELLAS from HEATWAVE
Holland-Dozier-Holland sizzler that shows off the classic Hitsville backing-vocal sound.

❸ **GET READY** THE TEMPTATIONS from GETTING READY
Solid, driving soul from the Motown backbone.

❹ **NEEDLE IN A HAYSTACK** THE VELVELETTES from BEST OF THE VELVELETTES
Catchy three-girl harmony, backed up with a rhythmic playground feel.

❺ **BABY LOVE** THE SUPREMES from WHERE DID OUR LOVE GO
Shimmering pop–soul crossover from Berry's brightest stars.

❻ **HEARD IT THROUGH THE GRAPEVINE** GLADYS KNIGHT AND THE PIPS from EVERYBODY NEEDS LOVE
Lowdown and languourous. A stunning version of the Marvin Gaye hit.

❼ **THIS OLD HEART OF MINE (IS WEAK FOR YOU)** THE ISLEY BROTHERS from THIS OLD HEART OF MINE
Weeping string and double drums underpin this #1 ballad.

❽ **TEARS OF A CLOWN** SMOKEY ROBINSON & THE MIRACLES from MAKE IT HAPPEN
Inspired by the opera I Pagliacci, Smokey takes the circus sound four to the floor.

❾ **GOTTA GIVE IT UP (PART 1)** MARVIN GAYE from LIVE AT THE LONDON PALLADIUM
Skin-tight 1970s party groover.

❿ **LIVIN' FOR THE CITY** STEVIE WONDER from INNERVISIONS
Motown gets funky on the wrong side of the tracks.

Rachel Coldicutt

Mott The Hoople & Ian Hunter

Most famous for that excellent smash hit, these glammy hard rockers enjoyed reasonable success in the 1970s before splintering. Ace songwriter Ian Hunter is still packing 'em in though.

MOTT THE HOOPLE

❶ **ALL THE WAY FROM MEMPHIS** from MOTT
Some fantastic ivory-bashing from Hunter, plus snazzy saxophone and guitar interplay give this a cool vintage rock'n'roll flavour.

❷ **ALL THE YOUNG DUDES** from ALL THE YOUNG DUDES
It looked like the end of the line for the lads before David Bowie revived them with this classic anthem. Listen carefully and you might catch him on backing vox.

❸ **CRASH STREET KIDDS** from THE HOOPLE
Look out, they're dressed to kill! And just when you think it's finished early, those guitars suddenly jump all over you.

❹ **THE GOLDEN AGE OF ROCK'N'ROLL** from THE HOOPLE
There's tons going on here. Ian Hunter gives the vocals some serious welly amid the piano, parping saxophones and glamorous backing vocals.

❺ **SATURDAY GIGS** from GREATEST HITS
The band's last hit single, and the biographical lyrics are tearjerkingly nostalgic – worth it just to hear them name check Croydon!

IAN HUNTER

❻ **ONCE BITTEN TWICE SHY** from IAN HUNTER
One of Hunter's best lyrics, with some great bar-room piano and Mick Ronson guitars.

❼ **WHO DO YOU LOVE** from IAN HUNTER
Another real cracker, with a terrific bouncy bass, and Mick Ronson conjuring up some fiery fretboard magic. Love the cool finger-clicking intro too.

❽ **ALL AMERICAN ALIEN BOY** from ALL AMERICAN ALIEN BOY
Very cool and funky autobiographical tune with some great female backing vox. Ends with an awesome rapidfire list of Native American chiefs' names.

⑨ CLEVELAND ROCKS from YOU'RE NEVER ALONE WITH A SCHIZOPHRENIC

A staple tune in the Hunter live set to this day, this is a storming melodic rocker with an irresistible hook.

⑩ SHIPS from YOU'RE NEVER ALONE WITH A SCHIZOPHRENIC

Bizarrely, Barry Manilow covered this and had a huge US hit. A gentle ballad that is genuinely touching without wallowing in schmaltz.

Essi Berelian

Mozambique

The world comes together in the music of Mozambique. Down on the shores of the Indian Ocean, influences from Indonesia, Brazil, the Congo, New York, India and the Middle East (to name just a few) meet a wealth of traditional styles and instruments and are born again.

① ELISA GOMARA SAIA ORCHESTRA MARRABENTA STAR DE MOÇAMBIQUE from INDEPENDANCE

The original marrabenta outfit, complete with Wazimbo on vocals and a full horn section. Here with steam coming out of their ears.

② RAMBANANE TIMBILA MUZIMBA from CONTA PROPRIA

Timbila Muzimba turn sax, drums, bass and a defiantly jazz outlook onto traditional *timbila* music.

③ MARIA TERESA DILON DJINDJI from DILON

A recent recording of a 1950s classic about a man caught between two women, by the man they call the King of Marrabenta.

④ NUNO MAALANI EYUPHURO from MAMA MOSAMBIKI

The great Zena Bakar leads this group from Nampula, in the Islamic north of the country. Her voice flies in this song about motherhood.

⑤ MBHOLE MBHOLE NA YONE DJAAKA from MBHOLE MBHOLE NA YONA

Rootsy brilliance from Beira's finest. A bit like Zimbabwean *chimurenga*, but built around the patterns of Mozambican *timbila* (traditional Chopi xylophones).

⑥ M'TSITSO VENANCIO MBANDE from TIMBILA TA VENANCIO

The king of timbila, Mbande performs a call and response with his 32-piece orchestra.

⑦ WUKATI LAKUKAWA HINENGUE FELICIANO GOMES from FORGOTTEN GUITARS FROM MOZAMBIQUE

Proper *marrabenta* of the 1950s, featuring acoustic guitars, drums and a traditional form of rap.

⑧ A FÚRIA DAS ÁGUAS FACE OCULTA from ATENÇÃO: DESMINAGEM!

Studio Kandonga (Underground) is the mainstay of Mozambique's hip-hop scene. Chilled beats and floating voices, but the fury's never far beneath the surface.

⑨ TOMA QUE TI DOU ZAIDA E CARLOS CHONGO from HOMENAGEM À ZAIDA

Irresistible Mozambican pop, with the late, much-lamented Zaida Chongo on lead vocals and Carlos Chongo playing that dreamy lead guitar. Best served with lots of sunshine!

Tom Bullough

Oliver Mtukudzi

No one in African music makes you want to dance, weep and laugh at the same time quite like the great "Tuku". The biggest star in Zimbabwe for years, he has now taken over on the international stage as well, playing his soulful, socially conscious songs. He's released 48 albums to date, and here are some good places to start.

① NDIMA NDAPEDZA from TUKU MUSIC

This is the album that broke him internationally, and if any one track swung it…

② RAKI from BVUMA/TOLERANCE

More about weeping than dancing. That great, deep voice over layers of delicate guitar and wailing backing singers.

③ CHIDO CHENYU from THE OTHER SIDE

A 1970s classic, this is stomping dance music about "those who sleep in the forest": that is, the guerrillas in the war of independence.

④ PINDIRAI from NHAVA

Among the first recordings made at his new studio in Norton, Zimbabwe, this 2005 number is the sound of Tuku at home.

⑤ ZIWERE from ZIWERE MUCOPENHAGEN

This live standard, originally released on 1978's *Ndipeiwo Zano*, is one of Oliver's most playful, joyful songs.

m

❻ NERIA from NERIA

The lovely, gentle theme song from Tuku's award-winning soundtrack to Zimbabwe's second feature film, in which he also starred.

❼ NDAKUVARA from VHUNZE MOTO

His voice cracks with passion. The bass rocks and thunders. The dancefloor fills up (if it isn't full already).

❽ UCHAROYA CHETE from KUVHAIRA

With a rare *marimba* (xylophone) playing in the band, Ucharoya Chete points straight to Tuku's roots.

Tom Bullough

Mudhoney

Nirvana had the hits, but Mudhoney kept it real. This is grunge as it was first conceived, an unholy sub-Stoogian racket filtered through the prism of punk.

❶ A THOUSAND FORMS OF MIND
from TOMORROW HIT TODAY

The loping riff could almost have been written by Black Sabbath's Tony Iommi circa 1971. The organ flourishes add a cool vintage vibe.

❷ HATE THE POLICE from HERE COMES SICKNESS, THE BEST OF THE BBC RECORDINGS

Mudhoney's infamous Dicks cover captured at the Reading festival is far more dangerous and frenetic than its studio version.

❸ IN 'N' OUT OF GRACE from SUPERFUZZ BIGMUFF

A completely unhinged riff and a fabulously discordant guitar solo compete to give you the migraine of your life. Welcome to grunge, baby.

❹ INTO THE DRINK from EVERY GOOD BOY DESERVES FUDGE

There's a 1960s pop song lurking somewhere beneath the garage grease and grime. It must be the acoustic guitar way down in the mix.

❺ JUDGEMENT, RAGE, RETRIBUTION AND THYME
from MY BROTHER THE COW

You've got to love the excellent Simon and Garfunkel title piss-take, while that scything, sliding guitar could easily have your ears off.

❻ LET IT SLIDE
from EVERY GOOD BOY DESERVES FUDGE

Is that a guitar solo ending the song or is it a drunken fingers-jammed-through-the-strings job? Sounds great either way.

❼ SUCK YOU DRY from PIECE OF CAKE

The band reckon this turned out just as they intended it. The spirit of 1960s garage rock condensed into a mere two-and-a-half minutes.

❽ THIS GIFT from MUDHONEY

A sinister but tuneful little ditty featuring an understated reverbed guitar motif burbling away underneath the verses.

❾ TOUCH ME I'M SICK from MARCH TO FUZZ

The drums sound like they're being thrown downstairs, and the guitars grind under industrial levels of distortion.

❿ YOU GOT IT from MUDHONEY

This sounds almost controlled and tuneful by Mudhoney standards, which is to say, it's merely chaotic rather than utter bedlam.

Essi Berelian

Murakami's music

With his wife Yoko, the Japanese novelist Haruki Murakami ran a jazz club in Tokyo for seven years, and is said to have a collection of six thousand records and CDs. Music permeates his novels and stories, even shapes them to a degree, and many of his characters discuss music with passion and knowledge.

❶ THE GIRL FROM IPANEMA STAN GETZ AND ASTRUD GILBERTO from GETZ-GILBERTO

Murakami wrote a whole story about this song, musing – riffing, you might call it – on how the girl looks at the sea in 1963, and, unchanging, two decades later.

❷ NORWEGIAN WOOD THE BEATLES from RUBBER SOUL

In Japan, *Norwegian Wood* was titled *Forest In Norway*, which is how the Beatles' song was originally translated. The novel's three million sales led to a light orchestral version of the song going to #1 in Japan.

❸ DEAR HEART HENRY MANCINI from DEAR HEART & OTHER SONGS

The main character in *Norwegian Wood*, Watanabe, gives a copy of this to Naoko, and it is the first song that Reiko plays to him before the two make love near the book's end.

❹ DANCE, DANCE, DANCE THE DELLS from OH WHAT A NIGHT: THE VERY BEST OF THE DELLS

The Dells' song –"I gotta dance dance dance now the beat's really hot right on the spot" – later covered by

The Beach Boys – gave Murakami the title of his next novel.

❺ STAR CROSSED LOVERS DUKE ELLINGTON

Hajime, the jazz bar owner in *South Of The Border, West Of The Sun*, has his club pianist play this over and over again (*Casablanca*-fashion) until suddenly it no longer moves him.

❻ THE THIEVING MAGPIE ROSSINI from ROSSINI OVERTURES CONDUCTED BY CLAUDIO ABBADO

The "monotonous melody" of Rossini's overture preoccupies Toru Okada, protagonist of *The Wind-Up Bird Chronicle*.

❼ TARA'S THEME THE PERCY FAITH ORCHESTRA from THE COLLECTION

Again in *The Wind-Up Bird Chronicle*, Okada hears this at the dry cleaners. The tune brings him good memories of taking his girlfriend to see the movie *A Summer Place*.

❽ D MAJOR (HEAVENLY) SONATA FRANZ SCHUBERT

Oshima, the leading character in *Kafka On The Shore*, listens to Schubert's D Major Piano Sonata when he's driving, so as to "feel the limitations of what humans are capable of" in its imperfect performance.

❾ THE ARCHDUKE TRIO BEETHOVEN performed by THE MILLION DOLLAR TRIO

Hoshino, the truck driver, falls for the Archduke Trio, and tells Oshima of this recording. Oshima rates it, though he himself prefers the version by the Czech group, The Suk Trio.

❿ FIVE SPOT AFTER DARK CURTIS FULLER from BLUESETTE

Asked " What musical pieces would you include on a Murakami playlist?", the novelist replied: "Whenever I write a novel, music just sort of naturally slips in… When I was writing my newest novel, *After Dark*, the melody of Curtis Fuller's "Five Spot After Dark" kept running through my head."

Mark Ellingham

Muse

Bombastic, ferociously loud, magnificent and unbeatable at conjuring up stadium rock, it's hard to imagine Muse back in the clubs.

❶ PLUG IN BABY from ORIGIN OF SYMMETRY

Matt Bellamy howls with love and fear over a dirty-sweet bass, distorted like it's wearing a sneer.

❷ BUTTERFLIES AND HURRICANES from ABSOLUTION

The first encounter between Muse and their by now enormous audience, this is a typical slow building rocker – owing much to Queen – technically accomplished, full of inviting singalong, heroic rock clichés and beefed up with a proper string section. Delicious.

❸ HYSTERIA from ABSOLUTION

Boasting the greatest opening riff of the 21st century and a power-chord pre-vocals intro that will bounce the gallery of any theatre they play, Hysteria drips with glittering hooks that audiences found hard to resist. Try it, you know it already, and you'll love it even more as your personal theme tune.

❹ STOCKHOLM SYNDROME from ABSOLUTION

A song whose pedigree goes way back to Deep Purple and Black Sabbath, and Queen, again. Melodramatic, swaggering – it requires a wind machine off stage just to ruffle the singer's hair adequately.

❺ SONG FOR ABSOLUTION from ABSOLUTION

Muse are at their best doing a "nuts to the grinder" rock-out but, for variety, their own longevity and the audience's need of a breather, they occasionally drift towards an eerie ballad such as this Zippos-aloft beast.

❻ SUPERMASSIVE BLACK HOLE from BLACK HOLES AND REVELATIONS

Strutting their stuff like some white-boy tribute to Prince, Muse hustle up falsetto lead, a sauce of sweet, singalong backing vocals and a spicy slice of funk.

❼ HOODOO from BLACK HOLES AND REVELATIONS

You've gotta love the Spanish acoustic meets surf rock guitar intro. You have to smile with joyful amusement at the lovelorn cowboy vocals. There's no resisting the mutation into a smoky nightclub torch song. In waltz time yet!

❽ KNIGHTS OF CYDONIA from BLACK HOLES AND REVELATIONS

Set all guitars to eleven! Fire up the killer synthesizers! Crank up the horsie sound effects! Unchain that guy behind the drums and let's go! Chaaaaaaaaaarge!

❾ INVINCIBLE from BLACK HOLES AND REVELATIONS

Space guitars and semi-military drumming set the scene for this anthem. A hell-spawned bass/keyboard/drums interlude gives way to keyboard and fret-disturbing high-velocity.

❿ CITY OF DELUSION from BLACK HOLES AND REVELATIONS

The album's most intriguing track, melding hugely diverse musical styles and influences into a powerful, yet subtle piece of work.

Al Spicer

Charlie Gillett rates
Muscle Shoals

DJ and writer CHARLIE GILLETT is best known for his ever-intriguing *World of Music* shows on BBC World Service. But he remains a big soul and R&B fan, having begun his career with the now-classic book on American music, *The Sound Of the City*. He says "The studios of Muscle Shoals, Alabama – Fame, Muscle Shoals, Quinvy – have produced many of the greatest R&B songs of all time. Here are ten classic singles."

❶ **I'LL TAKE YOU THERE** THE STAPLE SINGERS (MUSCLE SHOALS)

❷ **I NEVER LOVED A MAN** ARETHA FRANKLIN (FAME)

❸ **WHEN A MAN LOVES A WOMAN** PERCY SLEDGE (QUINVY)

❹ **STEALING IN THE NAME OF THE LORD** PAUL KELLY (MUSCLE SHOALS)

❺ **IT'S BETTER TO HAVE AND DON'T NEED** DON COVAY (MUSCLE SHOALS)

❻ **I'D RATHER GO BLIND** ETTA JAMES (FAME)

❼ **YOU LEFT THE WATER RUNNING** MAURICE & MAC (FAME)

❽ **HOLD WHAT YOU GOT** JOE TEX (FAME)

❾ **YOU BETTER MOVE ON** ARTHUR ALEXANDER (FAME)

❿ **UP TIGHT, GOOD MAN** LAURA LEE (FAME)

My Bloody Valentine

The undisputed kings of UK indie noise, MBV released few albums, but when they did appear, the results were stupendous and groundbreaking. The group has now all but dissolved, with frontman Kevin Shields only occasionally resurfacing for remix and production work.

❶ **SOFT AS SNOW (BUT WARM INSIDE)** from ISN'T ANYTHING
A machine gun of drums paves the way for luscious whale-song guitars and a silky Shields vocal.

❷ **SEVERAL GIRLS GALORE** from ISN'T ANYTHING
So good. The guitars phase and chug over Shields' vocal foil Belinda Butcher.

❸ **YOU MADE ME REALISE** from ISN'T ANYTHING
A single that saw thousands of mop-headed indie kids shaking their thing on student-union dancefloors up and down the nation during the late 1980).

❹ **SAFE IN YOUR SLEEP** from ECSTACY AND WINE
An early jangler that's very much of its time, though all the elements of the band's future glories are already in place.

❺ **SLOW** from YOU MADE ME REALISE
Basslines don't come much dirtier and sexier than this. A great B-side, and with lyrics that'll either make you blush or head straight to the bedroom.

❻ **CIGARETTE IN YOUR BED** from YOU MADE ME REALISE
A beautiful song that introduced many to MBV when it appeared on the Creation Records *Doing It For The Kids* LP – a classic indie playlist in itself.

❼ **SOON** from LOVELESS
This single (the A-side of the *Glider* EP) broke the band's mould and presented a radical collision of guitar-loop chaos and a killer dance-break.

❽ **TO HERE KNOWS WHEN** from LOVELESS
This whole album is a sumptuous fest of guitar texture and angelic vocals, and should really be taken as a whole … regularly. But if we have to single out one cut, this one's a corker.

❾ **COME IN ALONE** from LOVELESS
The guitars are dense and uplifting, creating a wall of sound that would send Phil Spector running for cover.

❿ **GLIDER** from GLIDER EP
This instrumental B-side doesn't make for relaxing listening – the guitar loops grind and whine like dental drills looking for soft root pulp. Hypnotic and extreme.

Peter Buckley

My Chemical Romance

Despite the band's disavowal of the label, My Chemical Romance make music that has all the rage and power of Emo (the music that dare not speak its name), and owes much to the visceral punch of punk rock – albeit lightly dusted with sweet pop sensibilities.

❶ SKYLINES AND TURNSTILES from I BROUGHT YOU MY BULLETS, YOU BROUGHT ME YOUR LOVE
MCR formed in response to the 9/11 outrage, with this song their first overwrought musical outpouring.

❷ OUR LADY OF SORROWS from I BROUGHT YOU MY BULLETS, YOU BROUGHT ME YOUR LOVE
There's a black humour in this track, as in much of MCR's early music, set precisely to disguise the heart-felt rage that inspired it.

❸ HONEY, THIS MIRROR ISN'T BIG ENOUGH FOR THE TWO OF US from I BROUGHT YOU MY BULLETS, YOU BROUGHT ME YOUR LOVE
It can be so irritating trying to get made up at the same time as your boyfriend, can't it?

❹ I'M NOT OKAY (I PROMISE) from THREE CHEERS FOR SWEET REVENGE
Screaming blue murder set to a rock'n'roll rhythm. Irresistible.

❺ HELENA from THREE CHEERS FOR SWEET REVENGE
Standout track from the second album boasting the clever lyrics and twisted guitar that won them a major label deal.

❻ THE GHOST OF YOU from THREE CHEERS FOR SWEET REVENGE
Whiny and undeniably "Emo", but in a good way, this has echoes of Placebo, tourmates Linkin' Park and even a hint of The Misfits.

❼ WELCOME TO THE BLACK PARADE from THE BLACK PARADE
First single and proud statement from their third full length album. This is MCR making glorious overblown pompous rock like few have attempted since Queen.

❽ FAMOUS LAST WORDS from THE BLACK PARADE
Another track owing much to Freddie Mercury's troupe but with a roar of its own strong enough to dry your hair after a thunderstorm.

❾ I DON'T LOVE YOU from THE BLACK PARADE
Much more tentative than anything they've released before as a single, "I Don't Love You" verges at time on the delicate, and features vocal harmonies that wouldn't shame a more traditional boy band.

❿ TEENAGERS from THE BLACK PARADE
One of the best adolescent rebel songs in a long, long time. Now then, all together for the chorus: "Teenagers scare the living shit out of me! They could care less as long as someone will bleed."

Al Spicer

N

Nashville divas

Reactionary as Nashville's business and political pursuits may be there's a long tradition of strong women making their presence felt. Many of their songs are declarations of love. Others reproach bad male behaviour. Dolly and Loretta may be the Queens who survived but let's not overlook those who also stood on the domestic frontline...

① IT WASN'T GOD WHO MADE HONKY TONK ANGELS KITTY WELLS from THE GOLDEN YEARS
Stone classic 1952 answer song to Hank Thompson's "The Wild Side Of Life" with Kitty stating it's men who lure women into the honky tonk life.

② TWO WHOOPS AND A HOLLER JEAN SHEPARD from HONKY TONK HEROINE
Shepard sang with an insider's perception about what the honky tonk life involved and her clipped, tough voice suggested you don't mess with Jean.

③ CRAZY PATSY CLINE FROM Greatest Hits
Willie Nelson's ballad became one of the 20th century's classic love songs with Cline's gorgeously plaintive voice wrapping itself around producer Owen Bradley's luscious arrangement.

④ STAND BY YOUR MAN TAMMY WYNETTE from GREATEST HITS
Tammy married five times, suggesting she tucked her tongue firmly in cheek while singing this, Still, she possessed a wonderfully tearful voice, the song has a huge hook, and any tune Hilary Clinton denounces must be OK, right?

⑤ ODE TO BILLIE JOE BOBBIE GENTRY from THE GOLDEN CLASSICS
Perhaps the strangest #1 country and pop hit ever; 1969 narrative tune, drenched in eerie strings, finds the molasses-voiced Gentry suggesting something unsettling happened on the Talahatchie Bridge.

⑥ MAMA HE'S CRAZY THE JUDDS from THE JUDDS
Mama and daughter duo who dominated the country charts across the 1980s sing a lush and lovely song about adolescent crushes.

⑦ HOW BLUES REBA MCENTYRE from GREATEST HITS VOL 1
Reba's smooth, emotive singing kept her near the top of the country charts across the 1980s and 90s. Bland? Sure. But many working class, white American women responded to Reba like no other.

⑧ SEVEN YEAR ACHE ROSANNE CASH from SEVEN YEAR ACHE
Johnny's daughter was a consistent hit-maker across the 1980s with a highly intelligent form of country song. Here she sings of then husband Rodney Crowell's wayward habits.

⑨ THAT DON'T IMPRESS ME MUCH SHANIA TWAIN from COME ON OVER
Twain was a working class Canadian singer struggling for success until she hooked up with producer Mutt Lange. The result made her a superstar and this snappy pop ditty demonstrates just why she is currently the biggest selling artist on Earth.

⑩ TIME THE REVELATOR GILLIAN WELCH from REVELATOR
Welch and guitar playing partner David Rawlings run their own label and own their own studio. For East Coast preppies they certainly make a good shot at conjuring up that old mountain music sound.

Garth Cartwright

Youssou N'Dour

Senegal's Youssou N'Dour is arguably the most successful African artist of the last quarter-century.

① JALO from ÉTOILE DE DAKAR VOL 1 – ABSA GUEYE
Slow, slinky, understated gem recorded live in 1979 in a Dakar nightclub. As with much of Youssou's early work, the accompanying players and vocalists (especially the gruff voiced El Hadji Faye) are key to its appeal.

② THIAPA THIOLY from ÉTOILE DE DAKAR VOL 2 – THIAPA THIOLY
A restless twelve-minute epic, complete with wildly clattering *tama* (small talking drum), spidery guitar, Cuban timbales and chopping *mbalax* rhythms.

❸ IMMIGRÉS/BITIM REW from IMMIGRÉS

The breakthrough hit, which gained an international release in 1984. This is Youssou at his white-hot artistic peak, on a creative roller coaster ride.

❹ RUBBERBAND MAN from NELSON MANDELA

Youssou puts a different spin on The Spinners' hit. A memorable and truly peculiar piece from a largely forgotten album.

❺ SHAKING THE TREE from THE LION

Youssou puts a different spin on The Spinners' hit. A memorable and truly peculiar piece from a largely forgotten album.

❻ SEVEN SECONDS from THE GUIDE (WOMMAT)

Easily Youssou's biggest hit, this 1994 duet with Neneh Cherry addressed the insidious nature of racism and struck a chord worldwide.

❼ GUISS GUISS from NE LA THIASS

Proving he's not just a great lead singer, Youssou does ghostly chorus vocals on this hypnotic collaboration with dreadlocked protégé Cheikh Lô.

❽ BIRIMA from JOKO

The best track on a much-derided album. Does not feature any guest appearance by Sting, Peter Gabriel, or Wyclef Jean. Fortunately.

❾ MBËGGÉÉL NOONU LA (BECAUSE LOVE'S LIKE THAT) from NOTHING'S IN VAIN

Back to mbalax basics, on this surging upbeat number from an album that signalled a return to form.

❿ TIJANIYYA from EGYPT

A great cut from an album celebrating Youssou's devotion to the Mouride faith.

Jon Lusk

Willie Nelson

These days Willie Nelson is an elder statesman, but he was the original country-music rebel, growing his hair and turning against the slick Nashville establishment that made his name. The last decade has seen him on better form than ever – releasing great albums, working with big names from all genres, and with his trademark throaty quaver and studiedly artless guitar-picking never better.

❶ CRAZY from CRAZY: THE DEMO SESSIONS

Patsy Cline made this great, great song famous, but this 1960s demo version is still the best.

❷ BLUE EYES CRYIN' IN THE RAIN from RED-HEADED STRANGER

Willie's first country number #1, from the pared-back *Red-Headed Stranger* album.

❸ GETTING OVER YOU from ACROSS THE BORDER

Willie may be a duet tart, but this recording, with Bonnie Raitt, is one of his best, and a highlight of the 1992 album that initiated the last great blooming of his genius.

❹ ME AND PAUL from THE ESSENTIAL WILLIE NELSON

This picaresque ballad details the adventures of Willie and his sidekick Paul English on the road in the late 1950s.

❺ NIGHTLIFE from THE ESSENTIAL WILLIE NELSON

Written on his way to a gig in Pasedena – "It ain't no good life, but it's my life".

❻ FUNNY HOW TIME SLIPS AWAY from THE ESSENTIAL WILLIE NELSON

Again, a bigger hit for someone else, but Willie's voice and the deliberately low-key arrangement of this version is the benchmark.

❼ YESTERDAY'S WINE from THE ESSENTIAL WILLIE NELSON

Crooning classic from the RCA years.

❽ BLOODY MARY MORNING from THE ESSENTIAL WILLIE NELSON

Still pop, still country, but closer to the narrative songs and spartan arrangements of later Willie.

❾ NEVER CARED FOR YOU from TEATRO

Willie's 1960s classic updated with a Latin tilt – a perfect example of just how dynamic his output has been in recent years, both with regard to his own songs and others.

❿ SOMEBODY PICK UP MY PIECES from TEATRO

A late, great Willie song that draws a great performance from Emmylou Harris, and the band is totally on the button. A fine example of Willie's uneducated, snap-gut guitar style.

Martin Dunford

The Neville Bros & The Meters

The preternaturally funky Neville Brothers have been at the forefront of New Orleans music for more than fifty years, as solo artists and in bands like The Meters, as well as in the Neville Brothers group itself – still going strong with the addition of various offspring and other relations.

❶ MARDI GRAS MAMBO THE HAWKETTS from TREACHEROUS
Eldest brother Art Neville's debut offering, from 1954, remains a carnival classic.

❷ TELL IT LIKE IT IS AARON NEVILLE from TREACHEROUS
Brother Aaron's astonishingly pure voice propelled this enduring soul classic to a US #1 in 1967.

❸ CISSY STRUT THE METERS from FUNKIFY YOUR LIFE
Art's "other" band, The Meters, were at their funkifying best on this 1969 instrumental.

❹ MEET DE BOYS ON THE BATTLEFRONT THE WILD TCHOUPITOULAS from THE WILD TCHOUPITOULAS
Joining up with their uncle's Mardi Gras Indian tribe marked a return to their New Orleans roots for the Nevilles in 1976.

❺ BROTHER JOHN / IKO IKO THE NEVILLE BROTHERS from FIYO ON THE BAYOU
Throughout the 1980s, the Nevilles profitably mined a deep vein of New Orleans funk/R&B.

❻ PLEDGING MY LOVE AARON NEVILLE from ORCHID IN THE STORM
Aaron's transcendent tones were perfect for a 1986 EP of doo-wop covers.

❼ MICKEY MOUSE MARCH AARON NEVILLE from STAY AWAKE
Just to prove that Aaron could move you to tears singing the phone book, he delivered this show-stopping rendition on a 1988 album of Disney covers.

❽ DON'T KNOW MUCH AARON NEVILLE AND LINDA RONSTADT from CRY LIKE A RAINSTORM
The soaring duet that made Aaron an unlikely pop star once again in 1989.

❾ YELLOW MOON THE NEVILLE BROTHERS from YELLOW MOON
Also in 1989, the Nevilles made a superb comeback album with hip producer Daniel Lanois, of which this was the title track.

❿ AMAZING GRACE AARON NEVILLE from GOSPEL ROOTS
Aaron continues to bring the house down each year in the gospel tent at New Orleans' Jazzfest; this 2003 recording shows he's still at his peak.

Greg Ward

New Order

New Order were seen as the pretty pop butterfly that emerged from the dour chrysalis of Joy Division after Ian Curtis's suicide. Despite a back catalogue impressively peppered with limited releases, alternative mixes, and ultra-rare imports from around the globe, they remain best loved as a singles band, knocking out hits for a chemically enhanced generation of new pop kids.

❶ TRUE FAITH from SUBSTANCE 1987
Available in a good half-dozen remixed flavours – all delicious, but with The Pet Shop Boys' at the top of the pile – this is the most divine evocation of the ecstasy experience.

❷ BIZARRE LOVE TRIANGLE from BROTHERHOOD
The soundtrack to some elegant night club where disco and electronica hook up for a few friendly drinks with rock'n'roll. Bernard's vocals take continual dives at the right note, occasionally scoring bang on target.

❸ THIEVES LIKE US from THE BEST OF
Masterful swirling keyboards and a slow funk groove make this track an unwitting tribute to The Human League's own brand of electro-lounge music.

❹ RUINED IN A DAY from REPUBLIC
Massive acoustic guitar chords establish a lush minor-key carpet where the finest of beats and keyboard swirls are displayed, and Bernard waxes melancholy.

❺ BLUE MONDAY from POWER, CORRUPTION AND LIES
Factory agreed to release this track in such a bewildering combination of remixes, deluxe sleeves and different formats that it lost money on every copy sold. Great tune though, no matter which version you load.

❻ PERFECT KISS from LOW-LIFE
Funky, in the way the chalk-white Mancunians have made their own, with superb right-on-the-money beats and bass working in harmony. A perfect piece of dance music.

❼ REGRET from REPUBLIC
There's joy, celebration and a bunch of pop hooks in this track that will always brighten the mood into a warm-summer-day feeling.

❽ VANISHING POINT from TECHNIQUE
Not as obvious a tribute to the speed-thriller of the same title as Primal Scream's, but a good, heavy, asphalt-pounding driver of a tune.

Nik Cohn's
New Orleans Bounce

Nik Cohn damn near invented pop-rock criticism with his seminal 1968 text *Awopbopaloobop Alopbamboom*. Since then he's often been in the right place at the right time – he wrote the story that would become *Saturday Night Fever* – while his most recent book, *Triksta*, is the result of several years spent living and working amongst the New Orleans rap scene. *Triksta* may just be Cohn's finest text yet so we asked Nik for a Top 10 of the tunes they call "bounce". Having conferred with the legendary DJ Chicken ("King of the bounce clubs"), Nik came back with the following: "Bounce is the New Orleans variant of rap. Patterned on the call and response of Mardi Gras Indian chants, its basic rhythm is the Triggerman beat (stolen from the Showboys' "Drag Rap"), spiced with second-line bass riffs, attack dogs barking, and New Orleans funk. A music of summer block parties and swelter, it's raw sex in dance. These tracks were released as singles and were local New Orleans (but not national) hits. Some were later anthologized on two albums entitled *The Greatest Rap Hits From Downsouth New Orleans, Vols 1 & 2*."

❶ **WHERE THEY AT** MC T.T. TUCKER & DJ IRV

❷ **GOT'S TO BE REAL** PIMP DADDY

❸ **GET THE GAT** LIL ELT

❹ **MONKEY ON THA DICK** MAGNOLIA SHORTY

❺ **THE PAYBACK** MIA X

❻ **TAKE IT TO THE HOLE** 5TH WARD WEEBIE

❼ **BOOTIE BOP** U.N.L.V.

❽ **BUCKJUMP TIME** GREGORY D & MANNIE FRESH

❾ **TWERK SOMETHIN'** CHEEKY BLAKK

❿ **PUNK UNDER PRESSURE** KATEY RED

❾ **CONFUSION** from SUBSTANCE 1987

The mix used in the *Blade* soundtrack comes ready for an in-car rave, with beats to focus the mind on the white lines dividing the lanes of traffic. Wiser to stick with the plain-vanilla version that went into *Trainspotting*.

❿ **EVERYTHING'S GONE GREEN**
from SUBSTANCE 1987

Written soon after Ian's departure from both Joy Division and this mortal coil, this sounds like a younger, less electronic version of Blue Monday.

Al Spicer

New Orleans R&B

When it comes to music, New Orleans has always been a law unto itself. During the 1960s in particular, the birthplace of jazz was home to some of the funkiest musicians on the planet, and the Crescent City produced a stream of insanely catchy R&B hits.

❶ **BIG CHIEF – PART 2** PROFESSOR LONGHAIR from FESS – THE PROFESSOR LONGHAIR ANTHOLOGY 1964

The definitive Mardi Gras dance number from the demented genius of the keyboard, though the song it self was written by Earl King.

❷ **MOTHER IN LAW** ERNIE K-DOE from HIGHLIGHTS FROM CRESCENT CITY SOUL

On the strength of this 1961 US #1 hit, the flamboyant Ernie remained the self-proclaimed "Emperor of the Universe" until his dying day – and he's still gigging as much as ever posthumously, though that's another story.

❸ **RULER OF MY HEART** IRMA THOMAS from SATURDAY NIGHT FISH FRY

Though Otis Redding and the Rolling Stones had bigger hits with the song as "Pain In My Heart", the mighty-voiced Irma got here first, in 1962.

❹ **I LIKE IT LIKE THAT** CHRIS KENNER from I LIKE IT LIKE THAT

Clocking in at well under two minutes, a glorious anthem to a long-vanished club.

❺ OOH-POO-PAH-DOO JESSIE HILL from HIGHLIGHTS
FROM CRESCENT CITY SOUL
Eccentric even by Nawlins standards, Hill does just
what he says he's going to do: "create disturbance in
your mind".

❻ IKO IKO THE DIXIE CUPS from SATURDAY NIGHT FISH FRY
Based on a Mardi Gras Indian chant, and backed
merely by minimal but madly infectious percussion,
this was a massive worldwide hit.

❼ EVERYTHING I DO GONH BE FUNKY LEE DORSEY from
THE BEST OF LEE DORSEY
Allen Toussaint wrote the songs, but nobody could
sound as downright cool as former middleweight
boxer Lee Dorsey.

❽ WHO SHOT THE LA LA ? OLIVER MORGAN from NEW
ORLEANS PARTY CLASSICS
Speculating about the real-life murder of singer Prince
La-La in 1964, Morgan manages to rule out various
suspects, including himself, but is still left with three
names to ponder.

❾ SEA OF LOVE PHIL PHILLIPS from SEA OF LOVE
Part doo-wop, part proto-soul, Phil Phillips' solitary
1959 hit was haunting enough to inspire its own
movie.

❿ BAREFOTIN' ROBERT PARKER from HIGHLIGHTS FROM
CRESCENT CITY SOUL
Parker's infectious dance hit from 1966 saw New
Orleans meeting soul.

Greg Ward

New Wave

**Often thought of as skinny guys in skinny ties,
New Wave is basically the more tuneful and
experimental power-pop cousin of punk rock.
Here's the scoop from both sides of the Atlantic.**

❶ ANOTHER GIRL, ANOTHER PLANET THE ONLY ONES
from DARKNESS & LIGHT: THE COMPLETE BBC RECORDINGS
A highly influential single from a band that could have
been so much more. The BBC sessions are considered
by some to be superior to the band's own album work.

❷ BACK OF MY HAND THE JAGS from EVENING STANDARDS
A great start to a career that fizzled soon after. A super,
zesty single with singer Nick Watkinson doing a very
good impression of Elvis Costello.

❸ GOT THE TIME JOE JACKSON from LOOK SHARP!
This is the closing track on a great album and a mad
dash for the finish line, featuring a genius chorus and
lashings of hooky power-pop guitar.

❹ GUT FEELING DEVO from Q: ARE WE NOT MEN? A: WE
ARE DEVO!
Time to dig out your yellow boiler suits and bug-eye
shades. This just seems to get faster and faster with its
spiralling keyboards and cool guitar thrashing.

❺ HEART OF GLASS BLONDIE from PARALLEL LINES
Sheer, immaculate pop perfection. A nice 'n' icy vocal
from Debbie Harry and some great throbbing synths.

❻ MY BEST FRIEND'S GIRL THE CARS from THE CARS
With its understated guitar and hand claps the intro
alone is wonderful. The beat is crisp and driving while
the main riff sounds almost country & western.

❼ MY SHARONA THE KNACK from GET THE KNACK
It may be the only tune Doug Fieger and co will be
remembered for, but what a tune it is. Wanton adolescent filth set to a thrusting, grinding beat

❽ PSYCHO KILLER TALKING HEADS from
TALKING HEADS: 77
Quirky and completely compelling, this economical
early track features a fantastic muscular bass line and
Dave Byrne's voice teetering on the edge of cracking.

❾ THE 15TH WIRE from 154
Arty and unashamedly weird, Wire were masters of
tension and off-kilter melody. Revel in the reverbed
layers of guitar and soothing synths.

❿ THIS IS POP XTC from WHITE MUSIC
Loud, raucous and just a little bit off the wall, this is
one of Andy Partridge's best early tunes – absolutely
buzzing with youthful brio.

Essi Berelian

New York rockers

**The Big Apple has long been fuelled by the
dialectic between glitter and grime and nowhere
more so than in its rock. These are the ten records
that best walk that perilous tightrope.**

❶ HELIUM HEAD SIR LORD BALTIMORE from SIR LORD
BALTIMORE (MERCURY, 1970)
The term "heavy metal" was coined to describe the
sound of this Big Apple train wreck.

❷ WALK ON THE WILD SIDE LOU REED from TRANSFORMER
The definitive New York rock'n'roll record.

❸ PERSONALITY CRISIS NEW YORK DOLLS from NEW YORK DOLLS
They may have squawked in doltish New Yawkese, but they were palookas with wit, hooligans with a sense of irony, dandies with chutzpah.

❹ NEXT BIG THING THE DICTATORS from THE DICTATORS GO GIRL CRAZY!
What the Dolls would have sounded like if they wore wrestling gear instead of makeup.

❺ BLITZKRIEG BOP THE RAMONES from THE RAMONES
Let Malcolm McLaren and Johnny Rotten have their delusions – this is the first punk-rock record.

❻ DON'T FEAR THE REAPER BLUE ÖYSTER CULT from AGENTS OF FORTUNE
Proof you don't have to wear corpse paint or have infernal croaking vocals to be truly scary.

❼ LOVE COMES IN SPURTS RICHARD HELL & THE VOIDOIDS from BLANK GENERATION
Legendary guitarist Robert Quine at his best.

❽ NEW YORK GROOVE ACE FREHLEY from ACE FREHLEY
Indomitable glitter disco stomp.

❾ HOT WIRE MY HEART SONIC YOUTH from SISTER
Blistering downtown guitar rave-up, even if the song was originally from San Francisco.

❿ YÜ GUNG PUSSY GALORE from SUGARSHIT SHARP
New York scuzz punk dares to make a rapprochement with hip-hop.

Peter Shapiro

New Zealand

The small nation at the bottom of the South Pacific is famous for producing rugby icons, hobbit movies and fine white wine. It's also managed to turn out some very respectable tunes.

❶ DANCE AROUND THE WORLD BLERTA from NATURE'S BEST: NEW ZEALAND'S TOP 30 SONGS OF ALL-TIME
Wildly imaginative hippie music-theatre troupe scored a hit with this in 1971. Blerta gave birth to noted character actor Bruno Lawrence and film director Geoff Murphy.

❷ ARE YOU OLD ENOUGH DRAGON from GREATEST HITS
Hard living, hard rocking Kiwi glam band who, in late-keyboardist Paul Hewson, possessed a master songwriter. This, their biggest hit – NZ and Oz #1 – is a glorious rush of mid 1970s rock.

❸ I GOT YOU SPLIT ENZ from TRUE COLOURS
Teenage guitarist Neil Finn was drafted in to save the Enz so he goes and writes this, their only international hit and one of the best songs of the New Wave era.

❹ DON'T ASK ME TOY LOVE from TOY LOVE
Monstrously talented, Toy Love were the Kiwi punks who saw beyond imitating US/UK outfits and so helped lead much Kiwi rock into maturity.

❺ NO NO NO DAVID KILGOUR from SUGARMOUTH
Ex-Clean guitarist delivers a dreamy rush of Dunedin psychedelia.

❻ DON'T DREAM ITS OVER CROWDED HOUSE from RECURRING DREAM
Epic, lovelorn ballad that became a huge American hit and finds Neil Finn pushing his singing and songwriting skills to the max.

❼ IN THE NEIGHBOURHOOD SISTERS UNDERGROUND from PROUD
New Zealand is now overflowing with Polynesian rappers yet this early, acoustic slice of urban wisdom remains the high water mark for South Pacific hip-hop.

❽ RIGHT ON OMC from HOW BIZARRE
Uplifting slice of Polynesian soul with great harmonies, Maori strummed guitar and a "aint-it-great-to-be-alive" vibe that was championed by BBC DJ Charlie Gillett.

❾ RUNGA SWAY BIC from DRIVE
Bic's fine Maori-Malay features, gift for melody and gorgeous voice made her the biggest selling Kiwi artist in NZ history. "Sway" was used as the soundtrack to *American Pie*'s seduction scene but it's a lot more subtle (and seductive) than that suggests.

❿ CAY'S CRAYS FAT FREDDYS DROP from BASED ON A TRUE STORY
Rolling dub grooves, fat jazzy horns and Polynesian soul all come together to create an organic dance music like no other. 21st century Kiwi musical culture begins here.

Garth Cartwright

Randy Newman

If you only know Newman from quirky but fundamentally warm movie soundtracks such as *Toy Story*, the acerbic cynicism and sheer emotional nakedness of his classic albums might just blow you away.

❶ MAMA TOLD ME NOT TO COME from 12 SONGS
Newman casts himself as the quintessential outsider; it's as though the Mr Jones who didn't know what was happening in Dylan's "Ballad Of A Thin Man" gets to sing his own song.

❷ REDNECKS from GOOD OLD BOYS
Singing as a redneck and flaunting the "n" word in every chorus, Newman lambasts Southern racism and lazy Northern liberalism in equal measure.

❸ LOUISIANA 1927 from GOOD OLD BOYS
A glorious, wistful account of the Mississippi flood of 1927.

❹ BIRMINGHAM from GOOD OLD BOYS
A beautifully realized character sketch of blue-collar life in Alabama, with the delicious line "my daddy was a barber, a most unsightly man".

❺ SAIL AWAY from SAIL AWAY
The stunning title song from Newman's finest album; a ballad extolling the joys of slavery, sung in Africa by a recruiter for the slave trade. As Newman put it "How else could I do it – slavery is bad?"

❻ YOU CAN LEAVE YOUR HAT ON
from SAIL AWAY
Adopted as the bump-and-grind anthem of strippers everywhere, but never more sleazy than in its original form.

❼ GOOD MORNING
from GOOD OLD BOYS (REISSUE)
Newman sings both voices in a duet between two estranged parents on their child's birthday; the father's malignant litany of "fuck offs" might explain why it was left off the original release.

❽ GOD'S SONG (THAT'S WHY I LOVE MANKIND) from SAIL AWAY
In which God, backed by some elegiac piano, explains why he just can't help loving us: "I take from you your children, and you say 'how blessed are we.'"

❾ POLITICAL SCIENCE from SAIL AWAY
Newman at his most sardonic; given that the rest of the world hates Americans, "Let's drop the big one now" and see what happens.

❿ MY LIFE IS GOOD from TROUBLE IN PARADISE
The definitive skewering of Tinseltown aggression, pretension and paranoia in the coke-fuelled LA of the early 1980s.

Greg Ward

Nirvana

It's Kurt Cobain's grunge pioneers who still cast the longest shadow over today's indie outfits. Partly the music, partly the myth.

❶ RAPE ME from IN UTERO
Controversial, aggressive and innocent. Atop a typically simple and effective four-chord riff, loveable Cobain cries out to be abused.

❷ SLIVER from INCESTICIDE
A futile attempt by Cobain to leave his grandparents' house is split between a whiny guitar as he pleads to go home and Chris Novoselic's upbeat bass riff as his grandparents attempt to cope with him.

❸ ABOUT A GIRL from BLEACH
Bleach's only indication of Nirvana's progressively more poppy sound: the girl is probably Cobain's former lover Tracy, who complained that he never wrote about her.

❹ HEART-SHAPED BOX from IN UTERO
A gentle arpeggiated riff sets the tone as Cobain writes about a child with cancer.

❺ FLOYD THE BARBER from BLEACH
Typical of Nirvana's early metal sound: a trip to the hairdresser goes horribly wrong.

❻ WHERE DID YOU SLEEP LAST NIGHT?
from MTV UNPLUGGED
Cobain makes this Leadbelly cover his own, growling over clean acoustics.

❼ COME AS YOU ARE from NEVERMIND
The bellowing guitar riff shrouds the song's mad undercurrent as Cobain tempts an old friend to pay one last visit.

❽ LITHIUM from NEVERMIND
Novoselic's finest bassline echoes all the way through what has to be Nirvana's most optimistic song.

❾ THE MAN WHO SOLD THE WORLD
from MTV UNPLUGGED
Bowie's epic, strung out on acoustic and gawd knows what else.

❿ SMELLS LIKE TEEN SPIRIT from NEVERMIND
The unmistakeable riff that brought Nirvana to the mainstream. If this is all you know, you'll love the songs above.

Ben Garfield

Stina Nordenstam

Swedish-born Stina Nordenstam has one of the most distinctive voices you'll hear: breathy, indefinably delicate, and at times so impenetrable you wonder if she really is singing in English. But the texture of her sound is sensational, and her writing is as atmospheric as anything in rock music.

❶ I SEE YOU AGAIN
from AND SHE CLOSED HER EYES
This gorgeous soundscape should hook you on Stina for life, with its opening of seductive obscurity, and a trumpet break to die for.

❷ LITTLE STAR from AND SHE CLOSED HER EYES
Little Star featured, memorably, in Baz Luhrmann's *Romeo + Juliet*. It begins with just guitar and voice, and builds to a huge sound, with Latin chant, before vanishing into thin air.

❸ SAILING from PEOPLE ARE STRANGE
Yes – the Rod Stewart song. But you'd never believe it could be this great, reduced to a handful of piano chords, rain, and voice.

❹ PURPLE RAIN from PEOPLE ARE STRANGE
Another wonderfully idiosyncratic reading on this album of covers. The Prince song is slowed down, stripped down, to strange beauty.

❺ CLOTHE YOURSELF FOR THE WIND from THIS IS STINA NORDENSTAM
1 minute 35 seconds. And yet it feels like a whole movie. One of the great tracks on Stina's finest album to date.

❻ EVERYONE ELSE IN THE WORLD
from THIS IS STINA NORDENSTAM
The saddest, most harmonious chorus – "Everyone else in the world would love me by now/Would love

me from day one/But not you." And the song needs hardly another word.

❼ FROM CAYMAN ISLANDS WITH LOVE
from THE WORLD IS SAVED
Much of Stina's recent work is pared down, with the voice carrying songs: this by contrast is almost orchestral, yet miraculously restrained.

❽ THE END OF A LOVE AFFAIR
from THE WORLD IS SAVED
"A scene from a movie", Stina sings, and doesn't it just feel that way? A song with this poise and power cries out for use in an indie film.

Mark Ellingham

Northern Soul

That strange phenomenon in which young men from the industrial wastelands of the north of England worshipped American soul records – the rarer and more obscure the better – with a zeal and piety that would shame anyone but the most devout religious followers. These ten records will make believers out of anyone.

❶ DO I LOVE YOU (INDEED I DO) FRANK WILSON from NORTHERN SOUL CONNOISSEURS
The most expensive record in the world, but also one of the best.

❷ PLEASE LET ME IN JJ BARNES from THE GROOVESVILLE MASTERS
As impassioned as, and grittier than, anything released by Ric-Tic's more famous crosstown Detroit rivals.

❸ STORM WARNING THE VOLCANOS from NORTHERN SOUL: ON THE PHILADELPHIA BEAT
Woefully underrated early Philly soul, rescued by British soul fans.

❹ HIT & RUN ROSE BATISTE from THE GOLDEN AGE OF NORTHERN SOUL
Certainly more soulful and sassy than The Supremes.

❺ EXUS TREK LUTHER INGRAM ORCHESTRA from HIPSHAKER
Big, bold colours and dramatic arrangement make for a three-minute instrumental epic.

❻ (COME ON BE MY) SWEET DARLIN' JIMMY (SOUL) CLARKE from THE GOLDEN AGE OF NORTHERN SOUL
As uplifting and joyful as any record in the Northern soul canon.

❼ TAINTED LOVE GLORIA JONES from **THE WIGAN CASINO STORY: FINAL CHAPTER**

One of the better examples of dancing as exorcism.

❽ SLICED TOMATOES JUST BROTHERS from **THE GOLDEN TORCH STORY**

Sounds like it was recorded for a 1960s surf flick, but so groovy that it was sampled heavily by Fatboy Slim.

❾ KEEP ON KEEPING ON N.F. PORTER from **THE GOLDEN TORCH STORY**

The driving but ghostly arrangement keeps this track shrouded in mystery.

❿ IT REALLY HURTS ME GIRL THE CARSTAIRS from **DAZZLE: DISCO DELIGHTS FROM NEW YORK CITY**

The record that tore the Northern Soul scene asunder, but at least it's worth fighting over.

Peter Shapiro

Ted Nugent/Amboy Dukes

While the Amboy Dukes were psychedelic warriors of America's 1960s acid culture, their motormouth guitarist Ted Nugent was raring to let his guitar run wild in a solo career.

AMBOY DUKES

❶ BABY PLEASE DON'T GO THE AMBOY DUKES from **THE AMBOY DUKES**

One of the killer cuts in the Amboy Dukes' armoury was a smoking rendition of this rock'n'roll classic.

❷ JOURNEY TO THE CENTER OF THE MIND THE AMBOY DUKES from **JOURNEY TO THE CENTER OF THE MIND**

Clean living Ted claims he never understood the stoner sentiments of this psychedelic classic. Just look at all those amazing colours ma-a-a-aaaan…

❸ LOADED FOR BEAR THE AMBOY DUKES from **MIGRATION**

Super-scary jungle noises kick off this funky rocker. Great percussion, awesome organ and some truly sizzlin' guitar work.

TED NUGENT

❹ JUST WHAT THE DOCTOR ORDERED from **TED NUGENT**

You want to hear the Motor City Madman spank his plank for all he's worth? Slap this on, turn it up and let your jaw drop.

❺ MOTOR CITY MADHOUSE from **TED NUGENT**

A neck-snapping encapsulation of what the Nuge is all about: a vivacious bad boy boogie driven by a relentless bass line.

❻ DOG EAT DOG from **FREE FOR ALL**

Kicks off with a howl for blood and a barnstorming riff before piling into a powerful chorus and yet another great set of guitar solos.

❼ CAT SCRATCH FEVER from **CAT SCRATCH FEVER**

What a stonking riff! "Well, I make a pussy purr with the stroke of my hand…" reckons our Ted. Pure rock'n'roll filth from start to finish.

❽ WANG DANG SWEET POONTANG from **CAT SCRATCH FEVER**

Worth checking out for the fabulously un-PC title alone. This is a love song, according to Ted – one loaded with attitude and about a zillion guitar solos.

❾ YANK ME, CRANK ME from **DOUBLE LIVE GONZO**

"I need ya baby, like a dog needs a bone!" bawls Ted wantonly. A testosterone-soaked stormer, absolutely buzzing with live atmosphere.

❿ WANGO TANGO from **SCREAM DREAM**

Nugent entered the 1980s with this to-the-point, grinding riff, leading into an infectious chorus and one of his infamous mid-song raps.

Essi Berelian

Laura Nyro

Prophetically named after a song, Laura Nyro had talent to burn, and then some. Her late 1960s and early 70s work is peerless and hugely influential. What a loss to music when her life was cut short in 1997.

❶ WEDDING BELL BLUES from **MORE THAN A NEW DISCOVERY (A.K.A. THE FIRST SONGS)**

Like several of Laura's best songs, this is probably most familiar from one of many anaemic covers, none of which can touch the original.

❷ AND WHEN I DIE from **MORE THAN A NEW DISCOVERY (A.K.A. THE FIRST SONGS)**

Laura wrote this memorable gospel-flavoured piece at the age of 17. Its maturity is a staggering testament to her imagination and "a certain folk wisdom that teen-agers have", as she put it.

❸ STONED SOUL PICNIC from ELI AND THE THIRTEENTH CONFESSION

Captures the magical bohemian spirit of the 1960s counterculture like nothing else. Another song many tried to cover. Roy Ayers and The 5th Dimension, eat your heart out!

❹ TIMER from ELI AND THE THIRTEENTH CONFESSION

Breathtaking tempo changes, a crazily brilliant, free-ranging song structure and an extraordinary exuberance. This is Laura's Bohemian Rhapsody.

❺ NEW YORK TENDABERRY from NEW YORK TENDABERRY

Just Laura, accompanying herself on piano. The stark and soulful title cut from her third album, an oddly austere soundtrack to what she calls her "wild years".

❻ SAVE THE COUNTRY from NEW YORK TENDABERRY

Peace and love, Nyro style. This became an anthem for a generation. It's still painfully relevant.

❼ WHEN I WAS A FREEPORT AND YOU WERE THE MAIN DRAG from CHRISTMAS AND THE BEADS OF SWEAT

This album gave notice that the fiery creativity of Laura's muse was on the wane. But it still has a handful of songs to die for, like this one.

❽ MET HIM ON A SUNDAY/THE BELLS from GONNA TAKE A MIRACLE

In 1971 Laura teamed up with Labelle to revisit some of her favourite soul songs. That choice proved an inspired move, as this fantastic double-barrelled intro shows.

❾ YOU REALLY GOT A HOLD ON ME from GONNA TAKE A MIRACLE

Smokey Robinson must have been proud of such a radical reworking. Unlike lesser artists who piggy-backed on the genius of her work, Laura added something unique to her covers.

❿ OH YEAH MAYBE BABY (THE HEEBIE JEEBIES) from WALK THE DOG AND LIGHT THE LIGHT

Laura's last studio album has some pretty resonant echoes of former glories, and this is the clearest of them all.

Jon Lusk

Oasis

At their peak, Oasis were the finest rock band in the UK, and they remain so steeped in their own myth that, even at their worst, they still seem to believe it. Recent recordings hint at a return to form, but in truth, it's only their earliest material that continues to sheeeee-iiiiine.

❶ ROCK 'N' ROLL STAR from DEFINITELY MAYBE
A song so full of itself, reeking of testosterone, cheap aftershave and bottled lager, that it might challenge you to go outside for a fight somewhere between the second and third verses.

❷ LIVE FOREVER from DEFINITELY MAYBE
When they meshed together in their earliest days of success, the Gallagher brothers had the world by the balls, knew it, and could write songs about it too.

❸ SUPERSONIC from DEFINITELY MAYBE
The protagonist of this little gem believes himself king of the world for the short time that his wrapper of happiness lasts him.

❹ WONDERWALL from (WHAT'S THE STORY) MORNING GLORY
The hypnotically obscure and enigmatic lyrics place the loved one in the role of saviour surrounded by an impermeable barrier of tongue-tied adoration.

❺ DON'T LOOK BACK IN ANGER from (WHAT'S THE STORY) MORNING GLORY
Never more Lennon-esque than in the rambling first verses, Noel suddenly gives the game away in the chorus, turning it into a majestic love song.

❻ CHAMPAGNE SUPERNOVA from (WHAT'S THE STORY) MORNING GLORY
Sure, it's replete with the atmosphere of "you'll all be sorry when I'm dead, won't you?", but even if it positively reeks of spoilt teenagers storming off to bed, there's a more mature, bitter taste under the surface

❼ I AM THE WALRUS (LIVE) from THE MASTERPLAN
The set-closer that rewarded only the most appreciative of crowds. Anthemic, monumental, bloody loud and, of course, a tune The Beatles themselves never played to a live audience.

❽ MORNING GLORY from (WHAT'S THE STORY) MORNING GLORY
Despite its anthemic, 1980s rock-guitar run, this is a bleak slice of misery and jaundiced self-loathing.

❾ SHE'S ELECTRIC from (WHAT'S THE STORY) MORNING GLORY
Cheerful, harmless, pop rock of the instantly memorable yet totally meaningless jauntiness school.

❿ CAST NO SHADOW from (WHAT'S THE STORY) MORNING GLORY
The strongest, most musicianly track from the early years, and an excellent, well-crafted lyric of maturity and poignancy.

Al Spicer

Sinéad O'Connor

Born to be a star? Sinead O'Connor has always had a difficult relationship with her fame. She may not want what she hasn't got, but what she has got is a voice with few equals.

❶ MANDINKA from THE LION AND THE COBRA
The first real hit – a driving rocker that owes little in the way of musical influence to its West African namesake.

❷ NOTHING COMPARES 2 U from I DO NOT WANT WHAT I HAVEN'T GOT
Certainly, Prince's version doesn't compare to Sinéad's. This is the song that really propelled her into the mega-league – and not just because of that tear-jerking video.

❸ THE LAST DAY OF OUR ACQUAINTANCE from I DO NOT WANT WHAT I HAVEN'T GOT
Sinéad's songwriting and storytelling genius really came into their own on her second album, from which this is a key cut.

❹ BEWITCHED, BOTHERED AND BEWILDERED from AM I NOT YOUR GIRL?
Phil Ramone's extravagant orchestral arrangements never upstage Sinéad's delicate vocal delivery.

Sinéad O'Connor's
Roots reggae

It was Bob Marley's *War* that longtime reggae fan SINÉAD O'CONNOR was singing on American TV in 1992 when she notoriously tore up that picture of the Pope, an incident that came close to ending her career in the US. Yet she still loves the song enough to include a version of it on her latest album *Throw Down Your Arms*, recorded in Jamaica with reggae veterans Sly & Robbie. Unsurprisingly, it heads her list of her ten favourite roots reggae tracks...

❶ **WAR** BOB MARLEY AND THE WAILERS from RASTAMAN VIBRATION

❷ **DOWNPRESSOR MAN** PETER TOSH from EQUAL RIGHTS

❸ **MARCUS GARVEY** BURNING SPEAR from MARCUS GARVEY

❹ **VAMPIRE** LEE PERRY from ARKOLOGY

❺ **Y MAS GAN** THE ABYSSINIANS from SATTA MASSAGANA

❻ **PROPHET HAS ARISE** ISRAEL VIBRATION from THE SAME SONG

❼ **UNTOLD STORIES** BUJU BANTON from 'TIL SHILOH

❽ **CURLY LOCKS** JUNIOR BYLES from BEST OF JUNIOR BYLES AND THE UPSETTERS

❾ **THROW DOWN YOUR ARMS** BURNING SPEAR from DRY AND HEAVY

❿ **DOOR PEEP** BURNING SPEAR from BURNING SPEAR

❺ **IN THIS HEART** from UNIVERSAL MOTHER
Staggeringly beautiful a capella track featuring the backing vocals of the little known but wonderful Irish trio Voice Squad. But what a patchy album, otherwise!

❻ **THIS IS TO MOTHER YOU** from THE GOSPEL OAK
A typical cri de coeur on the theme of motherhood, with the line "what your own mother didn't do" hanging heavy in the air. The *Gospel Oak* EP should really have been an album.

❼ **THIS IS A REBEL SONG** from I DO NOT WANT WHAT I HAVEN'T GOT
Perhaps the most perfect marriage of the political and the personal she's ever recorded. Like her best writing, this sounds like it could almost be a traditional song.

❽ **RELEASE** from COLLABORATIONS
This joint effort with Afro Celt Sound System is one of her better collaborations. If you really must jump up and down in a field, you could do a lot worse than do it to this.

❾ **NO MAN'S WOMAN** from FAITH AND COURAGE
An uplifting pop-rocker and a strong statement of independence – the soundtrack to Sinéad's controversial "coming out" in the media.

Jon Lusk

Will Oldham

Oldham's worldview is peculiar, and his songs are strange and beautiful in equal measure. For well over a decade he has pedalled his alt.country creations under numerous monikers, most famously Bonnie "Prince" Billy and the various incarnations of the "Palace" franchise. Oldham is a true American songwriter to be cherished.

❶ **RIDING** PALACE BROTHERS from THERE IS NO-ONE WHAT WILL TAKE CARE OF YOU
Oldham's plaintive voice lazily sings a tale of incest and damnation over distant drums and a gently twanging guitar.

❷ **HORSES** PALACE MUSIC from LOST BLUES AND OTHER SONGS
The vocal strains and cracks over mellow country atmospherics, before the electrics kick in with an hilariously noodling solo.

❸ **I SEE A DARKNESS** BONNIE "PRINCE" BILLY from I SEE A DARKNESS
He sure does. This woefully sung ballad pulls piano and bass together into a masterful, surprisingly uplifting composition.

④ DEATH TO EVERYONE BONNIE "PRINCE" BILLY from I SEE A DARKNESS

Console yourself, as Will does, in the fact that we're all gonna be worm food sooner or later.

⑤ I AM A CINEMATOGRAPHER BONNIE "PRINCE" BILLY from SINGS GREATEST PALACE MUSIC

A jaunty, full-country-band version of an old Palace number, from a great album of full-country-band versions of old Palace numbers.

⑥ BEAST FOR THEE BONNIE "PRINCE" BILLY & MATT SWEENEY from SUPERWOLF

This gorgeous track stands as Oldham's most memorable of recent times; the delicate guitar work skates along beneath a subtle lyric.

⑦ YOU HAVE CUM IN YOUR HAIR AND YOUR DICK IS HANGING OUT PALACE from ARISE THEREFORE

With a title like that how could this song not be worth hearing?

⑧ O LORD ARE YOU IN NEED? PALACE BROTHERS from THERE IS NO-ONE WHAT WILL TAKE CARE OF YOU

A simply strummed guitar and pendulum drum-track waltz into the sunset as Oldham's lyric drifts downriver.

⑨ COME IN PALACE BROTHERS from LOST BLUES AND OTHER SONGS

From a strangely disjointed beckoning at the song's opening, the instrumentation rises to accompany another quiet classic.

Peter Buckley

Olympian vocals

For some singers and their voices, bigger is invariably better. Hitting those high notes and trying to nail every other on the way back has become their life's work, it seems. For that perseverance and their impressive vocal chords, we salute them. The Olympic medallists in warbling are:

GOLD

① EMOTIONS MARIAH CAREY from EMOTIONS

Mariah's five-octave range is used to great effect here (were it seven octaves – as some enthusiasts believe – she'd have as many notes as a grand piano). Just don't put the kettle on while this is playing.

② MY HEART WILL GO ON CELINE DION from LET'S TALK ABOUT LOVE

The *Titanic* theme tune was a heartfelt weepie and the French–Canadian songbird delivered the lip-quivering goods, emoting to a staggering fifty million record buyers with every fibre of her being.

③ I WILL ALWAYS LOVE YOU WHITNEY HOUSTON from THE BODYGUARD

After landing a starring role in *The Bodyguard*, Whitney's memorable theme tune revisited Dolly Parton's classic in spectacular fashion. She and her reverberations ended up stealing not only Kevin Costner's heart, but the whole show.

SILVER

④ WUTHERING HEIGHTS KATE BUSH from THE KICK INSIDE

Kate Bush's update of Emily Brontë's novel won over a legion of adolescent fans. Even now, the damsel-in-distress's melodramatic vocals make men of a certain age tremble in admiration.

⑤ BELIEVE CHER from BELIEVE (WARNER, 1998)

Cher's dazzling reinvention as a modern disco diva employed a welter of writers and technical jiggery-pokery. The "wibbly" bits of the chorus were distorted via a Vocoder, creating clubby electro-pop perfection.

BRONZE

⑥ HUMAN BEHAVIOUR BJÖRK from DEBUT

On "Human Behaviour", Björk's staccato enunciation and alternately quiet and loud singing found the wide audience she deserved. She has since cornered the market in quirky power-yodelling.

⑦ LORELEI COCTEAU TWINS from TREASURE

Liz Fraser's ethereal warbling became a hallmark of The Cocteau Twins' oeuvre. On "Lorelei", swirling guitars enhance her vocals to create an otherworldly sound.

Ed Wright

On the road

A classic road song doesn't just roll down some anonymous road, it should name the road, the route and point out the roadside attractions. We can make exceptions.

① ROUTE 66 BOBBY TROUP from KICKS ON 66

The Stones made it their own, but whoever sings it – see our separate Route 66 list – this is the classic road song. Route 66 remains the place to get your kicks, anywhere from Chicago to LA, more than 2000 miles all the way.

❷ RUNNING ON EMPTY JACKSON BROWNE from RUNNING ON EMPTY
In 1965 Jackson Browne was 17 and running up 101, the inland road between Los Angeles and San Francisco. He rolled down 295 out of Portland, Maine, on the same album.

❸ DEEP WATER RICHARD CLAPTON from GOODBYE TIGER
There were plenty of road stories during Richard Clapton's late-1970s moment in the sun, but sitting out on the Palm Beach Road (it runs north from Sydney), drunk and with a car that won't go, was a peak.

❹ LAKE CHARLES LUCINDA WILLIAMS from CAR WHEELS ON A GRAVEL ROAD
Travelling down the Louisiana Highway, across Lake Ponchartrain, and in a yellow El Camino listening to Howlin' Wolf, Williams turns a road trip into a tragedy.

❺ THE LAST CHANCE TEXACO RICKIE LEE JONES from RICKIE LEE JONES
Tiptoeing along I-9, Rickie Lee Jones turns that last Texaco gas station into a metaphor for all our last chances.

❻ VENTURA HIGHWAY AMERICA from HOMECOMING
It was in the sunshine and the days were longer; the real highway is the coast stretch of 101 out of Los Angeles, before it turns inland.

❼ GRACELAND PAUL SIMON from GRACELAND
The actual road is never specified, but we know it follows the river, and since it's in the cradle of the Civil War it's clearly in the Deep South, even before we're told it runs to Graceland.

❽ ROLL ME AWAY BOB SEGER from THE DISTANCE
He's heading west, he's on a big motorcycle and when he picks up the girl who rides with him awhile, he's twelve hours out of Mackinaw City in Michigan – what more do we need to know?

❾ 24 HOURS FROM TULSA GENE PITNEY from THE VERY BEST OF GENE PITNEY
Apart from being a day's drive from Tulsa, Oklahoma, it's unclear where Gene met that temptress, but this is a road song warning about motels, cafés and jukeboxes.

❿ AUTOBAHN KRAFTWERK from AUTOBAHN
The German techno pioneers never name which

autobahn they're on but no matter, "wir fahr'n fahr'n fahr'n auf der Autobahn."

Tony Wheeler

The Orb

The Orb provided the interface at which prog rock met ambient: the chill-out zone, where whacked-out ravers – still grinning but too messed up to dance attractively – sat their twitching spines down for some recuperation time.

❶ POMME FRITZ (MEAT 'N' VEG) from U. F. OFF
At its best, The Orb's music will calm you down, take your mind off your problems, give you a gurgling keyboard sound to play with and put that smile back on your face.

❷ BLUE ROOM from U. F. OFF
Too beat-drenched to hold its own in the chill-out room, this is the track that grabs you by the lapel and leads you back to the dancefloor for one more cheeky half and a bit of a dance.

❸ HUGE EVER GROWING PULSATING BRAIN ... from ADVENTURES BEYOND THE ULTRAWORLD
Masterful, like Pink Floyd for a new generation taking different drugs. Classy, involved and deeply interesting music that makes you want to sit down, skin up and really think about things.

❹ LITTLE FLUFFY CLOUDS from ADVENTURES BEYOND THE ULTRAWORLD
Sampling Rickie Lee Jones reminiscing about her early life somewhere on a distant planet, this is always a trip, and a real floor-filler.

❺ OOBE from UFORB
This is The Orb at the meatier end of the spectrum. A harmless, unpretentious, four-to-the-floor dancehall stomper.

❻ PERPETUAL DAWN from ADVENTURES BEYOND THE ULTRAWORLD
Just plain silly. Vulgar mouth-noises made by a man with the voice of a 1950s radio presenter and back-to-basics beats make this totally irresistible.

❼ SPANISH CASTLES IN SPACE from ADVENTURES BEYOND THE ULTRAWORLD
Alex Patterson and the studio working together as one to show just how psychedelic a track can be.

⑧ TOWERS OF DUB from UFORB
Youth (ex-Killing Joke) made his contribution to the album most felt on this track, reflecting both his massive bass and taste for dub.

⑨ TOXYGENE from ORBLIVION
Late-period Orb single, which came as a double CD set of endless remixes. For once, however, they're all worth more than a single spin.

⑩ U. F. ORB from UFORB (ISLAND; 1996)
Immense low-frequency throbbing from Youth and a swirl of highly tweaked computer-generated keyboard effects from Alex.

Al Spicer

Roy Orbison

The high priest of romantic paranoia and rock's first monarch of miserabilism, whose soaring songs were as dark as his shades. He has even been compared to John Dowland by no less a luminary than Harrison Birtwistle.

① IN DREAMS from ALL TIME GREATEST HITS
If Roy Orbison hadn't existed, David Lynch would have had to invent him. This song, which haunts Lynch's *Blue Velvet*, is one of rock'n'roll's great dream songs.

② SHE'S A MYSTERY TO ME from MYSTERY GIRL
Written by Bono, this is the greatest work of the Big O's 1980s comeback and one of his greatest vocal performances, ending with a flourish that recalls his soaring climax to "Crying".

③ BLUE BAYOU from ALL TIME GREATEST HITS
Another classic dream song, the product of Orbison's productive partnership with Joe Melson. Almost as familiar through the cover versions – by Linda Ronstadt and Mireille Mathieu – as the original.

④ OH, PRETTY WOMAN from ALL TIME GREATEST HITS
A strutting, rocking, rollicking tale of a man who turns a pretty woman's head on the street. Since 1964, men on streets all over the world have replayed this scenario.

⑤ RUNNING SCARED from ALL TIME GREATEST HITS
A paranoid bolero, with a Mexican ambience, and a twist ending – to his own obvious disbelief, Roy gets the girl. Marvellous.

⑥ IT'S OVER from ALL TIME GREATEST HITS
You get the full Orbison *Sturm und Drang* here: lonely sunsets, falling stars, weeping rainbows and betrayal. Impassioned and overblown, this is a truly chilling ballad, as the wronged lover faces a life sentence of lovelessness.

⑦ BLUE ANGEL from ALL TIME GREATEST HITS
Though this was initially dismissed as too much of a clone of "Only The Lonely", the passages where Roy wordlessly sympathizes with his blue angel's heartbreak are simply out of this world.

⑧ CRYING from ALL TIME GREATEST HITS
An iconic song of heartache, this is based on a real encounter between Orbison and an old flame.

⑨ YOU GOT IT from MYSTERY GIRL
A late, insistent, celebration of love, almost a companion piece to "Oh, Pretty Woman", which shows that, even in the late 1980s, the Big O still had, as Barry Gibb said, "the voice of God".

⑩ DANNY BOY from MEMPHIS
Almost everybody has recorded this tear-jerking Irish folk standard, but Orbison's cover is exceptionally powerful.

Paul Simpson

Outkast

Big Boi and Dre, two Georgia rapper-producers, blended musical idioms like no one since Prince and gave the Dirty South a soul New Orleans thugs lacked.

① HEY YA from THE LOVE BELOW/SPEAKERBOX
"Shake it like a Polaroid picture", commands Dre. The world obliged. The best party tune of the twenty-first century? Easy.

② PLAYERS BALL from SOUTHERNPLAYALISTICADILLACMUZIK
A celebration of a pimps' and hustlers' convention. Ghetto-fabulous? This is it.

③ ROSA PARKS from AQUEMINI
Civil rights icons are rarely celebrated in hip-hop. Perhaps understandably: Rosa Parks sued them for using her name!

④ MS JACKSON from STANKONIA
Over an organ drone and staccato drum-pattern, Dre and BB celebrate their babies while asking for peace from the mamas.

❺ SO FRESH, SO CLEAN from STANKONIA

"We are the coolest motherfuckers on the planet/The sky is fallin', aint no need to panic", raps Big Boi in this slow-jam hymn to their fine selves.

❻ SOUTHERNPLAYALISTICADILLACMUZIK from SOUTHERNPLAYALISTICADILLACMUZIK

This early track saw Outkast mouthing gangsta clichés, yet the groove, languid as an Atlanta summer afternoon, means ya gotta love it.

❼ ELEVATORS (ME & YOU) from ATLIENS

A 1996 reflection on early days. "They're raking green, yeah, but there's a long way to go", says Dre. Some understatement.

❽ SPOTTIEOTTIEDOPALISICIOUS from AQUEMINI

Rough gigs, falling in love, raising a daughter and failing a Post Office drug test are among the concerns tackled here.

❾ THE WHOLE WORLD from BIG BOI & DRE PRESENT ... OUTKAST

Outkast celebrate their own success. The closest they've come to a conventional hip-hop tune.

❿ CRUMBLIN' ERB from SOUTHERNPLAYALISTICADILLACMUZIK

A hymn to getting high. Message: smoking herb is better than doing drive-bys.

Garth Cartwright

Outlaw Country

"Outlaw Country" took its name from Waylon Jennings' 1972 album *Ladies Love Outlaws* and soon came to apply to a host of artists who refused to play the Nashville game. Partly it was about image, but the movement's main objective was creative control for the artists and songwriters who came to be associated with it. Here are ten who refused to toe the line…

❶ BLUE EYES CRYIN' IN THE RAIN WILLIE NELSON from RED HEADED STRANGER

So stripped-down and low-key that at first Columbia refused to release the album, this song eventually gave Willie his first #1.

❷ ARE YOU SURE HANK DONE IT THIS WAY? WAYLON JENNINGS from DREAMING MY DREAMS

The song that summed up the frustration with how Nashville had lost touch with its roots.

❸ PANCHO AND LEFTY TOWNES VAN ZANDT from THE LATE, GREAT TOWNES VAN ZANDT

More than any of the outlaws, Townes lived the life he made in song. Willie Nelson, Merle Haggard and Emmylou Harris all covered this classic.

❹ SOLD AMERICAN TOMPALL GLASER from CHARLIE

A fantastic version of Kinky Friedman's bottomed-out cowboy lament from the least celebrated of the quartet who recorded the classic *Wanted! The Outlaws* album.

❺ YOU MEAN TO SAY JESSI COLTER from WANTED! THE OUTLAWS

Waylon's wife and one of the few female "outlaws", she achieved immortality by appearing on *Wanted! The Outlaws* alongside with Waylon, Willie and Tompall.

❻ ME AND BOBBY MGEE KRIS KRISTOFFERSON from ME AND BOBBY MCGEE

Covered by everyone from Janis Joplin to The Grateful Dead, the song that was the bridge between Hank Williams and Bob Dylan.

❼ LONGHAIRED REDNECK DAVID ALLAN COE from LONGHAIRED REDNECK

An outlaw anthem if ever there was one, from the man whose other songs included "Willie, Waylon And Me" and "Take This Job And Shove It".

❽ HONKY TONK HEROES BILLIE JOE SHAVER from HONKY TONK HEROES

Waylon recorded an entire album of Shaver's songs, of which this was the title track. But Shaver was a fine performer in his own right.

❾ DESPERADOS WAITING FOR A TRAIN GUY CLARK from OLD NO 1

A Texas compadre of Townes Van Zandt, this is the best-known of his eloquent country-folk narratives.

❿ UP AGAINST THE WALL, REDNECK MOTHER JERRY JEFF WALKER from VIVA TERLINGUA

Although Jerry Jeff wrote Mr Bojangles, this classic Texas bar-room sing-along was penned for him by Ray Wylie Hubbard.

Nigel Williamson

Oz Rock

Australia has long harboured a high-energy rock scene to rival any in the world. Here are eight of the most visceral rockers from Down Under, along with two wild cards to prove that they're not all he-man surfer dudes.

❶ YOU'RE DRIVING ME INSANE THE MISSING LINKS from THE MISSING LINKS

Totally unhinged maximum R&B.

❷ FRIDAY ON MY MIND THE EASYBEATS
from FRIDAY ON MY MIND

Even better than Loverboy's "Working For The Weekend".

❸ (I'M) STRANDED THE SAINTS
from I'M STRANDED

Snarl, groove, venom, hooks, momentum – is this the best rock record ever?

❹ NEW RACE RADIO BIRDMAN from RADIOS APPEAR

The faint right-wing gang overtones are a bit scary, but my god does this move.

❺ WILD WEEKEND PSYCHO SURGEONS
from DO THE POP!

Don't let the hint of melody at the beginning fool you, this is pure Neanderthal stomp.

❻ DO THAT DANCE PRIMITIVE CALCULATORS
from PRIMITIVE CALCULATORS

Spiky, agitated post-punk with electronics that owe a large debt to Cabaret Voltaire.

❼ 24 HOURS (SOS) THE CELIBATE RIFLES
from SIDEROXYLON

An awesome combination of jingle-jangle and high-voltage rifferama.

❽ BE MY GURU HOODOO GURUS
from STONE AGE ROMEOS

Big, dumb and stoopid – perfect trashy surfer rock.

❾ CATTLE AND CANE THE GO-BETWEENS
from BEFORE HOLLYWOOD

Gorgeous melancholia from Oz's greatest troubadours.

❿ BYE BYE GIRL HARD-ONS from DO THE POP!

Two minutes of thrashy perfection.

Peter Shapiro

P

Pacifica

... or Polynesian music, if you like. And that includes New Zealand, even though it's hardly tropical, because so many artists have made their homes there. See also the Hawaii playlist.

① FRENCH LETTER HERBS
from LISTEN: THE VERY BEST OF
1983's defining moment for this multicultural Pacific Island/Maori group, telling French nuclear testers to get out of the Pacific in no uncertain terms.

② ALOHA MEANS I LOVE YOU TAU MOE FAMILY WITH BOB BROZMAN from THE TAU MOE FAMILY WITH BOB BROZMAN
The globe-trotting family band with hyperactive hippy Brozman in tow. A truly charming collaboration.

③ HAWAI'I '78 INTRODUCTION ISRAEL KAMAKAWIWO 'OLE from FACING FUTURE
Bittersweet recollections of family life from "Iz", the unlikely giant of Hawaiian music, who died in 1997 at the age of 38.

④ HOW BIZARRE OMC from HOW BIZARRE
A worldwide hit by the Otara Millionaires Club, aka Pauly Fuemana. You couldn't avoid this song in 1996, but where is he now?

⑤ THE DAVID TUA THEME BROTHER D
from URBAN PACIFIKA: PIONEERS OF A PACIFIKAN FRONTIER
Crunching hip-hop tribute to Samoa's diminutive boxing star: "He packs a punch … He made the big nations aware of little islands."

⑥ MIHI TUATAHI WAI from WAI 100%
Innovative Maori music for the new millennium, by singer Mina Ripia and programmer/producer Maaka McGregor.

⑦ MISTY FREQUENCIES CHE FU from NAVIGATOR
A smoother-than-satin vocal treat by the leading light of Pacific/Kiwi soul, hip-hop and R&B … Che Fu is a hard man to pigeonhole.

⑧ FOR THE PEOPLE NESIAN MYSTIK
from POLYSATURATED
Upbeat Pacific R&B by a boy band with a difference.

⑨ LAKILUA TE VAKA from TUTUKI
Chunky, rootsy log-drums from Pan-Polynesian group who are worldwide festival favourites.

⑩ HOPE FAT FREDDY'S DROP
from BASED ON A TRUE STORY
Deeply soulful, urban-Pacific reggae grooves, featuring the amazing velvet vocals of Dallas Tamaira, aka Joe Dukie. This seven-piece are currently the hottest thing in New Zealand.

Jon Lusk

Paisley underground

This loose amalgamation of early 1980s Californian bands were seen as a "movement" thanks to their allegiance to late-60s artists like Pink Floyd, Jimi Hendrix and Neil Young – plus their sartorial tendencies. They reinvigorated underground rock just as commercial music reached its new-wave nadir.

① DAYS OF WINE AND ROSES DREAM SYNDICATE from DAYS OF WINE AND ROSES
This potent blast starts at a frenetic clip with Dennis Duck's pounding drums, and ends as lead guitarist Karl Precoda rings every last jolt of electricity out of the air.

② THIS CAN'T BE TODAY RAIN PARADE
from EMERGENCY THIRD RAIL POWER TRIP
A rare uptempo song from Rain Parade, who epitomized the gentler end of the scene, with a keyboard-driven sound that was a dead ringer for early-1970s era Pink Floyd.

③ HE'S GOT A SECRET THE BANGLES
from ALL OVER THE PLACE
This compelling song from the debut album by The Bangles is built around pile-driving power chords from guitarist Vicki Peterson.

④ NARCOLEPSY GREEN ON RED
from GRAVITY TALKS
Riding that mid-1960s garage sound hard, this nugget incorporates swelling organ and chiming rhythm guitar in its hypnotic palette.

❺ HOLOCAUST RAINY DAY from RAINY DAY

Big Star tune, drawn from loose-knit supergroup Rainy Day's 1984 covers album, and sung by Kendra Smith of The Dream Syndicate.

❻ FELL FROM THE SUN SMITH, ROBACK AND MITCHELL from FELL FROM THE SUN

After leaving The Dream Syndicate, Kendra Smith teamed up with David Roback of The Rain Parade and drummer Keith Mitchell. When Smith left, they morphed into Mazzy Star.

❼ ROCKET MACHINE OPAL from HAPPY NIGHTMARE BABY

This grinding, chugging T-Rex pastiche opened Opal's debut album.

❽ JET FIGHTER THE THREE O'CLOCK from SIXTEEN TAMBOURINES

Bassist/vocalist Michael Quercio's helium-pitched vocals carry this soaring song from the LA band most wed to mid-1960s soft-rock.

❾ TOO CLOSE TO THE LIGHT THE LONG RYDERS from NATIVE SONS

A sweetly melodic song from hard-core Byrds fanatics The Long Ryders.

❿ SOME VELVET MORNING THIN WHITE ROPE from WHEN WORLDS COLLIDE

An intense version of Lee Hazlewood's totally strange 1968 composition.

Butch Lazorchak

Parental controls

Even Roxy Music's "Teenage rebel of the week" was sometimes lost for words when it came to setting the folks straight. Trust the magicians of pop to provide both outlets for frustration and advice on what to say when the wheels fall off your wagon.

❶ PAPA DON'T PREACH MADONNA from IMMACULATE COLLECTION: THE BEST OF MADONNA

The young Mrs Ritchie kicked open many doors in her early career. Taking unplanned teen pregnancy into suburban homes through radio play and one of her finest videos, she assisted who knows how many young parents-to-be through that heart-stopping time just after the stick changes colour.

❷ WHITE RABBIT JEFFERSON AIRPLANE from SURREALISTIC PILLOW

Arguably the most powerful of the San Francisco hippy bands, the Airplane neatly netted the average parent's next worst nightmare – the kid gets into drugs – with this clever weave of *Alice In Wonderland* against domestic prescription pill-popping, and the undeniable appeal of heaven in a sugar lump.

❸ SHE'S LEAVING HOME THE BEATLES from SGT PEPPER'S LONELY HEARTS CLUB BAND

One of the lads' more potent heartstring-tuggers, and based in part on the true story of an escape from suburban suffocation into the liberal and free air of 1960s swinging London, this is the pop world's best ever attempt to show both the reason for leaving and the sudden eviscerated loss experienced by those left deserted, bereft and too old to understand.

❹ STRAY CAT BLUES THE ROLLING STONES from BEGGARS BANQUET

Recorded way after their manager's infamous "Would You Let Your Daughter Marry A Rolling Stone?" press stunt and before they turned into old, grizzled lechers in Lycra, this ode to pre-legal groupies and their persuasive ways made the blood of right-thinking folks turn to ice-cold fear.

❺ EMBARRASSMENT MADNESS from COMPLETE MADNESS: REMASTERED

Another look at the eternal pickle that tormented Madonna (see above), but here viewed from the back streets of working class North London. In a welcome return to Victorian Values, the strumpet is thrown out of the house to make her way as best she can in a cold hard world.

❻ SWEET SIXTEEN IGGY POP from LUST FOR LIFE

Scoring high on the average parent's list of night sweats is the prospect of a beloved child falling in with a bad crowd, staying out all night, turning feral, to addiction, and perhaps thence to prostitution. After all, those street girls sniffing away the cold and humiliation are, each and every one, somebody's baby, no? So if your little girl is out in leather boots and a plastic raincoat, and comes home reeking of white wine, looking older than she really is, maybe it's time for some tough love and positive intervention.

❼ BOHEMIAN RHAPSODY QUEEN from GREATEST HITS: REMASTERED

"Mama, just killed a man" is probably the worst way in history of starting a message from prison. Going on to whine about how life had just begun and how Beelzebub has a devil put aside for you isn't going to ease the poor woman's pain at all. Still, it might fill in the time until she can breathe again.

p

❽ YES, MY DARLING DAUGHTER DINAH SHORE from
YOU'D BE SO NICE TO COME HOME TO
From an altogether more innocent era when dancing
and the remotest possibility of romancing required
explicit parental permission, today's cynical audience
is inclined to bridle at mum's complicity in pimping
out her girl. Forget your worldly grown reluctance to
join in and surrender to the anticipation and excitement. It'll all end in tears mind, you mark my words.

❾ SONNY'S LETTAH LINTON KWESI JOHNSON
from **FORCES OF VICTORY**
Dating from an era when institutional racism was seen
as part of the job by many serving officers, Sonny's
letter from jail coats the bitter fight he joined to
protect his brother from the police battering he was
receiving, and the death that resulted from it, in a soft,
sweet pastry of respectful filial greetings and regret.

❿ TEENAGE DEPRESSION EDDIE & THE HOT RODS
from **TEENAGE DEPRESSION**
In which the Rods celebrate the lighter side of inter-
generational friction. "I'm spending all my money and
it's going up my nose" is a promising start, but having
the parents find out is a dumb thing to do. When
they tear up all your best clothes as a result, teenage
depression arrives as night follows day. Play it loud,
dress down, head on out and celebrate the weekend.
To hell with them and their geriatric ways.

Al Spicer

Charlie Parker

**Every jazz musician who came after Charlie Parker
(1920–55) was influenced by him – even in the
(rather unlikely) event they hadn't heard him.
Dating from the era of 78rpm singles and largely
pre hi-fi, his music enormously repays listening
through the crackles. All the following are drawn
from Proper's 4CD box-set, *Boss Bird*.**

❶ KO-KO
An astonishing virtuoso display from the first real
bebop recording session, in 1945. Parker soars over
the complex chords with a freedom and audacity then
quite new to jazz.

❷ NIGHT IN TUNISIA
Based on a bass riff, built around two exotic chords
and ending on a fade, Gillespie's 1946 composition
was a first in many ways. Parker's vertiginous four-bar
solo-break still thrills, and every solo which follows is
a classic.

❸ KLACTOVEESEDSTENE
The first of two takes of this tune, from 1947. Parker
reaches new levels of abstraction, building a solo
out of a jigsaw of motifs while drummer Max Roach
pushes him on.

❹ EMBRACEABLE YOU
Again producing his masterpiece on the first of two
1947 takes, Parker recomposes Gershwin's tune completely, working from a limpid five-note phrase into a
breathtaking solo.

❺ BIRD OF PARADISE
Recorded on the same day as "Embraceable You", and
featuring a solo so inspired and logical that it has
often been transcribed and played as a melody in its
own right.

❻ PARKER'S MOOD
Parker was always a great blues player, and this 1948
track is one of his best – a slow Kansas City blues
framed by a haunting minor-key cry on the alto.

❼ JUST FRIENDS
1949's "with strings" sessions still divide fans – but
once you get used to the sweet-and-sour sound, you
can hear one of Bird's great solos.

❽ BLUE'N'BOOGIE
The live 1951 reunion of Bird, Dizzy and pianist Bud
Powell is less well known than the Massey Hall concert
of a couple of years later, though it produced better
music.

❾ FINE AND DANDY
Most live Parker "airshots" offer poor recording quality;
this remarkably clear 1953 one shows the altoist fronting an excellent big band.

❿ NOW'S THE TIME
Revisiting one of his 1945 blues riffs in 1953, Parker
sounds like his old self. From now on, until his death
less than two years later, it was all downhill.

Alex Webb

Gram Parsons

**In a tragically short but intense career, stretching
from The International Submarine Band, via The
Byrds, The Flying Burrito Brothers and even The
Rolling Stones to his own beautiful, ethereal
solo records, and ended by his untimely death in
1973, Gram Parsons can take credit as the leading
progenitor of country rock.**

❶ SHE from GP

Parsons' voice is at his most poignant in this gently insistent examination of his quasi-Christian beliefs.

❷ HOT BURRITO #1
from THE GILDED PALACE OF SIN

A choked and vulnerable ballad that shows off Gram's voice to great effect.

❸ A SONG FOR YOU from GP

The sparse arrangement of this gospel-ish song perfectly offsets Gram's throaty quaver.

❹ RETURN OF THE GRIEVOUS ANGEL
from GRIEVOUS ANGEL

An acid-driven road movie of a song, full of sadness for brief encounters and long-lost soulmates.

❺ $1000 WEDDING from GRIEVOUS ANGEL

Gram's voice soars sublimely with Emmylou Harris's on this bitter lament.

❻ IN MY HOUR OF DARKNESS
from GRIEVOUS ANGEL

A medium-tempo country lament for the deaths of three close friends. Great playing, and gorgeous singing from Emmylou.

❼ HICKORY WIND
from SWEETHEART OF THE RODEO

Parsons' ode to his Southern roots, and a general commentary on good ole American lonesomeness.

❽ LOVE HURTS from GRIEVOUS ANGEL

Not a Parsons song, but a great one, showcasing Gram and Emmylou Harris at their very best.

❾ DARK END OF THE STREET
from THE GILDED PALACE OF SIN

The Flying Burritos Brothers' yearning interpretation of a Southern soul classic – perhaps the ultimate evocation of Parsons'"Cosmic American Music".

❿ DO YOU KNOW HOW IT FEELS TO BE LONESOME?
from THE GILDED PALACE OF SIN

Originally cut for *Safe At Home*, Gram's first venture with The International Submarine Band, and reprised in this slicker version with the Flying Burritos.

Martin Dunford

Dolly Parton

Larger than life but the real deal, country music has never seen anything quite like Dolly Parton. Singer, songwriter, country traditionalist and pop-crossover superstar, she was never a dumb blonde.

❶ COAT OF MANY COLORS
from COAT OF MANY COLORS

Moving autobiographical account of Dolly's dirt-poor upbringing in the Smokey Mountains.

❷ JUST BECAUSE I'M A WOMAN
from JUST BECAUSE I'M A WOMAN

Despite her male-pleasing image ("It costs a lot of money to make me look this cheap", she once cracked), she always had a strong streak of feminism.

❸ DADDY WAS AN OLD TIME PREACHER MAN from
ONCE MORE

Among the finest of the many duets Dolly recorded with Porter Wagoner.

❹ JOLENE from JOLENE

Her first big hit after splitting from Porter had to be something special. And it was.

❺ I WILL ALWAYS LOVE YOU from JOLENE

Forget Whitney Houston. Dolly wrote this as a tribute to Wagoner, who took her desertion from his show as a personal betrayal.

❻ MY TENNESSEE MOUNTAIN HOME
from MY TENNESSEE MOUNTAIN HOME

Dolly was never better than when singing about her Appalachian roots.

❼ HERE YOU COME AGAIN from HERE YOU COME AGAIN
The one that crossed her over into the pop charts.

❽ 9 TO 5 from 9 TO 5 AND ODD JOBS
The infectious title song written for the 1980 film of the same name.

❾ MULE SKINNER BLUES
from THE ESSENTIAL DOLLY PARTON

Dolly's first solo hit in 1970 was this vivacious interpretation of Jimmie Rodgers' classic song.

❿ THOSE MEMORIES OF YOU from TRIO
Magnificent, mournful bluegrass from a 1987 album with Emmylou Harris and Linda Ronstadt.

Nigel Williamson

Stephen Malkmus
Esoterica

The main man with Pavement, one of America's most influential alternative rock acts of the 1990s, STEPHEN MALKMUS created a suitably esoteric and alternative playlist for us, right down to opting for just the nine numbers. Less is the new more.

❶ DRIFTING LEIGH STEPHENS
from RED WEATHER

❷ SWEETIES THE HANDSOME BEASTS
from THE BEASTIALITY

❸ SPARE CHAYNGE JEFFERSON AIRPLANE
from AFTER BATHING AT BAXTERS

❹ KEEP ON TRYING ENGLISH GYPSY
from ENGLISH GYPSY

❺ BUY CHISWICK RECORDS RADIO STARS
from SONGS FOR SWINGING LOVERS

❻ THE ROYAL PLAN ABNER JAY
from SWANNEE WATER AND COCAINE BLUES

❼ PREPARE TO LIVE SECTION 25
from FROM THE HIP

❽ BEAT THE REAPER LAURIE STYVERS
from SPILT MILK

❾ OUR SONG STRAY from STRAY

Pavement

College rockers supreme, Stephen Malkmus and Scott "Spiral Stairs" Kannenberg became reluctant leaders of the alt.rock school of indie music in the 1990s. Their band Pavement created quirky beauty and elegance from the ugliest and most mismatched of musical components. Funny, deadpan and unique.

❶ FROM NOW ON
from WESTING (BY MUSKET AND SEXTANT)
Pavement's earliest declaration of how they planned to take on the world and win.

❷ ANGEL CARVER BLUES/MELLOW JAZZ DOCENT
from WESTING (BY MUSKET AND SEXTANT)
Epic, twisted mountain pathway of a tune that leads you blindly on until boom, revelation comes as you reach the summit.

❸ SUMMER BABE from SLANTED AND ENCHANTED
An early crowd-pleaser, encouraging fans to join in and help out with the harmonizing.

❹ CUT YOUR HAIR
from CROOKED RAIN, CROOKED RAIN
Comparatively straightforward rocker with the anthemic "No Big Hair" hook.

❺ HIT THE PLANE DOWN
from CROOKED RAIN, CROOKED RAIN
Scott goes all Mark E. Smith, one last, magnificent time.

❻ RANGE LIFE from CROOKED RAIN, CROOKED RAIN
Laid-back musings on the life of an averagely successful college band – the tours, the gigs, the petty rivalries – to a gentle acoustic setting.

❼ RATTLED BY THE RUSH from WOWEE ZOWEE
A four-minute exploration of the inside of Stephen's brain, beautifully illustrated with odd-job guitars and deadpan delivery.

❽ STEREO from BRIGHTEN THE CORNERS
The first single from this set, an art-rock jam guaranteed never to bother the charts.

❾ THE HEXX from TERROR TWILIGHT
While Pavement never quite evolved away from their roots as garage band and studio kids, by now they could turn small ideas into major workouts like this ominous heavy rocker.

❿ FLUX=RAD from WOWEE ZOWEE
Pavement's take on music to cruise by – groovy singalong lyrics and, hey, it's a toe-tapper!

Al Spicer

Peel faves

Long-standing champion of the weird and wonderful in modern music, DJ John Peel made the occasional bad choice, but when he threw his weight behind an act, you could guarantee it was something special. Though Peelie's gone, his work will live on, as long as there are "Peel Sessions" tapes to be unearthed and reissued.

❶ INDUSTRIAL ESTATE THE FALL
from COMPLETE PEEL SESSIONS
John claimed The Fall set a yardstick by which all other acts had to be judged. They played so many Peel sessions that the collection clocks in at six tightly packed CDs. This track captures their spiky, brilliant, enigmatic appeal.

❷ TEENAGE KICKS THE UNDERTONES
from THE BEST OF
The best single ever, according to the great man, recorded on zero budget by what was then the only punk band in Ireland.

❸ IRK THE PURISTS HALF MAN HALF BISCUIT
from TROUBLE OVER BRIDGEWATER
Permanently funny, shambling and amateurish, no matter how dour the delivery, HMHB were the consummate Peel band. This is by several lengths their best track.

❹ DOWN DOWN STATUS QUO from XS ALL AREAS
Controversial, quirky and possibly the only Quo track in this entire volume, "Down Down" was John's "if all else fails" dancefloor filler. From student discos to the Reading Festival, Peel exhorted the crowds to get down, deeper and down. Apparently it never failed.

❺ SURE 'NUFF & YES I DO CAPTAIN BEEFHEART & THE MAGIC BAND from SAFE AS MILK
John loved the Captain and would regularly play his 1968 live rerecording of this track, despite its appalling quality.

❻ 19 HEADACHES AUTECHRE
from THE PEEL SESSIONS VOL 2
Clearing the mental palate like sandpaper on a furred tongue, Autechre's aural assaults were a frequent delight on John's shows. This suitably titled track pokes into all the electro-noise closets and rattles the contents of our pleasure.

❼ YOU DON'T SEND ME BELLE AND SEBASTIAN from DEAR CATASTROPHE WAITRESS
Nothing if not eclectic in his musical tastes, our hero had his moments of gentle whimsy, as shown by this late slice of B&S.

❽ PAWN SHOPPE HEART THE VON BONDIES from LET PAWN SHOPPE HEART
Detroit noise-mongers like the Von Bondies, with their bad attitude and dirty habits, were meat and drink to John. Blast your brains with this slice of raw power.

❾ MR BLUE SKY THE DELGADOS
from ALL YOU NEED IS HATE
The none-more-indie Glasgow miserablists performed this ELO cover on the show, but this version has more gloss and finesse.

❿ Y CONTROL THE YEAH YEAH YEAHS
from FEVER TO TELL V
To the end of his life, John Peel championed the over-driven, raw end of the rock'n'roll circus. Finishing this list with The Yeah Yeah Yeahs' loudest, most distorted and glorious track to date seems only right.

Al Spicer

Art Pepper

Altoist par excellence Art Pepper made the transition from California cool cat to harrowing balladeer via a lifetime of heroin addiction.

❶ SUZY THE POODLE from SURF RIDE
Bop, West-Coast-style; Pepper comes on like a slick, suntanned Charlie Parker on his intricate 1952 variation on the chord sequence of Indiana.

❷ BEGIN THE BEGUINE from ART OF PEPPER
From a splendid series of Blue Note albums made after returning from prison on narcotics charges, this charged, hypnotic 1957 performance proved he'd lost none of his sparkle.

❸ IMAGINATION
from MEETS THE RHYTHM SECTION
Unprepared, undernourished and without a decent instrument, Pepper wings it in 1957 with Miles's rhythm section, and triumphs with playing of spirit and surprise.

❹ SHAW 'NUFF from MODERN JAZZ CLASSICS
The 1959 album featured beautifully hip, rich arrangements for an eleven-piece band; at the centre an insouciantly brilliant Pepper dances through Gillespie's fiendish bop flagwaver.

p

George Pelecanos'
Soul off the Dial

George Pelecanos has written thirteen crime novels, for lack of a better name, though they have a lyricism that defies simple genre definition. His characters inhabit a DC far from the scrubbed American capital many are familiar with. They also tend to listen to a wide range of music, from 1980s new wave to lost treasures like the ones you'll find below (they get their original single details – few are to be found on CD or download). More lists – of music, movie and literature recommendations – can be found on the writer's webpage (www.georgepelecanos.com).

❶ IT'S WHAT YOU GIVE
JIMMY CASTOR from JET SET 1002
Before Jimmy Castor led the Bunch, before "Troglodyte", he was a real soul man, evidenced by this track, recorded in DC Big horns, strong female background singers, and an insanely stoked J.C. going off in falsetto will disabuse you of the notion that Castor was "just" a novelty act.

❷ I'LL STEP ASIDE
BEN ATKINS AND THE NOMADS from STATUE 7001
Quavering, barely controlled vocals from Atkins and subtle production make this one of the great "sacrifice" records. I bet this one made men cry as they drove down those empty Southern roads late at night.

❸ REMONE
LINDELL HILL FROM from ARCH 1302
Basic track and blue-eyed soul vocals recorded in St Louis, horns added in Memphis by Stax man Steve Cropper. The background ladies sound like they're up on something good.

❹ SOMETIMES A MAN WILL SHED A FEW TEARS TOO JOHNNY ADAMS from PACEMAKER 249
Out of New Orleans, "The Tan Canary" had an erratic career with the big boys, but was never as powerful as he is here, singing for a tiny label. Listen to Adams hit those high notes.

❺ JUST A LITTLE OVERCOME
NIGHTINGALES from STAX 0091
A dramatic horn introduction leads to one of the most bitter opening lines ("Here's a toast to the both of you") in the deep soul canon, followed by a for-the-ages performance from vocalist Sir Mack Rice. Seek this out from the Best-of, under the original group name, Ollie and the Nightingales.

❻ SEPARATION LINE
LAURA LEE from COTILLION 45-44054
She had a hit with "Rip Off" in 1972, but this is the shining moment of Ms Lee's career – a ruminative, knowing, backward glance that is best heard while staring into a shot glass in your local, darkened neighbourhood bar.

❼ THESE AIN'T RAINDROPS
JAMES CARR from GOLDWAX 340
Troubled soul man Carr takes a simple premise ("These ain't raindrops in my eyes/but they are tears") and sells it with his from-the-gut vocals, aided by bluesy atmosphere and Memphis horns.

❽ THAT'S HOW STRONG MY LOVE IS
O.V. WRIGHT from GOLDWAX 106
The Roosevelt Jamison-penned stunner should have made Overton Vertis Wright a star, but a contract dispute kept this off the charts, later to be recorded and popularized by Otis Redding and The Stones. Much as I love Otis, Wright's version shreds.

❾ TRIED SO HARD TO PLEASE HER
THE KNIGHT BROTHERS from MERCURY 72829
Richard Dunbar and Jimmy Diggs, out of Washington DC, here display the smooth vocal interplay and harmonies that were a hallmark of the very best soul recordings of the 1960s.

❿ RAINBOW ROAD
ARTHUR ALEXANDER from WARNER BROS BS-2592
In the great tradition of story songs, this Penn/Fritts compositions cuts deep ("like my dreams, I've grown old") due to the way Alexander underplays it with his steady, world-weary style. A movie in three minutes and twenty five seconds.

⑤ TEARS INSIDE from SMACK UP

A rigorous reading of the Ornette Coleman tune from a 1960 session featuring some particularly limber work from pianist Pete Jolly.

⑥ GONE WITH THE WIND from INTENSITY

This 1960 collection of ballads and standards was the last in a tremendous series of albums for Contemporary. The smooth, West Coast approach was already transforming into something more rugged and ragged.

⑦ THE SUMMER KNOWS from THE TRIP

By 1975, the long, hard haul back into shape plus the influence of Coltrane had made its impact on Pepper, but his ballads – like this bruised, sobbing reading of the Michel Legrand tune – were a compelling experience.

⑧ BLUE BOSSA from SAN FRANCISCO SAMBA

Pepper's late-period passion and intensity were particularly potent on Latin grooves, as on this Kenny Dorham classic, recorded live in 1977.

⑨ WHEN THE SUN COMES OUT
from WINTER MOON

Not until 1980 did Pepper get to rhapsodize over a string orchestra. It was worth the wait, with Bill Holman providing the arrangements and Pepper playing like a man set free.

⑩ DON'T LET THE SUN CATCH YOU CRYING
from GOIN' HOME

Months from death in 1982, and alone with pianist George Cables, Pepper was in unflinching mood on this Joe Greene heartbreaker.

Chris Ingham

Pere Ubu & David Thomas

Emerging from the urban wasteland of Cleveland, Ohio in 1975, Pere Ubu are as edgy and confrontational today as they were 30 years ago. David Thomas remains an exceptional performer, his lyrics rooted deeply in the American landscape.

PERE UBU

❶ 30 SECONDS OVER TOKYO from TERMINAL TOWER

Their first single; even when the band were just feeling their way, they managed to produce an uncategorizable post-punk classic. Easy listening it ain't.

❷ STREET WAVES from THE MODERN DANCE

The Modern Dance has become an almost absurdly influential album; this is one of its more straighforward cuts, with Thomas slowly finding his unique voice.

❸ NAVVY from DUB HOUSING

"I've got these arms and legs that flip-flop": the opening lines of an album often rated as their best. Haphazard, disjointed, almost thrown together, but immensely powerful.

❹ MISERY GOATS from THE ART OF WALKING

"A challenging stew of inside-out song structures" is how *Art Of Walking* is described in the Ubu biography; the perky "Misery Goats" is its poppiest moment, if you can believe that.

❺ MY THEORY OF SPONTANEOUS SIMULTUDE from APOCALYPSE NOW

Ubu's early gigs were notoriously terrifying, but this live acoustic version of a David Thomas solo track reveals the warmth and humour of their live performances.

❻ FOLLY OF YOUTH from RAY GUN SUITCASE

"Back to the beeps" was the slogan for 1995's *Ray Gun Suitcase* album, and this track certainly heralded a return to the edgy, unpredictable EML synthesizer sound of the late 1970s.

❼ SAD.TXT from PENNSYLVANIA

A subtle, almost pastoral highlight of one of the band's most recent albums. "One day, I will be your man," whispers Thomas. "One day, I will be the best that you can do…"

❽ CONFUSE DID from SOUND OF THE SAND

Thomas's first solo album certainly didn't see him mellowing; this is an exhilarating merry-go-round of brass, percussion and slide guitars.

DAVID THOMAS

❾ SURFER GIRL AROUND THE FIRE from MONSTER

This barely recognisable but deeply affectionate tribute to Brian Wilson, accompanied by midi guitar and trumpet, was a highlight of Thomas's live shows in the late 1990s.

❿ BRUNSWICK PARKING LOT from 18 MONKEYS ON A DEAD MAN'S CHEST

So minimal, it's barely there at all; a gently wheezing melodeon propping up Thomas's haunting tale of Ohio's mysterious Blue Hole of Castalia.

Rhodri Marsden

Lee Perry productions

In his 1970s heyday at the mixing desk in the legendary Black Ark Studio – which he ultimately burned down – reggae producer Lee "Scratch" Perry was responsible for an astonishing range of seminal recordings. All were infused with his bizarre imagination and seemingly intuitive technical wizardry.

❶ BEAT DOWN BABYLON JUNIOR BYLES
from **TROJAN JAMAICAN HITS**
Perry's early collaborations with Byles, like this one from 1972, have seldom been surpassed.

❷ BETTER DAYS CARLTON & THE SHOES
from **JUNGLE LION**
An uplifting Rasta-inspired chant from 1972.

❸ WORDS OF MY MOUTH THE GATHERERS
from **JUNGLE LION**
Eerie, inspirational sounds from 1973, with the vocals pushed back behind some trademark dub ex-Perry-mentation.

❹ POLICE AND THIEVES JUNIOR MURVIN
from **POLICE AND THIEVES**
The big hit of 1976, later reinterpreted by The Clash.

❺ WAR IN A BABYLON MAX ROMEO
from **WAR IN A BABYLON**
Another 1976 hit, titled "Sipple Out Deh" ("slippery out there") on its original Jamaican release.

❻ PROPHET LIVE PRINCE JAZZBO
from **ITAL CORNER**
Freeform toasting from the underrated Jazzbo in 1976.

❼ RASTA TRAIN RAPHAEL GREEN AND DR ALIMANTADO
from **ARKOLOGY**
One of the very best of the Upsetter's 12" vocal-plus-DJ singles, from 1977.

❽ ARK OF THE COVENANT THE CONGOS
from **HEART OF THE CONGOS**
This 1977 album has to be Perry's finest hour: magnificent falsetto harmonizing, atop astonishing rhythms.

❾ TO BE A LOVER (HAVE SOME MERCY) GEORGE FAITH
from **ARKOLOGY**
The title track of a totally successful 1977 album that synthesized heavy dub with Philly soul.

❿ TALK ABOUT IT THE MIGHTY DIAMONDS
from **TROJAN ROOTS**
More delightful harmonies from 1977; the dub version, featuring Perry's caterwauling kids, is less appealing.

Greg Ward

The Pet Shop Boys

The Pet Shop Boys are a byword for pop of outstanding beauty – elegant crooning over cutting-edge electronica that veers from ethereal wispiness to amyl-fuelled techno.

❶ WEST END GIRLS (DANCE MIX) from **PLEASE** [ENHANCED]
The first the world heard of Neil Tennant and Chris Lowe: so good they had to release it twice before the public could believe its ears. Pop perfection, with that trademark slightly bitter taste already in place.

❷ ALWAYS ON MY MIND / IN MY HOUSE from **INTROSPECTIVE [ENHANCED]**
Neil sacrilegiously applies his Noël Coward routine to an Elvis song, then Chris kicks off a blasphemous house-inspired keyboard'n'computer workout. Guaranteed to have the King revolving in his grave (or wherever he is).

❸ BEING BORING (EXTENDED MIX) from **BEHAVIOUR** [ENHANCED]
The boys have a unique ability to whip up frothy concoctions that are somehow robust enough to support the crushing lyrics of regret, farewell and shame that are draped over them.

❹ CAN YOU FORGIVE HER? from **VERY [ENHANCED]**
Lyrics this arch deserve to be viewed in a grand public square, surrounded by fountains. The jaunty melody sugars an extremely bitter pill of confused sexuality and denial.

❺ SO HARD (EXTENDED DANCE MIX) from **BEHAVIOUR** [ENHANCED]
Ever fallen in love with someone you shouldn't have fallen in love with? Of course you have. And did they cheat on you? Of course they did. And did you love them all the same? This one's for you, sucker.

❻ RENT from **ACTUALLY [ENHANCED]**
Majestic, awesome, heartbreaking and enigmatic lyrics, telling either of true love or of the oldest financial transaction in the world. When the protagonist declares "I love you. You pay my rent", is that missing "and" or "because"?

⑦ DJ CULTURE from BEHAVIOUR [ENHANCED]
Knowing words of vacuous 1980s disco/nightclub lifestyle, set to one of Chris's most deliberately soulless arrangements.

⑧ OPPORTUNITIES [LET'S MAKE LOTS OF MONEY] (12" MIX) from PLEASE [ENHANCED]
Many pop bands write a declaration of their intent to rule the world; few match this for brazenness, elegance or wit.

⑨ HEART (DISCO MIX)
from ACTUALLY [ENHANCED]
A shirts-off, poppers-huffing muscle-mary of a tune, all red-faced, steroid-toned and ever-so-slightly menacing.

⑩ I WOULDN'T NORMALLY DO THIS KIND OF THING (BEATMASTERS EXTENDED NUDE MIX) from DISCO 2
Neil's tongue is so far in his cheek as he delivers a lyric so blatantly untrue that, like the song's character, you might also want to burst out laughing and dance naked in the rain.

Al Spicer

The Philly sound

Under the guiding hands of producers like Kenny Gamble, Leon Huff and Thom Bell, Philadelphia soul – with its warmth, pinsharp instrumental definition and gently uplifting momentum – marked a new direction for African-American music in the late 1960s and early 70s.

❶ YES, I'M READY BARBARA MASON
from YES, I'M READY
With its gushing string cascades, this 1965 torrent of virginal teen longing served as a prototype for the emerging genre.

❷ THE DELFONICS LALA MEANS I LOVE YOU
from LA LA MEANS I LOVE YOU
The most unctuous record ever made?

❸ ONLY THE STRONG SURVIVE JERRY BUTLER from THE ICEMAN COMETH
With its creamy guitar licks and resonant vibraphone, the production on this 1969 classic is like slipping on a smoking jacket and relaxing in front of the fire with a snifter of brandy.

❹ DROWNING IN THE SEA OF LOVE JOE SIMON from DROWNING IN THE SEA OF LOVE
The contrast of Simon's foghorn vocals and the roling

waves of strings, horns and guitar is one of Philly's greatest glories.

❺ BACK STABBERS THE O'JAYS
from BACK STABBERS
Perhaps the best introduction in the history of popular music – and things only get better.

❻ HAROLD MELVIN & THE BLUE NOTES
THE LOVE I LOST from BLACK & BLUE
Drummer Earl Young basically invents disco with his snare pattern and hi-hat work on this 1973 gem.

❼ I'LL ALWAYS LOVE MY MAMA
THE INTRUDERS from SAVE THE CHILDREN
An almost African-sounding guitar line makes this sheer delight, even if lead singer Little Sonny Brown wanders off pitch like a drunk trying to walk a straight line.

❽ LOVE IS THE MESSAGE MFSB
from LOVE IS THE MESSAGE
The fast section is the national anthem of disco.

❾ DO IT ANY WAY YOU WANNA
PEOPLE'S CHOICE from BOOGIE DOWN USA
Philly at its funkiest.

❿ LIFE ON MARS DEXTER WANSEL
from LIFE ON MARS
The cosmic synths of keyboardist Wansel take Philly into outer space .

Peter Shapiro

Wilson Pickett

Handsome, arrogant, sensual and owner of one of the most raw and powerful voices in 1960s soul, Wilson Pickett was nicknamed "The Wicked Pickett". Cutting hit after hit in Memphis and Muscle Shoals, he ranks as one of the great soul men.

❶ IN THE MIDNIGHT HOUR from IN THE MIDNIGHT HOUR
Wilson blew the charts apart in 1965 with this storming party anthem.

❷ NINETY-NINE AND A HALF (WON'T DO) from THE EXCITING WILSON PICKETT
Backed by Booker T & The MGs, the leather-lunged Pickett's declaration of perfection suggested how Southern soul was facing up to Motown's pop onslaught. Hardcore!

❸ LAND OF 1000 DANCES
from THE EXCITING WILSON PICKETT

Not the first version of a tune since covered by a thousand bands – but the chart-topper everyone remembers.

❹ 634-5789 from THE EXCITING WILSON PICKETT

"If you need a little lovin'/Call on me" boasts the Wicked Pickett over a funky groove and snarling horns.

❺ MUSTANG SALLY from THE WICKED PICKETT

Hard rhythms, snorting horns and fat'n'greasy organ – what a groove! – allow Wilson to lay back and tell Sally to leave her Mustang alone.

❻ FUNKY BROADWAY from THE SOUND OF WILSON PICKETT

Sizzling proto-funk, as Pickett struts down Broadway like he owns the goddam street.

❼ HEY JUDE from HEY JUDE

Atlantic Records made their soul singers tackle Beatles tunes to win over the white audience, usually to dire effect. Here Wilson, with Duane Allman in tow, fries Lennon/McCartney in boiling soul juice.

❽ I'M IN LOVE from MIDNIGHT MOVER

Wilson takes his buddy Bobby Womack's tune and sings it slow and soulful. If he wasn't such a badass stud you'd almost believe him.

❾ GET ME BACK ON TIME, ENGINE NUMBER 9
from WILSON PICKETT IN PHILADELPHIA

Mutant funk that still sounds spacey today.

❿ DON'T KNOCK MY LOVE
from DON'T KNOCK MY LOVE

Pickett's last big hit: driving bass, surging horns and a vocal that pleads and threatens.

Garth Cartwright

Pink Floyd

From psychedelic dandies to space-rock adventurers to stadium-sized chroniclers of the human condition… let's stop before we get to the 1990s reformation.

❶ SEE EMILY PLAY from RELICS

The peak of the Syd Barrett era, a perfect summations of Summer of '67 psychedelia: yearning, childlike, chock-full of ideas.

❷ ECHOES
from MEDDLE

This 25-minute oceanic "tone poem" features some of the most gorgeous melodies and harmonies in the Floyd canon.

❸ TIME
from DARK SIDE OF THE MOON

The explosion of clocks was a handy demo for 1970s hi-fis, but the song is a demonstration of melodic songcraft that's entirely timeless. Nice tuned tom-toms too.

❹ US AND THEM
from DARK SIDE OF THE MOON

Rippling with organ, sax and harmonies; rarely has anger – against war, poverty and racism – been couched in such laid-back music.

❺ BRAIN DAMAGE/ECLIPSE
from DARK SIDE OF THE MOON

An epic conclusion to an epic album: one minute deep in the madness of Syd Barrett, the next a shopping list of, well, life itself.

❻ WISH YOU WERE HERE
from WISH YOU WERE HERE

An irresistible acoustic riff, while Gilmour's impassioned vocal on this country pastoral transforms a cliché into a cry for help.

❼ SHINE ON YOU CRAZY DIAMOND PARTS 1–5
from WISH YOU WERE HERE

Barrett's madness inspires both Waters' fractured lyric and some brilliant space-blues guitar from Gilmour.

❽ NOBODY HOME
from THE WALL

A simple piano ballad, boasting one of Water's most touching – and funny – lyrics.

❾ COMFORTABLY NUMB
from THE WALL

Immune to camp cover-versions, this epic account of crack-up and retreat into fabled childhood boasts not one but two of the greatest guitar solos ever.

❿ ANOTHER BRICK IN THE WALL (PART TWO)
from THE WALL

A Christmas #1. The disco beat and children's choir weren't typical; the contrasting scathing lyric/liquid guitar solo combo were, though.

Toby Manning

The Pixies

Frank Black and Kim Deal's soaring guitar riffs and surreal lyrics fizz with energy. Forget the small name: The Pixies are a giant of a band.

❶ DEBASER from DOOLITTLE
Classic Pixies, from the first hopping bassline to the strained, sing-scream of an impassioned Black. Who knows what the hell a debaser is anyway? Who cares?

❷ ALLISON from BOSSANOVA
Synthy effects, strumming rhythms, a tale about Allison. All in one minute and twenty seconds. A real rollercoaster.

❸ MONKEY'S GONE TO HEAVEN from DOOLITTLE
One of their biggest hits, this is a dark environmental plea, brought to life by The Pixies' sharply rendered melodies and thumping bassline.

❹ CACTUS from SURFER ROSA
A dark, almost bloodthirsty love song. Black's vocals sound desperate, while scratchy guitars and pounding drums conjure up a dry desert heat.

❺ PLANET OF SOUND from TROMPE LE MONDE
Dark, edgy and raw, this fine cut builds to an eponymous wall of noise.

❻ GOUGE AWAY from DOOLITTLE
Gruesomely raw lyrics gouge away at your brain. This is Black at his punchiest.

❼ TAME from DOOLITTLE
Whispering, naughty, screaming, clashing guitars. No other band sounds like this.

❽ GIGANTIC from SURFER ROSA
The title says it all: one of the band's biggest hits, sung by Kim Deal. Wonderful layers of sound build up to give that Pixies DNA.

❾ HEY from PIXIES AT THE BBC
The Pixies do soft, kicking off with a gloriously moody Black and bass guitar. It all gets loud again at the end of this BBC session, though. They wouldn't have it any other way.

❿ WHERE IS MY MIND from SURFER ROSA
Rightfully one of The Pixies' best loved tracks. By turns hauntingly beautiful and surprising even when you hear it for the hundredth time. Medicine for the soul.

Tim Pollard

Pizza pie

Those sentimental guys with the easy manner and the smooth voices: ladies and gentlemen, the crooners.

❶ DEEP NIGHT RUDY VALLEE from VINTAGE VALLEE
With a straightforward style, a megaphone and a "Heigh Ho, everybody", Vallee invented pre-microphone crooning, and also co-composed this 1929 hit.

❷ THREE LITTLE WORDS BING CROSBY
from 1926–1932
The new-fangled microphone, invented just months before Crosby's recording debut, did much to transmit his warmth and intimacy into the hearts of millions. This relaxed take on Kalmer/Ruby's early-1930s hit is classic early Bing.

❸ PRISONER OF LOVE RUSS COLUMBO
from PRISONER OF LOVE
A rival for Crosby's crooning crown, with his louche-style Columbo, as heard on his self-penned early-1930s hit, was almost as influential as Bing on those who followed.

❹ THE VERY THOUGHT OF YOU AL BOWLLY
from THE AL BOWLLY STORY
Britain's most popular singer during the 1930s, Bowlly was lighter and stiffer than Crosby, but as pleasing on the ear in his own way.

❺ EMBRACEABLE YOU FRANK SINATRA
from THE BEST OF THE COLUMBIA YEARS
Though Frank loved Bing, he went out of his way to develop a distinctively legato style, as on this archetypically sensual 1946 hit.

❻ STRANGER IN PARADISE TONY BENNETT
from TONY'S GREATEST HITS
A little hotter and more spontaneous than the average crooner, Bennett nevertheless has his roots in the idiom, as his massive 1954 hit with the *Kismet* song displays.

❼ THAT'S AMORE DEAN MARTIN
from BEST OF
Filtering Crosby's approach through Italy and lacing it with booze, Martin brought a whole new detachment to novelty balladeering, as on his mid-1950s hit.

❽ PAPA LOVES MAMBO PERRY COMO
from PERRY COMO
The man who in Bing Crosby's words "invented relaxed" scored many solo hits in the 1940s, but this kind of silly-but-sweet novelty was his style in the 50s.

⑨ STARDUST NAT "KING" COLE
from **20 GREATEST HITS**

A jazz pianist who made his fortune wrapping his silky tonsils around ballads. Some were corny, some, like his immaculate 1957 reading of "Stardust" – composer Hoagy Carmichael's all-time favourite version – were classics.

⑩ YOUNGER THAN SPRINGTIME VIC DAMONE from **ON THE STREET WHERE YOU LIVE**

A singer cited by his biggest influence Sinatra as having "the best set of pipes in the business", Damone has produced decades of mellow, musical vocals on high-quality material, including this *South Pacific* ballad from 1964.

Chris Ingham

The Pogues/ Shane MacGowan

The Pogues didn't so much creep into the limelight in early 1980s London, but emerged seemingly fully formed with a pint of stout in one hand and an attitude in the other. At the band's core was the UK-born, but of Limerick stock, singer and lyricist Shane MacGowan who, at his peak and before his love of pints of Martini set in, produced a stream of stupendously poetic songs, all rooted in the Irish tradition. The band still reforms for Xmas and New Year shows, but nothing can ever repeat the sheer brio of their mid-1980s gigs. You really had to be there!

① STREAMS OF WHISKEY
from **RED ROSES FOR ME**

The stand-out track from the band's debut album, a tub-thumping corker with Spider Stacy's whistle well to the fore and the rhythm section not so much driving hell for leather as refurbishing an entire shoe shop.

② THE BOYS
from **THE COUNTY HELL FROM RED ROSES FOR ME**

A song title which many reckoned summed up the band itself, though the lyrics here reveal more about MacGowan's absorption in the Irish ballad tradition.

③ THE OLD MAIN DRAG from **RUM SODOMY & THE LASH**

Far more reflective than its predecessor, The Pogues' second album includes a welter of stunning songs from MacGowan, including this superb paean to his teenage experiences in Soho.

④ A PAIR OF BROWN EYES
from **RUM SODOMY & THE LASH**

The song that revealed MacGowan as his generation's foremost balladeer provides also the most rousing chorus in the entire Pogues canon.

⑤ SALLY MACLENNANE
from **RUM SODOMY & THE LASH**

Wilder than wild (and a major element in the band's live set) the song's lyrics incorporate one of MacGowan's finest choruses in a raging tale of drink, sex, gambling and lost love.

⑥ STREETS OF SORROW/BIRMINGHAM SIX
from **IF I SHOULD FALL FROM GRACE WITH GOD**

New arrival Terry Woods' sumptuous ballad proves a telling precursor to MacGowan's most political song, a condemnation of the criminal "justice" meted out to those found guilty (and later exonerated) of the Birmingham and Guildford pub bombings "for being Irish in the wrong place and at the wrong time".

⑦ FAIRYTALE OF NEW YORK
from **IF I SHOULD FALL FROM GRACE WITH GOD**

The most unlikely UK singles chart Xmas #1 ever sees Shane waxing lyrical about a drunken Christmas Eve romance in New York City, gloriously captured by a stirring duet with the late Kirsty MacColl. The song includes the astonishingly acerbic couplet "I could have been someone/So could anyone" – a veritable classic.

⑧ THE IRISH ROVER (WITH THE DUBLINERS)
from **THE DUBLINERS' SPIRIT OF THE IRISH**

The old Irish rebels and the then new ones combined to perfection on this rambunctious ballad.

⑨ WHITE CITY
from **PEACE AND LOVE**

The cracks in MacGowan's relationship with the rest of the band were becoming ominous by the time of this 1989 album (on which banjo player Jem Finer wrote much of the material), but there was still place for this punchy tale about betting on the dog races in West London.

⑩ THE SNAKE AT THE GATE OF HELL
from **THE RARE OUL' STUFF**

MacGowan's battle with the bottle is all too audible on much of this album with his new band The Popes, but this song, replete with many an Irish metaphor, is certainly among his best.

Geoff Wallis

Iggy Pop & The Stooges

Detroit's heaviest industry since they closed down the car plants, The Stooges swooped out from under the wing of The MC5 to unleash some of the mightiest riffs in dumb-ass rock'n'roll. When the drug-induced haze cleared, Iggy Pop was a solo artist, godfather of punk, ready to stomp the world in his dinosaur boots.

❶ I WANNA BE YOUR DOG from THE STOOGES
The Stooges' masterwork, boasting the Midwest's biggest, bestest riff ever. Iggy slips into his submissive role while the boys work up a four-chord hymn to degradation and bad behaviour of the most enjoyable kind.

❷ NO FUN from THE STOOGES
A cooler response to teenage boredom than that offered by the Sex Pistols' cranked-up cover, implying that whatever the boys do, they'll get into trouble doing it.

❸ SEARCH AND DESTROY from RAW POWER
The rock'n'roll equivalent to the evil helicopter-driven assault in *Apocalypse Now*. Skinny little Iggy describes himself as "a street-walking cheetah with a heart fulla napalm", and gets away with it.

❹ GIMME DANGER from RAW POWER
Iggy gets all Midwestern vampire, doom-mongering in his echoing baritone before the aforesaid cheetah persona claws its way out of the sack and he bites the throat out of the tune while the band pummels its body into pulp.

❺ FALL IN LOVE WITH ME from HIPPODROME PARIS 77
Put Iggy in front of a crowd, set the tape rolling and watch the magic unfold. Recorded while the man was still in recovery from a terrible pill habit, this shows him pulling out a big showbiz production from a distinctly shaky start.

❻ FUNTIME from THE IDIOT
A sordid little slice of emotionless, twitchy desire, based on the cocaine and drag-queen debauches of Iggy and Bowie in Berlin, and shining a tight beam of peculiarly coloured light on desires best left in the dark.

❼ NIGHTCLUBBING from THE IDIOT
Follows on perfectly from "Funtime" by leading you, drunk and befuddled, on a head-spinning tour of the seedy side of urban entertainment. Sleazy horn music for all you sleazy whores.

❽ PASSENGER from LUST FOR LIFE
A killer riff and a perfect lyric of life as a rock star, insulated by cocaine and armour-glass both from reality and those forced to inhabit it.

❾ JOHANNA from KILL CITY
A classic Iggy melodrama, a love song of passion and commitment wrenched from a man who could barely feel his face.

❿ REAL WILD CHILD from BLAH-BLAH-BLAH
Recorded at an age when most rock stars of his generation are looking forward to a free bus pass and reduced-rate haircuts on a Wednesday, Iggy hunts down a wild, untamed, rockabilly tune and wrestles it to the ground.

Al Spicer

Prefab Sprout

As skinny indie kid or hirsute man-mountain, Paddy McAloon has remained a consistent songwriting force over nearly 25 years, coupling stunning melodies with intelligent lyrics – if you ignore "hot dog, jumping frog, Alberquerque", of course.

❶ LIONS IN MY OWN GARDEN EXIT SOMEONE
from 38 CARAT COLLECTION
Their debut single neatly contrasts a pretentious title (the initials spell Limoges, where Paddy's then girlfriend had just moved to) with a gorgeous, stripped-back pop tune.

❷ CUE FANFARE from SWOON
The primitive production fails to mask a beguiling song, running off in a dozen different directions before reuniting for a memorable chorus about chess grandmasters.

❸ APPETITE from STEVE MCQUEEN
A typical cut from an unashamedly lovelorn album, all dripping piano chords, precise rhythms and the sugar icing of Wendy Smith's backing vocals.

❹ WHEN LOVE BREAKS DOWN
from STEVE MCQUEEN
It took four re-releases, but this track eventually became the band's first hit in the winter of 1985 – and deservedly so.

⑤ THE WORLD AWAKE from PROTEST SONGS
The opening song on the album that CBS weren't that keen on releasing; it's brittle in comparison with much of their output, but its myriad charms are revealed through repeated listens.

⑥ ENCHANTED from LANGLEY PARK TO MEMPHIS
Bouncing bass, perky keyboards and an unexpected didgeridoo show Paddy's playful side, while the allusions to *Romeo and Juliet* keep the romance quotient high.

⑦ NIGHTINGALES from LANGLEY PARK TO MEMPHIS
Prefab Sprout at their most sickly sweet, with shimmering violins and sleighbells underpinning a Stevie Wonder harmonica solo. How did they get away with it?

⑧ DOO WOP IN HARLEM
from JORDAN: THE COMEBACK
The exquisite closing track on a skewed concept album embracing love, Elvis, god and death.

⑨ IF YOU DON'T LOVE ME
from 38 CARAT COLLECTION
An unashamededly Pet Shop Boys-esque stab at a pop hit, which may only have scraped the Top 40 but remains one of their finest moments.

⑩ PRISONER OF THE PAST
from ANDROMEDA HEIGHTS
Booming timpani and sweeping orchestral lines signal another majestic McAloon opus, as memorable and mesmerizing as any of his earlier work.

Rhodri Marsden

Elvis Presley

Rock's one essential star, without whom so much else – such as The Beatles, Bob Dylan, and Cliff Richard – might never have come to pass. Uh-huh-huh…

① LAWDY MISS CLAWDY from ELVIS PRESLEY
Elvis sounds confusingly chirpy as he bemoans the faithlessness of his partner in his scintillating cover of Lloyd Price's classic, egged on by Shorty Long's pounding piano.

② MYSTERY TRAIN from ELVIS AT SUN
A confident, almost insolent, appropriation of Junior Parker's mournful tale of a love leaving town on a train sixteen coaches long. Scotty Moore and Bill Black supply the locomotion to back Elvis's cheeky vocal.

③ LONG BLACK LIMOUSINE
from FROM ELVIS IN MEMPHIS
Soulful backing singers, Chips Moman's finest production values, and Elvis' most impassioned indignant vocal make this country song sound like a protest number.

④ HIS LATEST FLAME from No1s
Apparently effortless, yet brilliantly studied and executed, this classic slice of love-gone-wrong popshuffles along to a beautiful Bo Diddley beat, driven by Floyd Cramer's fine piano and a wonderfully judged vocal.

⑤ TOMORROW IS A LONG TIME
from TOMORROW IS A LONG TIME
Gentle, hypnotic and unaffected, Bob Dylan's favourite cover version of one of his songs is utterly unlike anything else Elvis ever recorded.

⑥ GOOD ROCKING TONIGHT from ELVIS AT SUN
As writer Nick Tosches said, not a song so much as an invitation to a holocaust. A rawer, heavier, urgent precursor to "Jailhouse Rock".

⑦ I'M LEAVIN' from BURNING LOVE
The King's most chilling ballad – experimenting with his voice, he sounds almost suicidal as he contemplates life without his love.

⑧ IN THE GHETTO from FROM ELVIS IN MEMPHIS
A white multi-millionaire singing about a black ghetto? Come off it! But Elvis carries it off, sounding majestic, compassionate and sincere, pointedly – and subtly – underlining the double meaning in the line "Well the world turns".

⑨ HEARTBREAK HOTEL from No1s
If Edgar Allan Poe had cut a pop record, it would have sounded like this.

⑩ ONE NIGHT from No1s
While they cleaned up the lyrics of Smiley Lewis's lament, they couldn't hide the intensity and the passion in Elvis's vocal as he stutters and spits out the words.

Paul Simpson

The Pretenders

Chrissie Hynde's Pretenders survived death and disaster to created some of the finest love songs in pop history, delivered by one of its finest voices: equal parts honey and heartache.

❶ TALK OF THE TOWN from PRETENDERS II

An epic ballad of yearning and unrequited love – not to mention oh-no-everybody-knows paranoia. Worth the price of admission for the jangly guitar intro alone.

❷ BRASS IN POCKET from PRETENDERS

Even though Chrissie's telling you exactly how she's going to make you notice her, she's still going to succeed in seducing you – and there's nothing you can do about it.

❸ 2000 MILES from LEARNING TO CRAWL

Possibly the best Xmas record of all time. If you've ever been separated from your loved one at that time of year, this'll send shivers up your spine.

❹ DON'T GET ME WRONG from GET CLOSE

By this point, Chrissie had distilled the self-deprecating love song to a fine art – and this is very fine indeed. If the middle eight doesn't get you, then you've never really been in love.

❺ BACK ON THE CHAIN GANG
from LEARNING TO CRAWL

After half her band had killed themselves with overdoses, Chrissie came up with this: a statement of pride in her own survival, and a recognition of the necessity of starting to live again.

❻ HYMN TO HER from GET CLOSE

A pagan celebration of womanhood as the Triple Goddess of maiden, mother and crone.

❼ KID from PRETENDERS

Is it about the problems of single motherhood, or the problems of having a much younger lover? Either way, it works, and it's wonderful.

❽ POPSTAR from VIVA EL AMOR!

In which Chrissie amusingly trashes the (younger) competition and current pop/media trends. They don't make 'em like they used to? Damn right.

❾ STOP YOUR SOBBING from PRETENDERS

How to take a minor Kinks song that nearly everyone had forgotten and turn it into one of the 1970s' most impressive pop debuts. Having Nick Lowe as producer certainly didn't hurt.

❿ I'LL STAND BY YOU
from LAST OF THE INDEPENDENTS

Love, loyalty and commitment: an epic teen love ballad for grown-ups.

Pete Hogan

Primal Scream

The band that broke the rock'n'roll mould of the 1990s by throwing dance, techno and house into the mix.

❶ MOVING ON UP from SCREAMADELICA

Producer and DJ Andrew Weatherall doused Gillespie's rock'n'roll jangly guitars with dance and techno, and the ambitious, innovative "Moving On Up" exploded onto the dancefloor.

❷ LOADED from SCREAMADELICA

Slugging a powerful bass groove at "I'm Losing More Than I'll Ever Have" and removing most of its original instruments, Weatherall scorched decks for miles around.

❸ ROCKS from GIVE OUT BUT DON'T GIVE UP

Primal Scream returned to their 1970s hard-rock roots with this catchy, stay-up-all-night party anthem.

❹ TRAINSPOTTING from VANISHING POINT

Scream's reaction to poor reviews for *Give Out But Don't Give Up* was to come back with the dark theme to 1996's *Trainspotting*, richly laced with exotic trance.

❺ KOWALSKI from VANISHING POINT

A unique mix of Gillespie's creepy vocals and a menacing beat that propelled the Scream to their highest UK chart place – #3.

❻ IF THEY MOVE, KILL 'EM
from VANISHING POINT

This instrumental mix of acid house, rock and a banging beat, along with a crushing brass section, transports you to the hazy drug-fuelled ride of a 1970s road trip.

❼ KILL ALL HIPPIES from XTRMNTR

Scream go all political on their last Creation album.

❽ SWASTIKA EYES from XTRMNTR

A raucous lyrical loop, pounding along at high speed.

❾ SHOOT/SPEED/KILL LIGHT from XTRMNTR

If this dark euphoric melody makes you think of Joy Division, that's because of Bernard Sumner's unmistakable guitar riff.

❿ SOME VELVET MORNING
from EVIL HEAT

Lee Hazlewood and Nancy Sinatra made it a cult and now Gillespie has his muse Kate Moss to whisper and warble along with him in much the same way.

⓫ 99TH FLOOR from RIOT CITY BLUES

Bobby and the crew take on the Thirteenth Floor Elevators, and give them a punk rock makeover: wrestle 'em to the ground and get 'em to cry "Uncle".

⓬ DOLLS (SWEET ROCK 'N' ROLL) from RIOT CITY BLUES

…They know better than to try anything more risky than an unabashed tribute to the might and myth of the New York Dolls though.

Lisa-Jane Ellis

Prince

High on God and sex, the Minneapolis imp reinvented soul, funk, rock and pop throughout the 1980s.

❶ I WANNA BE YOUR LOVER
from PRINCE

Prince's first hit, a tasty funk number where he croons "I wanna be your lover/The only one who makes you come … running."

❷ DIRTY MIND from DIRTY MIND

Minimalist punk-funk, on which Prince sets out his manifesto for dominating women and the world.

❸ WHEN YOU WERE MINE from DIRTY MIND

On this rockin' tune, Prince pleads to a girl who's dumped him that, hey, he now loves her more than when she was his.

❹ 1999 from 1999

"Life is a just a party and parties weren't meant to last", intones Prince, mantra-like, over a huge, funked-up rip of The Band's *Chest Fever* riff.

❺ LITTLE RED CORVETTE from 1999

In which Prince wonders if he's man enough for his latest conquest, the used condoms in her pocket unsettling him. "A body like that's on the verge of being obscene", he observes, then leaps in.

❻ WHEN DOVES CRY
from PURPLE RAIN

Epic, spacey funk-rock that sounds like nothing recorded before or since. Prince contrasts his relationship with that of his parents – them ole dysfunctional blues never sounded better!

❼ KISS from PARADE

Stunning hard funk with one of Prince's funniest lyrics. "Act your age not your shoe size", he commands his latest paramour.

❽ SIGN O' THE TIMES
from SIGN O' THE TIMES

Urban horror show detailed over dubby keyboard, tough drum-machine and nasty guitar licks. No one in popular music was making music that came anywhere near this in 1987.

❾ IF I WAS YOUR GIRLFRIEND
from SIGN O' THE TIMES

Prince talks dirty, sings tender and uses a speeded-up voice to make one of his strangest and most entertaining of songs.

❿ ALPHABET STREET from LOVESEXY

A car-wreck of funk, in which sounds and voices come from everywhere. Altogether now: "Cat, we need you to rap!"

Garth Cartwright

The Prodigy

Liam Howlett and co have produced some of the finest (and most controversial) dance tracks of the past fifteen years, and continue to evolve with each album. Here are ten of the highlights so far…

❶ BREAK AND ENTER
from MUSIC FOR THE JILTED GENERATION

Breaking glass, cinematic strings, rumbling bass and a Baby D sample combine with melodic keyboard riffs and acid-tinged knob-twiddling to create an atmospheric opening track for The Prodigy's second album.

❷ EVERYBODY'S IN THE PLACE
from THE PRODIGY EXPERIENCE

Still exhilarating, despite the abundant old-school ravey daftness.

❸ FIRESTARTER from THE FAT OF THE LAND

Another distinct musical departure, from their third album. Keith Flint's more-rotten-than-Rotten vocals espouse the joys of being a wrong-un. A *Daily Mail* favourite.

❹ MEDUSA'S PATH
from ALWAYS OUTNUMBERED, NEVER OUTGUNNED

An incredibly rich and multi-layered soundscape of syncopated rhythms, epic strings, distorted keyboard riffs and dubby basslines. Perhaps the best movie theme that never was.

❺ POISON from MUSIC FOR THE JILTED GENERATION

Hip-hop drums, demented yelping and screeching

Liam Howlett's
Prodigious selections

When The Prodigy snarled their way through their number one hit "Firestarter" on *Top Of The Pops* in 1996, it was probably the most menacing sight seen in our living rooms since the Pistols outraged Middle England twenty years earlier. This playlist from the band's mainman Liam Howlett ranges from the pre-punk garage of The Third Bardo to classics from The Stranglers and The Jam and on through PiL to the insurrectionary street hip-hop of Noreaga and Method Man.

❶ I'M FIVE YEARS AHEAD OF MY TIME THE THIRD BARDO from THE EP I'M FIVE YEARS AHEAD OF MY TIME

❷ PEACHES THE STRANGLERS from RATTUS NORVEGICUS

❸ IN THE CITY THE JAM from IN THE CITY

❹ A MESSAGE TO YOU RUDY THE SPECIALS from THIS ARE TWO TONE

❺ RISE PIL from PIL

❻ I CHASE THE DEVIL MAX ROMEO from WAR IN A BABYLON

❼ WELCOME TO THE TERRORDOME PUBLIC ENEMY from FEAR OF A BLACK PLANET

❽ NOTHING NOREAGA from GOD'S FAVORITE

❾ RELEASE YO' DELF METHOD MAN from TICAL

❿ FEEL GOOD HIT OF THE SUMMER QUEENS OF THE STONE AGE from RATED R

vocals with a hint of didgeridoo, served up on a platter of teeth-rattling bass.

❻ OUT OF SPACE from THE PRODIGY EXPERIENCE
Manic mix of classic Prodigy rave beats and skanking reggae, topped off with helium-tinged vocals.

❼ DIESEL POWER from THE FAT OF THE LAND
Hardcore hip-hop featuring long-standing Howlett favourite Kool Keith of the Ultramagnetic MCs on vocals.

❽ CHARLY from THE PRODIGY EXPERIENCE
Often imitated, never bettered, The Prodigy's break-through tune represents the pinnacle of the crossover rave tunes bothering the charts in the early 1990s.

❾ SPITFIRE
from ALWAYS OUTNUMBERED, NEVER OUTGUNNED
Juliette Lewis takes over from Keith Flint on angry lyric-spouting duties and manages to surpass even him for rawness.

❿ NO GOOD (START THE DANCE)
from MUSIC FOR THE JILTED GENERATION
The classic Prodigy template of strings, speeded-up vocals and rave-inspired keyboard riffs, given a darker edge thanks to its clanking, industrial drums. The benchmark for British dance music in the mid-1990s.
Brendan Waller

The producers

Producers are to music what directors are to films: essential but rarely as celebrated as those fronting the music. Here are ten who shaped the sounds of their eras.

❶ JOHN HAMMOND: DON'T THINK TWICE BOB DYLAN from THE FREEWHEELING BOB DYLAN
Visionary producer whose ear for brilliance helped Bessie Smith, Benny Goodman, Billie Holiday, Bob Dylan and Stevie Ray Vaughan (among many others) cut classic recordings. "DTT" is a great performance by the young Dylan with Hammond capturing all the singer's energy and arrogance.

❷ SAM PHILLIPS: MYSTERY TRAIN JUNIOR PARKER from THE SUN BOX
Pioneering electric blues producer (Howling Wolf, Junior Parker) who swore he'd make a million dollars if he could find "a white boy who sang like a Negro". Did he ever! MT is a spooky blues shuffle demonstrating Phillips' brilliance at conveying atmosphere.

❸ JERRY WEXLER: AINT NO WAY ARETHA FRANKLIN from QUEEN OF SOUL
Ray Charles, Solomon Burke, Aretha Franklin and Wilson Pickett all benefited from his production. Also took Dusty to Memphis and helped Dylan go gospel. "ANW" may be Aretha's most pure and emotive vocal ever.

❹ ALLEN TOUSSAINT: EVERYTHING I DO GOHN BE FUNKY LEE DORSEY from SOUL MINE

No city ever had a sound quite so distinct as New Orleans and Toussaint was there from the late-1950s on to write, arrange and produce many of its greatest R&B hits. High points? For starters: Irma Thomas, Aaron Neville, Lee Dorsey, The Meters. "EIDGBF" finds Lee and The Meters stretching that New Orleans groove out.

❺ PHIL SPECTOR: BE MY BABY THE RONNETTES from PHIL SPECTOR'S GREATEST HITS

Claimed he created "little symphonies for the kids" and his recordings of The Ronnettes and Crystals are just that. Also did good work with John Lennon. "Be My Baby" is pop at its most epic and yearning.

❻ GEORGE MARTIN: STRAWBERRY FIELDS FOREVER THE BEATLES from MAGICAL MYSTERY TOUR

Parlophone staff producer whose musical and engineering skills, matched with a fierce intelligence, helped shape The Beatles' sonic ambitions. Has produced little else of note but his 1960s work remains a touchstone for rock-pop excellence. The recording of "SFF" is a testament to Martin's genius.

❼ WILLIE MITCHELL: LOVE AND HAPPINESS AL GREEN from AL GREEN'S GREATEST HITS

The consummate Southern soul producer. Took the Memphis sound to its apotheosis with Al Green while sprinkling magic dust on Ann Peebles, O.V. Wright, Syl Johnson and others. "LAH" finds Al philosophising over a superb arrangement. Listen to how Willie records Al Jackson's drums!

❽ MUTT LANGE: HIGHWAY TO HELL AC/DC from HIGHWAY TO HELL

Uber-producer whose immaculately crafted rock productions (AC/DC, The Cars, Brian Adams, Def Leppard) made him the most successful producer ever. He then married a struggling country singer called Shania . . . "HTH" rolls forth with immense precision and power.

❾ BILLY SHERRILL: HE STOPPED LOVING HER TODAY GEORGE JONES from GEORGE JONES GREATEST HITS

Nashville master who took notes from Owen Bradley and Chet Atkins' sweeping country politain sound so giving Tammy Wynette, Charlie Rich and George Jones their greatest hits. "HSLHT" is regarded by many as not just Jones' greatest recording but the greatest country song ever!

❿ DR DRE: GIN & JUICE SNOOP DOGGY DOG from DOGGY DOG WORLD

Hip-hop has no shortage of beat masters but Dre's dominated the genre. He shaped NWA in his Mom's apartment, scouted The DOC and Snoop Dog on the streets of LA and helmed Eminem and 50 Cent's mega-success; thus Dre's the godfather. Gin & Juice captures Dre's G-funk groove at its lazy, seductive best.

Garth Cartwright

Prog rock

Always critically reviled, despite selling bucketloads in the 1970s, prog rock has been reevaluated post-Radiohead and now stands as restlessly experimental music that, at its best, remained intensely melodic. The Moody Blues are deliberately excluded.

❶ CINEMA SHOW GENESIS from SELLING ENGLAND BY THE POUND

Inspired by T.S. Eliot's *Wasteland*, the poetic acoustic section gives way to cinematic instrumental. Tony Banks on keyboards and Phil Collins on drums vie to see who can avoid playing the same thing twice.

❷ HEART OF THE SUNRISE YES from FRAGILE

Who knows what Jon Anderson is warbling on about on this bonkers epic? But with its spooky atmospherics, attention-deficit tempo shifts and glorious melody, who needs to?

❸ EPITAPH KING CRIMSON from IN THE COURT OF THE CRIMSON KING

The future Mr Wilcox's outfit pretty much invented prog with their debut, a feast of song-suites, like this eccentric power-ballad, bristling with pipers, witches and mellotrons.

❹ ECHOES PINK FLOYD from MEDDLE

An "epic tone poem", apparently. Which is to say 25 blissful minutes of oceanic effects, bird cries and – naturally – lots of guitar solos.

❺ DARKNESS VAN DER GRAAF GENERATOR from THE LEAST WE CAN DO IS WAVE TO EACH OTHER

One of Peter Hammill's most perfect distillations of mood (crepuscular, creepy) and melody (cyclical, ever-building).

❻ MOCKING BIRD BARCLAY JAMES HARVEST from BARCLAY JAMES HARVEST

Posh prog's unsung poor cousins, BJH did a lovely line in prog pastoral. This delicately anthemic orchestral ballad is among their best.

❼ LOCOMOTIVE BREATH
JETHRO TULL from **AQUALUNG**
The piano intro manages to combine Beethoven and blues, before revving up to the riff-tastic folk-prog from which the band made an entire career.

❽ THE MOON IN JUNE
SOFT MACHINE from **THIRD**
Robert Wyatt's sidelong, near-solo evocation of exile from home and love, simultaneously aching and chatty, epic and cosy, and absolutely stickled with hooks.

❾ THE GOLDEN VOID **HAWKWIND**
from **WARRIORS AT THE EDGE OF TIME**
Prog's darker, scarier, more primitive wing show they could do grandiose if they chose – and create hitherto unheard Hoover noises to boot.

❿ FANFARE FOR THE COMMON MAN **EMERSON LAKE AND PALMER** from **WORKS VOL 1**
Ironically, the prog supergroup hit biggest in the summer of punk, the video finding them in furs in chilly Canada, blasting out this hard-rock attack on Copeland's classic.

Toby Manning

Protest songs

Every protest movement produces its own songs, but from "We Shall Overcome" on, the best have tended to have a universality that transcends the specific circumstances of their writing. No Dylan because he's got his own separate list, but here are ten that tried to change the world…

❶ STRANGE FRUIT
BILLIE HOLIDAY from **THE BEST OF BILLIE HOLIDAY**
Abe Meeropol's song about lynching, so powerful some couldn't even sing it without their voices breaking.

❷ TRAMP THE DIRT DOWN
ELVIS COSTELLO from **SPIKE**
"When England was the whore of the world, Margaret was her madam." Not a big fan of Mrs Thatcher, then…

❸ OHIO **CROSBY, STILLS, NASH AND YOUNG** from **SO FAR**
When four protesting students were shot dead at Kent State University, Ohio, in 1970, this Neil Young song was written, recorded and in stores as a single within days.

❹ WAR **EDWIN STARR** from **WAR AND PEACE**
"War…huh. What is it good for? Absolutely nothing." Not exactly subtle, this rare protest from the avowedly apolitical Motown stable.

❺ FOR WHAT IT'S WORTH **BUFFALO SPRINGFIELD** from **BUFFALO SPRINGFIELD**
Written by Steven Stills after a 1966 riot on Sunset Strip, like all good protest songs this went on to become an all-purpose clarion call.

❻ GIVE PEACE A CHANCE **PLASTIC ONO BAND** from **LENNON**
Had you told John and Yoko the song was simplistic, they'd have responded that the choice between war and peace was, indeed, very simple.

❼ B.O.B. **OUTKAST** from **STANKONIA**
B.O.B. stood for Bombs Over Baghdad, and was symptomatic of the way in which the second Gulf War repoliticized American music.

❽ WHAT'S GOING ON? **MARVIN GAYE** from **WHAT'S GOING ON?**
The smoothest protest song of them all.

❾ POLITICAL SCIENCE **RANDY NEWMAN** from **SAIL AWAY**
A devastating critique of American foreign policy, all the more potent for its rapier-like wit.

❿ BOB MARLEY AND THE WAILERS
GET UP STAND UP from **BURNIN'**
A universal anthem for the dispossessed and downtrodden.

Nigel Williamson

Protest is back

The events of 9/11 inspired a few patriotic, flag waving songs, but its real impact on the music world was to resurrect the protest song – against Bush's response and the war on Iraq…

❶ JOHN WALKER'S BLUES **STEVE EARLE** from **JERUSALEM**
Maybe only Steve Earle could write a song from the perspective of an American-born Taliban fighter – and make it work.

❷ NOT READY TO MAKE NICE
DIXIE CHICKS from **TAKING THE LONG WAY**
Banned and persecuted by American radio and the country music establishment for criticizing Bush and the Iraq war, this was the Dixie Chicks' defiant, rock-

ing, Rick Rubin-produced response – and the 2006 album it came from went straight to #1 in America.

❸ LET 'S IMPEACH THE PRESIDENT
NEIL YOUNG from LIVING WITH WAR

One of several direct and self-explanatory such sentiments on an entire album of anti-Bush songs.

❹ WHERE IS THE LOVE?
BLACK EYED PEAS from ELEPHUNK

"Overseas we tryin' to stop terrorism, but we still got terrorists here livin' in the USA – the big CIA, the Bloodz and the Crips and the KKK…"

❺ WHEN THE PRESIDENT TALKS TO GOD
BRIGHT EYES CD single

"When the president talks to God do they drink beer and go play golf while they pick which countries to invade, which Muslim souls still can be saved?"

❻ 9-11 FOR PEACE
ANTI-FLAG from MOBILIZE

Incendiary agit-pop from America's most subversive band (despite being signed to corporate monster Sony-BMG), complete with a sample of Martin Luther King's "I have a dream" speech.

❼ RADIO BAGHDAD
PATTI SMITH from TRAMPIN'

A coruscating twelve-minute assault on Bush's campaign of "shock and awe" combined with a timely celebration of Iraq's contribution to world history.

❽ AMERICAN IDIOT
GREEN DAY from AMERICAN IDIOT

Hardly subtle but it packed an undeniable punch and four million Americans bought it to stand up against idiocy.

❾ DEVILS AND DUST
BRUCE SPRINGSTEEN from DEVILS AND DUST

A subtle but pointed observation on how you can become the very thing you profess to hate.

❿ 11:11
RUFUS WAINWRIGHT from WANT ONE

"Woke up this morning and something was burning, realized that everything really does happen in my lifetime." Eloquent and passionate, never mawkish.

Nigel Williamson

Psychedelic guitar

Tune in the air-guitar. Turn on the music. Drop out somewhere the other side of sanity.

❶ VOODOO CHILE JIMI HENDRIX
from ELECTRIC LADYLAND

The original, the best; in fact, the sound of Jimi chopping down a mountain. With the edge – or is that "ledge"? – of his hand.

❷ I'M ALIVE PEARL JAM from TEN
Grunge rockers find redemption in mindwarp guitar.

❸ IN EVERY DREAM HOME A HEARTACHE ROXY
MUSIC from FOR YOUR PLEASURE

Ferry languidly relates a tale of fetishistic obsession; then Phil Manzanera kicks in and attacks his guitar in a fashion that borders on the psychotic.

❹ HEY JOE SPIRIT from SPIRIT OF 76
Submit to Randy California's sublime riffing swathed in echo. On headphones if possible.

❺ DOWN BY THE RIVER ROY BUCHANAN
from SWEET DREAMS

He may have looked like a geography teacher, but he played this Neil Young song from some very dark corner of his soul.

❻ LIKE A HURRICANE NEIL YOUNG from DECADE
… and Neil himself gets lost in a fog of loneliness.

❼ MAGGOTBRAIN FUNKADELIC
from MAGGOTBRAIN

Those funk boys certainly knew how to get down, and also how to seriously come down. And then some.

❽ SAFESURFER
JULIAN COPE from PEGGY SUICIDE

Flawed genius from the megalithic sage. Bonkers, of course.

❾ COMFORTABLY NUMB PINK FLOYD from PULSE
Dave Gilmour sets the controls for the heart of the storm.

❿ BIRD SONG THE GRATEFUL DEAD
from WITHOUT A NET

This tribute to Janis Joplin is a vehicle for Jerry Garcia to go to the places that only he could reach. And that's not a flute – just Jerry's guitar.

Chris Coe

Pub rock

Punk was not the only reaction against the bloated rock music of the 1970s. The bands who emerged on London's pub-rock circuit registered their dissatisfaction by playing rootsy R&B and country-tinged music in small rooms above insalubrious boozers. A few, like Ian Dury and Joe Strummer, made the transition from pub rock to punk, and Dire Straits somersaulted from a Deptford tavern to Wembley Stadium. But many more were lost by the wayside when punk threw the baby out with the bathwater.

❶ (WHAT'S SO FUNNY 'BOUT) PEACE LOVE AND UNDERSTANDING? BRINSLEY SCHWARZ from THE NEW FAVOURITES
The Brinsleys practically invented pub-rock and gave us the sainted Nick Lowe, who never guessed in 1974 that this song would one day make his fortune, via its inclusion in *The Bodyguard*.

❷ HOWLIN' WIND GRAHAM PARKER & THE RUMOUR from HOWLIN' WIND
Perhaps the most unlucky of all the pub-rockers whose careers were curtailed by punk. Tracks like this suggest Parker could have been a rival to Van Morrison.

❸ ROXETTE DR FEELGOOD from DOWN BY THE JETTY
Canvey Island's finest played Estuary rock'n'roll with menace, even if their amphetamine-fuelled compulsion was perhaps never captured as well on record as live.

❹ CINCINATTI FATBACK ROOGALATOR from RIDE WITH YOUR ROOGALATOR
Led by American guitarist Danny Adler, Roogalator played this sort of James Brown riff better than any white boys had a right.

❺ KEYS TO YOUR HEART THE 101ERS from ELGIN AVENUE BREAKDOWN
The Clash were not so much new-wave radicals as old-school traditionalists, and Joe Strummer's roots lay in pub rockers The 101ers, whose high-octane originals included this early antecedent of White Riot.

❻ UPMINSTER KID KILBURN AND THE HIGH ROADS from HANDSOME
The late, great Ian Dury first essayed his vignettes of Essex lowlife in the Kilburns, and long before Billericay Dickie and Plaistow Patricia there was the Upminster Kid.

❼ CHOO CHOO CH'BOOGIE CHILLI WILLI AND THE RED HOT PEPPERS from BONGOES OVER BALHAM
Seminal country-rockers Chilli Willi even had a song called Goodbye Nashville, Hello Camden Town, but they usually opened their sets with a riotous version of this Louis Jordan number.

❽ LITTLE DOES SHE KNOW KURSAAL FLYERS from BEST OF THE KURSAAL FLYERS
Named after their home town Southend's most famous landmark, the Flyers signed to Jonathan King's label and made the Top 20 with this 1975 Mike Batt-produced single.

❾ DO ANYTHING YOU WANT TO DO EDDIE AND THE HOT RODS from THE BEST OF ... THE END OF THE BEGINNING
The Hot Rods' R&B-fuelled energy almost shaded into punk on this strident 1977 hit.

❿ HOW LONG ACE from FIVE-A-SIDE
Most thought Paul Carrack's song was a simple tale of romantic infidelity. In fact, it was about a rival band attempting to steal their guitarist.

Nigel Williamson

Public Enemy

When they first hit the scene, PE seemed like the most revolutionary thing to hit popular culture since the electric guitar. Time hasn't blunted their best records, which still sound – as they put it – "Louder Than A Bomb".

❶ YO! BUM RUSH THE SHOW
from YO! BUM RUSH THE SHOW
It may actually be about sticking it to the bouncers, but it sounds like a universal call for the disenfranchised to seize the means of production. Maybe that's all down to what sounds like a piano being dropped from a great height on the chorus.

❷ PUBLIC ENEMY NO.1
from YO! BUM RUSH THE SHOW
Still one of the best examples of hip-hop's "less is more" credo, using little more than a flatlining moog and dusty old drums to challenge the world's woofers, tweeters and sucker MCs.

❸ BRING THE NOISE
from IT TAKES A NATION OF MILLIONS TO HOLD US BACK
The omnivorousness of the sampler ("Beat is for Sonny Bono/Beat is for Yoko Ono") and the perilous contingency of the black male ("How low can you go? Death row") are just two of this track's furious asseverations.

❹ COLD LAMPIN' WITH FLAVOR from IT TAKES A NATION OF MILLIONS TO HOLD US BACK

"Ya eatin' death … ya pick ya teeth with tombstone chips", accuses Flavor Flav gleefully, some bumptious funk transfiguring him into hip-hop's one and only voodoo avatar.

❺ DON'T BELIEVE THE HYPE from IT TAKES A NATION OF MILLIONS TO HOLD US BACK

"Teach the bourgeois/And rock the boulevard" – PE party like it's Paris '68, barking out another boast-cum-manifesto over hyper-inflated sax squeals and paramilitary funk guitar.

❻ FIGHT THE POWER
from FEAR OF A BLACK PLANET

"Most of my heroes don't appear on no stamps", asserts Chuck, smashing a few icons to the accompaniment of pneumatic funk and the insistent tocsin of a digital alarm clock.

❼ BROTHERS GONNA WORK IT OUT
from FEAR OF A BLACK PLANET

The familiar tropes of rock guitar and funk yelp are isolated, atomized, ruthlessly estranged and brutally disorientated by producers The Bomb Squad, until they become inimical spanners for petrified works.

❽ POLYWANNACRACKA
from FEAR OF A BLACK PLANET

Sardonic whistling, snide scratching and a laidback creep of a pace help narrate a parable about interracial relationships.

❾ BY THE TIME I GET TO ARIZONA
from APOCALYPSE 91: THE ENEMY STRIKES BLACK

A massive sludge of frazzled acid guitar that Funkadelic would have been proud of and a testifyin' gospel choir make this a moving tribute to the individual's power of protest.

❿ SHUT 'EM DOWN (PETE ROCK REMIX)
from SHUT 'EM DOWN

The album version (from Apocalypse 91) is stirring stuff, but this remix single really made the most of an uplifting anthem, one that inspires rather than hectors.

Matt Milton

Public Image Ltd

Originally genuine art-rock pioneers and purveyors of the deepest dub and darkest cynicism, PIL grew first into John Lydon's own personal soapbox, then after collaborations with

Afrika Bambaata and bids for chart success, into just another rock band.

❶ ANNALISA from PUBLIC IMAGE FIRST ISSUE

Annalisa dates back to when John Lydon was still beating Johnny Rotten out of his soul; its percussive nature shows how hard that was.

❷ PUBLIC IMAGE from PUBLIC IMAGE LIMITED

Perched miraculously on a fence where it could be seen by the old punk-rockers and by the new audience facing the bleak moorland of the 1980s, this swaggers with pride, berates the audience, and bigs up the band all at once.

❸ SWAN LAKE / DEATH DISCO from METAL BOX

Keith Levene had no time for idols, and showed little respect when he stole the melody from Tchaikovsky's ballet score. Set to a groovy disco beat, it was written by John for his mum who had cancer. She thought it was very funny.

❹ MEMORIES from METAL BOX (SECOND EDITION)

Heaven forbid anyone should say so to his face, but Lydon's lyric stands on its own as poetry. Keith and Wobble weave a hybrid of dance tune and devotional work, while his echoing mystic wail suddenly bursts into a confidential closeness, stripped of all studio effects.

❺ CAREERING from METAL BOX (SECOND EDITION)

Not so much "dated" as "identifiably of its time" due to the synth-drum assault and the whirring of dangerously overloaded electronics.

❻ FLOWERS OF ROMANCE
from FLOWERS OF ROMANCE

This track kicks off like something by The Creatures, its lyrics pointing to a pastoral afternoon of birdwatching out at Box Hill – an extra-urban adventure Johnny Rotten would have found unimaginably boring.

❼ THIS IS NOT A LOVE SONG (12" REMIX) from PLASTIC BOX

PiL's dance remixes always had a hint of self-parody in them and this one hints heavily at Trevor Horn's work with Frankie Goes To Hollywood.

❽ RISE from ALBUM

Lydon gets back to his roots on this late classic, with a refrain based on an old Irish farewell.

❾ WARRIOR (12" VERSION) from PLASTIC BOX

Lydon warbles and blusters his rebellious way while the production team rifles the sound-effects box; then the rhythm track kicks in and we're off on the nearest PiL ever got to trance.

⑩ THE SUIT from METAL BOX (SECOND EDITION)

A simple boom-chik on drums and a single bass riff repeated until it burrows into your mind for the rest of the day.

Al Spicer

Pull yourself together

Ever since the Blues, a miserable tradition has flourished. Warning: these songs of self loathing and auto-accusation may induce severe wallowing and affect your ability to operate heavy machinery.

❶ I'M A CREEP RADIOHEAD from PABLO HONEY

Lugubrious and poignant, a song for anyone ever shut out of the "popular group".

❷ I'M AN ASSHOLE

DENNIS LEARY from NO CURE FOR CANCER

Novelty song spoken word comedy routine, complete with lager-lout style sing-along chorus.

❸ CALL ME

BLONDIE from BEST OF BLONDIE

Embarassingly grovelling lyrics with begging French thrown in from a girl who needs some self-respect. Thank God you can dance to this 1980s punky-pop.

❹ LOSER BECK from MELLOW GOLD

American indie star delivers inpenetrable non-sequiturs, including "I'm a loser baby, so why don't you kill me? (get crazy with the cheese whiz)" and then tries again in Spanish. Nope, still confused.

❺ GET A LIFE AND LIVE IT LOSER

THE QUEERS from HOPELESSLY DEVOTED TO YOU TOO

Punk stalwarts The Queers give somebody a complete bollocking.

❻ BOYS DON'T CRY

THE CURE from BOYS DON'T CRY

Robert Smith may not actually weep during this trade-mark hits, but that's probably because it would have played merry hell with all that eyeliner.

❼ ONE BOURBON ONE SCOTCH ONE BEER JOHN LEE HOOKER from THE VERY BEST OF JOHN LEE HOOKER

Since his baby left him, the blues master growls his beverage order just so.

❽ POOR ME COLDPLAY from EXTRA SONGS

At least they got over self centredness for a moment to add the lyric "poor you" as well. Manners.

❾ POOR POOR PITIFUL ME LINDA RONSTADT from THE VERY BEST OF LINDA RONSTADT

Warren Zevon wrote it, and the ever-adventurous Linda Ronstadt gave it a rollicking, Californian coun-try-rock sound.

⑩ CRYING ROY ORBISON from CRYING

Who wouldn't? An exquisite voice and one of the most simple, beautiful and heartbreaking songs ever. (And it's not about his haircut.)

Kaz Cooke

Pulp

The Sheffield misfits who triumphed over adversity to make it – all too briefly – as the most eloquent observers of social awkwardness.

❶ COMMON PEOPLE from A DIFFERENT CLASS

Truly an anthem of the 1990s, combining all the things the band did best – lust, bitterness, jokes and melody.

❷ SORTED FOR E'S AND WIZZ from A DIFFERENT CLASS

The last word on the Summer of Love: one moment you're flying, the next your brain's destroyed.

❸ MIS-SHAPES from A DIFFERENT CLASS

Jarvis Cocker writes his biography, and suggests that people in weird clothes can indeed rule the world.

❹ DO YOU REMEMBER THE FIRST TIME? from HIS 'N' HERS

Oh, teenage crushes and fumblings, remembered from a position of maturity.

❺ BAR ITALIA from A DIFFERENT CLASS

The perfect come-down tune, a tender Soho waltz as the day dawns and the sugar in the coffee replaces the chemicals in your veins.

❻ THE FEAR from THIS IS HARDCORE

Creepy stuff, plus an oblique reference to Paul Daniels.

❼ BABIES from HIS 'N' HERS

The joy of older sisters, as observed from inside a wardrobe. No one says "all right" quite like JC.

❽ I SPY from A DIFFERENT CLASS

More dark voyeurism, a stalking quest for revenge among the haves and have-nots.

❾ DISHES from **THIS IS HARDCORE**
A house-husband's lament, another brutally touching tune about simple lives.

Simon Garfield

Punk originals

Young, loud and snotty to the core, punk's trailblazers lived as fast as they played, dressed to kill and thrill only themselves.

❶ SATELLITE **THE SEX PISTOLS** from **KISS THIS**
Big kids from the big city sneering at the better-heeled suburban teens who'd go on to make them rich and famous. With a guitar line that has all the aggression of stuffing shells into a shotgun, and Rotten doing his worst, this is pure punk venom.

❷ I DON'T WANNA WALK AROUND WITH YOU THE **RAMONES** from **THE RAMONES**
Written and learnt in desperation one afternoon when all the cover versions they tried proved too damn difficult to play, this has all the essence of The Ramones' appeal – a simple idea, stated simply, with a simple riff to follow.

❸ NEW ROSE **THE DAMNED** from **DAMNED DAMNED DAMNED**
The First-Ever Punk Rock Single and still one to set the goose-flesh tingling. Every pop kid knows the thrill of

Moby's Punk picks

Once labelled the "Iggy Pop of techno", there are few musical genres Moby has not embraced in his career. No surprise, then, that he came up with perhaps our most eclectic list…

❶ BANNED IN DC **BAD BRAINS** from **BANNED IN DC**
One of the best hardcore punk songs ever recorded. I remember listening to this over and over when I was in high school and missing a class as a result of my obsession with this song.

❷ MY RULES **VOID** from **FAITH/VOID**
Another DC hardcore band. Incredibly sloppy and chaotic, but somehow embodying that perfect punk ethos of sounding as if it's about to implode.

❸ WHITE MAN IN HAMMERSMITH PALAIS
THE CLASH from **THE CLASH**
Arguably the best Clash song every written, and that's saying something, as the Clash wrote and recorded about one hundred flawless songs. But this is epic, and it's almost like five songs in one. Kind of like the 'Bohemian Rhapsody' of punk rock."

❹ WHY **DISCHARGE** from **WHY**
I remember first hearing this and thinking that it sounded like the end of the world. I recently went back and listened to it again, and yes, it still sounds like the end of the world.

❺ SO WHAT? **ANTI-NOWHERE LEAGUE** from **WE ARE THE LEAGUE**
OK, a bit of comedy. Well, I assume it's comedy. Every time I hear this song it makes me laugh. I hope that was the intention…

❻ SEX BOMB **FLIPPER** from **SEX BOMB**
Another big slice of chaos. With the only lyric being "she's a sex bomb my baby, yeah", in the early 1980s this was the punk rock version of 'Louie, Louie' with every hardcore band doing their own version of it live.

❼ TRASH **NEW YORK DOLLS** from **NEW YORK DOLLS**
Is this punk rock? In my mind it is. It's degenerate and fun, as most good punk rock should be. And without the Dolls you never would've had the Sex Pistols.

❽ COMMUNICATION BREAKDOWN **LED ZEPPELIN** from **LED ZEPPELIN**
I'm sorry, but this is punk rock. Go back and listen to it – punk rock before there was punk rock. Even the title sounds like something that the Ramones or the Dead Boys would've come up with.

❾ LOS ANGELES **X** from **LOS ANGELES**
X's first three albums have held up amazingly well and they still stand as probably the best lyricists in the history of punk rock. This is still, in my mind, their signature song.

❿ FUCK CHRISTMAS, FUCK YOU
PORK GUYS from a limited edition single
OK, I'm just throwing this into the list for the hell of it. I played drums in the Pork Guys, and we were funny and noisy and absurd. The only lyric to this song is "fuck christmas, fuck you". Good luck trying to find it, as we only made a hundred copies.

Mark Perry's
Punk picks

Mark Perry launched the first British punk fanzine *Sniffin' Glue* in July 1976 after seeing the Ramones and also formed the band Alternative TV. His playlist concentrates on the period 1976–77 when *Sniffin' Glue* was briefly the most important music publication in Britain…

❶ **1977** THE CLASH from SUPER BLACK MARKET CLASH

❷ **LONDON'S BURNING** THE CLASH from THE CLASH

❸ **GOD SAVE THE QUEEN**
SEX PISTOLS from NEVER MIND THE BOLLOCKS

❹ **NOW I WANNA SNIFF SOME GLUE**
THE RAMONES from THE RAMONES

❺ **RIGHT TO WORK**
CHELSEA from CHELSEA: PUNK SINGLES

❻ **INCENDIARY DEVICE** JOHNNY MOPED from BASICALLY: THE BEST OF JOHNNY MOPED

❼ **ONE CHORD WONDERS** THE ADVERTS from CROSSING THE RED SEA WITH THE ADVERTS

❽ **BLANK GENERATION**
RICHARD HELL from BLANK GENERATION

❾ **NOBODY'S SCARED**
SUBWAY SECT from A 1978 SINGLE

---

a meaningless love story shouted out loud with high-speed guitar accompaniment and a drum beat to set the heartbeat racing.

❹ **WHITE RIOT** THE CLASH from THE CLASH
In retrospect, more than a little dumb and earnest but it kicks open the doors with wailing police sirens, knocks out the windows with a roaring football-chant chorus and sets up tactical positions from which to lay down swathes of punk-rock electric guitaaaaaaaaaaaarrrrrrr!

❺ **RISE ABOVE** BLACK FLAG from DAMAGED
One of the hardest mosh pit anthems of all time, originally by The Misfits but here pimped up like a stolen ride on steroids. The tune now probably accompanies more gently jogging gymnasium freaks than tattooed skate-punks out to scare the straight world.

❻ **CALIFORNIA ÜBER ALLES** DEAD KENNEDYS from FRESH FRUIT FOR ROTTING VEGETABLES
Jello Biafra and the boys posit an eerie future where a celebrity takes control of the most powerful state in the Union (so terribly prophetic, and to think we used to laugh at the DK's paranoia), predating The Cramps' voodoo rockabilly acquisition of doolally reverb and beautifully encapsulating the band's unique blend of outrage and fear.

❼ **ALL THIS AND MORE** DEAD BOYS from YOUNG, LOUD AND SNOTTY
One of punk's greatest love songs – smutty, sleazy and rotten to the bone.

❽ **SUSPECT DEVICE** STIFF LITTLE FINGERS from INFLAMMABLE MATERIAL
Urgent, shocked lyrics of urban terrorism and a guitar line that sounds like all the emergency services arriving at once make SLF's greatest hit as relevant today as it was three decades ago.

❾ **(I'M) STRANDED** THE SAINTS from I'M STRANDED
Riding in on a Pacific wave like the biker-surf dudes from hell, The Saints perfected the turbine-whine guitar roar, cranked up the volume then bellowed the lyrics into the maelstrom.

❿ **BLANK GENERATION** RICHARD HELL & VOIDOIDS from BLANK GENERATION
The New York punk anthem – nihilist and jerking around like a spiky-head at CBGB, overwrought by speed and Breaker Malt Liquor.

Al Spicer

Punk's new kids

Punk headed underground in the 1980s and stayed there, with all the best and most inventive acts doing the right thing and making the most of the small-scale joys that accompany limited success. Writing million-sellers and accumulating trust funds, groupie scabs and drug habits just isn't punk rock. Still, the kids seem to lap it up.

❶ OLYMPIA WA RANCID
from AND OUT COME THE WOLVES

Rancid may well sell zillions of CDs and it's been some time since any of the band saw the inside of a trailer park, but this memoir of a less glamorous past life rings as true as pure gold.

❷ GONE AWAY THE OFFSPRING
from IXNAY ON THE HOMBRE

Too intellectual, too rich to be punk? Very possibly, but they do make a most convincing attempt at an authentic angry punk sound.

❸ AMERICAN IDIOT GREEN DAY from AMERICAN IDIOT

Now into their second decade of teenage rebellion, Green Day decided at the outset to sound like The Clash's kid brothers, and have no reason to change things now.

❹ EASY TARGET
BLINK-182 from BLINK-182

Great stuff about a female serial killer, turning the highways of southern California into her own twisted charnel house.

❺ A.K.A. I-D-I-O-T
THE HIVES from BARELY LEGAL

High-quality pop punk from the best dressed band in town – any town. Not quite as authentically "street" as the average leather-clad mohican, but a lot more fun to be with.

❻ TAKE IT OFF
THE DONNAS from SPEND THE NIGHT

Yeah! Hot girl lust from The Donnas, a band that knows the future is female, plays guitar, and has issues with traditional notions of masculinity. Loud, raw, dirty music. It doesn't get any better than this.

❼ STILL WAITING
SUM-41 from DOES THIS LOOK INFECTED?

Some reviewers detected the slow advance of a social conscience in Sum-41's follow-up to "All Killer No Filler", but it doesn't take much effort to ignore it.

Al Spicer

Put that red dress on

Or take it off. Why are there so many songs where the singer instructs his girlfriend on what she should be wearing?

❶ WRECKING BALL NEIL YOUNG from FREEDOM

Somehow, something pretty and white doesn't ring true with the aging grungemeister – but that's what he wants her to wear.

❷ ALISON ELVIS COSTELLO from MY AIM IS TRUE

The problem with Alison's party dress, from Costello's viewpoint, is that somebody else got to take it off.

❸ HI-HEEL SNEAKERS
TOMMY TUCKER from HI-HEEL SNEAKERS

Assorted versions of this rock classic offer instructions to put on not only those footwear classics, but also a red dress, a wig hat and possibly some boxing gloves.

❹ THE HEALING HAS BEGUN
VAN MORRISON from INTO THE MUSIC

Van shows he can worry about fashion with the best of them; here it's instructions to put on a particular summer dress (the pretty one) and add an Easter bonnet as the finishing touch.

❺ ONE OF US CANNOT BE WRONG
LEONARD COHEN from SONGS OF LEONARD COHEN

Predictably Leonard Cohen does a different take on the what-to-wear question. He
doesn't want her to put on or take off that see-through dress, just to confess that he tortured it.

❻ ROSIE FAIRPORT CONVENTION from ROSIE

All Rosie has to take off is her coat (and settle down and listen to the band), but it remains one of Fairport's, and particularly Dave Swarbrick's, classics.

❼ CACTUS THE PIXIES from SURFER ROSA

This is undressing by remote control, with instructions to "take off the dress and send it to me", preferably soaking wet after wandering around in the desert.

❽ YOU CAN LEAVE YOUR HAT ON
RANDY NEWMAN from SAIL AWAY

The coat, the shoes, the dress all have to come off and there are even instructions on how to do it – real slow. But the hat? That can stay on.

❾ ROXANNE THE POLICE
from OUTLANDOS D'AMOUR

Well, this is more democratic; Sting's instructions are that you don't have to wear that dress, or put on the red light for that matter.

❿ PASTIES & A G-STRING
TOM WAITS from SMALL CHANGE

The gravel-voiced-one is totally straightforward in this ode to a beer-soaked strip joint: take 'em all off.

Tony Wheeler

Qawwali

The word means "utterance", the style is perhaps the world's most swinging religious music. Live performances regularly last over three hours, with listeners falling into trance as they understand the deeper meaning of the words.

❶ MUNADJAAT NUSRAT FATEH ALI KHAN
from EN CONCERT À PARIS VOL 2
Long a star in India and Pakistan, Nusrat launches his worldwide career performing this beautiful poem by the great Sufi Rumi at the studios of Radio France, in November 1985.

❷ HAAZYR HEIN HAAZYR HEIN SABRI BROTHERS
from QAWWALI MASTERWORKS
The mighty two, Ghulam Farid (bass) and Maqbool Ahmed Sabri (tenor), caught in full flight on a wicked rhythm.

❸ THE FACE OF LOVE NUSRAT FATEH ALI KHAN & EDDIE VEDDER from DEAD MAN WALKING – THE SCORE
One of Nusrat's most striking collaborations, based on the ghazal Tery Bina, and featuring Ry Cooder on bottleneck guitar.

❹ ALLAH HU NUSRAT FATEH ALI KHAN
from THE ECSTATIC QAWWALI II (JVC)
While it's not quite appropriate to speak of qawwali "hits", Allah Hu was always much requested when Nusrat performed.

❺ YA SAHIB-UL-JAMAL
SABRI BROTHERS from YA HABIB
"O Beloved of God, so luminescent is your beauty that even the moon, the sun and the stars are shy in your presence." A moving tribute to the prophet Mohammed (PBUH).

❻ MUSTT MUSTT – DUCK POND DUB MIX
NUSRAT FATEH ALI KHAN REMIXED BY MASSIVE ATTACK
from MUSTT MUSTT
Classic proof that qawwali works on the dancefloor too. The dramatic beats on the tabla work well with Massive Attack's tight reggae rhythm.

❼ GEET BAHAUDDIN QUTBUDDIN QAWWAL & PARTY
from FLIGHT OF THE SOUL
A good example how qawwali is traditionally performed at the shrines of Sufi saints.

❽ ALLAH HI JANE KAUN BASHAR HAI AZIZ MIAN
from ALLAH HI JANE
Aziz Mian stretches his incredible voice to the limit; some liken his music to punk, but, rest assured, it's still traditional qawwali.

❾ LAGI WALIAA NU NEEND NIA ONDHI ABIDA PARVEEN from HOMMAGE À NUSRAT FATEH ALI KHAN
A moving tribute to Nusrat, from the female voice of a genre largely dominated by men.

❿ NIGHT SONG NUSRAT FATEH ALI KHAN WITH MICHAEL BROOK from NIGHT SONG
Nusrat sings a kind of alaap that sounds like a lament, against a very dark synth drone.

Jean Trouillet

¿Que? Rock hits not in English

English is the universal language of rock'n'roll – wherever you come from, record companies the world over will tell you that's the tongue you have to sing in if you want international success. Here are ten that slipped under the wire…

❶ LA BAMBA RITCHIE VALENS
from HIS GREATEST HITS
A pop hit several times over since this 1958 version, the song actually comes from nineteenth-century Veracruz, Mexico. In truth, the lyric is nonsense in any language.

❷ MI TIERRA
GLORIA ESTEFAN from MI TIERRA
Few artists have combined English and Spanish releases more successfully; the Mi Tierra album even made the British Top 10 in 1993.

❸ NON, JE NE REGRETTE RIEN EDITH PIAF
from L'IMMORTELLE
And then Sony crassly went and reissued it on an album they called I Regret Nothing…

❹ JE T'AIME…MOI NON PLUS
JANE BIRKIN & SERGE GAINSBOURG
from JANE BIRKIN & SERGE GAINSBOURG
French was indeed the loving tongue, as this piece of aural eroticism went to #1 all over Europe in 1969.

❺ MACARENA LOS DEL RIO
from MACARENA NON STOP
Los Del Rio had recorded more than thirty albums of traditional Spanish music when this became a freak international hit in 1996.

❻ OYE COMO VA SANTANA from ABRAXAS
Written by Tito Puente, but brilliantly covered by Carlos and his band in 1970.

❼ GUANTANAMERA THE SANDPIPERS
from GUANTANAMERA
The much-covered Cuban classic gave this trio of Californian singers a Top 10 hit in Britain and America in 1966.

❽ PATA PATA
MIRIAM MAKEBA from PATA PATA
According to Makeba, the lyric, sung in Xhosa, is "meaningless". That didn't prevent it being an international hit in 1967.

❾ DIDI KHALED from KHALED
The first song in Arabic to chart in France in 1991, it was also a hit in Israel, Egypt and Saudi Arabia – and even, in Hindi, in India.

❿ HAVA NAGILA
SPOTNIKS from HAVA NAGILA
All right, this one's a cheat. This Swedish band took the Jewish folk song into the British Top 20 in 1963, but they left out the words and turned it into an instrumental.

Nigel Williamson

Queen

Queen – Freddie Mercury, Roger Taylor, John Deacon and Brian May – made the rocking world go round for much of the 1970s. Their flamboyant epicentre, Mercury, had a rare genius for vaudeville, lyrics, music and crowd psychology.

❶ MARCH OF THE BLACK QUEEN from QUEEN II
In tempo, harmony and key changes, this fans' favourite – more of a poem than a song – is as ambitious as "Bohemian Rhapsody".

❷ MELANCHOLY BLUES
from NEWS OF THE WORLD
2am, drink in hand, alone and slumped over in some lousy piano bar, say no more.

❸ SOMEBODY TO LOVE
from A DAY AT THE RACES
Full-throttle Freddie. The "Find me somebody to love" chant, alternately bombastic and desperate, provided the blueprint for many brilliant ballads to come.

❹ LOVE OF MY LIFE
from A NIGHT AT THE OPERA
A heart-rending tale of unrequited love with Freddie's poignantly simple piano accompaniment. Get the hankies.

❺ GOOD OLD FASHIONED LOVER BOY
from A DAY AT THE RACES
The band's last true vaudeville number fulfils Freddie's declared ambition that Queen songs should be works of brilliant escapism.

❻ SPREAD YOUR WINGS
from NEWS OF THE WORLD
Perhaps the second-finest contribution by John Deacon, the band's most overlooked member, to their work.

❼ KILLER QUEEN
from SHEER HEART ATTACK
One of the cleverest pop songs Freddie ever wrote, with nicely syncopated piano, and entertaining show-off lyrics.

❽ DROWSE from A DAY AT THE RACES
You're feeling sleepy, very sleepy. Talk about winding down, this Roger Taylor number, a secret favourite among Queen aficionados, will have you melting into the floor .

❾ BOHEMIAN RHAPSODY
from A NIGHT AT THE OPERA
This redefined the pop single, popularized the pop video, featured the longest lead melody of any single in its day, and left millions of schoolkids wondering who Scaramouche was and what he had to do with the fandango. Almost too familiar, but still plenty listenable.

❿ I WANT TO BREAK FREE from THE WORKS
Does he, doesn't he? Make your own mind up whether Freddie really wants to be out on his own or not. John Deacon's finest four minutes.

Lesley Simpson

Questions, questions...

Like all great artists, musicians down the centuries have always been renowned for asking the truly important questions in life.

① DO YOU LOVE ME? THE CONTOURS
from **GREATEST HITS**
Perhaps the crucial question in all pop music; their follow-up "Can You Jerk Like Me?" seemed somehow less important.

② WHO DO YOU LOVE? BO DIDDLEY
from **BO DIDDLEY**
Bo dares to push the questioning a little further.

③ WHAT IS LIFE? GEORGE HARRISON
from **ALL THINGS MUST PASS**
Trust George to tackle the really big issues.

④ WHY DON'T WE DO IT IN THE ROAD? THE BEATLES
from **THE WHITE ALBUM**
And trust Paul to bring things back down to the gutter.

⑤ CAN YOU PLEASE CRAWL OUT YOUR WINDOW?
BOB DYLAN from **BIOGRAPH**
And trust Dylan to turn surreal on us.

**⑥ ARE YOU EXPERIENCED? THE JIMI HENDRIX
EXPERIENCE** from **ARE YOU EXPERIENCED?**
Jimi gets straight to the point. By the next year, the drugs had taken their toll, and he was demanding "Have You Ever Been (To Electric Ladyland)?"

**⑦ WHAT'S THE UGLIEST PART OF YOUR BODY? THE
MOTHERS OF INVENTION** from **WE'RE ONLY IN IT FOR THE MONEY**
Couldn't we just gloss over that one, Frank?

⑧ DO YOU KNOW WHO I AM? ELVIS PRESLEY from **FROM
NASHVILLE TO MEMPHIS**
By the end of the 1960s, Elvis had never been bigger...

⑨ WHO AM I? ELVIS PRESLEY from **FROM NASHVILLE TO
MEMPHIS**
Even if his memory was not what it had been.

⑩ DO YOU WANT TO TOUCH ME?
GARY GLITTER from **GLITTERING GREATS**
If ever a question begged the answer "no", this was the one.

Greg Ward

R

R&B Divas

THE QUEENS

Aretha may be soul music's undisputed Queen but there's been a great number of fabulous black American singers who cut equally outstanding music from across the decades. Here are ten to remember.

❶ YOUNG HEARTS RUN FREE
CANDI STATON from THE BEST OF
Candi gained R&B fame for the raw throated hits she cut at Alabama's Fame studios but it's with this proto-disco classic that she got to express her personal struggle and gained international fame.

❷ HOME IS WHERE THE HATRED IS FROM
ESTHER PHILLIPS from A WHISPER TO A SCREAM
Beginning as Johnny Otis protégé Little Esther, Phillips' tough, nasal voice conveyed immense emotional power. Gil Scott Heron's song finds her conveying not so much a soul suffering as one traumatized.

❸ I CAN'T STAND THE RAIN
ANN PEEBLES from GREATEST HITS
Paired with Memphis uber-producer Willie Mitchell, Peebles scored one of the great 1970s soul hits with this sizzling ballad.

❹ I'D RATHER GO BLIND ETTA JAMES from TELL MAMA
Has there ever been a singer to match Etta for pure two-fisted emotional toughness? This raw soul ballad finds Etta wailing with such intensity there's no doubting her.

❺ I DON'T CARE ANYMORE
DORIS DUKE from I'M A LOSER
"I married a man who treated me like he bought me by the pound," sang Duke in this bleak yet awesome minor 1969 hit. Her career never took off and Duke's life has, it seems, been like one of the songs she sang so convincingly.

❻ YOU'LL LOSE A GOOD THING
BARBARA LYNN from THE GIRL'S GOT SOUL
Lynn was a precocious guitar playing, songwriting teen from West Texas who topped the R&B charts in 1962 with this gorgeous soul ballad.

❼ FOR YOUR PRECIOUS LOVE
LINDA JONES from HYPNOTIZED: 20 GOLDEN CLASSICS
Jones never enjoyed much commercial success before dying from diabetes in 1972 but her distraught performance of Curtis Mayfield's song suggests a singer on the very edge of sanity.

❽ YOUR GOOD THING IS ABOUT TO END
MABLE JOHN from THE STAX STORY
Mable's the brother of doomed R&B pioneer Little Willie John, learned from Billie Holiday, was Motown's first female signing and cut this classic when first signed to Stax. Put down songs don't come much tougher.

❾ IF LOVING YOU IS WRONG I DON'T WANT TO BE RIGHT MILLIE JACKSON from CAUGHT UP
Largely ignored today because of her preference for talking dirty (rather than singing), Jackson was once an exceptional singer whose ability to stretch a song into a monologue proved hugely influential.

❿ HIS HANDS CANDI STATON from HIS HANDS
Candi made a spectacular 2006 comeback with this country soul ballad, penned by Will Oldham, that deals with domestic violence.

THE PRINCESSES

Contemporary American R&B may seem a world away from its gospel roots with pop productions, hip-hop cameos and heavy emphasis on sex appeal. Yet among the gloss some of the smartest contemporary music is R&B. Here are ten worth referencing.

❶ CRAZY IN LOVE BEYONCE from DANGEROUSLY IN LOVE
From leading Destiny's Child to mega-platinum success on through even greater solo success, Beyonce Knowles is the singer all female R&B singer currently aspire to. Here she breathlessly declares her lurve assisted only by boyfriend Jay-Z tossing wild rhymes and fat Chi-Lites horn samples.

❷ NO SCRUBS TLC from FANMAIL
Huge 1999 hit from R&B's wildchild trio that slaps down men who don't measure up to T-Boz, Left-Eye and Chilli's very high expectations.

❸ CALL MY NAME
DESTINY'S CHILD from **THE WRITING'S ON THE WALL**

Having watched TLC implode through bad behaviour, Beyonce's band won an even larger audience without making the same mistakes. This fab slab of synthe-sized soul was as good as DC got.

❹ WE NEED A RESOLUTION **AALIYAH** from **AALIYAH**

The niece of Gladys Knight and protégé of R. Kelly and, briefly, his 15-year old wife came into her own when rap producer Timbaland matched his stuttering beats with her confident vocal. Aaliyah looked to be an R&B superstar but a 2001 plane crash ended the 22-year old's already hit-packed life.

❺ REAL LOVE **MARY J. BLIGE** from **WHAT'S THE 411**

The godmother of all contemporary R&B singers, Blige's 1992 debut hit showed a new way of blending soul vocals and hip-hop beats. Blige's strong, tough voice and unapologetic persona has ensured she remains black America's favourite diva.

❻ THE RAIN **MISSY ELLIOT** from **SUPA DUPA FLY**

Although primarily a rapper, Elliot's mix of singing and rhyming over Timbaland's innovative beats and slices of synths made this the de rigour sound of R&B at the start of the 21st century.

❼ MILKSHAKE **KELIS** from **TASTY**

The feisty NY singer-rapper with the multi-coloured afro rose to fame shouting "I Hate You So Much Right Now!!!" This 2003 hit, produced by The Neptunes, best demonstrates her extremely urban approach to singing.

❽ OOPS OH MY **TWEET** from **SOUTHERN HUMMINGBIRD**

With Timbaland and Missy Elliot at the controls Tweet voiced one of the most sexually knowing songs ever sung by a woman. A one-hit wonder? But, oh, what a hit . . .

❾ FALLIN' **ALICIA KEYS** from **SONGS IN A MINOR**

When music biz mogul Clive Davis presented Alicia as his new discovery in 2001 he proved to have found the perfect replacement for long awol Whitney Houston. Keys is undeniably gifted yet bland enough not to scare off the masses who find much R&B "too black".

❿ SOS **RIHANNA** from **A GIRL LIKE ME**

As of writing this was the biggest US hit of 2006 with the green-eyed teenage beauty from St Michael par-ish in Barbados gaining even greater success than her 2005 debut Pon De Replay.

Garth Cartwright

Radiohead

Radiohead is one of those rare bands who can lift listeners to the heights yet also scare the pants off them, all while staying true to their utterly unique vision.

❶ CREEP from **PABLO HONEY**

The anthem of self-loathing that launched a towering career. Once abandoned by the band, it's now at least sometimes embraced again on stage.

❷ THE BENDS from **THE BENDS**

Classic loud-soft-louder Radiohead. Feel the catharsis when Thom pleads "I wanna live, breathe. I wanna be part of the human race!"

❸ POLYETHYLENE (PARTS 1 & 2)
from **AIRBAG/HOW AM I DRIVING?**

A proto-*OK Computer* song (about plastic), the first part mumble-sung over picked acoustic, the second wailed over *Bends* bombast.

❹ PARANOID ANDROID
from **OK COMPUTER**

Pure Radiohead DNA, in all its millennial glory and technofear. Thom Yorke and the band sound positively, perfectly, blissfully unhinged.

❺ EVERYTHING IN ITS RIGHT PLACE
from **KID A**

After *OK Computer*, big things were expected from Radiohead – and they delivered on *Kid A*'s surreal, synth-heavy, alienating opener.

❻ IDIOTEQUE from **KID A**

Between *OK* and *Kid A*, the band reportedly listened to a lot of Warp Records stuff; this frenetic, freaked-out "dance" song is proof.

❼ PYRAMID SONG from **AMNESIAC**

Over a looping, stumbling piano line, Thom conjures "black-eyed angels" in a dream of life – or something like it – after death.

❽ LIFE IN A GLASS HOUSE from **AMNESIAC**

Bizarre New Orleans funeral dirge with sultry horns, shot through with Thom's paranoia that "someone's listening in".

❾ A WOLF AT THE DOOR
from **HAIL TO THE THIEF**

Classic closer, summing up in breathless, schizo-phrenic fashion – "dance you fucker don't you dare" – Thom's ongoing lyrical concerns.

⑩ TRUE LOVE WAITS from I MIGHT BE WRONG
For all Radiohead's fear and paranoia, they believe in humanity's essential, if embattled, dignity. This delicate fan favourite is proof.

Hunter Slaton

⑩ WHO AM I BEENIE MAN
from MANY MOODS OF MOSES
The record that alerted hip-hoppers to the sounds coming out of the dancehall.

Peter Shapiro

Ragga

In the simplest terms, ragga is reggae made with electronic instruments. The form has dominated Jamaican music since it emerged in 1985.

① UNDER ME SLENG TENG WAYNE SMITH
from SLENG TENG
The computerized portamento bassline that is the genesis of ragga.

② RING THE ALARM TENOR SAW
from STALAG 17, 18 AND 19
While not strictly ragga – it uses 1973's "Stalag 17" riddim – the uncompromising attitude is pure ragga.

③ TEMPO ANTHONY RED ROSE
from FIREHOUSE REVOLUTION
Menacing, creeping ragga with ice water in its veins.

④ GREETINGS HALF PINT from 20 SUPER HITS
The record that gave the new genre its name – "raggamuffin" shortened to two syllables.

⑤ BORDER CLASH NINJAMAN
from REGGAE ANTHOLOGY
The Don Gorgon of the dancehall shows off one of ragga's unique vocal deliveries.

⑥ BANDOLERO PINCHERS from BANDOLERO
Utterly bewitching Wild-West bravado.

⑦ MURDER SHE WROTE CHAKA DEMUS & PLIERS from ALL SHE WROTE
Sly Dunbar's "bhangra" riddim propelled this irresistible record to transatlantic pop success.

⑧ OH CAROLINA SHAGGY from PURE PLEASURE
The perfect postmodern Jamaican record, reaching back to the burro drums of the first Rastafarian rituals and to Cold War spy flicks.

⑨ LIMB BY LIMB CUTTY RANKS
from DANCEHALL 101 VOL 1
Breathtaking rockstone boasting – will take out any soundbwoy.

Rai music

Rai developed as the music of Algeria's underclass, with values diametrically opposed to the cultural mainstream, speaking boldly of drinking, sex and teenage kicks. Twenty years on, its biggest stars, notably Khaled, have moved up to world concert halls and festivals. They may no longer be dangerous, but their music retains its power and romance.

① MAGHBOUN CHEB KHALED
from POP-RAI AND RACHID STYLE
Before global fame beckoned, young Khaled sang his heart out for producer Rachid Baba – with a bottle of wine in his hand.

② DIDI KHALED from KHALED
Produced by Don Was, the bombastic bass-driven Didi, and the *Khaled* album, blew rai wide-open for thousands of non-Maghrebis, charting from Europe to India.

③ SIDI MANSOUR CHEIKHA REMITTI
from SIDI MANSOUR
The ultimate rock-rai mix? In her 1970s, Remitti collaborates with Robert Fripp on one of the most adventurous of crossovers.

④ ROCK EL CASBAH RACHID TAHA from TÉKITOI
Taha takes The Clash to Oran, cranks up the percussion and strings, and brings in a football-terrace chorus. The perfect reinvention.

⑤ BAÏDA FAUDEL from BAÏDA
Brought up in the grim Parisian suburb of Maintes-la-Jolie, Faudel is the new voice of rai, with sights set firmly on seducing "le grand public" in the manner of his childhood hero, Khaled. He's got the voice to do it.

⑥ YA RAYAH KHALED, TAHA, FAUDEL
from 1, 2, 3 SOLEILS
The three modern champions of Algerian music together, bringing the music full circle.

Chris Nickson

Raindrops keep falling

There's a song for every happy occasion, but sometimes, when it rains on your parade, you need a song for that, too.

❶ I CAN'T STAND THE RAIN ANN PEEBLES
from HOW STRONG IS A WOMAN
Also memorably covered by Eruption and Tina Turner, this Memphis diva's original version is arguably the finest.

❷ SINGING IN THE RAIN
GENE KELLY from SINGING IN THE RAIN
And dancing too, to come to think of it.

❸ I DON'T CARE IF THE SUN DON'T SHINE
ELVIS PRESLEY from SUNRISE
Young Elvis had better things to do than worry about the weather.

❹ RAINDROPS KEEP FALLING ON MY HEAD
B.J. THOMAS from BACK-FORWARD
Hal David's sad but optimistic lyric must have struck a chord with this performer, who had a long struggle with drug and alcohol dependency. His is the best-known cover of this song.

❺ IT'S RAINING MEN
THE WEATHER GIRLS from SUPER HITS
No need for an umbrella; they wanna get "absolutely soaking wet"! And who can blame them? A well-deserved camp classic from Izora Rhodes and Martha, err… Wash.

❻ AIN'T NO SUNSHINE BILL WITHERS from GREATEST HITS
A particularly lugubrious, not to say drenching, classic.

❼ IT'S RAINING IRMA THOMAS
from HIT SOUNDS OF NEW ORLEANS
Complete with highly authentic "drip, drop" effects, this anthem to misery could bring anyone down.

❽ RAINING IN MY HEART BUDDY HOLLY
from GREATEST HITS
Buddy can't have seen too much of the stuff in Lubbock, Texas. As he says, the sky was blue…

❾ RAINY NIGHT IN GEORGIA RAY CHARLES
from GENIUS & SOUL, THE 50TH ANNIVERSARY COLLECTION VOL 4
Mr Soul knew all about hard times; he pours his heart into this one, as many others have since.

❿ IT'S A RAINY DAY, SUNSHINE GIRL
FAUST from SO FAR
Gloriously minimalist Krautrock; Faust are rendered so dumbstruck by the unanticipated clemency that they merely chant the title for seven thumping minutes.

Greg Ward & Jon Lusk

The Ramones

Life-affirming, good-natured, high-speed pulse-racing jollity from the kings of New York punk. This is the band that invented it, so sit back and rock rock rock all the way to Rockaway Beach.

❶ BEAT ON THE BRAT from THE RAMONES
Inspired by an exasperated mom's novel approach to discipline, as observed from Dee Dee's front steps in Queens. Everything there is to know about punk rock in one quick hit, for today's hurried, time-short listener.

❷ SHEENA IS A PUNK ROCKER from ROCKET TO RUSSIA
A perfect, buzzsaw-guitar-powered drive through four chords of urban landscape. New York City really has it all!

❸ PINHEAD from LEAVE HOME
This touching tale of a pinhead's transformation by the healing power of love, inspired by Tod Browning's 1932 cult movie *Freaks*, gave the world the expression "Gabba Gabba Hey!".

❹ BLITZKRIEG BOP from THE RAMONES
Possibly the dance we'd all be doing if the Third Reich had won World War II, though the lyrics are too meaningless to tell, this is the *über*-dumb punk-rock theme performed by the undisputed masters of the scene.

❺ ROCKAWAY BEACH from ROCKET TO RUSSIA
Surf music for the scummy expanses of urban grit spread out along the East Coast, this track celebrates sunburn in a heady atmosphere of petrol fumes and decaying marine life.

❻ I WANNA BE YOUR BOYFRIEND from THE RAMONES
A slow, romantic ballad in the Shangri-Las' vein – they may have been lobotomized, but they still had big, dumb, fragile hearts.

❼ WE'RE A HAPPY FAMILY
from ROCKET TO RUSSIA
Hilarious, frenzied cartoon portrait of life back home at the Ramone family apartment: dysfunctional living at its modern best, ten floors up in the worst housing project in New York.

❽ I WANNA BE SEDATED from ROAD TO RUIN

Sooner or later, most bands that tour as much as The Ramones record a song about getting back home to the one you love. Of course, if you're Dee Dee, then the one you love comes powdered in bundles, and will sit you flat down on the base of your spine, drooling.

❾ TEENAGE LOBOTOMY from ROCKET TO RUSSIA

There was a dark, personal side to the band's fixation with mental illness, but it never crept into the music, which totally celebrated the brighter side of brain surgery and the fun to be had gobbling down the thorazines.

❿ JUDY IS A PUNK from THE RAMONES

Sheena's best pal and the perfect girlfriend for any right-thinking scion of the clan Ramone. The second verse is the same as the first.

Al Spicer

Red Hot Chili Peppers

The band that made it and lost it in the 1990s is now one of the world's greatest rock bands.

❶ BY THE WAY from BY THE WAY

A brooding opening bassline, followed by a crisp opening verse, which then explodes and pulls you into a chorus that leaves a lasting impression.

❷ UNDER THE BRIDGE
from BLOODSUGARSEXMAGIK

The classic track that made them famous and cata-pulted them to superstardom still stands the test of time.

❸ AEROPLANE from ONE HOT MINUTE

A great uplifting, track from a time when the band was dogged by tragedy.

❹ KNOCK ME DOWN from MOTHER'S MILK

A memorial track to Hillel Slovak, who overdosed on heroin the year before. The upbeat pop melodies testify to Slovak's influence.

❺ OTHERSIDE from CALIFORNICATION

Another soft ballad, delivered in a way that makes you want to turn the volume up and belt it out.

❻ UNIVERSALLY SPEAKING from BY THE WAY

This track transports you back to the 1960s, if not in style then in the feel of the lyrics.

❼ DOSED from BY THE WAY

A beautiful track where Kiedis truly lets go, unleashing his voice on a quasi-ballad built on guitar lines that almost become an addiction.

❽ CALIFORNICATION from CALIFORNICATION

One of their strongest tracks. The catchy bridge into the strong chorus leaves the listener wanting more.

❾ CAN'T STOP from BY THE WAY

A great return to funk rap, right down to the last note. Great drums, great riffs, great stuff.

❿ PARALLEL UNIVERSE from CALIFORNICATION

Upbeat and uptempo number, building into a wailing crescendo of rock.

Mike Symons

Red Hot Mamas

Sex sells and it always has. In fact, from the vaudeville of Sophie Tucker to the jazz-blues of Bessie Smith, there were probably more women singing sexually suggestive songs in the early decades of the last century than in our own. Here are ten of our favourite red hot mamas from the not-so-buttoned up years before World War II…

❶ I NEED A LITTLE SUGAR IN MY BOWL
BESSIE SMITH from THE ESSENTIAL BESSIE SMITH

" What's the matter, hard papa, come on and save you mama's soul 'cos I need a little sugar in my bowl…"

❷ I WANT A TALL SKINNY PAPA
SISTER ROSETTA THARPE from THE GOSPEL OF THE BLUES

"He's got to be all right, learn to fight all night, mama will do the rest…."

❸ I'M A MIGHTY TIGHT WOMAN
SIPPIE WALLACE from COMPLETE RECORDED WORKS VOL 2

" If you're a married man you ain't got no business here, 'cos when you're out with me I might make your wife shed a tear…"

❹ SHAVE 'EM DRY #2 LUCILLE BOGAN
from SHAVE 'EM DRY: BEST OF LUCILLE BOGAN

"I'm going to turn back my mattress, and let you oil my springs / I want you to grind me daddy 'til the bells do ring…"

❺ ORGAN GRINDER BLUES
VICTORIA SPIVEY from QUEEN VICTORIA 1927–37

" Your sweet music seems to ease my mind, it's not your organ, but it's the way you grind…"

➏ IF IT DON'T FIT DON'T FORCE IT
BARRELHOUSE ANNIE from **THE VARIOUS ARTISTS COMPILATION, SUGAR IN MY BOWL**
"It may stretch, it may not tear at all, but you'll never back that big mule up in my stall…"

➐ HOT NUTS GET 'EM FROM THE PEANUT MAN
LIL JOHNSON from **HOTTEST GAL IN TOWN**
" You see that man all dressed in brown, he's got the hottest nuts in town…"

➑ HE'S JUST MY SIZE **LILLIE MAE KIRKHAM** from **THE VARIOUS ARTISTS COMPILATION, SUGAR IN MY BOWL**
"He makes my biscuit rise, he uses the best baking powder and his biscuit's just my size…"

➒ NOBODY LOVES A FAT GIRL, BUT OH HOW A FAT GIRL CAN LOVE **SOPHIE TUCKER** NOT AVAILABLE ON CD
"I'm just a truck upon the highway of love, the only game I can get the boys to play is have 'em sit around and guess how much I weigh …"

➓ SALTY PAPA BLUES
DINAH WASHINGTON from **THE ESSENTIAL DINAH WASHINGTON**
"I said papa, why you so salty, why do you bring me down, there's no complaint when my other man comes around…"

Nigel Williamson

Otis Redding

The greatest male soul singer of all time? And then some. Redding was only 26 when he died tragically in a plane crash in 1967, and so never had to go disco or sing duets with Phil Collins. Here are ten of his mightiest and most pitiful.

❶ MR PITIFUL from SINGS SOUL BALLADS
Despite its title, the song that gave him his nickname is actually one of his more upbeat numbers.

❷ I'VE BEEN LOVING YOU TOO LONG from OTIS BLUE
The self-penned breakthrough that gave Otis his first Top 40 single.

❸ RESPECT from OTIS BLUE
Aretha's version is better known but Otis wrote it, and his version, sung from a man's perspective, makes a fascinating contrast.

❹ I CAN'T TURN YOU LOOSE
from THE COMPLETE STAX SINGLES
Otis at his earthiest on a song that was covered by The Rolling Stones.

❺ (I CAN'T GET NO) SATISFACTION from OTIS BLUE
At the time, Mick and Keith reckoned being covered by Otis was one of the greatest thrills of their young lives.

❻ A CHANGE IS GONNA COME from OTIS BLUE
We can argue all night whether Sam Cooke or Otis recorded the definitive version. Fact is, both are genius.

❼ FA-FA-FA-FA-FA (SAD SONG)
from THE OTIS REDDING DICTIONARY OF SOUL
Backed – as on most of his Stax sides – by the peerless Booker T and the MGs.

❽ TRY A LITTLE TENDERNESS
from THE OTIS REDDING DICTIONARY OF SOUL
From the slow goose-bump-inducing beginnings to the storming, stomping finale, the all-time perfect soul song.

❾ TRAMP from KING AND QUEEN
A wonderfully witty duet with Carla Thomas about his backwoods upbringing in rural Georgia.

❿ (SITTIN' ON) THE DOCK OF THE BAY
from DOCK OF THE BAY
Rendered more potent by being released posthumously. If you're ever in San Francisco, you can visit the dock of the bay where he wrote it, just over the Golden Gate Bridge, in Sausalito.

Nigel Williamson

Lou Reed

The Dark Prince of the Velvet Underground continued to impress with his solo work – though often erratic, it proved he was capable of writing about much more than just low life, S&M and hard drugs.

❶ WALK ON THE WILD SIDE
from TRANSFORMER
Reed soliloquizes about the bad habits of Andy Warhol superstars Holly (Woodlawn), Candy (Darling), "Little" Joe (Dallesandro) and the Sugar Plum Fairy (Joseph Campbell) – and turns it all into an irresistible pop song.

❷ PERFECT DAY
from TRANSFORMER
The title says it all – a gentle description of true love and a perfect date (or is it heroin?), revivable twenty years later for an all-star charity version.

Werner Pieper's
Reefer songs

WERNER PIEPER writes, publishes and compiles CDs under the name Grüne Kraft (Green Power) in Heidelberg, Germany. He was described by Timothy Leary as a "cyber-shamanic-psychedelic-performing-publisher and founding father of the European Green movement". His series of Flashback CDs include a marvellous volume of reefer songs. As he asserts, "Smoking dope and singing about it didn't start (or end) with the hippies."

❶ MUGGLES
LOUIS ARMSTRONG from DOPE & GLORY
One of the most famous pre-hippy dopers stretching his notes. What a wonderful music-world he opened up.

❷ THE U.S.S. TITANIC JAMIE BROCKETT from REMEMBER THE WIND AND THE RAIN
Well, finally we know why the drama happened: the captain took a toke. The finest fourteen minutes of this mid-1960s Boston singer-songwriter.

❸ KNOCKIN' MYSELF OUT BIG BILL BROONZY & JEAN BRADY from HIGH & LOW
One of the most recorded reefer-songs of all time, as if folks were smoking skunk sixty years ago.

❹ THE HASHISHIN RY COODER & BUFFY ST MARIE from PERFORMANCE SOUNDTRACK
A Jack Nitzsche song from the movie *Performance*, with Buffy on the mouth-bow and help from Jack Nitzsche.

❺ MARIHUANA THE FUGS from THE FUGS
A medieval Gregorian chant, celebrating the herb in dozens of languages. A global statement.

❻ AFRICAN REGGAE NINA HAGEN BAND from UNBEHAGEN
This hymn to African dope is partly rapped in German, sung in English, with some yodelling thrown in – an oddly powerful mix.

❼ GRUENZEUGKRISTALLE ISCHEN IMPOSSIBLE from DANCEHALLFIEBER 3
An unbelievably fine debut recording by four girls from Cologne. A teenage opera in under five minutes.

❽ PANAMA RED PETER ROWAN from PETER ROWAN
Recorded solo by Peter, with "Old And In The Way", by the New Riders and others. As long as the stuff is illegal, we should have more songs about dealers. (OK, let's not forget Traffic's "Dealer, Dealer".)

❾ VIPERS DRAG FATS WALLER from DOPE & GLORY
"Dreamed about a reefer five feet long … the sky is high and so am I" … Louis and Fats stand for all those 1930s and 40s musicians like Sidney Bechet, Mezz Mezzrow and Cab "Reefer Man" Calloway who recorded more dope songs than the hippies ever managed in the 1960s.

❿ PSYCHEDELIC KINGDOM COMEE SEEED from NEW DUBBY CONQUERORS
A Howard Marks favourite from Berlin's multi-bulti band.

❸ SATELLITE OF LOVE
from TRANSFORMER
The lilting tune – and David Bowie's sublime production – make it easy to forget that this is actually a song about serial infidelity and the pain it can cause.

❹ DIRTY BLVD from NEW YORK
Celebrating the mean streets of New York City, and the lives of the downtrodden and neglected who reside there; even if no one else cares about them, Reed does.

❺ A DREAM
from SONGS FOR DRELLA: A FICTION
Sung by John Cale but written by Reed, this is masterful: a reverie in the mind of the dying Andy Warhol. It's Reed's most moving tribute to his mentor.

❻ CAROLINE SAYS II
from BERLIN
A disturbing portrait of domestic abuse and a disintegrating relationship – and quite probably a tribute to Reed's former lover Nico (as is the whole *Berlin* album).

❼ GROWING UP IN PUBLIC from GROWING UP IN PUBLIC
Proof positive that Reed can be downright funny, while also taking a scathing swipe at his own short-comings. Shortly after this, he gave up both drugs and alcohol.

❽ THE BELLS from THE BELLS
Lengthy (nine minutes), jazzy and strange. Supposedly influenced by both Ornette Coleman and Edgar Allan Poe (there's arty), this improvised piece about a rooftop suicide is utterly compelling.

❾ I LOVE YOU, SUZANNE from NEW SENSATIONS
For all his literary merit, Reed can still also write great throwaway pop songs with dumb guitar riffs and dumber lyrics.

❿ MAGIC AND LOSS from MAGIC AND LOSS
In the last decade or so, Reed has frequently tackled a subject that other rock songwriters avoid like the plague: death. A tribute to dying friends that's as mature as rock will ever get.

Peter Really

Reggae: strictly the best

The ultimate reggae playlist is something of a tall order: ten tunes from the thousands made in a dozen styles over nearly fifty years on three different continents. But this is it, the unequivocal Ten Best Reggae Records Ever Made. Or at least this is what they are this afternoon.

❶ JOHNNY TOO BAD THE SLICKERS
from THE HARDER THEY COME
A cautionary tale of a rude boy's potentially sticky end, told with an appropriately swaggering early-reggae style.

❷ KING TUBBY'S MEETS ROCKERS UPTOWN
AUGUSTUS PABLO from KING TUBBY'S MEETS ROCKERS UPTOWN
Probably the most famous dub track ever committed to vinyl, and deservedly so, as inherent swing and discreetly persuasive echo set up a matchless per-petual motion.

❸ MONEY IN MY POCKET (2ND VERSION) DENNIS BROWN from THE BEST OF
This cut has a more rounded-out bass, a harder work-ing Hammond and springing percussion, brilliantly framing DB's subtle phrasings inside an apparently simple rhythm.

❹ ROCK (ALBUM MIX) MATUMBI
from THE BEST OF
Deep, grumbling, awesomely musically literate roots reggae that bases itself in Biblical prophecy and still involves a few minutes of jazzy flute and sax break that sounds suspiciously like Courtney Pine.

❺ SWING & DINE THE MELODIANS
from RIVERS OF BABYLON
At that beautiful junction where rock steady meets reggae, you'll find The Melodians' gentle harmonizing.

❻ THE BORDER GREGORY ISAACS from LIVE
Testament to the steamrolling power of the best reggae stage shows: The Cool Ruler at his uptempo, Jah Jah-praising best; the taut Roots Radics driving him to new heights; and an ecstatic crowd singing the choruses for him.

❼ BY HIS DEEDS VC from BY HIS DEEDS
Peter Tosh-level anger as, over the simplest beat-box backing, VC rips into those who are doing the country and its people wrong. He recorded this tune with his redundancy pay when he was laid off; catch-ing the mood of Jamaica, it was the biggest record of 2001.

❽ IT'S ME AGAIN JAH LUCIANO
from WHERE THERE IS LIFE
Although the sounds are as sparse and seemingly hard-edged as anything else in the dancehall, Luci's stylish gospel-ish tones give this nu roots classic a genuine ital glow.

❾ THE LIQUIDATOR HARRY J ALL STARS
from TROJAN'S GREATEST HITS
A snapping, bubbling, popping, bouncing, Hammond-happy poptastic smash in 1969.

❿ LOVE A DUB RANKING DREAD from LOVE A DUB
Springy, eternally cheerful slice of dancehall nonsense, with the DJ sticking that longstanding reggae tradi-tion and celebrating the music, himself and the dance in which the two have come together.

Lloyd Bradley

Roots reggae

More than simply loading up the chalice and praising Jah Rastafari, roots reggae had an earthy, almost organic feel to it that the best tunes expressed from beneath the palpable. It meant a vibe that was as close to Rasta's back-to-nature philosophy as was possible in a 1970s

Dennis Bovell's
Sound system

DENNIS BOVELL: founder and leader of Matumbi, musical director and bandleader for Linton Kwesi Johnson, leader of Dennis Bovell's Dub Band, and producer of acts as diverse as Orange Juice, The Slits and Bananarama. He says: "If I still ran my Jah Sufferer sound system, and we were playing before the band (Matumbi) did their set, these are ten tunes I'd play and the order in which I'd play them."

❶ RASTAMAN VIBRATION BOB MARLEY
from RASTAMAN VIBRATION

❷ GET TO LOVING DENNIS BROWN
from GET TO LOVING

❸ SLAVERY DAYS BURNING SPEAR
from MARCUS GARVEY

❹ GROOVING IN LOVE INNER CIRCLE
from THE CAPITOL YEARS 1976–1977

❺ ONE WHEELIE WHEEL EARLY B
from ONE WHEELIE WHEEL

❻ Y MAS GAN THE ABYSSINIANS
from SATTA MASSAGANA

❼ MAN IN ME MATUMBI from MUSIC IN THE AIR

❽ ONCE AGO GREGORY ISAACS
from THE BEST OF GREGORY ISAACS VOL 2

❾ 54-46 WAS MY NUMBER TOOTS AND THE MAYTALS
from ANTHOLOGY (1964–2000)

❿ THE HARDER THEY COME JIMMY CLIFF
from THE HARDER THEY COME

Jamaican recording studio... and why there are a disproportionate number of Lee Perry productions in this particular playlist.

❶ AFRICA ASWAD from CRUCIAL TRACKS
Instrumentally complex, solidly rocking, cleverly harmonized and sound in its sentiments: who says British roots struggled to keep up?

❷ SATTA MASSA GANA THE ABYSSINIANS
from SATTA MASSA GANA
The ultimate in roots reggae, combining classic Jamaican three-piece harmony with a biblical epic of a song, atop big brass, a chugging rhythm and a bassline of awesome authority.

❸ CROAKING LIZARD PRINCE JAZZBO
from SUPER APE
A version of "War In A Babylon" in which Jazzbo's seemingly nonsensical righteousness is as artfully delivered as the cleanly cut-up chaos of Perry's production, taking the tune to an even higher level of reggae genius.

❹ THE GHOST BURNING SPEAR
from GARVEY'S GHOST
Lightly dubbed, hi-stepping instrumental cut of Marcus Garvey, all the more dread for allowing the horns and percussion to take centre stage, showing off the intrinsic atmospherics.

❺ COUNTRY LIVING THE MIGHTY DIAMONDS
from COUNTRY LIVING
So bright and breezy and altogether wholesome, this could almost qualify as easy listening, but it's exactly such peace'n'harmony that gives the song true roots consequence.

❻ SMALL AXE (LEE PERRY PRODUCTION)
THE WAILERS from COMPLETE WAILERS 1967–72
Jaunty Hammonded-up "traditional" reggae backing leaves plenty of space for early-Perryisms, but, most importantly, there's room to frame the trio's totally sweet but entirely militant vocalizing.

❼ MOVE OUTTA BABYLON
JOHNNY CLARKE from DREADER DREAD 1976–78
Gently bubbling generic reggae beat supports Clarke's plaintive vocals; his touch is so delicate he could be crooning lovers' rock.

❽ CURLY LOCKS JUNIOR BYLES from CURLY LOCKS
The original roots/lovers' rock crossover sets Byles' voice off against a seemingly endless mount of subtly melodic touches going on waaaay back in the mix.

⑨ EAST OF THE RIVER NILE AUGUSTUS PABLO from EAST OF THE RIVER NILE

Slowing the rockers' pace down slightly, Pablo's melodica duels with a guitar to create a shifting-sand lullaby of a tune, which uses minimum dub techniques to maximum effect.

⑩ RICO CHILDREN OF SANCHEZ from ROOTS TO THE BONE

The wooziest, in-sight-of-Addis-Ababa jazz-influenced roots, with layering so clever it creates the illusion of dub. A masterpiece from the man who studied trombone under Don Drummond.

Lloyd Bradley

UK reggae hits

Britain's love affair with Jamaican music began well before Bob Marley. Despite the anti-reggae bias of the BBC at the time, all the records listed here made the UK Top 50. All these are available on the Trojan albums *Young, Gifted And Black*.

❶ MY BOY LOLLIPOP MILLIE

Based on a 1950s R&B song by Barbie Gray, Millie Small's worldwide hit was actually recorded in London, with a pop-ska arrangement by top Jamaican guitarist Ernest Ranglin.

❷ 007 (SHANTY TOWN) DESMOND DEKKER

Classic Dekker ska song from the original rude boy era.

❸ AL CAPONE PRINCE BUSTER

The gangster gimmick and sound effects gave the record novelty appeal, but it's the brilliant brass work – notably by tenor-sax player Val Bennett – that makes this an enduring classic.

❹ TRAIN TO SKAVILLE THE ETHIOPIANS

Despite the title, the suitably chugging rhythm is rock steady rather than ska. Apparently the horn riff derives from Johnny Cash's "Ring Of Fire", of all things.

❺ ISRAELITES DESMOND DEKKER

This topped the charts in half a dozen countries, and reached #9 in the US – not bad for a song that compared the plight of Jamaicans "slaving for bread" to that of the Israelites in Egypt/Babylon!

❻ RETURN OF DJANGO THE UPSETTERS

Nominally inspired by a spaghetti western, this perennial party favourite turned out to be an instrumental version of a cover of Chris Kenner's R&B tune "Sick And Tired". The sax solo is by the great Val Bennett.

❼ YOUNG, GIFTED AND BLACK BOB AND MARCIA

Sweetened with strings for its UK release, this pop-reggae version of the Nina Simone song remains a joyous affirmation of black potential.

❽ DOUBLE BARREL DAVE AND ANSELL COLLINS

Dave was Dave Barker, a fine falsetto singer who also specialized in vocal interjections, the keyboardist was Ansell Collins, and a young Sly Dunbar was on drums.

❾ EVERYTHING I OWN KEN BOOTHE

Boothe transforms David Gates' sensitive song about the death of his father into a timeless and super-soulful lovers' tune.

❿ IRIE FEELINGS (SKANGA) RUPIE EDWARDS

Whether because of the initial reference to "feeling high", or because it was just too weird, the BBC initially refused to play this, but it became mainstream Britain's first exposure to the deeply dippy delights of dub. Skanga… skanga… skanga… skanga.

Neil Foxlee

Euro-reggae

Reggae is alive and well in Europe, with committed scenes in both France and Germany, where local producers and musicians are creating strange hybrids.

❶ SEE MI YAH WILLI WILLIAMS from RHYTHM & SOUND

Old hero Willi Williams meets two cutting-edge Berlin-based techno producers. The result is Germany's deepest and most spiritual reggae sound.

❷ NE DANS LES RUES DE PARIS PIERPOLJAK from JE FAIS C'QUE J'VEUX

Opening with melancholic accordion, this sounds real French, with Bob Marley lurking around the corner.

❸ DEM GONE GENTLEMAN from JOURNEY TO JAH

Would you believe this is by a German reggae artist? Tilmann Otto sings in perfect Jamaican patois, using studios and riddims from the loudest island in the world.

❹ LA FILLE DU SELECTOR MASSILIA SOUND SYSTEM from 3968 CR 13

A soundsystem from Marseille that blends local roots music and dancehall. Here they sing in troubadour style about a girl who is cursed by a selector.

311

⑤ DICKES B SEEED from NEW DUBBY CONQUERORS
From a big-band who perform with three singers and a mighty horn section comes maybe the best hymn to Berlin ever written.

⑥ TOMBER LA CHEMISE ZEBDA
from TOMBER LA CHEMISE MAXI
Multi-culti outfit from Toulouse with a dancefloor stomper that went to #1 in France.

⑦ MEI GUADA FREIND HANS SÖLLNER from OIWEI I
He's been listening to the two Bobs – Marley and Dylan – and you can hear echoes of "Chimes Of Freedom" in this moving ballad about a departed friend.

⑧ STOP DA WAR SERGENT GARCIA
from BEST OF SERGENT GARCIA
Overtly political "salsamuffin" in dancehall style, with Latin horns and vocal stints by famous French rapper Bionik and Hector Caramelo.

Jean Trouillet

Reggaeton

A Latino original, reggaeton is infecting the world with its hybrid of hip-hop and dancehall reggae fused to a hefty load of Latino beats. At its best, it's a thrilling, thumping backing to the vocalists, interspersed with catchy rhythmic breaks from "live" or sampled *bachata* guitars, *vallenato* or *merengue* accordions, classic salsa piano riffs and catchphrases; at its worst, it's a cheap, repetitive, Latin imitation of the worst of gangsta rap and dancehall, oozing mysogyny and obscenity. Conceived in Panama, nurtured in Puerto Rico, there's always a local musical ID tag. Top cats include Daddy Yankee, DJ Omar and Ivy Queen. These are some of the best.

❶ PU TUN TUN EL GENERAL single
Inspired by the rhythm of Shabba Ranks' dancehall reggae hit, "Dem Bow", this reggaeton prototype led Puerto Ricans Vico-C and DJ Negro to create the real thing. Wobbly basslines soften the Jamaican beats, and the infectious melody inspired scores of covers, particularly among the merengue-hip-hoppers.

❷ LA INGLESA VICO-C from VICO-C GREATEST HITS
The bass still isn't prominent enough for pure reggaeton, but it's almost there: Vico-C's early hit sees "Sabrina, the Inglesa" initiated in Spanglish by the Hispanic posse, via Latin dancehall rhythms and infectious boogaloo whistles and handclap samples.

❸ GASOLINA DADDY YANKEE from DADDY YANKEE EN DIRECTO (LIVE)
Puerto Rican superstar, Daddy Yankee put reggaeton on the world map with this catchy hit, whose catchy swingbeat-like rhythm and tinkling keyboards match the risqué girls' chorus "Give me the gas."

❹ DILE IVY QUEEN from RUDE GIRL
The feisty blonde backing singer with New York's DLG re-born as a favourite reggaetonista. With her commanding, throaty voice, she gives the woman's answer to Don Omar's hit "Dile", while the aggression builds in cymbal beats emphasizing her questionable line that men should pay for what they want.

❺ ECHALE AGUA CHAKA from REGGAETON SESSIONS
Chaka's percussive feast is also melodic delight, the dynamic, bucking groove created from snare drum beats accompanying humming electronic basslines and rhythmic outbursts of sampled trumpets.

❻ DILE DON OMAR from THE LAST DON
One of many seminal hits by one of the Puerto Rican Kings. Omar's reggaeton is more musical than most, incorporating salsa piano, guitars and brass with the dancehall beats; it's like being in two clubs at once.

❼ TRAICIONERA DJ LOCO AND MC MAGICO from REGGAETON SESSIONS
London Colombians from La Raza Crew strut their stuff in phone conversation style, with vocalist Magico (a fine, sweet voice) hissing "Traicionera" (traitor) and "Mentirosa" (Liar) as "she" mumbles excuses. Machico's soulful voice and the pealing *bachata* guitar contrast well with Loco's tense, minimalist, urban production.

❽ MORDIDITA CANDYMAN from REGGAETON SESSIONS
Underlying this (relatively) minimalist hit by Cuba's leading reggaeton vocalist is the hypnotically aggressive, highly influential, "Bim Bim" rhythm from Chaka Demus and Pliers' "Murder She Wrote". Candyman's penchant is minimalizing words in the Cuban way; hence Mididita – little bite, as in, "Where did you get that little bite?" – and "she" answers, "In my casita". Everything ends in –ita, and everything rhymes.

❾ SE VAN VOLTIO FEATURING TEGO CALDERON from REGGAETON SESSIONS
Top Puerto Rican reggaeton singer Calderon joins young producer Voltio in a compulsive, sophisticated number: sampled salsa piano dropped in edgy rhythmic chunks onto synthesized snare drums and tinny timbales beats.

⑩ MI CORAZON EDDIE G from REGGAETON NIGHT

Shimmering *bachata* guitar riffs, hissy *merengue* cymbals, and an almost military timbales rhythm set the mood for the sweet-voiced Dominican singer Eddie G's lament about lost love.

Sue Steward

Nu Roots Reggae

You may not know it, but there's been a revival in roots reggae over the last fifteen years or so, spearheaded by the late great Garnett Silk who died in 1994. The music may sometimes be digital and the rhythms second-hand, but the results can be just as rewarding as in the 1970s.

❶ LORD WATCH OVER OUR SHOULDERS GARNETT SILK from REGGAE ANTHOLOGY

Killed in a gas-canister explosion at the age of just 28, Silk shows complete conviction on this lovely song.

❷ JAH IS BY MY SIDE TONY REBEL from IF JAH

Singjay Rebel draws on Psalm 23 for inspiration over an anthemic original rhythm.

❸ PSALM 24 LUCIANO & MUTABARUKA from LUCIANO: REGGAE MAX

Luciano and dub poet Mutabaruka on a brilliant Xterminator production that reworks Alton Ellis's "I Can't Stand It" to thrilling effect.

❹ PRAISE YE JAH SIZZLA from RAGGA ESSENTIALS

Bobo-dread deejay on fearsomely righteous form over a storming Xterminator rhythm, well before the homophobia controversy.

❺ PUT DOWN YOUR WEAPON YAMI BOLO & CAPLETON from FAT EYES PRESENTS: A DANCEHALL TWOFER

Another remarkable adaptation: a slowed-down version of a 1958 South African tune, Little Kid Lex's "New Year Rock", better known as Bert Kaempfert's "Afrikaan Beat".

❻ DOWN BY THE RIVER MORGAN HERITAGE from UNIVERSAL MESSAGE

Why this Jamerican family group didn't cross over with this pop-friendly monster is a mystery.

❼ JAH BLESS ME JAH CURE from UNIVERSAL MESSAGE VOL 3

Jamaica's currently most popular roots singer has a yearning quality to his voice, as well he might: he's been in prison since 1998.

❽ LIVING IN LOVE I WAYNE from UNIVERSAL MESSAGE VOL 3

His debut album disappointed, but this Jamaican radio #1 has instant and enduring appeal.

❾ WELCOME TO JAMROCK DAMIAN JR. GONG MARLEY from WELCOME TO JAMROCK

May not appeal to his father's fans, but this shows that one of his sons hasn't lost touch with the streets.

⑩ WORD, SOUND AND POWER MACKA B from WORD, SOUND AND POWER

Probably the most articulate, thoughtful and witty DJ around – and he's from Birmingham.

Neil Foxlee

Django Reinhardt

Django Reinhardt 1910–1953 was the first European jazz musician to win international respect with his remarkably fluid, expressive guitar playing. Django was a Romani Gypsy who mastered guitar even though his left hand had been crippled in a caravan fire; he cared little for polite society and played as he lived – wild and free. Hugely influential, his musical legacy lives in countless jazz, blues and Gypsy musicians. All selections are from *Retrospective Django Reinhardt 1934-53*.

❶ DINAH

A pioneering 1934 recording of the Hot Club Of France finds Django and his violin-playing partner Stephane Grappelli seducing Paris with their fast string interplay.

❷ ST LOUIS BLUES

Reinhardt takes on the famous Louis Armstrong tune in 1937 and stretches out on guitar, his playing lyrical, dramatic and unlike anyone else then recording. B.B. King cites Django as an influence and here's a fine example of how musicians listen and build.

❸ MINOR SWING

Original Reinhardt/Grappelli tune that was a huge pre-War hit and remains a classic swing tune "à la française".

❹ HONEYSUCKLE ROSE

The Fats Waller tune gets boiled in French oil and oh does it smoke! Listen to Django's solo and shout with joy.

❺ BLACK AND WHITE
Fabulous duet between Grappalli and Reinhardt that finds both stretching out further and further.

❻ LES YEUX NOIRS
Based on a Gypsy folk melody, this begins with a banging drum before a clarinet plays the melody then Django follows with an extended solo that's among his very finest.

❼ SWING 42
Joyous jazz rampage aimed at lifting French spirits 1941 and all that that finds Django at his most spirited.

❽ BLUES EN MINEUR
Django starts this one off on violin so revealing his campfire Gypsy roots then swaps to guitar.

❾ PLACE DE BROUCKERE
1949 recording finds Django picking out a distorted electric guitar solo that suggests what a musical radical he was.

❿ NUAGES
Django's most famous composition and a jazz classic. With its modernist melody, descending chords and fine soloing, one can hear Reinhardt building European jazz. No surprise then that Duke Ellington was a fan.

Garth Cartwright

R.E.M.

The original 1980s college radio jangle-pop band that just won't quit. Michael Stipe's lyrics remain an oblique, enigmatic highlight.

❶ RADIO FREE EUROPE from MURMUR
Irresistibly jangly and definitively obscure, with a call-to-arms chorus: "Calling all out in transit!" (We think.)

❷ SO. CENTRAL RAIN (I'M SORRY) from RECKONING
Looks forward to Michael Stipe's later-period apology-songs to an unnamed third person – possibly a lover?

❸ FALL ON ME from LIFE'S RICH PAGEANT
Bassist Mike Mills sings beautiful harmonies with Stipe and takes a solo turn too, revealing him to be R.E.M.'s secret vocal weapon.

❹ IT'S THE END OF THE WORLD AS WE KNOW IT (AND I FEEL FINE) from DOCUMENT
A tongue-twister party anthem if there ever was one, this has become R.E.M.'s concert-closing warhorse.

❺ COUNTRY FEEDBACK
from OUT OF TIME
This brooding, impressionistic tone poem essays deep sadness with "a paperweight, a junk garage, winter rain, a honey pot".

❻ NIGHTSWIMMING
from AUTOMATIC FOR THE PEOPLE
Piano-driven and heartbreaking, this nostalgic ode to the lost innocence of youth is maybe the best song from R.E.M.'s greatest album.

❼ E-BOW THE LETTER
from NEW ADVENTURES IN HI-FI
In the vein of Country Feedback, E-Bow looks hard at fame and decides, appropriately for R.E.M., that "adrenaline tastes like fear".

❽ DAYSLEEPER from UP
Delicate and fuzzy-headed, Stipe here takes on the persona of one who works anonymous nights "colored headache grey".

❾ SATURN RETURN from REVEAL
With a drifting, cosmic piano line, Saturn Return shifts in the middle from canned to live drums, giving the listener a feeling of lift-off.

❿ FINAL STRAW from AROUND THE SUN
Though spare and acoustic, Final Straw is R.E.M.'s most politically pointed song ever, as Stipe implores George W. Bush to "tell me why".

Hunter Slaton

Rembetika

Songs of sorrow, betrayal and hashish made famous by the so-called *manges*, rebellious characters who adorned themselves with fancy wardrobes, hated the police and loved the holy smoke and beautiful ladies.

❶ TA HANOUMAKIA
RÍTA ABADZÍ from GREEK-ORIENTAL REMBETICA – THE GOLDEN YEARS: 1911–1937
This is great Smyrna, Rembetiko in Asia Minor style, celebrating the "Hashish Harem", the girls taking care of the *narghile* (or hookah).

❷ MANA MOU ELLAS
STAVROS XARCHAKOS/NIKOS GATSOS from AMAN-AMIN
Taken from Kostas Ferris's stellar movie *Rembetiko*, this sings the desperation of exile.

❸ EGO MANGAS PHENOMOUNA MICHALIS JENITSARIS & PROSECHÓS from SALTADOROS

This song was a scandal, because it was written by a youngster: "I was born to be a *mangas*, I liked it, I learned to play bouzouki instead of going to school." The last surviving hero of Rembetiko, Jenitsaris died in May 2005.

❹ TO VAPORI APO TIN PERSIA – THE BOAT FROM PERSIA VASILIS TSITSANIS
from FÜNF GRIECHEN IN DER HÖLLE

In this *zeybekiko*, Tsitsanis, a bouzouki player from Piraeus, mourns the loss of eleven tons of the finest hashish.

❺ I FONI TU ARGILE
STELLAKIS PERPINIADIS from REMBETIKA – SONGS OF THE GREEK UNDERGROUND 1925–1947

"The voice of the *narghile*", recorded in 1935 using a real hookah, evokes the sorrow and relief of an imprisoned *mangas*.

❻ EMAI ORFANOS APO PAIDHI
NIKI TRAMBA, ROSS DALY & LABYRINTH from CAFÉ AMAN

Star vocalist of the Rembetiko revival Niki Tramba describes with personal metaphors the fate of the Greeks uprooted from Asia Minor.

❼ BAYAT (TRADITIONAL ARRANGEMENT) BRATSCH
from NOMADES EN VOL

French lovers of the genre, who even enchant Greek aficionados with their skilful playing.

❽ YEDIKULE KUDSI ERGUNER ENSEMBLE
from ENSEMBLE REMBETIKO FROM ISTANBUL

What a great idea: Greek and Turkish musicians have come together in this band to pay respect to the roots of the genre, which lay in Asia Minor from where the Greek population had to flee in 1922.

❾ O PINOKLIS CAFÉ AMAN AMERICA ORCHESTRA
from GREEK-AMERICAN SONGS REVISED AND REVISITED

Another great idea: a Greek producer digs into material recorded during the 1920s and 30s in the US, with a special focus on the then-used language of Gringlish.

❿ ZEYBEKIKO DIONYSSIS SAVOPOULOS
from THE DIASPORA OF REMBETIKO

Famous rock singer who has expressed through his music the struggles and dreams of the generation of 1968, singing with two parallel mirrored voices as if one were broken.

Jean Trouillet

The Replacements

Louder, catchier, and drunker than most, the 'Mats were in some ways the most popular band that never was – always on the verge of a breakthrough or falling apart.

❶ LEFT OF THE DIAL from TIM

A gorgeous rocker that masterfully evokes late nights, lonely highways, and missed connections – without actually saying much about any of them at all.

❷ WE'RE COMING OUT from LET IT BE

Running the gamut from hardcore thrash to nightclub swing, the 'Mats get in your face while hopped up on something.

❸ JOHNNY'S GONNA DIE from SORRY MA, FORGOT TO TAKE OUT THE TRASH

Many remember their late-career tribute to patron saint Alex Chilton; fewer this snot-nosed thumb-in-the-eye to Johnny Thunders.

❹ GO from STINK!

Compared with the rest of this short, revved up and thrashy EP, it sounds positively spaced out and draggy. But some of the melodic and echoey touches tell you there's a pop band waiting to break free.

❺ COLOR ME IMPRESSED from HOOTENANNY

Westerberg nails the social scene of the time; just note his sneer of the title line or, better yet, the double-edged plea "Can you stand me on my feet?"

❻ LITTLE MASCARA from TIM

Three minutes of perfect power pop.

❼ UNSATISFIED from LET IT BE

A soaring, searing statement with Westerberg at his emotional peak; the best thing the band ever did.

❽ WITHIN YOUR REACH from HOOTENANNY

Westerberg points the way to a future path with an intensely personal confession on which he plays all the instruments; if you didn't know better, you could almost hear a Cars tune in there somewhere.

❾ SIXTEEN BLUE from LET IT BE

Growing up never seemed harder; a song never seemed prettier.

❿ CAN'T HARDLY WAIT from PLEASED TO MEET ME

If you're going to spit and polish your sound, you may as well throw some horns in there for good measure.

Andrew Rosenberg

Jonathan Richman

Having started out as not only the Velvet Underground's most obsessive fan, but also, with the Modern Lovers, their greatest emulator, Jonathan Richman soon turned both more whimsical and more emotionally revealing. He continues to release excellent albums, and puts on a great live show.

❶ MONOLOGUE ABOUT BERMUDA from HAVING A PARTY WITH JONATHAN RICHMAN
The perfect encapsulation of the live Richman experience, this 1991concert recording entertainingly describes the musical and personal growth of the Modern Lovers.

❷ VELVET UNDERGROUND from I, JONATHAN
In which the mature Jonathan reflects on his youthful obsession, and tackles the issue of "How in the world were they making that sound?" with a brief rendition of "Sister Ray".

❸ I WAS DANCING IN THE LESBIAN BAR from I, JONATHAN
A hymn to the sheer joy of being – and dancing – in the right place at the right time, given a lovely twist by the technique of repeating crucial lines at high speed.

❹ ROADRUNNER (ONCE) from ROCK'N'ROLL WITH THE MODERN LOVERS (REISSUE)
Subtler than the punk thrash on the first Modern Lovers album, this glorious celebration of driving "with the radio on" gave Jonathan an unexpected chart hit in the UK.

❺ PABLO PICASSO from THE MODERN LOVERS
A bona fide punk classic – "Girls would turn the colour of an avocado/When he would drive down the street in his El Dorado/Pablo Picasso never got called an asshole." Producer John Cale even recorded his own cover version.

❻ I'M STRAIGHT from THE MODERN LOVERS
Few indeed were the rock musicians in 1972 who could so unabashedly beg the girl of their dreams to leave "Hippy Johnny" because he's always stoned, and let the "straight" Jonathan take his place.

❼ GIRL FRIEND from THE MODERN LOVERS
Tiring of his lonely walks through the Museum of Fine Arts in Boston, young Jonathan yearns instead for a G-I-R-L-F-R-E-N.

❽ THE NEIGHBORS from JONATHAN GOES COUNTRY
One of the great songs about serious adult relationships, even if Jonathan himself sounds remarkably truculent.

❾ YOU'RE CRAZY FOR TAKING THE BUS from JONATHAN GOES COUNTRY
Greyhound buses never sounded so appealing as in this highlight from Jonathan's successful 1990 foray into the world of rhinestones and cowboy boots.

❿ HEY THERE LITTLE INSECT from JONATHAN RICHMAN AND THE MODERN LOVERS
Jonathan's at his most child-like and innocent, but you can't help suspecting that if the little insect does come down to fool around, it may come to a sticky end.

Greg Ward

Riffs

The Stranglers said it best when they invited a "stranger from another planet" to just strap on his guitar and "play some rock'n'roll" (Get A Grip On Yourself). This list celebrates the riff – the simple yet magic combination of chords and rhythm that brings the guts, sweat and blood to rock music. Solos are for wimps!

❶ BAD TO THE BONE GEORGE THOROGOOD AND THE DESTROYERS from 30 YEARS OF ROCK
With this as your soundtrack, you could kick open the saloon door, stride up to the bar and order a sarsaparilla like Bob Hope in *Paleface*, and no man would dare bat an eyelid.

❷ WILD THING THE TROGGS from THE GREATEST HITS
The most powerful application of three chords known to man. Play air guitar to this by all means, just don't try to do a sexy dance.

❸ MY GENERATION THE WHO from MY GENERATION
"Hope I die before I get old", they sang. Is it bad taste to say "Two down, and two to go"?

❹ REBEL REBEL DAVID BOWIE from DIAMOND DOGS
Mick Ronson was the best rock'n'roll guitar-slinger that the old dame ever worked with, and this is the best riff he ever produced.

❺ SMELLS LIKE TEEN SPIRIT NIRVANA from NEVERMIND
The tune that took over from Deep Purple's "Smoke On The Water" as the one most despised by guitar-shop employees.

⑥ JUMPING JACK FLASH
THE ROLLING STONES from **40 LICKS**

Rule #1: Don't try to copy Keef's guitar licks. They don't call him "The Human Riff" for nothing, and his skills will leave yours crying in the dust. Rule #2: If you must, then you'll need to re-tune your guitar. Look it up on the Internet.

⑦ SHOULD I STAY OR SHOULD I GO? THE CLASH from
THE ESSENTIAL

Mick and Joe made this one with spare parts from 1960s pop hits, vintage R&B and a degree of cheek unmatched in the annals of pop.

⑧ SCHOOL'S OUT ALICE COOPER from THE DEFINITIVE

Magnificently snotty stuff from a band who were a parent's worst nightmare back in the innocent days of the 1970s.

⑨ OH PRETTY WOMAN ROY ORBISON
from ALL TIME GREATEST HITS

It's not hard to copy Roy's deceptively easy walking bassline once or twice, but it takes skill and stamina to keep it up all the way through the song.

⑩ I WANNA BE YOUR DOG THE STOOGES
from THE STOOGES

This riff descended into Ron Asheton through a haze of drugs and exploded in his guitar-playing fingers with a burst of white-hot inspiration.

Al Spicer

Riot Grrrl

While the indie boys had Seattle grunge, the girls had Riot Grrrl – a venomous explosion of feminist fury, punky guitars, tangled hair, big boots and babydoll dresses. These sisters clawed their way into the media spotlight, but after being all the alternative rage for a brief interlude in the early 1990s, the grrrowling faded. Sleater-Kinney and Le Tigre are among the few still carrying the torch.

① TEENAGE WHORE HOLE
from PRETTY ON THE INSIDE

Never knowingly understated, former teen stripper Courtney Love lays bare her muddled psyche in this insolent adolescent tirade.

② REBEL GIRL BIKINI KILL from PUSSY WHIPPED

A primal howl of a record from America's undisputed queens of Riot Grrrl, with toxic screeching from Kathleen Hannah.

③ PRETEND WE'RE DEAD L7 from BRICKS ARE HEAVY

The poppiest and most famous Grrrl song, this entered the UK Top 20 (helped along by Donita Sparks' on-stage antics).

④ HER JAZZ HUGGY BEAR
from TAKING THE ROUGH WITH THE SMOOCH

As spiky as it is earnest, this is punked-up revolutionary-preaching from Britain's foremost Riot Grrrl band.

⑤ BRUISE VIOLET BABES IN TOYLAND
from FONTANELLE

On their accomplished third album, chief Babe Kat Bjelland ear-bashes a former bandmate with her alternately sweet and snarly vocals.

⑥ THE DAY I WENT AWAY SLEATER-KINNEY
from SLEATER-KINNEY

Tight, harmonious garage-punk reigns on the Olympia, Washington, trio's debut LP.

Ed Wright/Claire Fogg

Rivers

Rivers have few peers as a rich source of pop song imagery… though things may not always be what they seem…

① CRY ME A RIVER JULIE LONDON from THE BEST OF JULIE

See what I mean? Water under the bridge! One great version among many.

② BIG RIVER JOHNNY CASH from THE MAN IN BLACK

This one's really about a woman. Johnny doesn't say how big she was, but apparently she loved "Big River" more than him.

③ GREEN RIVER CREEDENCE CLEARWATER REVIVAL from
GREEN RIVER

These California city boys did nostalgia for imagined roots far better than many more authentic bands.

④ BLACK RIVER FALLS CATHAL COUGHLAN from BLACK
RIVER FALLS

Typically opaque but spookily compelling number from the underrated former lead singer of Microdisney. Check him out!

⑤ RIVER BOY WILLIE NELSON from THE COMPLETE LIBERTY
RECORDINGS 1962–1964

An evocative early song about fishin' and longin' from the "good for nothin' River Boy". Yep, this one's actually about a girl.

❻ RIVER MAN NICK DRAKE from WAY TO BLUE
A suitably flowing tune by the tragic singer-song-writer, who achieved posthumous cult fame. Like the possible reasons for his death, the song is wide open to interpretation.

❼ RIVER DEEP, MOUNTAIN HIGH IKE AND TINA TURNER
from PROUD MARY: THE BEST OF IKE & TINA TURNER
Pees from a great height over other covers by Eric Burden, Deep Purple, Neil Diamond and… The Shadows.

❽ MANY RIVERS TO CROSS JIMMY CLIFF
from THE MESSENGER
The definitive original of a much-covered classic, Cliff's homesick, lonely lament resonates with washed-up losers everywhere. Always.

❾ RIVERS OF BABYLON THE MELODIANS from THE BEST OF
The most lovely of Jamaican songs, later perverted into 1970s disco by the German Caribbeans of Boney M.

❿ THE RIVER BRUCE SPRINGSTEEN from THE RIVER
The river in question is just a muddy backdrop to this sorry tale of teenage pregnancy, economic downturn and lurve gone cold.

Jon Lusk

Smokey Robinson

Motown's most consistent hit writer penned classics for The Temptations, Marvin Gaye and many others. But he saved his very finest songs for The Miracles.

❶ SHOP AROUND from HI, WE'RE THE MIRACLES
Leading The Miracles, Smokey's pumping 1960 tune about not going for the first girl who puts out provided Motown with its first national hit.

❷ YOU'VE REALLY GOT A HOLD ON ME from ANTHOLOGY
It's 1962 and this silky love ballad tops the R&B charts and sits at #2 in the pop charts. The master at work.

❸ MICKEY'S MONKEY from ANTHOLOGY
Remember the scene in *Mean Streets* where De Niro dances around Harvey Keitel's Cadillac to MM? The Miracles could cut dance tunes to match the best of them.

❹ GOING TO A GO-GO from GOING TO A GO-GO
Smokey's celebration of dancing remains one of the most infectious party tunes ever. Drop the needle and hit the dancefloor.

❺ THE TRACKS OF MY TEARS
from GOING TO A GO-GO
Marv Tarplin's guitar lines are as poetic as the lyrics Smokey sings. Pop music doesn't get any more divine.

❻ OOO BABY BABY from GOING TO A GO-GO
This is the Motown soul ballad at its zenith and Smokey at his most silky: just listen to those voices harmonize and wrap around his high tenor.

❼ I SECOND THAT EMOTION from ANTHOLOGY
"If you feel like loving me/If you got the notion/I second that emotion." No wonder Dylan called him America's greatest living poet.

❽ THE TEARS OF A CLOWN
from THE TEARS OF A CLOWN
Co-written with Stevie Wonder in 1966. Smokey sings sad while James Jamerson and The Funk Brothers keep the music pulsing.

❾ CRUISING from WHERE THERE'S SMOKE…
Smokey's so laid-back here he's near horizontal. Gorgeous bedroom ballad that hit #4 in the pop and R&B charts in the US.

❿ BEING WITH YOU from BEING WITH YOU
A hymn to love from the Detroit love god. Perfect soundtrack for a relaxed evening with your other half.

Garth Cartwright

Rocksteady

During this period in between ska and reggae (the late 1960s) the beat slowed down, vocals made a comeback and not (quite) all the good stuff was produced by Duke Reid.

❶ BA BA BOOM THE JAMAICANS from DUKE REID'S TREASURE CHEST
Something of a rock steady theme song, as the vocal trio celebrate the dance over muted horns and a crisp, percolating bass.

❷ FEEL LIKE JUMPING
MARCIA GRIFFITHS from FEEL LIKE JUMPING
Produced by Coxsone at Studio One, the rhythm for this glorious workout was later used for The Maytals' "54-46 That's My Number".

❸ LOVING PAUPER DOBBY DOBSON from DUKE REID'S TREASURE CHEST
A genuine rock steady classic, as the deeply soulful

Dobson croons a tale of love that may be poor but is certainly true.

❹ ILYA KURYAKIN IKE BENNETT & THE CRYSTALITES from FEEL LIKE JUMPING

Derrick Harriot's studio band, in an organ-led tribute to one of the Men from U.N.C.L.E.

❺ THE TIDE IS HIGH THE PARAGONS
from DUKE REID'S TREASURE CHEST

A hit for Blondie and then the Sugarbabes, this John Holt-led trio's original remains the one they will always be judged against.

❻ I'LL GET ALONG WITHOUT YOU NOW THE MELODIANS from DUKE REID'S TREASURE CHEST

A brilliant example of the Impressions-ish Jamaican three-part harmonizing as one of the style's greatest groups effortlessly swaps the lead with each other and background trumpet.

❼ RANGLIN ON BOND STREET ERNEST RANGLIN & TOMMY MCCOOK from DUKE REID'S TREASURE CHEST

McCook's sax and Ranglin's guitar languidly chase each other around a beat that sustains itself on some wonderful Hammond organ riffs.

❽ RIVERS OF BABYLON THE MELODIANS
from THE HARDER THEY COME

Rasta-sympathizing Melodians had to convince producer Leslie Kong this was a Christian song before he'd record it, then radio banned it for the "Oh Fari" chorus.

❾ I'M STILL IN LOVE WITH YOU
ALTON ELLIS from SINGS ROCK & SOUL

This original version of the tune that, after several reincarnations – including a radio jingle – became the Althea & Donna "Uptown Top Ranking" hit, remains a rock steady gem.

❿ PRETTY LOOKS ISN'T ALL THE HEPTONES from ON TOP

A much sampled and re-used bassline, holds up a fabulous, poignant harmony performance from Studio One's top vocal trio.

Lloyd Bradley

Rockabilly

It's 1950s America: Eisenhower is president, Reds hide under beds, all is normal… Until a greasy hillbilly called Elvis seduces the youth with his hopped-up mix of country and blues: rockabilly.

❶ THAT'S ALRIGHT MAMA ELVIS PRESLEY
from THE SUN SESSIONS

Elvis, Scotty and Bill start messing around with an Arthur Crudup blues. The world begins to shake, civilization collapses.

❷ DIXIE FRIED CARL PERKINS
from ORIGINAL SUN GREATEST HITS

Carl celebrates a gone cat who pulls razors "but he aint shavin'". Primal rockabilly from the genre's poet laureate.

❸ WHOLE LOTTA SHAKIN' GOIN' ON JERRY LEE LEWIS
from 18 ORIGINAL SUN GREATEST HITS

"Shake baby, shake", commands the Killer over frantic, manic piano. Who would dare disagree?

❹ BE BOP A LULA GENE VINCENT
from CAPITOL COLLECTORS SERIES

Gene purrs the vocal; Cliff Gallup pulls out a sexy, menacing solo. John Lennon heard this and knew destiny lay in such a sound.

❺ TWENTY FLIGHT ROCK EDDIE COCHRAN
from LEGENDARY MASTERS

Fast, funny and hip, Eddie was a boy genius with hot guitar. Paul McCartney sang this to Lennon on their first meeting.

❻ THAT'LL BE THE DAY BUDDY HOLLY
from 20 GOLDEN GREATS

Holly's hiccuping vocal and ripping guitar solos sounded a call to teenage arms, and the kids took this to #1 on the US charts in 1957.

❼ FUJIYAMA MAMA WANDA JACKSON
from ROCKIN' WITH WANDA

In the 1950s Wanda was the toughest white chick singing and Fujiyama Mama continues to detonate. A girl so gonzo even Elvis was in awe.

❽ TRAIN KEPT A ROLLIN'
JOHNNY BURNETTE TRIO from TRAIN KEPT A ROLLIN'

Mad, distorted music that inspired many a 1960s guitar hero. Go, cat, go!

❾ SUSIE-Q DALE HAWKINS
from ROCK'N'ROLL TORNADO

Lusty rockabilly anthem from the Louisiana wildman. The guitar solo from a teenage James Burton chewed up the ears of all who heard it.

❿ RUNAWAY BOYS THE STRAY CATS
from THE STRAY CATS

The 1980s revivalists debuted with this roaring ode to a place "that the cops don't know". What's the address?

Garth Cartwright

Jimmie Rodgers

"The Singing Brakeman" was discovered by producer talent scout Ralph Peer in 1927 at the same auditions as The Carter Family in Bristol on the Tennessee–Virginia border. One of American music's first superstars and celebrated as "the father of country music", Rodgers died aged 35 of TB in 1932. All selections appear on Rounder's magnificent First Sessions which gathers Rodgers' complete recordings.

❶ SLEEP, BABY, SLEEP
Rodgers' initial recording for Peer is not one of his best but stands as the recording where so much American music flowed from.

❷ BLUE YODEL ALSO KNOWN AS T FOR TEXAS
The song that established Rodgers as a huge star, this features his glorious yodel.

❸ IN THE JAILHOUSE NOW
Raucous celebration of having too much of a good time so ending up locked up.

❹ MISS THE MISSISSIPPI AND YOU
Gorgeous love song finds Jimmie on the road and missing his home and sweetheart.

❺ MY ROUGH AND ROWDY WAYS
Jimmie liked to play up the wild side of life and this song celebrates such.

❻ FRANKIE AND JOHNNY
Fabulous interpretation of the early blues song about Frankie shooting her lover 'cos "he done her wrong".

❼ MY GOOD GAL'S GONE-BLUES
Rodgers was as much a blues as country artist and this cut pairs him with the rockin' Louisville Jug Band.

❽ PISTOL PACKIN' PAPA
And you thought the likes of Tupac were the first to invent a hard man, gun slinging persona?

❾ WHIPPIN' THAT OLD T.B.
Instead within a year of recording the T.B. had whipped Rodgers. Features an unearthly blues fiddle solo by Clayton McMichen.

❿ JIMMIE RODGERS LAST BLUE YODEL
Recorded just days before he died, this is not only his last Blue Yodel but literally his last breath.

Garth Cartwright

Keith Richards
In the mood

Over more than forty years as a professional guitar slinger, Richards has remained remarkably true to the music that originally inspired him. All ten of his picks here were recorded before The Rolling Stones even formed.

❶ PREACHIN' BLUES (UP JUMPED THE DEVIL) ROBERT JOHNSON from KING OF THE DELTA BLUES

❷ ROLLIN' STONE MUDDY WATERS from FEEL LIKE GOIN' HOME

❸ THE MIDNIGHT SPECIAL LEADBELLY from THE DEFINITIVE LEADBELLY

❹ GOOD GOLLY MISS MOLLY LITTLE RICHARD from HIS GREATEST RECORDINGS

❺ YOU WIN AGAIN HANK WILLIAMS from THE COMPLETE COLLECTION

❻ MOANIN' AT MIDNIGHT HOWLIN' WOLF from HOWLIN WOLF RIDES AGAIN

❼ EVERYDAY I HAVE THE BLUES BB KING from THE VINTAGE YEARS

❽ I'M IN THE MOOD JOHN LEE HOOKER from THE LEGENDARY MODERN RECORDINGS

❾ TALKIN' TO YOUR MAMA BLIND WILLIE MCTELL from THE DEFINITIVE BLIND WILLIE MCTELL

❿ MARDI GRAS IN NEW ORLEANS PROFESSOR LONGHAIR & HIS SHUFFLING HUNGARIANS from AN INTRODUCTION TO PROFESSOR LONGHAIR

The Rolling Stones

Of course we're all delighted to find The Rolling Stones still chugging away into the 21st century, but there's no denying that the (very strong) case for seeing them as the greatest rock'n'roll band of all time rests entirely on their first ten years together, up to 1972.

❶ NOT FADE AWAY from THE ROLLING STONES
The sheer energy of this Buddy Holly song made it stand out among the many cover versions on the Stones' first album in 1964, before Jagger and Richards had got into their stride as songwriters.

❷ (I CAN'T GET NO) SATISFACTION from HOT ROCKS
Keef's archetypal riff gave the Stones their crucial breakthrough hit in the US in 1965.

❸ PAINT IT, BLACK from HOT ROCKS
The creative stimulus of their rivalry with The Beatles spurred the Stones to this 1966 gem.

❹ STREET FIGHTING MAN from BEGGARS BANQUET
In retrospect, LSE graduate Jagger as socialist revolutionary no longer rings quite true, but in the heady days of 1968 anything seemed possible.

❺ PRODIGAL SON from BEGGARS BANQUET
It was the Stones' love of the blues that got them started in the first place; their 1968 rendition of the Rev. Robert Wilkins "That's No Way To Get Along" remains one of their finest moments.

❻ GIMME SHELTER from LET IT BLEED
The Stones' most perfectly realized album found them flirting with darkness, murder and mayhem; on its most atmospheric track, Keef's riffing is positively demonic.

❼ YOU CAN'T ALWAYS GET WHAT YOU WANT
from LET IT BLEED
Kicking off with a children's choir, this 1969 classic is a magnificent anthem to negativity.

❽ HONKY TONK WOMEN from HOT ROCKS
The Stones were at their peak in 1969: at the same time as turning out complex albums of genuine depth and subtlety, they were still releasing perfect singles like this.

❾ BROWN SUGAR from STICKY FINGERS
The last of the truly great Rolling Stones singles one-dimensional, sure, but majestic in its simplicity.

❿ HAPPY from EXILE ON MAIN STREET
While it's hard to pick out stand-out tracks from the quintessential Stones album, "Happy" represents Keith at his definitive best.

Greg Ward

Route 66

Jazz pianist Bobby Troop wrote the song "(Get Your Kicks On) Route 66" while on the road, arriving in LA with a tune celebrating the highway that brought everyone from dustbowl migrants to Chicago mobsters to California. Troop's song quickly became a standard, fuelling much of the mythology behind Americana.

❶ NAT KING COLE
The first to record "Route 66". His version, leading on piano, is jazzy, light, a hipster's delight.

❷ ANITA O'DAY
Anita's a jazz singer but a tough, sassy one and the kicks she suggests getting are those best not mentioned in polite company.

❸ CHARLES BROWN
The smoothest blues singer going also took the song for a spin.

❹ CHUCK BERRY
More than any other song, "Route 66" probably showed Chuck how to write detailed, witty songs. He rocks up Troop's tune until it sounds like a Berry original.

❺ THE ROLLING STONES
A stomping take on their 1964 debut album suggested the Stones saw "Route 66" as the highway that lead to all kinds of American kicks.

❻ THEM
A young Van Morrison ripped through "Route 66" on Them's debut album. Has any singer ever sounded hungrier to get on that highway?

❼ ASLEEP AT THE WHEEL
On *Wheelin' And Dealin'* the Western swing band cut a roaring version, accompanied by several veteran musicians from Bob Wills' Texas Playboys. Smokin'!

❽ MARCIA BALL
Ball's a classy blues pianist and singer who lives on the road. Listen to her name those towns and realize she knows them all too well.

Garth Cartwright

Geoff Travis's
Rough Inspirations

Geoff Travis opened the Rough Trade shop in London's Notting Hill in 1976, and it swiftly became the place for punk records on tiny labels not stocked by the mainstream stores, and hard-to-find American imports. Two years later, Travis launched the Rough Trade label, whose signings included Stiff Little Fingers, Scritti Politti and The Smiths. The label went under in 1991 but was reborn in 2000 to unleash such bands as The Libertines, The Strokes and Belle & Sebastian. Or as Travis himself puts it: "We are an independent label trying to make some records that will stand the test of time and hopefully hold a candle to the type of music you see on my playlist."

❶ **BEECHWOOD 4-5789**
THE MARVELETTES from GREATEST HITS
Groove and sass, wonderful playing and city sophistication wrapped up in silver paper.

❷ **LET'S GET MARRIED** AL GREEN from GREATEST HITS
When Al sings "Let's get married … might as well", Camus finds an existentialist rival of the first order.

❸ **BUILDING STEAM FROM A GRAIN OF SALT** DJ SHADOW from ENTRODUCING
How to rearrange all the musical debris of the last forty years into a brand new weave. A bit like Portobello Market on a Friday morning, you always discover something new.

❹ **SPIRIT IN THE DARK**
ARETHA FRANKLIN from SPIRIT IN THE DARK
Gospel translated through sublime pop.

❺ **FLESH OF MY SKIN**
KEITH HUDSON from FLESH OF MY SKIN
Jamaican sorcery. A bit like the eccentric carnival barker with a profound heart sitting at the end of the alley, gently haranguing any stray.

❻ **HYPOCRITE** THE HEPTONES from 22 GOLDEN GREATS
If Leroy Sibbles had of been born in Detroit we would be praising him just like Smokey or David Ruffin.

❼ **ALFIEB** ROBERT WYATT from ROCK BOTTOM
Interesting how a partnership sustained over a lifetime can enrich the work: good on you, Alfie.

❽ **SUGAR HICCUP** COCTEAU TWINS from LULLABIES TO VIOLAINE
Elizabeth Fraser deserves to be knighted, so says Antony of the Johnsons. He should know.

❾ **MY SHADOW IS A MONDAY** LAVENDER DIAMOND from FIRST ALBUM
Balm for the cynical soul, love can ward off a great deal of evil. A new artist from LA by way of Tennessee.

❿ **JUST LIKE HONEY**
THE JESUS AND MARY CHAIN from PSYCHOCANDY
My history – and a thrilling collision of melody and electricity.

Roxy Music

The definitive art-rock group, whose work contained everything from 1950s rock to the Velvets to Can to the poetry of John Donne, the wit of Dorothy Parker and the romantic genius of Humphrey Bogart. The definitive line-up – Bryan Ferry, Brian Eno, Phil Manzanera, Andy Mackay and Paul Thompson – only lasted two albums. But the band were reinvented as masters of elevator smooch music, while Ferry established an alternate career as lounge lizard, pop vampire and tuxedoed crooner.

❶ **MOTHER OF PEARL** from STRANDED
Ferry's finest lyric, Roxy's most versatile song – at times, too noisy for its own good, at others, inducing a trance-like state – this is the number where Ferry really does sound as if he's about to sink his teeth into your neck.

❷ **IN EVERY DREAM HOME A HEARTACHE**
from FOR YOUR PLEASURE
Pre-dating – and anticipating – both Talking Heads'

Phil Manzanera's
Latin list

"People tend to need a bit of help in the area of Latin music", says Roxy Music guitarist PHIL MANZANERA, who grew up in pre-Castro Cuba in the 1950s. "So, given my background, here's my alternative Latin playlist." He even plays on a couple of 'em.

❶ YOLANDA PABLO MILANES from CLASICOS DE CUBA

❷ PLAYA GIRON SILVIO RODRIGUEZ from CUBA CLASSICS 1 – CANCIONES URGENTES

❸ GUITARRA Y VOZ JORJE DREXLER from ECO

❹ J19 NOVIEMBRE CARLOS VIVES from VARIOUS SONGS OF CARLOS VIVES

❺ AMANECIO OTRA VEZ ANA BELEN Y CHAVELA VARGAS

❻ LA VACUNA ORISHAS from EL KILO

❼ CUCURRUCUCU CAETANO VELOSO from THE BEST OF CAETANO VELOSO

❽ HASTA SIEMPRE 801 LATINO from 801 LATINO

❾ PARA TI NENGON CORONCHO from CORONCHO

❿ CHAN CHAN BUENA VISTA SOCIAL CLUB from BUENA VISTA SOCIAL CLUB

---

bleak vision "Once In A Lifetime" and the Police's silly "Be My Girl", this is Roxy's most ambitious song.

❸ BEAUTY QUEEN from FOR YOUR PLEASURE
When Roxy started, no one knew quite how to take Ferry's vocals – was he serious or what? Here he deploys every trick, sounding at times grandiose, indecipherable, cynical and impassioned.

❹ IF THERE IS SOMETHING? from ROXY MUSIC
As strange a song as Roxy ever cut – with the possible exception of Bitters End, the closer on the same album.

❺ THE THRILL OF IT ALL FROM COUNTRY LIFE
There are those who say that Duran Duran made a whole career out of rewriting this haunting anthem.

❻ MORE THAN THIS from AVALON
Quiet, lavish, efficient, heartfelt, chilling – the ultimate late Roxy performance, such a great song that even Bill Murray's karaoke performance couldn't destroy it in *Lost In Translation*.

❼ THESE FOOLISH THINGS from THESE FOOLISH THINGS
The first – and greatest – evidence that Ferry wasn't joking about his ambition to become a white tuxedoed nightclub singer.

❽ OH YEAH from FLESH AND BLOOD
This is a subtly played, brilliantly sung, ode to lost love, in which the lyrics move with startling economy – an

expression in her eyes is all it takes to surprise and enchant the narrator. A master class in radio-friendly romantic pop.

❾ BOTH ENDS BURNING from SIREN
The finest fruit of Roxy's brief disco phase, which also gave us the glory that is "Love Is The Drug".

❿ DO THE STRAND from FOR YOUR PLEASURE
A tribute to a dance craze's ability to distract us from mash potato schmaltz, and to Roxy's ability to give a work of pure satire such genuine power. The tumbling piano interlude is one of the song's underrated highlights.

Paul Simpson

Rick Rubin

"Reduced by Rick Rubin" read the original Def Jam production credits and Rubin's minimalist style has reinvented rap, rock and country. Rubin dropped out of law school to set up Def Jam Records and follow his very individual instincts as a producer. Instantly successful, he's taken hip-hop into the mainstream, promoted thrash metal, resurrected Johnny Cash and made the Red Hot Chili Peppers superstars. He's done his share of forgettable money jobs (Mick Jagger, Melanie C, The Cult) yet rarely rests on his laurels...

❶ I NEED A BEAT LL COOL J from RADIO

Def Jam's debut finds 14-year old James Smith busting rhymes over a propulsive drum machine and furious scratching.

❷ RHYMING & STEALING THE BEASTIE BOYS from LICENSED TO ILL

Self-proclaimed metal head Rubin employed a Black Sabbath guitar riff and Led Zep's Levee Breaks drum patterns for rap's 3 Stooges to shout insults at everyone within earshot.

❸ ROCK THE BELLS LL COOL J from RADIO

One of hip-hop's defining singles: LL furiously rhymes over Rubin's raw, minimalist production so unleashing a detonation of sound.

❹ WALK THIS WAY RUN-DMC from RAISING HELL

Rubin calculated he could sell black rappers to white kids if he wrapped them in heavy guitars. In doing so he made Run-DMC stars, invented rock-rap and breathed life into Aerosmith's moribund stadium rock.

❺ CROSS YOUR HEART THE RED DEVILS from KING, KING

Rubin's produced a lot of rock, much of it tending towards the extreme end of thrash metal, but this offering from a tough white blues band is up there with his best.

❻ UNDER THE BRIDGE THE RED HOT CHILLI PEPPERS from BLOOD SUGAR SEX MAGIC

Rubin clears the clutter so freeing punk funk veterans to create a subdued homage to addiction and LA.

❼ THE BEAST IN ME JOHNNY CASH from AMERICAN RECORDINGS

Brooding Nick Lowe song is captured by Rubin as just voice and guitar. This marked Cash's artistic resurrection.

❽ BY THE WAY THE RED HOT CHILLI PEPPERS from BY THE WAY

Huge, rushing sound with a Beatlesque chorus finds Rubin pushing the Chilli Peppers into ever more dynamic territory.

❾ HURT JOHNNY CASH from AMERICAN IV

The Nine Inch Nails smack tune remoulded by Rubin as the most brooding and autobiographical ballad Cash ever sang.

❿ OH MARY NEIL DIAMOND from 12 SONGS

Rubin strips Diamond of strings so forcing him to reach into his huge arsenal of pop hooks and thus delivering the moody, broody Neil of legend.

Garth Cartwright

Run-DMC

The self-appointed "Kings from Queens" reinvented New York hip-hop with their minimalist sound and sportswear look.

❶ IT'S LIKE THAT from RUN-DMC

Existential statement about how things are in Reagan's America. Message: they ain't gonna change so get used to it.

❷ SUCKER MCS from RUN-DMC

Back in 1983 no one shouted louder or boasted harder than Run and DMC.

❸ HARD TIMES from RUN-DMC

Rhyming over a blunt drum machine, the duo unleashed the new sound of young black America.

❹ CAN YOU ROCK IT LIKE THIS from KINGS OF ROCK

Fame and all its illicit fruit celebrated over big beats and power chords.

❺ MY ADIDAS from RAISING HELL

Product placement? Yeah. But if only all ads cut so fresh and hard.

❻ WALK THIS WAY from RAISING HELL

Producer Rick Rubin reinvents rap and rehabilitates Aerosmith. Everyone involved makes millions.

❼ IS IT LIVE from RAISING HELL

Furious rhyming, wild percussion and raw scratching.

❽ IT'S TRICKY from RAISING HELL

"It's tricky to rock a rhyme/To rock a rhyme/That's right on time."

❾ MARY MARY from TOUGHER THAN LEATHER

The Monkees' tune gets a hip-hop makeover. Ridiculous? Sure. But fun.

Garth Cartwright

Todd Rundgren

Rundgren is a polymath genius, at his best when he's at his most succinct, most tuneful and most vulnerable in affairs of the heart. You want adult pop? This is how it's done

❶ OPEN MY EYES from NAZZ

Exhilarating 1968 Anglophile rocker from his days in The Nazz, a Philadelphia power quartet.

❷ I SAW THE LIGHT from SOMETHING/ANYTHING?

A neat Carole King pastiche and a great song about the belated recognition of love.

❸ HELLO IT'S ME from SOMETHING/ANYTHING?

A tender song about trying not to trample on hurt feelings in an affair that won't last.

❹ CAN WE STILL BE FRIENDS?
from SOMETHING/ANYTHING?

A strained relationship comes to a good end.

❺ IT WOULDN'T HAVE MADE ANY DIFFERENCE from SOMETHING/ANYTHING?

Amazing the bite a bit of bitterness can add. Defiance in the face of getting dumped.

❻ LOVE IS THE ANSWER
from OOPS! WRONG PLANET

Unusually restrained – and touchingly soulful – universal truth from the misbegotten Utopia.

❼ A DREAM GOES ON FOREVER from TODD

The military hint and "life's greatest tragedy" puts a new, wider slant on loved and lost.

❽ BE NICE TO ME
from THE BALLAD OF TODD RUNDGREN

Seeking short-term escape from the long-term expectations of a relationship.

❾ MARLENE from SOMETHING/ANYTHING?

"I'm in trouble if your folks get mean…" A jaunty but (fairly) innocent infatuation with a 17-year-old.

❿ TINY DEMONS from I SAW THE LIGHT (BEST OF)

"They won't ever leave, but they won't show their faces to me…" Todd on insecurities. A 1981 gem (from the *Healing* sessions) but relegated to a B-side, for goodness sake.

Ian Cranna

S

Salsa

You can't pin salsa down to one style or dance or rhythm, so even these brilliant dance tracks can't do justice to a continent and some's worth of dazzling music. Wherever you stand in the Latin world, you'll hear a very different playlist.

❶ LA NOCHE JOE ARROYO from 32 CAÑONAZOS
All the ingredients of Arroyo's *caribeño* sound: lilting Colombian–Caribbean salsa, shot through with trumpets and topped by his unmistakeably, earthy, rhythmic voice.

❷ DECISIONES RUBEN BLADES from BUSCANDO AMÉRICA
The revolutionary singer-songwriter who turned salsa inside out with his social-realist lyrics never abandoned the dancers. This song broke every rule, weaving doo-wop and Cuban *son* with reggae and New York salsa.

❸ DECARGA CACHAO CACHAO from CACHAO MASTER SESSIONS VOL 1
The Latin world's greatest double-bass player leads a funky jam (*descarga*) with a glorious band of legendary soloists, produced by Hollywood's Andy Garcia.

❹ CALLE LUNA, CALLE SOL WILLIE COLON & HECTOR LAVOE from LA EXPERIENCIA
The sheer brilliance of these 20-something Nuyoricans, in 1973, is still astonishing. Role models for two generations of salsa musicians, Colon and Blades shine in this song of Old San Juan: Lavoe's fabulously emotive vocals, Colon's raw trombone, and the sparkiest percussionists in town.

❺ DIOSA DEL RITMO CELIA CRUZ & FANIA ALL STARS from CELIA CRUZ WITH FANIA ALL STARS
The irrepressible, eternal voice of La Reina, the Queen of Salsa, backed by the greatest American salsa band ever. This is packed with solos, and rocks to Cuban–American rhythms.

❻ ESENCIA DIEGO GALE from ESENCIA LATINA
Bright, brassy, youthful Colombian salsa, led by the reckless timbales player, Diego Gale.

❼ CHOCO'S GUAJIRA RUBEN GONZALEZ & IBRAHIM FERRER from CHANCHULLO
Elegant Cuban *guajira* from the Buena Vista dream team, recreating a classic with young conga wizard, Anga Diaz, and *tres* player, Papi Oviedo. Gonzalez's effortlessly rhythmic piano and Ferrer's yearning vocals are pure bliss.

❽ CALCULADORA OSCAR D'LEON from ESENCIALES: THE ULTIMATE COLLECTION VOL 1
Luscious and swoony, this cover of a classic Cuban cha-cha-cha gets the Venezuelan, D'Leon treatment with swathes of violins and trombones.

❾ EL CHIVO DE LA CAMPANA ISMAEL RIVERA from ISMAEL RIVERA: EL SONERO MAYOR
Classic old-school Puerto Rican salsa, driven by Rafael Cortijo's congas, and a showcase for the voice of Rivera (the island's equivalent to Al Green or Sam Cooke).

Sue Steward

Samba

Samba from Rio's *favelas* is the soundtrack to the world's favourite carnival, and you never tire of it.

❶ YAYA MASSEMBA MARIA BETHÂNIA from BRASILEIRINHO
Bethania is a glorious Bahian singer with a rich, androgynous voice, here describing the unspoiled tropical landscapes, painted by the guitars and percussion.

❷ REFAVELA GILBERTO GIL from REFAVELA
Gilberto Gil – singer, composer, now Minister of Culture – scored with this song in the 1970s, and it's still greeted with cheers. Rippling guitar melodies open for Gil's gloriously honeyed voice in a deceptively harsh story of *favela* life.

❸ SAO VICENTE MILTON NASCIMENTO from CLUBE DA ESQUINA 2
Brazil's greatest lyrical singer with his "Corner Club" group. Nascimento combines the legacy of choral singing with samba-esque guitars, and his unmistakeably African ancestry.

❹ GODDESS OF EBANO VIRGINIA RODRIGUEZ from NOS
The exquisite operatic voice of this singer from Salvador, Bahia, pays homage to the Afro–Brazilian

deities of *candomble* goddess Ebano as Celso Fonseca's guitar ripples, and a sublime chorus rises to join her.

❺ VELHA INFANCIA TRIBALISTAS
from TRIBALISTAS

This recent supergroup featuring singers Marisa Monte and Arnaldo Antunes, and percussionist Carlinhos Brown, raised Brazilian
pop to new heights with gorgeously hypnotic harmonies and inventive arrangements. This song was an instant classic.

❻ CANTO DO CIDADE DANIELA MERCURY
from SWING TROPICAL

Bahia's best-loved young singer, Mercury has brought pop-sambas to the electronic-beat generation. Canto Do Cidade is a heavy, rocking, street samba, which forces her voice to soar high above the crowds of revellers.

Sue Steward

San Francisco

"If you're going to San Francisco/Be sure to wear some flowers in your hair", waxed Scott McKenzie in 1967. These days, wannabe hippies still hang out in the Haight, but Silicon Valley exudes a much greater influence. Which may be why it's no longer a major music city.

❶ WHITE RABBIT JEFFERSON AIRPLANE from SURREALISTIC PILLOW

Acid-tinged soundtrack to the Summer of Love, with Grace Slick convincingly suggesting wisdom may be found in Lewis Carroll.

❷ DANCE TO THE MUSIC SLY & THE FAMILY STONE from GREATEST HITS

Sly's male/female, black/white, psychedelic soul sound blew minds. Including Sly's once he'd shifted to LA.

❸ I-FEEL-LIKE-I'M-FIXING-TO-DIE-RAG COUNTRY JOE & THE FISH from WOODSTOCK

Haight Ashbury's ambassador provides Woodstock's muddy masses with their anti-war anthem.

❹ BLACK MAGIC WOMAN SANTANA from SANTANA

San Francisco has a large Mexican community, although Carlos Santana is the only sonic evidence. Tasty Latin flavouring of the Fleetwood Mac tune.

❺ A WOMAN LEFT LONELY JANIS JOPLIN from PEARL

JJ was a Texan blues-soul shouter who rose to fame fronting SF's psychedelic warriors Big Brother And

The Holing Company. But this slow-burning Dan Penn tune shows she really could sing.

❻ RIPPLE GRATEFUL DEAD from AMERICAN BEAUTY
Zen country-rock for the tie-dyed masses.

❼ FORTUNATE SON CREEDENCE CLEARWATER REVIVAL
from WILLIE AND THE POOR BOYS

Roaring, rockin' prole anger directed at those who declare war then send po' boys off to fight.

❽ LOAN ME A DIME BOZ SCAGGS from BOZ SCAGGS
Another transplanted white Texan who could sing the blues. Here Boz stretches out while Duane Allman sets fire with slide guitar.

❾ CALIFORNIA ÜBER ALLES DEAD KENNEDYS from FRESH FRUIT FOR ROTTING VEGETABLES

"You will jog for the master race": political satire of the highest order. Jello Biafra was the smartest, sharpest San Franciscan rocker.

❿ BASKET CASE GREEN DAY from DOOKIE
MTV-friendly punks won a huge adolescent audience with this celebration of being stoopid.

Garth Cartwright

Santana

Carlos Santana's fusion of Latin rhythms and blues-rock was way ahead of its time, and his band's electrifying performance at Woodstock was one of the highlights of the festival. In the mid 1970s he discovered jazz and Indian spiritualism, changed his name to Carlos Devadip and recorded John Coltrane tunes. By the end of the 1990s he'd sunk into semi-obscurity, but then surprised everyone by storming back with the best-selling album of his career and winning eight Grammies.

❶ SOUL SACRIFICE from WOODSTOCK
This explosive piece also appeared on the band's first album but the "three days of love, peace and music" version is the one to go for.

❷ BLACK MAGIC WOMAN/GYPSY QUEEN from ABRAXAS
You wouldn't have thought anyone could improve on Fleetwood Mac's version of the Peter Green song… but you'd be wrong.

❸ SAMBA PA TI from ABRAXAS
A contender for the greatest instrumental track ever as Carlos rings every last drop of emotion out of his guitar.

4 OYE COMO VA from ABRAXAS
A crash course in salsa for rock fans who'd never heard of the song's author, Tito Puente.

5 EVIL WAYS from SANTANA
The other standout track from the band's 1969 debut – and Santana's first big hit.

6 SHE'S NOT THERE from MOONFLOWER
The old Zombies number gets the Black Magic Woman treatment

7 EVERY STEP OF THE WAY from CARAVANSERAI
A bit unfair to single out one track from the band's fourth and most ambitious album, because it's really one long suite that deserves to be listened to in its entirety. But if you're looking for a soundbite, try this.

8 THE HEALER JOHN LEE HOOKER from THE HEALER
Santana's blistering guitar work on the title track of John Lee Hooker's 1989 comeback album had him sounding bluesier than in years.

9 INCIDENT AT NESHABUR from LOTUS
Early Santana were a magnificent live ensemble and although this jazz-rock masterpiece first appeared on the immaculate *Abraxas*, their sixteen-minute version recorded live in 1973 is awesome.

10 SMOOTH from SUPERNATURAL
On which the 50-something Carlos is reinvented as a modern pop star with this monster hit featuring Matchbox 20 singer Rob Thomas.

Nigel Williamson

Scots rock

We're not talking Harry Lauder and Andy Stewart's White Heather Club here and sadly we also have to pass over the vibrant Scottish folk and roots scene. We're talking Scottish rock'n'roll. Here are ten who came over Hadrian's Wall to rock the world…

1 SHOUT LULU from THE BEST OF
Scotland never had its own Beatles. But it did have Marie MacDonald McLaughlin Lawrie, who recorded this rasping version of the Isley Brothers' song in 1964 when she was just 15.

2 FALLING AND LAUGHING ORANGE JUICE from THE HEATHER'S ON FIRE
Strange to think that the Burroughs cut-up technique could play a part in this shimmering, delicate beauty.

Arty but not fey or contrived – a thing of beauty and a joy for ever.

3 DOWN THE DIP AZTEC CAMERA from HIGH LAND, HARD RAIN
Written in a matter of minutes, this song of devotion is unusually direct for the unpredictable Roddy Frame, but it's the most memorable song on a memorable debut album.

4 NEXT! THE SENSATIONAL ALEX HARVEY BAND from NEXT
A Jacques Brel song about prostitutes and soldiers in wartime, given a powerful rendition by the godfather of Scottish punk.

5 MOLLY'S LIPS THE VASELINES from THE WAY OF THE VASELINES
Lanarkshire's finest with a song good enough to be covered by Nirvana.

6 SAY WHAT YOU WANT TEXAS from WHITE ON BLONDE
A 1997 Top 10 hit from band led by Sharleen Spiteri, Scotland's sexiest singer since Lulu.

7 SING TRAVIS from THE INVISIBLE BAND
For a brief while, their radio-friendly angst made them the biggest band in the UK – a unique achievement for a bunch of Scots.

8 PARTY FEARS TWO THE ASSOCIATES from SULK
Classic 1980s post-punk pop from Billy MacKenzie, who tragically took his own life in 1997.

9 TAKE ME OUT FRANZ FERDINAND from FRANZ FERDINAND
The art-school dance goes on for ever. Clever imagery and the spiky, angular rhythms of post-punk are reworked into something shiny and postmodern.

10 AN TOLL DUBH RUNRIG from RECOVERY
They even sang in Gaelic. McRespect.

Nigel Williamson/Ian Cranna

Screaming Trees/ Mark Lanegan

For a decade the Screaming Trees, rated higher than Nirvana by the grunge faithful, were intrinsic to the Seattle scene. They always had more going for them than just grunge. Singer Mark Lanegan has subsequently made a series of fine solo albums and collaborated with the mighty Queens Of The Stoneage and former Belle & Sebastian vocalist, Isobel Campbell.

SCREAMING TREES

① IVY SCREAMING TREES from INVISIBLE LANTERN
Relentless and irresistible, this opener typifies the wall of sound and rough edges of the band's early efforts. The vocals froth over the wah-wah guitar.

② BLACK SUN MORNING SCREAMING TREES from BUZZ FACTORY
Vocals as harsh as Oregon logging saws as the Trees rage about ecological destruction. Van Conner's luscious bass runs maintain order.

③ BED OF ROSES SCREAMING TREES from UNCLE ANESTHESIA
The poppier side of the band is showcased, as Gary Lee serves up some disarmingly sweet riffs while Lanegan croons nonchalantly.

④ WINTER SONG SCREAMING TREES from SWEET OBLIVION
Honey-throated spirituality, honeycombed in jagged jangles and backwards guitars. Piercing hooks, too.

⑤ ALL I KNOW SCREAMING TREES from DUST
Hop, skip and boom – the Trees launch us into a helter-skelter rush of whirling guitar and bouncy melodies.

⑥ DYING DAYS SCREAMING TREES from DUST
The acoustic intro is blown away by a blast of Zep-like proportions. Lanegan manfully bares his soul for the end times, while Gary Lee soars. Superb.

MARK LANEGAN

⑦ EL SOL from WHISKEY FOR THE HOLY GHOST
Heartfelt and divine lament to the loss of sun and heaven. Lanegan's voice could make the angels weep as he wrenches out the simple refrain about waiting for some warmth a-coming down.

⑧ STRANGE RELIGION from BUBBLEGUM
A folk/blues lullaby touching Lanegan's favourite topic of redemption meets road movie. Aided by Izzy Stradlin and a backing choir.

ISOBEL CAMPBELL & MARK LANEGAN

⑨ HONEY CHILD, WHAT CAN I DO from BALLAD OF THE BROKEN SEA
Collaborating with Isobel Campbell was an inspired move and this sweet country-hued song sounds like you've known it forever.

⑩ DO YOU WANNA COME WALK WITH ME? from BALLAD OF THE BROKEN SEA
More delicious country duetting from the Nancy Sinatra and Lee Hazlewood of our days.

Nick Edwards

Scritti Politti

From disciple of Martin Carthy to hip-hop devotee, Green Gartside has embraced innumerable genres along the way, but a few consistent elements bring together his whole career. Beautifully constructed melodies, lyrics veering wildly between philosophical references and disarmingly simple love songs, and of course his voice – one of the most gorgeous of the modern era.

① SKANK BLOC BOLOGNA from EARLY
The very first single, opening with shards of guitar and a hesitant rhythm section, growing into a glorious six-minute opus of unhinged ska and clattering xylophones.

② CONFIDENCE from EARLY
Scratch the surface, and you'll find a hint of what was to come several years later; Green's vocal is softening and the tempo gently relaxing in this understated summery lament.

③ JACQUES DERRIDA from SONGS TO REMEMBER
Scritti Politti never sounded so gleeful, with a hup-2-3-4 march effortlessly segueing into a hip-hop coda, shoehorning in a deliberate mispronounciation of the French philosopher's surname along the way.

④ THE SWEETEST GIRL from SONGS TO REMEMBER
Green's melodies never go quite where you expect, but you're always glad that they did. This standout track on the NME's *C81* cassette propelled Green from post-punk outsider to pop contender.

⑤ THE WORD GIRL from CUPID & PSYCHE '85
Their biggest UK hit, and deservedly so. The phrase "perfect pop" was never more appropriate: slick, sweet, not a note out of place, but still managing to avoid every cliché in the book.

⑥ WOOD BEEZ from CUPID & PSYCHE '85
Magically crafted for both AM radio and the dancefloor, this homage to Aretha Franklin fuses a leaping synth bass with the "ker-ching" that became Scritti's trademark guitar lick.

7 OH PATTI from PROVISION

On an album which made the previous studio master-piece sound like a four-track demo, this single was the highlight, with the trumpet of Miles Davis adding icing and marzipan to the cake.

8 BRUSHED WITH OIL, DUSTED WITH POWDER from ANOMIE & BONHOMIE

A fan's favourite, tucked away at the end of a largely hip-hop influenced album. Strings, harps and acoustic guitar give the track a sweeping, epic majesty.

9 SNOW IN SUN from WHITE BREAD, BLACK BEER

A beautifully multi-layered vocal intro gives way to the most direct and honest love song Green ever recorded. "You will never need to doubt me, you will never be without me…" Stunning.

10 MRS HUGHES from WHITE BREAD, BLACK BEER

Less of a song, more of a three-piece suite: Beach Boys harmonies, squealing guitar solos and a squelching hip-hop fade are all scribbled down in the Scritti sketchbook. "That's just the way that you are…"

Rhodri Marsden

Seattle

The Northwestern city is famous for hosting Bill Gates' Microsoft empire and the Starbucks chain but it's also long been home to a very raw rock scene.

1 TALL COOL ONE THE WAILERS from THE ORIGINAL GOLD CREST MASTERS

Primal garage band formed in 1958. All Seattle's guitar madness spills, more or less, from this gonzo combo.

2 WALK DON'T RUN THE VENTURES from WALK DON'T RUN: THE BEST OF THE VENTURES

The world's biggest guitar-instrumental band formed just outside Seattle in 1959, and this is their twangy theme tune.

3 PSYCHO THE SONICS from PSYCHO-SONICS

Truly psychotic garage band legends. Cut in 1965, Psycho rocks harder than 99 percent of punk bands. Guaranteed.

4 LOUIE LOUIE THE KINGSMEN from THE BEST OF THE KINGSMEN

OK, they're from Portland, Oregon, but their cut on Louie is such a classic that every band in the North West learned it, so spiritually they're from Seattle.

5 BARRACUDA HEART from LITTLE QUEEN

Sisters Ann and Nancy Wilson delivered this hard rocking ode to fast cars while leading the biggest band to come out of Seattle in the 1970s.

6 TOUCH ME, I'M SICK MUDHONEY from SUPERFUZZ BIGMUFF

Grunge godfathers punk anthem. Mudhoney never got rich and never lost their soul; true Seattle heroes!

7 BLACK HOLE SUN SOUNDGARDEN from SUPERUNKNOWN

Doom … doom … on MTV and going platinum … doom. Soundgarden were real fun guys.

8 SMELLS LIKE TEEN SPIRIT NIRVANA from NEVERMIND

Has rock'n'roll ever sounded so good again? Crank it up and let it loose.

9 RAIN WHEN I DIE ALICE IN CHAINS from DIRT

Heavy smackheads unleash huge Sabbath riffs while vocalist Layne Staley wails about impending doom. Before the decade was out heroin fulfilled Layne's prophecy.

10 HIT THE CITY MARK LANEGAN BAND from BUBBLEGUM

Wonderful weary rumble of a rocker from former Screaming Trees vocalist. Give the guy a venti espresso, yeah?

Garth Cartwright

Sex Pistols

When you absolutely definitely want to knock out the upper register of your hearing, there's no better way than with the noisiest, naughtiest boys ever to swagger out of West London and into the limelight.

1 HOLIDAYS IN THE SUN from NEVER MIND THE BOLLOCKS HERE'S THE SEX PISTOLS

A paramilitary drum beat intro leads into a crashing guitar and a dive-bomber riff – sounding just like Slade's angry little brothers, the Pistols released this track at the height of their pomp and never again reached this peak.

2 SATELLITE from SPUNK

Raw and primitive. Jones and the band have all the equipment set on "SNARL" and Rotten is swigging a bottle of poison in between lines of lyric, the better to spit it back in the face of the audience.

Steve Jones's
Punk picks

Improbable as it may sound, these days former Sex Pistols guitarist Steve Jones is a DJ running a Los Angeles radio show called "Jonesy's Jukebox" on the Clear Channel-owned station, Indie 103.1 Studio guests on his show have included Brian Wilson, Nancy Sinatra and Courtney Love but he still finds time to play plenty of punk classics and sent us this typical playlist from the West Coast.

❶ SPELLBOUND SIOUXSIE & THE BANSHEES from JUJU

❷ I'M STRANDED THE SAINTS from (I'M) STRANDED

❸ I DON'T WANNA GROW UP THE RAMONES from HEY HO LET'S GO: THE ANTHOLOGY

❹ TOP OF THE POPS REZILLOS from CAN'T STAND THE REZILLOS

❺ DIRTY PICTURES RADIO STARS from a 1977 single

❻ PILLS NEW YORK DOLLS from NEW YORK DOLLS

❼ AMERICAN NIGHTS THE RUNAWAYS from THE RUNAWAYS

❽ CRUEL TO BE KIND SPACEHOG from RESIDENT ALIEN

❾ WHAT EVER HAPPENED? THE STROKES from ROOM ON FIRE

❿ NEVER TURN YOUR BACK ON MOTHER EARTH SPARKS from PLAGIARISM

❸ NO FEELINGS from NEVER MIND THE BOLLOCKS HERE'S THE SEX PISTOLS
By the time they got round to recording the final album version, this song had slowed down a little allowing for the lyrics to get through.

❹ SEVENTEEN (2ND VERSION) from SPUNK
Multi-tracked vocals mean Johnny sounds even more rotten, but this is one track that definitely shows the benefits of Malcolm's strong black coffees. Drums raining down like hailstones, sheets of cymbals, guitar trickery – the full English.

❺ NEW YORK (LOOKING FOR A KISS) from SPUNK
Chunkiest guitar line that Jonesy ever conjured and the perfect bass accompaniment – the kind you don't notice – from Matlock provide just the background needed for Rotten to lay into the New York Dolls, safe in the knowledge that David Jo and Johnny Thunders were still hanging out on the other side of the Atlantic.

❻ LIAR from SPUNK
The phased speakers on the guitar and crisp drumming are all very well but what makes this the definitive version of the Pistols' most vitriolic is, of course, Rotten's delivery.

❼ SUBMISSION (2ND VERSION) from SPUNK
Punk's only hymn to the delights of going down Mexico Way, and the only song ever to feature a solo blown on the whistle of an old-fashioned kettle.

❽ NO FUTURE (GOD SAVE THE QUEEN) from SPUNK
The occasional wrong note can be excused as a sign of the artists' desperate sincerity, the lyrics are best described as still to be finalized and it is quite obviously bolted together from two different takes, but this once-bootleg version sparks with more energy than that finally released on the album and as a single.

❾ PRETTY VACANT from NEVER MIND THE BOLLOCKS
Opening with the most crucial three-note alarm in the history of punk, "Pretty Vacant" hangs the guys out to dry – warts, haemorrhoids and all – as a dumb but lovely boy band.

❿ ANARCHY IN THE UK (1ST VERSION, AKA NOOKIE) from SPUNK
All guns firing at once, this is the definitive version of the song that made them famous. It bursts with red-faced rage, as Rotten roars like a very pissed-off caged beast, Jones hacks a Dolls-esque path through the chord chart, and Cook beats the fear of gods into his kit.

Al Spicer

Sheffield

They came out of Yorkshire armed with synthesizers and tape loops, wanting to kill rock music. Instead, they managed to rejuvenate it.

Here are nine songs that celebrate their noble experiment.

❶ NAG NAG NAG CABARET VOLTAIRE from THE LIVING LEGENDS
The guitar riff may have been straight out of the garage, but the dentist-drill synths and mosquito vocals bore a hole in your skull.

❷ BEING BOILED HUMAN LEAGUE from REPRODUCTION
Post-industrial doom-saying never sounded so good.

❸ LOVE ACTION (I BELIEVE IN LOVE) HUMAN LEAGUE from DARE!
A landmark of plasticity, garish artifice and shimmering surfaces, this made synth-pop's sangfroid the soundtrack to the look-but-don't-touch 1980s.

❹ (WE DON'T NEED THIS) FASCIST GROOVE THING HEAVEN 17 from PENTHOUSE AND PAVEMENT
Ex-Human Leaguers Ian Craig Marsh and Martyn Ware proved that you didn't have to give up politics to be catchy.

❺ POISON ARROW ABC from THE LEXICON OF LOVE
Instead of embracing industrial decay, ABC tried to kill rock by drowning it in smarm and decadence.

❻ BREAKDOWN CLOCK DVA from ADVANTAGE
Terrifyingly bleak avant-funk noise collage.

❼ TRACK WITH NO NAME FORGEMASTERS from WARP 10
Minimalist, brutalist house music that kicked off Sheffield's finest label, Warp.

❽ TESTONE SWEET EXORCIST from WARP 10
Spartan electronic masterpiece from Cabaret Voltaire's Richard H Kirk that became one of the building blocks of British Hardcore.

❾ PHOTOGRAPH DEF LEPPARD from PYROMANIA
Proof that no matter how hard they tried, Sheffield's electronic naysayers just couldn't kill the beast.

Peter Shapiro

Shoegazing

A droning, distorted sound, and mumbled, introspective lyrics were de rigueur amongst a cohort of English bands that emerged in the late 1980s. The *NME* dubbed them "shoegazers" after their onstage appearance, preoccupied as they generally were staring down at their effects pedals.

❶ ONLY SHALLOW MY BLOODY VALENTINE from LOVELESS
The opening cut from an album best listened to as a whole. Kevin Shield's hugely influential, multi-layered guitar masterpiece nearly bankrupted a pre-Oasis Creation Records. A huge, beautiful bruised sound.

❷ LISTEN, THE SNOW IS FALLING GALAXIE 500 from THE PORTABLE GALAXIE 500
Though from Boston, this group's reverb-laden laments, Velvet Underground influence and label (4AD) often saw them tagged shoegazers. A lovely epic piece, with vocals by Naomi Yang.

❸ VAPOUR TRAIL RIDE from NOWHERE
Like the Stone Roses on mogadons, this floaty drone-pop anthem is a highlight of Ride's best album.

❹ SIGHT OF YOU THE PALE SAINTS from 1980 FORWARD
Before the term "shoegazing" came into use, this much derided Leeds-based band ("middle class ninnies") were an influence on Ride with songs like this.

❺ LEAVES ME COLD LUSH from GALA
The airy vocal harmonies of Miki Berenyi and Emma Anderson drowning in jangle on this cut pretty much epitomize this group's early output.

❻ WHEN THE SUN HITS SLOWDIVE from LIKE A DAYDREAM. A SHOEGAZING GUIDE.
Anthemic for no apparent reason, as we can't really hear what Neil Halstead is on about. Does it matter? No! Get lost in a lovely shimmering wall of sound…

❼ YOU KNOW IT'S TRUE SPIRITUALISED from LAZER GUIDED MELODIES.
A seductively hazy psychedelic intro to the debut by the band Jason Pierce formed after Spacemen 3 – a seminal influence on many shoegazers.

❽ GIRL ON A BIKE SWERVEDRIVER from MEZCAL HEAD
An unusually pensive number from this otherwise rocked-up band.

❾ THE MERCY SEAT ULTRA VIVID SCENE from LIKE A DAYDREAM. A SHOEGAZING GUIDE
American shoegazing "imposter", aka Kurt Ralske, at his most memorable.

❿ WAKE UP BOO! THE BOO RADLEYS from WAKE UP!
By the time this Liverpool band delivered their quintessential pop thrill (1995), shoegazing was more or less history. The band soon would be too. Dream over.

Jon Lusk

Shop 'til you drop

Diamonds, dosh and designers provide plenty of scope for songwriting indulgence.

❶ GIVE, GIVE, GIVE ME MORE, MORE, MORE IT'S YER MONEY I'M AFTER BABY THE WONDER STUFF from THE EIGHT-LEGGED GROOVE MACHINE

In the glossy, airbrushed 1980s, the snotty scowling of Miles Hunt was a refreshingly honest look at the era's materialistic sheen. Stourbridge's finest produced this acerbic pair of tunes about greed, personal and global.

❷ MATERIAL GIRL MADONNA from LIKE A VIRGIN

Money-themed puns and inuendo litter the lyrics, and the video memorably promoted sassy Ms Ciccone camping and vamping as a thoroughly modern Marilyn (reverting to girl-next-door, backstage).

❸ HEAD LIKE A HOLE NINE INCH NAILS from PRETTY HATE MACHINE

Opening Trent Reznor's dissonant debut album, this track boils with rage at corporate greed, as a growling torrent of contempt is spat at the listener. Extensive MTV airplay boosted the single's unexpected success.

❹ FOR THE LOVE OF MONEY THE O'JAYS from THE ESSENTIAL O'JAYS

A Gamble & Huff collaboration with Anthony Jackson spawned this funky comment on the root of all evil, expertly rendered by the Ohio trio. Jackson's sublime bassline has been sampled by Grandmaster Flash and the Happy Mondays, among others, while the track found a new audience via US TV show The Apprentice.

❺ MONEY, MONEY, MONEY ABBA from ARRIVAL

Bjorn and Benny wrote this ode to ambition in response to critics who dubbed ABBA more of a business than a band. Taut, unfussy lyrics offset a rich backdrop that hints at stage musicals.

❻ FAVOURITE THINGS BIG BROVAZ from NU FLOW

Injecting fun into hip-hop's often angry, dispossessed stance on materialism, the London outfit supersize Rodgers and Hammerstein's genteel singalong with a wish list including "Gucci dresses and drop-top Kompressors". A far cry from Maria's schnitzel and strudel tastes.

❼ DIAMONDS ARE A GIRL'S BEST FRIEND MARILYN MONROE from GENTLEMEN PREFER BLONDES

Gold-digging Lorelei Lee makes no effort to disguise her first love, while trying to snag a rich husband in the 1953 musical. You've got to admire her attention to detail, even namedropping specific jewellers to make her point.

❽ OPPORTUNITIES (LET'S MAKE LOTS OF MONEY) PET SHOP BOYS from PLEASE

With aspirations of living the dream in Thatcher's Britain, the narrator's hollow embrace of all things capitalist is tinged with pathos, as Neil Tennant waxes satirical to a multi-layered cocktail of a backing track.

❾ RICH GIRL GWEN STEFANI from LOVE.ANGEL.MUSIC.BABY

Reworking Topol's turn from Fiddler on the Roof into a wry modern clarion call to consumption, Stefani targets Hollywood mansions and designer labels. With rapper Eve and producer Dr Dre on board to rev up the poppy dancehall beat, there's not a biddy-biddy-bum in sight

❿ MONEY SONG MONTY PYTHON from MONTY PYTHON SINGS

"There is nothing quite as wonderful as money", Eric Idel pronounces. "You can keep your Marxist ways, for it's accountancy that makes the world go round."

Ed Wright

Wayne Shorter

One of the great exponents of the soprano and tenor saxophone, Shorter is also an outstanding composer, his output on the Blue Note label and then as part of the legendary Miles Davis quintet of 1965–67 leaving a legacy of stunning compositions and even better performances. After co-founding the fusion group Weather Report, Shorter retired from live performance but in recent years has returned to the stage with a new quartet and a series of fantastic concerts.

❶ FREE FOR ALL ART BLAKEY AND THE JAZZ MESSENGERS from FREE FOR ALL

An example from 1960 of Shorter's emerging and original style of composition as part of Blakey's school for future greats.

❷ FEE-FI-FO-FUM from SPEAK NO EVIL

A laid-back setting for Shorter and Freddie Hubbard to chat.

❸ DELUGE from JUJU

With Elvin Jones supplying joyous support, Shorter takes all the time he needs to say his piece.

❹ MAHJONG from JUJU

Another beautiful melody demonstrating Shorter's ability to use all his musicians to create a distinctive and coherent sound.

⑤ IRIS MILES DAVIS from E.S.P.

Shorter's first compositional effort for the Miles Davis quintet shows him at his most mournful and languid.

⑥ FOOTPRINTS MILES DAVIS from MILES SMILES

The fluid and loose sound which set this group apart is demonstrated to perfection on this lovely track.

⑦ ADAM'S APPLE from ADAM'S APPLE

Shorter gets funky with one of his more conventional popular-sounding tracks. No one does it better.

⑧ SANCTUARY MILES DAVIS from BITCHES BREW

Shorter's contribution to the groundbreaking album retains the swelling, epic abstractness of his earlier writing. He plays mean soprano, too.

⑨ PALLADIUM WEATHER REPORT from HEAVY WEATHER

An example of Shorter's composition for the influential fusion group. While the overall sound is unrecognizable from the acoustic material, the haunting timbre of Shorter's sax remains.

⑩ JUJU from FOOTPRINTS LIVE!

Shorter's present-day group gives a startling new flavour to this self-penned classic. Collective improvization at its most impressive.

Nat Defriend

Shouters, screamers and belters

The missing link between the blues and rock'n'roll, the shouters developed their strident vocal style in order to be heard above the uptempo swing and front-line horns of the big bands and raucous jump combos of the 1940s. Although most were male, a parallel school of screamers – big-voiced female divas – was also closely related. Here are ten who turned the volume up to eleven…

❶ SHAKE, RATTLE AND ROLL BIG JOE TURNER from GREATEST HITS

By 1954, Turner was a 43-years-old jazz-blues veteran, but this brought him a new audience and teen adoration, even if Bill Haley's toned down cover version was a bigger hit.

❷ ALL SHE WANTS TO DO IS ROCK WYNONIE HARRIS from BLOODSHOT EYES: THE BEST OF WYNONIE HARRIS

All the pounding, honking raucousness of Little Richard – recorded way back in 1949.

❸ JUICE HEAD BABY EDDIE "CLEANHEAD" VINSON from HONK FOR TEXAS

Wheezy blues shouter and bebop sax player was an unusual combination, but tracks like this made Vinson a jump blues giant in the late 1940s.

❹ DOWN THE ROAD APIECE AMOS MILBURN from CHICKEN SHACK BOOGIE MAN

One of the great unsung post-war rockers, Milburn embodied the spirit of good living, booze and fast women on this romping party track, later covered by the Rolling Stones.

❺ GOOD ROCKIN' TONITE ROY BROWN from GOOD ROCKIN' TONIGHT: THE BEST OF ROY BROWN

This 1948 R&B hit helped established the language of "rocking" and "rolling" in popular music. Alas, others would benefit more than Brown. By the late 1950s, he was reduced to selling encyclopaedias door-to-door.

❻ 'TAINT NOBODY'S BUSINESS IF I DO JIMMY WITHERSPOON from JAZZ ME BLUES

Was he a blues singer, an R&B shouter or a jazz crooner? On this 1949 hit he straddled the lot…

❼ GOIN' TO CHICAGO JIMMY RUSHING from THE ESSENTIAL JIMMY RUSHING

Fifteen years shouting with Count Basie's band taught Rushing to pitch his high tenor against a hard-blowing horn section and it held him in good stead on his exuberant signature tune.

❽ HOUND DOG BIG MAMA THORNTON from HOUND DOG: THE PEACOCK RECORDINGS

One of the great female shouters, she will always be remembered for her raucous 1952 version of this Jerry Leiber and Mike Stoller song, not recorded by Elvis until some four years later.

❾ JIM DANDY LA VERN BAKER from ATLANTIC R&B VOL 3: 1955–57

The term shouter was for the most part applied to male singers but Baker's big voice on this 1956 hit was totally in keeping with the style.

❿ WHOLE LOTTA SHAKIN' BIG MAYBELLE from THE COMPLETE OKEH SESSIONS

Another R&B diva in the tradition of the male shouters, Big Maybelle scored with this storming version in 1955, two years before Jerry Lee Lewis's hit.

Nigel Williamson

Jane Siberry

Siberry should be a star on a par with Kate Bush, possibly even fellow Canadian Joni Mitchell. Her caring insights into love and nature can be complex and deeply emotional, yet are strongly visual, engagingly conversational and leavened with gentle humour.

❶ MIMI ON THE BEACH from NO BORDERS HERE

An early landmark: an eight-minute mini-movie with two spoken monologues (Siberry exhorts a young surfing girl to do something with her life), yet almost a hit in Canada.

❷ RED HIGH HEELS from THE WALKING

A small church, snow on the fields and a girl going home, thinking of a past love. Sweet and spirited.

❸ THE WALKING AND CONSTANTLY from THE WALKING

"Your shoes, you left your hat/ It's on the bed or else the chair/I don't know, I don't know, I…" The pain and confusion of being unable to let go of a failed romance.

❹ THE LOBBY from THE WALKING

"So I go down to the lobby and everybody stares/ They say, take off that foolish hat, put down that chair…" Spellbinding, slow-motion song about failure to connect.

❺ BOUND BY THE BEAUTY from BOUND BY THE BEAUTY

"The slowness of the falling leaves across this warm November door/And the geese flying southness the arms out evermore…" A loving hymn to Mother Earth.

❻ EVERYTHING REMINDS ME OF MY DOG from BOUND BY THE BEAUTY

A jaunty song of affection to the world that makes you laugh every time you hear it.

❼ LOVE IS EVERYTHING
from WHEN I WAS A BOY

A cry of pain and dismay turns into a determination to love bigger and better still. This Eno-produced flood of emotion is one of her most heartfelt.

❽ CALLING ALL ANGELS
from WHEN I WAS A BOY

"We're hoping, we're trying, we're hurting, we're loving, we're crying… because we're not sure how this goes" – a song of supplication, a duet with KD Lang, and her biggest hit.

Ian Cranna

Simon & Garfunkel

At their best, they recast the Everly Brothers' harmonies for a brighter, more optimistic generation. At their worst, they rehashed the Everly Brothers' incessant squabbling.

❶ THE SOUND OF SILENCE from WEDNESDAY MORNING 3AM

Later souped up with a drum track, but just right in this quiet acoustic form.

❷ I AM A ROCK from WEDNESDAY MORNING 3AM

As solipsistic as they come, but done with enough conviction to stick in the memory.

❸ HOMEWARD BOUND from GREATEST HITS

Allegedly written on Widnes railway station during Simon's sojourn as a struggling songwriter in England. Again, look for this version, without a drum track.

❹ KATHY'S SONG from SOUNDS OF SILENCE

While in England, Simon learned at the feet of the English folk revivalists, notably Martin Carthy. His influence and that of Bert Jansch can be heard here.

❺ THE 59TH STREET BRIDGE SONG (FEELIN' GROOVY) from PARSLEY, SAGE, ROSEMARY AND THYME

Not sure whether to be grandiose or finger-clickin'; eventually, happily, plumps for the latter.

❻ AMERICA from BOOKENDS

A Greyhound bus journey becomes a quest for the soul of the nation itself. As they do.

❼ A HAZY SHADE OF WINTER from BOOKENDS

The Bangles made this into pure power-pop: listening to the original, it's striking how little they had to do.

❽ MRS ROBINSON from BOOKENDS

Works as a song even for those who haven't graduated.

❾ CECILIA from BRIDGE OVER TROUBLED WATER

John Lennon thought this the most carnal song imaginable: what could be more decadent than making love in the afternoon?

❿ MY LITTLE TOWN from OLD FRIENDS

A few years after going their separate ways, Simon wrote this cynical, brass-driven song for Art's sake. They sang it together and it appeared on both their solo albums of the time.

David Honigmann

Paul Simon

Paul Simon strained at the leash as the better half of a duo with Art Garfunkel: his interest in developing a broader palette could be heard in songs like "El Condor Paso". Solo, he gave this compulsion full rein, covering New Orleans jazz, embryonic reggae, South African township music, Braziliana and points south. His lyrical preoccupations, however, remained firmly rooted in New York.

❶ FATHER AND DAUGHTER from SURPRISE
A chiming African guitar call opens this charming meditation on a father's love for his daughter – composed for *The Wild Thornberrys* kids movie, but as good as anything from his solo career.

❷ DARLING LORRAINE from YOU'RE THE ONE
The story of a marriage, it patters on happily until it runs into rocky ground in the penultimate verse, rocked by tiny brass stabs like slaps to the face; but it comes through smiling.

❸ THE OBVIOUS CHILD from RHYTHM OF THE SAINTS
A rainstorm of drumming from Olodum, a Brazilian carnival bloc, heralds this opening track from *Rhythm Of The Saints*, an attempt to do for South America what Graceland had done for South Africa. As a whole, the album is less successful, but this is musically forceful and lyrically elliptical in true Simon style.

❹ CAN'T RUN BUT from RHYTHM OF THE SAINTS
This, by contrast, ripples quietly, folding back on itself as it goes so that it seems to have no beginning and no logical end.

❺ BOY IN THE BUBBLE from GRACELAND
Groaning opening accordion chords kick off this unmistakable Lesotho stormer before massive drumbeats usher in a bassline like floorboards being ripped up with a crowbar. Across the world, the sound of 1986 was the sound of South Africa.

❻ DIAMONDS ON THE SOLES OF HER SHOES from GRACELAND
As light as "Boy In The Bubble" was heavy, this married the breathy choral singing of Ladysmith Black Mambazo to trilling guitar.

❼ RENÉ AND GEORGETTE MAGRITTE WITH THEIR DOG AFTER THE WAR from HEARTS AND BONES
Belgian surrealism meets 1950s doo-wop.

❽ STILL CRAZY AFTER ALL THESE YEARS from STILL CRAZY AFTER ALL THESE YEARS
An exaggerated lazy calm, rising into a truncated saxophone solo, serves as defence against the tough talk from an old flame.

❾ 50 WAYS TO LEAVE YOUR LOVER from STILL CRAZY AFTER ALL THESE YEARS
Only Simon could turn a light ditty to teach rhyming schemes to a child into a tale of romantic desolation.

❿ LOVES ME LIKE A ROCK from THERE GOES RHYMIN' SIMON
Joyful gospel, backed by the Dixie Hummingbirds, harking back to the soundtrack of Simon's 1950s childhood.

David Honigmann

Nina Simone

She set her heart on being a classical pianist and never wanted to be a singer at all. But, despite her reluctance, she could sing her laundry list and make it sound soulful becoming one of the great vocal stylists of the last fifty years. These ten span jazz, blues, pop, swing and soul.

❶ FEELING GOOD from I PUT A SPELL ON YOU
The High Priestess of Soul at her mid-1960s peak.

❷ MY BABY JUST CARES FOR ME from LITTLE GIRL BLUE
From her very first album in 1959 – though it wasn't a hit untl 1987.

❸ MISSISSIPPI GODDAM from IN CONCERT
She sang a lot of covers but she was also a fine songwriter. This was one of her most potent civil rights anthems.

❹ I PUT A SPELL ON YOU from I PUT A SPELL ON YOU
With one of the best scat passages you will ever hear – copied note for note by Van Morrison and Them.

❺ STRANGE FRUIT from PASTEL BLUES
Simone found this song so harrowing that she broke down every time she sang it and eventually had to drop it from her repertoire.

❻ I WANT A LITTLE SUGAR IN MY BOWL from SINGS THE BLUES
At her most delightfully risqué…

❼ I WISH I KNEW HOW IT WOULD FEEL TO BE FREE
from SILK & SOUL

Effortlessly swinging and now forever associated with Barry Norman's TV programme.

❽ TO BE YOUNG GIFTED AND BLACK from BLACK GOLD

Another of her own compositions, dedicated to her late friend, the playwright Lorraine Hansberry, and typical of her growing militancy in the late 1960s.

❾ SAVE ME from SILK & SOUL

Originally released as the B-side of "Young Gifted And Black", this version of the Aretha Franklin classic was the funkiest thing she ever recorded.

❿ FOUR WOMEN from WILD IS THE WIND

This hymn to black feminism is one of her most moving compositions.

Nigel Williamson

The Simpsons

One of the funniest, longest-running shows on TV is also chock-full of great music. You can track down the episodes – which will yield plenty of musical material unavailable elsewhere – or just grab *Songs In The Key Of Springfield* and *Go Simpsonic With The Simpsons*.

❶ FLAMING MOE'S from FLAMING MOE'S

A great TV theme gets the Simpsons' overhaul. *Cheers'* famous tune didn't have lyrics quite this close to the bone, however.

❷ HAPPY BIRTHDAY MR BURNS from ROSEBUD

Short and sweet, just like their own songs, The Ramones put the boot into both Mr Burns and one of the best known tunes in the world.

❸ IN A GADDA DA VIDA
from BART SELLS HIS SOUL

Bart decides to play a prank, and the Iron Butterfly heavy rock classic gets the big church organ treatment. Sounds entirely appropriate.

❹ SCORPIO END CREDITS
from YOU ONLY MOVE TWICE

Spot the Bond theme. Imagine *Goldfinger* with ace lyrics about a homicidal megalomaniac providing his employees with great pensions and health plans.

❺ SEÑOR BURNS from WHO SHOT MR BURNS?

The legendary Tito Puente & His Latin Jazz Ensemble sizzle and swing with no small amount of style.

❻ THE GARBAGEMAN from TRASH OF THE TITANS

Candyman gets remodelled into a hilariously over-the-top tune about the joys of collecting trash.

❼ THE SIMPSON'S END CREDIT THEME
from HOMERPALOOZA

Insanely discordant and awash with ear-bleeding feedback, Sonic Youth thrash through the final credits.

❽ THE SIMPSON'S END CREDIT THEME
from THE SIMPSONS CONNECTION

There's nothing quite like a spot-on homage: the familiar theme is delivered in the style of Mike Post's classic *Hill Street Blues*.

❾ WE PUT THE SPRING IN SPRINGFIELD
from BART AFTER DARK

The entire Simpsons cast pitch in with this fabulous ragtime romp of a show tune recalling *The Best Little Whorehouse In Texas*.

❿ YOUR WIFE DON'T UNDERSTAND YOU
from COLONEL HOMER

A terrific Tammy Wynette tears-in-your-beer country homage. The lyrics mirror Homer's domestic woes, and that pedal steel could make a grown man cry.

Essi Berelian

Frank Sinatra

The Voice of the Century with his greatest collaborator, the arranger Nelson Riddle.

❶ I'VE GOT THE WORLD ON A STRING from THIS IS SINATRA!

After the crooner of the 1940s, this 1954 variety of Sinatra, with a gleaming Riddle swing arrangement, was a strutting, swinging optimist.

❷ GET HAPPY from SWING EASY

Discreet modern tonalities and a roaring mid-point climax from Riddle with Frank in a freewheeling rhythmic mood, a highlight of his 1954 album.

❸ ILL WIND from IN THE WEE SMALL HOURS

At the other end of the emotional spectrum, both Riddle and Sinatra hit compelling depths in 1955 on Harold Arlen's Cotton Club ballad.

❹ I'VE GOT YOU UNDER MY SKIN from SONGS FOR SWINGIN' LOVERS!

The most overt example of Riddle's arranging following the intensity arc of sexual foreplay: Sinatra understands, and after this flawless 1956 reimagining of Cole Porter's song, so do we all.

❺ YOU MAKE ME FEEL SO YOUNG from SONGS FOR SWINGIN' LOVERS!
In which an unassuming 1947 romantic ditty is turned for all time by Riddle and Sinatra's *Swingin' Lovers* masterpiece into a swaggering, lusty celebration of senses awakened.

❻ I GOT PLENTY O' NUTTIN' from A SWINGIN' AFFAIR!
An audacious 1956 reworking of the Gershwins' song from *Porgy And Bess* in which Riddle's brilliantly reharmonized bass-trombone interlude shoots way off the hip-o-meter.

❼ ONE FOR MY BABY from ONLY THE LONELY
The 1958 treatment of the ultimate saloon song blends Bill Miller's bar-room pianistics with hazy strings and a deep Sinatra vocal to devastating effect.

❽ NICE 'N' EASY from NICE 'N' EASY
Relaxed, swinging, with a hint of sleaze, this 1960 arrangement of a modern song is a rare example of a Sinatra/Riddle classic not built on a standard of the previous generation.

❾ SUMMER WIND from STRANGERS IN THE NIGHT
Sinatra is stately on Johnny Mercer's weather meditation "Summer Wind", and the intro riff alone – played on organ on a chord of mysterious properties – is worth the price of the otherwise rotten 1966 album.

❿ SOMETHING from TRILOGY
Riddle's wondrous recasting of George Harrison's *Abbey Road* ballad in lush impressionist strings coaxes one of Sinatra's best late-period performances in 1979.

Chris Ingham

Ska

As Independence fever swept the island at the start of the 1960s, ordinary, working-class Jamaicans rejected US R&B, or what was fed to them on the BBC-based national radio, in favour of a vociferous homegrown sound. This was ska – and as an intrinsic expression of Jamaican-ness, it is music that is always going to be hard to beat.

❶ BOOGIE IN MY BONES LAUREL AITKEN from STORY SO FAR
A gloriously hard-partying example of ska's R&B-based forerunner, "JA boogie". Rest assured, the Trades Description Laws clearly won't be troubling this title.

❷ TEAR UP THE SKATALITES (FEATURING ROLAND ALPHONSO) from STRETCHING OUT
This simplest of ska riffs is so uplifting you can hear Alphonso smiling through his saxophone as he blows some ridiculously cheerful solos.

❸ SIMMER DOWN THE WAILERS from THE WAILING WAILERS
Teenage Wailers with the naked power to come out on top of an arrangement so raw it's probably been served its own ASBO.

❹ CARRY GO BRING COME JUSTIN HINDS & THE DOMINOES from ANTHOLOGY 64–74
Big bass drum drives this song, meaning that Hinds's perfectly weighted vocals can motor along with hardly any cause for fuss or strain.

❺ EASTERN STANDARD TIME DON DRUMMOND from TROJAN INSTRUMENTALS
Contemplative, cool-tempo instrumental ska from the master of the minor key, trombonist Don Drummond.

❻ MADNESS PRINCE BUSTER from HUSH UP!!!
The Prince takes it easy with this hiccupping, rollicking riff, but it's the ultra-affability of his vocals that makes this such an infectious piece of music.

❼ SKA-ING WEST SIR LORD COMIC & HIS COWBOYS from FROM THE DYNAMIC TREASURY VOL 2
Rudimentary Western-flavoured ska that jumps to the beat like a jack rabbit on the prairie, presided over by one of the first, and still the most laid-back, toasters on record.

❽ BROADWAY JUNGLE THE MAYTALS from THE BEST OF
Background shouting, jungle noises, chugging beat and a wailing trumpet. It's the perfect platform for Toots and the boys at their raucous, rasping best.

❾ STORM WARNING LYNN TAITT & HIS COMETS from TROJAN MOD REGGAE (BOX)
A subtly melodic instrumental, that manages to sound optimistic in spite of the rumbling menace in the bassline. Duke Reid really should have produced more ska.

❿ RAIN OR SHINE THE SKATALITES (FEATURING DON DRUMMOND) from SKA AUTHENTIC VOL 2
Three minutes of wild-style Eastern promise, as Drummond's mournful 'bone blows all the way to Addis Ababa, and the backing keeps up with a woozy, wavey brass-heavy extravaganza.

Lloyd Bradley

Slade

At the height of 1970s Slademania these cheerfully rocking glamsters were Top Of The Pops regulars, amassing seventeen consecutive top 20 hits and six number ones.

❶ ALL THE WORLD IS A STAGE from NOBODY'S FOOLS
Almost a Wall Of Sound-style production job here. Melodic and wistful verses erupt in a storm of pyrotechnic guitar riffing on the choruses.

❷ COZ I LUV YOU from SLADEST
The band's first number one hit created in just half an hour, this was the first tune Noddy Holder and Jim Lea wrote together. Dig that crazee violin solo!

❸ CUM ON FEEL THE NOIZE from SLADEST
This has party time writ large all over it and boasts one of Slade's best ever football terrace choruses. A thundering classic with some cool maracas lurking in the mix!

❹ GET ON UP from NOBODY'S FOOLS
Lots of energy, a hooky riff and a marked transatlantic feel on the rousing chorus as female backing singers complement Nod's rasping bark.

❺ HOW DOES IT FEEL from IN FLAME
Noel Gallagher reckons this is one of the best songs ever written. Noddy's heartfelt lyrics are superb and the addition of brass provides a distinct Beatlesy atmosphere.

❻ LOCK UP YOUR DAUGHTERS from TILL DEAF US DO PART
Part of Slade's major 1980s renaissance after a period out of the limelight. This is pounding melodic metal through and through.

❼ MAMA WEER ALL CRAZEE NOW from SLAYED?
Silly boots, awesome mutton chops, mirrored top hats…One of the definitive glam singles of the early 1970s and a benchmark vocal performance from Noddy.

❽ STANDING ON THE CORNER from IN FLAME
A raucous old fashioned rock'n'roller complete with a hot sax and brass section parping away and a ridiculously tongue-twisting chorus.

❾ THEM KINDA MONKEYS CAN'T SWING from IN FLAME
A scorching, superfast rocker driven hard by a fat and rumbling bass line and featuring some truly blistering guitar.

❿ WE'LL BRING THE HOUSE DOWN from WE'LL BRING THE HOUSE DOWN
A real heavy bruiser, this feels like Nod's jumping up and down on your head with his enormous boots. There's a marked "Ballroom Blitz" feel to the drums.

Essi Berelian

Slapp Happy/Peter Blegvad

"Naive rock", Slapp Happy defined their style as they embarked on a consciously low-key career in the mid-1970s. They were madly out of time, coming at the height of prog rock, but their songs of "sinister whimsy", delivered by the marvellous Dagmar Krause, retain their magic. And in Peter Blegvad, they had a songwriter of most peculiar genius.

SLAPP HAPPY

❶ JUST A CONVERSATION from SORT OF
The quirkily joyous opener from their debut has Krause singing a chorus line over oddball lines of chat from Blegvad and Anthony Moore.

❷ CASABLANCA MOON from ACNALBASAC NOOM
"He used to wear fedoras but now he sports a fez, Cabalistic innuendoes in everything he says", begins this very catchy, surreal narrative.

❸ A LITTLE SOMETHING from ACNALBASAC NOOM
There's a perfection to this breathy love song, strummed on electro-acoustic, with its tale "from the tip of Alaska to the edge of Spain…"

❹ THE DRUM from ACNALBASAC NOOM
A quirky rocker, covered by Bongwater two decades on. The Slappy original was recorded by the trio with Faust in Germany.

❺ SLOW MOON'S ROSE from CASABLANCA MOON
Virgin got Slapp Happy to re-record their UK debut album, and on this song, with its sweet, wistful sax break, they got it right.

PETER BLEGVAD

❻ GOLD from CHOICES UNDER PRESSURE
This song is a huge country hit in waiting: a tale of the uselessness of gold, "the lowliest of metals, too soft for serious use, pretty of course…"

Peter Blegvad's
Rx (är'e˘ks')

n 1. A prescription for medicine or a medical appliance. 2. A remedy, cure, or solution for a disorder or problem.

❶ SANTA CLAUS SONNY BOY WILLIAMSON from THE CHESS YEARS

A shot of pure adrenaline in which Williamson tears his baby's crib apart (not his tot's cot, you dig) trying to find out "what did she bought me for Santy Claw". He leaps into each verse, piling the fantastic language up, the combo swinging harder and harder until finally he vents a happy "oh yeah!" and lets his harp wail.

❷ TIME FOR THE SUN TO RISE EARL KING from SEXUAL TELEPATHY

The haunting guitar has something of the sweetness of Hendrix's "Little Wing", but with more primitive mystery and depth. The song evokes a mood of dreamy longing – "Sunrise, why must you come so soon/Sunrise, you don't suit me like the moon."

❸ WHO WILL SING FOR ME THE STANLEY BROTHERS from 16 GREATEST GOSPEL HITS

Songs by the Stanley Brothers are sinister yet full of light. Heap good goose-bump medicine.

❹ MA'S DREAM BLUES MICHAEL HURLEY from WATERTOWER

One of the ruefullest songs ever, vulnerably voiced by the troubadour, cartoonist, former Holy Modal Rounder and occasional *loup garou* known as Snock, Wood Bill and other handles to his devotees. Records can be got direct from the man himself at snockonews.com. In this song, Blind Willie McTell and Ma Rainey appear to the dreamer; Willie has regained his sight; Snock starts dancing but when he turns around he realizes…

❺ UP THE LAZY RIVER LOUIS ARMSTRONG

I lost my copy of this years ago. But as soon as I'm asked about all-time favourite tracks I hear it in my head. The scat solo in which Satchmo amazes himself: "Boy am I riffin' tonight, I hope sumpin'." The trumpet solo which comes up like glory, raising the dead. But memory swerves. Could it really be THAT stately and great? So I order a new copy, wait days, it arrives, I play it, and … that's me, prostrate, acknowledging the transcendent made manifest in my living room.

❻ I MUST HAVE THAT MAN BILLIE HOLIDAY from LADY DAY, THE BEST OF

My dad is a great jazz buff. I like to hear him tell how in the 1960s Teddy Wilson came to our London flat after a gig and tickled the ivories on our out-of-tune upright. Wilson leads the classic line-up on this celebrated track. Lady Day at her youthful peak, transforming what would otherwise be a mere ditty into a masterpiece. Lester "Nijinsky of the saxophone" Young's solo is one of my favourite moments in music.

❼ MUSIC FOR GLASS HARMONICA (K617)
W.A. MOZART from MUSIC FOR GLASS HARMONICA

Mozart's last piece of chamber music. The glass harmonica is a series of tuned glasses spinning on an axle and played with wet fingers. Devised by Benjamin Franklin, it makes an unearthly, ethereal sound. In the eighteenth century, people were warned of its effect on sensitive temperaments. Mesmer used it as part of his "animal magnetism" treatments. Necromancers used it to summon the dead. Some of the instrument's most popular players went mad, and by the mid-nineteenth century the instrument had been banned. In fact, it was probably poisoning from the lead in the glass which toppled their reason, so it's perfectly safe to listen to – though this piece does have addictive, narcotic properties.

❼ DAUGHTER from JUST WOKE UP

An unusually straight but affecting song on parenthood. It was covered by Loudon Wainwright for the movie *Knocked Up*.

❽ KING STRUT from KING STRUT

Blegvad's rocking narrative of a dreamer, featuring the terrific line "imagination like a muscle will increase with exercise".

❾ MEANTIME from KING STRUT

A train song with a difference: destination meantime, where you could wait for ever.

❿ WASTE OF TIME from CHOICES UNDER PRESSURE

Perversely, Blegvad prefaced his retrospective album with this tale of "a devil in my cranium who wants to see me fail". Splendid, nonetheless.

Mark Ellingham

Slide guitar

Tune your guitar to some sort of chord, stick a glass or metal tube over a finger or hold some sort of metal bar in your hand, and slide it up and down the strings. It's a sound associated most strongly with the blues, is claimed by some to have started in Hawaii, but in truth crops up all over the world.

❶ WRITE ME A FEW LINES FRED MCDOWELL from MISSISSIPPI DELTA BLUES

"I don't play no rock'n'roll", claimed Fred, all the while pounding out driving, rattling, awesome country blues like this that made most rockers sound like pale ninnies.

❷ DHUN KEHARWA BRIJ BUSHAN KABRA from EXOTIC SOUNDS ON GUITAR

The father of Hindustani slide guitar, carried to the levels of musicianship required by Indian classical music.

❸ CAN'T BE SATISFIED MUDDY WATERS from THE ANTHOLOGY

He took the acoustic blues of Son House and Robert Johnson onto electric guitar and into the Chicago clubs. The world changed and his mojo henceforth worked.

❹ CAY TRUC XINH KIM SINH from THE ARTISTRY OF…

The master of slithery Vietnamese guitar has adapted its sound to the lap Hawaiian version too.

❺ SONG OF THE RANGE JIM & BOB, THE GENIAL HAWAIIANS from HAWAIIAN STEEL GUITAR CLASSICS

They recorded very little in the early 1930s, but their extraordinary version of "Home On The Range" is one of the all-time great slide guitar masterpieces.

❻ COLUMBUS STOCKADE BLUES DARBY & TARLTON from COMPLETE RECORDINGS

These days country music is awash with Dobros and pedal steel guitars, but that slidey sound was pioneered in the old-timey music of the 1920s.

❼ PALOLO SOL HOOPII from HAWAIIAN STEEL GUITAR CLASSIC

The hottest of the hot Hawaiians from the golden age in the 1920s and 30s.

❽ ALALAKE SEKOU "DIAMOND FINGERS" DIABATÉ from THE SYLIPHONE YEARS

Slide guitar reached Africa too: the aptly nicknamed Diabate showcased it in Guinea's mighty Bembeya Jazz, and it's used in Nigerian juju bands as well.

❾ KOLOPA BOB BROZMAN (WITH LEDWARD KAAPANA) from KIKA KILA MEETS KI HO'ALU

The world's greatest binge collaborationist has blended his virtuoso slide talents with those of players from Okinawa, India, Guinea, La Réunion, Hawaii and beyond.

❿ THE LOVER'S GHOST MARTIN SIMPSON from THE BRAMBLE BRIAR

One of England's finest acoustic guitarists adapts techniques learned from the blues to melodic English and Celtic folk tunes.

Ian Anderson

Sly Stone

The Beatles, The Rolling Stones, The Temptations and James Brown may have had more hits, but no one epitomized the late 1960s/early 70s more than Sly & the Family Stone. While other bands paid lip service to such 1960s ideals as racial integration, sexual equality and fighting the establishment, the erstwhile Sylvester Stewart and his clan of brothers, sisters and ofays put the rhetoric into practice with some of the most radical, perfectly crafted, galvanizing music ever.

❶ DANCE TO THE MUSIC from DANCE TO THE MUSIC

Blends James Brown and The Who so seamlessly that you can't figure out where the rock stops and the soul begins.

❷ M'LADY from LIFE

Churning funk almost identical to "Dance To The Music", but the groove is so ferocious you won't care.

❸ I WANT TO TAKE YOU HIGHER from STAND!

Boom-lacka-lacka-lacka-boom.

❹ EVERYDAY PEOPLE from STAND!

Sly took pop's great subject, "everybody is a star", and made it a political statement of empowerment, belonging and belief.

❺ STAND from STAND!

In which Sly desperately tries to apply the solipsism of acid rock to the real world.

❻ THANK YOU (FALETTINME BE MICE ELF AGIN) from GREATEST HITS

Far removed from the anthemic heights of old, this is a snarling vamp that is the group's most uncompromisingly funky record.

❼ FAMILY AFFAIR from THERE'S A RIOT GOIN' ON
Perhaps Sly's best record about being trapped by fate.

❽ QUE SERA SERA (WHATEVER WILL BE, WILL BE) from FRESH
In which Sly turns the sickly sweet Doris Day chestnut into a gospel hymn.

❾ IF YOU WANT ME TO STAY from FRESH
As savage and brutal a kiss-off as Bob Dylan's "Positively Fourth Street".

❿ LOOSE BOOTY from SMALL TALK
A record that pops with weird energy, but what do Shadrach, Meshach and Abendego have to do with loose booty?

Peter Shapiro

The Small Faces & other mods

Though the mods were famous for masculine peacock finery of the most paisley-patterned rainbow-coloured kind, styles that look good even now were just the icing on the cake of the youth movement, which thrived on soul, bluebeat, ska, Tamla Motown and the ear-cracking chimes Rickenbacker guitars fed without mercy into overdriven amplifiers.

❶ ALL OR NOTHING THE SMALL FACES from THE ULTIMATE COLLECTION
Marriott had the voice, the attitude and credit in Carnaby Street strong enough to permit him this most macho of mod lyrics. Not a dance tune, but the perfect accompaniment to your tenth cup of cappucino in the caff opposite the Flamingo Club.

❷ THE KIDS ARE ALL RIGHT THE WHO from THE ULTIMATE COLLECTION
They should have played more Motown covers and they never mastered bluebeat, but The Who managed to define mod for a generation. In the lyrics hides a world of teenage confusion and turmoil, locked away behind a cool exterior of blocked (ho! ho!) emotions.

❸ THE "IN" CROWD DOBIE GRAY from THE ULTIMATE COLLECTION
A song so cool that even Bryan Ferry couldn't totally mess it up. It delivers a concentrated distillation of the whole mod ethos painlessly and in less than three minutes.

❹ LET'S GO BABY (WHERE THE ACTION IS) ROBERT PARKER from THE WARDELL QUEZERGUE SESSIONS
Ultimate mod sentiments from a man who, oddly enough, wouldn't recognize a mod if one bit him on the leg. It's all about finding yourself the good times, where the beat goes on and the people don't care about too much but their clothes. A great dance tune, of course.

❺ THESE HANDS (SMALL BUT MIGHTY) BOBBY BLAND from ANTHOLOGY
Bland's unmistakeable voice yells his soul out to the skies on wings of sweet, sweet brass from the tightest horn section in the town of Memphis.

❻ DON'T BRING ME DOWN THE PRETTY THINGS from THE BBC SESSIONS
Stereotypical cool classic British R&B from the band that gave the Stones bad dreams and cold sweats. This song of Saturday-night love affairs was banned by the BBC for the suggestion contained in the lyric "…and when I laid her on the ground,/My head was spinning round…". What can they have been thinking of?

❼ HOLD ON I'M COMIN' THE CHORDS from THIS IS WHAT THEY WANT
The mod revival that sprouted in the late 1970s produced some truly forgettable music. This version of the Sam & Dave soul classic was the exception. Mod was all about music like this; fast, sweaty, wearing a huge beaming grin and so cranked up that the boys can't blink.

❽ WACK WACK THE YOUNG HOLT TRIO from LOOKING GOOD (VARIOUS ARTISTS)
Time to break it down and bust yourself a move or two to the piano stylings of a hot, shuffling instrumental. Nothing's cooler than singing along to the bassline like the guy who's playing it, then freestyling across the floor to the drum break.

❾ I'M GONNA RUN AWAY FROM YOU TAMI LYNN from AT THE CLUB (VARIOUS ARTISTS)
Lynn's coldly emotional vocal echoes like it was recorded in the enormous freezer beneath a meat warehouse, and the melody seems ready to turn to ice with her. You treated her wrong, you dog, and even though it breaks her heart, she's gonna find someone better.

❿ I GOT A WOMAN (PARTS 1 & 2) JIMMY MCGRIFF from GREATEST HITS
A cool groove with the swinging Hammond sounds of the man McGriff. Finish off your set now, sprinkle that talcum on the floor and slide your stride, but mind my mohair threads, OK?

Al Spicer

Smashing Pumpkins

Seattle's post-grunge four-piece produced three breathtaking records (and, it has to be said, some dross) before imploding.

❶ DISARM from SIAMESE DREAM
Church bells, strings and acoustic guitar back Billy Corgan's bellow of rejection and isolation.

❷ ZERO from MELON COLLIE AND THE INFINITE SADNESS
The definitive Pumpkins grungey rock song, a rough ride through self-obsessed lyrics, heavy bass and gnarly riffs.

❸ 1979 from MELON COLLIE AND THE INFINITE SADNESS.
The years without responsibility and consequence recalled over a slurry riff-and-drum track.

❹ TONIGHT TONIGHT from MELON COLLIE AND THE INFINITE SADNESS
A marching snare complements a string quartet as Corgan enthuses "the impossible is possible tonight."

❺ SIVA from GISH
From the Pumpkins' often forgotten first album, Siva scruffs its way between soft melodies and wailing solos.

❻ TODAY from SIAMESE DREAM
The typical Pumpkins dynamic range, juxtaposing a sweet riff against distorted guitar.

❼ BULLET WITH BUTTERFLY WINGS from MELON COLLIE AND THE INFINITE SADNESS
Squealing guitars and desperate lyrics: "Despite all my rage/I am still just a rat in a cage."

❽ AVA ADORE from ADORE
Like much of the band's later work, a more electronic and less gritty noise for Corgan to sing of selfish, uncompromising desires.

Ben Garfield

Elliott Smith

Having tragically died at the height of his powers, Smith left behind a clutch of albums that constitute a songbook of such quality that his name will not quickly be forgotten.

❶ NEEDLE IN THE HAY from ELLIOTT SMITH
Guitar and voice, simple and effective. The lo-fi production and Smith's near-whisper almost place him and his tape machine in the same room as you.

❷ ROMAN CANDLE from ROMAN CANDLE
A quiet song about anger like no other. An acoustic guitar boils while Smith softly spits venom.

❸ LAST CALL from ROMAN CANDLE
Perhaps this songwriter's finest moment: an unrivalled analysis of the troubled aftermath of a relationship.

❹ INDEPENDENCE DAY from XO
An altogether sunnier number that bounces along in a Beatles-esque fashion.

❺ SOMEBODY THAT I USED TO KNOW from FIGURE 8
Another uptempo amble through Smith's head. He can pretend all he wants that he doesn't care. It's clear that he does.

❻ COAST TO COAST from FROM A BASEMENT ON THE HILL
This opening cut of Smith's posthumously released final collection is a full-throttle stomper that's hard to shake out of your head.

Peter Buckley

Patti Smith

You can forget Tony Soprano and Bruce Springsteen. New Jersey's toughest export is Patti Smith – poet, artist, performer. Although she can occasionally be irritating and scattershot in her work, when she gets it right, there's nobody to match her for purity, intensity and the mystic quasi-religious mania of genius.

❶ GLORIA from HORSES
The song that started it all for Patti begins with the best line she ever wrote – "Jesus died for somebody's sins, but not mine". Her version of Van Morrison's song blossoms into a bump and grind that climaxes in a breathless ascent of the highest bell tower in the universe.

❷ REDONDO BEACH from HORSES
The band's incongruously chirpy white reggae at first hides the unfolding story of love gone wrong, arguments, tantrums and suicide down at the beach.

❸ FREE MONEY from HORSES
This should be the National Lottery Show theme tune. It's a blue-collar, coupon-clippers' hymn, poignant in

its desperate reliance on the gods of chance for a way out of their miserable lives, that builds to a fantastic, liberating peak of release.

❹ BREAK IT UP from **HORSES**
Hallucinatory lyrics from childhood fever dreams take the listener up a staircase built from Tom Verlaine's

swooping guitar, in one of Patti's greatest moments. Inspiration struck her at Jim Morrison's grave, so the story goes.

❺ KIMBERLY from **HORSES**
Named after Patti's sister, the one who found it even harder to escape the many tentacles of love in the

---

Ed Smith's
Pavilion playlist

Middlesex and some time England cricketer **ED SMITH** compiled this list of the music he listens to before going out to bat. Smith is also a broadcaster and author of *On And Off The Field*. He writes of his list: "A pavilion, particularly the dressing room, witnesses just about every human emotion: joy, affection, despair, rage, hope, laughter, tears. Team sport leads us to experience the full range, alongside our peers, and music provides a great bond along that journey."

❶ BORN TO RUN BRUCE SPRINGSTEEN
from BORN TO RUN
Adrenalin-driven but intelligent rock'n'roll. Makes you feel anything is possible.

❷ INTO THE MYSTIC VAN MORRISON
from MOONDANCE
Cricket attracts Van Morrison fans. My old Kent team-mate Graham Cowdrey has seen him 187 times (seriously). "Into The Mystic" perfectly captures Morrison's plaintive mysticism. I don't know what it's about and that's just fine.

❸ THE RESCUE BLUES RYAN ADAMS from GOLD
"Everybody wants you to be special" runs the opening line, reminding us sports people that we all once harboured hopes of being the best. And for almost everyone, that hope is slowly dashed.

❹ TINY DANCER ELTON JOHN from MADMAN ACROSS THE WATER
There are few happier moments than a win followed by a team sing-song. This is the most sing-along-able I know.

❺ IT MAKES NO DIFFERENCE
THE BAND from THE LAST WALTZ
In making *The Last Waltz*, Martin Scorsese not only captured a great concert, but also the whole essence of life on the road. Sportsmen, just like musicians, understand the road only too well. While providing a constant stream of new adventures, it makes us vulnerable to nostalgia and introspection.

❻ EVERYBODY'S CHANGING
KEANE from HOPES AND FEARS
Tim Rice-Oxley, Keane's keyboardist, played with me in the same Tonbridge School First XI (bowling handy inswingers). He was the same brilliant musician and intelligent, modest man that he is now. Ten years on, Keane was an instant hit in the pavilion – catchy, evocative, moody – and this song is my favourite.

❼ SIMPLE TWIST OF FATE BOB DYLAN from BLOOD ON THE TRACKS
Luck, destiny, fate – sport's recurring themes.

❽ EAST MARAH
from 20,000 STREETS UNDER THE SKY
Sometimes you need straight-shooting, no bullshit rock'n'roll. The question is: does anyone make it these days? Marah do, and East is their best – like an early Springsteen song.

❾ FIRE AND RAIN JAMES TAYLOR from YOU'VE GOT A FRIEND, THE BEST OF JAMES TAYLOR
Bitter-sweet and melancholic but not depressing, "Fire And Rain" makes people stop talking and listen (for about a minute).

❿ MOST OF THE TIME BOB DYLAN
from OH MERCY
Dylan sings this brilliantly: no irony, no bitterness, just straight heartache. Four decades of emotion expressed in five minutes.

Smith household, this song hangs in the memory like a promise of rescue left by an escaped cellmate.

❻ AIN'T IT STRANGE from RADIO ETHIOPIA
While the band click out some precise, uneasy reggae, Patti jolts and stumbles through a trip of imagery all her own, with girls in white dresses, boys shooting white stuff and books of gold.

❼ ROCK 'N' ROLL NIGGER from EASTER
The Patti Smith group has no peers when it comes to tales of life in the music world. This track celebrates and glorifies the outsider status of true-blue dyed-in-the-wool rockers. Takes guts to drop the "N-bomb", too, if you're a white woman outta NJ.

❽ BECAUSE THE NIGHT from EASTER
Smith's magnificent take on this Bruce Springsteen song takes it to an entirely different place with lyrics of her own.

❾ PEOPLE HAVE THE POWER from DREAM OF LIFE
So when we've burned down all the lottery ticket outlets, let's move on to overthrow the system and fight the power. This shall be our rallying song. Patti leads the band and the audience into a singalong, out onto the streets and, waving flaming torches, up to City Hall.

❿ SMELLS LIKE TEEN SPIRIT from TWELVE
Aside from Patti, the only people to attempt Nirvana covers are kids in guitar stores. But even the boldest of them would hesitate to chuck electric banjo plucking and a burst of their own free-range poetry into the mix. Old enough to know better, Smith delivered a dozen decent tributes on this album of covers, with this particular cut being the weirdest and the best.

Al Spicer

❸ THE QUEEN IS DEAD from THE QUEEN IS DEAD
"I know you, and you cannot sing", the monarch announces. To which Morrissey would now respond "But you should hear Camilla play piano."

❹ HEAVEN KNOWS I'M MISERABLE NOW from HATFUL OF HOLLOW
Desolation, blushing, genuinely funny lyrics and a falsetto. When people parody The Smiths, this is the song they use.

❺ MEAT IS MURDER from MEAT IS MURDER
The most complete example of The Smiths as a band rather than simply a Moz/Marr duet. And the one that made young vegetarians of thousands.

❻ THE HEADMASTER RITUAL from MEAT IS MURDER
Cold showers and pupil abuse in all guises – Morrissey sings as if he enjoyed school a great deal.

❼ A RUSH AND A PUSH AND THE LAND IS OURS from STRANGEWAYS HERE WE COME
A revolutionary call to stand up for yourself in an uncaring world.

❽ HAND IN GLOVE from THE SMITHS
A mouth-organ heralds a defiantly happy private love story. But not to worry: it's all dashed at the end.

❾ I KNOW IT'S OVER from RANK
A heartbreaking confessional, it's also the band's most stirring live performance.

❿ PANIC from THE WORLD WON'T LISTEN
"Hang the DJ" was the singalong, but "The music that they constantly play/Says nothing to me about my life" summed up precisely why The Smiths stood out.

Simon Garfield

The Smiths
The ultimate student bedsit to Los Angeles poolside story: the misery of Manchester still sounds sublime.

❶ THERE IS A LIGHT THAT NEVER GOES OUT from THE QUEEN IS DEAD
The most romantic traffic pile-up in the world – car, ten-ton truck and double-decker bus – with a string section and Morrissey at his sweetest as it unfolds.

❷ HOW SOON IS NOW from HATFUL OF HOLLOW
Johnny Marr cascades and stutters in a tribute to crippling social inadequacies.

Snoop Dogg
After losing his way in the chronic haze and misplacing his dignity in his porno-producer persona, the Dogg is back like he never went away. If you're sitting in his place sucka, you'd best move before he pops a cap in yo'ass. Fo'shizzle!

❶ AIN'T NO FUN (IF THE HOMIES CAN'T HAVE NONE) from DOGGY STYLE
One of the least misogynistic of the cuts on this album of filth and funky degradation, "Ain't No Fun" is still breathtakingly foul-mouthed and bad in attitude. Like all Snoop's best cuts, this one swings and grooves

along like an open-topped Lexus on the Pacific Coast Highway. When the rap kicks in, all kinds of @&%#%$!! flood the vocals and you're left amazed that there are so many novel ways of saying things you shouldn't. .

❷ MIDNIGHT LOVE from DEATH ROW'S GREATEST SNOOP DOGG HITS
Beware girl! There's a Dogg on your tail. Snoop plans to steal a sweet girl away from her lover man, turn her out and earn money from her life of shame. Don't even think about trying to get the li'l darling back once the Snoop's put his stamp on her.

❸ GIN AND JUICE from DEATH ROW'S GREATEST SNOOP DOGG HITS
Wonderful, warm afternoon cruising tune. Presumably safely belted into his seat behind a designated sober driver, Snoop celebrates smoking menthol (mixed with an ounce of the chronic), hooking up with Dr Dre and hanging with willing sweethearts from the noble city of Compton.

❹ NUTHIN BUT A G THANG from DEATH ROW'S GREATEST SNOOP DOGG HITS
The first of many outstanding collaborations between Snoop and the once-lost, now rediscovered champion of the hip-hop world, Dr Dre. Masterful beats courtesy of the good Doctor give Snoop a rich polyrhythmic set of platforms to skip between.

❺ ROUND HERE from THA BLUE CARPET TREATMENT
Compelling meditation on the darker side of fame and fortune. A double edged blade at the best of times, when success hits a performer who gets his tales and credibility from the streets it can be dangerous.

❻ A BITCH I KNEW from THA BLUE CARPET TREATMENT
Reminiscing to the night of the Sugar Ray fight, Snoop feels obliged to lead us graphically along the path of his early female partners. Despite them doing him ALL kinds of favours, he never really learned to respect womankind.

❼ GANG BANGING 101 from THA BLUE CARPET TREATMENT
Snoop plans to meld the Crips into one solid posse. He's gonna call together all the Bloods too. And, once he gets them to stop killing one another he's going to take over the world with this unstoppable "We Will Rock You" beat.

❽ WHO AM I (WHAT'S MY NAME) from FROM DEATH ROW'S GREATEST SNOOP DOGG HITS
Snoop's calling card, winding up the crowd into a call and response work of mass hypnosis. He works the "Mo-Fo" word, in all its charming variety of forms, so densely into the lyric that it becomes a vocal tic.

❾ THINK ABOUT IT from THA BLUE CARPET TREATMENT
A much longer, considered and laid-back meditation. When the backing track drops Snoop matches it beat for beat, drumkick for cymbal clash with a spray of syllabology that shoots down all comers.

❿ CRAZY from THA BLUE CARPET TREATMENT
Nate Dogg, vintage Don of the G-Funk scene, adds his cred, slick vocals and classic style to a cool stroll along the beach. Snoop's finest lazy accented pimpspeak glints his eyes at you over a pair of sunglasses too fashionable for you to wear … ever.

Al Spicer

Snow Patrol

None more sincere indie chaps, originally from Ireland but now based in Scotland, Snow Patrol polished up soft rock for the 21st century. They didn't really hit their stride until 2004's *Final Straw* but comitted fans interested in where they come from should check out *Songs For Polarbears* and *When It's All Over We Still Have To Clear Up*.

❶ WOW from FINAL STRAW
Earnest commitment seeps from every word, the guitar line begs for understanding, even the drums wear puppy dog eyes. This track rocks, but with a hint of regret.

❷ CHOCOLATE from FINAL STRAW
No added milk or sugar here, this is darkly bitter chocolate, intended for adults.

❸ GRAZED KNEES from FINAL STRAW
Haunting vocals from Gary Lightbody, who sounds like he's grazed his entire soul.

❹ TINY LITTLE FRACTURES from FINAL STRAW
A classic straightforward rocker that demonstrates the band's more muscular side.

❺ YOU'RE ALL I HAVE from EYES OPEN
The perfect upbeat Snow patrol confection: fantastic guitar riff, descended from The Velvet Underground's "Waiting for the Man", superbly phrased singing from Lightbody, and spot-on falsetto backing vocals.

❻ SET THE FIRE TO THE THIRD BAR from EYES OPEN
Martha Wainwright's vocal input turns this song around from dirge into something soaring way up into the realm of heart-freezing beauty.

Al Spicer

Gary Lightbody picks
Influential songs

Currently bestriding the world and giving U2 a run for their money in the "biggest band from the island of Ireland" stakes, Snow Patrol has captured the knack of creating outstandingly powerful stadium-sized ballads from the intimate minutiae of personal tragedies and sobbed regrets. So, Gary, where did all the crazy ideas come from?

❶ BAD MICHAEL JACKSON from BAD
I was about 10 and musically it had no effect on me at all. But it was a great pop song and I liked it image-wise – lots of sparkly costumes and fantastic dance moves. I knocked all the ornaments off the walls trying to copy them.

❷ ROCK'N'ROLL DAMNATION AC/DC from IF YOU WANT BLOOD
The first record I loved that my parents hated. They didn't understand the noise and they really thought it was the devil's music.

❸ TERRITORIAL PISSINGS NIRVANA from NEVER MIND
A clarion call. When I first heard it, I felt my whole future was mapped out.

❹ MELLOWED OUT TEENAGE FAN CLUB from GRAND PRIX
When it came out I thought the whole album was the most perfect pop record I'd ever heard. But if I had to chose one song from it I'd say "Mellowed Out".

❺ HOMETOWN UNICORN SUPER FURRY ANIMALS FROM FUZZY LOGIC
I was 18 years old, I'd just left home and it was terrifying. The Super Furries first album was about to come out and it was preceded by this single…

❻ OVER THE OCEAN LOW CD SINGLE
The first time I heard it was on a John Peel show . He just said "listen to this" and put on this wonderful, orchestral-sounding nothingness. I'm not a spiritual person but it was a very spiritual moment.

❼ TRANSATLANTICISM DEATH CAB FOR CUTIE from TRANSATLANTICISM
The lyrics are amazing, building up into the mantra "I need you so much closer". It breaks my heart and mends it, then breaks it and mends it again, over and over but the cycle always ends with mending. It never lets you down.

❽ SET THE FIRE TO THE THIRD BAR SNOW PATROL from EYES OPEN
This is the song of ours that I'm proudest of, not because of us but because Martha Wainwright sings on it. I wrote it as a love song to her voice. I'd never met her but she sounded like a dangerous angel. Then we called her and invited her to sing it.

❾ CHICAGO SUFJAN STEVENS from ILLINOIS
That record was the soundtrack to 2005 for me.

❿ USE IT THE NEW PORNOGRAPHERS from TWIN CINEMA
It contains the line, "Heads down, thumbs up, two sips of the cup of human kindness and I'm shit-faced." Now that's genius, isn't it?"

Solos sans guitar

Sick of boring old air guitar getting all the publicity? This playlist is for the ignored instruments of rock and pop's less obvious solos!

❶ MY BOY LOLLIPOP MILLIE from THE REGGAE BOX
This harp solo (played by Rod Stewart!) is made all the more satisfying because of the hints of which hum in the background of the song's earlier verses like a circling shark, before BAM! Air harmonica!

❷ C'EST LA VIE B*WITCHED from B*WITCHED
One of the finest moments in the late-1990s Irish pop explosion – if an "explosion" can entail all of, oh, four artists – the tin whistle solo in "C'est La Vie" is all the more arresting because of the almost entirely synthesized arrangements it explodes out of.

❸ HIP TO BE SQUARE HUEY LEWIS & THE NEWS from FORE!
The blazing saxophone solo that responds to the call of the synth brass is heaven: out of the midst of The News' overproduced 1980s arrangement springs a moment of pure saxophonal madness.

❹ CALIFORNIA DREAMIN' THE MAMAS & THE PAPAS from GREATEST HITS

Of course it's a flute solo – what other instrument suggests the mournfulness of grey skies made gloomier by regrets and heartache?

❺ IF ONLY HANSON from THIS TIME AROUND

The great thing about Taylor Hanson's harmonica work in "If Only" is the way the harp swings from the dinkily upbeat opening riff to that absolutely sublime Toots Thielemans-ish post-middle eight solo, packed with yearning and throbbing emotion.

❻ LOUIE, LOUIE TOOTS & THE MAYTALS from THIS IS REGGAE MUSIC

"Toots" Hibbert gets in two sneaky solos in this brillo take on the garage standard; the first is a perfectly wonderful saxophone solo, but the second comes at the outro, a completely crazy garbled Hammond organ riff that sounds like someone gargling into a flanger.

❼ LONG WAY TO THE TOP AC/DC from T.N.T.

Only Bon Scott could make the bagpipes seem like the most natural choice for a rocking middle eight solo.

❽ HURRICANE BOB DYLAN from DESIRE

Scarlett Rivera's frankly electric work on the fiddle provides this song's emotional might. It swirls about the song like Ruben Carter's adopted namesake, whirring with barely reserved intent during the verse and then bursting out all over, then retreating back into the shadows.

❾ ROUNDABOUT YES from THE ULTIMATE YES

Rick Wakeman's nimble-fingered Hammond work ushers in guitar, bass and drum solos, though rightfully installing the organ as the star of the song by continually popping up again, just in case we needed a reminder.

❿ MOONLIGHT FEELS RIGHT STARBUCK from MOONLIGHT FEELS RIGHT

And just when you thought you'd heard all that non-guitar solos have to offer, up jumps Starbuck, with the jauntiest vibraphone solo you've ever heard this side of the hit parade. Just try to resist its air-vibe charms.

Clem Bastow

Sonic Youth

Sonic Youth are more of a New York institution than a rock band. Their catalogue is vast and largely essential; as such, this list barely scrapes the surface.

❶ DEATH VALLEY 69 from BAD MOON RISING

Thurston and special guest Lydia Lunch scream their way through this blood-shedding aural road movie while hallmark super-fast open-tuned guitar scree falls all around them.

❷ TEENAGE RIOT from DAYDREAM NATION

It's impossible not to get swept away by this song; the opening bars gently tuck you in before a whirlwind of killer riffs rip the roof off your house.

❸ SUPERSTAR from IF I WAS A CARPENTER

The Youth have tackled many covers over the years. This take on the Carpenters' classic is brilliant, and surprisingly faithful.

❹ SCHIZOPHRENIA from SISTER

This radical rework of an old Skip Spence song opens an entire album that no home should be without. Guitars duck and dive and tempos shift with every single note and sound slotting into place like parts of a jigsaw.

❺ I DREAMED I DREAM from SONIC YOUTH

An early excursion of menacing power and precision. Could be the soundtrack to a creeping lava flow.

❻ EXPRESSWAY TO YR SKULL from EVOL

A slow burning excuse for some amplifier abuse hidden behind a great hook and tune.

❼ BULL IN THE HEATHER from EXPERIMENTAL JET SET, TRASH AND NO STAR

From 1994, this single finds Kim Gordon at the mic for a stripped-back stab at angular weirdness.

❽ COTTON CROWN from SISTER

Kim and Thurston duet over layers of crunching guitar.

❾ SKIP TRACER from WASHING MACHINE

When he's not been busy melting guitar scratch plates, Sonic Youth's Lee Ranaldo has taken the time to write and sing some of the band's most memorable lyrics. This one is a prime example.

❿ WALKING THE COW LUCKY SPERMS from WALKING THE COW EP

Track down this SY offshoot project (featuring Mike Watt) if you can. The track was originally by Daniel Johnston and this version of it is genius.

Peter Buckley

Classic soul

The best of it all came from the same place, the heart, and ended up in roughly the same vicinity, the bedroom. But it was never merely a seduction tool – the soul ballad is the epitome of soul music itself, no matter what era it was recorded in.

❶ THE FIRST TIME EVER I SAW YOUR FACE ROBERTA FLACK from THE VERY BEST OF...
Straightforward and almost startling in its purity of voice and instrumentation. Ballads don't get more soulful than this.

❷ MY GIRL THE TEMPTATIONS from THE ULTIMATE COLLECTION
In spite of all the Motown sophistication in the backing, the Temps still manage to sound touchingly naive, as if they can hardly believe their collective luck.

❸ MUNCHIES FOR YOUR LOVE BOOTSY'S RUBBER BAND from AHH ... THE NAME IS BOOTSY, BABY!
This bonkers, viscous, all-embracing love song practically oozes out of your speakers.

❹ ORDINARY PEOPLE JOHN LEGEND from GET LIFTED
By taking a satisfyingly lo-fi approach, Legend ensures none of his inherent soulfulness gets lost in whatever's going on around him.

❺ GYPSY WOMAN CURTIS MAYFIELD from LIVE IN EUROPE
On this cool updating of an Impressions' classic, Curtis and his guitar are backed by bass, drums, another guitar and a hyperactive bongo player. It's all over much too soon.

❻ I CAN'T STAND THE RAIN ANN PEEBLES from I CAN'T STAND THE RAIN
The other half of the Hi sound, with that Hammond organ, the Memphis horns and a Willie Mitchell production buoying up one of the 1970s' finest voices.

❼ JOY & PAIN MAZE from GREATEST HITS
Always a Saturday night anthem, it has to be the live version for this chunky, funky, philosophical approach to lurrrve to make any sense.

❽ ALONE JODECI from BACK TO THE FUTURE
Slowed-down swingbeat that allows the group's post-hip-hop attitude to square itself with their no-nonsense notions of seduction to create a true love song for the 1990s.

❾ HOMELY GIRL THE CHI-LITES from THE BEST OF...
This has a bizarre country feel to it, backed up by an almost military beat, yet the simple sentiments and smooth harmonizing pull it all together into a pop-soul masterpiece.

❿ SHE'S SO GOOD TO ME LUTHER VANDROSS from THE ESSENTIAL
Crisp, percussion-laden and tied up with just the right amount of strings, Luther's voice leads us around a celebration of his love.

Lloyd Bradley

Seventies soul

This decade had a great deal going for it. After the social upheavals of the 1960s, black music had an enormous confidence and sense of purpose, and was yet to gobbled up by the mainstream record industry and spat out as disco. Musicians controlled the technology, so 1970s soul had a good few years to please nobody but itself.

❶ WHO IS HE AND WHAT IS HE TO YOU? CREATIVE SOURCE from CREATIVE SOURCE AND MORE
Almost twelve minutes of shimmering percussion, wood-chopping wah-wahs, darting horns and towering vocals, building into a crescendo of paranoia that's borderline psycho.

❷ THE LOVE I LOST HAROLD MELVIN AND THE BLUE NOTES from THE ESSENTIAL...
Probably the ultimate Gamble & Huff tune: Teddy Pendergass on lead vocal; seemingly random four-part backing harmonies; broken-hearted subject matter; and a bassline that takes no prisoners.

❸ LOVE'S THEME LOVE UNLIMITED ORCHESTRA from BARRY WHITE AND LOVE UNLIMITED ORCHESTRA: BACK TO BACK
A forty-piece orchestra works hard to keep up with a rhythm section urged on by a relentless wah-wah guitar in a production as big as Barry White himself. More bling than this and we'd all go blind.

❹ BE THANKFUL FOR WHAT YOU GOT WILLIAM DEVAUGHN from BE THANKFUL FOR WHAT YOU GOT
Cool, breezy and delicately put together, this easy-rocking hymn to the virtues of poverty is so infectious it makes not having a car sound like a good idea.

❺ FAMILY AFFAIR SLY & THE FAMILY STONE from THERE'S A RIOT GOIN' ON
Larry Graham percolates his bass under the sparsest organ and guitar, while Sly oozes over everything with lyrics quite scary in their whacked-out, self-absorbed pointlessness.

Jazzie B's
Soul set

A bit of a polymath, JAZZIE B. The founder of Soul II Soul – who have a good claim to putting British soul on the international map – he has also worked as a producer (James Brown is among his credits), a label boss, and sometime DJ with Kiss FM. "This", he says, "is a playlist of ten records that would be played in my set, and the order in which I'd play them."

❶ FLIP-JACK HUSTLERS OF CULTURE from FAT JAZZY GROOVES
A cult club track, I've been playing this for over five years now and it still commands dancefloor respect.

❷ ONE SWEET LOVE TO REMEMBER ROY AYERS from SOUTHPORT WEEKENDER VOLUME 3
One of those classic Ayers tracks that is such a big boogie tune.

❸ YOU MAKE LOVE LIKE SPRING TIME TEENA MARIE from IRONS IN THE FIRE
The Lady of Soul. So full of passion, heart, emotion.

❹ AS GENE HARRIS from THE WONDER OF STEVIE
A Stevie Wonder tune, and this updated version really works for me.

❺ LET'S GET IT ON MARVIN GAYE (PAUL SIMON REMIX) from LET'S STEP IT ON
A classic that has been given a new lease of life with an updated backing track, and the original vocals re-spun on top.

❻ SUNNY JAMES BROWN from LIVE IN JAPAN
The great Mr Brown with a Japanese remake that totally blows up the dancefloor.

❼ BATTLE WOOKIE from BATTLE (SINGLE)
His greatest commercial track.

❽ DUTCH PTA MIX BOOTLEG
A Missy Elliot remake. This bootleg gets respect.

❾ AS IF YOU READ MY MIND STEVIE WONDER from HOTTER THAN JULY
The don… 'nuff said!

❿ BACK TO LIFE (SPECIAL MIX) SOUL II SOUL from BACK TO LIFE (SINGLE)
How could my set be complete without this?

❻ GHETTO: MISFORTUNE'S WEALTH 24-CARAT BLACK from GHETTO: MISFORTUNE'S WEALTH
A classical-type orchestra and choir that moved protest soul into a new, symphonic world, this is an intimidating, bubbling funk slice of a revolutionary opera.

❼ RIVERS OF MY FATHERS GIL SCOTT-HERON/BRIAN JACKSON from WINTER IN AMERICA
Brian Jackson's centre-stage piano, the lowest-profile bass and drums, and a world-weary Gil all yearn for a better life. There was always much more to Heron than anger and irony.

❽ THE GHETTO DONNY HATHAWAY from EVERYTHING IS EVERYTHING
Built almost entirely on an electric piano that doesn't know how to stop and lyrics that limit themselves to "the" and "ghetto". These are eleven minutes of the soul of Donny Hathaway.

❾ GYPSY MAN WAR from THE VERY BEST OF WAR AND MORE (REMASTERED)
A groove so relentless it could crumble concrete is peppered with percussion and laced with electronica, but it's the harmonica that grabs the tune by its lapels and hurls it into a place beyond street funk.

❿ WHATCHA SEE IS WHATCHA GET THE DRAMATICS from WHATCHA SEE IS WHATCHA GET
There's a riot going on in the background as the instrumentation works against itself. The delivery is mad as hell and the lyrics are a veiled rallying cry, yet it's one of the smoothest soul songs you'll ever hear.

Lloyd Bradley

Soul pride

After the upheavals of the 1960s, for every soul song protesting conditions and situations there was another one that celebrated being black with a rousing self-assured optimism. Naturally, James Brown led the way in such matters.

❶ SAY IT LOUD, I'M BLACK AND I'M PROUD JAMES BROWN from SAY IT LOUD I'M BLACK AND I'M PROUD
You're spoilt for choice as far as JB's concerned in this category, but, musically and lyrically, you won't find anything more to the point than this.

❷ CHOCOLATE CITY PARLIAMENT from CHOCOLATE CITY
The revolution as viewed from the Mothership was always going to be more fun, and this goes as far as to install Richard Pryor as Minister for Education.

❸ WHATCHA SEE IS WHATCHA GET THE DRAMATICS from WHATCHA SEE IS WHATCHA GET
OK, so we had this 1970s classic in the previous list, and it is ostensibly a love song – but it took on soul power anthemic status after being the theme song for the movie *Wattstax*.

❹ IDLE HANDS HARLEM RIVER DRIVE from HARLEM RIVER DRIVE
This Latin-tinged call to arms from Eddie Palmieri's big band divorces the past from the present, to negate any excuses for not getting involved.

❺ MISS BLACK AMERICA CURTIS MAYFIELD from CURTIS
Curtis's tribute to the beauty of black womanhood is as delicate of instrumentation and delivery as it is of sentiment, but really you'd expect nothing less.

❻ RED BLACK AND GREEN ROY AYERS UBIQUITY from RED BLACK & GREEN
A deft jazz funk tribute to (and explanation of) the colours of the flag of black liberation.

❼ THE YEAR OF DECISION THE THREE DEGREES from THE BEST OF THE THREE DEGREES
Either you're part of the solution or you're part off the problem – get off the fence! The Philly label delivered a great far more soul pride anthems than people give it credit for.

❽ RIVERS OF MY FATHER GIL SCOTT HERON from WINTER IN AMERICA
An eloquent, if slightly oblique hymn to black self help, delivered with a beautiful wistfulness not seen too often.

❾ MESSAGE FROM A BLACK MAN THE TEMPTATIONS from PUZZLE PEOPLE
A remarkably in yer face statement from the group who, two years earlier, in 1967, were wearing tuxedos while they crooned "Old Man River".

❿ AIN'T NO STOPPING US NOW MCPHADDEN & WHITEHEAD from MCPHADDEN & WHITEHEAD
Another Philly Sound anthem that took optimism to new levels – of danceability as well as sensibility.

Lloyd Bradley

Blue-eyed soul

In essence, this is soul music made by white singers with great voices, although the lines tend to blur into pop, blues and rock.

❶ REASON TO BELIEVE ROD STEWART from EVERY PICTURE TELLS A STORY
Surely the king of British blue-eyed soul, in splendid form with this majestic cover of the Tim Hardin classic.

❷ GROOVIN' YOUNG RASCALS from GROOVIN'
Magnificent mid-1960s American group who managed to cross musical boundaries and successfully merge soul and pop. Those voices…

❸ BREAKFAST IN BED DUSTY SPRINGFIELD from DUSTY IN MEMPHIS
If Rod's the British King then Dusty is his Queen. Written by the great Eddie Hinton, this is from perhaps the greatest blue-eyed soul album of them all.

❹ YOU'VE MADE ME SO VERY HAPPY BOBBIE GENTRY from ODE TO BOBBIE GENTRY
Bobbie Gentry crossed several different musical styles from country to pop to soul and always managed to make it sound great. This is a storming cover of the Blood, Sweat & Tears hit.

❺ EVERY KIND OF PEOPLE ROBERT PALMER from DOUBLE FUN
Underrated in his lifetime but held by many as a great lost talent. Palmer liked to experiment with styles, but rarely sounded better than when he was singing soul.

❻ SHE'S GONE HALL & OATES from ABANDONED LUNCHEONETTE
Massively influenced by soul, especially the sound of Philadelphia, Hall & Oates' early work is as good as blue-eyed soul gets.

❼ HARD LUCK GUY EDDIE HINTON from HARD LUCK GUY
Eddie Hinton was a fantastic songwriter, arranger, musician and singer, but never found much fame in his lifetime. Far more a background musician than a star, he died penniless in 1995.

❽ SOUL QUEEN OF NEW ORLEANS AVERAGE WHITE BAND from SOUL SEARCHING
Scottish soul music? Yes indeed and damn fine it is, too. These boys could play funk, soul, and even disco.

❾ 20 MILLION THINGS TO DO LOWELL GEORGE from THANKS I'LL EAT IT HERE
The late leader of the great Little Feat only managed to record one solo album. Buy it – you won't regret it. Beautiful voice, stirring tune and lyrics to break your heart.

❿ HOW LONG ACE from FIVE A SIDE
Led by Paul Carrack, owner of a great set of pipes, this was Ace's biggest hit and it has hardly aged at all.

Dave Atkinson

Sounds familiar

A selection of songs with stories to tell about the intricacies of copyright law.

❶ MY SWEET LORD GEORGE HARRISON from ALL THINGS MUST PASS
Harrison was successfully sued for subconsciously plagiarizing The Chiffons'"He's So Fine" when writing this tune.

❷ YOU SHOWED ME THE TURTLES from THE TURTLES PRESENT THE BATTLE OF THE BANDS
De La Soul sampled a significant portion of this tune in their song "Transmitting Live From Mars", and found themselves on the wrong end of one of the most significant early copyright cases regarding sampling.

❸ PRETTY WOMAN 2 LIVE CREW from GREATEST HITS VOL 2
This parody version of the Roy Orbison classic was the subject of a lawsuit that went all the way to the US Supreme Court.

❹ OLD MAN DOWN THE ROAD JOHN FOGERTY from CENTERFIELD
This contentious song formed the basis of a lawsuit filed by Fogerty's former label Fantasy Records, in which they claimed that he was plagiarizing himself, and by extension, his former band Creedence Clearwater Revival, whose catalogue they owned.

❺ DAZED AND CONFUSED JAKE HOLMES from THE ABOVE GROUND SOUND OF JAKE HOLMES
Jake Holmes' 1967 recording undoubtedly influenced Led Zeppelin's better-known version, which appeared on their 1969 debut album, though for unknown reasons he received no songwriting credits.

❻ THE QUEEN AND I JUSTIFIED ANCIENTS OF MU MU from 1987 (WHAT THE FUCK IS GOING ON?)
Abba discovered that the JAMS had borrowed liberally from their track Dancing Queen in the construction of this song, and subsequently sued, forcing the band to destroy the remaining copies of the records (a process the band documented on the cover of their *History Of The Jams* album).

❼ U2 NEGATIVLAND from U2
Negativland appropriated and reassembled U2's "I Still Haven't Found What I'm Looking For", leading to a lawsuit that almost bankrupted the band and their label.

❽ BITTERSWEET SYMPHONY THE VERVE from URBAN HYMNS
The British band was forced to forfeit its songwriting royalties from this massive hit, due to an unauthorized sample of the Andrew Oldham Orchestra's 1966 instrumental version of the Rolling Stones'"The Last Time".

❾ 99 PROBLEMS DANGERMOUSE from THE GREY ALBUM
This ingenious mash-up of The Beatles' *White Album* and Jay-Z's *The Black Album* garners cease-and-desist orders, but stays alive via Internet downloads.

❿ 100 MILES AND RUNNIN' N.W.A. from 100 MILES AND RUNNIN'
N.W.A's three-note sample from Funkadelic's "Get Off Your Ass And Jam" provided the subject matter for a 2004 case that effectively raised the possibility that any unauthorized music sampling would be illegal under US law.

Butch Lazarchak

Soundtracks

Modern movies are often overloaded with music shovelled in as product placement – but on occasion directors' have chosen tunes that reflect a film's characters, to potent effect.

❶ 20 FLIGHT ROCK EDDIE COCHRAN from THE GIRL CAN'T HELP IT
Eddie shimmies, sings and picks his Hofner guitar in one of many majestic scenes from the great 1950s rock'n'roll movie. For many teens this was a call to arms.

② BORN TO BE WILD STEPPENWOLF from EASY RIDER

"Get your motor running . . ." with Steppenwolf's grungy anthem blaring, Hopper and Fonda hit the road on their hogs. Millions roared approval and followed their lead.

③ BE MY BABY THE RONNETTES from MEAN STREETS

Harvey Kietel wakes up with the night sweats as The Ronnettes' anthem echoes through the Brooklyn projects. So opens the finest ever movie soundtrack.

④ FREDDIE'S DEAD CURTIS MAYFIELD from SUPERFLY

Superfly glamorizes Priest, a hip drug dealer, yet Curtis chooses to concentrate on Freddie, a messy minor dealer who ends up dead. "Freddie's dead/pushin' drugs for the Man" sings Curtis with pathos and compassion over the toughest funk imaginable.

⑤ STAYING ALIVE THE BEE GEES from SATURDAY NIGHT FEVER

John Travolta struts down the street to "Staying Alive" as the ultimate celebration of NY disco begins. Pure cinematic testosterone.

⑥ PASSION PETER GABRIEL from THE LAST TEMPTATION OF CHRIST

Gabriel's soundtrack to Scorsese's tough, provocative telling of Christ's last days employs the voice of the great Pakistani qawwali singer Nusrat Fateh Ali Khan to suggest the man's soul leaving Christ's body.

⑦ MY WAY SID VICIOUS from GOOD FELLAS

Sid's seminal take on Sinatra's theme tune was originally part of the chaos of The Great Rock'N'Roll Swindle but it takes on a greater life when employed over the credits of Scorsese's malignant mafia feature.

⑧ LUST FOR LIFE IGGY POP from TRAINSPOTTING

Iggy's thumping celebration of the wild life proved the perfect theme tune for cinema's take on Irvine Welsh's tales of messy Scottish junkies.

⑨ O DEATH RALPH STANLEY from O BROTHER WHERE ART THOU

This offbeat movie was imbued with seductive mountain music. Here Ralph Stanley sings a grim Dock Boggs lament and ends up with the greatest success of his fifty-years-plus career.

⑩ WOKE UP THIS MORNING ALABAMA 3 from THE SOPRANOS

Admittedly, not a movie soundtrack but the greatest TV series ever has employed music brilliantly and the Brixton cowboys' electro-gospel hymn makes for the perfect theme tune.

Garth Cartwright

South African jazz

In the 1950s, Sophiatown in Johannesburg and District Six in Cape Town played host to an African renaissance in art, music and writing. The jazz scene combined American bop influences with the driving marabi rhythms to create a defiant music that was both fresh and doomed: most of its leading lights went into exile, and many met premature deaths.

① CHOBOLO SPOKES MASHIYANE from KING KWELA

Street-corner pennywhistle jive from the master.

② SWITCH CHRIS MCGREGOR AND THE CASTLE LAGER BIG BAND from JAZZ – THE AFRICAN SOUND

Chris McGregor would be a mainstay of South African expatriate jazz throughout the 1970s with the Brotherhood of Breath. Here he leads a stellar big band on an insomniac recording session, with a tune by the outstanding altoist Kippie Moeketsi.

③ NDENZENI NA? THE FATHER HUDDLESTONE BAND from DRUM: SOUTH AFRICAN JAZZ AND JIVE

Trevor Huddlestone was an unlikely jazz impresario as the headmaster of St Peter's, Sophiatown. This is an early outing for Hugh Masekela and Jonas Gwangwa.

④ BLUES FOR HUGHIE THE JAZZ EPISTLES from VERSE 1

Masekela, Gwangwa, Moekestsi in the frontline, with Abdullah Ibrahim (then still Dollar Brand) on piano. South African jazz groups don't come much more stellar than that.

⑤ SAD TIMES, BAD TIMES KING KONG CAST from THE KING KONG SOUNDTRACK

… unless it's here, in a musical based on the rise and fall of a celebrity black boxer. Starring Miriam Makeba and Nathan Mdledle of The Manhattan Brothers, and with musical support from Masekela and others, this Sophiatown take on Guys And Dolls led, indirectly, to most of its cast going into exile.

⑥ MIRIAM AND SPOKES PATA PATA THE SKYLARKS from THE BEST OF MIRIAM MAKEBA AND THE SKYLARKS

Makeba and Spokes Mashiyane team up for a *kwela* jive, topped by some studio backchat in Zulu.

⑦ MANNENBERG ABDULLAH IBRAHIM from VOICE OF AFRICA

Ibrahim's seven-note piano riff forms the base over which Basil Coetzee solos endlessly on saxophone. Halfway between township and Harlem, this track sums up South African jazz.

8 INGUGA HENRY ZUMA from JAZZ OFFERINGS FROM SOUTH AFRICA

South Africans will recognize this as the theme from the excellent polemical documentary series, *Beckett's Trek*. Everyone else can warm to its scratchy violin jive.

9 UDF CHRIS MCGREGOR AND THE SOUTH AFRICAN EXILES from THUNDERBOLT

Dudu Pukwana joins McGregor and a scratch band of exile talent in 1986: a brief recapitulation of all that had been lost.

10 IDUBE POPS MOHAMMED from ANCESTRAL HEALING

A modern *mbaqanga* stomper that builds from tiny pinpricks of thumb piano to a headlong torrent, in celebration of the 1994 elections.

David Honigmann

South African pop

South Africa has a hugely diverse pop music culture, dominated, currently, by gospel and *kwaito* – the home-grown hip-hop. Here are some (mostly) modern sounds.

1 FASSIE VUL' NDLELA BRENDA FASSIE from MEMEZA

Brenda's biggest-ever hit, with a great lyric about two gossips at a wedding, set to a classic rousing *mbaqanga* beat.

2 THATH'ISIGUBHU BONGO MUFFIN from THE CONCERTO

Great feel-good *kwaito* number, perfect for line-dancing, township style.

3 KHULA TSHITSHI LAMI BUSI MHLONGO from FREEDOM

Haunting Zulu ballad, beautifully arranged and produced, from a true maestro of urban roots.

4 NDIHAMBA NAWE MAFIKIZOLO from SIBONGILE

Surely one of the all-time great SA dance tunes, from one of the most potent groups on the *kwaito* scene today.

5 NKALAKATHA MANDOZA from NKALAKATHA

Definitive stomp-rock/*kwaito* combo that was a huge and deserved cross-over hit for Mandoza on release in 2000, and is still very popular.

6 LELILUNGELO ELAKHO LADYSMITH BLACK MAMBAZO from THE VERY BEST OF

Exquisite vocals from Joseph Shabalala and crew, with a subtle and poetic lyric too.

7 MBUBE SOLOMON LINDA'S ORIGINAL EVENING BIRDS from FROM MARABI TO DISCO

Recorded in 1939, and unquestionably one of the great South African tunes, frequently plagiarized (as "Wimoweh/The Lion Sleeps Tonight") but never bettered.

8 IT IS WONDERFUL H2O from EXPRESSIONS: WORDS UNLIMITED

Lovely tune that re-works an old Ella Fitzgerald line, adding mellow, well-paced hip-hop lyrics.

9 KUKE KWAGIJIM' IVENI MFAZ' OMNYAMA from NGISEBENZILE MAMA

A superb example of the Zulu maskanda style, ultra-masculine, yet graceful and melodic.

10 SONDELA RINGO from SONDELANI

One of the finest SA love songs of recent years, beautifully rendered by the Xhosa heart-throb.

Greg Salter

Southern rock

Southern rock relies on whiskey-fuelled guitar solos to propel the blues into an elongated boogie that still attracts fans from Atlanta to Aberdeen; despite multiple tragic band-member deaths over the years, the genre is still dominated by the Allmans and Skynyrd.

1 SWEET HOME ALABAMA LYNYRD SKYNYRD from SECOND HELPING.

With its irresistible chorus, defiant lyrics and nifty guitar/piano interplay, this was the highpoint of southern rock's foray into the charts.

2 JESSICA ALLMAN BROS from BROTHERS AND SISTERS

This slide-driven instrumental is the sound of summer, Georgia-style…and TV's *Top Gear*.

3 FREEBIRD LYNYRD SKYNYRD from PRONOUNCED LEH-NERD SKIN-NERD

A plaintive ballad that develops into the most fiery guitar duel ever recorded. Truly awesome.

4 GREEN GRASS HIGH TIDES THE OUTLAWS from THE OUTLAWS

The only song to come close to Freebird in fret-burning intensity; guitarist Hughie Thomassen later joined Skynyrd.

❺ MIDNIGHT RIDER ALLMAN BROS from IDLEWILD SOUTH
Much-covered ballad romanticizing southern outlaws.

❻ THAT SMELL LYNYRD SKYNYRD
from STREET SURVIVORS
Burns with indignation that friends could drink and
drug themselves to death.

❼ THE DEVIL WENT DOWN TO GEORGIA CHARLIE
DANIELS BAND from CHARLIE DANIELS BAND
A crossover hit that tells of a musical duel between
the devil and some hapless hick. The fiddle playing is
fiendish and, needless to say, the hick wins.

❽ THE WAY LYNYRD SKYNYRD from VICIOUS CYCLE
Never the rednecks of popular imagination, Skynyrd
reference the Iraq debacle in this recent epic, as powerful as anything from their heyday.

Chris Coe

Space rock

Sonic properties receive the same emphasis
as melody to create an otherworldly feel to
the music. Space is the place where music and
hallucination fused together.

❶ 2000 LIGHT YEARS FROM HOME THE ROLLING
STONES from THEIR SATANIC MAJESTIES REQUEST
From the most unusual album in the Stones catalogue
comes the one song that all space-rock music can
trace its roots back to. Over thirty years later, this still
ranks as one of the best Rolling Stones songs.

❷ LOST IN MY DREAM SPOOKY TOOTH from SPOOKY TWO
Back when Gary Wright was a real rock singer, Spooky
Tooth wrote one of the spaciest songs ever. With dark,
dreamy vocal imagery and frazzled guitars this is some
spooky space indeed.

❸ MYOPIC VOID CAPTAIN BEYOND from CAPTAIN BEYOND
Captain Beyond came out of nowhere in 1972 and
blasted the music scene with rock music that could
only be described as "power space".

❹ A SPRINKLING OF CLOUDS GONG from GONG YOU
Just about any track from Gong's recordings are as
spacey as you can get. Gong's history spans over thirty
years and nearly as many albums.

❺ SANDOZ IN THE RAIN AMON DÜÜL II from YETI
"Sandoz In The Rain" is the album's closer and is considered by many to be the birthplace of space rock.

❻ SEA NATURE STEVE HILLAGE from GREEN
"Sea Nature" opens what many consider his best
album and harkens to the desire for undersea life first
explored by Jimi Hendrix on *Electric Ladyland*.

❼ SET THE CONTROLS FOR THE HEART OF THE SUN
PINK FLOYD from A SAUCERFUL OF SECRETS
Following the departure of Syd Barrett (who took a
space trip and never returned), Pink Floyd gave eve-
ryone in the 1960s a creative reason for hallucination.
This is a space classic.

❽ DAMNATION ALLEY HAWKWIND from QUARK,
STRANGENESS & CHARM
A tad more polished than previous releases, the band
was obviously trying to tighten their sound and
become a little more accessible.

**❾ THE PSYCHEDELIC WARLORDS (DISAPPEAR IN
SMOKE)** HAWKWIND from THE HALL OF THE MOUNTAIN GRILL
Irresistible sentiment from the undisputed kings of
space rock.

❿ PSYCHEDELEKTRIKA TRIP SEQUENCE NUKLI from
THE TIME FACTORY
Caution! Put this into your playlist at your own risk.
There's no map for the return trip from Nukli's sojourn
into deep space!

Geoff Colquitt

Spacemen 3 / Spiritualized

Notorious for their fondness for strong cough
syrups, Spacemen 3 often found it simpler to sit
down to play live rather than attempt to balance
on two legs and stay conscious at the same time.
Spiritualized, Jason's post-Spacemen project,
by contrast went on to major success. Sonic
Boom resurfaced briefly as Spectrum but soon
disappeared without leaving much of an echo.

❶ WALKIN' WITH JESUS SPACEMEN3 from THE PERFECT
PRESCRIPTION
If the Velvet Underground had ever got into surf
music, as well as chemicals, then the music they made
would sound just like this.

❷ COME DOWN EASY SPACEMEN3 from THE PERFECT
PRESCRIPTION
The best sassy, drug-addled strut they ever produced.

Sing up at the back there: "1987, all I wanna do is get stoned!"

❸ TRANSPARENT RADIATION SPACEMEN3 from THE PERFECT PRESCRIPTION

Even when attempting garage rock Spacemen 3 were never in much of a hurry – and this, their cover of the Red Krayola's classic, is very pleasantly languid indeed.

❹ SUICIDE SPACEMEN3 from PLAYING WITH FIRE

The band's most perfect concoction, just over eleven minutes of smack-rock drone. It should be finishing about the same time you loosen the tourniquet and stop puking.

❺ MAY THE CIRCLE BE UNBROKEN SPACEMEN3 from PLAYING WITH FIRE

Calling up the best stoner voice since a 1974 New York Dolls bootleg, this is enough to send fans of traditional music running for the hills – and no bad thing either.

❻ SYMPHONY SPACE SPIRITUALIZED from LAZER GUIDED MELODIES

Pure, pharmaceutical quality shoegazing, lovingly cooked up in Jason's own lab. Addictive, enveloping and desirable.

❼ TAKE YOUR TIME SPIRITUALIZED from LAZER GUIDED MELODIES

Epic, swooning and, surprisingly for one so numbed from the cerebral cortex downwards, sexy.

❽ THINK I'M IN LOVE SPIRITUALIZED from LADIES AND GENTLEMEN, WE ARE FLOATING IN SPACE

Funny. An undeniably humorous, self-deprecating look at the delusions that come with rock star life.

❾ SHE KISSED ME (IT FELT LIKE A HIT) SPIRITUALIZED from AMAZING GRACE

Smashing pun on the old Shangri-Las' ode to spousal abuse – their's was "He hit me (and it felt like a kiss)" – Spiritualized open all throttles to full and pinprick new scars across the sordid, emaciated arms of rock'n'roll. Trashy, sleazy, badly-behaved guitar music and delightful for all the wrong reasons.

❿ ROCK AND ROLL SPIRITUALIZED from COMPLETE WORKS VOL 2

This version – from the Steve Lamacq radio show session – shows Spiritualized at their lushly romantic, full-orchestra best.

Al Spicer

Spandau Ballet

From electro-synth New Romantic idols to cool and suited white soul aficionados, Spandau Ballet were one of the key UK chart bands of the 1980s.

❶ ALWAYS IN THE BACK OF MY MIND from PARADE

A sublime rhythm track, some bright funk guitar stylings and Tony Hadley's voice sounding incredibly assured. Got to love Steve Norman's sax blowing too.

❷ COFFEE CLUB from DIAMOND

If you tried to dance to this you might just break your legs. The memerizing, stuttering beat makes room for a seriously intense Latin-style mid-section.

❸ GOLD from THE TWELVE INCH MIXES

Running at a fantastic seven minutes plus, this just builds and builds with some amazingly groovy percussion and string arrangements.

❹ FIGHT FOR OURSELVES from THROUGH THE BARRICADES

Beautifully structured strings, bold stabs of synth and a strident gospel-style chant make this an upbeat highlight of a particularly polished album.

❺ I'LL FLY FOR YOU from PARADE

One to enjoy with an icy Martini or two, while watching the sun set from the balcony of a luxury hotel in the Bahamas – pure jet-setting pop, you get the picture.

❻ REFORMATION from JOURNEYS TO GLORY

Fantastically overblown and self-important, the martial beat and synth landscape is almost clinically perfect. A sure-fire New Romantic dancefloor pleaser.

❼ THE FREEZE from THE TWELVE INCH MIXES

Starts like a robot sneezing before launching into an irresistible rhythm and some mad squelchy synth effects Martin Kemp's bass never sounded twangier.

❽ TO CUT A LONG STORY SHORT from JOURNEYS TO GLORY

Short and sweet, this is the one that turned them into New Romantic poster boys, tartan on *Top Of The Pops* and all.

❾ TRUE NEW MIX from REFORMATION

An intriguing new mix of one of their biggest hits, this is slightly longer than before and features the original mellow 'n' soulful intro.

❿ THROUGH THE BARRICADES from THROUGH THE BARRICADES

Just Tony Hadley's voice and some beautifully played acoustic guitar glide towards the grand pay off and some gorgeous sax melodies.

Essi Berelian

Sparks

The most English act to have come out of America (hell, they even do irony!), the Mael brothers have influenced virtually every UK singer/synthesizer duo from Depeche Mode to Pet Shop Boys, while other devout fans include XTC, The Associates and early Simple Minds. Here's a joyful selection of their cleverest wit and snappiest melodies.

❶ TALENT IS AN ASSET from KIMONO MY HOUSE
"We're his parents/Everything's relative…" The young Albert Einstein is the focus of this precursor to XTC's "Making Plans For Nigel" with a dancing hook that sticks for days.

❷ AMATEUR HOUR from KIMONO MY HOUSE
Teenagers discover puberty in Sparks' second UK hit, though with lyrics like "lawns grow thick in the hinterland" it's amazing it got any airplay. One of the best of their glam-rock era.

❸ THE NUMBER ONE SONG IN HEAVEN from NO. 1 IN HEAVEN
"Gabriel plays it/God how he plays it…" Giorgio Moroder's driving electro-rhythms provided the perfect foil for the brothers' witty pop, with a neat twist of cynicism.

❹ BEAT THE CLOCK from NO. 1 IN HEAVEN
"Went to school when I was two/PhD that afternoon…" Not a new idea but wonderfully executed as Sparks are reborn with a production partnership that no one saw coming.

❺ WHEN I'M WITH YOU from TERMINAL JIVE
"I never feel like garbage when I'm with you…" Sparks could hit tender areas under that deadpan humour: this moving, unexpectedly vulnerable love song is pure genius.

❻ I WISH I LOOKED A LITTLE BETTER from IN OUTER SPACE
More self-mockery set to a piping Farfisa organ, driving beat and superb tune – a great lost hit from a great lost album.

❼ ROCKIN' GIRLS from IN OUTER SPACE
"You're the only girl I ever met named Linda Lou/

Maybe that's the reason I'm so in love with you…" Clever synth-pop reworking of rock'n'roll's tropes that works in its own right.

❽ A FUN BUNCH OF GUYS from IN OUTER SPACE
"On our TVs in the sky/Your re-runs come in fine…" Slower deadpan humour as aliens introduce themselves ("here to get a tan and infiltrate") and sneak in a sly comment or two.

❾ MUSIC THAT YOU CAN DANCE TO from MUSIC THAT YOU CAN DANCE TO
"… that and that alone is enough for me." Sparks' elegantly sardonic response to being rejected by London Records for not making simple enough dance music.

❿ WHEN DO I GET TO SING MY WAY? from GRATUITOUS SAX AND SENSELESS VIOLINS
"When do I get to feel like Sinatra felt?" A neatly worked yet wistful look at the younger generation, who gained the success that eluded Sparks yet borrowed so heavily from them.

Ian Cranna

The Specials & Two-Tone

Although its revivalist ska and pop-art checkerboard logo were retro in style, Jerry Dammers' label embodied the sound and culture of Britain in the late 1970s and early 80s.

❶ GANGSTERS THE SPECIALS from THE SPECIALS
Prince Buster + punk energy = a revolution.

❷ ON MY RADIO THE SELECTER from GREATEST HITS
A bouncy and irresistible pop classic.

❸ A MESSAGE TO YOU RUDY THE SPECIALS from THE SPECIALS
It may have been a pretty straight cover of Dandy Livingstone's twelve-year-old song, but it captured the tenor of the times perfectly.

❹ TEARS OF A CLOWN THE BEAT from THIS ARE 2 TONE
The group's only single for the label is one of the few Motown covers that actually work.

❺ THE SPECIALS TOO MUCH TOO YOUNG from THE SPECIALS
This souped-up version of Lloyd Charmers' Birth Control was the label's first #1.

S

6 TOO EXPERIENCED THE BODYSNATCHERS from THIS ARE 2 TONE
Wavering, charming cover of Winston Francis's teen reggae classic.

7 MIRROR IN THE BATHROOM THE BEAT
from I JUST CAN'T STOP IT
Savage, scornful, politically engaged – The Beat's finest.

8 GHOST TOWN THE SPECIALS from THE SINGLES COLLECTION
One of the all-time great pop singles and the label's crowning achievement.

9 THE BOILER RHODA & THE SPECIAL A.K.A.
from THIS ARE 2 TONE
A chilling record about date rape that was unjustly ignored at the time.

10 NELSON MANDELA THE SPECIAL A.K.A.
from THE SINGLES COLLECTION
That rarest of political records – one that is as joyous as it is earnest.

Peter Shapiro

Phil Spector

The producer who originated the wall of sound, matching dense clusters of orchestration with rock-solid rhythms, fervently emotional singers, and a knack for amazingly catchy songs.

1 BE MY BABY THE RONETTES from THE BEST OF THE RONETTES
Grabs you by the collar with that echoing opening drumbeat, after which Ronnie Spector's heart-tugging vocal won't let you go.

2 HE'S A REBEL THE CRYSTALS from THE BEST OF THE CRYSTALS
A foot-stomping, almost martial beat anchors an anthem of devotion that's both proud and rebellious.

3 YOU'VE LOST THAT LOVIN' FEELIN' THE RIGHTEOUS BROTHERS from ANTHOLOGY 1962–1974
Operatic and booming orchestral pop, delivered as if it's announcing not just the end of a relationship, but the end of the world itself.

4 DA DOO RON RON THE CRYSTALS from THE BEST OF THE CRYSTALS
Where nonsense syllables say more about the thrill of an onrushing new romance than the most eloquent poetry. Great scampering piano, too.

5 RIVER DEEP, MOUNTAIN HIGH IKE & TINA TURNER from RIVER DEEP, MOUNTAIN HIGH
A maze-like mini-epic, jam-packed with ascending and descending riffs, rattling percussion, and ardent declarations of passion.

6 AWAITING ON YOU ALL GEORGE HARRISON from ALL THINGS MUST PASS
Harrison's pious religious sermonizing sounds like a call to party rather than prayer, owing to a mini-wall of thunderous percussion and chanting voices.

7 THEN HE KISSED ME THE CRYSTALS from THE BEST OF THE CRYSTALS
The insistent three-note riff that opens and motors this hit might be simple, but you'll never tire of it.

8 BABY I LOVE YOU THE RONETTES from THE BEST OF THE RONETTES
Another great, unstoppable hook in the wordless moaned chorus, Ronnie Spector's quivering voice melting the hardest hearts to jelly.

9 UPTOWN THE CRYSTALS from THE BEST OF THE CRYSTALS
Cinematic, Latin-tinged drama of American urban life, where the tenement changes from symbol of ghetto squalor to palace of sexual fulfillment.

10 WALKING IN THE RAIN THE RONETTES from THE BEST OF THE RONETTES
Complete with actual thunder effects, as dank and tempting as an actual wet walk huddled with your honey, with an especially anthemic chorus.

Richie Unterberger

Spirit

Spirit's West Coast psychedelia blended Randy California's guitar pyrotechnics with the jazz drums of father-in-law Ed Cassidy, earning a cult following on both sides of the Atlantic.

1 NATURE'S WAY from THE 12 DREAMS OF DR SARDONICUS
Randy's gentle ecology ballad became an instant hippy anthem.

2 LIKE A ROLLING STONE from SPIRIT OF 76
One of the great Dylan covers; the interplay between whispered vocals and delicate guitar refrains subverts the vitriol of the original.

3 MR SKIN from THE 12 DREAMS OF DR SARDONICUS
Founder-member Jay Ferguson's brassy attack on pornographers.

❹ **RUN, RUN, RUN** from JO JO GUNNE

OK, strictly speaking this isn't Spirit, but it would be a shame to ignore one of the all-time great rock singles, produced by Ferguson's solo project.

❺ **HAPPY** from SPIRIT OF 76

The Stones re-invented with reverb and distortion.

❻ **HEY JOE** from SPIRIT OF 76

Hendrix taught California guitar, and this trippy tribute to his mentor shimmers relentlessly under the weight of some mind-bending licks.

❼ **FARTHER ALONG** from FARTHER ALONG

An instant classic from Spirit's period of re-invention in the late 1970s.

❽ **THE OTHER SONG** from SON OF SPIRIT

Cosmic blues interspersed with light jazz, and the kind of time changes that make Spirit so distinctive.

Chris Coe

Spoken word

The Beats kicked off that mysterious sub-genre Spoken Word, as they encouraged jazz (and later rock) musicians to jam behind their readings. Today, it encompasses everything from the riffs of doomed comedians – Bruce, Pryor and Hicks are icons – to wannabe rappers and weary punk veterans. Here are ten pioneer wordsmiths.

❶ **OCTOBER IN THE RAILROAD EARTH** JACK KEROUAC from THE JACK KEROUAC COLLECTION

Kerouac reads lyrically from *On The Road* backed by Steve Allen's fluid jazz piano. Exquisite stuff from a time when all things appeared possible.

❷ **FATHER DEATH BLUES** ALLEN GINSBERG from FIRST BLUES

Ginsberg was Spoken Word's prophet, recording albums as well as appearing with Dylan, The Clash and others. Here he accompanies himself on harmonium as he sing-speaks a striking ode to mortality.

❸ **THE PRIEST** WILLIAM BURROUGHS from "THE PRIEST" THEY CALLED HIM

Burroughs snarls a tale of an altruistic junkie giving away his fix as it's Xmas eve, while fanboy Kurt Cobain distorts and mutates "Silent Night" on guitar. A bleak and funny meeting of deranged talents.

❹ **NIGGERS ARE SCARED OF REVOLUTION** THE LAST POETS from THE LAST POETS

Three ex-cons gathered in 1970 to rap the angriest rhymes ever heard in America and, amazingly, had a hit album! So potent that they found themselves on President Nixon's subversives list.

❺ **WINTER IN AMERICA** GIL SCOTT HERON from WINTER IN AMERICA

Across the 1970s no other voice proved as eloquent in its critique of US racism as that of novelist-poet Scott Heron. Backed by Brian Jackson's jazz funk band, GSH is at his most poignant on this track.

❻ **BEASLEY STREET** JOHN COOPER CLARKE from SNAP CRACKLE (&) BOP

The "punk poet" combined lyrical wordplay with a fierce Manc wit. Wrapped in a brilliant soundscape by producer Martin Hannett, JCC's survey of British decay remains his tour de force.

❼ **SONNY'S LETTAH** LINTON KWESI JOHNSON from FORCES OF VICTORY

Pioneering Brixton dub poet LKJ lays out an unrelenting tale of police brutality and racism in this prison letter from a youth charged with murder. Dennis Bovell's dub band keep things dread.

❽ **FOUR CORNERED ROOM** LYDIA LUNCH from WIDOWSPEAK

While fronting NY No-Wave bands Lydia Lunch made un-listenable "music" – yet when performing Spoken Word she can be both articulate and confrontational. Here she chats an urban hell tale over an atmospheric groove from LA Latino-funk fusionists War.

❾ **THOSE DUMB PUNK KIDS (WILL BUY ANYTHING)** JELLO BIAFRA from SIEG HOWDY

While ex-Black Flag vocalist Henry Rollins may have won a large audience with his star-fucking rants the former Dead Kennedys vocalist is more interesting, matching subversive politics and droll wit. Backed by The Melvins, this is a loud, funny blast at punk lemmings.

❿ **NU BLUE SUEDE SHOES** BENJAMIN ZEPHANIAH from HEADING FOR THE DOOR

No one has worked as hard to take poetry to people around the world as Birmingham born Benjamin Zephaniah. Here, over Back To Base's jazzy-electro groove, he chats wise word games.

Garth Cartwright

Dusty Springfield

The queen of British blue-eyed soul, embracing everything from lowdown R&B to show tunes with grace and grit.

❶ I ONLY WANT TO BE WITH YOU from THE VERY BEST OF DUSTY SPRINGFIELD

Her first solo hit was not just dynamite soulful pop, but also among the most credible emulations of Phil Spector's "Wall of Sound".

❷ YOU DON'T HAVE TO SAY YOU LOVE ME from THE VERY BEST OF DUSTY SPRINGFIELD

Overblown it might be, but it's overblown to a purpose, and reined in by Dusty's ultra-commanding vocal.

❸ WISHIN' AND HOPIN' from THE VERY BEST OF DUSTY SPRINGFIELD

The Merseybeats had a British hit with this Bacharach/David classic, but Springfield landed an American one with one of her most wistful performances.

❹ I JUST DON'T KNOW WHAT TO DO WITH MYSELF from THE VERY BEST OF DUSTY SPRINGFIELD

More peerless Bacharach/David interpretation, Dusty unsurpassed in maintaining determined dignity as her love life falls to pieces.

❺ SON OF A PREACHER MAN from DUSTY IN MEMPHIS

Justly acclaimed as one of the all-time 1960s soul classics, from her much-vaunted recordings with genuine Memphis soul musicians.

Richie Unterberger

Bruce Springsteen

The new Boss is much the same as the old Boss: for more than thirty years Bruce Springsteen has been delivering a spectacular rock'n'roll show that touches on masculinity, working-class solidarity and the quest for romance (in the widest sense) in an unromantic world.

❶ THUNDER ROAD from BORN TO RUN

A carillon peal gives a carousel spin to this energetic opener to Springsteen's first really huge album.

❷ MEETING ACROSS THE RIVER from BORN TO RUN

A short story of self-deception and doom, with a melancholy trumpet running through it like an undertow.

❸ BADLANDS from DARKNESS ON THE EDGE OF TOWN

A thumping rocker: you'll be too busy chanting along to even wave a lighter in the air.

❹ PROMISED LAND from LIVE 1975/85

In the studio (on *Darkness At The Edge Of Town*), this was fine, but a bit thin; the live version lifts it into another dimension.

❺ THE RIVER from THE RIVER

The river starts as a symbol of liberation and end up as an emblem of despair: the narrator who starts off swimming comes to dream of drowning. A stark harmonica riff seals the leaden atmosphere.

❻ SEEDS from LIVE 1975/85

Only available in this live version, Seeds sets the travails of redundant oil workers to a spring-heeled bass lead.

❼ BECAUSE THE NIGHT from LIVE 1975/85

A collaboration between Springsteen and Patti Smith: his version is smoother and easier than hers, and you can hear the whole stadium singing along.

❽ TUNNEL OF LOVE from TUNNEL OF LOVE

Springsteen bids farewell to his first marriage in this tale of a relationship that begins as a tunnel of love and ends as a haunted house.

❾ THE GHOST OF TOM JOAD from THE GHOST OF TOM JOAD

Springsteen's quieter acoustic songs tend to favour lyrics over melody and are an acquired taste. But this one, about illegal immigrants into the border states, rises from a whisper into a barely sung chorus, precisely capturing its subjects' combination of invisibility and pride.

❿ EYES ON THE PRIZE from WE SHALL OVERCOME: THE SEEGER SESSIONS

Latter-day Springsteen in full-on 1960s political mode, with a classic civil rights anthem.

David Honigmann

Staple Singers

A family that prayed together and played together, the Staples' greatest assets were Pops Staples' reverb-drenched blues guitar and daughter Mavis's deep, erotic contralto. Like Sam Cooke, they are most powerful on the gospel numbers (1–4 on this list).

❶ ON MY WAY TO HEAVEN from GLORY IT'S THE STAPLE SINGERS

It may be gospel, but Mavis – on breathy bass lead – is passionate as they come.

❷ I'M COMING HOME from GLORY IT'S THE STAPLE SINGERS

Six minutes and forty seconds of slow, stark, stunning vocal and guitar interplay.

❸ TOO CLOSE from GLORY IT'S THE STAPLE SINGERS

Rough sound-quality, but this five-minute live recording is the Staples at their spellbinding best.

❹ WILL THE CIRCLE BE UNBROKEN from GLORY IT'S THE STAPLE SINGERS

The original and superior 1960 Vee Jay cut of the great country-gospel standard about a mother's funeral.

❺ WHY? AM I TREATED SO BAD from THE ULTIMATE STAPLE SINGERS

Quiet but forceful Pops-led call to resist racial injustice "in the Master's name".

❻ FREEDOM HIGHWAY from FREEDOM HIGHWAY

Live civil rights song with a funky Pops guitar riff, full of handclapping churchy atmosphere.

❼ RESPECT YOURSELF from THE ULTIMATE STAPLE SINGERS

The lyrics may not always repay close attention, but the overall message and vibe come through loud and clear.

❽ I'LL TAKE YOU THERE from THE ULTIMATE STAPLE SINGERS

Pop-soul perfection, over a reggae bassline borrowed from the Harry J. Allstars' Liquidator instrumental.

❾ YOU'RE GONNA MAKE ME CRY from THE ULTIMATE STAPLE SINGERS

A superb Stax production that more than matches O.V. Wright's deep-soul original. As Mavis's ad-lib about "putting those needles in your arm" makes clear, the underlying issue is the human cost of a heroin habit.

❿ IF YOU'RE READY COME GO WITH ME from THE ULTIMATE STAPLE SINGERS

Another great uplifting number with a reggae vibe.

Neil Foxlee

The Stax sound

From the early 1960s to the early 70s, Stax studios in Memphis were responsible for some of the greatest soul and blues music ever created.

❶ GREEN ONIONS BOOKER T & THE MGS from GREATEST HITS

The definitive funky soul instrumental.

❷ SOUL FINGER THE BAR-KAYS from GREATEST HITS

A magnificent 1965 dance groove from the Bar-Kays, several of whom died in the plane crash that killed Otis Redding.

❸ IN THE MIDNIGHT HOUR WILSON PICKETT from GREATEST HITS

An early classic of Southern soul, superbly delivered by the wicked Mr Pickett in 1965.

❹ HOLD ON, I'M COMIN' SAM & DAVE from THE BEST OF

Yet another solid-gold slide of deep soul, co-written by Isaac Hayes in 1966.

❺ KNOCK ON WOOD EDDIE FLOYD from KNOCK ON WOOD

Floyd's barnstorming 1967 hit was written with Steve Cropper in Memphis's Lorraine Motel, where Martin Luther King later died.

❻ (SITTIN' ON) THE DOCK OF THE BAY OTIS REDDING from THE OTIS REDDING ANTHOLOGY

Otis was the heart and soul of Stax; his biggest hit was recorded shortly before he died in 1967.

❼ PRIVATE NUMBER WILLIAM BELL & JUDY CLAY from THE BEST OF WILLIAM BELL

Sublime soul duet from 1967.

❽ THEME FROM SHAFT ISAAC HAYES from SHAFT

"Black Moses" established himself as the funkiest man on the planet with this 1971 movie soundtrack.

❾ I WANNA GET FUNKY ALBERT KING from I WANNA GET FUNKY

The title track of a great 1972 album by the finest of Stax's small roster of blues artists.

❿ RESPECT YOURSELF THE STAPLE SINGERS from THE ULTIMATE STAPLE SINGERS

The song may be listed above, but you can't ignore this uplifting gospel/soul fusion.

Greg Ward

Steely Dan

There really are no half measures with Steely Dan. You either love the three ages of Dan or you hate them. From the first recordings 33 years ago through to the most recent, nothing revolutionary happens, it's just a quest for studio perfection and the ultimate rhythm and blues pop groove.

❶ AJA from AJA
If you love drums, enjoy; if you play them, cry, as Steve Gadd shows you how.

❷ THROUGH WITH BUZZ from PRETZEL LOGIC
It's short, it's sweet, it swirls. Quit drugs in 1 minute 32 seconds.

❸ DIRTY WORK from CAN'T BUY A THRILL
Early genius, with Dave Palmer taking a rare non-Fagen lead vocal. All the elements are there that made everything that followed great.

❹ BAD SNEAKERS from KATY LIED
If the lyrical picture-painting doesn't get you, Michael Macdonald's backing vocals will sweep you away. His voice was amazing back then.

❺ COUSIN DUPREE from TWO AGAINST NATURE
The big return after twenty years, and they were as clean and clever as ever. Fagen reminds us that our cousins can grow up to be sexy women.

❻ DEACON BLUES from AJA
The perfect late-1970s song. There are no obvious clues to what it's all about and it doesn't really matter. It just takes you somewhere else.

❼ ANY MAJOR DUDE from PRETZEL LOGIC
Listen to the words and it's very dark, but the style and vibe are very light indeed. Lyrics that include phrases like "superfine" and "my funky one" just seem to work so well.

❽ MY RIVAL from GAUCHO
It rolls and grooves its way along with an extended fade-out that suggests an assured confidence. They had nothing left to prove.

❾ THE THINGS I MISS THE MOST
from EVERYTHING MUST GO
Fagen is doing his best to cope with divorce, but he is rather more obsessed with his material loss than any emotional one. It's nasty, funny and honest all at the same time.

❿ THE FEZ from THE ROYAL SCAM
The keyboard and guitar work are just superb. Who the hell cares what it's about – it just makes you smile. A song that could go on for forty minutes instead of four.

John Duhigg

Al Stewart

If he sounded less like Neil Tennant and had less of a weakness for Andrex-soft-rock he would be taken as seriously as he deserves. When they were both penniless Soho folk singers in the mid 1960s, Paul Simon offered to sell Stewart his entire song catalogue. Stewart refused.

❶ ROADS TO MOSCOW from LIVE AT THE ROXY
An epic song by pop standards, but a lot shorter than *A Day In The Life Of Ivan Denisovitch*. The studio original starts with a botched cross-fade; this live version is flawless.

❷ ON THE BORDER from YEAR OF THE CAT
The title track of this album has become dulled by overfamiliarity, but this short, sharp, urgent tale of nocturnal gun-running still hums.

❸ OLD ADMIRALS from PAST, PRESENT & FUTURE
Probably the only song to have been inspired by "First Sea Lord Jackie Fisher", a lament for old admirals who feel the wind but never put out to sea.

❹ NIGHT TRAIN TO MUNICH from BETWEEN THE WARS
The album tells the history of 1930s Europe dancing into 1939 in a series of vignettes: this one comes on like a long-lost collaboration between Django Reinhardt and Eric Ambler.

❺ TRAINS from FAMOUS LAST WORDS
Steve Reich would explore the same imagery in "Different Trains": a symbol of escape and freedom becomes the way to the death camps, the whole 20th century racing headlong down the tracks.

❻ ANTARCTICA from LAST DAYS OF THE CENTURY
An icy flute motif frames an obsessive, busy song.

❼ FIELDS OF FRANCE from LAST DAYS OF THE CENTURY
A delicate tale of World War I aviation, set to a fragile piano and flute duet.

❽ POST WORLD-WAR TWO BLUES from PAST PRESENT AND FUTURE
British history from 1945 to 1973 condensed into a rollicking torrent.

⑨ SOHO (NEEDLESS TO SAY) from RHYMES IN ROOMS

If "Subterranean Homesick Blues" had been written in London, it would have sounded like this.

⑩ FLYING SORCERY from YEAR OF THE CAT

Vanished aviatrix as erotic touchstone.

David Honigmann

Stiff Records

"If it ain't Stiff it ain't worth a fuck" was the pioneering London independent label's motto. From 1975 to 77 it almost held true.

❶ WHAT'S SO FUNNY ('BOUT PEACE, LOVE AND UNDERSTANDING?) NICK LOWE from PURE POP FOR NOW PEOPLE

Cynical or serious? Nick never let on. Covered on *The Bodyguard* soundtrack, it made Lowe a millionaire. One imagines he laughed all the way to the bank!

❷ NEW ROSE THE DAMNED from DAMNED DAMNED DAMNED

The first 45 of the UK punk movement unleashed Rat Scabies and Captain Sensible on the world. Moronic but brilliant.

❸ WATCHING THE DETECTIVES ELVIS COSTELLO from THIS YEAR'S MODEL

The girlfriend's hooked on TV cop shows; Costello's full of malice. His best-ever song got to #15 in the UK charts in 1977.

❹ SWEET GENE VINCENT IAN DURY AND THE BLOCKHEADS from NEW BOOTS & PANTIES

From a misfit to a misfit: Ian celebrates Gene in what could be cited as one of the few love songs of the punk era.

❺ NEAT NEAT NEAT THE DAMNED from DAMNED DAMNED DAMNED

Even faster and funnier than "New Rose". British rock'n'roll has rarely been so exhilarating.

❻ ONE CHORD WONDERS THE ADVERTS from CROSSING THE RED SEA

The Adverts only had one chord, but they made good use of it on this attempt at a punk anthem.

❼ MY GIRL MADNESS from ONE STEP BEYOND

"My girl's mad at me," sang Suggs, and the nation wanted to give him a cuppa and a cuddle.

❽ HIT ME WITH YOUR RHYTHM STICK IAN DURY AND THE BLOCKHEADS from DO IT YOURSELF

Mix cockney innuendos, soft disco groove, screeching sax solo and proto-rap rhyming and what do you get? #1 UK for two weeks. Those were the days…

❾ WHITE LINE FEVER MOTORHEAD from THE BEST OF

The metal lepers were given a break by Stiff in 1977, so they recorded a salute to amphetamine. Music to grind teeth to.

❿ HOLE WIDE WORLD WRECKLESS ERIC from WRECKLESS ERIC

Eric thinks his dream girl just might live in Tahiti. He packs his lunch and heads off to find her.

Garth Cartwright

Sting/The Police

Not known for not taking himself seriously enough, the former teacher is also a sharp songwriter. The Police married tight white reggae to irresistible pop hooks; Sting's solo career spiced things up with jazz and world flavours.

THE POLICE

❶ ROXANNE from THE SECRET POLICEMAN'S BALL (VARIOUS ARTISTS)

OK, this is actually a solo version of the Police hit but then that's Sting for you – and he brings out the song's cheeky pathos.

❷ MESSAGE IN A BOTTLE from REGGATTA DE BLANC

Ferociously energetic punk-reggae where hook and central image mesh like cork and bottleneck.

❸ WALKING ON THE MOON from REGGATTA DE BLANC

Slow and spacey in the right way, with Andy Summers' guitar defying gravity as Sting walks home dancing on air.

❹ DON'T STAND SO CLOSE TO ME from ZENYATTA MONDATTA

Now they were unstoppable enough to rhyme "shake and cough" with "Nabokov". For the time being, they got away with it. But the pretension police were noting it all down in Sting's criminal record.

❺ INVISIBLE SUN from GHOST IN THE MACHINE

The thumping bassline that runs through the verse drops away into a chasm for the chorus of this song

Michael Stipe's
Support network

R.E.M. always chose their support acts with great care, and most of the artists on Michael Stipe's list have at one time or another supported the band on tour.

❶ **IN THE SUN** JOSEPH ARTHUR from **COME TO WHERE I'M FROM**

❷ **WING** PATTI SMITH from **GONE AGAIN**

❸ **WE ARE NOWHERE AND IT IS NOW** BRIGHT EYES from **I'M WIDE AWAKE IT'S MORNING**

❹ **HIDDEN SONG** ANGELA MCCLUSKEY from **THE THINGS WE DO**

❺ **MERCEDES CHILDREN** THE CHEEKS from **WHAT YOU HEARD**

❻ **AUNT AVIS** VIC CHESNUTT from **DRUNK**

❼ **REVERSE** NOW IT'S OVERHEARD from **FALL BACK OPEN**

❽ **FAVOURITE WRITER** MAGNAPOP from **MAGNAPOP**

❾ **NIGHTS OF THE LIVING DEAD** TILLY AND THE WALL from **WILD LIKE CHILDREN**

❿ **H THE PRESIDENT** FLASH TO BANG TIME from **GLO**

---

about Northern Ireland, banned from radio broadcast on its first release.

❻ **EVERY LITTLE THING SHE DOES IS MAGIC** from **GHOST IN THE MACHINE**
Two minutes of pure joy from an otherwise dark album.

STING

❼ **FORTRESS AROUND YOUR HEART** from **DREAM OF THE BLUE TURTLES**
Schoolbook Sting, taking an outlandish metaphor and treating it seriously. Branford Marsalis is indispensable on saxophone.

❽ **FRAGILIDAD** from **NADA COMO EL SOL**
A quarter of *Nothing Like The Sun* was devoted to songs about human rights abuses in South America. This version of "Fragile" does the logical thing and recasts the song in Spanish. It has deservedly become a standard.

❾ **I BURN FOR YOU** from **BRING ON THE NIGHT**
Looser than the Police's version on the *Brimstone And Treacle* soundtrack, an impeccable slow blues.

❿ **HELLHOUND ON MY TRAIL** from **JOURNEY TO THE LABYRINTH**
From the concert version of Sting's unfairly derided lute album; Robert Johnson's blues are as icy as ever in this Elizabethan setting.

David Honigmann

The Stone Roses

At the end of the 1980s, Ian Brown and cohorts were the messiahs of Manchester, delivering one of the greatest debut albums of all time. Contractual disputes and procrastination meant the long-awaited follow-up largely fell between the two stools of Led Zep and Happy Mondays, so they broke up.

❶ **I WANNA BE ADORED** from **THE STONE ROSES**
The band announce their intent as rumbling bass emerges from some quiet noodlings before a tasty riff and a pop/psych tune take over.

❷ **SHE BANGS THE DRUMS** from **THE STONE ROSES**
A lovely bass run and shimmering guitars make this 1960s-style paean to Lady Love flow like a paisley dress in the breeze.

❸ **ELIZABETH MY DEAR** from **THE STONE ROSES**
If the composer of "Scarborough Fair" were around he would have sued for royalties on the intro. The ensuing pop masterpiece is closer to The Beatles by the end.

❹ **SUGAR SPUN SISTER** from **THE STONE ROSES**
The finest hook on the album precedes Brown's swing into "Sometimes I Fantasise". There's even a touch of Latin semi-acoustic and a wailing electric solo.

❺ THIS IS THE ONE from THE STONE ROSES

Byrds jangles and a sudden three-chord stab surround Brown's plaintive vocals about what he's been waiting for all his life.

❻ I AM THE RESURRECTION from THE STONE ROSES

The tour de force album-closer is almost a mini rock-opera with offbeat drums, honeyed bass, killer riffs and pure psych vocals of punk vitriol. And they return for more just when you think they've done.

❼ TEN STOREY LOVE SONG from SECOND COMING

A quasi-Eastern intro dissolves into the album's finest moment – pop magic with a haunting tune and the customary psychedelic sensibilities.

❽ HOW DO YOU SLEEP from SECOND COMING

Not a cover of the Lennon tirade against Macca but just as nasty, albeit wrapped in sugary tones and West Coast guitar fluidity.

Nick Edwards

The Stranglers

Previously known as the Guildford Stranglers, the "meninblack" had a head start on the competition when punk kicked off – they were already competent musicians, they had a mean way with a lyric and blended boyish smut with testosterone-induced rage in a manner most appealing.

❶ GET A GRIP (ON YOURSELF) from IV RATTUS NORVEGICUS

This jaundiced but jerkily energizing song contemplates life on the rock-and-roller-coaster: no money, no privacy, no appreciation, no personal hygiene, just the endless routine of turning up, tuning up and playing the same set night after night after night.

❷ HANGIN' AROUND from IV RATTUS NORVEGICUS

There's a bad-taste pun lurking somewhere in the lyric about Christ "hanging around" on the cross, but the song's main aim is to illustrate the boredom, listlessness and ennui of life on a 1970s street corner.

❸ NO MORE HEROES from NO MORE HEROES

Two-fisted macho growling about one of punk's strongest articles of faith.

❹ SKIN DEEP from AURAL SCULPTURE

Hugh Cornwell croons a lyric of cynical disappointment, betrayal and friendship turned sour. He left the band shortly after.

❺ GOODBYE TOULOUSE from IV RATTUS NORVEGICUS

Harmonies in the backing vocals and a fiercely complicated rhythm meant this track stood out from the flood of punk rock that hit the streets in 1977.

❻ DUCHESS from THE RAVEN

Posh porno fantasy lyric of a naughty aristocrat with a taste for both quality and quantity in her desires. Frothy and lacking in social comment, but a damn fine tune and chortle-along refrain of "And the Rodneys are queueing up, God forbid".

❼ NICE 'N' SLEAZY from MENINBLACK

In a cellar club, people of indeterminate gender are removing their clothes while dancing. Somebody charges you a huge price for a watered-down drink and then you hear the music. As a hand slips into your jacket removing your wallet, you recognize it as this old-time Stranglers' classic.

❽ GOLDEN BROWN from LA FOLIE

There's simply not enough harpsichord in rock music. Let's all listen to the delicately traced butterfly wing of a guitar solo and pretend it is nothing more than a gentle waltz-time song written to please a gently tanned lover.

❾ STRANGE LITTLE GIRL from LA FOLIE

A re-treading of the ground covered by The Beatles in "She's Leaving Home", but updated for a later and more dangerous period. Keyboards, strings and electric guitars all chip in to stop the heroine getting too bruised by the cold dark world she moved into.

❿ SOMETHING BETTER CHANGE from NO MORE HEROES

Now a dad-rock classic track that provokes inappropriate dancing with the first run-through of its instantly recognizable opening riff, this is J.J. Burnel's best-known vocal and still one of the best of the punk-rock originals.

Al Spicer

The Strokes

The band that transformed the musical landscape back in 2001, just when everyone thought rock was dead.

❶ HARD TO EXPLAIN from IS THIS IT

Music condensed to claustrophobic essentials: verse as catchy as chorus, chorus like a runaway train, inarticulacy as "fuck you" attitude.

② LAST NIGHT from IS THIS IT

The perfect meeting point between the Velvet Underground and Iggy Pop, but entirely Strokes in its compressed syncopation and shrugging melodicism.

③ SOMEDAY from IS THIS IT

This melodic midpacer neatly combines melancholy and exuberance, the line "All my fears come back to me in threes" lunges straight for your pacemaker.

④ REPTILIA from ROOM ON FIRE

Heed not those who slag off the second album. A great catcalling vocal, and a scorching Nick Valensi guitar solo make this a Strokes classic.

⑤ 12:51 from 12:51

This Cars-influenced single is slow medicine, but over time its infectious synth-guitars, machine drums and mechanical claps become addictive.

⑥ THE MODERN AGE from IS THIS IT

Where it all started: those stuttering Lou Reed vocals and a heady sense that rock music was suddenly visceral and vital again.

⑦ TRYING YOUR LUCK from IS THIS IT

The nearest these cynics get to sounding romantic. Yearning, almost delicate in its intricacy, with another fantastic Valensi solo.

⑧ BARELY LEGAL from IS THIS IT

A typically dismissively misanthropic Julian Casablancas lyric wedded to totally exuberant music, clipped but excitable, concluding in a headrushing climactic lift.

⑨ WHAT EVER HAPPENED? from ROOM ON FIRE

Business-meaning opener to the second album: Casablancas at his most splenetically throaty and disaffected.

⑩ THE END HAS NO END from ROOM ON FIRE

More synth-like guitars criss-crossing Casablancas' megaphone vocal, just as the delicate verse and crescendoing chorus criss-cross in turn.

Toby Manning

Studio One

Clement "Coxsone" Dodd's Studio One label launched the careers of many of Jamaica's greatest stars, including Bob Marley and Burning Spear. For many aficionados, the bass-heavy sound of Studio One's much-recycled rhythms is the definitive sound of classic reggae.

① WHAT KIND OF WORLD? THE CABLES from WHAT KIND OF WORLD?

The perfect Studio One formula: contemplative harmonizing backed by a metronomic bass beat.

② BOBBY BABYLON FREDDIE MCGREGOR from STUDIO ONE ROCKERS

Despite his later success, McGregor never really topped his early Studio One hits, like this Rasta anthem.

③ HOW CAN I GO ON? THE GAYLADS from SOUL BEAT

This young vocal trio cut a superb album for Studio One in the 1960s.

④ FATTIE FATTIE THE HEPTONES from FATTIE FATTIE

Perhaps the Studio One group to beat them all, in fine voice.

⑤ MR BASSIE HORACE ANDY from NICE UP THE DANCE – STUDIO ONE DISCOMIXES

Still going as strong as ever in the 21st century, the high-voiced Horace produced a string of Studio One classics.

⑥ SET ME FREE KEN BOOTHE from STUDIO ONE SOUL

A gloriously mellifluous extended version of The Supremes classic.

⑦ NICE UP THE DANCE MICHIGAN AND SMILEY from NICE UP THE DANCE – STUDIO ONE DISCOMIXES

Rollicking nonsense from the DJ duo at their youthful peak, once again backed by the Real Rock rhythm.

⑧ YAHO THE VICEROYS from RESPECT TO STUDIO ONE

Short and sweet, a lovely little piece of piratical nonsense.

Greg Ward

Summertime

Of the hundreds of versions in myriad styles of the song written in 1924 as part of Gershwin's "folk-opera" *Porgy And Bess*, here are ten crackers.

① SIDNEY BECHET from JAZZ ANTHOLOGY 1939

Bechet's soprano sax had an almost primeval howl, perfectly suited to the crying Gershwin melody.

S

❷ THE ZOMBIES from THE ZOMBIES
Revered British beat combo turned it into a hip jazz waltz on their 1964 debut album.

❸ THE THREE SOUNDS from HERE WE COME
Excellent relaxed swinging jazz trio from 1960, featuring the deeply groovy Gene Harris on piano.

❹ SANTO AND JOHNNY from SANTO AND JOHNNY
Best known for their 1959 instrumental hit "Sleepwalk", the Farina brothers' version is hauntingly twangsome.

❺ ELLA FIZGERALD AND LOUIS ARMSTRONG from PORGY AND BESS
Two entirely different vocal approaches – the smooth and the rough – yet equally resonant and affecting.

❻ JONI MITCHELL from GERSHWIN'S WORLD
The first appearance of Joni as smoky jazz singer; the vocal is lived-in and luscious, and there's a gorgeous harmonica solo by Stevie Wonder.

❼ ALBERT AYLER from MY NAME IS ALBERT AYLER
A torrential highlight from the avant-garde primitivist saxophonist's 1963 session.

❽ MILES DAVIS from PORGY AND BESS
Set among Gil Evans's cloudy Dorian horns, Miles's 1959 reading has an icy cool modality.

❾ LARRY ADLER from GENIUS OF LARRY ADLER
No one could tease out the beauty of his old friend George's melody like harmonica virtuoso Larry, or so Larry says anyway.

❿ PAUL McCARTNEY from CHOBA B CCCP
Part of his Russia-only rock'n'roll release from 1988, a loose bluesy jamming attitude gives Macca a chance to tear into a risky vocal.

Chris Ingham

Sun Records

The Memphis label did more than any other company to start white rock'n'roll with its rockabilly artists, most famously Elvis Presley. Sun Studio also cut some crucial early electric blues before Elvis took off.

❶ THAT'S ALL RIGHT MAMA ELVIS PRESLEY from THE SUN SESSIONS
Presley's mid-1954 debut single was the first great rock'n'roll record by a white artist, and the one that virtually invented rockabilly.

❷ BLUE SUEDE SHOES CARL PERKINS from ORIGINAL SUN GREATEST HITS
The ultimate fusion of country, rhythm & blues, and pop is on this exuberant 1956 rockabilly classic, which made on-the-surface ridiculous imagery into the hippest of poetry.

❸ I WALK THE LINE JOHNNY CASH from THE SUN YEARS
The prototype for Cash's persona, never surpassed: a stolid righteousness that's both Biblical and humble in tone, imprinted here by the slow train-chugging rhythm and hymnal wordless humming.

❹ WHOLE LOTTA SHAKIN' GOIN' ON JERRY LEE LEWIS from 18 ORIGINAL SUN GREATEST HITS
Pounding piano, cocky-as-get-out vocals, a leering spoken passage, and an electrifying rockabilly guitar solo made this one of the all-time greatest 1950s rockers.

❺ MYSTERY TRAIN ELVIS PRESLEY from THE SUN SESSIONS
All ten of the tracks on Elvis's five mid-1950s Sun singles were great, but this almost supernaturally eerie adaptation of a Junior Parker blues song was the greatest.

❻ MYSTERY TRAIN JUNIOR PARKER from MYSTERY TRAIN
Speaking of which, here's the Junior Parker original, whose irregular beats and smoky, woozy tone makes for a nice contrast with Presley's hepped-up cover.

❼ BEAR CAT RUFUS THOMAS from THE BEST OF RUFUS THOMAS: DO THE FUNKY SOMETHIN'
An "answer" record to the original "Hound Dog," this playfully nasty, lean'n'mean electric blues novelty gave the Sun label its first big seller in 1953.

❽ ROCKET 88 JACKIE BRENSTON from THE SUN STORY
There was no definitive "first rock'n'roll record", but this 1951 thumper with boogying Ike Turner piano, fuzzy electric guitar, and car-cruising lyrics is often cited as the one.

❾ RED HOT BILLY LEE RILEY from RED HOT: THE BEST OF BILLY LEE RILEY
"My girl is red hot, your girl ain't doodly squat!" declares Riley's raw buzz of a vocal on this cult rockabilly favorite. And really, what more needs to be said?

❿ MONA LISA CARL MANN from MONA LISA: THE VERY BEST OF CARL MANN
A Jerry Lee Lewis-like rockabilly overhaul of this Nat "King" Cole pop evergreen gave Sun Records its last big hit in 1959.

Garth Cartwright

The Supremes & Diana Ross

Sweet sounds from the Queen Bees of Motor City.

❶ BUTTERED POPCORN THE SUPREMES from MEET THE SUPREMES
Florence Ballard delivers sexy, sassy, soul worthy of Etta James.

❷ WHEN THE LOVELIGHT STARTS SHINING THROUGH HIS EYES THE SUPREMES from WHERE DID OUR LOVE GO
Holland-Dozier-Holland get the girls on the dancefloor for their first proper pop song.

❸ WHERE DID OUR LOVE GO THE SUPREMES from WHERE DID OUR LOVE GO
Diana's barely-there vocal backed up with the Motown double-drum sound and a thousand "baby babys". Their first #1.

❹ LOVE IS LIKE AN ITCHING IN MY HEART THE SUPREMES from SUPREMES A GO-GO
Catchy as love hives.

❺ NO MATTER WHAT SIGN YOU ARE DIANA ROSS AND THE SUPREMES from LET THE SUN SHINE IN
The Supes get psyched. "I don't care about your rising sign", indeed.

❻ LOVE CHILD DIANA ROSS AND THE SUPREMES from LOVE CHILD
Funky-feeling delirious tenement-dwelling fantasy.

❼ STORMY THE SUPREMES from NEVER-BEFORE-RELEASED MASTERS
Sensitive rework of the easy-listening classic. Sweet enough to make a grown man cry.

❽ UP THE LADDER TO THE ROOF THE SUPREMES from RIGHT ON
New recruit Jean Terrell takes the helm for this Diana-alike wah-wah fest.

❾ SURRENDER DIANA ROSS from SURRENDER
Stripped down and serious. Ashford & Simpson deliver a soul classic for Diana's pre-disco album.

❿ LOVE HANGOVER DIANA ROSS from DIANA ROSS
Breathless disco two-parter that sees Diana pull out the stops. She don't need no cure …

Rachel Coldicutt

Surf's up

The soundtrack to coastal Californian life in the early-to-mid 1960s, whether it was instrumentals with oceanic guitar reverb or chipper odes to beach bumming by the Beach Boys and Jan & Dean.

❶ SURF CITY JAN AND DEAN from SURF CITY: THE BEST OF JAN & DEAN
Two girls for every boy – the ultimate pre-women's lib male teenage fantasy. But what great falsetto harmonies from Beach Boy (and co-writer) Brian Wilson.

❷ SURFIN' USA THE BEACH BOYS from SURFIN' USA
The tune was taken from Chuck Berry's "Sweet Little Sixteen", but the sun-baked harmonies and utopian ode to surf culture were all Beach Boys.

❸ WIPE OUT THE SURFARIS from SURFIN' HITS
Infectious maniacal laughter, a drum-roll solo copied by garage bands the world over, and an up-and-down guitar riff that won't quit.

❹ PIPELINE THE CHANTAYS from SURFIN' HITS
Rubbery bass, pre-Doors mysterioso electric keyboards, and guttural guitar twang evoke both the majesty and fatal danger of the deep.

❺ SURFIN' SAFARI THE BEACH BOYS from SURFIN' SAFARI
Their first big hit matches the guitar chug of Eddie Cochran with impeccably timed harmonized exhortations to get on the surfing bandwagon.

❻ MISIRLOU DICK DALE from SURFIN' HITS
Latin and Mddle Eastern melodies collide, and wet staccato riffs mimic swelling waves, on the signature tune by the king of surf guitar. Later used by Quentin Tarantino to open *Pulp Fiction*.

❼ SURFER GIRL THE BEACH BOYS from SURFER GIRL
Every surfing stud needs another half, lovingly idealized on this arching ballad with another great falsetto vocal from Brian Wilson.

❽ SURFIN' BIRD THE TRASHMEN from SURFIN' HITS
Two-chord jitter with delightfully moronic strangled vocals, taking an off-the-wall turn into the unaccompanied gargles of a drowning man halfway through.

❾ CATCH A WAVE THE BEACH BOYS from SURFER GIRL
Riding the surf is made to sound like an almost holy experience, the vocal harmonies on the chorus rising like a tidal wave.

⑩ MAR GAYA THE FENDER IV from GUITAR PLAYER PRESENTS LEGENDS OF GUITAR: SURF VOL 1

Phenomenal machine-gun-fire surf guitar on this obscurity, which roars with the menace of an oncoming tsunami.

Richie Unterberger

Swingers

New Swing, or Jump Jive, was briefly huge in America in the late 1990s and was further popularized by the cult movie *Swingers*. The new breed of big-band swing has produced some of the finest music to dance to in years.

❶ GO DADDY O BIG BAD VOODOO DADDY from BIG BAD VOODOO DADDY

This is seen by many as the essential track of the genre. "Go Daddy O" provides a high point in the cult film *Swingers*, delivered by one of the most exciting live bands of the time. It's a killer.

❷ RED LIGHT! INDIGO SWING from RED LIGHT!

Johnny Boyd has a beautiful, sweet, soulful voice and on "Red Light!" he croons for all he's worth.

❸ ZIP GUN BOP (RELOADED) ROYAL CROWN REVIEW from THE CONTENDER

With a blistering mix of film noir, bebop and punk, "Zip Gun Bop" fair races along. Anyone trying to dance to this one is likely to end up in traction. They call it gangster bop, and I'm not arguing.

❹ JUMP JIVE & WAIL THE BRIAN SETZER ORCHESTRA from DIRTY BOOGIE

Ex-Stray Cats mainman Setzer updates Louie Prima's classic jump jive tune. It turned up in an advert, sold thousands of chino trousers and put Setzer's amazing live band at the forefront of the New Swing movement in America.

❺ BOOZIN' AND A CRUISIN' DEM BROOKLYN BUMS from THERE GOES THE NEIGHBOURHOOD

More gangster bop from another New York band. A live favourite that swings like the devil.

❻ SHE COULD BE A SPY SWINGERHEAD from SHE COULD BE A SPY

Band leader Michael Andrew *is* swing, from the collar of his leopard-print jacket to the very tips of his shoes. You can hear his love of Sinatra, Burt Bacharach and Bobby Darin in every second.

❼ EVERY SINGLE DAY JET SET SIX from LIVIN' IT UP

New York City's finest exponents of kitschy, lounge-lizard cool mix hipster swing and some good ol' 1960s melodies with killer tunes and a great horn section.

❽ MR WHITE KEYS CHERRY POPPIN' DADDIES from ZOOT SUIT RIOT

Formed way back in 1989 by ex-punk rockers, The Daddies have a huge, ska-inspired sound and masses of attitude.

❾ RENAISSANCE IN HARLEM COMFY CHAIR from PARTY ON THE TITANIC

A band from San Francisco who play as either an acoustic three-piece or a hard rockin' four-piece. This one is from their debut album and shows just a hint of their full cabaret madness.

⑩ HE JUST WANTS TO CHA CHA (SHE JUST WANTS TO TWIST) SWINGERHEAD from SHE COULD BE A SPY

Another utterly charming number from the swing-tuned mind of Michael Andrew. It delivers just what the title says. A song that is funny as well as fun, and catchy as hell.

Gavin McNamara

Syliphone

"The elephant's label" as it was known, was one of the most important and influential African labels of all times. What was published here was avidly listened to by fans and musicians alike throughout West Africa.

❶ INTRODUCTION/TENTEMBA BEMBEYA JAZZ NATIONAL from L'ANS DE SUCCÈS

The band starts a long intro and takes you on a maelstrom while the track progresses. Bembeya should be known as one of the best pop bands of all times!

❷ LA GUINÉE MOUSSOLOU ORCHESTRE DE LA PAILLOTE from VOLUME 1

Track one of the very first LP on Syliphone. Opened by a shady guitar, this is a bolero which sings the praises of Guinean women.

❸ N'NA KOUYATÉ SORY KANDIA from KOUYATÉ SORY KANDIA

Most of the recordings of this giant singer are with his ensemble traditionnel, but this one perfectly blends electric guitar, saxophone and balaphon and the powerful mezzo soprano.

❹ **KADIA BLUES** ORCHESTRE DE LA PAILLOTE from 40ÈME ANNIVERSAIRE SYLIPHONE VOL 2

A spooky tune reminiscent of Louis Armstrong: a muffled trumpet, bluesy notes from a guitar, the snare played with brushes.

❺ **PETIT SEKOU** BEMBEYA JAZZ NATIONAL from DISCOTHÈQUE 76

A guitar scorcher from Sekou "Bembeya" Diabaté, a.k.a. Diamond Fingers. With an irresistible groove and calm, Diabaté shows off his talents.

❻ **SO I SI SA** SUPER BOIRO BAND from 40ÈME ANNIVERSAIRE SYLIPHONE VOL 1

Unbelievable keyboard playing, with a pumping rhythm section that leads you straight to the dance-floor.

❼ **WHISKY SODA** DEMBA CAMARA WITH BEMBEYA JAZZ NATIONAL from HOMMAGE À DEMBA CAMARA

This adaptation of a highlife rhythm is pure fun: a guy is singing the virtues of whisky soda and getting tipsier throughout the song.

❽ **MALOUYAME** MIRIAM MAKEBA from DISCOTHÈQUE 73

Little is known about Miriam Makeba's stay in Guinea, where she was looking for shelter with husband Stokely Carmichael. This one is also known as the widely popular "Bani", a traditional tune.

Jean Trouillet

David Sylvian

After leading the arty pioneers of the early 1980s New Romantic explosion, the highly talented Sylvian headed off on an avant-garde odyssey of his very own.

❶ **FORBIDDEN COLOURS** from SECRETS OF THE BEEHIVE

More graceful than the *Merry Christmas, Mr Lawrence* version, Ryuichi Sakamoto also tinkles the ivories on this simple and beautiful song.

❷ **GHOSTS** JAPAN from TIN DRUM

Who'd have thought something so oblique and odd could be a hit? Electronic bleeps and spectral chimes decorate a sparse vocal and haunting synth melody.

❸ **JEAN THE BIRDMAN** DAVID SYLVIAN & ROBERT FRIPP from THE FIRST DAY

David Sylvian sounding almost playful? Who'd have thought it possible? An upbeat vocal bounces around a cool Robert Fripp guitar melody.

❹ **LATE NIGHT SHOPPING** from BLEMISH

Icily detached yet bizarrely intimate, Sylvian's vocals are eerily perfect. The stark electronic handclap rhythm is particularly spooky.

❺ **MIDNIGHT SUN** from DEAD BEES ON A CAKE

A weird amalgam of creaking Delta blues and Sylvian sound art. Ryuichi Sakamoto provides the off-kilter brass arrangements.

❻ **MOTHER AND CHILD** from SECRETS OF THE BEEHIVE

The acoustic bassline is simply divine and provides a perfect foil for Sylvian's dusty croon. The fractured jazz of the mid section is superb too.

❼ **NIGHTPORTER** JAPAN from GENTLEMEN TAKE POLAROIDS

Sylvian sounds almost supernaturally miserable and lonely here. His fragile voice floats above a lost piano and ghostly cello.

❽ **QUIET LIFE** JAPAN from QUIET LIFE

A more dancefloor-oriented effort, with a crisp beat and some artfully drawn guitar lines weaving around the synth and bass interplay.

❾ **RIVER MAN** from GONE TO EARTH

Robert Fripp provides strange and ethereal guitar textures while Sylvian sounds particularly contemplative. Great sax midway through, too.

❿ **TALKING DRUM** JAPAN from TIN DRUM

Pop music as abstract art. Mick Karn's slippery fretless bass sounds as though it's turning to jelly in his hands.

Essi Berelian

June Tabor

The great tragedy queen of English folk, with a well-nigh infallible ear for a song. Most of her albums begin with A, like a taxi firm trying to be first in the Yellow Pages.

❶ A PLACE CALLED ENGLAND from A QUIET EYE
This Maggie Holland song argues for an English nationalism based on landscape and botany rather than ethnicity. Tabor's reading comes with a full jazz orchestra and is the highpoint of a wonderful album.

❷ STRANGE AFFAIR from A CUT ABOVE
Tabor – here with Martin Simpson, folk guitarist extraordinaire – takes on a song from Richard and Linda Thompson. Electric from the very first line.

❸ I WONDER WHAT'S KEEPING MY TRUE LOVE TONIGHT from ALEYN
Also known as "Green Grass It Grows Bonny", this song is common to both Scottish and Irish traditions: Tabor claims it for the English, too.

❹ SIR PATRICK SPENS from AN ECHO OF HOOVES
The album collected border ballads of horse thievery, kidnap and murder from the English–Scottish badlands. Sir Patrick Spens's doomed sailing expedition was top of these pops.

❺ DI NAKHT from ALEYN
On *Aleyn* Tabor cast her net wider than folk, including this Yiddish song of the 1920s that acquired a darker, sadder context over the coming decades.

❻ FALSE, FALSE from AGAINST THE STREAMS
Stark and accusing, with not a syllable wasted. Collected by Ewan MacColl and Peggy Seeger from an Aberdeenshire traveller called Christina MacAllister, who sounds formidable.

❼ A PROPER SORT OF GARDENER from ALEYN
Another Maggie Holland horticultural song, about familial love.

❽ MISSISSIPPI SUMMER THE OYSTER BAND from FREEDOM AND RAIN
Taking a break from solo work to pose as rock chick singer with the ever-reliable Oyster Band, Tabor brought life to this formerly arid Delta blues.

❾ ROSE IN JUNE from ROSA MUNDI
Rosa Mundi was (of course) a concept album about rose growing. Tabor found a full songbook to explore, and the highlight was this, with words by Bob Copper, and a spring in its piano line that leaves the listener smiling.

❿ SEND US A QUIET NIGHT from APPLES
A sailor's anxious plea, with words by the travel writer Christopher Somerville, that reminds Tabor of Murmansk convoys, Cornish fishermen, Ellen MacArthur, over a minimalist piano accompaniment.

David Honigmann

Talking Heads

David Byrne was half-geek, half-preacher; Chris Frantz and Tina Weymouth were an endlessly versatile rhythm section; Jerry Harrison had the funk. Together, they explored every style under the new wave sun, and still had time to make the only watchable concert film ever made.

❶ LOVE GOES TO BUILDING ON FIRE from SAND IN THE VASELINE: POPULAR FAVORITES
This early song has the nerdy plastic energy that drives all the band's early work.

❷ DON'T WORRY ABOUT THE GOVERNMENT from THE NAME OF THIS BAND IS TALKING HEADS
From the early, scratchy punk-funk Heads, a celebration of strong central government that sounds like the military-industrial complex set to the music of the 1950s.

❸ I ZIMBRA from FEAR OF MUSIC
Dadaist nonsense verse by Hugo Ball set to frenetic West African guitars.

❹ ONCE IN A LIFETIME from REMAIN IN LIGHT
The synthesizer riff gushes like a fountain as Byrne harnesses the demeanour of a charismatic preacher to a tale of alienation and anomie: "And you may ask yourself/How did I get here?" Eno chips in with the chorus.

❺ BURNING DOWN THE HOUSE from SPEAKING IN TONGUES
Began as a chanted Parliafunkadeliment chorus but evolved into one of the Heads' best-loved songs.

⑥ THIS MUST BE THE PLACE (NAIVE MELODY) from STOP MAKING SENSE

A tender song about domesticity: how un-rock can you get? In the film, Byrne can be seen at this point dancing with a standard lamp.

⑦ STAY UP LATE from LITTLE CREATURES

A song that ackles and bounces like a demented toddler – which is pretty much what it is about.

⑧ BLIND from NAKED

Central American menace pervades this jackhammer opener from the Heads' underrated sign-off album.

⑨ MR JONES from NAKED

Any relation to Dylan's Mr Jones, who didn't know what was happening? Either way, he's back in town.

⑩ (NOTHING BUT) FLOWERS from NAKED

Jocular guitar from Johnny Marr and backing vocals from Kirsty McColl sweeten this tale of a dystopian garden paradise.

David Honigmann

Tango

Though its musical treasures are many, Argentina has been associated with tango more than any other style for over a hundred years. This urban music with rural roots appeared in the late 19th century, when Buenos Aires became Argentina's capital city, but it's also experienced a thrilling revival of late, with dance beats and electronica.

Philippe Cohen Solal's
Go-Tango time

PHILIPPE COHEN SOLAL formed Gotan Project in 1999 with keyboard player Christoph H. Mueller and Argentinian guitarist Eduardo Makaroff. He is happy to pay homage to some of the sounds that inspired the trio and their associates.

① CITÉ TANGO ASTOR PIAZOLLA from TANGO ZERO HOUR

Piazolla was our way into tango. He wanted to bring tango to a seated audience who liked classical music and jazz; we wanted to take it back to the dancers. The *bandoneon* is the voice of tango – it can sing or whisper, shout or cry, and that's how such emotion was brought into tango music. This track is funky, very soundtracky.

② EL DIA QUE ME QUIERAS CARLOS GARDEL from CARLOS GARDEL, THE PASSION OF TANGO

Carlos Gardel was the creator of the *tango canción* – the tango song. He was, all his life, a myth. Then he died young, like Monroe and Dean. This shows what tango songs are about: always love. They are very politically incorrect, very macho, but it's great to listen and cry!

③ TRES Y DOS ANÍBAL TROILO from INSPIRACIÓN ESPIRACIÓN (PHILIPPE COHEN SOLAL'S REMIXES)

I'm a big fan of Aníbal Troilo, the *bandoneon* player. His music is very tango: energetic, nervous, urban. He brought something new, while keeping the tradition; like smart, intelligent dance music.

④ COMO DOS ESTRANOS ROBERTO GOYANECHE AND NESTOR MARCONI from THE BEGINNER'S GUIDE TO TANGO

Goyaneche was the Sinatra of tango, a fantastic singer, great personality – and a cocaine addict (the drug of tango). Eduardo says he's like Charles Aznavour: he's not only singing, he acts his music.

⑤ PERCUSIÓN (PART I) DOMINGO CURA from INSPIRACIÓN ESPIRACIÓN (REMIXES)

Our Remixes album contain collisions and collaborations from hip-hop and techno/house. Percussionist Domingo Cura was a starting point, as I was thinking of mixing urban tango and rural folk music.

⑥ PERFUME BAJOFONDO WITH ADRIANA VARELA from BAJOFONDO TANGOCLUB

Bajofondo are from Buenos Aires, and they are more popular there than Gotan because they released a CD before us. This is one of the two or three tracks on the album which are collaged – which we avoid ourselves.

⑦ LA CERCANO SE ALEJA JUAN JOSE MOSALINI Y QUATUOR BENAIM from MOSALINI AND QUATUOR BENAIM INTERPRETAN BEYTELMANN

Eduardo created the "New Tango" tango label, Mañana, in Paris. It includes this album. It's an interesting way to discover the new sounds. All the Mosalinis are bandoneon players and they are all called Juan Jose!

❶ MI BUENOS AIRES QUERIDO CARLOS GARDEL from BUENOS AIRES BY NIGHT

Thanks to his operatic, the most famous tango singer ever became a global phenomenon during tango's golden age in the 1920s and 30s. Then he died in a plane crash, ensuring immortality.

❷ LA CUMPARSITA JUAN D'ARIENZO Y SU ORQUESTA TIPICA from 100 AÑOS EN 100 TANGOS

The most popular instrumental tango of all time. Much covered (you'll recognize it!) the first recording of it dates from 1916, but this 1937 version is superbly atmospheric.

❸ RESPONSO ANÍBAL TROILO from 100 AÑOS EN 100 TANGOS

One of the stars of the 1940s, accordionist and composer Troilo gave Piazzolla his first break. Here he shows off his skills as a soloist on an intense, cinematic instrumental.

❹ SOBRE EL PUCHO TITA MERELLO from WOMEN OF TANGO

A gloriously dramatic, almost camp, number from 1964 by this little-known artiste. Despite the music's chauvinism, there have been plenty of excellent female tango singers.

❺ VUELVO AL SUR ROBERTO GOYENECHE from CAFE ARGENTINA

Goyeneche was hugely respected by generations of younger *tangueros*, and by the Argentinean public for his *garganta con arena* (throat with sand).

❻ MILONGA DEL ANGEL ASTOR PIAZZOLLA from LUNA

Like watching gravity hold its breath, this ghostly, drifting masterpiece by the Einstein of tango was recorded during his last-ever concert on July 26, 1989.

❼ CADA VEZ QUE ME RECUERDES ADRIANA VARELA from CORAZONES PERVERSOS

There is no other contemporary female tango singer who can touch Varela for sheer style and sultriness. This early 1990s piece is a highlight in a career still going strong.

❽ SANTA MARIA (DEL BUEN AYRE) GOTAN PROJECT from GOTAN PROJECT

Tango moves effortlessly into club lounge class with this imaginative piece of tango electronica. Grace Jones would be proud of it, having herself tackled Piazzolla.

❾ MULETA DE BORRACHO DANIEL MELINGO from SANTA MILONGA

A heavenly choir and a voice that sounds like it's been through hell make for a winning combination on this recent recording by an icon of tango's contemporary avant-garde.

❿ AY, DI MÍ CRISTÓBAL REPETTO from CRISTÓBAL REPETTO

A dazzling new vocal talent, whose take on this 1941 song is as old-school as 21st century tango gets. Repetto has also worked with electronic *tangueros* Bajofondo Tango Club.

Jon Lusk

Tarantino tunes

Quentin Tarantino's enthusiasm for making movies is matched by a love of inserting golden oldies into essential scenes. Here are ten that did the business.

❶ STUCK IN THE MIDDLE WITH YOU STEALERS WHEEL from RESERVOIR DOGS

Used for the unbearably savage ear-slicing scene, so lending what was a poppy Dylan-imitation an extremely sadistic overtone.

❷ MISIRLOU DICK DALE from PULP FICTION

This ripping surf guitar instrumental captured the excitement about to unfold, re-established Dale as a live draw, and gave surf music a cachet long overdue.

❸ GIRL YOU'RE GONNA BE A WOMAN SOON URGE OVERKILL from PULP FICTION

Neil Diamond ballad gets grunged up for Uma Thurman's mob missus to do the shimmy to.

❹ FLOWERS ON THE WALL THE STATLER BROTHERS from PULP FICTION

A country and pop hit in 1965 from the duo who toured for years with Johnny Cash, this goofy slice of hillbilly surrealism framed Bruce Willis' execution of John Travolta.

❺ JUNGLE BOOGIE KOOL & THE GANG from PULP FICTION

Tarantino likes mindless monosyllabic tunes (witness "Hooked On A Feeling" in *Reservoir Dogs*) and this slice of heavy funk worked nicely in a bar scene.

❻ ACROSS 110TH ST BOBBY WOMACK from JACKIE BROWN

Originally composed as theme for the extremely heavy 1972 blaxploitation film of the same name, Tarantino threw this across the opening credits to suggest Jackie's desire to escape a desperate situation.

❼ STAWBERRY LETTER 23 THE BROTHERS JOHNSON from JACKIE BROWN

Huge 1977 R&B hit originally cut by Shuggie Otis. The soft 1970s soul textures Tarantino employed throughout *Jackie Brown* were the closest he's come to giving a movie a thematic soundtrack.

❽ DIDN'T I BLOW YOUR MIND THE DELFONICS from JACKIE BROWN

"You like The Dells?" says Ordell with pleasant surprise to Max when he picks up a cassette.

❾ BANG, BANG MY BABY SHOT ME DOWN NANCY SINATRA from KILL BILL

Originally a hit for Cher, Nancy Sinatra's dramatic reading provided the perfect opening theme for a film where a man violently betrays a woman.

❿ WOO HOO THE 5, 6, 7, 8'S from KILL BILL

The liveliest scene in a gory yet dull film found Japanese female garage rock trio The 5, 6, 7, 8's rocking out while mayhem reigned

Garth Cartwright

James Taylor

JT created the template for the sensitive singer-songwriter and has found no need to depart from it in almost forty years.

❶ SOMETHING IN THE WAY SHE MOVES from JAMES TAYLOR

From his debut 1968 album on The Beatles' Apple label, it was this song that inspired George Harrison's "Something" (which Frank Sinatra famously declared the best ever Lennon and McCartney song).

❷ CAROLINA IN MY MIND from JAMES TAYLOR

Taylor at his sunniest – although before we get too carried away, the song does include the line "Ain't it just like a friend of mine/To hit me from behind."

❸ SWEET BABY JAMES from SWEET BABY JAMES

A lilting lullaby for his young nephew and the title track of the most perfectly sensitive singer-songwriter album of its time.

❹ FIRE AND RAIN from SWEET BABY JAMES

Was there ever a more heartbreaking opening line than "Just yesterday morning/They let me know you were gone"?

❺ YOU'VE GOT A FRIEND from MUD SLIDE SLIM AND THE BLUE HORIZON

Written by Carole King and with Joni Mitchell singing backing vocals. Nice, as Bob Harris, might say.

❻ MUD SLIDE SLIM AND THE BLUE HORIZON from MUD SLIDE SLIM AND THE BLUE HORIZON

On which he gets a little funky with guitarist Danny Kortchmar and a top-notch band.

❼ DON'T LET ME BE LONELY TONIGHT from ONE MAN DOG

And a thousand broken hearts in bedsitter-land sang along.

❽ SHOWER THE PEOPLE from IN THE POCKET

Tender sentiments with his then-wife Carly Simon on backing vocals.

❾ SECRET O'LIFE from JT

Words of wisdom from a 1977 album, made just as his own life was about to go off the rails into addiction and divorce.

❿ COPPERLINE from NEW MOON SHINE

It's perhaps unfair that this 1991 track is the only representation of Taylor's post-1970s output, because he's continued to make quality albums throughout his long career.

Nigel Williamson

The Teardrop Explodes

Brass-flavoured acid depravity and pop songs of searing, everlasting perfection from Julian Cope and his posse. The Teardrops took psychedelia back to the schoolkids, knowing they could be trusted to fry their own brains when the time came. Stardom wasn't to Julian's taste and he turned first odd, then solo (for more on which, see his individual playlist).

❶ BENT OUT OF SHAPE from WILDER

Spooky beats and deceptively jaunty brass introduce the Teardrops' unique mix of over-awing pop and nervous, inquisitive lyrics.

❷ BOUNCING BABIES from KILIMANJARO

Desperate-sounding yet still undeniably sweet and appealing, Baby Julian must have been a dear. He grew up to be a bouncing bomb, so he says here.

❸ COLOURS FLY AWAY from WILDER

Julian's skilled weave of strange yet compelling imagery instantly promoted him to the premier league of psychedelic explorers. This ream of slightly threatening nonsense hasn't dated in the least.

❹ KILIMANJARO from KILIMANJARO

Spinning around in a daze booted rhythmically in the rear by the band's most rock-solid beat, Julian pumps out the psychedelia like a man who's taken some kind of drug.

❺ LIKE LEILA KHALED SAID from WILDER
Ms Khaled hijacked her first airliner in the late 1960s and became a revolutionary pin-up for frustrated guerrillas all over the world – even in Julian's bedroom. The song has little to do with her life, but it's good to know who she was.

❻ PASSIONATE FRIEND SAINTS & SINNERS MIX BY LIQUID Single (original on WILDER)
Long before he was openly championing the lost majesty of Scott Walker, Julian was doing a fair impression of the man. This is pure 1980s but could so easily have been twenty years earlier. The Liquid remix of this already heavenly soulful tune lays on even more of the diva vocals.

❼ REWARD from THE COLLECTION
Horns blare, keyboard lines wiggle up and down the keyboard lines wiggle up and down the keyboard, then Julian lets rip: "Bless my cotton socks! I'm in the news!" This single was a rush.

❽ SEVEN VIEWS OF JERUSALEM from WILDER
The Teardrop Explodes, it must be remembered, was a band – not simply Julian and a set of session musicians. This is keyboardist Dave Balfe's highest achievement, an infinitely repeatable progression teased from nowhere.

❾ THE GREAT DOMINIONS from WILDER
Saint Julian's most glorious awesome sunset of melancholy.

❿ TREASON (IT'S JUST A STORY) from THE COLLECTION
Julian hides his poison in the sweet-smelling bouquet assembled and attractively wrapped by his ensemble.

Al Spicer

Techno

The robots are taking over! Dance music for a machine world. All tracks are singles, but they appear on various compilations.

❶ WARM LEATHERETTE THE NORMAL
This 1978 B-side could have been released into clubs today – though the lyrics (inspired by J.G. Ballard's automobile-erotic novel *Crash*) aren't exactly uplifting.

❷ FUTURE MODEL 500
"The future is here": so says the robotic voice on Juan Atkin's cold, metallic techno manifesto from 1985.

❸ ONE NIGHT IN NEW YORK CITY THE HORRORIST
Eerie music-box bells and a nauseating squelchy bassline underpin this twisted techno lullaby, telling the story of a sleazy night out.

❹ INNER CITY JUNKIES KEKTEX/SARCOBLAST
An anti-anthem of the nihilistic London squat techno scene, with its vocal cataloguing every conceivable drug abuse. Also, a typical example of London techno: fast and relentless.

❺ ENERGY FLASH JOEY BELTRAM
Representing the backlash to the second Summer of Love, this is a dark, uneasy blend of subtly filtered synths and handclaps, along with the famous "ecstasy…" vocal samples.

❻ DOMINATOR HUMAN RESOURCE
Notable for its effective early use of the "hoover" noise, which was later appropriated by a million terrible hard-house tunes.

❼ THE BELLS JEFF MILLS
With its remixes still causing mayhem in clubs now, The Bells boasts the most instantly recognizable hook in techno.

❽ MUTATE AND SURVIVE OLIVER HO
Weirdly looped backwards vocals gradually emerge over a backing of densely layered percussion. The blend is sweatily euphoric.

❾ SOMETIMES LEO LAKER
A perfect example of how minimalist techno should be done – warm and hypnotic, repetitive but never boring.

❿ SPASTIK PLASTIKMAN
A flurry of syncopated snare rolls, an insistent kick drum, and not much more. Richie Hawtin's finest moment.

Dan May

Teenage Fanclub

If you've never been seduced by the rich songwriting of Glasgow's Teenage Fanclub drop everything RIGHT NOW and listen up. Boasting three genius singer songwriters they have made album after album of mellifluous guitar driven rock.

❶ EVERYTHING FLOWS from A CATHOLIC EDUCATION
Lead track on their first album. Shades of Neil Young and a really great indication of the sound that was to become trademark.

❷ GOD KNOWS IT'S TRUE from DEEP FRIED FANCLUB
Densely melodic lead track from an early EP that's well worth the effort to track down.

❸ WHAT YOU DO TO ME from BANDWAGONESQUE
This was the favourite track of many from their break-through album. Grungy, repetitive and blissful pop.

❹ ALCOHOLIDAY from BANDWAGONESQUE
And this was the undoubted melodic highlight. Producer Kramer added layers of sound but the tune still shines through.

❺ RADIO from THIRTEEN
The band followed up the hugely successful *Bandwagonesque* with an album of difficult, darker sounding songs – a great collection, once absorbed, and this track in particular stands out.

❻ NEIL JUNG from GRAND PRIX
Perhaps the best track on arguably their best album, chock full of guitar-driven hyper tuneful pop rock.

❼ I'LL MAKE IT CLEAR from GRAND PRIX
Another belter from the genius that is Norman Blake.

❽ I DON'T WANT CONTROL OF YOU from SONGS FROM NORTHERN BRITAIN
Oh those Byrds-y harmonies.

❾ I NEED DIRECTION from HOWDY
A gem from their least satisfying album.

❿ SLOW FADE from MAN MADE
The band returned to form with this terrific album on their own label. A tad avant garde but it rocks.

Dave Atkinson

Telephonica

If you can't say it to your baby in person, maybe you could say it over the phone?

❶ SWITCHBOARD SUSAN NICK LOWE from LABOUR OF LUST
A leering Lowe gets a lot of mileage out of a very few notes and some amusing wordplay – "Can we be friends after six and at weekends?" – written by fellow British pub-rocker Mickey Jupp.

❷ ANSWERING MACHINE THE REPLACEMENTS from LET IT BE
Westerberg pours out his frustrated heart to a most unreceptive device; urgent, compelling stuff.

❸ RIKKI DON'T LOSE THAT NUMBER STEELY DAN from PRETZEL LOGIC
The band's biggest hit was a characteristically gorgeous jazz-rock piece, highlighted by the kind of guitar solo for which they were sorely underrated.

❹ 911 IS A JOKE PUBLIC ENEMY from FEAR OF A BLACK PLANET
The ultimate communication breakdown – a public service is indicted as racist, and Flavor Flav has a ton of fun serving the papers.

❺ 867-5309 JENNY TOMMY TUTONE from TOMMY TUTONE 2
Mindless power pop fun that had thousands calling up the number in their area code.

❻ OPERATOR (THAT'S NOT THE WAY IT FEELS) JIM CROCE from JIM CROCE
The operator gets cast in the traditional role of bartender, as Jim looks for a sympathetic ear and realizes it won't come if he actually places that call.

❼ YOUR PHONE'S OFF THE HOOK BUT YOU'RE NOT X from LOS ANGELES
An imagistic rave-up that sounds as good as the song's title reads.

❽ OFF THE HOOK ROLLING STONES from THE ROLLING STONES, NOW
The boys sound like they're having a good old time, despite the fact that it's late, their baby's number is busy, and lord only knows what the imagination can conjure up.

❾ MY LITTLE RED BOOK MANFRED MANN from ALL MANNER OF MANN: 1963–1969
Love also did a well known version of this Bacharach/David composition, but Mann's pulses and swells with tension.

❿ TELEPHONE LINE ELO from A NEW WORLD RECORD
Hopelessness usually doesn't sound this lush and sweet, but no one ever accused Jeff Lynne of under-production.

IF THOSE LINES ARE BUSY, TRY:

⓫ HANGING ON THE TELEPHONE BLONDIE from PARALLEL LINES

⓬ 634-5789 WILSON PICKETT from THE EXCITING WILSON PICKETT

⓭ ALEXANDER GRAHAM BELL RICHARD THOMPSON from
RT: THE LIFE AND MUSIC OF RICHARD THOMPSON

⓮ PENNSYLVANIA 65000 GLENN MILLER from THE
ESSENTIAL GLENN MILLER

⓯ YOU KNOW MY NAME LOOK UP THE NUMBER
THE BEATLES from ANTHOLOGY 2

Andrew Rosenberg

Television

Arty, poetic and capable of some of the most elegant and beautifully flowing guitar lines in rock, Television still get lumped in with primeval New York punk rockers like The Ramones. Tom Verlaine probably finds that slightly irritating.

❶ LITTLE JOHNNY JEWEL from THE BLOW-UP
Kicking off the list with a fifteen-minute virtuoso performance that makes strong male guitar players fall down on their knees and weep, and a lyric of four-word three-chord dumbness. The ultimate art-punk interface.

❷ PROVE IT from MARQUEE MOON
Laid-back New York swagger of a tune, with a cool Spanish-strolling guitar riff that leads you unsuspect-ing into a Verlaine ambush around the corner down the alley in the chorus.

❸ GUIDING LIGHT from MARQUEE MOON
So trippy and hallucinatory that the band, and finally you too, lose your place in the real world and float off to the land of Richard Lloyd's solo from paradise.

❹ TORN CURTAIN from MARQUEE MOON
Darkest of Television's epic ballad-expeditions to the core of inner space and one of Verlaine's most melo-dramatic moments. It's not surprising the rest of the band left him soon after.

❺ VENUS DE MILO from THE BLOW-UP
One of the best guitar riffs to come from the CBGB scene and a perfect example of the band's psych-edelic/jazz/punk/soul grooves.

❻ ELEVATION from THE BLOW-UP
The live take of this classic is the one to hold out for: it's dramatic and heart-wrenchingly gorgeous.

❼ MARQUEE MOON from MARQUEE MOON
Nine minutes long (the Ramones would be halfway through their set in that time), this has enough

confidence to stretch out forever and beyond, only kicking in with the full-on majesty when everybody's comfortable.

❽ FRICTION from MARQUEE MOON
Staccato guitar from Lloyd, like he's trying to machine-gun the first three rows of the crowd, making way for one of Verlaine's balletic whirls up and down the neck of his guitar.

Al Spicer

The Temptations

Motown's most versatile vocal group, blessed with several fine lead singers and the ability to handle both smooth ballads and socially conscious funk-psychedelia.

❶ SINCE I LOST MY BABY from THE ULTIMATE COLLECTION
A classy early Smokey Robinson production, the strings and call-and-response vocals dripping with reflective sorrow.

❷ AIN'T TOO PROUD TO BEG from THE ULTIMATE COLLECTION
A rough'n'ready David Ruffin vocal, and a fine example of how The Temptations could growl as well as purr.

❸ MY GIRL from THE ULTIMATE COLLECTION
An unforgettable upward-curling guitar lick, one of Smokey Robinson's best lyrics, and a magnificent uplifting chorus. What else do you need?

❹ (I KNOW) I'M LOSING YOU from THE ULTIMATE COLLECTION
Few other Motown productions emanate such angst, from both the foreboding piano riff and David Ruffin's straining lead vocal.

❺ THE WAY YOU DO THE THINGS YOU DO from THE ULTIMATE COLLECTION
The Temps' first hit was a mega-catchy mid-tempo groove, with a strutting swing impossible to resist.

❻ GET READY from THE ULTIMATE COLLECTION
Underrated mid-charting 1966 single had both a compulsive funky riff and a superb Eddie Kendricks falsetto lead vocal.

❼ I CAN'T GET NEXT TO YOU from THE ULTIMATE COLLECTION
Wonderful tag-team lead vocal trade-offs on this lusty 1969 American #1, as well as a surprise instrumental drum break.

t

❽ PAPA WAS A ROLLING STONE from **THE ULTIMATE COLLECTION**

Post-1960s gloom hits soul music with a vengeance on the grim percolating funk of this tale of a shiftless patriarch.

❾ CLOUD NINE from **THE ULTIMATE COLLECTION**

Psychedelia hits soul music on this late-1960s hit, both in the waves of wah-wah guitar and the drug-alluding lyric.

❿ PSYCHEDELIC SHACK
from **THE UNIVERSAL MASTERS COLLECTION**

Gimmicky but fun hit from the peak of the group's psychedelic excursions, with some positively searing guitar and electronic squeals on the chorus.

Richie Unterberger

T For Texas

Surely no other US state has been as celebrated? Here's a Rough Guide to the lone star state.

❶ T FOR TEXAS BLUE YODEL NO 1 JIMMIE RODGERS from **FIRST SESSIONS**

Country music's first superstar started out singing in a blackface "nigger minstrel" show. There he learned his mix of blues, folk and yodelling so leading to his first big hit in 1928 with this rollicking salute to his adopted home state.

❷ AMARILLO BY MORNING GEORGE STRAIT from **GREATEST HITS**

Strait is a proud Texan who often mentions his home state – "All My Ex's Live In Texas" was another of his hits – but this soulful ballad about a broke rodeo rider trying to make it to Amarillo is one of the definite celebrations of Texan cowboys.

❸ LUCKENBACH, TEXAS (BACK TO THE BASICS OF LOVE) WAYLON JENNINGS & WILLIE NELSON from **OL' WAYLON**

The two Texan leaders of the Outlaw movement scored a huge hit with this duet in 1977; so much so that the small town of Luckenback was inundated with tourists wanting to know where "Waylon and Willie were". Problem being, neither had ever visited.

❹ YELLOW ROSE OF TEXAS GENE AUTREY from **THE ESSENTIAL GENE AUTRY**

Autry was marketed as a singing cowboy and became one of America's most popular movie stars and singers in the 1930s and 40s. "Yellow Rose Of Texas" is a love song from this native Texan to his girl and his state.

❺ AMARILLO HIGHWAY TERRY ALLEN from **LUBBOCK ON EVERYTHING**

Allen is a sculptor and conceptual artist alongside being a surreal, highly entertaining country singer. This wry song is from an album that uses the city of Lubbock as a reference point to examine America.

❻ SAN ANTONIO ROSE BOB WILLS & THE TEXAS PLAYBOYS from **ANTHOLOGY, 1935–1973**

Waylon Jennings sang "when you're down in Austin/ Bob Wills is still the King" and the late Western Swing icon first scored in 1940 with "San Antonio Rose".

❼ THE BALLAD OF CHARLES WHITMAN KINKY FRIEDMAN from **SOLD AMERICAN**

Friedman led The Texas Jewboys and his brilliantly comic songs often involved such Texan absurdities as this one about a psychotic Austin sniper.

❽ LA GRANGE ZZ TOP from **TRES HOMBRES**

Texan power trio and one of America's most consistent and witty rock bands across the 1970s and 80s. Here they celebrate a border brothel.

❾ TEXAS RADIO & THE BIG BEAT THE DOORS from **LA WOMAN**

The Doors were Kings of the LA rock scene yet here Jim Morrison recalls how, as a child, border radio were sonic sorcerers playing blues, rock'n'roll and Tex-Mex.

❿ TEXAS FLOOD STEVIE RAY VAUGHAN from **TEXAS FLOOD**

Austin-born Vaughan's debut release was this 1983 recording of the Larry Davis song. His guitar broods and sizzles so conjuring up deep Texas blues.

Garth Cartwright

Texas singer-songwriters

Despite regional differences, Texas has produced a tight community of singer-songwriters who share a loyal, if not generally stadium-filling, fan base. They offer up a bit of everything: high plains and backland prairies, country and rock, western and folk, gypsy music and Mexicali blues.

❶ PANCHO AND LEFTY TOWNES VAN ZANDT from **THE LATE GREAT TOWNES VAN ZANDT**

Now that Van Zandt is gone, it's hard to see a show in which his cohorts don't cover at least one of his tunes. Recognized in his time as the great poet and lyricist he was, his songs made the rounds even then. "Pancho and Lefty", a hit for country outlaws Willie Nelson (Texan!) and Merle Haggard, was a favourite.

❷ DALLAS FLATLANDERS from MORE A LEGEND THAN A BAND
Jimmie Dale Gilmore, Joe Ely and Butch Hancock, each of whom could have a number of songs on this list, came together for one great album in 1972. Their spirited partnership, now renewed, brings out the best in each of them: Hancock's deft writing, Ely's imagery and Gilmore's ghostly quaver.

❸ STAR IN MY HEART BILLY JOE SHAVER from THE EARTH ROLLS ON
One of the lesser known of the Texans, cowboy-poet Shaver wears his rough life on his sleeve and in his music. Teamed here with his son Eddy just before Eddy's death in 2000, this glimpse of lost potential adds a raw ache to a song about unconditional love.

❹ GRINGO HONEYMOON ROBERT EARL KEEN from LIVE NO. 2
With a rough-hewn, almost monotone voice, Keen tells stories as much as sings them. Evocative details – hot sand and an old gut-string guitar – paint a tale of love on the border.

❺ LA FREEWAY GUY CLARK from OLD NO. 1
A gifted songwriter, Clark's "LA Freeway" was a hit for adopted Texan Jerry Jeff Walker. Here, native Clark gives it his own craggy treatment as he sings about disillusion and alienation.

❻ MR BOJANGLES JERRY JEFF WALKER from MR BOJANGLES
Born a New Yorker but a committed member of the Texas music scene, Walker made countless albums but is best known for this gentlest of songs, written about a former cellmate.

❼ LOVE AT THE FIVE AND DIME NANCI GRIFFITH from LAST OF THE TRUE BELIEVERS
Finally, a song by a woman. Sounding more like a folk singer than usual, Griffith has a pure, eternally youthful voice that graces this melodic tale about love in a small town and on the road.

❽ YOU'RE STILL STANDING THERE STEVE EARLE WITH LUCINDA WILLIAMS from I FEEL ALRIGHT
Another hard-living Texan with the songs to show for it. Here, Earle and Williams (Louisiana-born but a big part of the 1970s Austin scene) bring their voices and baggage together.

❾ HER FIRST MISTAKE LYLE LOVETT from ROAD TO ENSENADA
With one of the better singing voices of the Texas men, Lovett also has a sharp, self-deprecating wit

that blows through his lyrics like a prairie wind. That's evident here, along with his strong sense of regionalism and of people.

❿ I NEVER CARED FOR YOU WILLIE NELSON from TEATRO
Labelled "outlaw country", Willie Nelson predates Van Zandt and company by a few years. He *can* fill stadiums. But he's always been supportive of his fellow Texans, covering their songs, dueting with Lovett. On "I Never Cared For You" he toys with the beat, singing in front or behind his guitar, yet somehow keeping in time with backup vocalist Emmylou Harris.

Madelyn Rosenberg

Tex-Mex

The music of the Mexico–Texas border, known to Anglos as Tex-Mex and to Mexicans as *conjunto* (literally "group") is all about accordion-led dance music. Ain't nothing better for beer'n'chilli parties.

❶ MAL HOMBRE LYDIA MENDOZA from MAL HOMBRE
The first Mexican-American star, Lydia sang and played a twelve-string guitar, and began recording in San Antonio in 1934. This was her first hit and is a Tex-Mex classic.

❷ LA CHULADA NARCISO MARTINEZ from 15 REGIONAL MUSIC CLASSICS OF MEXICO
Narciso combined *bajo sexto* (twelve-string bass) with his accordion playing in the 1930s, so pioneering the sound now called *conjunto*. Thus "the father of *conjunto* music".

❸ MI ROSITA ISIDRO LOPEZ from EL INDIO
This lush ballad helped establish Isidro as the pioneer of Tejano (the Texan music that blended big bands and *conjuntos*) and the Mexican–American Sinatra.

❹ VALENTE QUINTERO SANTIAGO JIMENEZ JR from CORRIDOS DE LA FRONTERA
This is a classic "hard times" *corrido* from the son of the master accordionist (Santiago Sr) and brother of Flaco Jimenez.

❺ JUAREZ FLACO JIMENEZ from AY TE DEJO EN SAN ANTONIO
Flaco became the world's most famous Tex-Mex musician after his Arhoolie recordings led him into Ry Cooder's band. Here he pumps out a lovely *danzon* on his button accordion.

❻ OAXACA STEVE JORDAN from EL HURRACAN
The one-eyed, accordion-pumping Texan wildman cooks up the musical chilli peppers here.

⑦ UNA MAS CERVEZA THE TEXAS TORNADOS from THE BEST OF
Late, great Texan rocker Doug Sahm blended *conjunto* into his sound for this anthem to beer. Formed The Texas Tornados with Flaco Jimez, organ blaster Augie Meyers and Chicano country singer Freddy Fender.

⑧ SI UNA VEZ SELENA from 12 SUPER EXITOS
Huge hit from the Tex-Mex Madonna, shot to death by the former president of her fan club in 1995. Her conjunto-pop is an acquired taste but huge fun.

⑨ WAVE ALEJANDRO ESCOVEDO from A MAN UNDER THE INFLUENCE
Lyrical reflection on how Mexicans arrived in Texas, kept moving by the legendary Chicano rocker.

Garth Cartwright

Richard Thompson

Thompson's sinuous, Celtic-influenced guitar sound has become the trademark of his long, prolific career – that and the lashings of burnt sugar he tends to pour over his love songs.

① WHEN I GET TO THE BORDER RICHARD AND LINDA THOMPSON from I WANT TO SEE THE BRIGHT LIGHTS TONIGHT
A short encyclopedia of musical styles, this hymn-like march bristles with mandolin solos and bursts of electric guitar, and has a delightfully shouty chorus.

② BEESWING from MIRROR BLUE
So delicately fingerpicked, this sweet folk number about innocence and love transports you to places usually only depicted in soap commercials.

③ WALKING ON A WIRE RICHARD AND LINDA THOMPSON from SHOOT OUT THE LIGHTS
You can almost hear Richard and Linda's marriage dissolving in the background, as she delivers the hammer blows; the tension is nearly unbearable, the up-and-down guitar soloing unimpeachable.

④ NOBODY'S WEDDING from HENRY THE HUMAN FLY
Cheeky and folky, this seems casually tossed off, especially when it breaks into rockin' its little jigs, but it manages to dig deeper, thanks largely to his earnest, almost shy vocals.

⑤ SO BEN MI CA BON TEMPO from 1000 YEARS OF POPULAR MUSIC
Thompson's transforms this sixteenth-century Italian trifle (translated: "I know a lucky fellow") into a hypnotic, nearly religious incantation. The whole album, in which he covers the highlights of Western music from 1068 AD on, including Britney Spears, is priceless.

⑥ NIGHT COMES IN from POUR DOWN LIKE SILVER
The last three minutes of this spellbinding epic could be the closest he's ever sounded to Pink Floyd.

⑦ I MISUNDERSTOOD from RUMOUR AND SIGH
The coolly detached delivery works almost too well

Richard Thompson's
1000 Years of Popular Songs

"In late 1999, I was asked for a list of the greatest songs of the millennium," Richard Thompson recalls. "Hah! I thought, they don't mean millennium, they mean the last twenty years. I'll call their bluff and do a real thousand-year selection." The magazine declined to print his list – so he turned it into a live show. Here are ten from down the centuries you might hear him cover on a good night.

① SUMER IS ICUMEN IN TRADITIONAL

② KING HENRY V'S CONQUEST OF FRANCE TRADITIONAL

③ WHEN I AM LAID IN EARTH HENRY PURCELL

④ SHENANDOAH TRADITIONAL

⑤ THERE IS BEAUTY... GILBERT & SULLIVAN

⑥ OLD ROCKING CHAIR'S GOT ME HOAGY CARMICHAEL from HOAGY SINGS CARMICHAEL

⑦ DRINKING WINE SPO-DEE-O-DEE STICKS MCGHEE from ATLANTIC RHYTHM AND BLUES, 1947–74

⑧ KISS PRINCE from PARADE

⑨ MONEY, MONEY, MONEY ABBA from GOLD

⑩ IT WON'T BE LONG THE BEATLES from WITH THE BEATLES

– though the lyric is about being taken by surprise by a lover's departure.

❽ WHEN THE SPELL IS BROKEN
from ACROSS A CROWDED ROOM

In between the snaking, ominous guitar opening and the final, repeated warning that "you can't cry if you don't know how", comes a punchy, acerbic take on a relationship, with surprising doo-wop female harmonies.

❾ ONE DOOR OPENS from THE OLD KIT BAG

Positively a toe-tapper by Thompson standards, this bright rhythm – somewhere between Celtic and Arabian – gets a lift from Judith Owen's harmonies. .

❿ SHOOT OUT THE LIGHTS from SHOOT OUT THE LIGHTS

From its opening, distorted note through two barely controlled guitar solos, words and music have rarely combined to communicate such sustained menace.

Andrew Rosenberg

Thrash Metal

Take some straight-ahead heavy metal and inject a lethal dose of speed and brutality. Headbang to this list and you'll end up in a neckbrace...

❶ AS THE WORLD BURNS KREATOR from TERRIBLE CERTAINTY

There's nothing quite like a global apocalypse to fan the flames of thrash. This is efficient, deadly and to-the-point.

❷ BLOOD OF THE SCRIBE LAMB OF GOD from ASHES OF THE WAKE

Intelligent, twisted and technical, this abrasive monster of a song displays both speed and virtuosity in equal measure.

❸ DISASTERPIECE SLIPKNOT from IOWA

Extreme thrash given a brutal and downtuned nu-metal twist, this sounds like it's raining anvils pure and simple. Not for wimps.

❹ I AM THE LAW ANTHRAX from AMONG THE LIVING

2000 AD's harsh but fair lawman Judge Dredd gets all thrashed up. Mosh-friendly verses and a megafast mid-song break make this a thrash classic.

❺ LEGIONS OF THE DEAD TESTAMENT from THE GATHERING

Vocalist Chuck Billy sounds like his soul is being ripped apart. A heads-down, no messing speedfest.

❻ PEACE SELLS MEGADETH from PEACE SELLS...BUT WHO'S BUYING?

One of the crunchiest, chewiest riffs in mid-1980s thrash. An awesome chugging opening leads to a frenzied dash for the finishing line.

❼ RAINING BLOOD SLAYER from REIGN IN BLOOD

So scary this will have you crying for your mummy. Thunder rolls and a riff forged by Satan himself bludgeons you into submission.

❽ RATAMAHATTA SEPULTURA from ROOTS

The band's Brazilian heritage takes them beyond the realms of mere brutality to create a cool amalgam of world music and crushing metal.

❾ REVELATION THE HAUNTED from THE HAUNTED MADE ME DO IT

Can you stand the pace? Intense, savage and extremely violent, this lot cram an entire song into one and a half minutes.

❿ THE STORM WITCHERY from SYMPHONY FOR THE DEVIL

A title that promises exactly what the band delivers. Tornado-scale riffs and licks whip around you with flesh-ripping intensity.

Essi Berelian

Tindersticks

Nottingham's kings of soul-tinged, booze-drenched melancholy.

❶ A MARRIAGE MADE IN HEAVEN from DONKEYS

Stuart Staples croons with Isabella Rossellini like they were Nancy & Lee. The original Rough Trade single is even better.

❷ RENTED ROOMS (SWING VERSION) single

A track with more sleaze, feathers and swinging brass than your average night out in Soho.

❸ KATHLEEN from LIVE IN AMSTERDAM

An amazing take on the Townes Van Zandt classic. Just when you thought the song couldn't get any better.

❹ HER from TINDERSTICKS (THE FIRST ALBUM)

A quick flourish of Spanish guitar and a dollop of self-loathing add up to a live favourite. It's the scraped strings. They get you every time.

❺ TINY TEARS from TINDERSTICKS (THE SECOND ALBUM)

A kitchen-sink drama of a song, it might just be the perfect early Tindersticks track. It swoons.

6 SHE'S GONE from TINDERSTICKS (THE SECOND ALBUM)
You could never accuse the first couple of albums of lacking melancholy, but this ode to missing your daughter is as poignant as they come.

7 PATCHWORK from TINDERSTICKS (THE FIRST ALBUM)
Wonky glockenspiel with a tapped tambourine could only hint at what was to come on this early and glorious single.

8 CAN WE START AGAIN from SIMPLE PLEASURE
Out went the suits and the indie miserablism. In came some heartbroken soul and some serious yearning. With handclaps.

9 PEOPLE KEEP COMIN' AROUND from CAN OUR LOVE
The transformation into a bruised soul band is almost complete, with the merest hint of funky bass, female backing singers and less crooning.

10 TRAVELLING LIGHT from TINDERSTICKS (THE FIRST ALBUM)
More from the Nancy and Lee school of brooding male vocal and wry and infuriated female response. Topped off with a trumpet. What more do you need?

Gavin McNamara

Toasters

Rather than DJs in today's accepted sense of the word, these are old-school, pre-1980 toasters whose primary job was to big up whatever sound system they were working on at the time. This was done live to whatever record the selector was spinning, so lyrical dexterity and a nimble train of thought was a given. These records reflect such qualities, and the ability to turn nonsense into a dancefloor delight.

1 WEAR YOU TO THE BALL U-ROY from VERSION GALORE
Classic, old-school rocksteady toasting, with U-Roy whooping, yelping and talking nonsense on top of The Paragons' immaculate harmonizing.

2 NUMBER ONE STATION DENNIS ALCAPONE from GUNS DON'T ARGUE: THE ANTHOLOGY 1970–77
Fabulous illustration of the glorious self-servingness of early toasting: Alcapone's sprightly, musical tones do little other than celebrate his environment and the assembled company.

3 COOL BREEZE BIG YOUTH from RIDE LIKE LIGHTNING: THE BEST OF 1972–1976
On top of a dub cut of Keith & Tex's "Stop That Train", Big Youth swings wildly between a yearning love song and a tribute to the blaxploitation hero of the title, before tying up the two.

4 UNDER HEAVY MANNERS PRINCE FAR-I from UNDER HEAVY MANNERS
Deep roots steppers' beat and Far-I warning mankind in a voice that sounds like a bear abruptly woken up from hibernation at the back of a very deep cave.

5 THREE PIECE SUIT AND T'ING TRINITY from LOVE OF THE COMMON PEOPLE (JOE GIBBS)
Mad toast detailing what it takes to be a ladies man – "diamond socks and t'ing" – over the top of a dub of "I'm Still In Love With You", the tune that also became "Uptown Ranking".

6 COCAINE IN MY BRAIN DILLINGER from COCAINE IN MY BRAIN
Maybe the maddest reggae record ever made: built on the central riff from the Philly funk classic "Do It Any Way You Wanna", the hardest-working lyric is "A knife, a fork, a bottle and a cork/That's the way you spell New York". Draw your own conclusions.

7 WELDING I-ROY from VARIOUS ARTISTS: THE CHANNEL ONE STORY
Back on more familiar turf with a lazily phrased piece of slackness, as I-Roy rides a classic rub-a-dub rhythm while he sorts out the battle of the sexes, aided only by his "welding iron".

8 MR HARRY SKANK PRINCE JAZZBO from GLEN BROWN & FRIENDS: RHYTHM MASTER VOLUME ONE
The portentous dread of the backing beat – heavy heavy bass and drum, spiked with a scary sax – Jazzbo's gruff delivery and hymn to a sound system operator make the perfect counterpoint.

9 DRAW YOUR BRAKES SCOTTY from THE BEST OF SCOTTY
Coming very close to singing, and with a remarkably cogent narrative, Scotty delivers the smooooovest of lyrical laments over the original "Stop That Train".

10 JACK OF MY TRADE SIR LORD COMIC from LOVE OF THE COMMON PEOPLE (JOE GIBBS)
Simple, totally infectious old-time reggae groove, complementing Comic's easy action stream-of-consciousness good-naturedness.

Lloyd Bradley

Toots & The Maytals

Frederick "Toots" Hibbert remains one of reggae's most compelling performers, almost four decades after the string of dance hits that made his name.

❶ SIX AND SEVEN BOOKS OF MOSES from TIME TOUGH-THE ANTHOLOGY
The first Toots classic, recorded at Studio One in 1963.

❷ DO THE REGGAY from TIME TOUGH
The first record to mention the word "reggae", from 1968.

❸ 54-46 WAS MY NUMBER from TIME TOUGH
Inspired by his incarceration for marijuana possession, this guaranteed floor-filler from 1968 has to be Toots's finest hour.

❹ PRESSURE DROP from TIME TOUGH
A driving reggae number from 1969, which builds to a frenzied climax and was later covered by The Clash.

❺ MONKEY MAN from TIME TOUGH
A quintessential Maytals romp from 1969.

❻ FUNKY KINGSTON from TIME TOUGH
By 1973, Toots was achieving global success, hard on the heels of Bob Marley.

❼ REGGAE GOT SOUL from TIME TOUGH
Evidence from 1975 of Toots' ongoing fascination with fusing reggae with American soul music.

❽ (I'VE GOT) DREAMS TO REMEMBER from TIME TOUGH
A sublime tribute to Otis Redding, from 1988's *Toots In Memphis* album.

Greg Ward

Trains

Oddly, the best songs about trains make no reference whatsoever to Thomas the Tank Engine. Mind you, tots should like a decent number of these, all the same.

❶ LAST TRAIN TO CLARKSVILLE THE MONKEES from BEST OF THE MONKEES
Some deft songwriting (by Boyce & Hart; not by any actual Monkees) made this an easy hit for the band.

❷ MONKEY AND THE ENGINEER THE GRATEFUL DEAD from RECKONING
A monkey jumps in the driver's seat of a train and drives off at 90 miles per hour. The original comes from bluesman Jesse Fuller; the Grateful Dead remake speeds it up and smooths it out.

❸ MYSTERY TRAIN ELVIS PRESLEY from THE KING OF ROCK'N'ROLL: THE COMPLETE 50s MASTERS
From a quick chug to the long, sweeping toot of a train whistle, Presley varies the lengths of his notes to great effect in this fast blues recorded for Sun in 1955.

❹ NEW RIVER TRAIN BILL MONROE from THE ESSENTIAL
The New River is said to be the world's second oldest railroad, and this song, too, dates back to the turn of the last century. In this speedy version, Monroe and company give it the bluegrass treatment.

❺ NIGHT TRAIN JAMES BROWN from NIGHT TRAIN
"HELLO, BOISE!" Some performers shout out the name of the city they're performing in. The Godfather of Soul namechecks all of the major cities on the East Coast, plus New Orleans, with soulful hollers.

❻ ORANGE BLOSSOM SPECIAL JOHNNY CASH from ORANGE BLOSSOM SPECIAL
Written about a real, Miami-to-New York train and recorded as a bluegrass song in the 1940s (and probably every year since). Cash's boozy 1965 version makes the song less about the fiddle and more about voice.

❼ LAST OF THE STEAM-POWERED TRAINS THE KINKS from THE KINKS ARE THE VILLAGE GREEN PRESERVATION SOCIETY
Good hooks and harmonies, with a riff that stands the test of time.

❽ THE TRAIN IS COMING KEN BOOTHE from A MAN AND HIS HITS
A rock steady classic from 1966, Boothe's melodic voice is full of both yearning and comfort.

❾ TRAIN KEPT A ROLLIN' TINY BRADSHAW from THE GREAT COMPOSER
The Yardbirds recorded it. So did Aerosmith. But Bradshaw did it first and better with throaty vocals, a big band, and a swinging blast of sax.

❿ WABASH CANNONBALL DAN ZANES WITH BOB WEIR from HOUSE PARTY
There must be a thousand versions of this song, first made popular by the Carter Family. Former Del Fuego Dan Zanes put it on his perfect-formula kids' record with vocal help from Weir.

Madelyn Rosenberg

T Rex

Marc Bolan sold his soul and all his hippy threads for the chance of three years in the spotlight as the prettiest star in UK pop history – where Tyrannosaurus Rex had dallied in sun-dappled glades, T Rex stomped in the spotlight. Primarily a singles band, the best of their material is always available on whichever Best Of collection is at your local store.

❶ 20TH CENTURY BOY
from THE ESSENTIAL COLLECTION
Stomping all over London like some cocaine-crazed killer reptile from before the dawn of history, with Flo & Eddie providing bad influences and soprano-pitch backing vocals.

❷ KING OF THE RUMBLING SPIRES from THE ESSENTIAL COLLECTION
One of the earliest T Rex (as opposed to Tyrannosaurus) tracks, and one where Marc still had to completely ditch his Tolkien fantasies. Very dark, bass-heavy and stardust-sprinkled.

❸ SOLID GOLD EASY ACTION from THE ESSENTIAL COLLECTION
Easy action is a technical term that describes the closeness of guitar strings in relation to the neck of the instrument. Of course, with Bolan at the helm, it turned into a fast-paced song about fucking.

❹ METAL GURU from THE SLIDER
The bopping elf of the 1960s had traded in his fairy cloak for teen superstardom, T Rextasy in the newspapers and fame so unassailable that he could knock out rubbishy lyrics like this and still take them to the top of the charts. Magnificent nonsense.

❺ CHILDREN OF THE REVOLUTION
from THE ESSENTIAL COLLECTION
"You won't fool the children of the revolution! No Way! Hey!" Oh the powers that be must have quaked at this powerful polemic. Great riff though, great solo too.

❻ HOT LOVE from THE ESSENTIAL COLLECTION
Bolan and the band never surpassed this early bopping classic, a standard twelve-bar blues stripped down for the pre-teen audience. Hot love, indeed!

❼ JEEPSTER from ELECTRIC WARRIOR
The jury is still out on what exactly Bolan meant by Jeepster, but when he claims to be "A vampire for your love", all the little girls understand.

❽ RIDE A WHITE SWAN
from RIDE A WHITE SWAN
Another transitional tune from the late hippy-early glam period, and another dead simple tune suitable for someone like Marc, new to the electric instrument. If he'd lived long enough to write a guitar tutor manual, this would have been on page one.

❾ TELEGRAM SAM from THE SLIDER
Sam, according to legend, was a dealer; a man who delivered drugs to the stars. Bolan apparently "wrote" this in the lift at the BBC, on his way to record a Peel session.

❿ GET IT ON from ELECTRIC WARRIOR
Three chords, a sympathetic photographer and a winning, pants-melting smile will get a boy a long way in the music business. This song was banned in America because of the "bang a gong" line. Evidently percussion is still frowned on over there.

Al Spicer

Trojan reggae

Although the Trojan label is historically associated with pop-reggae and now specializes in reissues, its original subsidiaries released some of the finest Jamaican music of the late 1960s and 70s. Here's a selection to put some reggae in your jeggae.

❶ YOU DON'T CARE THE TECHNIQUES from LET'S DO ROCKSTEADY
A.k.a. Curtis Mayfield and the Impressions'"You'll Want Me Back", this is rocksteady perfection.

❷ WAKE THE TOWN U ROY from VERSION GALORE
Produced by Duke Reid in 1970, this was the record that started the deejay revolution.

❸ LOCK JAW DAVE BARKER from DAVE AND ANSELL COLLINS - DOUBLE BARREL
Exemplary Jamaican funk.

❹ BLOOD AND FIRE NINEY from NINEY AND FRIENDS (BLOOD AND FIRE REISSUE)
Classic rebel music from 1970. A good name for a reggae reissue label.

❺ BEAT DOWN BABYLON JUNIOR BYLES from I AM THE UPSETTER
An understated sufferer's lament over a gently insinuating Lee Perry rhythm.

K.T. Tunstall
Takes Twelve

Part-Chinese, part Scottish, K.T. Tunstall sung with Oi-Va-Voi before releasing her debut solo album *Eye To The Telescope* at the end of 2004. Hailed as one of the most exciting new British singer-songwriters in many a year, the album has gone platinum and gained a Mercury nomination. "I know there's twelve on this list, but I really can't live without any of them," she insists.

❶ **INNER MEET ME** THE BETA BAND from THE 3 EPS

❷ **FOLSOM PRISON BLUES** JOHNNY CASH from JOHNNY CASH AT FOLSOM PRISON

❸ **COUNTRY CASSETTE** HALFCOUSIN from THE FUNCTION ROOM

❹ **BULLITT: MAIN TITLE THEME** LALO SCHIFRIN from BULLITT SOUNDTRACK

❺ **BE MY HUSBAND** NINA SIMONE from PASTEL BLUES/LET IT ALL OUT

❻ **ROOT DOWN** BEASTIE BOYS from ANTHOLOGY

❼ **LOST CAUSE** BECK from SEA CHANGE

❽ **JIMMY T** DAVID AXELROD from DAVID AXELROD

❾ **PATIENCE** MICAH P HINSON from AND THE GOSPEL OF PROGRESS

❿ **WHO ARE YOU** TOM WAITS from BONE MACHINE

⓫ **PERFECT DAY ELISE** PJ HARVEY from IS THIS DESIRE?

⓬ **SEGA** RY COODER & ALI FARKA TOURE from TALKING TIMBUKTU

❻ **COW THIEF SKANK** CHARLIE ACE AND THE UPSETTERS from I AM THE UPSETTER
Perry anticipates hip-hop in 1973 by splicing three rhythms together, adding mooing sounds for good measure. Absolutely barking, absolutely brilliant.

❼ **SCREAMING TARGET** BIG YOUTH from SCREAMING TARGET
Tuff version of the "No No No" rhythm by the don of cultural DJs.

❽ **NONE SHALL ESCAPE THE JUDGEMENT** JOHNNY CLARKE from A RUFFER VERSION
Top roots singer tackles Earl Zero's righteous warning. Jonathan Richman borrowed the rhythm for Egyptian Reggae.

❾ **NOTHING IS IMPOSSIBLE VERSION** TECHNIQUES ALL STARS from KING TUBBY'S FINE STYLE
Dubfather King Tubby (a.k.a Osbourne Ruddock) triumphantly takes on the Interns'/Viceroys' "Mission Impossible".

❿ **THE BIG RIP OFF** AUGUSTUS PABLO & KING TUBBY'S from KING TUBBY'S IN FINE STYLE
Dynamic duo deconstruct Jacob Miller and Inner Circle's formidable "Forward Jah Jah Children".

Neil Foxlee

Ike & Tina Turner

Ike Turner creates the "first" rock'n'roll record with Rocket 88 in 1950, marries Annie Mae Bullock and transforms her into Tina Turner, discovers cocaine and becomes Mr Nasty. Still, they cut some fine tunes before Tina fled for superstardom.

❶ **RIVER DEEP MOUNTAIN HIGH** from RIVER DEEP MOUNTAIN HIGH
Phil Spector throws the proverbial sink in for this epic blast of orchestrated pop.

❷ **NUTBUSH CITY LIMITS** from NUTBUSH CITY LIMITS
Fuzz guitar, funk keyboard, sleazy horns and Tina in a rage over small-town life. Didn't they just rock so hard?

❸ **I THINK IT'S GONNA WORK OUT FINE** from IKE & TINA TURNER
Stomping slice of soulful optimism. Hear this and you can believe they loved one another back in 1961.

❹ **PROUD MARY** from IKE & TINA TURNER
The Creedence tune gets slowed down, given some soul flavour, then builds into a R&B hurricane.

❺ FUNKIER THAN A MOSQUITO'S TWEETER from
WORKIN' TOGETHER
Tina dismisses a sleazy admirer: "You got a mouth like a head o' bo-weevils". Go git 'em, girl!

❻ I'VE BEEN LOVING YOU TOO LONG from WHAT YOU
SEE IS WHAT YOU GET
Extraordinary live version of the Otis Redding song. Tina sucks Ike. Ike eats Tina. Or so they strongly hint.

❼ A FOOL IN LOVE from THE SOUL OF IKE AND TINA TURNER
Their first single. This 1960 tune is tough southern soul, steeped in blues and grits.

❽ BABY – GET IT ON from ACID QUEEN
Ike and Tina engage in another mutual bout of lust.

Since this was 1975, it's hard to believe they still shagged each other. Nonetheless, they make out good and proper on a tough, sexy disco-flavoured rocker.

❾ SWEET RHODE ISLAND RED from
SWEET RHODE ISLAND RED
Tina recycles the Nutbush riff to tell this semi-auto-biographical tale of being a very hot, young mulatto woman.

❿ UP IN HEAH from IKE & TINA TURNER
Tina sings in the voice of a girl who left her church background to become a "daughter of evil". Cut in 1972 when Ike was coked up and strung out, this has to be a cry for help.

Garth Cartwright

U2

Pious Irish godbotherers turned anthemic political campaigners turned fly hipsters turned anthemic godbothering hipsters again. No wonder U2 have *Vertigo*. Still setting the standard for the biggest band in the world: pretenders beware.

❶ SUNDAY BLOODY SUNDAY from WAR
Not a rebel song, said Bono famously, but the flag-bearer for the militant pacifism of *War*, set to a martial drum tattoo.

❷ NEW YEAR'S DAY from WAR
A bleak piano figure drips like an icicle through the angular post-punk funk of this concert favourite.

❸ PARTY GIRL from UNDER A BLOOD-RED SKY
Under A Blood-Red Sky, a live mini-album recorded in the aftermath of a Colorado rainstorm, is the perfect distillation of the early, utterly sincere U2. "Party Girl", a jerky B-side, is here reimagined as an autumnal elegy for misspent youth.

❹ PRIDE (IN THE NAME OF LOVE) from THE UNFORGETTABLE FIRE
All right, so they got the time of day of Martin Luther King's assassination completely wrong. (To their credit, they resisted any temptation to silently fix it: as their mentor Eno said, honour your mistakes.) And you can hear the grinding gear-change in the chorus. But what a chorus.

❺ IN GOD'S COUNTRY from THE JOSHUA TREE
The Joshua Tree was where U2 hit the big time. Side 1 of the LP had all the hit singles, side 2 all the best songs, including this furiously strummed slice of American mythology.

❻ UNTIL THE END OF THE WORLD from ACHTUNG BABY
Achtung Baby was a swerve towards Bowie's sound-track for *Christiane F*. U2 made pretty convincing

children of Zoo Station, never more so than on this title-tune from Wim Wenders' messy futuristic pica-resque ramble of a film. Listen closely, and this is the Garden of Gethsemane from Judas's point of view.

❼ ZOOROPA from ZOOROPA
It's Mitteleuropean pomp and circumstance all the way in this majestic opener from a dodgy album, knocked together on tour.

❽ IF YOU WEAR THAT VELVET DRESS TONIGHT from POP
Pop was a stinker. But if it can be redeemed, this carnal whisper over a stuttering drum machine loop is the song to do it.

❾ BEAUTIFUL DAY from ALL THAT YOU CAN'T LEAVE BEHIND
By the end of the 1990s most people thought U2 were fogged in the incense of their own pretensions. But this perfect single, whose chorus goes off like dyna-mite, proved them wrong.

❿ SILVER AND GOLD from SUNCITY (ARTISTS UNITED AGAINST APARTHEID)
An early shot at setting the world to rights, from a polemical anti-apartheid benefit album. This dry-as-dust version is Bono and The Edge with Ron Wood; the full band version on *Rattle And Hum* is overblown by comparison.

David Honigmann

Uncle Tupelo

Alt.country's own Lennon & McCartney, Jeff Tweedy and Jar Farrar, with drummer Mike Heidhorn, wedded traditional country themes – depression, drinking, God, and manual labour – to punk vitriol, energy and anger. The results were revolutionary.

❶ NO DEPRESSION from NO DEPRESSION
This update of the 1930s Carter Family classic was the song that kick-started alt.country. "Depression" here meaning something else.

❷ SCREEN DOOR from NO DEPRESSION
A laid-back early track; you can hear the youth in Tweedy's voice as he sings "Sometimes it snows/But when it does/It doesn't last long".

❸ FALL DOWN EASY from STILL FEEL GONE
On Tupelo's more punky second album, this rant against "the moral stare of Big Brother" is driven by Mike Heidhorn's martial drumming.

4 STILL BE AROUND from STILL FEEL GONE

Sung by Jay Farrar, this is a gentle, acoustically strummed number in which "The Bible is a bottle/And the hardwood floor is home".

5 SAUGET WIND from 89/93: AN ANTHOLOGY

With its towering, wailing build-up, it's amazing this song was never properly released until *Anthology*. A cathartic epic.

6 CRIMINALS from MARCH 16–20, 1992

On *March*, Tupelo pulled a reverse-Dylan and went acoustic, baiting George Bush Sr with the line "They want us kinder and gentler… at their feet."

7 MOONSHINER from MARCH 16–20, 1992

An old standard lamenting the hard-luck life of a moonshiner, in good company on back-to-basics *March*; Dylan's version is also fantastic.

8 NEW MADRID from ANODYNE

Tweedy began to come into his own on Tupelo's last album, showing hints here of the surrealist imagery he'd later use to such success in Wilco.

9 WE'VE BEEN HAD from ANODYNE

This explosive rocker careens from the "Marshall stack", stopping to indict "Republicans and Democrats" and shout about how "we've been had".

10 STEAL THE CRUMBS from ANODYNE

A career-ending track as fitting as The Beatles'"The End", as Jay and Jeff harmonize the heartbreaking line, "No more, no more will I see you."

Hunter Slaton

USA Today

There's been a profound change in the rock scene stateside over the last couple of years. Bands have stopped peering over their shoulders to the UK post-punk school of the late 1970s and focused instead on a dark style all of their own.

1 BLACK CADILLACS MODEST MOUSE from GOOD NEWS FOR PEOPLE WHO LOVE BAD NEWS

An ideal introduction to these angry young men. Far from mouse-like, frontman Isaac Brock growls into the microphone like a vampire tucking into a good looking neck.

2 PHANTOM LIMB THE SHINS from WINCING THE NIGHT AWAY

Showcases The Shins' own brand of alt.country.folk. rock – a winning way with melody, subtle instrumentation and pure, fine vocals.

3 FIRE EYE'D BOY BROKEN SOCIAL SCENE FROM BROKEN SOCIAL SCENE

Delicate and mournful as the band's cryptic name suggest, this salute to the fire eye'd boy is a jangle-pop dream. Yes, OK, they're from Canada, not the US…

4 IN THIS HOME ON ICE CLAP YOUR HANDS SAY YEAH FROM CLAP YOUR HANDS SAY YEAH

More jangling guitar pop – this time inspired more by the shoegazers than the surfers – with a delicious insecurity in the vocal and a lyric so shy it probaby hides behind one of the amplifiers.

5 NORTH AMERICAN SCUM LCD SOUNDSYSTEM FROM SOUND OF SILVER

Who said Yanks can't do irony? A bittersweet meditation on becoming famous across Europe when it's hard to get arrested in your home town.

6 ROSCOE MIDLAKE from THE TRIALS OF VAN OCCUPANTHER

Marvellous slow-paced evocation of the Mid West. Moody and impressionistic, it's like the soundtrack to a pointless interstate drive on a slow road in the rain.

7 WOLF LIKE ME TV ON THE RADIO from RETURN TO COOKIE MOUNTAIN

TV On The Radio jump out of any pigeonholes that try to contain them. They blurt out raw energy and understand the majesty of rock and mystery of roll like few other new arrivals on the scene.

8 RED RIVER WALKMEN from SPIDER-MAN 3: THE OFFICIAL SOUNDTRACK

Rolls as deep as the river of the title, with drums coming and going like the wash of a passing steamer hitting the bank and guitars issuing a satisfying stream of smoke from all funnels.

9 WHOO! ALRIGHT – YEAH … UH HUH THE RAPTURE from PIECES OF THE PEOPLE WE LOVE

A fun-loving, strange but delightful piece of cynical pop frothiness.

10 STANDING IN THE WAY OF CONTROL (LE TIGRE REMIX) GOSSIP from GSSP RMX EP

This track always sounded angry, but this version is simply incandescent, with Le Tigre stripping it back to the bone and welding on a hard-assed drum track.

Al Spicer

Ray's singing that most peers and rivals lacked. Curse the fade-out on this studio recording, then go looking for the live versions.

❼ CROSSFIRE from IN STEP

Cleaning up can do terrible things to a musician. But an unstoppable low-down groove embellished with steely Albert King-style fills puts those worries to rest.

❽ TIGHTROPE from IN STEP

And if you thought that was good, wait until you hear the solo on this.

❾ LOVE ME DARLIN' from IN STEP

Wonderfully exuberant cover of an old Howlin' Wolf track. Wolf's original may be hard to beat, but Stevie Ray is on exhilarating, joyful form.

❿ LITTLE WING from THE SKY IS CRYING

Hendrix was such a unique talent that there aren't many who can get away with covering his music, let alone make his songs sing and soar like this one does.

Rowland White

Stevie Ray Vaughan

He had the chops, for sure, but it was Stevie Ray's soulfulness that marked him out from the crowd. Then he was cut off in his prime by an air crash after beating the addictions that nearly killed him. Asked the secret of his success, he said: "Use heavy strings, tune low, play hard and floor it."

❶ PRIDE AND JOY from TEXAS FLOOD

From the first album – overseen by the legendary John Hammond. This signature tune is a statement of intent, and a great solo displays all of Stevie Ray's warmth, attack and tone.

❷ TEXAS FLOOD from TEXAS FLOOD

Another song Stevie Ray made his own. Nothing better demonstrates the rich, full-bodied tone he pulled out of "Number One", his battered old 1959 Sunburst Stratocaster guitar.

❸ THINGS THAT I USED TO DO from COULDN'T STAND THE WEATHER

There's fierce competition, but when it comes down to it, this wins the vote for best slow blues from Stevie Ray. Thrilling.

❹ COULDN'T STAND THE WEATHER from COULDN'T STAND THE WEATHER

The genuinely funky title-track of the second album. Tight and loose, it's a showcase for his razor-sharp rhythm-guitar playing.

❺ CHANGE IT from SOUL TO SOUL

This stinging, often overlooked track is as tough as sun-baked saddle leather. It's from an album that is grossly underrated.

❻ LIFE WITHOUT YOU from SOUL TO SOUL

As well as thick slabs of rich, crying guitar over the coda, this displays the sweetness and soul in Stevie

The Velvet Underground

Blasting out a furious counterpoint to the complacencies of the hippy era, The Velvet Underground burned themselves out in a few short years at the end of the 1960s. But they still sound contemporary.

❶ HEROIN from THE VELVET UNDERGROUND & NICO

It's the sheer tender wistfulness of Lou Reed's hymn to the joys of heroin – "it's my wife, and it's my life" – that makes the original version so much more shocking than his histrionic 1970s renditions .

❷ I'LL BE YOUR MIRROR from THE VELVET UNDERGROUND & NICO

Somehow, the fact that Teutonic ice maiden Nico is at her most dispassionate only serves to heighten the power of one of Reed's most beautiful love songs.

❸ SISTER RAY from WHITE LIGHT/ WHITE HEAT

The Velvets at their most unrelenting; a seventeen-minute duel between Cale on organ and Reed on guitar that only Cale's ultimate departure from the band could resolve.

❹ SWEET JANE from LOADED

On their last true album, the Velvets sounded much

more like other rock bands of the era – but this carefully crafted Reed classic ranks among their finest moments.

5 BLACK ANGEL'S DEATH SONG
from THE VELVET UNDERGROUND & NICO

Lou Reed intones darkly portentous lyrics atop the cacophonous barrage of John Cale's electric viola – exactly the sound for which the Velvets were born.

6 WHAT GOES ON? from LIVE 1969 VOL 1

By the time of this live album, Cale's viola had been replaced by what sounds very like a fairground calliope – and weirdly, it works, to superbly hypnotic effect.

7 I'M STICKING WITH YOU from VU

This frivolous but affectingly romantic little song languished in the vaults for years, until the Velvet's so-called "lost" fourth MGM album was finally released.

8 PALE BLUE EYES
from THE VELVET UNDERGROUND

The Velvet's third album came as an oasis of calm after the storm of their first two, and never more so than on this sublime, gentle love song.

9 WHITE LIGHT/ WHITE HEAT
from WHITE LIGHT/ WHITE HEAT

For once, the original Velvets manage to cram all their power and ferocity into less than three minutes, though as a paean to heavy drug use, it was never going to make the pop charts.

10 VENUS IN FURS from THE VELVET UNDERGROUND & NICO

It may turn up in TV ads these days, but this S&M epic had an erotic, fetishistic charge that emphasized just how far removed Andy Warhol's New York really was from the West Coast's Summer of Love.

Greg Ward

W

Rufus Wainwright

Is there a better singer-songwriter right now? That's a purely rhetorical question. Rufus Wainwright writes and sings with a daring that takes your breath away. His albums are modern treasures, laden with songs that could grace the classic American songbook.

❶ CIGARETTES AND CHOCOLATE MILK
from POSES

Start here for an enduring love affair. Great tune, hint of a lisp, enticing sense of excess and danger ("everything it seems I like is a little bit harmful for me").

❷ APRIL FOOLS from RUFUS WAINWRIGHT

A story-song that could almost be prime Lennon/McCartney, this was promoted with a wonderful pop video of Rufus racing round town to rescue fallen opera divas.

❸ IMAGINARY LOVE from RUFUS WAINWRIGHT

"Every kind of love, or at least my kind of love, must be an imaginary love to start with": now what kind of miracle of an opening line is that?

❹ POSES from POSES

Rufus, accompanying himself at the piano, sings of "wearing flip-flops on Fifth Avenue". You will it to go on forever.

❺ DINNER AT EIGHT from WANT ONE

"No matter how strong, I'm going to take you down with one little song… see what you're really worth to me." A song about his dad, Loudon, that delivers its promised knock-out, dwarfing Wainwright Sr's entire oeuvre.

❻ GO OR GO AHEAD from WANT ONE

Rufus has operatic ambitions – but he was surely there already with this lavish howl of emotion. If you hear him perform it live, you hold your breath – despite the characteristic arch introduction ("let's just say it's a ski jump instead of a cliff!").

❼ OH WHAT A WORLD from WANT ONE

The audacity of it! A beautiful lyric about life's passing beauty, with an arrangement that begins as monkish hum and escalates to a full-blown orchestral rendition of Ravel's *Bolero*.

❽ OLD WHORE'S DIET from WANT TWO

Virtuoso singing from Rufus and androgynous pal Anthony (of Anthony & The Johnsons), on this anthemic gay wake-up call. Rufus's sister Martha helps them rock out.

❾ GOING TO A TOWN from RELEASE THE STARS

A wonderful song on an album packed with jewels: catchy yet subtle, and with lyrics that effortlessly forge personal concerns and broader politics. Not to mention the brilliance of a protest song that langorously choruses "I'm so *tired* of you, America."

❿ BETWEEN MY LEGS from RELEASE THE STARS

This is another (relative) rocker, with instantly classic hooks. It's an odd tale, with Rufus offering escape from an apocalyptic New York to a transvestite whore. He has a tunnel from his house, running right beneath the city, you see.

Mark Ellingham

Tom Waits

He can be sentimental and he can be fiercely avant-garde, but to call Tom Waits a singer-songwriter has never seemed a remotely adequate description.

❶ OL' 55 from CLOSING TIME

The Eagles covered it, but ol' Tom's was the definitive version.

❷ TOM TRAUBERT'S BLUES from SMALL CHANGE

Another song famously covered, this time by Rod Stewart. But the peerless, tormented original was again the best.

❸ THE PIANO HAS BEEN DRINKING (NOT ME) from SMALL CHANGE

Louis Armstrong meets Jack Kerouac in a twilight world of late-night whiskey bars.

❹ SOMEWHERE from BLUE VALENTINE

Waits' improbably brilliant reinvention of Bernstein's *West Side Story* standard is one of the warmest songs he's ever recorded. Makes you wish he'd have a longer crack at the classic American songbook.

Tom Waits
For No Man

A typically eclectic ten from TOM WAITS, one of rock's most singular figures.

❶ IN THE WEE SMALL HOURS OF THE MORNING FRANK SINATRA from IN THE WEE SMALL HOURS

❷ DEE'S DINER COLONEL LES CLAYPOOL'S FEARLESS FLYING FROG BRIGADE from PURPLE ONION

❸ THE DELIVERY MAN ELVIS COSTELLO AND THE IMPOSTERS from THE DELIVERY MAN

❹ I SHOULD CARE THELONIOUS MONK from SOLO MONK

❺ I JUST WANT TO SEE HIS FACE ROLLING STONES from EXILE ON MAIN STREET

❻ JESUS BLOOD GAVIN BRYARS from THE SINKING OF THE TITANIC

❼ DIRTY OLD TOWN THE POGUES from RUM SODOMY AND THE LASH

❽ LUCILLE LITTLE RICHARD from THE SPECIALTY SESSIONS

❾ CIRCLING PIGEONS WALTZ TEXAS-CZECH from BOHEMIAN-MORAVIAN BANDS

❿ NESSUN DORMA FRANCO CORELLI WITH THE ROME OPERA THEATRE ORCHESTRA & CHORUS

❺ THIS ONE'S FROM THE HEART from ONE FROM THE HEART
An oil-and-water duet with Crystal Gayle (of "Don't You Make My Brown Eyes Blue" fame), written and recorded for Coppola's 1982 film.

❻ SHORE LEAVE from SWORDFISHTROMBONES
Surrreal soundscapes played by a junkyard orchestra on this sailor's tale.

❼ DOWNTOWN TRAIN from RAIN DOGS
Rod Stewart knew a good song when he heard one and he covered this, too. But once again, he couldn't match the grit and honesty of Waits' intuitive original.

❽ WHAT'S HE BUILDING from MULE VARIATIONS
In which Tom wittily ventriloquizes conservative small-town paranoia in the face of introspective kookiness.

❾ ALL THE WORLD IS GREEN from BLOOD MONEY
Even as his later music grew ever more angular and dissonant, Waits remained capable of bittersweet serenades of haunting beauty such as this.

❿ LONG WAY HOME from BIG BAD LOVE
A little-known and understated masterpiece from the soundtrack of Arliss Howard's 2001 film, recently covered by Norah Jones.

Nigel Williamson

Walk don't run

Ten tracks to put the power in your powerwalk.

❶ TAKE A WALK ON THE WILDSIDE LOU REED from TRANSFORMER
Reed's tale of cross-dressing – pulled out of the underground by the impossibly catchy doo-doo-doo chorus.

❷ WALK THIS WAY AEROSMITH from TOYS IN THE ATTIC
This sex-fuelled cut may lack subtlety ("You ain't seen nothin' till you're down on a muffin"), but it will get your pulse racing and your legs moving.

❸ I WALK THE LINE JOHNNY CASH from LIVE FROM FOLSOM PRISON
The sober end of the walking genre. A classic Man In Black combination of resonant voice, understated lyrics and chugging guitar.

❹ I'M WALKIN' FATS DOMINO from WALKING TO NEW ORLEANS
Nothing says 1950s quite like The Fat Man and this lively, rolling jukebox staple was one of his best.

❺ WALK LIKE AN EGYPTIAN THE BANGLES from DIFFERENT LIGHT
A hugely catchy, novelty hit by the pre-eminent LA girl band.

❻ THESE BOOTS WERE MADE FOR WALKING NANCY SINATRA from BOOTS

Snarling sex kitten Nancy Sinatra gives her all in this foot-stomping classic. (But run, don't walk, from Jessica Simpson's pouty, "updated" version.)

❼ STRAY CAT STRUT THE STRAY CATS from BUILT FOR SPEED

Speaking of kittens… Recognizing that the 1980s were a dark period for rock'n'roll, The Stray Cats turned back the clock and shot up the charts.

❽ I'M GONNA BE 500 MILES THE PROCLAIMERS from SUNSHINE ON LEITH

Scots Craig and Charlie Reid meld their voices to show off rudimentary maths skills in a jaunty song about love and drunkenness. Perfect for a volksmarch.

❾ WALK THE DINOSAUR WAS (NOT WAS) from WHAT UP DOG?

Fast and fresh, Detroit's genre-blending group Was (Not Was) take a little silliness and turn it into a dance hit. Boom boom acka lacka!

❿ WALKIN' AFTER MIDNIGHT PATSY CLINE from PATSY CLINE'S GREATEST HITS

Time for the cool down. An unparalleled singer with a strong, throaty voice, Cline seems as if she'd be too self-possessed to moon the way she does in this witching-hour sojourn, the first of her hits.

Madelyn Rosenberg

Scott Walker/ Walker Brothers

The golden-throated Walker's journey from quality MOR pop-rock (with the Walker Brothers) to darkly theatrical singer-songwriterisms, and out-there electronic landscapes, is unique in popular music.

WALKER BROTHERS

❶ MAKE IT EASY ON YOURSELF from TAKE IT EASY WITH THE WALKER BROTHERS

Walker was once a master at delivering relatively big pop numbers, as this 1965 chart-topping Bacharach/David cover proves.

❷ AFTER THE LIGHTS GO OUT from PORTRAIT

Flip the British #1 smash "The Sun Ain't Gonna Shine Anymore" to find this stellar B-side, the Spectorian

production bringing to mind a moodier Righteous Brothers.

❸ IN MY ROOM from PORTRAIT

No relation to The Beach Boys' classic of the same name, with a grand mock-classical opening theme leading into heart-rending operatic crescendos on this opus of isolation.

❹ ORPHEUS from IMAGES

An early indicator of the artier pop Scott would sing in his solo career, with its swirling pseudo-classical air.

SCOTT WALKER

❺ PLASTIC PALACE PEOPLE from SCOTT 2

Swimming strings waver between dreamland and reality, Walker observing his fellow men and women with a wry inside-the-fishbowl detachment.

❻ TIME OPERATOR from 'TIL THE BAND COMES IN

Desperate for romantic connection, Scott croons his come-on to a telephone operator. She doesn't listen, just keeps announcing the time. Beyond creepy.

❼ THE OLD MAN'S BACK AGAIN from SCOTT 4

"Dedicated to the Neo-Stalinist Regime", this is almighty gothic obscurity from the King of Brood, accented by Aeolian chanting.

❽ THE SEVENTH SEAL from SCOTT 4

The inspiration from the classic Ingmar Bergman film might be transparent, but the sweeping intimation of oncoming calamity in this melodramatic song is entirely Walker.

❾ THE ROPE AND THE COLT from IN FIVE EASY PIECES

Riveting extract from an obscure French movie that ranks as the best Ennio Morricone spaghetti-western-styled theme not penned by Morricone himself.

❿ MATHILDE from SCOTT

Walker tucks into this lively Jacques Brel tune – one of many he'd cover – with the exultant elan of a starving man at the banquet table.

Richie Unterberger

Dionne Warwick

Let's get this straight: Dionne Warwick may no longer make great records, nor thrill in concert. But in her heyday, debuting a string of Bacharach/David compositions, she was sensational.

James Walsh's
Barbecue songs

JAMES WALSH's band Starsailor burst on to the scene in 2002 with their debut album *Love Is Here*. Clearly owing a debt to such 1970s troubadours as Tim Buckley (one of whose albums gave the band their name) and Van Morrison, the band marked a return to pre-Britpop indie values.The sun must have been shining in Ireland where Walsh lives, because the list he supplied was headed "best songs for a summer barbecue".

❶ **A DAY IN THE LIFE** THE BEATLES from SGT PEPPER'S LONELY HEARTS CLUB BAND

❷ **LAST GOODBYE** JEFF BUCKLEY from GRACE

❸ **WHERE THE STREETS HAVE NO NAME** U2 from THE JOSHUA TREE

❹ **SYMPATHY FOR THE DEVIL** THE ROLLING STONES from BEGGAR'S BANQUET

❺ **RING OF FIRE** JOHNNY CASH from RING OF FIRE

❻ **RIVERMAN** NICK DRAKE from FIVES LEAVES LEFT

❼ **JUST WHEN YOU'RE THINKIN' THINGS OVER** THE CHARLATANS from THE CHARLATANS

❽ **THE NIGHT THEY DROVE OLD DIXIE DOWN** THE BAND from THE BAND

❾ **THE BUCKET** KINGS OF LEON from AHA SHAKE HEARTBREAK

❿ **TINY DANCER** ELTON JOHN from MADMAN ACROSS THE WATER

Download these old recordings from a good compilation such as *Walk On By: The Definitive Dionne Warwick Collection*; beware of remixed, modern or medley versions.

❶ **WALK ON BY** from WALK ON BY
Possibly Bacharach/David's greatest song, and certainly Dionne's most iconic. Who could be unmoved by the quiver, the mix of strength and despair, as Dionne instructs her former lover to walk on by as she starts to cry?

❷ **SOMEWHERE** from THE WINDOWS OF THE WORLD
There's a place for us. OK, the Tom Waits version runs it close, but this is a gorgeous, near-definitive take on the *West Side Story* number.

❸ **DO YOU KNOW THE WAY TO SAN JOSÉ** from WALK ON BY
Another Bacharach/David gem – and a perfect vehicle for Dionne, breathing the romance of the great big LA freeway.

❹ **ALFIE** from WALK ON BY
Dionne sung this first, then Cilla Black copied her intonation note by note for a #1 hit. But there really was no comparison.

❺ **THERE'S ALWAYS SOMETHING THERE TO REMIND ME** from WALK ON BY
Big voice, big horns, great song.

❻ **HASBROOK HEIGHTS** from DIONNE
One of Dionne's last Bacharach/David songs, from 1972, combining delicacy, spring and poignancy. Dionne's magic is made clear if you hear Burt ballsing it up on his own box set.

❼ **I JUST DON'T KNOW WHAT TO DO WITH MYSELF** from WALK ON BY
A Bacharach/David lament which builds into a triumphant barrage of melancholy.

❽ **YOU'VE LOST THAT LOVIN' FEELIN'** from SOULFUL
Soulful was a great Dionne album, taking a new R&B direction, and as the drum shuffle gives way on this number, Dionne lets rip.

❾ **THEN CAME YOU** from THEN CAME YOU
In 1973 Dionne's sound was again nicely updated, this time by The Detroit Spinners and a spot of funk guitar.

❿ **TRACK OF THE CAT** from TRACK OF THE CAT
Alas, 1974's *Track Of The Cat* album was the last time

Dionne got a sympathetic make-over. Tigers roar, flutes purr, as Thom Bell lays on the Philly sound on an irresistible track.

Mark Ellingham

Muddy Waters

The Rolling Stones famously took their name from one of his songs – and many others copped a whole lot of attitude from his pioneering Chicago electric blues.

❶ I JUST WANT TO MAKE LOVE TO YOU
from HIS BEST 1947 TO 1955

What doesn't Muddy want you to do, other than make love? Hear him count the ways on this elemental bump-and-grinder.

❷ I'M YOUR HOOCHIE COOCHIE MAN
from HIS BEST 1947 TO 1955

Another classic that seals Muddy's status as both a wholly uninhibited love-man and a genius messenger of the blues start-stop rhythm.

❸ GOT MY MOJO WORKING
from HIS BEST 1956 TO 1964

It's one of the most overdone bar band staples by now, but Muddy was the one who popularized this incessantly motoring, cocky (in all senses of the word) blues standard.

❹ I CAN'T BE SATISFIED
from HIS BEST 1947 TO 1955

Breathtaking slide guitar and agile bass were the only instruments Waters needed to get his point across on this breakthrough late-1940s single.

❺ I WANT TO BE LOVED from THE ANTHOLOGY

"I Just Want To Make Love To You" from the reverse viewpoint, with a defy-you-not-to-dance funky groove, mischievous vocals, and just-right dots of harmonica.

❻ TIGER IN YOUR TANK from ONE MORE MILE

Not far short of "Got My Mojo Working" if you want some quick rollin'n'honking Waters R&B, penned by ace blues-songwriter Willie Dixon.

❼ YOU NEED LOVE from HIS BEST 1956 TO 1964

An atypical organ is added to Waters's usual guitar-bass-drums combo on this pounder, (in)famously adapted by Led Zeppelin for "Whole Lotta Love".

❽ WALKIN' THRU THE PARK
from HIS BEST 1956 TO 1964

Shows how Muddy's 1950s bands electrified down-home blues with guileless ease, the harmonica, piano and guitar becoming more than the sum of their parts.

❾ I'M READY from HIS BEST 1947 TO 1955

Waters in a devious mood that leaves no doubt what he's ready for, with fine harmonica by fellow Chi-town blues giant Little Walter.

❿ TROUBLE NO MORE
from HIS BEST 1947 TO 1955

Celebratory promise of revenge that's more good-humoured than mean-spirited, ducking in and out of time like a light-on-his-feet boxer.

Richie Unterberger

Watersons

The Watersons – the first family of British folk – have dominated the trad scene for forty years and remain as prolific as ever, both solo and in various combinations. Our list includes classics from the Watersons and Waterson-Carthy, the group which superseded them, plus various off-shoots from Norma Waterson, Martin Carthy and their exuberant daughter, folk babe Eliza Carthy.

❶ JOHN BARLEYCORN from FROST AND FIRE

Sung by Mike, this arrangement was later covered by Steve Winwood and Traffic.

❷ THE WHITE COCKADE
from A YORKSHIRE GARLAND

Immaculate harmony singing from Lal, Mike, Norma and John Harrison.

❸ SOUND SOUND YOUR INSTRUMENTS OF JOY from
SOUND SOUND YOUR INSTRUMENTS OF JOY

With Martin Carthy now a fully paid-up member of the family group, has folk music ever sounded more vibrant than on this stirring rendition of the trad hymn?

❹ I BID YOU GOODNIGHT from OUT ON THE ROLLING SEA

The Joseph Spence song recorded by the Watersons and friends under the name Blue Murder.

❺ BLACK MUDDY RIVER from NORMA WATERSON

An improbable Grateful Dead cover from the solo album that saw Norma nominated for the Mercury Music Prize. She came second behind Pulp.

W

❻ BRIGHT PHOEBUS from BRIGHT PHOEBUS
The magnificent title track from a great album by Mike and the late-lamented Lal Waterson.

❼ THE GREY COCK from WATERSON:CARTHY
An early showcase for Eliza from the first album she made with the family.

❽ WORCESTER CITY from ANGLICANA
The stand-out performance on Eliza's 2002 album which won her four BBC Radio 2 Folk Awards.

❾ HEARTBREAK HOTEL from SIGNS OF LIFE
Anything is a folk song in Martin Carthy's hands, as he proved with this remarkable cover from a 1998 solo album.

❿ AIN'T NO MAN WORTH THE SALT OF MY TEARS from MIGHTY RIVER OF SONG
Norma sang this on her first solo album, but there's an even better a capella version by her and Eliza, that long remained unreleased until it saw the light of day in 2004 on a Watersons' four-disc career-retrospective box set.

Nigel Williamson

Weather news

In daily conversation, the weather's what you talk about when there's nothing left to say. In music, the weather's what you sing about when your true love's broken your heart or blown you away. Or when there's nothing left to say.

❶ PORTLAND WATER MICHAEL HURLEY
from LONG JOURNEY
From the fringes of folk comes the rough and ragged Michael Hurley, with a song that comforts like soft flannel on a grey day.

❷ BLACK SHEETS OF RAIN BOB MOULD from BLACK SHEETS OF RAIN
Mould's voice is too high to compare to thunder, but there's a storm of guitar and emotion.

❸ A HARD RAIN'S A-GONNA FALL BOB DYLAN from THE FREEWHEELIN' BOB DYLAN
Anointed spokesman for a generation, Dylan's keen observations are captured here as always: with poetry and precision.

❹ BLUE EYES CRYING IN THE RAIN
WILLIE NELSON from REDHEADED STRANGER
With a whiskey-warm voice that is as distinctive as the

songwriter himself, Nelson has the power to bring rain or sun, joy or sadness.

❺ GOOD DAY SUNSHINE THE BEATLES
from REVOLVER
The sort of mood-enhancing music you wish you could bottle, no prescription necessary.

❻ COLD RAIN AND SNOW THE GRATEFUL DEAD from THE GRATEFUL DEAD
Hardly recognizable as a traditional piece: more reminiscent of surf than mountain music – the weather apart.

❼ BIG RED SUN BLUES LUCINDA WILLIAMS
from LUCINDA WILLIAMS
The emotion behind Williams' voice comes through raw and uncut under the sun.

❽ WHO LOVES THE SUN VELVET UNDERGROUND from LOADED
A boppy, poppy – sunny – chorus makes Lou Reed sound all the more worn and woeful.

❾ WALKING ON SUNSHINE KATRINA AND THE WAVES
from WALKING ON SUNSHINE
Nothing says 1980s like an infectious pop tune. Here's one that could get cynics to roll down the car windows and sing.

❿ LIKE A HURRICANE NEIL YOUNG
from AMERICAN STARS 'N' BARS
A reedy voice that bends with emotion and an extended, wailing guitar solo make this song the obvious finale for a Neil Young show and, of course, for this weather set.

Madelyn Rosenberg

Easy does it: Jimmy Webb

Jimmy Webb achieved fame as a songwriter in his teens, but never matched it as a performer. He has often been compared to Burt Bacharach (his hero); if you want to extend the simile into metaphor, his Dionne Warwick was Glen Campbell.

❶ MACARTHUR PARK RICHARD HARRIS from TUNESMITH: THE SONGS OF JIMMY WEBB
What's it all about? There are a thousand theories for this way-over-the-top classic. Notably covered by Donna Summer.

❷ UP, UP AND AWAY FIFTH DIMENSION from
TUNESMITH: THE SONGS OF JIMMY WEBB

Cheese didn't come much riper than this in the 1960s: you know the one, "…in my beautiful, my beautiful, ball–oooon" (cue horns).

❸ EASY FOR YOU TO SAY LINDA RONSTADT from GET CLOSER

Linda Ronstadt was in top form on this beautiful bitter ballad.

❹ THE MOON'S A HARSH MISTRESS JOE COCKER from I CAN STAND A LITTLE RAIN

This is probably Cocker's best album, and his voice is put to amazing effect here.

❺ MET HER ON A PLANE IAN MATTHEWS from TUNESMITH: THE SONGS OF JIMMY WEBB

Fairly hard to find, but this version is gorgeous and haunting.

❻ WHEN CAN BROWN BEGIN? JIMMY WEBB from LETTERS

Regarded as Webb's finest album and this track has many of the elements of his greatest work with Richard Harris. Scott Walker did a cool version, too.

❼ CRYING IN MY SLEEP ART GARFUNKEL from WATERMARK

From an album consisting almost entirely of Jimmy Webb songs. Nearly a hit but a damn fine miss.

❽ HIGHWAYMAN THE HIGHWAYMEN from TUNESMITH: THE SONGS OF JIMMY WEBB

This track topped the country charts for a fine ensemble consisting of Waylon Jennings, Johnny Cash, Willie Nelson and Kris Kristofferson.

Dave Atkinson

Weird but great cover versions

Metal meets country, pop meets industrial, Tuvans take on Joy Division: whatever the clash there's nothing quite like a bizarre cover version that leaves you slack-jawed with amazement.

❶ ACE OF SPADES HAYSEED DIXIE from LET THERE BE ROCKGRASS

Motörhead's classic hymn to fast living gets the bluegrass treatment, complete with screeching fiddles and some fast'n'furious banjo mayhem.

❷ LOVE WILL TEAR US APART ALBERT KUVEZIN AND YAT-KHA from RE-COVERS

Tuvan throat singer Kuvezin and his band take on Manc misery, and pull it off royally. They also do a cracking version of Led Zep's "When The Levee Breaks" on the same disc.

❸ CHEERS THE WILDHEARTS from COUPLED WITH

The sentimental and nostalgic piano-led theme tune is turned into a pedal-to-the-metal, honest-to-goodness punk'n'roll romp.

❹ COMMON PEOPLE WILLIAM SHATNER from HAS BEEN

Captain Kirk back in *Transformed Man* territory, only this time with Joe Jackson, Ben Folds and an entire choir helping out. Quite astonishing.

❺ (I CAN'T GET NO) SATISFACTION DEVO from Q: ARE WE NOT MEN? A: WE ARE DEVO!

A (new) wave of nerdy ebullience permeates the Ohio quintet's revamped Rolling Stones standard, the shards of which get aurally rebuilt as if trundling down a production line.

❻ RAINING BLOOD TORI AMOS from STRANGE LITTLE GIRLS

Only a singular talent such as Tori Amos could take an evil mother of a thrash metal song and transform it into something so menacingly ghostly.

❼ SWEET DREAMS (ARE MADE OF THIS) MARILYN MANSON from LEST WE FORGET

Some of them want to abuse you, indeed. The Eurythmics' electro-pop hit gets metallicized with an industrial-sized boot up the backside.

❽ DON'T STOP MOVIN' THE BEAUTIFUL SOUTH from GOLDDIGGAS, HEADNODDERS & PHOLK SONGS

Ever imagined how the S Club would sound if they'd started drinking pints of bitter and smoking tabs in the local Working Men's Club? Wonder no more…

❾ LIVE IS LIFE LAIBACH from OPUS DEI

This brooding Balkan collective stepped out from relative obscurity to rework Opus's crowd-friendly anthem. The Austrians' original was a life-affirming singalong, but Laibach mutated it into a growled set of directives, backed by a pounding drum beat.

❿ APACHE MICHAEL VINER'S INCREDIBLE BONGO BAND from DJ POGO PRESENTS THE BREAKS

Just imagine The Shadows trying to do their crazy leg dance to this version of their hit. Sampled by countless rap artists, proving that Cliff Richard helped spawn hip-hop.

Essi Berelian/Ed Wright

Barry White

Affectionately known as the "Walrus of Love", Barry White rose from South Central LA's gangs to become a soul star, sex symbol and pop-culture icon.

❶ WALKING IN THE RAIN WITH THE ONE YOU LOVE
from LOVE SONGS
Barry's first hit found him lending his deep voice to female vocal trio Love Unlimited's tune. If Phil Spector had possessed a sexier voice he might have done this kind of thing with The Ronettes.

❷ I'M GONNA LOVE YOU JUST A LITTLE BIT MORE BABY from I'VE GOT SO MUCH TO GIVE
Blending Isaac Hayes' husky voice and Al Green's gentle seductiveness, Barry emerges as the cuddliest of all 1970s soul stars.

❸ NEVER GONNA GIVE YA UP from STONE GON'
Opens with hi-hat and strings – very Temptations – then Barry's deep breathing comes in and everything goes to disco wonderland.

❹ CAN'T GET ENOUGH OF YOUR LOVE from CAN'T GET ENOUGH
Considering Barry's girth, a more honest title may have been "Can't Get Enough Fried Chicken". But, hey, that's not likely to go down too well on Ally McBeal.

❺ YOU'RE THE FIRST, THE LAST, MY EVERYTHING
from CAN'T GET ENOUGH
Barry takes the most clichéd romantic couplets and inflates them until they're convincing. There's a certain genius in that.

❻ WHAT AM I GONNA DO WITH YOU
from JUST ANOTHER WAY TO SAY I LOVE YOU
If you listen to Barry's original early-1970s albums you will get to hear his sex raps, where the great man murmurs "take off that brassiere" and "I don't wanna see no panties".

❼ YOUR SWEETNESS IS MY WEAKNESS
from THE MAN
In Barry's world everything is love'n'lust and ecstasy is easily achieved. Which, I guess, makes him the black Barbara Cartland.

❽ PUT ME IN YOUR MIX from PUT ME IN YOUR MIX
Barry returns sounding slicker than ever: from disco to hip-hop he could do no wrong.

Garth Cartwright

The White Stripes

Garage-rock revivalists Jack & Meg White have what few other "The" bands can claim:

real talent, a massive sound, and Dylanesque inscrutability.

❶ SEVEN NATION ARMY from ELEPHANT

Opening the Stripes' post-big-break album, Seven Nation Army kicks things off confidently with a caveman-heavy rock'n'roll call to arms.

❷ HAND SPRINGS from WHITE BLOOD CELLS (JAPANESE IMPORT VERSION)

A 1950s garage-rock fight-song that sees Jack buy his girl a Coke before putting a bowling ball through the glass of a rival's pinball game.

❸ HELLO OPERATOR from DE STIJL

Classic Stripes blues-stomp, with wailing amplified harmonica and squawking guitar, as Jack tries to get the phone operator into bed.

❹ WHY CAN'T YOU BE NICER TO ME? from DE STIJL

With a bump-bump-BUMP beat that harks back to Hendrix's "Foxy Lady", Jack shows his sensitive side, wildly begging the song's title.

❺ JOLENE from BLACKPOOL DELUXE (LIVE)

Covering Dolly, Jack turns a plaintive cry for mercy into something from the depths of fear and jealousy.

❻ BALL AND BISCUIT from ELEPHANT

A dirty, slow-burn rave-up that sees Jack spouting blues-myth lines like "It's a fact that I'm the seventh son." Best Stripes guitar solo to date.

❼ FELL IN LOVE WITH A GIRL from WHITE BLOOD CELLS

Like Robert Johnson played by The Ramones, weighing in under two minutes.

❽ HOTEL YORBA from WHITE BLOOD CELLS

Jaunty, stomp-along front-porch number, among the Stripes' catchiest. In many ways the track that broke them to the world.

❾ FOREVER FOR HER (IS OVER FOR ME) from GET BEHIND ME SATAN

A big departure for the peppermint twins, flush with marimba, xylophone, egg shakers and a restraint not previously noted.

❿ ICKY THUMP from ICKY THUMP

One in the eye for anyone who thought Jack's side projects would be the end of the Stripes, this first cut from the new album references vintage British TV show The Goodies for no immediately obvious reason.

Hunter Slaton

If you like White Stripes…

The White Stripes have their own particular sound, but they're only one band in a long line of blues-mangling artists. If you like what Jack 'n' Meg have done, check out this common ground.

❶ DANG JON SPENCER BLUES EXPLOSION from ORANGE

Quite possibly a big influence on The Stripes. Two guitars, a sensational drummer and no bass. Very raw but incredibly funky.

❷ PREACHIN' THE BLUES THE GUN CLUB from FIRE OF LOVE

Vastly underrated in their day, The Gun Club were an awesome psycho-blues-swamp-punk band featuring the howling voice of Jeffrey Lee Pierce. This is a great cover of a Son House classic from their debut album.

❸ SHE'S THE ONE THAT'S GOT IT TAV FALCO PANTHER BURNS from BEHIND THE MAGNOLIA CURTAIN

Cult icon Tav Falco and the various Panther Burns incarnations have been making idiosyncratic blues and rock for more than thirty years. Here's a great example.

❹ HUMAN FLY THE CRAMPS from GRAVEST HITS

The Cramps will forever be associated with their love of 1950s and 60s kitsch, sleazy subject matter and utterly mad lead singer Lux Interior (Erick to his mum).

❺ SHE SAID HASIL ADKINS from CHICKEN WALK

A hero to The Cramps, Hasil Adkins was a one-man band, playing guitar with his hands and drums with his feet. His music was a mix of rockabilly and country – stripped down, strange and quite brilliant.

❻ GOIN' DOWN SOUTH R.L. BURNSIDE from A ASS POCKET OF WHISKEY

An original Delta country blues player, Burnside learnt his craft from some of the music's greats. He teamed up with Jon Spencer on this album to make some extraordinary, funky, juke-joint blues.

❼ BLACK EYED GIRL SPEEDBALL BABY from CINEMA

An arty New York rockabilly outfit with bizarre ranting lyrics and some terrific guitar work.

❽ WHEN YOU STOPPED LOVING ME THEE HEADCOATS from ELEMENTARY HEADCOATS

One of countless tracks by Billy Childish and co. Completely unrefined, it sounds like they've stumbled across a vault of long-lost Kinks B-sides and played them in a giant dustbin.

⑨ GIVE ME DAUGHTERS JONATHAN FIRE*EATER from TREMBLE UNDER BOOM LIGHTS

Organ-led, ferocious and strange. This short-lived American band made some great tunes and this EP showcases their best moments. Kind of blues, kind of indie, kind of intense…

⑩ EIGHT BALL SEASICK STEVE AND THE LEVEL DEVILS from CHEAP

Some time hobo, Steve Wold got a Mojo breakthrough award in 2007 – not bad after 40 years. This track from his 'solo' debut is a cracker, rocking out with the best.

Dave Atkinson

The Who

Power chords, aggressive rebellion, a wicked sense of humour, an underrated facility for both pop tunes and whimsical spirituality – and the most energetic stage show of their generation.

① MY GENERATION from MY GENERATION

From Roger Daltrey's defiantly sputtering vocal to the crazed climax of feedback and splashing drums, it was always going to be The Who's definitive statement.

② I CAN SEE FOR MILES from THE WHO SELL OUT

Both threat and the joy of revenge hang over this track like thunder splitting dark clouds, the crackling drums and bee-buzz guitar announcing that the Day of Judgement has come.

③ SUBSTITUTE from THE ULTIMATE COLLECTION

Power pop's greatest moment, especially in the opening declarative guitar chords. Its lyrics depicting confused identity and wilful illusion are great, too.

④ UNDERTURE from TOMMY

Ten-minute instrumental from *Tommy* whose pseudo-classical sweep has a grandeur seldom achieved by rock, underscored by wondrous guitar riffs and characteristically maniacally urgent drums.

⑤ ANYWAY, ANYHOW, ANYWHERE from THE ULTIMATE COLLECTION

A riot of feedback in the instrumental break, but a solid proto-power-pop tune underneath, delivered with appealing bluster by Daltrey.

⑥ THE KIDS ARE ALRIGHT from MY GENERATION

The power-chord youth anthem to beat all youth anthems, and an early hint of a sensitive heart beneath the group's pillhead toughness.

⑦ THE REAL ME from QUADROPHENIA

Quadrophenia's dynamic curtain-raiser launched this rock opera as surely as a mod kick-starts his scooter.

⑧ PICTURES OF LILY from THE ULTIMATE COLLECTION

Another great single from The Who's early career, one whose catchy tune and bouncy story-song masks penetrating tragicomedy.

⑨ I CAN'T REACH YOU from THE WHO SELL OUT

A relatively obscure album track, but one of Pete Townshend's most tender expressions of vulnerability and spiritual hunger.

⑩ I'M FREE from TOMMY

Ecstatic midtempo riff-driven rocker that works just as well removed from the context of the group's famous rock opera.

Richie Unterberger

Wilco

Having morphed from Uncle Tupelo also-rans to become the US Radiohead, Wilco's art-damaged Americana continues to dazzle, delight and confound.

① CASINO QUEEN from A.M.

Jeff Tweedy still managed to have a great time while burning out the last vestiges of Uncle Tupelo; this rollicking, reckless song is proof.

② MISUNDERSTOOD from BEING THERE

Announcing loud his new vision, Tweedy hollers "nothing" over the noise in this cathartic kick-off to the double album *Being There*.

③ SUNKEN TREASURE from BEING THERE

A sweet, sad ballad where Tweedy laments being "so out of tune with you", before the song collapses into squawking feedback.

④ A SHOT IN THE ARM from SUMMERTEETH

Wilco's third album is shot through with songs like this: irresistible technicolor pop juxtaposed with addict lyrics.

⑤ I AM TRYING TO BREAK YOUR HEART from YANKEE HOTEL FOXTROT

The first song by Tweedy the surrealist poet, with lyrics like "I assassin down the avenue" over a neo-tribal drumbeat.

❻ ASHES OF AMERICAN FLAGS from YANKEE HOTEL FOXTROT

A hymn to and a jeremiad against autumnal America, alongside a noisy self-immolation of one whose "lies are always wishes".

❼ SPIDERS (KIDSMOKE) from A GHOST IS BORN

The Chicago bar-band guitar heroes fight the Michigan Krautrock spiders from for eleven epic minutes!

❽ KICKING TELEVISION from A GHOST IS BORN BONUS EP

Whether it's a snotty throwaway rocker or the smart way forward for Wilco, this tongue-in-cheek anti-consumer rant still kicks.

❾ THE LATE GREATS from A GHOST IS BORN

Happily ending the masterful *A Ghost Is Born*, Wilco returns to their roots with this fence-straddling, winking bit of self-parody – or is it?

❿ BOB DYLAN'S 49TH BEARD from THE MORE LIKE THE MOON EP

Tossed-off but touching, a simple slice of odd, strummed-guitar genius, laced through with spacey, dreamlike, underwater murmurs.

Hunter Slaton

Hank Williams

The heart and soul of country music, Hank Williams burnt out young but left a vital, admired and much-covered legacy.

❶ MOVE IT ON OVER from 40 GREATEST HITS

The first Williams single is classic honky tonk with great words – and classic backing vocals.

❷ LOVESICK BLUES from 40 GREATEST HITS

The song that made Hank Willliams respectable enough to be invited to take the stage at the Grand Ol' Opry.

❸ LONG GONE LONESOME BLUES from 40 GREATEST HITS

Nihilistic yodel heaven.

❹ YOUR CHEATIN' HEART from 40 GREATEST HITS

One of his most famous and covered songs, written just after his divorce from Audrey Mae Sheppard.

❺ LOST HIGHWAY from 40 GREATEST HITS

The song that best embodies the rootless, drifting lifestyle that helped to kill Williams at the age of 29.

❻ COLD COLD HEART from 40 GREATEST HITS

Feel Hank's pain.

❼ JAMBALAYA from 40 GREATEST HITS

Popularized by The Carpenters, of course, but the original is the real deal.

❽ YOU'RE GONNA CHANGE from 40 GREATEST HITS

Band and voice in perfect harmony.

❾ MANSION ON THE HILL from 40 GREATEST HITS

Money and fame can't buy you happiness, as Hank knew better than anyone.

❿ I SAW THE LIGHT from 40 GREATEST HITS

Hank gets religion.

Martin Dunford

Lucinda Williams

"It's my belief that Lucinda Williams is the closest living counterpart to Hank Williams when it comes to writing from the heart with absolute economy", Elvis Costello reckons. "And it's a bonus that her rock'n'roll vocal style will shake up any band in a fashion that I can only compare to Keith Richards' guitar playing."

❶ LAFAYETTE from HAPPY WOMAN BLUES

Lucinda goes cajun on this early composition from 1980.

❷ PINEOLA from SWEET OLD WORLD

Knockout, literate southern story-telling in the Flannery O'Connor tradition.

❸ CAR WHEELS ON A GRAVEL ROAD from CAR WHEELS ON A GRAVEL ROAD

After a six-year silence following *Sweet Old World*, we'd just about forgotten her. Then she showed up in Nashville and came out with this 1998 masterpiece.

❹ CONCRETE AND BARBED WIRE from CAR WHEELS ON A GRAVEL ROAD

Blissful acoustic guitars embellished with, mandolin, slide and Steve Earle's harmonies on one of Williams' most perfect songs.

❺ LAKE CHARLES from CAR WHEELS ON A GRAVEL ROAD

Another exquisitely evocative southern vignette, from an album that really deserves to be heard in its entirety as an indivisible mood piece.

Lucinda Williams
On a roll

She's more country than almost anything out of modern Nashville and she's funkier than a mosquito's tweeter. What's more, LUCINDA WILLIAMS started making the best music of her life in her mid-40s with the release of 1998's classic *Car Wheels On A Gravel Road* and has been on a roll ever since. She does a list pretty good, too...

❶ IT MAKES NO DIFFERENCE THE BAND from NORTHERN LIGHTS SOUTHERN CROSS

❷ GOOD DAY PAUL WESTERBERG from EVENTUALLY

❸ MARY PATTY GRIFFIN from FLAMING RED

❹ THESE DAYS GREG ALLMAN from LAID BACK

❺ FAMOUS BLUE RAINCOAT LEONARD COHEN from SONGS OF LOVE AND HATE

❻ SYLVIA PLATH RYAN ADAMS from GOLD

❼ MY FUNNY VALENTINE CHET BAKER from MY FUNNY VALENTINE

❽ DON'T EXPLAIN NINA SIMONE from LET IT ALL OUT

❾ TEARS ARE IN YOUR EYES YO LA TENGO from AND THEN NOTHING TURNED ITSELF INSIDE-OUT

❿ NO OTHER LOVE CHUCK PROPHET from NO OTHER LOVE

❻ GET RIGHT WITH GOD from ESSENCE
A drop of country-gospel fervour that was one of the highlights of a fine 2001 album.

❼ AMERICAN DREAM
from WORLD WITHOUT TEARS
Williams turned 50 in 2003 and marked the occasion with the best album of her career, which included this coruscating alternative state-of-the-nation address.

❽ OVERTIME from WORLD WITHOUT TEARS
Classic heartbreak like a latter-day Patsy Cline, with a touch of Patti Smith thrown in.

❾ RIGHTEOUSLY from WORLD WITHOUT TEARS
You can get horny just listening to her moan her way through this.

❿ REAL LIVE BLEEDING FINGERS & BROKEN GUITAR STRINGS from LIVE AT THE FILLMORE
The rocking studio version on *World Without Tears* is blistering – but this live take is nuclear.

Nigel Willamson

Winners & losers

Maybe most writers are afraid to boast: a lot of winning songs sound an awful lot like they're songs about losing (unless they were written by Freddy Mercury). On the other hand, some songs about losing can sound oddly triumphant...

❶ WINNER TAKES IT ALL ABBA from THE NAME OF THE GAME
Not the song to put on after a hard-earned victory (it tells of the band's dissolution through failed marriages). But the chorus swells with that Abba magic.

❷ BEAUTIFUL LOSER BOB SEGER from BEAUTIFUL LOSER
Seger's smoke-and-leather voice carries this glorious ballad; he makes coming up short sound inevitable and universal.

❸ LOSER BECK from MELLOW GOLD
Theme song for a slack generation, this was the world's introduction to Beck.

❹ I'M A LOSER BEATLES from BEATLES FOR SALE
John at his self-deprecating best, and you can't help but want to shout it along with him.

❺ YOU WIN AGAIN HANK WILLIAMS from THE ORIGINAL SINGLES COLLECTION
Ol' Hank suffers a gut-wrenching blow at the hands of a low-down cheatin' lover. The final stanza is a killer: "You have no heart/you have no shame . . . I love you still/You win again."

⑥ WE ARE THE CHAMPIONS QUEEN from NEWS OF THE WORLD

Yes, you've heard it a thousand times before, but that elegant piano line keeps it listenable for 1000 more.

⑦ EVEN THE LOSERS TOM PETTY from DAMN THE TORPEDOES

Like Seger, Petty wrote rockers that sounded ripped from some mythic American heartland; this song's anthemic quality has everything to do with sentiment over bombast.

⑧ (I KNOW) I'M LOSING YOU THE TEMPTATIONS from THE TEMPTATIONS WITH A LOT 'O SOUL

A spirited blast of heartache from the masters of 1960s soul.

⑨ YOU LOSE THE REPLACEMENTS from HOOTENANNY

While they claim "Winners, losers, all the same", you certainly don't hear Paul Westerberg gleefully and repeatedly shouting "Yeah, you win", over that galloping riff and backbeat.

⑩ SUCCESS GRAHAM PARKER from THE MONA LISA'S SISTER

When you've got the kind of success that leaves you "alone with a wristful," the words" pyrrhic victory" begin to come to mind. Parker's iconoclastic career has suffered for the fact he's never suffered fools gladly; it makes for great material though.

Andrew Rosenberg

Steve Winwood & Traffic

Just 15 when he started singing with The Spencer Davis Group, Steve Winwood's genius was a freak of nature. His voice had barely broken, but he sounded like a veteran soul singer and could play organ, lead guitar, bass and drums with equal virtuosity. When he tired of playing R&B, he explored psychedelia with Traffic, formed the world's first supergroup, with Eric Clapton, and later reinvented himself for the dancefloor.

SPENCER DAVIS GROUP

① GIMME SOME LOVING from BEST OF THE SPENCER DAVIS GROUP

A searing, soul-drenched vocal and one of the killer rhythms of all time; only the Beach Boys' Good Vibrations kept it from #1.

② I'M A MAN from BEST OF THE SPENCER DAVIS GROUP

He was a 16-year-old boy, but he sounded like Ray Charles.

BLIND FAITH

③ CAN'T FIND MY WAY HOME from BLIND FAITH

Blind Faith could never sustain the weight of expectation that the supergroup tag imposed, but Winwood contributed three brilliant songs to their sole album, of which this is the best.

TRAFFIC

④ DEAR MR FANTASY from MR FANTASY

The spirit of 1967 personified in the lead track from Traffic's stellar debut.

⑤ NO FACE, NO NAME, NO NUMBER from MR FANTASY

Traffic invented the notion of "getting it together in the country", and this vulnerable, melancholic ballad was one of the finer results of Steve's rural idyll.

⑥ JOHN BARLEYCORN from JOHN BARLEYCORN MUST DIE

Having tired of being the white Ray Charles, he then turned into a more soulful Martin Carthy on this magnificent and mysterious rendition of the old folk ballad.

⑦ LOW SPARK OF HIGH-HEELED BOYS from LOW SPARK OF HIGH-HEELED BOYS

Twelve minutes of inspired improvisation over a jazz-tinged groove. Traffic had never sounded more fluid than they did on this.

SOLO

⑧ VALERIE from TALKING BACK TO THE NIGHT

A tune so memorable that 22 years after its release, Eric Prydz borrowed it for his 2004 number one single, "Call On Me".

⑨ HIGHER LOVE from BACK IN THE HIGH LIFE

Not even the horribly dated synths and programming can ruin this irresistible dance groove that ruled the airwaves in 1986.

⑩ ROLL WITH IT from ROLL WITH IT

Backed by the Memphis Horns, Winwood paid tribute to the Motown beat on a song that rolled back the years and sounded as if it could have come from his Spencer Davis years.

Nigel Williamson

Wire

One of the quirkier and more interesting bands to emerge from the late 1970s British punk scene, Wire were largely ignored at the time, but have been consistently referenced since by bands as diverse as Elastica and Franz Ferdinand.

❶ MANNEQUIN from PINK FLAG

Chosen as a single for its pop tune and harmonies, its chunky chords and vicious lyrics belie the rosy exterior in sinister fashion.

❷ OUTDOOR MINER from CHAIRS MISSING

It takes genius to squeeze such a delicious pot pourri of melodic hooks into 1:45. Lyrics like "Face worker, a serpentine miner, a roof falls, an underliner, of leaf structure the egg timer" defy criticism.

❸ I SHOULD HAVE KNOWN BETTER from 154

Staccato bell effects and downbeat spoken lyrics help issue the salutary warning intended.

❹ LOWDOWN from PINK FLAG

The Stooges' guitar pauses for Newman's punk musings.

❺ MAROONED from CHAIRS MISSING

Sporadic bass rumbles and ice-cool guitar stabs summon up the plight of being stranded on a melting iceberg. Newman remains stoic throughout the ordeal.

❻ 15TH from 154

The poppiest cut on the album could almost be a precursor of The Cure.

❼ FEELING CALLED LOVE from PINK FLAG

A brief blast of garage with dashes of Louie Louie and angelic harmonies thrown in.

❽ ANOTHER THE LETTER from CHAIRS MISSING

Frenetic Flight Of The Bumblebee synth and staccato drop-tone vocals show where the lines between Colin Newman and Gary Numan occasionally got blurred.

❾ ON RETURNING from 154

A Buzzcocks-like jaunt. Punk of the first order with chopped guitars, runaway synth and furious vocals.

❿ MR MARX'S TABLE from SEND

In this effort from their recent reformation, Newman sounds incongruously tuneful over a wall of sound that could be Spacemen 3.

Nick Edwards

Bill Withers

Navy vet Withers brought an adult understanding to 1970s soul and many of his beautifully literate songs have become standards.

❶ AIN'T NO SUNSHINE from JUST AS I AM

One of the most perfect songs ever written. Dig it when Bill goes into his mantra "I-know-I-know-I-know-I-know-I-know."

❷ USE ME from STILL BILL

One of the few truly smart songs about sexual pleasure that our sex-obsessed culture has ever produced.

❸ GRANDMA'S HANDS from JUST AS I AM

A meditation on his grandma, whose hands "would sometimes ache and swell". Who else in popular music has written with such natural observation?

❹ WHO IS HE (AND WHAT IS HE TO YOU?) from THE BEST OF BILL WITHERS

Bill gets a little uneasy when he and his partner pass a man who tries to stare Bill down. The confusion grows and the paranoia builds.

❺ LEAN ON ME from STILL BILL

Songwriting rarely gets better than this hymn to solidarity between friends and lovers. Bill obviously paid attention at church.

❻ I CAN'T WRITE LEFTHANDED from BILL WITHERS LIVE AT CARNEGIE HALL

Bill sings from the perspective of a Vietnam veteran who has lost his right arm and is struggling to fit back into society.

❼ HARLEM/COLD BALONEY from BILL WITHERS LIVE AT CARNEGIE HALL

Bill's encore is a slice of social reality that's quietly understated yet builds until it's absolutely devastating.

❽ LOVELY DAY from MENAGERIE

A hymn to the simple pleasures of enjoying a day with the one you love.

❾ JUST THE TWO OF US from THE BEST OF BILL WITHERS

Bill teams up with saxophonist Grover Washington Jr in 1981 for an R&B Grammy.

❿ BETTER OFF DEAD from JUST AS I AM

Bill adopts the voice of a suicidal alcoholic whose wife has left taking the children. As good as a Raymond Carver short story.

Garth Cartwright

Bobby Womack

A master singer-songwriter-guitarist, Bobby Womack started out as a teenage protégé of Sam Cooke (whose widow he married), eased into shaping 1970s soul, and wrote classic songs for The Rolling Stones (It's All Over Now) and Wilson Pickett (I'm A Midnight Mover). Plus he plays all over Sly Stone's *There's A Riot Going On*. Respect is the word.

❶ THAT'S THE WAY I FEEL ABOUT CHA from THE VERY BEST OF
This was Womack's first big hit – an early 1970s number that sounds like it came straight out of Memphis soul. It's hard to get enough of this.

❷ FLY ME TO THE MOON from THE VERY BEST OF
Nobody makes a cover version their own quite like Bobby Womack. He adds a jazz sensibility to other folks' songs, and here, on this delicate flight of soul, he disregards both lyric and tune.

R. Crumb's
Hot women

Celebrated cartoonist, musician and collector R. CRUMB is a leading authority on regional music of the 78 era. His CD *Hot Women: Women Singers From The Torrid Regions* gathers 24 performances by female artists of the 1920s–50s. "Very little is known about some of these performers." says Crumb. "Many of them were only recorded because companies like HMV were trying to sell phonographs to the colonies so sent out engineers to record the local talent." All the selections listed here are from the CD.

❶ BLUES NEGRES CLEOMA FALCON
Louisiana's Cleoma played guitar and sang in an Arcadian French dialect while her husband Joseph Falcon played accordion. The Falcons were the first Cajuns to make phonograph recordings, beginning in 1927.

❷ MEXICO EN UNA LAGUNA LYDIA MENDOZA
Lydia belonged to a poor but musical family. They travelled throughout the Rio Grande Valley playing in a style later known as "norteno".

❸ EL CACAHUATERO TONA LA NEGRE
Tona was born in 1910 in Veracruz, Mexico, which might explain the Caribbean–Cuban flavour of her singing. She became a popular radio and recording artist and appeared in several Mexican films.

❹ LIVA LEONA GABRIEL
Born in Martinique in 1891, Leona sang in the thriving "Creole" musical scene until leaving for around 1920. She became a star of the Montparnasse clubs and performed until 1935.

❺ EL TAMBOR DE LA ALEGRIA GRUPO DE LA ALGERIA
Issued in 1928, I was unable to find any information on this group. Probably Cuban.

❻ QUERO SOSSEGO ARACI CORTES
Born in Rio de Janiero, the daughter of a musician, Araci left home aged 17 to join the circus as a performer and singer. She went on to have a successful career as a musical and theatrical performer and remained active in Brazil until the 1970s.

❼ LA PAPA ARAUCANA LAS CUARTO HUASAS
Chile's The Four Huasas were acclaimed singers of traditional songs in the 1930s. Almost nothing more is known about them.

❽ SEVILLANAS NO. 2 LA NIÑA DE LOS PEINES
One of flamenco's great icons, La Niña was born in Seville in 1890 and became the first female Gypsy singer to achieve prominence. Her nickname means "the girl of the combs" and she was always pictured with a comb in her hair.

❾ LU FISTINU DI PALERMO ROSINA TRUBIA GIOIOSA
American record companies issued hundreds of discs aimed at immigrant labourers. This Sicilian folk song – recorded for southern Italians living in New York, Chicago and elsewhere – is a good example. I have found no information on the singer.

❿ MIME STELIS MANA ANASTIN AMERIKI RITA ABADZI
Born in 1903 in Smyrna, Turkey, Rita became a refugee in Greece after the Turko–Greek war in 1922. She went on to become a key figure of the golden era of Greek music in the 1930s. The song's title translates as "Mother, Please Don't Send Me To America"!

❸ CALIFORNIA DREAMING from THE VERY BEST OF
Lush, beautifully evocative reading of The Mamas & The Papas hit. Gave Womack a surprise 2004 UK hit when it served as soundtrack for a car ad.

❹ ACROSS 110TH ST from ACROSS 110TH ST
Womack scored the extremely tough blaxploitation flick and his brooding title-tune is heavy with ghetto claustrophobia. So much so that Tarantino re-employed it for *Jackie Brown*.

❺ HARRY HIPPIE from UNDERSTANDING
Laidback soul hit with Bobby casting a cold eye at panhandlers. Features some of Womack's most beautifully fluid guitar playing.

❻ WOMAN'S GOTTA HAVE IT
from UNDERSTANDING
His biggest US R&B hit is a gorgeous hymn to loving and listening to your woman.

❼ I'M A MIDNIGHT MOVER
from THE MIDNIGHT MOVER
Bobby was a notorious party animal, so this anthem to sleeping all day and raising hell all night is possibly autobiographical.

❽ IT'S ALL OVER NOW from THE MIDNIGHT MOVER
Originally penned by the teenage Womack for his group The Valentinos, it gave The Rolling Stones their first #1. This 1970s remake is a funky feast.

❾ IF YOU THINK YOU'RE LONELY NOW
from THE POET
1981 comeback hit that proves Womack is among the greatest of soul men.

❿ LOVE HAS FINALLY COME AT LAST
from THE POET II
Bobby teams up with Patti LaBelle and they sing their asses off.

Garth Cartwright

Stevie Wonder

Born blind, Steveland Morris was signed to Motown aged 12 and named "Little Stevie Wonder" by Berry Gordy. That's foresight: Wonder developed into Motown's most talented and consistently successful artist. But his true genius was revealed in the groundbreaking albums he made in the early 1970s, from *Talking Book* through to *Songs In The Key Of*

Life – records on which he played just about everything himself.

❶ FINGERTIPS from THE DEFINITIVE COLLECTION
Little Stevie was just 13 when this came out: a blast of harmonica so exuberant, it still gets you standing to applaud.

❷ YESTER-ME, YESTER-YOU, YESTERDAY from THE DEFINITIVE COLLECTION
1969 hit that finds the mature – 19-year-old – Stevie delivering a gorgeous love song.

❸ SUPERSTITION from TALKING BOOK
The toughest groove, the most ferocious atmosphere: launched in 1972 and still keeping heads ringin'. Hats off to Jeff Beck, too, for whom Stevie wrote the song, and who puts in brilliant guest guitar on the album.

❹ YOU ARE THE SUNSHINE OF MY LIFE from TALKING BOOK
Whatever Stevie sang, he sang with such heartfelt appreciation it wins you over. But this was also the launch of the definitive Stevie Wonder rhythm, one he returned to time and again.

❺ LIVING FOR THE CITY from INNERVISIONS
"A boy is born in hard time Mississippi", begins the song and Stevie leads us through a tale of poverty and desperation as shaped by white American racism.

❻ VISIONS from INNERVISIONS
"I know that leaves are green/They only turn to brown when autumn comes around", sings a blind man as he demands Dr King's vision of equality be made real.

❼ SIR DUKE from SONGS IN THE KEY OF LIFE
Duke Ellington and co. are celebrated in this joyous hornfest. One of the highlights of an album that's part genius, part just a little too kitsch.

❽ HAPPY BIRTHDAY from HOTTER THAN JULY
Stevie's constant campaigning helped get Dr Martin Luther King's birthday made a national holiday. This was the campaign's glorious soundtrack.

❾ MASTERBLASTER (JAMMIN')
from HOTTER THAN JULY
Stevie acknowledges Bob Marley as a contemporary giant on a sizzling funky reggae groove.

❿ I JUST CALLED TO SAY I LOVE YOU from THE DEFINITIVE COLLECTION
Sentimental. Catchy as hell. Hugely popular. Agreed. Now what's your problem?

Garth Cartwright

Songlines'
World music landmarks

Nobody likes the term much, but "world music" has a rapidly growing audience, dozens of labels and a cluster of magazines (not to mention a two-volume Rough Guide). Here SIMON BROUGHTON, editor of *Songlines* magazine, picks some of world music's landmark hits – from African pop to Sufi soul.

❶ SINA SALIF KEITA from SORO
A great track from Keita's seminal 1987 album, which brought African music to a new international audience. The incantatory opening immediately evokes Mali's vibrant musical world.

❷ KALIMANKOU VOIX BULGARES from LE MYSTÈRE DES VOIX BULGARES
Bulgaria's Radio-TV choir had a surprise global hit with this recording. Yanka Rupkina's solo voice carries a beautifully ornamented melody through dangerous harmonic waters.

❸ MUSTT MUSTT NUSRAT FATEH ALI KHAN from MUSTT MUSTT
Nusrat, who died in 1997, was simply a phenomenon. Who'd have thought that a devotional song to a Pakistani Sufi saint could turn into such a worldwide hit? Who'd have thought religious music could be so funky?

❹ UTRUS HORAS ORCHESTRA BAOBAB from PIRATES CHOICE
With its spacey guitar and mellow sax, this is the 1982 signature track from one of Africa's greatest bands.

❺ MARIA LISBOA MARIZA from FADO EM MIM
With her debut recording in 2002, Mariza became the new voice of Portugal's bluesy fado music. This is wonderful version of an old fado classic.

❻ DIDI KHALED from KHALED
This storming track opened the Algerian rai star's first international release – and it's a song that he's been performing ever since.

❼ BALADA CONDUCATORULUI TARAF DE HAIDOUKS from MUSIQUE DES TZIGANES DE ROUMANIE
An extraordinary success story: poor Romanian Gypsies become ambassadors of their music round the world. This track tells of the fall of the dictator Ceausescu in 1989.

❽ LI MA WEESU YOUSSOU N'DOUR from NOTHING'S IN VAIN
Probably the biggest name in African music nowadays; this is one of his catchiest recent songs, from 2002.

❾ CHAN CHAN BUENA VISTA SOCIAL CLUB from BUENA VISTA SOCIAL CLUB
You only have to hear the first chord to know what's coming. The catchiest track from world music's greatest success story. Sublime music from Eliades Ochoa and Compay Segundo.

❿ CLANDESTINO MANU CHAO from CLANDESTINO
A great melody, snatches of conversation, street sounds and a whiff of subculture – this is distinctively Manu Chao, drawn from his groundbreaking 1998 album.

World jazz

The landscape of jazz music is changing dramatically as musicians from every corner of the globe adopt it, adding in elements of their own folk roots.

❶ FUSIC TOUFFIC FARROUKH from DRAB ZEEN
Lebanese sax man Farroukh has blended jazz and Arabic old and new together seamlessly, grooving all the way to the Kasbah.

❷ FUNK RAI NGUYEN LE from MAGREB & FRIENDS
Born in Paris to Vietnamese parents, Le has fast become one of the world's premier jazz guitarists. Funk Rai opens doors from Saïda to Vienna, Algiers to France, Hanoi to Sardinia and beyond.

❸ ENTRE CONTINENTES RENAUD GARCIA-FONS from ENTREMUNDO
When it comes to the acoustic bass, Garcia-Fons is in a class by himself. On Entremundo he fuses together brilliant jazz bass and the fiery heat of Flamenco.

Damon Albarn's
World grooves

"When I travel I find there's so much great music out there that isn't widely available outside the country where it was made," DAMON ALBARN says. "That's why we set up our own label, just to get some of it out there." The Blur/Gorillaz singer Damon Albarn, has become a fervent champion of world music in recent years and in 2002 co-founded the Honest Jon's label, which has since released recordings from Mali, Nigeria, Cuba, Trinidad and elsewhere. His current personal playlist contains several Nigerian funk tracks as he is presently in the studio finishing up an album of original songs he started recording in Lagos in 2004 with ex-Fela Kuti drummer Tony Allen.

❶ DENI KELENBE KOKO (LONELY GIRL BY THE RIVERSIDE) LOBI TRAORE GROUP from LOBI TRAORE GROUP

❷ OMELEBELE DR VICTOR OLAIYA from LAGOS CHOP UP

❸ PROFESSIONAL SUPER BANTOUS SUPER NEGRO BANTOUS from LAGOS ALL-ROUTES

❹ CALPYSO BLUES MONA BAPTISITE from LONDON IS THE PLACE FOR ME VOL 2

❺ CHOCOLATE EN C7 CHOCOLATE from SON CUBANO

❻ EL HOB KEDA OUM KALTHOUM from EL HOB KEDA

❼ EYA KA JO JIMMY SOLANKE AND THE JUNKERS from THE SHRINE PRESENTS AFROBEAT

❽ THE OLD ARK'S A-MOVERIN' ALPHABETICAL FOUR MOVERIN from COMPLETED RECORDED WORKS 1938–43

❾ SHAKE SUGAREE ELIZABETH COTTEN from SHAKE SUGAREE SMITHSONIAN FOLKWAYS

❿ MANKUNTO MAULA MEHR ALI AND SHEER ALI QAAWAALI from SACRED VOICES: SUFI PASSION

❹ LA ABUELITA AQUILES BAEZ from REFLEJANDO EL DORADO

Aquiles Baez is a national treasure in his homeland of Venezuela. It's easy to see, or rather hear, why. A brilliant guitarist, he brings together local traditions with jazz freedom.

❺ NEKEMTENEMMUTOGATOL ORO BESH 'O DROM from CAN'T MAKE ME

Besh 'o Drom from Budapest take the folk-driven Balkan Brass sound and makes it as jazz-filled as anything you've ever heard. Jazz *cimbalom*? Yessir!!

❻ WHITEWASH JASPER VAN'T HOF'S PILI PILI from HOTEL BABO

Pili Pili span twenty years of world jazz music. Dutch jazz pianist Van't Hof built this band with musicians from all over Africa – Mali, Senegal, Congo, South Africa, Guinea – and discovered Angélique Kidjo, who performs on this track.

❼ BIEL ANNA MARIA JOPEK WITH PAT METHENY from UPOJENIE

With one of the most beautiful jazz voices of our time, Polish jazz vocalist Anna Maria Jopek teamed up with guitarist Pat Metheny to create this extraordinary album. Who cares if the vocals aren't in English?

❽ JUNGLE ME MUNGLE FREE WINDS from INDIAN AIR

German sax-player Heinrich Von Kalnein recorded two albums with Indian Air, this being the most special. It features Kanjira master V. Selvaganesh along with tabla master Jatinder Thakur, and the blend of modern jazz and Indian rhythms is utterly intoxicating.

❾ THE HAPPY SHEIK RABIH ABOU-KHALIL from THE SULTAN'S PICNIC

Oud master Rabih Abou-Khalil adapts traditional folk melodies to great jazz effect.

❿ VOL DE NUIT HADOUK TRIO from LIVE A' FIP

Literally a world-jazz super-group with Didier Malherbe, Steve Shehan and Loy Erlich, the trio creates something entirely fresh and new in the jazz realm. The trio takes its name from the two primary instruments used in these recordings, the doudouk and the hajouj.

Geoff Colquitt

World percussion

The best beats from around the world. Let the rhythm take you on a trip through South America, the Caribbean, West, Central and North Africa, the Middle East and the Far East.

❶ AGRUPACIÓN LUBOLA "C" ARMANDO LA LLAMADA from URUGUAY: TAMBORES DEL CANDOMBE
Montevideo's finest hammer out some classic Afro-Uruguayan candombe rhythms on this wonderful example of the carnival procession music that rules the city every February.

❷ LUZ E BLUES OLODUM from REVOLUTION IN MOTION
Powered by the boom of massive surdo drums, this is Brazil's best known "Afro Bloco". Their surging rhythms have been copied and sampled … but never bettered.

❸ KEYMAN WINGLESS ANGELS from WINGLESS ANGELS
The ancient chants and rhythms of *nyabinghi* Rastafarian drummers from the high hills of Jamaica. Recorded in situ with Keith Richards and a number of chirping tree frogs.

❹ YEMAYA CONJUNTO FOLKLÓRICO NACIONAL DE CUBA from CUBA I AM TIME
Spine-tingling call-and-response vocals honouring Yemayá – the Santería cult's deity of the sea – backed

---

Robert Wyatt's
Disques de France

"What this list's about", wrote ROBERT WYATT, "is the French take on a non-European culture during my lifetime: from exiled black American jazz musicians after the war to North African-influenced music. Europe beyond Europe. It's inadequately explained but from the heart."

He broke the key rule of this book by specifying albums rather than individual songs, but, hey, someone's allowed to do things different and Wyatt's the man.

❶ BOHEMIA AFTER DARK EDDY LOUISS
This – and the three choices below – are all on the wonderful French jazz label, Gitanes. So nostalgic! Louiss plays Hammond organ, in the style of Jimmy Smith or Shirley Scott.

❷ JAZZ SUR SEINE BARNEY WILEN
A French tenor sax player, accompanied by a group which is basically the (black American) rhythm section of The Modern Jazz Quartet.

❸ JOUE BUD POWELL RENÉ UTREGER
Utreger is a pianist who worked a lot with Kenny Clarke after he made his home in Paris. The French treated Black American musicians as real artists, not just entertainers. Americans couldn't play in Britain at the time because of our Musicians Union restrictions, which was maybe why all the guitar bands took over.

❹ JEUX DE QUARTES BOBBY JASPAR
Jaspar was actually Belgian. He played sax and flute

with a very light touch – each of his notes was very good.

❺ LUCKY IN PARIS MARTIAL SOLAL
A great session, featuring drummer Gerard Pochonet and sax player Lucky Thompson. But it's the Algiers-born pianist, Solal, who makes such a fresh sound. A master at work.

❻ POULINA ORCHESTRE NATIONAL DE BARBÈS
I love this. It's a big band of North Africans from Barbès, the Paris suburb.

❼ HADOUK DIDIER MALHERBE
Didier plays every wind instrument under the sun. He recorded this with Maghrebi players.

❽ LES RUES DE LA NUIT HÉLÈNE DELAVAUT
Totally French. She's a very sexy 1930s French opera singer, and this is just her and a pianist.

❾ PORTRAIT-ROBOT BERTRAND BURGALAT
Burgalat's a French pop producer who occasionally makes more personal, intimate solo records. Most recently with guest wordsmiths including her upstairs, Alfie (Benge – Robert's wife). It's a lovely record and a good example of French international inclusiveness. But he's used some of Alfie's lyrics on this one. So he's in!

❿ CHANSONS JOHN GREAVES & ÉLISE CARON
John lives in Paris, so this is a proper French record. He's a wonderful bass player, and songwriter. I did a very discreet bit on the album.

by gradually accelerating *batá* drummers Cuban music at its most enchanting.

⑤ LES FRÈRES COULIBALY DJANTO BADENYA from SÉNIWÈ
Djembe and *dun dun* drums lead this engaging stop-start "percussion discussion" by the brothers Coulibaly from Burkina Faso Catch one of their spectacular live shows if you can.

⑥ SONTAOULA KÉLÉTIGUI DIABATÉ from SANDIYA
Mali's leading master of the balafon – West Africa's wooden xylophone – duets here with star guitarist Djelimady Tounkara on this pensive and exquisitely melodic piece

⑦ UNTITLED THE DRUMMERS OF BURUNDI from THE DRUMMERS OF BURUNDI
A half hour tour-de-force by this tiny country's rhythmic ambassadors, who were famously featured on Joni Mitchell's track "The Jungle Line Here" they are without her.

⑧ NAGRISHAD EL DIN HAMZA from A WISH
The late "father of Nubian music" sings gently and plays *tar*, *doumbek* and *riq* over a complex and mesmerizing 48-beat cycle of handclaps. Music for an Egyptian wedding.

⑨ SAINT MAIME 1 CHEMIRANI TRIO from TRIO DE ZARB
The subtle roll and rumble of three Iranian zarb drums (played with the fingertips) in heady conversation.

⑩ MENARI SAMULNORI from SPIRIT OF NATURE
Korea's leading exponents of *nongak/pungmul* (farmers' percussion music) here use their *kkwaengwari* and *ching* gongs plus *changgo* and *puk* drums to play shamanic music.

Jon Lusk

Robert Wyatt

Robert Wyatt proclaims himself a true minimalist ("I really don't do a lot"), an assertion that flies in the face of a constantly inventive solo career since leaving Soft Machine in 1974. His is a unique voice that has integrity and heart and he has applied it to his own compositions as well as a memorable series of political songs and off-kilter covers.

① SEA SONG from ROCK BOTTOM
Rock Bottom is Wyatt's great work, recorded while recovering from the accident that left him paralysed and wheelchair-bound. It's not really an album to

excerpt, but this marine opener is a good way in, with his trademark wordless voice as primary instrument, set above a wonderful swirl of guitar from Mike Oldfield.

② AT LAST I AM FREE from NOTHING CAN STOP US
This was pretty special as a disco number by Chic. Wyatt slows it to a beat you couldn't even tap a foot to, and lets the words soar. Magic.

③ INSENSATEZ from CUCKOOLAND
Wyatt has an unerring instinct for the heart of a song, and Tom Jobim's lovely bossa nova suits him perfectly.

④ TE RECUERDO AMANDA from MID-EIGHTIES
Victor Jara, the Chilean songwriter murdered by Pinochet's regime, wrote this most tender love song. Wyatt's treatment, almost funereal, and in the original Spanish, renders it a song as much for Jara, as for itself.

⑤ LEFT ON MAN from DONDESTAN
Wyatt is a great percussionist: here his urgent beats and rhythm-chorus of "simplify, reduce, oversimplify" underpin a stark political message: "What we call freedom in the North is just freedom to use you…"

⑥ MARYAN from SCHLEEP
A dreamy highlight of this mid-1990s album, recalling *Rock Bottom* in mood, and with exquisite guitar work from Philip Catherine.

⑦ THE WIND OF CHANGE from FLOTSAM JETSAM
Long before African music grew popular in the West, and when Mozambique was a forgotten war zone, Wyatt enlisted the SWAPO singers, and a London big band, to assert a buoyant message of hope and liberation.

⑧ I'M A BELIEVER from GOING BACK A BIT
You have to grin as Wyatt launches into The Monkees' love-affirming number. An oddball UK hit, it even got him onto *Top of the Pops*.

⑨ O CAROLINE from MATCHING MOLE
An affecting song of lost love, recorded with Wyatt's post-Soft Machine band.

⑩ SHIPBUILDING from NOTHING CAN STOP US
Elvis Costello wrote this marvellous, subtle political song for Wyatt as the Falklands war gathered momentum. "Diving for dear life, when we could be diving for pearls" is the chorus, but really it's perfect from start to finish.

Mark Ellingham

Alternative Xmas

A few tunes that probably won't be blaring out of your stereo on Christmas Day, but probably should be.

❶ FAMILY COACH THE LILAC TIME from LOOKING FOR A DAY IN THE NIGHT
Over some deft finger-picking, Stephen Duffy recalls his own family Christmas in 1968, before comparing and constrasting it with that of the astronauts on Apollo 8.

❷ RIVER JONI MITCHELL from BLUE
It's Christmas, but Joni's lost the best baby she ever had. Cheer up, girl, there's some figgy pudding steaming on the stove.

❸ BACK DOOR SANTA CLARENCE CARTER from SNATCHING IT BACK
A solid soul groove and wailing horns underpin an unsavoury tale of a Father Christmas more interested in seducing women than eating mince pies.

❹ JINGLE BELL ROCK THE FALL from THE COMPLETE PEEL SESSIONS
"Laughing and dancing in jingle bell square," grunts Mark E Smith, sounding like he's just forced a child to hand over the controls of a new Playstation.

❺ COMMON COLD HAWKSLEY WORKMAN from ALMOST A FULL MOON
Over the course of a terrific Christmas album, Hawksley addresses our annoying susceptibility to illness over the chilly winter months.

❻ CHRISTMAS TREE KING STITT from TROJAN CHRISTMAS BOX SET
"Nice, nice, nice," yells Mr Stitt. "On the count of nine, drink wine/Feel fine, it's Christmas time/Wow!" A sentiment shared by us all.

❼ HAVE YOURSELF A MERRY LITTLE CHRISTMAS GLEN CAMPBELL from GLENN CAMPBELL CHRISTMAS
An extraordinary reworking of the classic Christmas standard – no, only joking, it's the same as any other version you've ever heard. Still gorgeous, though.

❽ JUST LIKE CHRISTMAS LOW from CHRISTMAS
"On our way from Stockholm it started to snow," sings Mimi Parker over a gentle shuffle and festive bells. You're in Scandinavia, Mimi, what do you expect?

❾ CHRISTMAS IN HOLLIS RUN DMC from TOGETHER FOREVER
Run DMC, chillin' & coolin' like snowmen, get to work and record what must surely be the only rap ever to rhyme "yule log" with "egg nog".

❿ CHRISTMAS AS I KNEW IT JOHNNY CASH from JOHNNY
A tale of depravation to make you feel bad about unwrapping an MP3 player earlier in the day. "Daddy killed a squirrel, and Louise made the bread." Yum.

Rhodri Marsden

X-Ray Spex

The greatest talent to rise up from a genuinely street background in the London punk scene, Poly Styrene was wise enough to step away from fame when she found it not to her taste. Before that, though, she knocked out one brilliant album and a bunch of superb, spirit-of-the-age singles.

❶ I AM A CLICHÉ from GERM FREE ADOLESCENTS
Classic punk tune from Poly and the band – played loud, played fast with one verse, one chorus, one repeat and a fade.

❷ THE DAY THE WORLD TURNED DAY-GLO from GERM FREE ADOLESCENTS
Apocalyptic in a streetwise manner that Patti Smith could only sigh at wistfully, Poly trips out on the sheer number of plastics, additives and E-numbers in her life.

❸ IDENTITY from GERM FREE ADOLESCENTS
Forget about identity fraud, Poly's talking about total identity crisis and personality breakdown. Punk rock of the highest quality, provoking thought and questioning the status quo.

❹ I AM A POSEUR from GERM FREE ADOLESCENTS
A charming piece of swagger that captures the sheer fun of shocking the straight world.

❺ GENETIC ENGINEERING from GERM FREE ADOLESCENTS

Way back before cloning, in a time when even photocopiers were still regarded as magic, Poly wrote this prophetic little nightmare of a bleak future still to come. A perspective on Aldous Huxley's *Brave New World*, as observed from the World's End in Chelsea.

❻ ART-I-FICIAL from GERM FREE ADOLESCENTS

Excellent meditation on the role of make-up, messed-up education and enforced reliance on domestic appliances in a woman's world. And you can dance to it too!

❼ I LIVE OFF YOU from GERM FREE ADOLESCENTS

Cats live off rats in Poly's world, where pimps beat whores and Freddie will try to strangle you with your own plastic popper beads. Life sucks.

❽ GERM FREE ADOLESCENTS from GERM FREE ADOLESCENTS

The ultimate western teenage love song, in which one's entire romantic life depends on the state of one's skin.

❾ OH BONDAGE! UP YOURS! from GERM FREE ADOLESCENTS

The band's anthem, and still unfortunately necessary as a rallying cry for the oppressed 51 percent.

Al Spicer

XTC

British pop's answer to Mr Pooter in *The Diary Of A Nobody*, the work of XTC shines a friendly light onto the niceties of British culture. Starting as thoughtful punks they progressed to a stately middle age of epigrams and anecdotes.

❶ SCIENCE FRICTION from FOSSIL FUEL

This song can be dated to the end of the 1970s just by listening to the angular guitar lines and tinny keyboards. A charming piece of harmless British New Wave perked up beyond jollity by Andy Partridge's super-clipped vocal delivery and the sheer joy of the twitchingly urgent tune itself.

❷ TOWERS OF LONDON from BLACK SEA

Deliciously twangy guitar and sloppy-sounding drumming are the instant hooks of this rather unusual musing on the city's long and distinguished pedigree.

❸ GENERALS AND MAJORS from BLACK SEA

This is as near as XTC ever got to a downbeat comment on the gloom of the Cold War and the militarized political scene of the 1980s. Of course, being one of Colin Moulding's compositions, it bops and bounces along as if it had just won a prize at a kid's birthday party.

❹ STATUE OF LIBERTY from WHITE MUSIC

A silly lyrical love song in tribute to New York's best-known attraction. Neatly sums up the emotional reaction of more than four million annual tourists to the big lass who stands on the island.

❺ SGT ROCK (IS GOING TO HELP ME) from BLACK SEA

Daytime radio favourite – and one of Andy's chirpiest, fruitiest tunes – this is a classic "coming of age" tune for boys in the vein of the Who's "Pictures Of Lily".

❻ LOVE ON A FARMBOY'S WAGES from MUMMER

A far more mature look at the world of romance from a chap having to make do on a cult musician's wages.

❼ BALL AND CHAIN from ENGLISH SETTLEMENT

Exuberantly anti-development singalong from one of the band's best albums. Lyrics are reduced almost to simple slogans as the group let the repetitive beat of chisel on masonry do the talking for him.

❽ MAKING PLANS FOR NIGEL from DRUMS AND WIRES

XTC's biggest chart hit was so successful that management at British Steel (damned by faint praise in the lyric) rounded up all the Nigels they could find on the payroll and paraded them, show-trial style, in front of the cameras to say just how happy they were to be in the industry.

❾ SENSES WORKING OVERTIME from ENGLISH SETTLEMENT

Delightful British psychedelia from a man who might not even need LSD to see the hidden charms in rainy old Swindon, Wiltshire.

❿ THIS IS POP? from WHITE MUSIC

Dating back to XTC's days of punkish attitude, this champions the band's own musical taste in the face of abuse from the normals. Snotty, teenage rebel music, but polite – Andy Partridge is nothing if not well brought up.

Al Spicer

Yes

Yes were always the most atmospheric, adventurous and loopily strange of prog acts. If they often lost sight of reality, they rarely lost sight of melody.

❶ STARSHIP TROOPER from THE YES ALBUM
Epitomizing the excitement of classic Yes, this three-part space-rock suite soars ever upward, from its arpeggiated opening to acoustic middle to sinister fade.

❷ LONG DISTANCE RUN AROUND from FRAGILE
Yes at their most direct and poppy: guitar and bass syncopate snappily around Jon Anderson's keening falsetto.

❸ GOING FOR THE ONE from GOING FOR THE ONE
Charging heavy rock lifted skyward by lightning steel guitar from Steve Howe and Anderson's jaw-droppingly dramatic vocal.

❹ HEART OF THE SUNRISE from BUFFALO 66
As featured in *Buffalo 66*, it's proto trip-hop with a huge bass riff and ambient synth washes. Only Anderson's bonkers lyrics ("SHARP, distance") belong firmly in prog.

❺ YOUR MOVE from THE YES ALBUM
Another simple, early Yes song: a lapping wave of acoustic beauty that is a modest precursor to the more pompous "And You And I".

❻ CLOSE TO THE EDGE from CLOSE TO THE EDGE
Twenty-minute pastoral epic that opens and closes with birdsong, that pulls and pushes in between with equal parts of excitement and beauty.

❼ ROUNDABOUT from FRAGILE
Take a simple R&B riff, add classical flourish courtesy of new boy Rick Wakeman, add a chorus classic rock fans could hum and – bingo! – an American breakthrough.

❽ GATES OF DELIRIUM from RELAYER
An epic anti-war song that goes from nippy opening via combative middle to swooning serenity at the end.

Toby Manning

Yo La Tengo

An indie-rock institution, Yo La Tengo have been around for over twenty years and have rarely repeated themselves. Feedback and folk are equal staples of their sound.

❶ BLUE LINE SWINGER from ELECTR-O-PURA
Yo La Tengo at their My Bloody Valentine-esque best: indistinguishable male/female vocals, a simple, nagging hook and layer upon howling layer of feedback.

❷ SHADOWS
from I CAN HEAR THE HEART BEATING AS ONE
YLT at their most delicate: drummer Georgia Hubley's wounded bird whisper makes you want to hug her as she approaches the high notes.

❸ ALYDA from PRESIDENT YO LA TENGO
An early, folk-rock mid-pacer, the first to feature Hubley's gorgeous backing vocals alongside Ira Kaplan's (Lou) reedy tones.

❹ TOM COURTENAY from ELECTR-O-PURA
Perfect pop, YLT style, with noisy guitars and oodles of "ba ba bas". Extra points for namechecking Julie Christie and Eleanor Bron.

❺ I HEARD YOU LOOKING from PAINFUL
Instrumental feedback freakout that keeps looping back to its original, cyclical catchy riff.

❻ BY THE TIME IT GETS DARK from LITTLE HONDA (SINGLE)
Hubley and Kaplan duet deliciously on this Sandy Denny ballad, like the Velvet Underground doing folk.

❼ YOU CAN HAVE IT ALL from AND THEN NOTHING TURNED ITSELF INSIDE OUT
An old disco cut milked both for campness and melancholy, Hubley's shy vocal wooed by the boys' ebullient "da-ba-das".

❽ FIVE-CORNERED DRONE (CRISPY DUCK) from MAY I SING WITH ME
One of many culinary titles from these notorious foodies: a rich repast of poppy melody and chiming guitars, plus eruptions of feedback.

Toby Manning

Neil Young

Part sensitive singer-songwriter, part guitar-thrashing axeman, Neil Young has been consistently releasing great records ever since he left Canada forty years ago. All his best work is characterized by the raw honesty that unites the two sides of his personality.

❶ MR SOUL from DECADE
This Buffalo Springfield hit shows Young's views on the record industry were already fully formed by 1967.

❷ CINNAMON GIRL from EVERYBODY KNOWS THIS IS NOWHERE
Backed by Crazy Horse on his second solo album in 1969, Neil Young perfected the technique of writing haunting love songs that also allowed space for over-amped guitar wig-outs.

❸ DOWN BY THE RIVER from EVERYBODY KNOWS THIS IS NOWHERE
Quite why Neil shot his baby when he seemed to like her so much is rendered no clearer by nine minutes of musical mayhem.

❹ ONLY LOVE CAN BREAK YOUR HEART from AFTER THE GOLDRUSH
A typically simple but damnably catchy song of the kind that brought Young-as-lonesome-troubadour his greatest commercial success.

❺ OLD MAN from HARVEST
Back in 1972, when being 24 seemed pretty old, Neil's willingness to admit his similarity to his father was both radical and touching.

❻ ON THE BEACH from ON THE BEACH
The title track from Young's bleakest album revealed that even worldwide acclaim had turned sour by 1974.

❼ TONIGHT'S THE NIGHT FROM TONIGHT'S THE NIGHT
A desolate 1975 lament for the way drugs had destroyed a generation.

❽ LIKE A HURRICANE from AMERICAN STARS'N'BARS
The rest of the album it's from is no great shakes, but this gloriously churning riff has been a live mainstay ever since.

❾ CRIME IN THE CITY from FREEDOM
The energy and intensity of this 1989 album made Neil Young seem relevant again for at least another decade.

❿ FARMER JOHN from RAGGED GLORY
Neil has never sounded happier than when reunited with Crazy Horse for this raucous 1990 singalong.

Greg Ward

Z

Townes van Zandt

Before there was alt.country there was Townes van Zandt (1944–97), self-effacing poet, songwriter and chronicler of lives. Once a military academy drop-out and latterly a recluse, he never had anything approaching a hit, but the list of country and folk stars who have recorded his troubadour's truthful songs is long and still growing.

❶ PANCHO AND LEFTY from THE LATE, GREAT TOWNES VAN ZANDT

It was Emmylou Harris's 1977 cover of this portrait of two ageing Mexican bandits – one dead, the other living in a cheap hotel – that brought van Zandt his first real recognition.

❷ TECUMSEH VALLEY
from OUR MOTHER THE MOUNTAIN

A miner's daughter finds a job in hard times, tending bar for Gypsy Sally, but finds she can never go home again – an early sad story, but poignant truth rather than country hard corn.

❸ MR MUDD & MR GOLD
from HIGH, LOW AND IN BETWEEN

Gripping, well-worked tale of playing cards conspiring to bring a gambler down – until the Queen of Diamonds is reminded of her lost son and starts to pray.

❹ LORETTA from FLYIN' SHOES

A travelling man finally acknowledges his undeclared love for his bar-room goodtime girl – "Keep your dancing slippers on/Keep me on your mind a while/I'm coming home."

❺ MARIE from NO DEEPER BLUE

From near the end of his career, a very different and deeply affecting monologue: of love on the welfare line, between a homeless drifter "with no one left to call" and his pregnant girl.

❻ TWO GIRLS from LIVE AT THE OLD QUARTER

"One's in heaven, one's below/One I love with all my heart and one I do not know." A typically intense, demanding portrait of a disturbed man wrapped up in his own world.

❼ I'LL BE HERE IN THE MORNING
from TOWNES VAN ZANDT

Like "Gentle On My Mind" in style, but the reverse in content: a drifter declares his lover is more important to him than his travelling – a gentle, charming, upbeat song of devotion.

❽ FRATERNITY BLUES from LIVE AT THE OLD QUARTER

Droll, talking-blues satire of the American college fraternity system, with barbed asides: "Besides, I figured if you want good friends, you gotta pay for them."

❾ WAITING AROUND TO DIE
from TOWNES VAN ZANDT

This wry collection of sad attempts to escape aimless lives of low expectations – and the hopeless alternatives – packs a powerful message: make the most of your opportunities.

❿ TWO HANDS
from HIGH, LOW AND IN BETWEEN

Delightful, uplifting Carter Family-style spiritual: a modest pastiche but its gospel-style simple avowal of faith – "I ain't gonna think about trouble any more" – hit's the spot.

Ian Cranna

Zimbabwe

Pungwe! In Zimbabwe, licensing laws do not apply. The music goes on all night, as loudly as possible. The arrival of Western instruments in the 1960s and 70s saw such pioneers as Thomas Mapfumo and Oliver Mtukudzi combine the traditional patterns of drum and *mbira* with soul and reggae to create styles like *jit*, *chimurenga* and *sungura* – music for drinking, dancing and easing troubled minds.

❶ CHITIMA NDITAKURE THOMAS MAPFUMO from CHAMUNORWA

"Train, take me away." Hypnotic and heavy on the *mbira*, this is as rootsy as it gets.

❷ NDIMA NDAPEDZA OLIVER MTUKUDZI
from TUKU MUSIC

The most beautiful moment on a beautiful album

Barry Miles selects
Frank Zappa

BARRY MILES has written key books on 1960s culture as well as biographies of such figures as Burroughs, Ginsberg and Paul McCartney. He knew Frank Zappa, attending many of his recording sessions and, in 1994, writing his biography. Selecting a playlist proved a challenge: "Zappa composed in a wide variety of styles, from post-Varesian sound clusters to retro doo-wop, from novelty ditties to jazz-inspired rockouts, protest music to spoken-word collages. With more than seventy CDs in print, many of them doubles, to choose just ten tracks would not even cover all his styles, let alone rank his output. There were certain melodies that he re-worked time and time again, and some other tracks that jump out for attention, so, in no particular order, here are ten great Zappa tracks."

❶ PEACHES EN REGALIA from HOT RATS
A beautiful instrumental number described by Zappa as "probably the ultimate across-the-board Frank Zappa song of all time. It's the only thing I've never heard anybody say they didn't like."

❷ UNCLE MEAT from UNCLE MEAT
Another instrumental, a favourite for string quartets and ensembles to cover. Zappa recorded it many times, but the original Uncle Meat album has the best version.

❸ WILLIE THE PIMP from HOT RATS
Another Hot Rats track, this a vocal sung by Captain Beefheart; it combines classy vocals, a classic example of Zappa's weird lyrics and terrific musicianship.

❹ THE JAZZ DISCHARGE PARTY HATS from THE MAN FROM UTOPIA
Zappa regarded this as one of his best. He

described it as coming "close to Schoenberg, with its jazz accompaniment to a *Sprechgesang* text presentation". Many people find the lyrics deeply offensive.

❺ BROWN SHOES DON'T MAKE IT from ABSOLUTELY FREE
Recorded by the original Mothers line-up, this shows exactly why Zappa got such a following in the first place.

❻ WATERMELON IN EASTER HAY from FRANK ZAPPA PLAYS THE MUSIC OF FRANK ZAPPA
Recorded many times. *Frank Zappa Plays…* has two versions, including the original from *Joe's Garage*. One of his most beautiful compositions, beautifully played.

❼ BLACK NAPKINS from FRANK ZAPPA PLAYS THE MUSIC OF FRANK ZAPPA
Another superb composition, also present on *Frank Zappa Plays…* alongside the original recording on the *Zoot Allures* album.

❽ VALLEY GIRL from VALLEY GIRL SOUNDTRACK
One of Zappa's few hits, and a song that shows his anthropological approach to pop culture, in this case the teenage girls of the San Fernando Valley, whose accents are wonderfully imitated by his daughter Moon Unit, then 14 years old.

❾ VALARIE' (SIC) from BURNT WEENIE SANDWICH
A cover version of Jackie And The Starlites' doo-wop original that shows how deep Zappa's roots were in West Coast R&B.

❿ G-SPOT TORNADOS from THE YELLOW SHARK
Another of Zappa's favourite tracks. This stark Ensemble Modern version is perhaps the most unusual and interesting.

– the perfect Tuku blend of soul and groove.

❸ KUROJA CHETE THE BHUNDU BOYS from SHABINI
Even the struggle to pay the rent sounds like a cause for celebration!

❹ MISORODZI DUMISANI MARAIRE from THE AFRICAN MBIRA
Pure *mbira* tradition. All the sorrow of Africa.

❺ AMAI VARUBHI ALICK MACHESO from SIMBARADZO
The biggest hit from the biggest-selling Zimbabwean

album ever. Macheso urges dialogue between wives and husbands over an unstoppable *sungura* beat.

❻ MAPIYEMANA STELLA CHIWESHE
from KUMUSHA

Mbira, voice, clapping, drums and *hosho* hand-rattle – you don't get much more trance-inducing than this.

❼ TORNADOS VS. DYNAMOES (3-3) REAL SOUNDS from VENDE ZOKO

An epic piece of rumba. Zimbabwe meets the Congo in the greatest football clash in African music history.

❽ KULELIYANI'ZWE LOVEMORE MAJAIVANA
from THE BEST OF LOVEMORE MAJAIVANA

The biggest star of the minority Ndebele tribe (an offshoot of the Zulu), steeped in South African *mbaqanga*.

❾ NDIVUMBAMIREIWO FOUR BROTHERS
from ROOTS ROCK GUITAR PARTY

Awesome, no-messing-about Shona guitar pop from the 1980s Golden Age.

❿ KUMAKORODZI MBIRA DZE NHARIRA from RINEMANYANGA HARIPUTIRWE

Probably Zimbabwe's best new band of the past few years, Mbira dze Nharira play stripped-down, ethereal mbira music.

Tom Bullough

ZZ Top

This hairy lil ol' blues outfit from Texas nearly took over world in the 1980s with their MTV-hogging videos. Possibly the only band ever to make beards look cool.

❶ A FOOL FOR YOUR STOCKINGS from DEGÜELLO

Billy Gibbons sounds like he's hurting real bad, baby. And just get a load of Dusty Hill's fantastic loping bass line.

❷ BALINESE from FANDANGO

A gloriously raucous party tune penned about the notorious Balinese Ballroom in Galveston. Gambling, drinking, dancing girls… it's got the lot.

❸ BEER DRINKERS AND HELL RAISERS from TRES HOMBRES

If there was one track to sum up early ZZ Top then this is it. Beer-drinking, bar-room-brawling boogie and then some.

❹ CHEAP SUNGLASSES from DEGÜELLO

A fabulously funky ode to that essential piece of ZZ face furniture. Billy Gibbon's guitar rarely sounded grimier or groovier.

❺ HEARD IT ON THE X from FANDANGO

A seriously soulful celebration of 1960s Texas pirate radio stations, pushing some major wattage. Superb drums and top hand clapping!

❻ I'M BAD, I'M NATIONWIDE from DEGÜELLO

Smooth, smoky and bad to the bone, this is about cars and girls, but not necessarily in that order. Makes you want to hit the road with the top down.

❼ LA GRANGE from TRES HOMBRES

A sleazy little tale about the Best Little Whorehouse In Texas, featuring one of the dirtiest riffs in rock'n'roll. A stone-cold classic.

❽ SHARP DRESSED MAN from ELIMINATOR

Hugely commercial robo-boogie for the MTV masses. Acres of guitars, some great solos and a riff to die for.

❾ SURE GOT COLD AFTER THE RAIN FELL from RIO GRANDE MUD

The Top are not noted for their lengthy compositions but this tear-jerking number clocks in nearly eight minutes of pure, bluesy beauty.

❿ TUSH from FANDANGO

One of the Top's most covered tunes, this cheeky hymn to hedonism is set to one of the band's finest boogie riffs.

Essi Berelian